D0215729

GOLDEN GATE SEMINARY LIBRARY

CHILDREN
and
YOUTH

PSYCHOSOCIAL DEVELOPMENT

CHILDREN and YOUTH 2nd edition

PSYCHOSOCIAL DEVELOPMENT

ELLIS D. EVANS
University of Washington

BOYD R. McCANDLESS

Holt Rinehart and Winston

New York   Chicago   San Francisco   Dallas
Montreal   Toronto

GOLDEN GATE SEMINARY LIBRARY

BF
713
M32
1978

Cover photograph by Marjorie Pickens.

Library of Congress Cataloging in Publication Data
Evans, Ellis D
   Children and youth.

   In the 1st ed. B. R. McCandless appeared first
on t. p.
   Includes bibliographical references.
   1. Developmental psychology.   2. Social psychology.   I. McCandless, Boyd R. Children and
youth.   II. Title.
BF713.M32   1978   155.4   77-26045
ISBN 0-03-019316-8

Copyright © 1973 by The Dryden Press
Copyright © 1978 by Holt, Rinehart and Winston
All rights reserved
Printed in the United States of America
8 9 0 1   039   9 8 7 6 5 4 3 2

PREFACE

Readers familiar with the original edition of this book will recognize that at least three major changes appear in this revised version. First, and basic, is a change in the conceptual framework of organization. The early exposition of theoretical accounts of human development in the first edition has given way to a framework organized around social influences upon learning and development. Not only does this provide us with a more consistent way to discuss empirical studies across major streams of human development, but it helps us to focus more sharply upon environmental conditions associated with variations in patterns of development. Thus, rather than discussing at the outset alternative and often competing theoretical interpretations of development, we focus on the theme of major social influences—parents, peers, schooling, mass media—throughout the entire book. We believe that this is important for understanding how the environment may be designed to promote positive human growth and development. And this understanding, we believe, is among the basic reasons for psychological study in the first place.

But we also believe that stressing the theme of social influences on development need not mean a deemphasis of the role of theory. In fact, our broad overview of major theoretical perspectives on human development, though its present placement differs from the original edition, has been retained. By providing this overview in Appendix A, the reader can benefit from greater flexibility in the use of theory. Such flexibility constitutes our second reason for organizational change. In other words, readers can now consider theoretical perspectives at any point along their course of study, depending upon their individual needs or the preferences of their instructors. For example, some users may wish to begin their study by considering broad theoretical perspectives from which to view the human development research literature. If so, Appendix A can be used as introductory material. Others may find it helpful to consult Appendix A in conjunction with or immediately following Chapter 2. Still others may prefer to delay their use of the appendix until after Parts II or III of this book. In short, reader discretion on this matter is both feasible and desirable; we encourage divergent ways of sequencing the content of this revision in relation to psychological theory.

A second basic change reflected in this revision has to do with the content itself. Of course, the very term *revision* implies an updating of content to indicate advances in our knowledge about a given subject matter. In addition to fresh research evidence on basic topics of human development (Part III), however, we have attempted to familiarize the reader with important and timely developments associated with developmental psychology. These include a growing emphasis upon cognitive aspects of development, changing concepts of sex-role development, the social significance of children's prosocial behavior, hazards of child abuse, cultural pluralism in socialization practices, and so on.

Many of the major additions appear as new chapters: Parents (Chapter 3), Schooling and Mass Media (Chapter 5), Physical-motor Development, including major developments of infancy (Chapter 6) and Achievement and Career Development (Chapter 10). Compared to our original version of this book, much greater attention has also been paid to concepts of benetics and learning, the measurement of behavioral development, and important *unknowns* as well as the presumed *knowns* about human development.

To maintain a book of reasonable length and cost and accommodate critics of the 1973 edition, these additions have required certain deletions. Largely in response to critics of the first edition, we have chosen not to repeat our discussion of political development and student activism, the structure of American schools, drug abuse among youth, school dropouts, and a few other topics about which the current research literature is less than strong. Certain other topics accorded full chapter status in the 1973 edition, including the self-concept and "dilemmas" in the study of development, have been integrated wherever appropriate within our new organizational framework. In the final analysis, of course, any book will represent selectivity in content. No one textbook either can or should be represented as all things to all people; we make no claim to universal comprehensiveness. We have, however, attempted to recommend helpful sources of information about topics we touch only lightly or in passing.

The third basic difference between the revised and original edition of the book concerns style. We have attempted to provide a more readable text in several ways. For one thing, less space is given to the technical details of specific studies; rather, their more general conclusions and their relevance to social issues about human development are stressed. For another, we have eliminated the "boxes" characteristic of the original edition, which many users apparently found distracting and often tangential to the main text. Still another stylistic difference is the more frequent use of case studies and concrete examples to illustrate important generalizations about human development. And yet another difference is in the language itself—a more explicit use of structuring comments for the purposes of introduction and summary, elimination of sexist language, less complex syntactic expression, and so on. It is hoped that our readers will find these stylistic changes a collective improvement over the first edition. In a further effort to reinforce major points and improve the visual appeal of this book we also offer a variety of figures and tables. In addition, each chapter has been provided with a portfolio of photographs related to the subject matter of the chapter. These illustrations have intentionally been left without "explanatory" captions—except for a few items of technical information. We believe that it is more important to train the eye of the observer by presenting "unexplained" scenes from real life than to decorate each picture by remarks that frequently and inevitably become vapid.

And now for the most difficult portion of this preface. In sadness and with a profound sense of loss I must inform the reader that the changes for this revision were discussed in only very general and preliminary terms before the untimely death in December 1975, of my colleague, close friend, and coauthor Boyd R. McCandless. Considering our carefully arranged working relationship, this shocking and unexpected event was a serious threat to any revision of this book. Thanks to the sustained support and encouragement of Professor McCandless' family—especially of his wife, Elinore—and the editorial staff at Holt, Rinehart and Winston—especially Richard C. Owen—I proceeded to detail our tentative revision strategy. The ensuing project was enormously challenging, often frustrating, never easy, but ultimately gratifying as an experience in professional growth. I have tried consistently to provide a breadth and level of scholarship of which my former coauthor would approve. But the final responsibility for organization, content, and style must be mine alone.

In addition to the assistance and cooperation of Elinore McCandless and Richard C. Owen, I wish to acknowledge several other invaluable contributions to this revision. Michael Roe provided the initial draft of Chapter 6 and the section on exceptionality in Chapter 12. Critic reviewers of the initial revised manuscript, though they remain anonymous to me, provided many constructive comments and suggestions. Considerable editorial refinements were supplied by Daniel Stein. My wife, Cindy, patiently and competently typed and retyped every word of the over 700 pages of original manuscript. Mary Todd assisted with the chapter bibliographies in a most competent fashion. And, of course, without the contribution of the scholars and researchers whose work I have cited, a book such as this is not possible.

To these persons I extend my heartfelt thanks. And to my departed colleague, Boyd R. McCandless, I extend a special gesture of gratitude. He, more than any single person, has provided both the inspiration and example of scholarship and humanism that were necessary for me to attempt, and eventually complete, a project of this kind. And so it is to the memory of Boyd R. McCandless that this book is dedicated.

Seattle, Washington   E.D.E.

CONTENTS

CHILDREN
and
YOUTH
PSYCHOSOCIAL DEVELOPMENT

PART I

INTRODUCTION

It seems paradoxical to many observers of the human condition that we understand more about supersonic travel, moonwalks, and space probes than we do about ourselves. Harnessing complex forces of nature through technology is a genuine wonderment. By comparison, our understanding of the forces that govern and influence human development and behavior, and our ability to harness them, seem pale. To be sure, some progress toward these goals has been made. If not, such a book as this could not be written. But we have come to recognize the incredible complexity of human behavior development during the short time we have applied the methods of science to its study. An enormous number of interactions make up this complexity—combinations of hereditary and environmental factors, evolving patterns of interpersonal relationships, and life circumstances that change over time and with social conditions.

We would be foolhardy indeed to claim that present knowledge permits these interactions to be neatly analyzed and presented, especially in a single volume. It is, therefore, with a keen awareness of the limitations of the behavioral sciences in general and ourselves in particular, that we set the stage in Part I of this book for a reasoned analysis of interaction and development. Our data come largely from the behavioral sciences, especially psychology. From these data and their interpretations, we gradually formulate ideas to improve understanding of human development.

Chapter 1 begins by discussing development as change through time. A model of interaction is presented and illustrated by three case histories. In turn, these case histories are used to establish some important points about development, including ideas about both diversity and commonality in human development. Overall, Chapter 1 provides an introduction to the concepts of development that are discussed in detail in subsequent chapters.

Chapter 2 extends this introduction to more technical aspects of developmental psychology. The emphasis upon interactionism continues throughout an examination of maturation and learning. The developmental roles of genetic factors and different kinds of learning are discussed. Chapter 2 also briefly presents the principal methods for studying development. Examples of these methods are sprinkled throughout the book. Chapter 2 concludes with an explanation of concepts of development that have evolved from the use of these methods of study.

chapter 1

A perspective on development

DEVELOPMENT AS CHANGE THROUGH TIME

The differences in behavior between a newborn infant and a 3-year-old child are obvious to the most casual observer. An elementary school child is strikingly different from a 15-year-old adolescent.

Children and youngsters with several years of age between them differ enormously in physical-motor, personal-social, and intellectual-academic skills. Newborn infants, for example, depend completely on others for survival. During the first few weeks of life they seem to respond to their environment and body tensions more than they initiate behavior or react to experiences. They cannot roll over or sit up, nor can they distinguish their mothers or principal caregivers from other adults or older children. About the only way they have to communicate their needs is to cry. Although their potential is enormous and wonderful, they show little organized behavior. Yet there is no doubt that they are learning, even in the first few days of life.

By contrast, normal elementary school children handle such complex matters as hopscotch and tetherball play; speak much like the adults they know best; and lead a sophisticated social life with family, peers, and such nonfamily adults as teachers and storekeepers. They have also learned how to compete and cooperate, how to please and offend, and how to lead and follow.

Differences like these that are associated with age may be viewed as the result of progressive changes over time. They represent successively higher degrees of differentiation and complexity in behavior. "Differentiation," as used here, means finer and usually more precise gradations of behavior. Increasing differentiation is usually accompanied by both increasing complexity and greater integration. For example, the 14-month-old child may call out, "Water." Interpreted as a one-word sentence, this may mean any number of things, which the child's caregiver must guess from intonation, gesture, and context. Within a year or two, the child's language will have become more differentiated and complex. The child can then supply a pronoun, an action verb, and a modifier—"I want some water," or "(You) see the water." In the first few months of life, infants may recognize and attempt to grab an object within their reach, but they can only swipe unsuccessfully at it. By age 6 months or so, they can make pincers of their thumb and fingers to grasp what is wanted with considerable efficiency.

Human development thus can be thought of as a process of continuous change through time. In many ways, these changes are predictable and sequential, that is, they take place in a fixed order. This is most easily illustrated by gross motor development. Infants, for example, can be expected to roll over before they sit, sit before they stand, stand before they walk, and walk before they run and walk. Throughout this book, developmental sequences will be observed in other areas of human functioning as well.

Interaction and the Whole Person

We can liken human development to a complex puzzle, the pieces of which are only gradually being identified and fitted together. Even so, the whole of human behavior and development may be greater than the sum of its individual parts. Certain more obscure aspects of humanness that contribute to the frequent unpredictability of behavior may never be unraveled. And because humans are *whole* beings, complete with poorly understood qualities, writing about people is enormously difficult.

As one step toward dealing sensibly with this difficult task it seems helpful to think about the "whole person" in terms of three broad categories of behavior and personal characteristics. One category, *physical-motor*, includes body build and configuration, size, strength, rate of physical maturation, motor skill coordination, physical health, and the like. Temperament, interpersonal relationship skills, emotional adjustment, and morality are included in a second category, *personal-social*. Within the third category, *cognitive-intellectual*, are included perception, memory, language, problem-solving and thinking abilities, academic achievement, and so on.

This way of viewing the whole person can be represented by the schematic diagram in Figure 1.1 The development of behaviors specific to each category is discussed in Part III of this book. Until then, we are concerned mostly with how these categories are interrelated and affect human interaction. At this time our point about interaction from this schematic diagram is twofold. First, children's physical-motor, personal-social, and cognitive-intellectual developments interact among one another to result in characteristic ways of behaving. For example, children's mobility and self-help skills (eating, dressing, toileting) are all based heavily on physical-motor development (corner A). But children's progress and satisfaction with these accomplishments may both reflect and affect certain related personal-social developments, such as a growing sense of autonomy or independence (corner B). These physical-motor accomplishments also make it possible to seek and enjoy advanced social relationships with other children, as in play. And, as noted in Chapter 4, play provides further opportunities for the acquisition and practice of problem-solving skills (corner C). Opportunities for and patterns of success (or failure) in games and social relationships may affect further development in several ways, as will become increasingly clear in later chapters of this book.

Our second point about interaction from Figure 1.1 is that development is a two-way street: just as children's development may be influenced by parents and other social forces (such as peers or the mass media), children influence their parents and the environment in which development occurs (Bijou, 1976). Some parents, for example, may expect their children to meet high standards of physical and intellectual performance. Rightly or wrongly, such parents may even attempt to accelerate the development of their children's capabilities.

Other parents may take no forceful role in shaping the course of development. Still others may actively interfere with such development by taking a negative attitude toward the task of parenting. Whatever pattern of influence is attempted by parents, children respond in turn, usually to influence the tempo and style with which their parents seek to "train" or "control" their young. Similarly, children's efforts to master their broader physical and social environment will produce effects which further influence development. We can thus think about the process of human development as a series of feedback loops whereby conditions of the individual and the environment operate continuously to produce change. The extent to which this interaction series is positive and constructive, or negative and destructive, depends largely upon a child's genetic make-up and environment for growth. Assuming that most children are genetically healthy and normal, and that most parents want the "best" for and from their children, a balanced set of interactions to promote well-rounded development is likely to prevail. Such parents will demonstrate skill in recognizing, providing for, and encouraging the growth of genuine individuality in their children. A bias in interactions is common, however. Bookish parents may concentrate heavily on corner C; parents strongly identified with athletics on corner A; and so on.

Even concentrations, if they are suitably tailored to the children's capacities, may lead to a constructive and healthy developmental history. If not, however, quite another and less pleasant life history may unfold.

It is unrealistic to think that as children proceed to the wider world of neighborhood and school all interactions will be balanced. Upon entering school, for example, children learn that teachers seldom concentrate much on corner A.

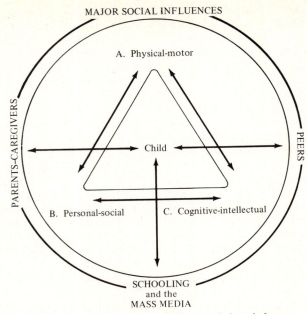

MAJOR SOCIAL INFLUENCES

A. Physical-motor

PARENTS–CAREGIVERS

Child

PEERS

B. Personal-social

C. Cognitive-intellectual

SCHOOLING
and the
MASS MEDIA

Fig. 1-1 A sketch of how children and their behavior and characteristics may be usefully viewed. The double-headed arrows indicate interactions. Major social influences are discussed in Part II of this book. Various aspects of physical-motor, personal-social, and cognitive-intellectual development are presented in Part III.

Children's physical-motor development is often only peripheral to their classroom work. Of course, children with physical handicaps compel attention. And qualitatively different teacher-child interactions may be shaped by teachers' perceptions of and responses to children's personal appearance and physical grace. But, in general, teachers mostly concentrate on corner C and build their interactions largely on children's intellectual merits or their lack of them. Because there are children and youth who present personality or conduct "problems," teachers sometimes are forced to concentrate on corner B, however ill-equipped they may be to establish appropriate beneficial personal–social interactions. Enter personnel workers, clinical and school psychologists, psychiatrists and social workers, all of whom usually are preoccupied with corner B, even to the relative neglect of corner C. In further contrast, doctors, nurses, dentists, and physical educators share a stronger concentration of thought and effort in corner A, with perhaps only modest attention, if any, to corners B and C.

In brief, the nature of the interactions that combine to affect children's development and, in turn, to influence children's impacts on adults will vary with the social setting. The cumulative effect of such interactions is to produce remarkable variations in developmental patterns and overall life styles, as the following brief cases illustrate. Each case is based upon the life circumstances of real persons, though of course names have been changed.

Illustrations of Interaction

The case of Lyle. Lyle was an active, healthy boy. His family—father, mother, and one older brother—lived in a small, rural midwestern community. His father, a third generation Anglo-American and a modestly successful farm implements dealer, provided the family with a comfortable but not luxurious existence. Lyle's mother was a well-educated woman who had reluctantly accompanied her husband from a larger city to build their independent business. This move had intensified her cool, aloof manner toward her family, except for her much-favored firstborn son, older than Lyle by three years. Lyle had been born a male instead of the female his mother wanted, which also affected his mother's response toward him.

Like most children, Lyle was anxious to please his parents and gain their approval. Perhaps as a result, he was an obedient and loyal son who did little to threaten his tentative acceptance in the family. This conformity extended to waiting on his brother, an aggressive child who always seemed to get the best of everything, from new clothes and special privileges to the more expensive toys at birthday and Christmastime. Lyle often felt angry and resentful about this unfairness, but learned to suppress his feelings so effectively that he could not even talk about them. Accordingly, both of Lyle's parents often complained about and criticized Lyle's frequent extended silences.

Parental dissatisfaction with Lyle was increased by his weak motivation to excel in school, although he clearly had the ability to do so. Lyle's brother, in contrast, brought great pleasure to his mother by consistently earning high marks in school. Lyle's father was so preoccupied with keeping his farm implements business afloat that he had little time left for either of his two sons.

When he was 10 years old, Lyle gained permission to join the local Boy Scout troop. His assets, a strong body and an interest in nature, were quickly recognized by the young Scoutmaster who was himself a dedicated family man. Lyle soon began to spend most of his leisure time with this second family. Over the next several years, a robust outdoor life was cultivated—hunting, fishing, trapping, and hiking—based upon a mutually rewarding friendship between Lyle and his new mentor. Now confident in his body and sure of its capabilities, Lyle went out for high school athletics and was most successful. However, his sports achievements were not enough to overcome a basic sense of inferiority to his brother, who by this time was in college. Largely because of parental pressure, Lyle followed his brother to college, where his early academic progress was marginal. Both football and a new romance took priority over his disliked studies.

Just as Lyle's grades began to improve during his sophomore year, he was stunned by news from home about the loss of the family business. His parents were no longer able to support both sons in college. Because his brother was well into medical school, Lyle's parents elected to continue financing that venture. His mother suggested that Lyle come home to help his father. Torn between his sense of family duty and a desire for independence, Lyle decided to stay on in school. He supported himself with part-time work while pursuing his studies. This required dropping football and other sports to make ends meet. Lyle's relationship with his parents deteriorated; he visited home less and less often.

Limited employment opportunities

when he graduated from college led Lyle to leave his native state in search of a satisfactory living. This exploration eventually took him to South America and a job with an American oil company. After several years of physical labor in oil fields in South America, Lyle returned to the U.S. to be groomed for public relations and sales work in the oil industry. By age 30 he was married to his college sweetheart, a marriage that yielded one son who was crippled by poliomyelitis in early adolescence.

A strong, healthy, athletic body (corner A) established early for Lyle a set of interactions dominated by physical-motor development. His rigorous outdoor life, followed by an intense involvement in sports, was increasingly rewarding, perhaps compensating in part for deficiency in the personal-social area at home (corner B). The friends and emotional satisfaction Lyle found in scouting and in team sports facilitated his personal-social development. Throughout his childhood and youth, these factors were associated with a lesser concentration upon intellectual-academic interactions (corner C). Although he completed college, Lyle's academic record was undistinguished. He was never noted for intellectual pursuits. His life had been dominated by physical activity. By young adulthood, Lyle had a generally positive, although not altogether satisfying, adjustment.

The case of Juan. Juan was the first-born in a family of four sisters and one brother. His parents as teenagers had come separately from Mexico to the southwestern United States community where they eventually met, married, and became naturalized citizens. Juan's father worked mainly as an unskilled laborer, moving on and off welfare fairly often, mostly because of poor health. At times, when he was able and seasonal conditions were favorable, the father followed the wave of migrant laborers that worked fruit and vegetable farms over a tri-state area.

The father's resulting low profile in the family was a contrast with Juan's mother's very active role. Largely because of her influence, the family became very close-knit, deriving emotional support from each other and from nearby members of the Catholic community in which the family resided. A fiercely proud woman, Juan's mother gradually became the family's sustaining force, perhaps at the expense of paternal guidance and influence.

Except for the hazards of poverty in ghetto-like urban surroundings, Juan's preschool years were uneventful. From the beginning, however, Juan was physically small for his age, lacking strength but not agility. Spanish, their native language, was exclusively spoken in the home. Juan's early school years were traumatic because English was the only accepted language for classroom learning. By the end of the second grade, having received little help from his teachers, Juan was diagnosed as a retarded learner and placed in a special classroom composed largely of similar ethnic-minority children. He remained in such classrooms throughout elementary school, advancing little in academic development.

Juan cared so competently for his younger siblings and survived so adeptly on the dusty streets of his small world that his mother never accepted the diagnosis of retardation. Finally, with the help of the family doctor, she was able to convince school personnel that Juan should receive a comprehensive re-evaluation of his mental development. A perceptive school psychologist reported that much of Juan's difficulty was rooted in specific second language inadequacy.

Meanwhile, Juan's father had died of tuberculosis. Juan's mother, now the sole source of family economic support, could ill afford remedial education for Juan. Moreover, the school district in which Juan's family lived was poorly equipped to do much more than provide a bare minimum of special instruction for "slow learners." Aware of his status in school, Juan was both humiliated and frustrated in his relationships with teachers and more favored pupils. His small size and comparatively slow physical maturation did little to help. As Juan's attitude toward school deteriorated, he began a pattern of truancy that further threatened his educational development. Largely because of his mother's persistence and emotional support, Juan remained in school and finally was reassigned to regular classes. By this time, however, Juan's primary sources of satisfaction and his sustaining interests were care for his younger siblings and street games with his peers. At age 16, Juan left school, with little thereafter to constructively occupy his attention and energies.

After a few mild brushes with the law—minor vandalism and petty theft as a member of a street gang—Juan was convinced by his parish priest that the best way out of his increasingly restricted world was the military. At the age of 18, he volunteered and was accepted for active duty with the U.S. Army. Shortly after Juan's basic training, the country was at war in Korea. His unit was prepared for combat and, within a few months, Juan was on the front lines facing the enemy in a foreign land.

Wounded by a burst of shrapnel, Juan spent the remainder of his service time as a medical aide. Able to identify closely with the plight of young, wounded, and disabled peers whom he served, Juan developed an expertise at his job that gained him several merit commendations and an enviable promotion record. Much of his salary was sent home to assist the family. After one reenlistment Juan returned home, secured a hospital job in a nearby community,

and assumed full responsibility for his family's welfare. Largely because of this, Juan married relatively late in life. Juan is now a well-established medical technician, the father of three children, and a well-liked member of his community.

Juan's development represents a series of interactions. His physical-motor development (corner A) permitted him little gratification during childhood. Limited by this in play and street gang activity, he sharpened his personal-social (corner B) and cognitive-intellectual skills (corner C) to survive on the streets of his community. A school that required proficiency in English, however, caused difficulties in Juan's formal learning. As a result, his classroom cognitive-intellectual interactions were unsatisfactory. Strong emotional support from the home strengthened further his surprisingly healthy personal-social development. Apparently his interactions in this area were sufficient to carry him through many difficult times and provided a good background for his eventual life work in the helping professions. His story illustrates the resiliency and verve, as opposed to the vulnerability, of children and youth.

The case of Rebecca. Rebecca is the only child of wealthy and highly educated Jewish parents living in the northeastern United States. Her mother, heiress to a large family fortune of her own, went to private schools and graduated from an exclusive eastern women's college. Rebecca's father is a brilliant corporate lawyer whose work brings him into contact with representatives of many foreign countries. Both Rebecca and her mother have often accompanied him on business trips around the world. From birth, Rebecca has had what many might call "everything"—the adulation of her parents and relatives, a rich childhood environment, and a financially secure household. Her early schooling was largely tutorial, including private French lessons, piano and ballet instruction, and skiing. Beginning about the age of 6, Rebecca became interested in riding horses. This led to the construction on the large family estate of a stable for several thoroughbred horses. Rebecca's native abilities flourished within her privileged surroundings, enhanced both by her parents' demands and by their rewards for excellence in performance.

When Rebecca was thirteen years old, a small stable fire which she rushed to help extinguish burned the left side of her face and neck. Although the scars were minor, Rebecca soon began to brood about what she saw as her disfigurement. She gradually withdrew from social activities and spent large periods of time alone in her room or with her horses. Her mother, by this time heavily involved in philanthropic work, was concerned and cultivated an even deeper emotional relationship with Rebecca. After an extended trip abroad with both parents, Rebecca decided to try plastic surgery for her cosmetic "problem." While healing, Rebecca plunged into a variety of academic studies, again with tutors instead of in a regular school. She learned French and Chinese, and studied creative writing and advanced mathematics. By the time she reached 16, several of her short stories had been accepted for publication by popular magazines. Throughout her adolescence Rebecca seldom saw boys, or even spent much time with other girls. Her few social relationships centered around riding and music.

Despite the success of her surgery and her intellectual-cultural achievements, Rebecca continues to be dissatisfied with her body and mind. She is subject to occasional bouts of depression and social withdrawal that even her parents are unable to alter. On the whole, however, her adjustment seems basically sound. Rebecca, now 17, is pondering decisions about her future. By her own admission she does not feel comfortable yet with boys, partly because she has little past experience upon which to build. Also, because of her many talents and skills, she believes she threatened most of the boys she has met.

Rebecca, too, represents a complex of interactions. Her high potential for cognitive-intellectual development (corner C) was enhanced by a rich, supportive, but achievement-demanding environment. This dominant pattern of interaction was balanced somewhat by invigorating physical-motor activity (corner A). Her slight facial disfigurement during early adolescence was followed by a shift in personal-social interactions (corner B) that temporarily set back her development in this area. It seemed to tip the scales further in the direction of cognitive-intellectual interactions. The net result remains unclear. Rebecca is still in a critical period of her development. We can speculate, however, that Rebecca's advantaged upbringing and impressive talents promise a relatively full and balanced development over her total life span.

Principles of Interaction

These brief case descriptions illustrate three important principles about interaction. First, *all aspects of development interact* within the individual. Lyle, Juan, and Rebecca were each affected in unique ways by complex interactions of physical-motor, personal-social, and cognitive-intellectual developments. Some features displayed by these interactions are clearer than others, although we can not make hard and fast generalizations about behavior and development. These collective interactions reinforce the idea of a *whole* person. Second, the notion that *experiences have a cumulative effect over time* is implicit in these case descriptions. This is exemplified most clearly by Lyle's athletic development, Juan's history of supportive personal-social interactions, and Rebecca's strong cognitive-intellectual development. Third, individuals are *active forces in their own development*. In all three case studies, behavior and development seemed largely shaped by environmental encounters, but these encounters were not simply a matter of reacting. They also involved an *acting on* the environment, which serves to further affect development. For example, just as Lyle, Juan, and Rebecca were influenced by their parents, so did they in turn significantly influence their parents. And sometimes this mutual individual-environment influence occurs in unpredictable ways. For instance, few (if any) would have predicted success for Juan, given his unfortunate public school experience and deprived socioeconomic background.

We have chosen to illustrate principles of interaction by describing real persons. These data are anecdotal, not the outcome of systematic research. Anecdotal reports, of course, cannot be taken as proof of any point. However, both clinical inference and controlled experiments have documented a wide-ranging reciprocity of parent–offspring effects (Harper, 1975). Most obvious are the physiological changes brought about in mothers by pregnancy and, in turn, the importance of maternal health and nutrition for prenatal development. How parents move in and use their living space is affected by the birth of children. Caregiving practices can be influenced by the emotional responsiveness, temperament, or general activity level of children. Parents even talk differently to their young than they do to each other. Furthermore, children and youth affect the very culture in which they live. Political activism and consumer power are but two examples of how the young affect their elders and thus the broader culture of which everyone is a part.

The case descriptions not only make explicit the significance of reciprocity but also provide a springboard to additional important ideas about development. These ideas are grouped according to some basic differences and similarities in the development of children and youth. All are rooted in the underlying idea that the development of behavior does not occur in a vacuum but rather in a fluid setting in which the immediate face-to-face interactions of daily living are embedded.

DIVERSITY AND THE CONTEXT FOR DEVELOPMENT

Some Factors Producing Diversity

The social context in which different children develop, especially in a pluralistic society like the United States, is a combination of many diverse factors. First, and perhaps most obvious, is the *cultural heritage*—that pattern of values, beliefs, information, social customs, and communication patterns around which a group of people organizes its life and which provides ways of dealing with common life problems (McCandless, 1967). Our case studies illustrate only three of the great variety of cultural heritages that are part of American society. Lyle's has historically been dominant—white, Anglo-Saxon, Protestant, with roots in the puritanism of Britain and colonial America. Juan's cultural heritage is Hispanic, sharing the Spanish language, Catholicism, and a combination of Mediterranean and native Mexican life styles. Rebecca's derives from eastern Europe, Judaism, and a long-standing oppression that is paralleled in some ways by the more recent cultural history of black Americans. In all three, however, the cultural heritage has been diluted by time and generational changes to the point where something

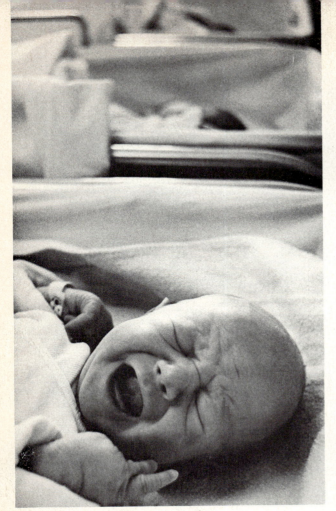

Photograph by Charles Harbutt, © 1965 Magnum Photos

Photo © Mimi Cotter

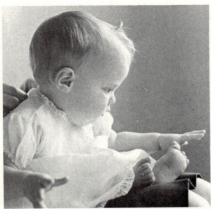

Photo by Suzanne Szasz

Photo by Suzanne Szasz

Photograph by Dorien Grunbaum

Kenneth Karp

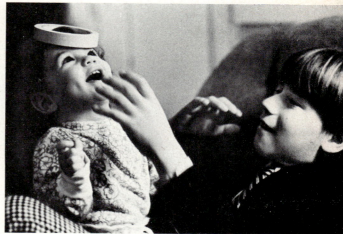

Fred Weiss

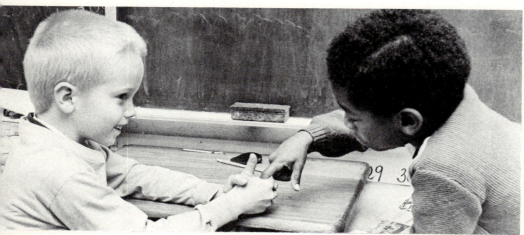

Joe Di Deo, NEA

Photo by Suzanne Szasz

Stephen H. Fritsch

Photo © Mimi Cotter

Photo by Suzanne Szasz

Photo by Suzanne Szasz

Photo © Mimi Cotter

Photo by Suzanne Szasz

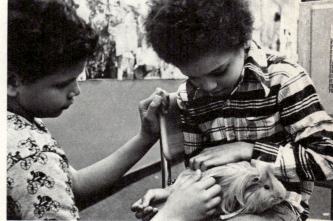

Kenneth Karp

Courtesy Moore Public Schools, Moore, Oklahoma

© George W. Gardner

"distinctly American" is shared by these individuals.

Second, these brief case descriptions indicate remarkable diversity in the *socioeconomic circumstances* of development, ranging from poverty and educational deprivation for Juan to wealth and educational opportunity for Rebecca. Countless studies of children and youth demonstrate the influence of socioeconomic status on nutrition, on general cognitive stimulation, on patterns of parental authority, and on other key aspects of development. Such studies will be sampled later in this book but for the moment, it is enough to say that differences in socioeconomic status usually mean differences in support systems and learning opportunities for children. Higher levels of parental income and education—the criteria for socioeconomic status—usually mean more favorable conditions for biological development and more alternatives for pursuing the individual goals and interests that are encouraged and rewarded in American society (Havighurst, 1976).

Third, the *family structures* into which these three individuals were born were also diverse. Family structures can be broadly conceived as nuclear, extended, or communal (see Glossary). By far the dominant form in American society is the nuclear, consisting of a mother, father, and their offspring living together in a single family dwelling. Our three individuals shared the nuclear family experience, although Juan early lost his father to death. Yet there are important structural variables within the nuclear family itself that may influence children's development. Examples include the presence or absence of a parent and its effect on children in that family; a child's birth order; and the number, sex, and spacing of other children in the family. These variables, their possible effects, and children's responses

to them are examined in later chapters of this book.

Fourth, and related to the first three factors, are *parental attitudes* toward emotional involvement with their children. Of the three individuals, Rebecca benefitted most from the love and support of *both* parents. Juan was sustained primarily by a strong positive maternal affection and by emotional intimacy with his sisters and brother. While Lyle was not actively rejected by his parents, neither was he warmly nurtured by either one. At least his physical needs were adequately met and there was no evidence of physical abuse by his parents. Unfortunately, even this cannot be said for many children in contemporary America. As we will see in Chapter 3, parental willingness and ability to provide overall support for their children's development are far from uniform in this era of presumed enlightenment about child-rearing.

Finally, although less clearly inferred from the bare essentials of the three case histories, the conditions for human development vary enormously over *time*. Lyle was born in 1906. On the whole, his childhood was less affected by the growth of large cities and technological change than was Rebecca's. Lyle's generation was too young to fight in the First World War, and too old, in many cases, for the Second. On the other hand, as Lyle and his peers reached young adulthood in the 1930s, they and their parents suffered the full impact of a severe economic depression.

According to recent analysis by Elder, the Depression (roughly from 1929 to 1936) was particularly stressful for families already poor or economically unstable (Elder, 1974). Lessened economic advancement through educational attainment, poorer adult health among children from deprived families of lower working class status, and a high value on family and child-rearing among men and women from deprived homes were among the most enduring effects of the Depression upon total life experiences.

Lyle and his family were not threatened with total financial catastrophe, but Lyle did face the dismal employment prospects of the Depression years, even for those like him who graduated from college. Lyle's immediate future and that of his peers were affected in important ways by the Depression. Although poverty has not disappeared, the overall living standard for a majority of American parents and their children has improved significantly since the 1930s. Barring another radical economic set-back, future generations may achieve economic security surpassing any since our republic was founded.

Surprisingly, increased wealth and luxury may also create or make worse certain hazards to psychological development. Robert Coles, for example, speaks of a mist of uncertainties, anxieties, and general uprootedness that surrounds children of the mobile rich (Coles, 1975). Parents of these children are described as aloof and trendy. They are said to depend on the acquisition of material goods for security, instead of on an ethic of sharing and commitment to common values. At worst, such parents may be caught in a web of despair which can too easily be transferred to their offspring, a despair thought to accompany the realization that affluence is no substitute for the more basic human values, including religion, that traditionally unite and are celebrated by members of a community.

These remarks are not intended to glorify poverty, even when it is accompanied by strong positive family and group ties and a shared identity. Juan's early upbringing, for example, was fraught with deep frustration and anxiety about basic subsistence. Material needs were generally unmet. Born in 1931, Juan's late childhood and early adolescence during the Second World War meant additional hardships because of food and other forms of rationing. Juan had to find his footing among the aftershocks of that war. Lyle entirely missed any military service, whereas Juan enlisted in 1949, shortly before the outbreak of the Korean conflict. Fortunately, Juan survived the Korean war and was able to develop his human potential in large part *because* of the army experience. Tragically, the same cannot be said for thousands of American youths, whose lives ended prematurely in wars.

Times have changed so drastically since the 1940s when Juan was growing up that it is hard for us to remember how widespread prejudice and discrimination against ethnic and racial minorities were in America. In many states, laws enforced segregation in public accommodations and in the public schools. Many Blacks and Hispanics were effectively prevented from voting. Bilingual education, based on the concept that children should get their early education in school in their mother tongue, was almost unheard of. The public schools tended to be rigid and inflexible, using intelligence tests based on standards derived from white, middle-class youths to arbitrarily classify many minority group children (including those who, like Juan, were not native speakers of English) as retarded or otherwise uneducable. Higher education was inaccessible for most minority youths.

Yet, despite all these social inequities, Juan fared well, as he is the first to admit. His father, for example, had no formal schooling at all in Mexico, was never able to support himself or his family for long, and died of a disease that has been almost eliminated in America. Juan, overcoming early deprivations, has become a self-supporting and self-respecting member of his community, able to take care of his family and to provide for his children far greater opportunities than were ever available to him.

Rebecca's developmental history is still unfolding. Like many other members of her generation, she was born to relative luxury and to a comparatively permissive and tolerant set of standards about the rights of women and of minorities. Even for those born in less favorable economic circumstances, there are more opportunities today for higher education than ever before. And America is at peace, so the anxieties and risks of war are not immediately present.

Social Change and Diversity

It is tempting to believe that the conditions for human development have been continuously improving and will go on doing so. We may think, for example, of medical advances and social welfare programs that have brought better nutrition and health care to many. At this writing, the average life expectancy for a newborn American infant is just over 72 years of age. The fatal, or crippling, effects of such diseases as poliomyelitis have been virtually eliminated. We have new ideas about humankind's relations to the physical environment, about racial relations, and about personal freedom and liberation.

Despite these improvements, recent surveys show that a majority of American adults are pessimistic about the future quality of life for their children (Campbell, 1975). The psychologist Urie Bronfenbrenner shares this pessimism and has written extensively about what he calls the "unmaking of the American child" (1970). Buttressed by some evidence from research and by personal observations, he questions the extent and sincerity of American society's commitment to bringing up children. Bronfenbrenner contends that parents and social institutions lack a master plan for promoting positive human development, including moral education. This lack has been intensified by rapid urbanization, technocracy, and physical and social mobility. Fathers work outside the home, at jobs largely unseen and ill-understood by children. Mothers have increasingly joined the work force. Added to this is a mushrooming divorce rate, creating hundreds of thousands of single-parent homes. Family instability and work commitments mean that parents no longer spend as much time as formerly with their children. Neglected children idle away excessive amounts of time watching television. Prompted by a system of age-grading in schools and segregated residential neighborhoods, children also are said to have become dominated by peer group influences. This, in combination with a general child-rearing philosophy of permissiveness and violence portrayed by the mass media, intensifies antisocial tendencies among the young. Adults in turn condemn the young for these destructive tendencies, thus widening the conflict between the generations. At worst, adults have abdicated their responsibilities for child rearing and seem unwilling to marshall available resources to turn the tide. Thus, the root cause of deterioration in interpersonal relations and in what is needed for personal-social development is a chaotic and uncoordinated, if not harmful, approach to child-rearing.

Not everyone agrees with this analysis. For example, R. T. Fruehling claims a different origin for these allegedly distorted patterns of social behavior (Fruehling, 1971). Instead of parental neglect and unchecked amoral influences, our problems are seen as the outgrowth of a core value that pervades American society as a whole: egocentric individualism or egocentric self-reliance. Competitiveness and aggressiveness are its principal attributes. Fruehling argues that children learn what they are taught: success in American society demands a continued search for ways to beat the competition. Little room is left for personal honesty, genuine respect for others, or helping relationships.

At least four issues are involved in this debate about social changes and human development. First is the extent to which either Bronfenbrenner or those who share similar views have accurately described various indicators of serious social problems in our society. If these descriptions are accurate and the indicators are valid, the second issue is whether the underlying causes have been correctly identified. The third issue is what, if anything, we should do about these "problems" within the context for human development, And the fourth issue is our capacity for change. Do we presently have the resources and technical know-how to establish more desirable conditions for development? For some, including Bronfenbrenner, the answer is affirmative. We shall consider some of these proposals for change throughout this book, but we do so with less alarm, more suspended judgment, and fewer broad generalizations about social problems and human development than does Bronfenbrenner.

SOME COMMONALITIES IN HUMAN DEVELOPMENT

Thus far, we have pointed to five basic factors that contribute to diversity in the social context for development: cultural heritage, socioeconomic status, family structure, family emotional climate, and time. Our broad themes have been diversity and change in the context for development. How diversity and contextual changes affect human development and how they are linked to individual differences in development are the core questions for the research psychologist. The methods and procedures available for this inquiry are complex and not altogether satisfactory but they can help us to know more about commonalities in the development of individual children and youth (Riegel, 1973).

Several of these commonalities are illustrated in our case histories of Lyle, Juan, and Rebecca. First, within their respective psychological worlds, all three of these individuals strived for competence in mastering the environment. Some psychologists (such as White, 1959) argue that such *competence striving* is the most fundamental human motive. Within American society, this striving is given direction by certain core values such as independence and personal achievement. In other societies, different basic values shape the direction and form taken by competence striving. Regardless of its form, striving is not without complications. For instance, all of our three individuals have encountered unique adversities and conflicts. But like a majority of human beings, they have demonstrated a capability for continued development without being overcome by damaging social-emotional problems. Unfortunately this cannot be said for some children and youths who, because of genetic defects, severe deprivation of physical and emotional needs, distorted learnings, or some combination of these, show the harmful effects of development going wrong. We examine some of these problems later in this book.

A second related commonality is that each individual encountered a set of tasks to be mastered at certain pivotal steps on the ladder of development. In other words, physical maturation, cultural pressures, and personal values and goals combine at each age to define specific problems to be solved (Havighurst, 1972). In the earliest years, such problems include learning to walk, talk, and control the body's excretory functions. They also include learning basic styles of human interaction, the differences between the sexes, and basic concepts of social and physical reality.

Problems older children must cope with include school, getting along with their peers, and developing thinking skills and concepts of moral conduct. Adolescents face key choice points involving sexuality, vocational planning, more advanced moral development, and emancipation from their parents. These problems were resolved differently by Lyle and Juan; Rebecca is still coming to terms with them.

These problems can be stated formally as *developmental tasks* that arise "at or about a certain period in the life of the individual, successful achievement of which leads to well being, positive adjustment, and success with later tasks, while failure leads to unhappiness, disapproval by society, and difficulty with later tasks" (Havighurst, 1972, p. 2). The developmental task idea reinforces the principles that all aspects of development interact and that experiences have cumulative effects.

As developmental tasks arise and are solved with varying degrees of success, all children and youth come to perceive and think about themselves in characteristic ways, just as did Lyle, Juan, and Rebecca. This represents a third basic commonality in human experience: the development of self-knowledge of ourselves as persons with strengths, limitations, and individual tastes (McCandless, 1977.) This self-knowledge generally is shown by a set of expectancies about how well a person can accomplish tasks and solve problems.

Self-knowledge and self-expectancies are accompanied by the development of self-evaluations. We all develop subjective evaluations about our self-worth, from positive to negative. Such evaluations taken together reflect our general self-regard, or self-esteem.

Self-knowledge, expectancies, and esteem make up the *self-concept*. The self-concept summarizes the net effect of total developmental experience on the individual and at the same time can serve as a major influence on further development. Juan, for example, achieved sufficient self-knowledge and esteem outside the classroom to continue the development of his human potential. Had he not, quite possibly Juan would be less personally fulfilled, perhaps even dependent upon society for basic subsistence. A cycle of positive or negative self-concept development illustrates the basic theme of interactionism in human development.

Competency striving, developmental tasks, self-concept learning—these are but a few factors of development that seem common to all children and youth. Still other commonalities, not explicit in our case history descriptions, can be mentioned. In fact, it may even be preferable to think that human beings are more alike than different. One prominent personality theorist (Sullivan, 1951), for example, has maintained that a critical factor for healthy emotional development is for children to discover within an intimate, trustworthy peer relationship that they are not unique in their human apprehensions, insecurities, puzzlements, and hungers. In a phrase, we can and should come to validate our subjective, common human experience by consensus with other people. Such may be part of the appeal of the group therapy experiences now so widespread in American society.

More concretely, it seems clear that most, if not all, children and youth travel a course of predictable stages in physical, linguistic, and mental development (Part III). And, in terms of developmental *processes*, children and youth are fundamentally subject to the joint effects of maturation and learning. We now proceed to Chapter 2, in which these basic processes are discussed in greater detail, together with the methods used by psychologists to chart the outcomes of this interaction.

SUMMARY

Development has been defined as change through time toward a higher degree of differentiation and complexity in behavior. As a process, development can be thought of as interaction. Two related ideas about interaction have been stressed. First, a continuous interaction of all major aspects of development gives a shape to the individual's behavior at any point in time. These major aspects of development include the physical-motor, the personal-social, and the cognitive-intellectual. Second, the changing individual continuously interacts with the environment to affect and be affected by major social forces such as parents, peers, schooling, and the mass media. A schematic diagram has been presented to symbolize these interactions. Case study material has been presented to illustrate further principles of interaction and development and especially to emphasize the notion that individuals are important factors in their own development. Though these basic principles apply to all persons, individual differences in development are widely observed. Important sources of diversity in development, such as the culture, the socioeconomic environment, family structure, parent-child relationships, and the passage of time, have been stressed. But though individuals can be remarkably diverse in their development, they also share basic commonalities. Competence striving, developmental tasks, and self-concept learning are but a few of many such commonalities to be explored at various points throughout this book.

REFERENCES

Bijou, W. S. *Child development: The basic stage of early childhood.* Englewood Cliffs, N.J.: Prentice-Hall, 1976.

Bronfenbrenner, U. *Two worlds of childhood.* New York: Russell Sage, 1970.

Campbell, A. *The perceived quality of life.* New York: Russell Sage, 1975.

Coles, R. The cold, tough world of the affluent family. *Psychology Today,* 1975, *9* (6), 67–77.

Elder, G. H., Jr. *Children of the great depression: Social change in life experience.* Chicago: University of Chicago Press, 1974.

Freuhling, R. T. Socialization, contract, and interpersonal relations. *Phi Delta Kappan,* 1971, *53,* 622.

Harper, L. V. The scope of offspring effects: From caregiver to culture. *Psychological Bulletin,* 1975, *82,* 784–801.

Havighurst, R. *Developmental tasks and education* (Rev. ed.). New York: McKay, 1972.

Havighurst, R. The relative importance of social class and ethnicity in human development. *Human Development,* 1976, *19,* 56–64.

McCandless, B. R. *Children: Behavior and development.* New York: Holt, Rinehart and Winston, 1967.

Riegel, K. F. Time and change in the development of the individual and society. In H. W. Reese (ed.), *Advances in child development and behavior* (vol. 7). New York: Academic Press, 1972.

Sullivan, H. S. *The interpersonal theory of psychiatry.* New York: Norton, 1953.

White, R. Motivation reconsidered: The concept of competence. *Psychological Review,* 1959, *66,* 297–333.

chapter 2

The language of development

A first and often frustrating task for students of human development is to learn the vocabulary of developmental psychology. All specialized fields or endeavors have their own unique vocabularies to enable those in the field to communicate clearly, efficiently, and precisely. This is as true of medicine, law, football, or farming as it is of developmental psychology. Such special vocabularies ("appendix" or "touchback") also serve to describe phenomena for which the common language is unsuitable or a common language term does not exist.

Developmental psychologists, unfortunately, do not always agree about the exact meanings of terms and concepts. Different psychologists may mean very different things when they talk about "intelligence," "cognition," "creativity," "anxiety," or "adjustment." Though universal agreement among developmental psychologists about their own professional vocabulary is sometimes lacking, we attempt in this book to provide conceptual meanings that are generally accepted within our discipline.

In one sense, we have already confronted the language of development issue. In Chapter 1, for example, the meanings of "development" and "interactionism" were discussed. We can now delve further into those concepts important for understanding the nature and scope of developmental psychology. We begin where Chapter 1 ended: a consideration of the interacting effects of maturation and learning in producing development.

MATURATION

Maturation refers to developmental changes that are extensively if not totally controlled by genetic or hereditary factors, including species-specific behavior. For example, all normal children, if exposed to other human beings who talk, learn to talk; but no other species possesses this elaborate formal language. All normal English hen sparrows build untidy nests of twigs, straw, and feathers, and lay brown speckled eggs in them. Few, if any, human beings build untidy nests of twigs, straw, and feathers; and no human beings lay brown speckled eggs. Instead, we apply our species-unique intelligence to a complex network of personal and collective problems. It is our genetic nature to develop successively higher, more complex and integrated patterns of neurological functioning for this purpose. This functioning, although affected by environmental

factors, is essentially the outcome of genetic action.

Genetic Forces at Work

The importance of genetic make-up to one's life experiences should not be underestimated. We had some inklings of this in our case history individuals. Lyle's body build and motor competence facilitated his development into an excellent athlete, a development that was significant for many of his personal-social interactions. Juan's comparatively small size and slow rate of physical maturation established for him a quite different set of learning experiences. It is even possible that genetic phenomena contributed to his second language learning difficulty. Certainly among the most important ways in which genetics affects development is by establishing our biological sex. The difference in Rebecca's physical structure creates for Rebecca a cycle of interactions that contrast with Lyle's and Juan's.

Gender-related interactions associated with differences in personal-social and cognitive-intellectual development are discussed in Chapter 9. We can note here, however, that the genetic underpinnings of gender go beyond physical structure; to a large extent they also determine glandular action. This means differences in both the regulation and type of hormonal activity. Hormonal activity, in turn, significantly influences behavior. For example, the class of male hormones called androgens are associated with aggressiveness, while the estrogens, or female hormones, are associated with maternal behavior and are usually at a peak following the birth of a child.

Hormonal factors are also involved with growth in height, weight, and bone ossification—a process of development from the flexible limbs of infancy to the brittle bones of old age. Genetic forces ultimately act to affect total life span.

Barring accidents and given equivalent health, physical care, and nutrition, Simon may die of natural causes at 65, Garfunkel at 85. Such different time-tables may be drastically modified by environmental variables—nutrition, health care, disease, accident, and perhaps even geographic climate and psychological stress. Biological maturational factors, however, seem less responsive to environmental effects than do social and psychological factors.

In the extreme, genetic factors can unalterably distort the normal pattern of development (Robinson & Robinson, 1976). At birth, Danny, now age 6, was born with a peculiarly shaped head and face. His head was flat on the backside, his eyes slanted upward, and his ears and nose were unusually small. Compared to normal infants, his neck was short and broad and his hands were square with short fingers, especially the little fingers. An odd spacing between the first and second toes of his feet, mottled skin, and generally "floppy" muscle tone added to a picture of abnormality. Danny was correctly diagnosed as having Down's syndrome. His developmental future is likely to be somewhat better now than it might have been in the past, but, in general, the quality of Danny's maturation and learning will not be as desirable as we would hope. His sexual development will probably be delayed or incomplete. His personal-social and cognitive-intellectual development have already been marked by deficiencies, and this pattern is likely to continue. Danny's life expectancy is also lower than normal, partly because of greater susceptibility to disease and especially because of a congenital heart problem. Danny's parents, by now adjusted to Danny's condition, recognize that his life chances are best enhanced by careful supervision and specially designed learning experiences.

Down's syndrome is but one of a number of developmental deviations about which more will be said later in this book. The syndrome has a genetic cause, so Danny's example raises the issue of how genetic forces work. Many of these workings still are cloaked by mystery and space limitations prevent a full, technical discussion, so we will review only their most basic aspects.

Basic Concepts of Genetic Influence

The essence of genetic influence is contained in deoxyribonucleic acid, or DNA. The molecules of this chemical substance harbor genetic information in the form of a code carried by the genes, those thousands of submicroscopic structures whose vast number of combinations determines individual human uniqueness. The genes, in turn, are carried in the chromosomes, microscopic rod-shaped bodies that are the active agents in human reproductive cells. Human reproductive cells include 23 pairs of chromosomes. Our biological gender is determined by one pair of sex chromosomes, symbolized as XX in the female and XY in the male. The remaining 22 chromosome pairs, called autosomes, are common to both sexes. At the time of human conception, the male sperm and female egg, having earlier undergone a special kind of cell division, each bring one chromosome from each of the 23 pairs to the union. This union makes possible an extremly large number of gene combinations, but the newly formed unit—the zygote—again has the normal complement of 46 chromosomes. The zygote, of course, quickly undergoes cellular transformation to develop into embryonic, then fetal form. If all goes well, a healthy infant will be born in roughly 280 days. Whether the infant is male or female will depend on the twenty-third chromosome combination.

The mother has transmitted only an X chromosome; the father has contributed either an X or a Y chromosome. An XX or XY union will establish femaleness or maleness, respectively.

Technically speaking, environmental influences on development, for example, nutrition and general health of the mother, begin at the moment of conception. It is therefore difficult to separate the relative effects of heredity (nature) and environment (nurture) on development even this early in the human life span. There are, however, many distinct human traits determined exclusively by genetic inheritance. Most of these traits are physical or biochemical—hair and eye color, bone structure, blood type, and male baldness, for example. Strictly hereditary defects can also be observed, such as glaucoma and hemophilia, anomalies of the eye and the blood-clotting function, respectively.

In contrast, other traits or defects can be genetically determined, though not inherited. This means that chromosomal balance is somehow upset in the process of cell division and reunion. Danny's Down's syndrome, for example, was not inherited. No history of this developmental deviation could be found in either side of his parents' families. His Down's syndrome is a genetic anomaly created by a chromosomal aberration, specifically an extra set of genes in the number 21 chromosome carried by the female ovarian egg. This has the effect of creating a third 21 chromosome, upsetting the normal balance for chromosomal distribution at time of conception. The result is a form of mutation that unfortunately limits rather than catalyzes the potential for human development. Certain cases of directly inherited Down's syndrome have been observed, though they are extremely rare. But Danny's case serves to distinguish between strictly hereditary and other ge-

netically determined human characteristics (Reed, 1975). In both cases, the fundamental nature of internal growth forces is at issue. How these gene-governed forces influence behavior is a fundamental question for the discipline called *behavior genetics*.

Behavior Genetics and Human Development

Behavior genetics can contribute to our understanding of development in three ways (Thompson & Wilde, 1973). First, it attempts to estimate accurately the extent of hereditary or genetic effects on behavior. Selective breeding studies with animals are examples of attempts to achieve this goal. It has been shown, for instance, that strains of bright and dull maze-learning rats can be bred gradually from a base population by careful selection of the fastest and slowest learners for mating with comparably fast or slow litter mates. Selectively controlled mating from subsequent litters continues as the strains begin to become more differentiated. Markedly different strains of learners are eventually created, demonstrating a strong hereditary component in maze-learning ability. Equivalent controlled human studies have never been possible, but this has not prevented researchers from developing elaborate means for estimating the significance of genetic factors in, for example, human intelligence (Chapter 8).

A second contribution of behavior genetics is the identification of specific genetic, biochemical, and physiological factors that mediate, or provide a setting for, particular effects on behavior. To continue our earlier illustration, a researcher might concentrate upon locating the immediate biochemical effects of genes known to be primarily responsible for fast or slow learning, high or low intelligence, and so on. Ultimately, such information might have implications for techniques of environmental control over body chemistry. At this writing, much is being said about the relationship of genetically influenced biochemical substances to motivation for learning and achievement (Kasal, 1974).

Third, behavior geneticists analyze how genetic factors are associated with the behavioral characteristics of entire populations and how such associations both mirror and affect evolutionary changes in those populations. This geneticist's goal is most practically pursued through animal studies. But many ideas from animal research generate parallel questions about human development and the evolution of our species. With rats, for example, it may be shown that the genetic components of maze-learning behavior are important for survival in some environmental circumstances. This might lead us to ask if there are certain human hereditary or genetic factors common to all, or only to some, forms of human intelligence or to inquire whether evolutionary mechanisms influence variations in human intelligence that are manifest in group differences. These are but two of a host of provocative questions which emerge from behavior genetics.

Genetic influence on behavior is not limited to the time of conception, of birth, or of any other single period in the human life span. As one authority puts it:

Developmental processes are subject to continuing genetic influence, and different genes are effective at different times—the timing of gene action for example is shown by the late age of onset of Huntington's chorea [a rare, heritable trait characterized by neural degeneration and accompanying mental-emotional pathology in adulthood]. The genes responsible for determining blood group, on the other hand, appear to have this effect early in fetal development, and [this]

remains unaltered throughout life. Yet another characteristic, hemoglobin type, changes very dramatically early in life, but remains stabilized thereafter ... [there is also] evidence for genetic control of growth rate and deceleration of growth rate, but not for length at birth (McClearn, 1970, p. 61).

Our knowledge about the workings of developmental genetics and its unequivocal effects on human behavior is meagre. Yet there is evidence that along with affecting the timing of developmental events, patterns of physical development and motor coordination are characteristic of families across generations (McClearn, 1970). This has special relevance to corner A of our interaction model, physical-motor development. Developmental genetic processes are also suggested by increasing degrees of resemblance in intellectual performance between parents and their progeny during the early years of life (Honzik, 1957). At this point, however, we find ourselves in a wide, grey area between heredity and learning.

The grey area between genetics and learning for cognitive-intellectual development, corner C of our interaction model, seems even wider when we consider corner B, personal-social development. Especially compared to corner A, physical-motor development, the role of maturational processes in personal-social development seems less direct. Yet some authorities (for example, Gottesman, 1965) argue for a strong heritable component in "personality" development along two major lines. One, *neuroticism*, is a general nervousness or fearfulness. The other is a general tendency to direct one's attention and interest outwardly or inwardly, to conduct oneself with relative ease or difficulty in social relationships, and to be open or secretive in thought and action. These tendencies are summarized by the terms *extraversion–introversion*. Together with neuroticism, they are thought to account for a considerable degree of variation in human personal-social behavior (Wiggins, 1968). We cannot be sure how much of this variation is genetically based; learning experiences can also contribute strongly to the development of these behaviors.

Questions about possible genetic programming in human behavior have been intensified recently by a growing interest in the science of ethology (Eibl-Eibesfeldt, 1975). Ethology is a biologically oriented discipline concerned with the comparative study of behavior across all animal species, including the human. Ethologists seek to identify inborn skills, drive mechanisms, dispositions to learn, and adaptation patterns common to various species that are relatively uninfluenced by individual experience. Our earlier reference to the English sparrow's nesting behavior is one example. Others include animals' warning and distress calls, curiosity behavior, play, imprinting, and territoriality.

The relevance of ethology to human behavior is perhaps most specifically marked by still more recent developments in the emerging and closely related discipline called *sociobiology* (Barash, 1977). Sociobiology confines its study to the biological basis of all forms of *social* behavior across species. Its purpose is to establish general principles of the evolution and biology of uniquely social behavior, again with an eye toward discovering patterns of potentials for such behavior that are "built in" to the heredity of a whole species. For example, humans everywhere—regardless of cultural membership—seem to use the same facial configurations to express basic emotions such as joy, fear, perplexity, and disgust. Likewise, humans everywhere show a strong tendency for social organization and have developed elaborate kinship rules for this purpose.

Sociobiology may ultimately clarify the exact construction of humankind's inherent social nature and distinguish distinctively evolutionary social traits from those that are determined more strongly by idiosyncratic learning experiences. From this, a more powerful science of human development and behavior may result.

We should not underestimate the influence of genetic effects and maturational processes upon development, nor should we underestimate the ability of learning experience to channel and even modify these effects. Even genetically equivalent or similar human beings, such as identical or fraternal twins, can develop dramatically different skills, interests, and life styles depending upon their unique learnings. We now consider some basic concepts of human learning that psychologists find useful in accounting for such differences.

LEARNING

We have indicated that maturation refers to any aspect of development that occurs independent of specific learning or practice (Ausubel & Sullivan, 1970). In contrast, learning refers to relatively enduring behavior changes that come about from experience, including practice. (Behavior changes caused by disease, drugs, fatigue, and the like are excluded from the domains of both learning and maturation.) The experience we call learning takes many forms. For example, arranged experiences, such as formal school lessons or specific tutoring in skills, are one way to provide learning. Other learning results from unarranged experiences, such as free play and random verbal interchange.

Learning also varies with the tasks involved. Some learning is academic, such as reading a book at grade level;

other learning is social, such as resolving a conflict about rule infractions during a game. Still other learning is perceptual-motor, such as learning to draw a triangle, make a dress for a doll, or catch a ball with a mitt. And yet other learning primarily involves feelings or emotions, such as a child's fear of monsters or love of animals. Some learning requires large amounts of time, for example, becoming proficient at piano-playing. Other learning can occur quickly in a single experience. Burning your fingers once over a flaming match, for example, is usually sufficient to learn a permanent avoidance response to open flame.

Beyond such dramatic experiences, much learning usually depends upon some combination of three factors: a person's maturational status, an opportunity to learn, and practice or repeated experience that is in some way personally satisfying or rewarding. Walking is a good example. Regardless of opportunity and practice, few if any 6-month-old children can learn to walk. Given only a little opportunity and practice, the average 15-month-old learns to walk quickly and well. Maturation, opportunity, and practice enter into successful learning of such diverse things as toilet training, bicycle riding, violin playing, and a foreign language. On the other hand, learning to avoid mother when she is angry seems to be less a matter of maturation and more a matter (from a very early age) of repeated experience.

Nonetheless, almost all behavior requires both "raw material that grows and matures" (maturation) and experience of one sort or another; both *readiness* and *opportunity* are needed. Readiness means possession of all the prerequisite skills and attitudes necessary for the mastery of a task at a new level of difficulty (Bruner, 1960). A fifth-grader's successful learning of fractions, for example, demands application of prior basic arithmetical skills as well as sufficient motivation to attend to the details of this more advanced task. Experiencing pleasant consequences for increasingly accurate and efficient mathematics responses will probably strengthen the new learning. These consequences may range from special rewards or privileges through praise from others to the simple satisfaction of doing something well. Such consequences are thus said to reinforce learning, or more accurately, to affect the performance of behavior, from which we infer that learning has occurred.

Given these general introductory comments we can move to a more technical discussion of learning and its role in development. The basis for our discussion is provided by two fundamental ideas. The first is implicit in the preceding few paragraphs: there are different kinds of learning, the effectiveness of which may be altered by the conditions under which the learning occurs. The second idea is that these different kinds of learning result in various complex and integrated learning outcomes, such as cognitive-intellectual, personal-social, and physical-motor skills. Both ideas are tied to our broader theme of interaction. Learning itself is a process of interaction during which an enormous amount of information from the environment is processed, or acted upon in some way by the learner.

Basic Concepts of Learning

Much, it not most, learning by children and youth occurs in natural social situations such as the home, peer group, and school. Important aspects of language acquisition, motor skills, social values and beliefs, and skills of social interaction are but a few examples. To account for these behavior changes, psychologists have developed a cluster of social-learning concepts based on stimulus-response, or S-R psychology (Baldwin, 1973).

Most simply, S-R psychology holds that the basic unit of analysis for any learned behavior is the association between stimulus and response. A stimulus can be defined as any object or event that arouses one or more of the senses; a response is any resultant activity, whether physiological, neural, or motor (Reese, 1976). In short, a stimulus activates, or excites; a response is a reaction to excitation. Some responses to stimuli occur automatically; others must be learned by repeated association. Examples of the former, often called reflexive or involuntary responses, include the startle, knee-jerk, eye blink, salivation, and galvanic skin responses. Responses over which we have voluntary control, but which nonetheless become associated with and are emitted in the presence of stimuli, comprise by far the largest part of such complex learning as reading and playing a musical instrument. In these two examples, printed symbols—configurations of letters and notes, respectively—serve as stimuli; our performance consists of a complex chain of responses that originates "inside the head."

Learning by Conditioning

We can further explore the details of the S–R model of learning through the following examples of learning in a social context. Of necessity, they are oversimplified for purposes of illustration. We begin by presenting the notions of classical and instrumental conditioning.[1]

Classical conditioning. Alan, a sensitive 18-month-old, is playing on the front porch of his home under the watchful eye of his mother. Suddenly, a large yellow cat appears on the porch. Alan, who

[1] The terms *classical* and *instrumental* conditioning are often used interchangeably with the terms *respondent* and *operant* conditioning, respectively.

has never before seen such an animal, reaches out to grab its tail. At this instant Alan's mother, very much afraid of cats, shouts a sudden loud "No!" Alan startles and whimpers as the cat runs away.

The next morning this incident is repeated, but in addition to being startled by his mother's shout, Alan is taken roughly from the porch and deposited in his playpen, where he cries for several minutes. Later the same day, the cat returns while Alan is playing in his sand box. As Alan reaches for the cat, the ever-watchful mother again shouts a warning. This time, however, Alan is spanked with the cat in full view. The spanking, thinks his mother, will teach Alan a lesson. As a well-thrown rock dispatches the cat, Alan retreats crying, to the safety of his home.

The following day, while in the front yard with his father, the cat comes bolting into view. Alan responds by crying and turns toward the house. Alan's father is puzzled by this behavior. Shortly thereafter, Alan's grandmother visits, bringing gifts for the whole family. Alan's present is a stuffed, yellow dog. Upon receipt of the toy, Alan drops it to the floor and begins to cry, much to his grandmother's dismay.

In this example, the aversive shouting and spanking behavior by Alan's mother represent stimuli whose net effect is an experience of pain for Alan. His startle, whimpering, and crying behavior are responses elicited unconditionally by such aversive stimuli. As these painful experiences are associated in space and time (contiguity) with the yellow cat, this initially neutral object (animal) has the effect of eliciting Alan's crying and general avoidance responses. Thus we say that the cat has become a conditioned stimulus for Alan's crying. The cat's salient physical properties—a small, four-legged, furry, yellow animal—are embodied in grandmother's present of a stuffed dog. Presumably because of this perceptual similarity to the cat, the toy dog is now capable of affecting Alan's behavior in a similar way. If so, this is an example of *stimulus generalization*: the general properties of the conditioned stimulus have been further and more broadly extended to similar, previously neutral stimuli.

Alan has been conditioned. The process whereby reflexive or automatic responses such as pain are associated with and eventually elicited by previously neutral responses is *classical conditioning*, so called because it was the first kind of conditioning to be studied and described. Our emotional responses to the environment are for the most part "learned" through this kind of conditioning. As one authority (Ringness, 1976) observed, children may "learn" stage fright in school as the result of being mistreated while attempting to speak in front of class. Others may develop a fearfulness about physical education from being forced to compete (and failing to do so successfully) with more competent peers. And the painful frustration of academic failure in attempting to master arithmetic is common. Again, painful emotional reactions are paired or associated with initially neutral stimuli in such cases. Of course, classically conditioned learning can be pleasant as well, as in an infant coming to respond with comfort and joy to a caregiver who has been associated with gentle, soothing attention to the infant's basic physical needs.

Instrumental conditioning. A second, more prevalent, form of conditioning is also crucial for an understanding of social learning principles. Consider this example of *instrumental conditioning*.

The parents of a precocious 14-month-old infant, Susan, are entertaining dinner guests. Anxious to make a good impression, they have taken great pains to see that the dinner party proceeds smoothly, and Susan is placed on display next to the dinner table but is securely strapped in her high chair. As the dinner progresses, Susan becomes very restless and suddenly emits a loud shriek. To keep her occupied and quiet, her mother immediately pops a mint candy into Susan's mouth. After the mint is eaten, Susan again becomes restless and emits a second shriek. Again, a mint candy finds its way into Susan's mouth. This pattern is repeated several times until Susan's mother determines that this shrieking dinner partner must be removed and placed in her nursery.

Susan's learning experience differs in important ways from Alan's. A pivotal event was her shrieking response, apparently a random, yet nonetheless voluntary event. Immediately *following* her shriek (response), a mint candy (stimulus) was delivered into her mouth. The presentation of this stimulus depended, or was contingent upon, the occurrence of Susan's response. Thus we can say that her shrieking was instrumental in gaining for her an apparently satisfying consequence. Subsequently, her shrieking became more and more frequent — the rate increased. When a response frequency is maintained or increased by presenting a contingent stimulus, we say that the response has been positively reinforced.

Instrumental learning is not restricted to primitive responses such as shrieking. It may occur *any* time an individual does something and gets something for having so behaved. It is not necessary for a reward or reinforcer to follow an action every time it occurs, but at least occasional reinforcement may be necessary to maintain a response. If a response, once learned, is never thereafter reinforced, a child may no longer volunteer the action. If this happens, the behavior has been *extinguished*.

Deliberate extinction may be desirable for annoying or unacceptable behavior. For example, few if any parents relish their children's temper tantrums. To extinguish such behavior would require that absolutely no reinforcement accompany a tantrum. Parents seem often to give their tantrumming children much attention, or wearily submit to their child's tantrum demands, thus inadvertently increasing the probability that tantrum behavior will reoccur. Inadvertent positive reinforcement is also seen in Susan's case. She was conditioned to shriek during the dinner party occasion; apparently the candy rewarded her for doing so.

Susan's example illustrates that her mother was also being instrumentally conditioned. The mother's voluntary response of delivering candy was followed by a cessation of shrieking, if only temporarily. In effect, the mother was being reinforced or rewarded by the cessation of Susan's presumably disruptive shrieking. But in the mother's case, the nature of the reward is different and demonstrates what is called *negative reinforcement*. This form of reinforcement occurs when a voluntary response (in this instance, candy delivery) has the effect of *removing* or attenuating an existing and usually unpleasant stimulus. In other words, if an antecedent stimulus, when removed from a situation following the occurrence of an instrumental response, increases the probability of response reoccurrence, we have negative reinforcement.

Susan at the dinner party illustrates mutual reinforcement, albeit in different forms. Susan quickly learned the relationship of her behavior to the consequences and thereby gained a form of control over her immediate environment. Just as the environment affects children, so do they affect their environment.

Edibles are but one of many classes of reinforcers that can affect the frequency and quality of voluntary or instrumental responses. Other classes, including social reinforcers (such as praise and recognition) and informational feedback (gaining knowledge about the correctness of a response), are important in naturalistic learning. Consistent with the idea of competence striving discussed in Chapter 1, the positive affect or feeling that comes from doing something well is among the most powerful of all reinforcements. The influence of reinforcement is affected by many factors, including the age of a learner, what is being learned, and the social context for learning.

The concept of reinforcement reminds us that much human behavior is a function of its consequences. This leads many psychologists to consider carefully both the kinds and the schedules of reinforcement to which children and youth are exposed in order to understand and modify any given behavior pattern. By kinds of reinforcement, we mean the many consequent events that have demonstrable effects on behavior: *consumables* (food and drink), *manipulables* (toys), *visual and auditory stimuli* (pictures and music), *social stimuli* (attention from others), and even *high strength behavior* (Bijou & Sturges, 1969; Premack, 1965). High strength behavior is that which occurs naturally or preferentially with high frequency (as compared to other behaviors) and can be used to reinforce behavior with lower natural frequencies. Algernon, age 10, may be observed to skateboard frequently but to infrequently pick up his clothes, books, and other personal items littered throughout his home. Skateboarding, then, could be used as an effective reinforcer to increase his cleanup behavior, should his parents so elect. The method of reinforcing low strength with high strength behavior is often referred to as "Grandma's Rule": "First the potatoes and gravy, then the ice cream!"

Schedules of reinforcement refer to

the extent to which reinforcement occurs continuously or intermittently. Reinforcement of a given response each and every time it occurs is a continuous schedule. Many laboratory studies indicate that the acquisition of new responses is more rapid or efficient when reinforcement is continuous (Ferster & Skinner, 1957). Teachers, for example, are advised to reinforce childrens' new learning continuously, especially in its early stages. Apart from carefully planned situations, however, this tactic is rarely possible. More typical of real-life situations is *intermittent* reinforcement, in which a reinforcing stimulus occurs only periodically. In some cases, intermittent reinforcement is determined by time intervals, such as receiving a salary on a weekly or monthly basis. In other cases, it is the number of responses that determine how reinforcement is scheduled, such as the familiar "piecework" method of payment in industrial settings. In fact, psychologists have described up to sixteen distinct reinforcement schedules based upon fixed or variable time intervals and response frequencies; each of these is associated with different response rates over time (Ferster & Skinner, 1957). Their specifics need not concern us here, but a general point about intermittent reinforcement is extremely important: behavior that comes under the control of intermittent reinforcement can be highly resistant to extinction. In grass roots terminology, "A simple *yes* can undo a thousand *nos*."

Punishment　So far we have stressed the powerful effect of positive reinforcement (attainment of satisfying consequences) and negative reinforcement (removal of a preexisting, usually noxious stimulus), on the development of behavior. But behavior *consequences* themselves often are conspicuously painful or aversive. If so, we can speak about *punishment* or a *punishing stimulus.*

Many S-R psychologists are careful to specify, however, that a consequence is punishing only if it has the effect of reducing the likelihood that the "punished" response will recur. Or, they may refer to an inhibiting effect of punishment, whereby a learner consciously refrains from performing a response that has previously resulted in aversive consequences. The earlier example of fingers burned by a flaming match illustrates this notion. Thus punishment can be distinguished from negative reinforcement. For punishment, an aversive stimulus *follows* and instrumental response; for negative reinforcement, an instrumental response must occur for the *removal* of an aversive stimulus.

A punishing stimulus can be either corporal or psychological (or both). Corporal punishment refers to the direct infliction of bodily pain, whereas psychological punishment may take the form of reproof, ridicule, social rejection, and the like. Understandably, comparatively little is known from systematic punishment research with human subjects. Animal study has yielded insights about physical punishment (such as electric shock) and its effects on learning. What little evidence can be offered about punishment and human learning comes from the use of fairly mild psychological punishment, for example, children being told they are wrong or criticized in some way about their performance on learning tasks. Beyond this, our beliefs about the effects of punishment must come from inferences from observation in the natural setting.

Even with this limited knowledge, two important points about punishment and learning can be made (Parke, 1972; Solomon, 1964; Travers, 1977). First, the consequences of punishment are generally less predictable than those of reinforcement. Sometimes punishment is effective and works to suppress or inhibit an "unwanted" response; sometimes it does not. In other words, the conditions under which punishment is effective in controlling or changing behavior are extremely complex. One condition is the timing of punishment. In general, the longer the time interval between the occurrence of a response and its punishment, the less obvious is the impact of that punishment; the swifter the punishment, the better. But the intensity of a punishing stimulus can be a factor as well. Usually, the more severe or intense a punishment is, the more likely it is to have an effect. Still another condition is the nature of the relationship between a person who delivers and one who receives the punishment. Punishment seems often to have greater meaning for behavior change in the context of a positive affectional relationship than otherwise. In other words, when a punishment indicates disapproval to an individual who desires approval from the punisher, that individual is more likely to take the punishment seriously. Another condition that may help determine the impact of punishment is the extent to which reasoning accompanies the application of a painful stimulus. In practical terms this means that if individuals are helped to understand why they are being punished and what they can do to avoid further unpleasantness (or to achieve positive reinforcement), punishment may be more effective over time. In all honesty, however, we must acknowledge that these statements are "iffy" and tell only a small part of a still incomplete story about punishment and learning.

Our second major point about punishment emphasizes the likelihood of its undesirable or negative side effects. Even if punishment weakens or inhibits a given response, it can backfire. We have seen one example of this when Alan learned to fear the cat after having been punished in its presence, and then generalized this fear response to the toy dog. Another common side effect of punishment is anger or hostility. Such feelings may be expressed directly by retaliating against a punisher (counteraggression), or they may be expressed less directly through attempts to "get a punisher's goat" or acting out aggressively against less-threatening persons or objects. Above all, it should be noted that persons who utilize physical punishment, especially as a tactic to control behavior, serve as explicit models for aggressive behavior. The implication of this for children's learning is obvious.

For these and other reasons, including moral considerations in human relationships, psychologists prefer to emphasize the use of reinforcement, especially positive reinforcement, for learning and nonreinforcement for "unlearning." The occurrence of punishing consequences can, of course, be functional for survival, as in learning to avoid hazards to personal health and welfare. However, punishment as a tactic for controlling human behavior is itself hazardous. Unfortunately, it is perhaps too widely used in childrearing (Chapter 12).

Observational Learning

We have briefly outlined how conditioning can occur in social situations. Both Alan and Susan, however, were subject to more than conditioning. They were also provided with an opportunity for observational learning (Bandura, 1977). Simply by watching others and given a capacity for enacting those watched behaviors, Alan and Susan will demonstrate an enormous amount of learning. Those persons whom they watch, be they parents, siblings, or friends, will be *models* for this learning. By shouting, spanking, and physically removing Alan from the porch, Alan's mother modeled a power-assertive approach to childrearing. Susan's mother modeled a distraction procedure—candy to occupy the child's attention and hopefully prevent Susan from further shrieking. If Alan and Susan on occasion repeat such maternal behaviors, they will have imitated their respective models.

Imitation—the actual performance of behavior that has been observed—is necessary to achieve efficiency in reproducing the many responses that we see other people enact. But imitation is not necessary for observational learning to occur (Baldwin, 1973). Once having witnessed a model's behavior, children are apparently capable of establishing a visual image or verbal code for the act. This image or code is stored in memory. Whether or not the code is eventually translated into the children's own behavior will depend upon their being both able and wanting to do so. This means that a certain degree of selectivity is involved in performing behaviors learned by observation.

Selectivity also seems to be affected by certain characteristics of models whom children observe. Obviously, children do not go about imitating everyone they see or hear. Rather, some models affect children more than others. Greater influence is most likely when children have a pleasantly warm relationship with a model. Technically speaking, this is usually called a nurturant relationship, or referred to as nurturant properties of a model. The extent to which a model is perceived as powerful, or as controlling resources or having access to privileges desired by children, is another important variable affecting imitation. Also significant may be the extent to which children perceive themselves as similar to a model in sex, race, interests, and the like. Accessibility to a model and the model's skill in helping children solve their problems may further influence impact.

Finally, the extent to which the consequences of a model's behavior are observed by children to be positive or negative may also make a considerable difference in subsequent imitation. Models, who by their behavior gain rewards or are punished, establish a condition for children known as *vicarious reinforcement*. Presumably this creates for an observing child some sort of expectation about behavioral consequences. The nature of these consequences thus can become a further factor in a child's motivation for imitation.

To conclude this section, we emphasize that different models vary in influence with different children. Furthermore, some children seem more generally prone to imitate, or to become "better" imitators than others, perhaps because of learning differentials in their interaction with parents (Hartup & Coates, 1970). These points are important as we consider how the potentialities for observational learning are realized, even exploited, in human relationships. Observational learning will occur, whether by design or not. Either way, it is crucial in the development of parent–child relationships, in selecting and training teachers of children and youth, and in the widespread modeling that occurs within peer group settings and from television. Both desirable and undesirable social behaviors can be learned via observations. For example, children can learn to help other people from having observed their parents as helpers. Similarly, many children may learn ways of aggressing against others by observing their parents' techniques of punishing them.

Cognitive Aspects of Social Learning

Taken together, conditioning and observational learning account for much social learning. However, other concepts of behavioral development are necessary to understand learning more completely. For instance, Alan and Susan, like all normally developing children, will come to conceptualize, or infer meanings about other people's thoughts, motives, feelings, intentions, and opinions. In a real sense, these children will behave as if they were psychologists by attempting to predict and explain other people's behavior. They will also act as amateur moral philosophers by making judgments about the goodness or badness of such behavior.

These explanations and judgments will occur primarily within the children's immediate network of interpersonal relationships. A lot of observational learning and attention to the distinguishing characteristics of others (their habits, beliefs, values, etc.) will also occur. There will be various role-taking episodes, in which children will assess "inside their heads" the viewpoints or perspectives of other people during such social give-and-take as arguments, conflicts of interests, self-justifications, or rationalizations for behavior. As such, a good bit of reasoning and even logical analysis will come into play. Thus, we step far beyond social learning by conditioning and imitation to the nature of children's mental abilities and their capacity for empathy with others.

Empathy in this context can be thought of in two ways: understanding what it is that another person feels under given circumstances (such as the elation of success or the depression of failure) and possibly even sharing with similar intensity the same emotion as another person (Hogan, 1973). Both empathy and the mental abilities for judging people's behavior according to standards are important ingredients in moral development, as we discuss in Chapter 11.

Conceptualizing and evaluating other people's behavior, social role taking, and empathy are associated collectively with the development of *social cognition* (Schantz, 1975). From a developmental process point of view, social cognition means how children come to know and to organize their knowledge about people. Like many aspects of development,

changes in social cognition are usually shown in children's verbal interchanges with others, and become increasingly differentiated, specific, and precise with age. Younger children, for example, seem to perceive and describe their teachers in very diffuse terms (Stephens & Evans, 1973). Teachers are simply liked or disliked. Disliked teachers are "mean," "cranky," "crabby," "unfair," or "bossy." Liked teachers are "nice," "fun," "neat," or "friendly." Young children seldom talk about their teachers' instructional behavior, such as intellectual stimulation or clear organization of material. They may mention "helps a lot," or "explains things well," but little else surfaces. In contrast, person perceptions become much more role specific among adolescents. By high school age, pupils seem able to both distinguish and verbalize qualities associated with teaching: knowledge of subject matter, encouraging students to learn, resourcefulness and variety in approach to instruction, accessibility to students, engaging students in decisions about course activities and goals, treating students as colleagues, and general ability to communicate (Evans, 1976).

Social cognition reflects important changes in behavior through time. Its outcomes are various aspects of social knowledge: coming to know about other people, understanding the social effects of behavior, standards of social conduct, and the nature of social roles, for example, what it means to be a father, mother, teacher, shopkeeper, policeman, and the like.

Verbal Reception and Discovery Learning

Thus far we have discussed three ways children learn: conditioning, observation, and organizing and testing their social cognitions. Learning also occurs in other ways. Much can be learned by listening to what other people say. *Verbal reception learning* occurs when words and sentences of varying length and complexity are received from other people, hopefully understood, and perhaps later acted upon. Psychologists use the generic term, verbal learning, to include tasks for which some sort of verbal performance is also required. Thus, a task that calls first for the memorization, then the recitation of a prose passage would constitute an act of verbal learning. The point is that verbal learning, as we discuss it here, is not synonymous with language development or limited to vocabulary acquisition (Chapter 7). Rather, it refers to the learning of verbal information which can be presented to an individual orally or in printed form (Gagné, 1974).

Much verbal material that can be "learned" may not be understood, or may even be misconstrued. Becky, age 5, was recently overheard talking about her sister's allergy. When asked what "allergy" meant, she admitted to not having the foggiest idea whatsoever. Marjo Gortner, now a film actor, delivered as many as seven different hour long evangelical speeches a week as a young child. His audiences apparently were mesmerized by the content and style of his communications. He now freely admits that his usually flawless performances were a product of rote memory skill and had no real personal meaning for him. The point is that verbal expression per se cannot always be taken as a measure of understanding. Nor can it be assumed that children fully understand our verbal messages, even when they appear to do so. Todd, age 6, anxious to help his mother bake a poundcake, quickly brought her a hammer from his father's workbench.

Limitations recognized, the use of words is both essential and desirable for much learning. Words serve as cues for guiding children's responses in learning such diverse tasks as cooking, bicycling, and writing. As means for coding experience, words provide a basis for the application of skills in problem solving and critical thinking. Words further provide the stuff for explaining game rules, storytelling, expressing human feelings, and so on.

Yet, perhaps too often, verbal learning is overemphasized by adults at the expense of children's comprehension of physical reality. Critics of schools, for example, often decry the dominance of verbal teaching techniques in the classroom, where instruction is often based solely upon lecturing and reciting. Systematic surveys of American classrooms have, in fact, revealed a strong bias for verbal techniques, as the "rule of two-thirds" aptly illustrates. That is, researchers (for example, Flanders, 1965) have revealed that two-thirds of the total time spent in a typical American classroom involves verbal discourse. Further, two-thirds of this verbal discourse is teacher talk. And still further, two-thirds of this teacher talk is lecturing, explaining, criticizing, giving directions, and justifying authority.

We dare not generalize the rule of two-thirds to all teachers or all classrooms, but the typical pattern reminds us of the importance of adult's efforts to promote children's learning by direct verbal means. At issue is the extent to which relatively abstract verbal communication is the best way to accomplish desired learnings, such as an understanding of cause-effect relationships or the effects of one's actions on objects in the environment. For these learnings, many psychologists (such as Bruner, 1961) emphasize the merits of *discovery learning*, where children are actively involved in constructing their own integrated clusters of knowledge from a rich diet of concrete, sensory experiences. This construction process need not be totally independent from other people, nor totally lacking language activity. Nor is it inevitably trial and error. Discovery can be facilitated subtly by an adult's discreet arrangement and sequencing of learning materials and experiences for children. The point, however, is that discovery learning is distinguished by a reliance upon first hand experience, observation, manipulation, and experimentation (Kolesnik, 1976).

The act of discovery is considered essential for developing two *kinds* of knowledge: physical knowledge and logical knowledge (Elkind, 1974). Physical knowledge concerns learning about the nature of matter. It includes knowledge about the physical properties of objects that children everywhere encounter in their environments: weight, form, texture, size, and so on. Physical knowledge also includes the development of a repertoire of actions that can be performed on objects and that have predictable effects. Squeezing, folding, pouring, shaking, and tearing are examples of such action. Logical knowledge is the development of thinking operations or processes of logical reasoning. It is conceptual and includes ideas about space, number, and time. Logical knowledge also includes the ability to group, or classify objects by their conceptual relationships, that is, on the basis of similarities and differences. And, logical knowledge includes the ability to compare and arrange objects in order along particular dimensions, say, of length, color, and weight. These early physical and logical knowledge learnings are significant, because they are said to provide the necessary foundation for such later abstract thinking as deducing conclusions from a set of hypothetical events. Consequently, verbal discourse about these learnings will be productive to the extent that it has a strong foundation in concrete experience. The structures of logical thought that gradually develop from this experience during childhood and adolescence also depend upon maturation and strategies for processing and storing information (Neimark, 1971).

The reader surely will appreciate that a full analysis of the kinds, processes, and outcomes of learning can consume entire volumes. We have, however, sketched out some major ideas about learning and development. From a social learning perspective, the importance of conditioning and observational learning has been stressed. Basic aspects of social cognition were introduced, followed by brief references to verbal learning and the discovery of physical and logical knowledge. Our intent has been to illustrate some major ways in which learning contributes to development and to show that different kinds or types of learning are pertinent to an understanding of different patterns of behavior.

We have not exhausted the major categories of such learning outcomes as verbal knowledge, motor skills, attitudes, and cognitive-intellectual skills. Nor have we dealt with the various conditions under which learning may occur more or less efficiently or effectively. Interested readers can explore these topics by consulting more advanced sources (Gagné, 1977; Travers, 1977). Now we move to a brief, but important, commentary about methods for describing and attempting to understand the interaction of maturation and learning which produces development.

A WORD ABOUT METHODS FOR STUDYING DEVELOPMENT

Basic Approaches to Observation

Our most useful descriptions of developmental change come from the careful observation of children and youth over time. Only through the systematic gath-

J. Appleton

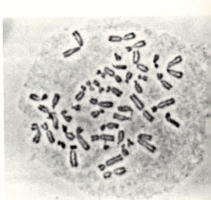

CHROMOSO

Photo © Shelly Rusten 1971

o by Suzanne Szasz

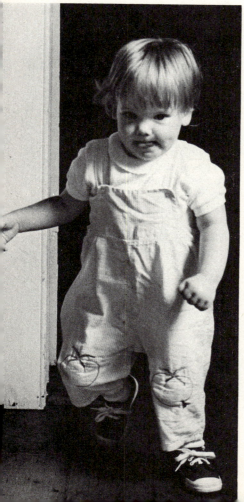

Photograph copyright © 1977 by Arthur Sirdofsky

Photo by Suzanne Szasz

ering and analysis of data from representative individuals and groups of people over time can we hope to succeed in charting behavior change and the conditions under which it occurs. Technical aspects of observational and other techniques for gathering information about development exceed the scope of this chapter. However, whatever its technical form, the scientific observation of behavioral development typically occurs in one or more of three ways. The first is the observation and recording of behavior as it occurs or has occurred at any given point in time in the natural environment. This natural environment could be the home, school, playground, or other settings where human beings normally congregate and interact. In many cases such observation simply describes the behavior or developmental status of children or youth, for example, similarities and differences in the form of children's play (Chapter 4). In other cases, an observer may attempt to describe associations or relationships between behavior or developmental status and environmental conditions which can be important for predicting or understanding individual differences in development. Thus, a research worker may study any possible relationships between children's play behavior and readily observed aspects of their home environment such as physical space for play, variety of play materials, and the extent to which parents or caregivers play with their children. The resulting description is necessarily limited to a statement of relationship—a *correlation*—between two or more of these variables[2] for example, the extent to which children's play behavior is related to frequency of adult involvement in play. We could not conclude anything about cause and effect in play from this information, but

we have important data from which to speculate and explore further the possibilities of a causal relationship.

A second approach to observation involves the use of interviews, questionnaires, or psychological tests to gather information directly from the individuals concerned. The discussion in this book about many topics of human development is based primarily on this kind of information. The study of children's intellectual behavior, for example, is mostly a description of their performances on intelligence tests. Similarly, self-concept study is largely determined by what children and youth are able and willing to say about themselves in response to various self-report measures. Even data about parent childrearing practices are often limited to adults' professed attitudes, beliefs, and recollections about raising their children. Descriptive data about intelligence, self-concept, or childrearing practices may be gathered in relation to other variables. Thus, one researcher may wish to assess the strength of a relationship (correlation) between parents' and their children's intelligence. Others may investigate the relationship between self-concept and school achievement. Still others may attempt to establish a relationship between parents' stated childrearing orientations and the actual behavior of their children. All such data can be important for a clearer understanding of development and behavior, but we must caution about inferring cause and effect from them. Correlation does not mean causation (see Appendix B).

The third basic approach involves observation in contrived or laboratory settings. In such settings it is usually possible for researchers both to exert greater control over what occurs and to observe behavior more carefully. Sometimes the objective is to determine how children or youth with differing characteristics or backgrounds respond to specific environmental conditions. We may find, for

---

[2] See Appendix B for an explanation of correlation and other basic statistical concepts.

example, that males and females from different socioeconomic or cultural backgrounds respond differently to conditions of material reinforcement for verbal learning, or tasks requiring individual competition vs. cooperation, or frustration induced by repeated failure to solve complex puzzles. In other cases, the objective may be to deliberately manipulate conditions in the environment (laboratory or otherwise) to produce some kind of behavior change, that is, to assess the effect(s) of some specified treatment upon children's behavior. Thus, we may wish to observe the effect of a training strategy designed to increase creativity, or decrease children's fear of animals, or modify their language behavior. Manipulation to create change or assess treatment outcomes is the definitive feature of *experimental* research in developmental psychology. Many results of experimental research are presented in later chapters. But we must note that experimental studies are greatly outnumbered by those based upon correlational methods. Both practical and ethical limitations on the study of humans have contributed to this relative imbalance. The net implication is clear: in the absence of amply documented and replicated cause–effect data from experimental study we must be cautious about making claims about conditions that facilitate or interfere with human development.

The Design of Developmental Study

The approaches to observation we have outlined vary in suitability depending upon the kinds of questions about development that psychologists hope to answer. Within *developmental* psychology, of course, a basic orientation is to describe behavioral change through time. This requires that observations occur at two or more points in time across given periods in the life span. The results of

such observation can then be reported as *age differences* or *sequential behavioral development* (see next section). Two designs for taking such observations are basic: the *longitudinal* and *cross-sectional* approaches (Bayley, 1965; Kessen, 1960).

Longitudinal Research

The *longitudinal* approach is the preferred strategy for gathering data about developmental change. It requires observing the same individual or group of persons (subjects) at different times as they mature and noting any changes in their behavior. Longitudinal studies enable us to examine both the rate and direction of behavior change over selected time periods, extending from several months to many years. Longer-term studies usually provide us with more complete and valuable perspectives on development. One of the most informative and significant longitudinal studies in psychology, for example, involved the periodic observation of "gifted children" exceptionally high in their measured intelligence (Terman, 1954). The study began in the 1920s and data from this group of people are still accumulating. These data have contributed much to our understanding of the intellectually talented and their life experiences.

Other advantages of the longitudinal method include its value in assessing how stable (or unstable) behavior patterns are over time and the extent to which early experiences and later development are related. (See last section of this chapter.) Moreover, many variations on the theme of longitudinal study are possible. For example, children and youth can be observed across cultures to tease out similarities and differences in development influenced by different patterns of cultural experience. Longitudinal comparisons of children within the same culture who differ in sex, racial-ethnic identity, social class, rural-urban upbringing, and type of schooling can also provide valuable information. But such comparisons are not without their problems. They require patience and enormous expenditures of money and effort. They also involve a high risk of attrition, that is, loss of subjects and, sometimes, of researchers themselves! It is extremely difficult for psychologists to keep track of people for lengthy periods of time, especially in today's highly mobile society.

Even so, the longitudinal method comes highly recommended for gaining the truest picture of development, because we observe the same persons through time. Equally important, the longitudinal method actually is required to answer certain kinds of questions about development (Ausubel & Sullivan, 1970). For example, if we wish to know the relationship between height or weight at successive ages from infancy to adulthood, we must take appropriate measures on the same individuals periodically from birth to age 18 or beyond. Similarly, if we are interested in the cumulative relationship between prenatal or birth complications and adult physical or mental status, a longitudinal design is advised for best results.

Cross-sectional Research

Because of the practical problems associated with longitudinal research, however, developmental psychologists frequently resort to a second approach, the cross-sectional method. In this method, developmental change is measured by observing different individuals (or groups) who differ in age at any given point in time. Its primary advantage is relative economy of time, money, and other resources. It is often easier to seek and gain the cooperation of large groups of subjects for research. The problem of subjects "dropping out" of the study is all but eliminated. Data

taken from subjects within a shorter time span can be much more quickly analyzed, interpreted, and reported. For example, suppose our interest is developmental changes in children's attitude toward school from elementary through the high school years. A longitudinal design would require successive measurements of school attitude among children over a period of up to 12 years. A cross-sectional design, in contrast, could involve a simultaneous comparison on a suitable attitude measure of school children and youth at different ages or school grade levels.

This example also illustrates a major problem with the cross-sectional approach. School attitude may be influenced by more than just aging and length of school experience. Broader cultural factors and the quality or kind of school experience are important factors. We could not be sure that the school experience of our older subjects was essentially the same as that the younger ones were now experiencing. Nor could we be sure that the younger subjects will necessarily encounter school experiences identical or even similar to that now occurring for the older ones. Furthermore, the older subjects may represent a more selective sample—especially if school attitude is related in any systematic way to learning or remaining in school as higher grades are reached. In other words, the comparability of subjects is a serious problem in cross-sectional research. Changes in cultural experience can influence different age groups in different ways. As comparability suffers, research results can become misleading or distorted.

Other weaknesses in cross-sectional study remind us of the strengths of longitudinal research. That is, cross-sectional research says little about the stability or durability of behavior through time. Rates—and perhaps even the direction—of growth are obscured by comparing different age groups of children. However, many questions about development are well suited to the cross-sectional approach. Much has been learned about age differences in intellectual functioning and moral judgments, for example, by applying the cross-sectional approach (Chapters 8 and 11). And, as we have suggested, this approach is often the only practical one to take in studying developmental change.

Most psychologists agree that both the longitudinal and cross-sectional designs provide meaningful though somewhat different information about human development. These designs can complement one another, so the important consideration is which is suited to the study of any given question about development. In fact, authorities in methodology continue to seek stronger designs for understanding behavior change through time. These designs may involve combinations of the best of both longitudinal and cross-sectional methods (Nesselroade & Baltes, 1974). Refinements in longitudinal methodology also show promise for understanding more thoroughly individual age changes in relation to change through time within the broadest context for development—society itself (Riegel, 1972).

Technical details about these refinements or improvements in methodology can be found in several sources (for example, Goulet, 1975). Our purpose is mainly to stress the importance of sound developmental research. Sound research must meet three basic requirements: the development of valid techniques for measuring human attributes, the selection and implementation of appropriate designs for obtaining data with those techniques, and the application of suitable means for analyzing the results obtained (Nunnally, 1973). Any generalizations about children's development and behavior are only as sound as the data—observed facts—upon which they are based. Because the facts themselves depend on the techniques or tools used to obtain them, we cannot emphasize too strongly the importance of precise measurement for the study of human development.

In empirical research, how a given behavior, trait, or characteristic is measured becomes its definition. Thus, intelligence is often defined (measured) by a score on an intelligence test; hunger motivation may be defined (measured) by a time span since last food intake; aggression may be defined (measured) by the number of times an individual hits, kicks, pushes, or otherwise acts out against other persons; and so on. Such quantifications of behavior for study constitute *operational definitions*, because they state the operations or procedures used to distinguish the behavior under study from other behavior or objects. Valid measurement operations are essential for research findings about which we can be confident.

BASIC CONCEPTS OF DEVELOPMENT

The use of longitudinal and cross-sectional approaches to the study of development among individuals has led to different ways of describing that development. In this section, we discuss the differences between two basic ways to describe development. The first, and more traditional, is based upon chronological age. The second is more directly concerned with sequential change and the processes of development; chronological age as such may be considered irrelevant from this perspective.

An Age Concept of Development

The most commonplace framework for describing development derives from the study of children and youth according to their chronological ages. For each age level, descriptions, averages, and ranges are presented (Baer, 1970). Thus, a generalized picture of children's developmental status is ordered by age typicalness and cross-age differences. A popularized example of this approach has resulted in labeling children successively as "terrible twos," "trusting threes," "fascinating fours," "frustrating fives," and so on (Gesell & Ilg, 1943).

Simplistic labels aside, such a way to order behavior development is sensible if for no other reason than that children do appear different and behave differently at successive ages. As they grow older, children learn new and more complex tasks. The skills required for the different tasks at the different ages can be analyzed. As we learn more about human development, predictions about what behaviors are likely to appear when become more accurate, so that it can be specified with fair confidence what the average child can do at any given point in his development.

Table 2.1 contains generalized age-based descriptions of behavior, usually called *norms*, emphasizing the first five years of life. Such norms refer to the average, or typical, case and do not explain developmental changes in behavior. Nevertheless, norms are useful to gain a general picture of normal development and as reference points for considering deviation from the average. Plans for

children and adolescents, such as schooling, can be made with only partial accuracy by the person's age, because emotional and intellectual maturity (to name only two factors) are responsible for wide variations in behavior among children of the same age. Since age alone provides only a general but convenient index for cataloguing developmental change, limitations in using age as a developmental index should be noted.

First, age is only a shorthand method of charting developmental change over time. A person's age does not specify the exact biological and cultural factors that contribute to development. The intellectual, problem-solving superiority of an adolescent over a preschool-age child is not explained at all by saying, "The adolescent is older." Specifying the precise characteristics of intellectual behavior at these two periods of development and charting the forces that produce these characteristics are much more helpful than a simple statement of age. What have been the different learning experiences? What have been the effects of pubescence and the changes in self-concept and social expectations that accompany sexual maturity? What is the effect of adolescents' increased strength and mobility within their environment?

TABLE 2.1   Normative Stages of Development

Physical and Language Development	Emotional Development	Social Development
BIRTH TO 1 YEAR		
0 to 1 Month		
Birth Size: 7–8 lbs., 20 inches	Generalized tension	Helpless
Feedings: 5–8 per day		Asocial
Sleep: 20 hours per day		Fed by mother
Sensory capacities: makes basic distinctions in vision, hearing, smelling, tasting, touch, temperature, and perception of pain		
Reflexes: sucking, swallowing, crying, hiccoughing, grasping, pupillary contraction		

TABLE 2.1   *Continued*

Physical and Language Development	Emotional Development	Social Development
2 to 3 Months Sensory capacities: color perception, visual exploration, oral exploration Sounds: cries, coos, grunts Motor ability: control of eye muscles, lifts head when on stomach	Delight Distress Smiles at a face	Visually fixates a face Smiles at a face May be soothed by rocking
4 to 6 Months Sensory capacities: localizes sounds Sounds: babbling, makes most vowels and about half of the consonants Feedings: 3–5 per day Motor ability: control of head and arm movements, purposive grasping; rolls over	Enjoys being cuddled	Recognizes his mother Distinguishes between familiar persons and strangers No longer smiles indiscriminately Expects feeding, dressing, bathing
7 to 9 Months Motor ability: control of trunk and hands, sits without support, crawls (abdomen touching floor)	Specific emotional attachment to mother Protests separation from mother	Enjoys "peek-a-boo"
10 to 12 Months Motor ability: control of legs and feet, stands, creeps, apposition of thumb and forefinger Language: says one or two words, imitates sounds, responds to simple commands Feedings: 3 meals, 2 snacks Sleep: 12 hours, 2 naps Size at one year: 20 lbs., 28–29 inches	Anger Affection Fear of strangers Curiosity, exploration	Responsive to own name Waves bye-bye Plays pat-a-cake Understands "no no!" Gives and takes objects
1 TO 1½ YEARS Motor ability: creeps up stairs, walks (10–20 months), throws a ball, feeds himself, builds a 2–3 cube tower (18 months), makes lines on paper with crayon	Dependent behavior Very upset when separated from mother Fear of bath	Obeys limited commands Repeats a few words Interested in his mirror image Feeds himself
1½ TO 2 YEARS Motor ability: runs, kicks a ball, builds 6 cube tower (2 yrs.) Capable of bowel and bladder control Language: vocabulary of more than 200 words Sleep: 12 hours at night, 1–2 hour nap Size at 2 years: 23–30 lbs., 32–35 inches	Temper tantrums (1–3 yrs.) Resentment of new baby Negativism (18 months)	Does opposite of what he is told (18 months)

TABLE 2.1 *Continued*

Physical and Language Development	*Emotional Development*	*Social Development*
2 to 3 Years Motor ability: jumps off a step, rides a tricycle, uses crayons, builds a 9–10 cube tower Language: starts to use short sentences, controls and explores world with language, stuttering may appear briefly Size at 3 years: 32–33 lbs., 37–38 inches	Fear of separation Negativistic (2½ yrs) Violent emotions, anger Differentiates facial expressions of anger, sorrow, and joy Sense of humor (plays tricks)	Talks, uses "I," "me," "you" Copies parents' actions Dependent, clinging Possessive about toys Enjoys playing alongside another child Negativism (2½ yrs.), resists parental demands Gives orders Rigid insistence on sameness of routine Inability to make decisions
3 to 4 Years Motor ability: stands on one leg, jumps up and down, draws a circle and a cross (4 yrs.) Language: asks questions, actively conceptualizes, complete sentences of 6–8 words (4 yrs.) Self-sufficient in many routines of home life Size at 4 years: 38–40 lbs., 40–41 inches	Affectionate toward parents Pleasure in genital manipulation Romantic attachment to parent of opposite sex (3 to 5 yrs.) Jealousy of same-sex parent Imaginary fears of dark, injury, etc. (3–5 yrs.)	Likes to share, uses "we" Cooperative play with other children Nursery school Imitates parents—beginning of identification with same-sex parent Practices sex-role activities Intense curiosity, asks questions Interest in other children's bodies (3 to 5 yrs.) Imaginary friends (3 to 5 yrs.)
4 to 5 Years Motor ability: mature motor control, skips, broad jumps, dresses himself, copies a square and a triangle (5 yrs.) Language: talks clearly, uses adult speech sounds, has mastered basic grammar, relates a story, knows over 2,000 words (5 yrs.) Size at 5 years: 42–43 lbs., 43–44 inches	Responsibility and guilt Feels pride in accomplishment	Prefers to play with other children Becomes competitive Prefers sex-appropriate activities
5 Years to Puberty Gets first permanent teeth (6 yrs.) Major increase in growth (10 to 11 yrs.) Puberty: girls 11–13, boys 13–15 yrs. Growth tapers off (17 to 20 yrs.)	Basic emotions all established Emotions continue to develop in subtlety and connotative richness	Independent of parents (5–6 yrs.) Clubs, comic books, TV (7 to 11 yrs.) Dating (12 yrs. on)

The contents of this table have been abstracted from a variety of sources including Gesell and Ilg (1943), McCandless (1961), and Mussen, Conger, and Kagan (1963). Adapted from Charles P. Smith, *Child Development* (1966), pp. 8–9. Reprinted by permission of Charles P. Smith.

A second limitation of age as a developmental index is the great variation in developmental status that exists even among children of the same age. We usually describe a 4-year-old or a 14-year-old according to characteristics of "average" 4-year-olds or "normal" 14-year-olds. But there are very wide variations around these averages. Some 14-year-olds, for example, are 5 feet tall; others are 6 feet 1 inch tall. Some 14-year-olds are fully mature sexually; others are not yet even pubescent. Some 14-year-olds are still in the fifth or sixth grade; others are in the tenth and eleventh grades. In other words, for an accurate picture of development, one must move beyond the *average* (or mean) and consider the range in developmental variation at different ages. As seen in Table 2.1, organizing data around the average, and the range of children and youth around this average, results in behavioral norms. For most human characteristics, the bell-shaped curve charts these norms.

In Figure 2.1, the curve for the distribution of intelligence quotients for physically and neurologically normal children is given. The high point of the curve (the largest single number of children or youth) defines the average, an IQ of 100. But as can be seen from pegging the altitude (height) of the curve, there are almost as many children and youth of 99 or 101 IQ; fewer of 95 or 105 IQ; and very few of 50 IQ or lower or 150 IQ or higher. "Normal IQ" is often considered to lie within a certain predefined range above and below the average for intelligence; and the standard range for intelligence quotients is usually set by test makers at 15 or 16 points. This means that about two-thirds of all children who are represented by the curve in Figure 2.1 have IQs between about 84 or 85 and 115 or 116. (Technically speaking, this represents the range from one standard deviation below to one standard deviation above the average.)[3]

A third limitation of age as a developmental index is that most of our information about behavior of children and youth comes from studying them where we find them. At least in the past, researchers have most often taken as their subjects for study "average" children in "normal" circumstances. The resulting descriptions indicate only what children are like under those conditions, not what they could be like or are like if the conditions are altered sharply for better or for worse.

Limitations aside, the universality of an age-dependent concept of development cannot be denied. In fact, judging by the way in which American society is organized, educationally, economically, and legally, it is tempting to suggest that developmental changes and expectancies for children's behavior are "programmed in" by virtue of pre-established chronological age-based standards. For example, such important life

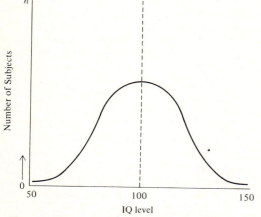

Fig. 2-1 The normal curve for the distribution of intelligence quotients.

---

[3] Readers unfamiliar with statistical terms such as *mean* and *standard* deviation should consult Appendix B for clarification.

events as school entrance, getting working papers for a full time job, marriage without parental permission, and voting usually are determined solely by chronological age. Why age should be the criterion for such wide-ranging privileges is not easily explained. Within our society and most others, however, chronological age seems to represent the best *single* indicator of successive levels of maturity. This age-consciousness is also reflected in the work of psychologists who study and chart the psychological development of children and youth. Chronological age, for example, is commonly viewed by psychologists as an index of relative homogeneity or commonality in behavior among children and youth; hence, the "shorthand" or "summarizing" function of age mentioned earlier.

An orientation to development based on chronological age has led many authors to organize their writings about children and youth by age level. That is, it is common for a textbook in developmental psychology to consist of generalized descriptions of children and youth by basic age categories: infancy (the first two years of life), the preschool years, the early school years, middle childhood, preadolescence, early adolescence, middle adolescence, late adolescence, and the like. This book selects an alternative framework in an effort to better preserve the *stream* of development in critical areas such as language, psychosexual development, moral development, and the like. Moreover, because individual children differ in their rates of development, the *range* of individual differences in behavior increases markedly with time. This makes it increasingly difficult to construct meaningful portraits of behaviors based only on an age-related concept of development. We do retain, however, a strong emphasis on *age-related trends* in the basic areas of psychological development.

Chronological age, then, is a popular, convenient, and useful way to describe developmental change. However, developmental change can be described and analyzed without depending on the age variable. This brings us to a second, major concept of development.

A Sequence Concept of Development

Suppose we observe three groups of infants: 3 months old, 6 months old, and 12 months old. We see that the first group is able to roll over, but not to sit up or walk with support; that the second group can all roll over and most of them can sit up with little or no support; and the third group can almost all walk a little bit with support. We conclude that we have exposed a sequence of motor development: rolling over precedes sitting up, and sitting up precedes walking. If no infant deviates from this sequence, we say it is fixed or constant and applies to most and perhaps all normal children.

This order, however, indicates only the outcome, or the typical timing of this kind of motor development (which some call antigravity postures) (Thompson, 1962). The processes or forces that have produced the motor changes cannot be determined from descriptive or normative information. Even less can the specific times when a given force or set of forces operates to produce change be selected. One may assume that biological maturation is the major factor involved in developing antigravity behavior. However, development of motor behavior can be greatly retarded and even prevented by severe malnutrition or total isolation of an infant or a young child. We might say, then, that norms, whether age norms or sequence-relevant norms, only describe. *Norms do not explain.*

Another example of a sequence-relevant aspect of development is discriminating left from right in a useful way in dealing with the environment. According to age norms, it is not until about age 7 that most children can manage this conceptual task. Few 4-year-olds have a clear general grasp of the meaning of left and right. The important question is, "What occurs between ages 4 and 7 that enables the older child to reach or surpass this developmental landmark?" If a sequence of learning experiences could be isolated so that we could bring a 4-year-old rapidly into mastery of left and right (say, in 30 minutes), we can certainly state that change through time has occurred. But we cannot say that the 4-year-old was older in the usual sense of age at the end of one-half hour than he was at the beginning. Age, in other words, does not explain the mastery of the left–right idea. We have to say that this change has resulted from training. Such condensing of what usually takes 3 years into a 30-minute training period is striking and leads us to infer that in many cases specific training can shortcut the inefficient learning that ordinarily would have taken place in the child's natural environment.

Developmental change in left–right learning has actually been produced much as described above (Baer, 1970). The sequence-dependent or sequence-relevant approach is based on the idea that changes that occur over extended time periods can sometimes be accomplished in a far shorter time through efficient training. If this is so, many developments within the natural environment may reflect comparatively inefficient or confusing programs of learning for most children and youth. Where speeding up is desirable, the assumption of sequence dependency may lead to a concentration on intervention and training with genuine advantages to a child or a youth. This idea is related to readiness, which is essentially the possession of the skills necessary to move on to the next level of behavior.

No one has yet demonstrated that all kinds of developmental change either can or should be achieved through precise learning technology, nor do psychologists and educators necessarily view the human being's natural environment as an enormous, imperfect program of learning (Sutton-Smith, 1970). In fact, many psychologists (for example, Kohlberg, 1968) maintain that there is no substitute for age-related natural experience, especially for intellectual development. If the child (or the adolescent) is not ready, many psychologists, educators, and philosophers state, no possible training procedure will produce change. Only when readiness exists (when the appropriate, usually age-related developmental stage has been reached) will there be a match between organism and environment so that the desired behavioral sequence can occur.

An approach to development that is not closely bound to chronological age has merit for at least three reasons. First, it suggests the possibility that some aspects of development are less dependent on the passage of time (increase in age) than on the timing of the specific learning experience. In other words, children do not necessarily have to be 6 years old before learning to read. Many 4-year-olds (or even younger children) are ready to read, will enjoy learning to read, and will profit from this new skill acquired at an early age. Of course, the methods and materials for learning to read used with 4-year-olds may be different from those typically used with 6-year-olds in the schools.

Second, an age-irrelevant approach to development opens up the possibility that more than one effective environmental sequence or program can facilitate a specific developmental outcome. Just as "many roads lead to Rome," so may many different but equally sound sequential programs of learning accomplish the same developmental task.

Third, it is quite possible that viewing development as sequence-dependent or sequence-relevant and studying it scientifically can lead to devising programs or training plans that will speed up a specific developmental process, if that is useful, or will remedy one that has lagged, as in such compensatory education programs as Head Start and Sesame Street. These ideas will concern us in later chapters of this book.

Such ideas are reflected in three broad, long-standing disputes about human development: the nature–nurture controversy, the critical-periods issue, and the question of behavioral stability. Since these disputes appear in various forms in studying almost every aspect of human development, we conclude Chapter 2 with a reference to each.

KEY ISSUES IN HUMAN DEVELOPMENT

The Nature–Nurture Controversy

A basic issue for developmental psychology is the degree to which nature (heredity) on the one hand and nurture (environment) on the other contribute to behavior development. Like the mythical Flying Dutchman doomed forever to sail the seven seas without ever coming into port, this dilemma has historically seemed fated to exist forever. One reason for this frustrating state of affairs is the way in which psychologists have approached the issue. In the 1930s and 1940s their questions took the form, "*Which* human traits or characteristics are determined mainly by heredity and which by environment?" Or, "*How much* of a given trait or characteristic is determined by heredity and *how much* by environment?" For some things the answer is relatively simple. Eye color is clearly determined by heredity. For others, such as mechanical or musical skills, keenness of abstract thinking, or

personal adjustment, the answer is far from simple. No one really knows what proportions of these characteristics are governed by heredity or environment.

As their scientific sophistication grew, psychologists moved away from *which* and *how much* questions, realizing that heredity is a necessary condition for environment, and vice versa. To ask which is most important for human development is like asking which is more important to water, H_2 or O, or asking if length or width is more important in calculating the area of a rectangle (Endler, Boulter, & Osser, 1976). More recently, scientists have moved to thinking about *how* heredity and environment combine and interact in behavior and development (Anastasi, 1958), although there is often logical and practical merit in trying to calculate the degree of influence exerted by one, the other, and both. Since there is little or nothing we can do about selective breeding (the only clear way known to influence heredity), we are now mainly preoccupied with discovering what environments permit optimum growth for individuals of all types of heredity.

The time, energy, and emotional commitment devoted to heredity and environment have not been totally wasted. We now know that identical twins, for example, are much more like each other than fraternal twins, who, in turn, resemble each other in some characteristics (for example, intelligence) more closely than nontwin siblings. Remarkable similarities continue to exist for identical twins, even when they have been reared apart, but, on the whole, they are less similar in psychological characteristics than identical twins reared together. Thus, we have evidence that both genetics and learning strongly influence many human characteristics (Gottesman, 1963; Shields & Slater, 1961).

Even more striking evidence comes

from studies of animals, whose rearing and breeding conditions can be more tightly controlled. For example, one authority reports that boxers and Scottish terriers differ markedly from many other breeds in aggressiveness and fearlessness. This difference is commonly considered to be constitutional (genetic). However, when rearing circumstances are sharply altered for these breeds, their normal fearlessness is markedly decreased.

Perhaps more significant still is a generalization, also based on animal research, that identical environmental treatment may result in very different outcomes for animals of different genetic makeup. Consider, for example, an experiment designed to examine the effects of "indulgent" and "disciplinary" training strategies with four breeds of dog: beagle, basenji, wirehaired fox terrier, and Shetland sheep dog (Freedman, 1958). Dogs from each breed were subjected to both strategies, beginning daily from the third week of life and continuing through the eighth week. *Indulged* pups were never punished and were encouraged to engage in exploratory and other active forms of behavior. In contrast, disciplined pups were restricted and were taught to "sit," "stay," and "come" at the trainer's command.

At the end of the eighth week, a test was given to each pup. A bowl of food was placed in front of each pup, but the pup was prevented from eating for three minutes, during which time a slap on the pup's hindquarters and a shouted "No!" were administered by the experimenter. After this, the experimenter left the room, and the elapsed time until the pup began to eat was recorded. This test situation was repeated for eight days.

Results of this experiment indicated that training strategy effects were large for beagles and terriers. For both breeds, the indulged pups delayed their eating behavior much longer than did their disciplined same-breed mates. In contrast,

kind of training seemingly had little effect for the other two breeds. All Shetland sheep dogs avoided the food entirely; all basenji pups ate quickly. These effects occurred whether an indulgent or a disciplinary approach to training had been taken.

These results seemingly have a parallel in childrearing. Most of us who have children or who have worked with children have observed them react differently to uniform treatment. Johnny, for instance, may respond calmly to a firm "No," whereas Bill may become physically agitated or openly emotional in response to the same firm "No." Such individual differences in reactivity demand more individualization of education (including types of control) than is typically provided in schools and often in homes for the different children in a family (Caspari, 1968).

The nature–nurture dilemma is by no means resolved or even fully understood. Given normal heredity, some behavior may depend on experience; or given normal environment, some behavior may depend on heredity. But the two determinants are interdependent (Hebb, 1966). One writer has summarized the interdependence in this simple equation: Genotype × Environment = Phenotype. "Genotype" refers to the sum of the individual's genetic endowment, and "phenotype" is the class name for the individual's observable qualities (Dobzhansky, 1950). All individuals except identical twins differ in genotype. This equation permits the obvious conclusion that the genetic potentialities of one person may be fully realized in environment A, only moderately well in environment B, and perhaps not at all in environment C.

The Critical-Periods Hypothesis

We have suggested that neither heredity nor environment alone yields behavior.

Rather, heredity yields structures which, under certain environmental conditions and depending on their state (for example, how mature they are and whether they have been damaged by disease or accident) are capable of a certain range of behavior (Endler, Boulter, & Osser, 1976). This notion of interaction leads us to another dilemma. Is the *timing* of environmental influence on genetic structure important? If so, in what ways? Are there periods during human development when the environment may affect the course and outcome of development in profound and permanent ways? These are questions about the reality and nature of critical periods in development — specific time spans during which crucial maturational and learning processes can (may) affect or alter subsequent development.

Three somewhat different themes in the literature about critical periods can be identified (Caldwell, 1962). One theme is that *organisms can be totally indifferent to, or resist certain forms or patterns of, stimulation after a critical point in time.* For example, the fetus is thought to be safe from danger of damage from rubella from three to four months after conception, but exceptionally vulnerable before then. The idea of indifference or resistance following the critical period is also supported by embryological studies (Hamburger, 1954). However, we have only speculative notions about whether the critical-periods hypothesis holds for almost any aspect of postembryological human development, especially psychological development.

A related hypothesis, that organization inhibits reorganization (Scott, 1968), is plausible in relation to resistance or indifference. This means that the more organized and established a set of responses becomes, the more difficult it is to change them. We speculated earlier that Americans typically wait too long to start their children on a second language; chronic underachievement after about the fourth grade has proved spectacularly resistant to remediation; persons trained on a conventional keyboard typewriter will usually encounter great difficulty learning another method, and so on.

A second theme in the mixed body of facts and theory that surrounds the critical-periods hypothesis is the notion of *maximum susceptibility*. If children are too young or too old, a set of experiences will have little effect on them. Again, this hypothesis is supported by research from embryology, but we are not at all sure either how or if it works in psychological development. Maria Montessori, for example, believe that 3 to 6 years is the critical period for muscular training; many ballet teachers seem to agree. Some authorities on perception hold that 4 to 6 years is the critical age period for perceptual training to facilitate later higher-order cognitive development (Frostig & Horne, 1964). For Piaget (1970) children must have a rewarding and rich set of experiences during infancy and the preschool years to move along well through the later stages in cognitive development. Another psychologist, Erikson (1963), maintains that the first two years of life are critical periods for the development of trust among human beings. An associated, moderately well grounded principle is that experience has more effect on an organism the more rapidly the organism is growing and developing (Bloom, 1964). The best evidence for this principle comes from the study of physical growth and brain development where devastating effects of severe early nutritional deprivation can be shown (Reed, 1971).

A third important theme within the critical-periods literature is the *cumulative deficit* hypothesis (Ausubel, 1964; Jensen, 1966). This means that deficiencies or distortions of experience pile up—cumulate—and progressively interfere with future development. This interference may be geometric, that is, become more severe at an accelerating tempo. For example, the consensus of research seems to be that at the end of the second grade, disadvantaged children are only a few months behind their advantaged counterparts in academic achievement; but after ten to twelve years of schooling, they are several years behind on the average. The cumulative-deficit notion lies behind much compensatory and early childhood education. Project Head Start, for example, was originally designed to provide children of an appropriate age (an age many now think was too old) with enriched experiences to prevent cumulative deficit.

In a moral society, we must ask further questions. Can cumulative effects of debilitating early experience be reduced or eliminated by enriching a child's later environment? Can "normal" development be restored without permanent aftereffects? When traumatic or debilitative early experience includes nutritional deficiency so severe as to interfere with neurological development, reversal or complete compensation is probably not possible. However, we are only beginning to gather sufficient firm data to permit us to move soundly in the area of compensation. Ideally, our society should be so constituted that compensation is not necessary. Compensation for early deprivation-debilitation is a bit like insurance compensation for one's house and furnishings after they have been burned. It is, by definition, inadequate, although better than nothing.

The critical-periods hypothesis raises a number of crucial questions for any industrial society. At what ages are what minimum and maximum amounts and types of environmental experience necessary for optimum social-personal development? Or for intellectual-academic development? Or for physical-motor development? After what time is it too late for adequate experience to produce optimum development or to remedy inadequate development? When is the best time to introduce a given type of learning skill (for example, learning to read, learning a second language, learning to play the piano)?

Stage theories of development are to some degree critical-periods theories. That is, many students of human development believe that sequential and qualitatively different periods of organized maturation and learning define progress from birth to maturity; each stage is a necessary forerunner of the next. Jean Piaget (1970), for example, suggests four major stages of intellectual development from birth to adolescence (see Chapter 8). Another stage theorist, Erik Erikson (1963), envisions *eight* successive stages of personality development throughout the human life cycle (see Appendix A). Also, events in the environment, such as death of a parent, may *create* critical periods. It should not be forgotten that "*all* periods in development are critical, but some may be more critical than others" (Caldwell, 1962, p. 42).

The Question of Behavioral Stability

The question "Is human development continuous and predictable and therefore stable, or is it typically in constant flux and therefore unpredictable and labile or inconstant?" has long intrigued students of human development. Underlying this question is confusion about the extent to which the human developmental system is closed, that is, patterned in advance and subject to an inevitable "upper limit" in its mature state. Hereditarians and constitutionalists are likely to view development as a closed system (Emmerich, 1967). An extreme hereditarian stance would be that genetic forces — relatively unaffected by variations in experience — persist and overwhelmingly determine major components of personality, cognition, and intellect. Assuming there is adequate nutrition and freedom from disease and accident, most of us see development in physical growth and in timing of physical (sexual) maturity as closed; environment may not much affect these conditions. More generally, a person who believes that the course of personality development is partially, perhaps totally, determined in the first six or seven years of life implicitly embraces a closed system of development. The belief that learning can result in major change at any time in the life span implies an open system of development.

Relative openness and closedness in development is basic to the stability (constancy)–lability (inconstancy) issue. Yet the observation of behavioral stability or lability is itself difficult. One meaning of stability/lability is based on the idea that a trait or some other aspect of development may be considered stable if members of a group keep the same ranking over their development span. If the most aggressive 2-year-old is still the most aggressive 14- or 44- or 84-year-old in the group, and if other members of the group all keep about their same rankings, one is inclined to say that aggressiveness among humans is stable. If our most aggressive 2-year-old is our least aggressive 44-year-old, and if all other individuals shift their ranking in the group as much as the most aggressive 2-year-old has done, we are likely to think of aggression as a labile trait.

A second meaning of lability–stability is more absolute. Our hypothetical 2-year-old has exactly the same amount of aggression at ages 14, 44, and 84. Such an absolute definition brings in horrendous problems of measurement, because aggression among 2-year-olds is a very different matter from aggression among 84-year-olds. No common "yardstick" is available, so it may be impossible to determine that the amounts of aggression are the same from one age to another.

To a considerable extent, any of the statements made at this time about the lability–stability question must be qualified by stating that our instruments for measuring complex human behavior are limited. Within such limits, research workers have found modest evidence of stability from preschool ages through adolescence for passivity–activity, social extraversion, and emotional responsiveness. Moreover, past research indicates that girls have been reasonably stable in their dependency behavior, boys less so (Kagan and Moss, 1960). Society does not take kindly to dependent adult males, but permits little boys to seek physical and emotional comfort from others. Social expectations, then, also affect stability. If organization inhibits reorganization, it follows that any set of behaviors which have been well learned (such as how to deal with aggressive, dependent, or sexual feelings) is likely to be persistent. Such persistence leads to behavioral stability. On the other hand, we are bombarded by social change. Paradoxically, in failing to change (or behave flexibly in different cultural contexts), we may also appear unstable. Once again we see that behavior must be interpreted in full view of the social context in which it occurs.

A reasonable position is that both genetic and experiential factors determine behavioral stability–instability. Scott can be "born" hyperactive. His calm, unflappable parents are not bothered. Eventually, not having been seriously frustrated and punished, Scott can learn the behavioral controls necessary for him to live without disturbing other people unduly. As a young man in business, Scott learns to pace around his desk, or to excuse himself frequently from long and confining meetings to "get a drink of water" or to make a quick telephone call. He copes constructively, or at least in a socially neutral manner. Other, equally hyperactive children, handled oppressively, can conceivably learn to handle their problems through violent delinquency or to retreat from them—one way of handling them passively—by using drugs.

Environmental consistency is certainly related to behavior consistency. When parents are calm and predictable and when home life is well organized, it is logical to predict that the children in that family will show greater behavioral consistency than children in a home where one day cannot be predicted from the preceding day. Because rapidly changing cultures affect all families, it also seems logical that there will be less behavior consistency in cultures that are changing rapidly than in those that are changing slowly (Emmerich, 1967).

This idea leads directly to the notion of cultural conditioning in childrearing. Some cultures are continuous, others discontinuous in the ways they arrange and reinforce children's learning experiences (Benedict, 1938). Cultures vary in the extent to which certain behavior patterns are encouraged and rewarded consistently from early childhood through adolescence and beyond. In a continuous culture, for example, expectations for children have much in common, whether the children are 2, 10, or 14 years old. The 2-year-old boy in a hunting culture is given a toy bow; at 10 he is given an instrument more appropriate to his age; and in another few years he is expected to be able to handle an adult hunting bow. Or at ages 2, 5, and 15, boys and girls are expected and encouraged to be interested in each other's sexuality. The interest—mild to indifferent

at 2 if we believe Freud (Appendix A), keen but nonfunctional at 5, and keen and functional at 15—is matter-of-factly accepted within a continuous culture at each age, whatever its manifestations. In contrast, with reference to sex (but not achievement), United States culture traditionally has been discontinuous. Children and unmarried adolescents are required (but not really expected) to be asexual, or to suppress their sexual urges. But immediately upon marriage expectations are high, perhaps unrealistically so, for mutual and profound sexual satisfaction. Similarly, many children in America seemingly are indulged, reinforced for dependency, and receive little training for personal responsibility. Later, especially during adolescence, we can observe strong pressures and expectations for the young to exercise self-reliance, and take responsibility for their own actions. The problem is that few helpful learning experiences may be provided for the young to make the transition smoothly. Thus, we can speak of socialization discontinuities as a possible source of instability. Children and youth may be unsure about exactly what they "should" do or how best to do it. Their actions can therefore be inconsistent across various situations.

To summarize, the question of behavioral stability is related to many issues: determinism versus free will; nature and nurture; critical periods; and the theory of measurement. Interaction is again apparent: stability and change are functions of both the nature of the individual human being, including gender, and the experiences and circumstances of learning. Thus, the variations in and potentials for development are enormous. At an even more abstract level, this behavioral stability issue, together with ideas about nature–nurture and critical periods, can be tied to arguments for and against stage theories of development.

We have reserved more abstract theoretical concerns for Appendix A, although some readers may prefer to examine them before moving to Part II of this book.

Chapter 2 provides an overview of some major terms and concepts for the formal study of human development. These terms and concepts can be grouped into three interrelated themes. First, following our ideas about interaction from Chapter 1, we have discussed the mutual influence of maturation and learning in producing development. Maturational processes are governed largely by genetic forces. Thus we have examined basic concepts of genetic influence, including mechanisms of heredity and the contributions of behavior genetics to our understanding of human development. Any full understanding of development is not possible, however, without an analysis of how learning occurs and how it affects development.

Among the most fundamental mechanisms of learning are classical and instrumental conditioning, each of which was defined and illustrated. Principles of reinforcement were discussed, with an emphasis upon how behavior is affected by its consequences. Ideas about social learning, including observational learning and cognitive aspects of learning in the natural environment, were presented. Finally, a distinction was made between verbal reception and discovery learning as a prelude to later chapters about language and cognitive-intellectual development.

A second theme of Chapter 2 is the methodology of developmental study. The formal study of human development is based upon systematic observation. Systematic observation can be conducted in several different ways, depending upon the kinds of questions about development that

SUMMARY

psychologists hope to answer. As objectives for study these questions describe developmental status, establish correlations between or among various aspects of development, and seek to document conditions that affect or create changes in development and behavior. Observational tactics in developmental study can be designed according to one or both of two fundamental methods or approaches, longitudinal and corss-sectional. These designs have specific strengths and limitations, with a general preference in favor of the longitudinal approach (or variation thereof).

These methods of developmental study lead to the third and final theme of Chapter 2: issues about the total concept of development itself. One way of conceptualizing developmental change involves chronological age. Development is described and interpreted by chronological age differences. A second way of thinking about development is specific to sequential changes in behavior for which chronological age is irrelevant. Taking this approach, psychologists strive to document the progressive differentiation and integration of behavior with greater precision. Either way, certain fundamental and unresolved issues or points of debate continue to dominate developmental psychology. These issues are the nature–nurture controversy, the critical-periods hypothesis, and stability–instability of behavior throughout the life span. These issues are encountered in various guises in every aspect of development.

REFERENCES

Anastasi, A. Heredity, environment, and the question, how? *Psychological Review,* 1958, *65,* 197–208.

Ausubel, D. P. How reversible are the cognitive and motivational effects of cultural deprivation? *Urban Education,* 1964, Summer, 16–37.

Ausubel, D. P., & Sullivan, E. V. *Theory and problems of child development* (2nd ed.). New York: Grune & Stratton, 1970.

Baer, D. M. An age-irrelevant concept of development. *Merrill-Palmer Quarterly,* 1970, *16,* 238–245.

Baldwin, A. S. Social learning. In F. N. Kerlinger (Ed.), *Review of research in education* (vol. 1). Itasca, Ill.: Peacock, 1973.

Bayley, N. Research in child development: A longitudinal perspective. *Merrill-Palmer Quarterly,* 1965, *11,* 184–190.

Bandura, A. *Social learning theory.* Englewood Cliffs, N.J.: Prentice-Hall, 1977.

Barash, D. P. *Sociology and behavior.* New York: Elsevier, 1977.

Benedict, R. Continuities in cultural conditioning. *Psychiatry,* 1938, *1,* 161–167.

Bijou, S., & Sturges, P. Positive reinforcers for experimental studies with children. *Child Development,* 1969, *30,* 151–170.

Bloom, B. S. *Stability and change in human characteristics.* New York: Wiley, 1964.

Bruner, J. S. *The process of education.* Cambridge: Harvard University Press, 1960.

Bruner, J. S. The act of discovery. *Harvard Educational Review,* 1961, *31,* 307–311.

Caldwell, B. M. The usefulness of the critical period hypothesis in the study of filiative behavior. *Merrill-Palmer Quarterly,* 1962, *8,* 229–242.

Caspari, E. W. Genetic endowment and environment in the determination of human behavior: Biological viewpoint. *American Educational Research Journal,* 1968, *5,* 43–55.

Cohen, S. *Social and personality development in childhood.* New York: Macmillan, 1976.

Dobzhansky, T. Heredity, environment, and evolution. *Science,* 1950, *11,* 161–166.

Eibl-Eibesfeldt, I. *Ethology: The biology of behavior* (2nd ed.). New York: Holt, Rinehart and Winston, 1975.

Elkind, D. *Children and adolescents* (2nd ed.). New York: Oxford University Press, 1974.

Emmerich, W. Stability and change in early personality development. In W. W. Hartup & N. Smothergill (Eds.), *The young child: Review of research* (vol. 1). Washington, D.C.: National Association for the Education of Young Children, 1967.

Endler, N., Boulter, L., & Osser, H. *Contemporary issues in developmental psychology* (2nd ed.). New York: Holt, Rinehart and Winston, 1976.

Erikson, E. *Childhood and society.* New York: Norton, 1963.

Evans, E. D. *The transition to teaching.* New York: Holt, Rinehart and Winston, 1976.

Ferster, C. B., & Skinner, B. F. *Schedules of reinforcement.* New York: Appleton, 1957.

Flanders, N. A. *Teacher influence, pupil attitudes, and achievement.* Washington, D.C.: U.S. Government Printing Office, 1965.

Freedman, D. G. Constitutional and environmental interactions in rearing of four breeds of dogs. *Science,* 1958, *127,* 585–586.

Frostig, M., & Horne, D. *The Frostig program for the development of visual perception.* Chicago: Follett, 1964.

Gagné, R. M. *Essentials of learning for instruction.* New York: Holt, Rinehart and Winston, 1974.

Gagné, R. M. *The conditions of learning* (3rd ed.). New York: Holt, Rinehart and Winston, 1977.

Gesell, A., & Ilg, F. *Infant and child in the culture of today.* New York: Harper & Row, 1943.

Gottesman, I. I. Genetic aspects of intelligent behavior. In N. Ellis (Ed.), *Handbook of mental deficiency.* New York: McGraw-Hill, 1963.

Gottesman, I. I. Personality and natural selection. In S. G. Vanderberg (Ed.), *Methods and goals in human behavior genetics.* Chicago: Aldine, 1965.

Goulet, L. R. Longitudinal and time-lag designs in educational research: An alternative sampling model. *Review of Educational Research,* 1975, *45,* 505–523.

Hamburger, V. Trends in experimental neuroembryology. In *Biochemistry of the developing nervous system,* 1954, 52–73.

Hartup, W. W., & Coates, B. The role of imitation in childhood socialization. In R. Hoppe et al. (Eds.), *Early experiences and the processes of socialization.* New York: Academic Press, 1970.

Hebb, D. O. *A textbook of psychology* (2nd ed.). Philadelphia: Saunders, 1966.

Hogan, R. Moral conduct and moral character: A psychological perspective. *Psychological Bulletin,* 1973, *80,* 217–232.

Honzik, M. P. Developmental studies of parent-child resemblance in intelligence. *Child Development,* 1957, *28,* 215–228.

Jensen, A. R. Cumulative deficit in compensatory education. *Journal of School Psychology,* 1966, *4,* 37–47.

Kagan, J., & Moss, H. A. The stability of passive-dependent behavior from childhood through adulthood. *Child Development,* 1960, *31,* 577–591.

Kasl, S. V. Biochemical correlates of achievement behavior and motivation. *Review of Educational Research,* 1974, *44,* 447–462.

Kessen, W. Research design in the study of developmental problems. In P. H. Mussen (Ed.), *Handbook of research methods in child development.* New York: Wiley, 1960.

Kohlberg, L. Early education: A cognitive-developmental view. *Child Development,* 1968, *39,* 1013–1062.

Kolesnik, W. B. *Learning: Educational applications.* Boston: Allyn and Bacon, 1976.

McCandless, B. R. *Children: Behavior and development.* New York: Holt, Rinehart and Winston, 1961.

McClearn, G. E. Genetic influences on behavior and development. In P. Mussen (Ed.), *Carmichael's manual of child psychology* (vol. 1). New York: Wiley, 1970.

Neimark, E. An information-processing approach to cognitive development. *Transactions of the New York Academy of Sciences,* 1971, *33,* 516–528.

Nesselroade, J. R., & Baltes, P. B. Adolescent personality development and historical change: 1970–1972. *Monographs of the Society for Research in Child Development,* 1974, *39* (154).

Nunnally, J. C. Research strategies and measurement methods for investigating human development. In J. R. Nesselroade & H. W. Reese (Eds.), *Life span developmental psychology: Methodological issues.* New York: Academic Press, 1973.

Parke, R. D. Some effects of punishment on children's behavior. In W. W. Hartup (Ed.), *The young child* (vol. 2). Washington, D.C.: National Association for the Education of Young Children, 1972.

Piaget, J. Piaget's theory. In P. H. Mussen (Ed.), *Carmichael's manual of child psychology.* New York: Wiley, 1970.

Premack, D. Reinforcement theory. In D. Levine (Ed.), *Nebraska Symposium on Motivation, 1965.* Lincoln: University of Nebraska Press, 1965.

Read, M. S. The biological bases: Malnutrition and behavioral development. In I. J. Gordon (Ed.), *Early childhood education.* Chicago: University of Chicago Press, 1972.

Reed, E. Genetic anomalies in development. In F. Horowitz (Ed.), *Review of child development research* (vol. 4). Chicago: University of Chicago Press, 1975.

Reese, H. W. *Basic learning processes in children.* New York: Holt, Rinehart and Winston, 1976.

Riegel, K. F. Time and change in the development of the individual and society. In H. W. Reese (Ed.), *Advances in child development and behavior* (vol. 7). New York: Academic Press, 1972.

Ringness, T. A. Whatever happened to the study of classical conditioning? *Phi Delta Kappan,* 1976, *57,* 447–455.

Robinson, N. M., & Robinson, H. B. *The mentally retarded child* (2nd ed.). New York: McGraw-Hill, 1976.

Schantz, C. The development of social cognition. In E. M. Hetherington (Ed.), *Review of child development research* (vol. 5). Chicago: University of Chicago Press, 1975, 257–324.

Scott, J. P. *Early experience and the organization of behavior.* Belmont, Calif.: Wadsworth-Brooks/Cole, 1968.

Shields, J., & Slater, E. Heredity and psychological abnormality. In H. J. Eysenck (Ed.), *Handbook of abnormal psychology.* New York: Basic Books, 1961.

Smith, C. P. *Child development.* Dubuque, Iowa: William C. Brown, 1966.

Solomon, R. Punishment. *American Psychologist,* 1964, *19,* 239–253.

Stephens, J. M., & Evans, E. D. *Development and classroom learning.* New York: Holt, Rinehart and Winston, 1973.

Sutton-Smith, B. Developmental laws and the experimentalists' ontology. *Merrill-Palmer Quarterly,* 1970, *16,* 253–259.

Terman, L. M. The discovery and encouragement of exceptional talent. *American Psychologist,* 1954, *9,* 221–230.

Thompson, G. G. *Child psychology.* Boston: Houghton Mifflin, 1962.

Thompson, W. R., & Wilde, G. Behavior genetics. In B. B. Wolman (Ed.), *Handbook of general psychology.* Englewood Cliffs, N.J.: Prentice-Hall, 1973.

Travers, R. M. W. *Essentials of learning* (4th ed.). New York: Macmillan.

Wiggins, J. S. Personality structure. In P. R. Farnsworth (Ed.), *Annual Review of Psychology,* 1968, *19,* 293–350.

PART II

MAJOR SOCIAL INFLUENCES

Our emphasis upon interaction and development is extended in Part II by examining the principal ingredients of the social context in which interaction occurs. These ingredients—supplied largely by parents, schools, and the mass media—all influence the developing individual by exerting *socialization* influences. Socialization can be thought about in two related ways. First, socialization refers to the process which influences children to behave acceptably or desirably within the larger social group of which they are a part. Accordingly, childrearing and educational methods are brought to bear upon this process by adults whose vested interests are at stake. Some of these methods are designed carefully, others seem to occur haphazardly with no detectable planning. Either way, many random learnings occur in a typical American child's life as the child grows older. As age increases, so usually does freedom to participate in an ever-widening circle of experiences over which parents and other primary agents of socialization have little control. Thus we can speak of children as active agents in their own socialization. By chance, choice, or some combination of both, children encounter learning opportunities that are not always consistent with parents' and educators' attempts at socialization. Viewed in this way, the socialization process extends beyond childrearing and education to peer group influences, including play interactions and other inputs from the child's culture such as the mass media.

A second, related way to think about socialization is in terms of the outcome, or product, of the influencing process. If we say the process occurs to establish socially acceptable or desirable behavior patterns, then we face the problem of defining exactly what these patterns are. Following one psychologist, Erik Erikson, we may argue that citizens of the United States, if not individuals in all Western cultures, are "well-socialized" when they are trusting, autonomous, possess initiative along socially approved lines, and share at least enough of the work ethic, so that they enjoy the "business" as well as the "play" parts of their lives. Another psychologist, Edward Shoben, projects similar socialization outcomes as desired: good self-control, personal and social responsibility, democratic social interest, and incorporation of ideals of principled conduct into everyday behavior. In United States society the notion of successful socialization would include economic self-sufficiency. Persons who fall short of minimum expectations in these areas by behaving impulsively, immorally, or dependently, instead of rationally, morally, or independently, may be labeled as poorly socialized or undersocialized. Persons whose behavior is imbalanced, for example, in the direction of compulsive work and constant fear of being rejected by others, might be thought of as oversocialized.

Whatever the desired outcomes of socialization, their achievement is seldom, if ever, an either-or matter. For instance, persons are not totally impulsive or rational, completely immoral or moral. Neither are they likely to be totally compulsive and fearful, as compared to completely flexible and confident. It is more accurate to speak about such personal characteristics in degrees. It may also be more useful for understanding to ask about the conditions under which specific behaviors occur, instead of labeling persons as generally impulsive, moral, fearful, or whatever.

The terms themselves are ambiguous. One individual's impulsiveness may be another's spontaneity; compulsiveness for one person may be persistence or dedication for another. Moreover, important questions must be answered. Are these characteristics largely learned, and therefore open to socialization influence? Or are they heavily determined by our genes, and thus less changeable by environmental forces?

Socialization is both process and product. Presumably, agents of socialization use methods that they believe are necessary to achieve desirable socialization outcomes. We will examine various interrelated aspects of the socialization process. Throughout the chapters in Part II, we highlight ways in which psychologists and others have studied and thought about these social influences on behavior and development.

chapter 3

Parents

Resolved: "If you spare the rod, you spoil the child." As a parent, or prospective parent, on which side would you prefer to debate this issue? If you argue pro, you would have to show which and what kinds and amount of physical punishment would be desirable or necessary for effective socialization. If you argue con, you would have to argue against punishment and for alternative tactics that would effectively socialize children. More straightforward punishment questions include, "What are the effects of corporal punishment?" and "Under what conditions is corporal punishment effective?" Even assuming clear answers to these questions were available, a nagging moral-ethical issue remains: Can the corporal punishment of children or youth be morally justified under *any* conditions?

This is but one of many perplexing and controversial issues about childrearing that are debated throughout American society. The punishment issue is part of the broader question of how best to raise children so as to promote their independence, achievement, social skills, sense of morality, self-esteem, or whatever else is established as an important goal of socialization.

CHILDREARING: A PERSISTENT DILEMMA

Some Reasons for Debate

Debate and uncertainty about how best to raise children seem to have intensified over the years. One author (Sunley, 1968) suggests three reasons for this intensification. First, there has been a steady, gradual, but increasingly obvious emphasis on children as extensions of parental ambitions and as symbols of their parents' status in society. Such children may be *extrinsically* valued, instead of valued as persons of inherent worth and dignity (Ausubel, 1958). It is, of course, a rare parent who does not take pride in seeing his or her child develop and secure social recognition. There is nothing wrong with such eminently normal behavior. But if this is *all* the child means to the parents, both parents and child may suffer.

At issue here is motivation for parenthood, an important foundation of the parental attitudes that eventually affect the quality of overall parent–child interaction. These attitudes can have effects on socialization that range from positive and growth-enhancing to negative and growth inhibiting. When parents see their children primarily as ways to get satisfactions they are missing or as instruments of self-gratification, there may be cause for concern about the consequences for child development. Several studies of college students (for example, Meade & Singh, 1973; Rabin, 1965) indicate that prospective fathers' dominant motivations for wanting children are often narcissistic, that is, their desire for children reflects needs to enhance or perpetuate the self, prove virility, or realize frustrated occupational or avocational pursuits through their childrens' successes. The behavior of many parents at children's sporting events, such as Little League baseball, and parental pressures upon youths to seek "prestigious" occupations ("My child the doctor") seem to illustrate such motivations.

There are, of course, other ways to think about children (Becker & Hill, 1955). Some parents view children primarily as a responsibility delegated by their deity, thus stressing caretaking functions and religious training. Other parents envision their children as a bundle of potentialities to be actualized through enriched childrearing experiences. Prospective mothers, in particular, seem to emphasize mutual love and joy in observing the development of individual potential (Meade & Singh, 1973). Still other parents, perhaps not wanting children in the first place but having them by accident or in response to social pressures, may consider their children a nuisance or see them as obstacles to personal freedom.

This nuisance view is often intensified by the increased economic pressure childbearing creates among many American families. According to the Health Insurance Institute of America, the cost in 1976 of a family's first baby was nearly $2,200.00 and rising fast, having increased 40 percent since 1974! Economic and other family stresses produced by children may partly account for recent evidence of marital unhappiness and dissatisfaction among parents. According to Campbell (1975), self-reports of happiness among married couples are highest before the birth of their children, lowest during the early years of childrearing, and increase positively, if slowly, as children grow older. Once children have "left the nest," marital and general life satisfactions return to or even exceed the prechild levels.

While not true of all parents, this does suggest that childrearing is not totally blissful. The nuisance or hassle factor for most parents is balanced or offset by personal gratifications and growth in self-understanding from the parenting experience. The question is how best to achieve such a balance.

A second reason for widespread uncertainty about childrearing technique is that many people have become convinced of their power to control their environment and to shape their futures, a conviction that includes the belief that children can be molded by their environments. This belief, in turn, leads directly to a concern about how conditions in the environment affect behavior.

This suggests a conception of the parental role that extends far beyond simple caretaking functions, such as feeding, cleaning, and protecting. It also means more than simply providing a model for children's learning, serving as disciplinarian, or meeting a child's emotional needs (Hoffman, 1975). It implies that parents are active teachers of their own children, even if much of the teaching is informal or in response to transitory curiosity or requests by children for help in solving their problems. Many parents also engage in proactive teaching, that is, they provide preplanned learning activities with definite purposes or goals in mind.

Including teaching in the parental role further clarifies an important distinction between control and training. Control can be seen in interactions between parents and children where the aim is to immediately maintain or change a specific behavior in a given situation. Such verbal parental exhortations as "Be quiet," or such threats as, "One more mistake like that and there's no television for a week," illustrate the immediacy of control attempts. Training, by contrast, involves deliberate and specific efforts to change a child's customary way of behaving in the future. For example, parents may spend considerable time discussing with their children why they "misbehaved," show how

the behavior was inappropriate, and point out how such behavior can cause problems for the child with others outside the family. More positively, training can include parental guidance to achieve desired goals, such as responsibility for pet care, household chores, and the like. In a phrase, the difference between control and training is in focus—"now versus next" (Sears, Maccoby, & Levin, 1956).

A third trend that has apparently intensified dilemmas about childrearing is the strong need for personal direction (values, ideals, and the like) that comes on the heels of rapid and extreme cultural change. When established patterns of living are disrupted by technological change, mushrooming bureaucracies, physical and social mobility, and philosophical and moral ferment, new patterns must take their places. The problem is deciding how to select new patterns that are appropriate, valid, and satisfying. Not only families, but churches, schools, communities, and state and national groups face these dilemmas.

Even a casual browse through library bookshelves or commercial bookstores reveals an abundance of published advice about "new and better ways" of childrearing. This advice varies in quality and specificity and is often contradictory. One "expert" may insist that parents firmly and consistently refuse to allow their young child into the parental bed, say, following a bad dream. Another expert may advocate full acceptance of the child's attempts to seek such snuggly comfort. Both will have reason(s) for their respective positions. The first may caution against fostering dependency and permitting children to invade their parents' privacy; the second may argue that acceptance is critical to soothe the child's fears and establish a relationship of trust and security. Who is more correct, if indeed either of them is?

Or might the first strategy be effective for one child, the second for another?

Research and Childrearing Practices

Psychologists believe that the answers to such questions will come only through empirical research in parental childrearing practices. This research takes several forms. The best is careful, systematic observation of parent–child interaction over time and across a wide variety of situations. Unfortunately, such naturalistic observation is not always practical or convenient. We often must satisfy ourselves with observing contrived laboratory incidents in which parents and their children voluntarily participate. Even more often, however, we must rely on reports from parents about their perceptions of interaction and influence, attitudes toward their children, or what they have done or would do for, with, or to their children under given circumstances. Occasionally children's perceptions of their parents' behavior are also explored through interviews or questionnaires. Such verbal reports, once removed from behavior, are subject to distortion by selective forgetting, or even through unwitting prompting by a researcher. We know that words can belie behavior—"You say you love me, but look how you treat me!" Caution and tentativeness must accompany our interpretations of even the most careful attempts to understand parenting and its effects.

Despite these limitations, we must do with what we have. The amassed research data about parenting does permit us the luxury of a few assured points. First, patterns of childrearing practice in America have undergone significant changes through time (LeMasters, 1977). Scientific observational data are not available, but a mass of anecdotal reports and historical accounts paint a picture of a comparatively austere emotional life and authoritarian childrearing throughout much of colonial America. The widespread Calvinistic belief that children were conceived in sin and born with a predisposition to evil was accompanied by strict, often punitive, methods to convert the child's nature to morality. Obedience and submission by the child to authority were sought by adults; indulging children was shunned.

Seeds of change were clearly apparent by the early-to-middle nineteenth century. Benevolent adult care of children was assigned a more significant role. Gentler treatment of the child was advocated in a budding literature about childrearing. Interest in the importance of children and parenting problems grew substantially (Sunley, 1968). Formal psychological theory, notably psychoanalysis and behaviorism (Appendix A), raised the levels of parental consciousness about the significant effects of early childhood experiences on children's later development. Children's adjustment and general mental health emerged as a high, if not the highest, goal of "proper childrearing." This value was also apparent in the strong efforts by educators to promote "life adjustment" education in American schools. In the words of one perceptive observer, a "fun morality" guided the experts' advice to parents. They should enjoy their children, play with them, be frivolous, and practice true egalitarianism in the home (Wolfenstein, 1951).

Recent Trends in Childrearing Practices

Formal research on childrearing developed gradually. By the 1950s, certain trends in parental behavior were apparent, corroborating less formal observations (Bronfenbrenner, 1961). These trends included an increased permissiveness toward children's "spontaneous desires," a freer expression of adult affection for children, and greater use of psychological techniques of discipline (reasoning, appeals to guilt, expressions of disappointment, isolation) rather than direct physical punishment and scolding. Taken as a whole, these early studies suggested that certain shifts were occurring in parental role relationships. Fathers were becoming more affectionate and less autocratic, and mothers were taking on a more significant role as disciplinarians, especially for boys.

Some authorities, including Bronfenbrenner (1961), speculate that permissiveness and the use of indirect disciplinary techniques were reduced somewhat by the space race triggered in 1958 by Russia's Sputnik. According to this view, intellectual achievement, as shown by technological competence, replaced social adjustment as the most important socialization value. Greater pressures for children's early school achievement—extended through the college years—were said to characterize American family life. Such pressures supposedly were accompanied by greater parental intolerance of error, mediocrity, and signs of dependency. The achievement obsession went hand-in-hand with charges from critics that America's schools were a great "educational wasteland." "Out with frills, in with basics," they said. Curriculum changes placed great emphasis upon science and mathematics. Efficiency experts championed educational technology (for example, "teaching machines") which were later accused of fostering depersonalization in schooling. All this was tied to a cycle of heightened failure—frustration, alienation, and eventually protest—among the young. Vietnam and Watergate symbolized aggressive achievement, depersonalization, conformity, and immorality. Brought into focus was a need to

reassess basic values. Altruism, empathy, creativity, and morality are values that have laced the newer rhetoric for childrearing (for example, Gordon, 1970).

This suggested chain of events, if accurate, suggests that socialization practice is largely reactionary. The pendulum swings, but only so far, before it is checked and begins to swing back. It is not, however, possible to speak about such changes in absolute cause–effect terms. We cannot assume that because one thing follows another, causation is proven. Instead, we try to make sense out of related or associated events. One basic point remains clear: for whatever reasons, childrearing practices change through time. To the extent that such practices affect children's development, we can anticipate alteration in the fabric of human development as well.

It is also apparent that the social context affects how questions about childrearing (and about human psychological functioning as a whole) are seen as relevant or important (Sears, 1975). Aspects of motivational development, for example, have surged to the top of investigators' concerns in relation to broader social issues. We have observed that America's economic depression focused research on the *hunger* drive, *aggression* became focal during the rise of facism, and a burst of research about *anxiety* occurred as America approached the Second World War. Prolonged family separation during the war was associated with research about *dependency*, the McCarthy era saw research on *conformity*, and, as noted, *achievement motivation* was studied when Soviet–U.S. space competition was at its height. Similarly, such current changes in family structure as the heightened divorce rate and an increase in the number of working mothers are associated with growing concerns about socialization practices, including the effects of single parenting, home versus group day care, and the like.

Evolution in Socialization Research

Socialization research itself has undergone stages of evolutionary change, each of which has contributed in its own way to our knowledge about parenting influences and parent–child interaction (Yarrow, 1973).

Early socialization studies dealt disproportionately with emotionally disturbed children, infants, and even animals in an attempt to establish causal relationships between stress factors, including early maternal deprivation and subsequent distortions in personality development. Generally speaking, these studies (for example, Spitz, 1945), while often provocative and dramatic, suffered from flaws in methodology and data analysis. The resulting ambiguities prevented any pronouncements about inevitable pathological outcomes of early stress. These earlier studies also failed to show definitive links between even very gross parental characteristics and the development of children's psychopathology (Frank, 1965). The net evidence does not rule out the possibility that links exist, only that they are at best obscure and equivocal.

More recent studies echo this. Wollins (1970), for example, has provided evidence that casts doubt on the belief that early separation of children from their parents and long-term institutionalization necessarily results in psychological impoverishment. Still another authority (Rutter, 1971), while conceding that separation of children from their families can bring about short-term distress, argues that it cannot be established as a cause of longer-term disorders. Rather, the relationships between separation and later problems, such as antisocial behavior, are more likely to be a function of the active family discord and lack of affection that precedes and accompanies separation.

The broader hypothesis about the importance of early experiences is not cast away. Ample data exist to show that sensory deprivation and restriction of opportunity for movement can retard infant development (Appleton, Clifton, & Goldberg, 1975). But strong claims about necessary relationships between early stresses and later emotional disturbances must submit to more explorations and limited explanations. Variables such as the timing, duration, intensity, and type of stress, lack of compensatory support, and constitutional predisposition to emotional reactivity or illness are among the interrelated factors that must be considered. Our clearest evidence about the origins of long term deviant development comes from the study of severe early physiological trauma (prenatally or in early postnatal life) combined with a deprived material environment (Sameroff, 1975).

This notion of interacting variables, however, did not at first guide the research that followed the early stress-pathology studies. Efforts to tease out environmental determinants on infants and children were focused on specific, and possibly too simple and isolated, aspects of childrearing; hence, the rash of studies of the comparative effects of nursing and other feeding practices. These studies were directed both to assessing practical decisions about rearing and to testing assumptions about emotional development in psychological theory, especially psychoanalysis (Appendix A). It has been claimed, for example, that the method of infant feeding—breast or bottle—profoundly affects security and other central aspects of personality. Breast feeding has often been favored. Related issues are when and how to wean the infant from breast or bottle to cup and spoon and the merits of demand feeding (when the child wants it) versus scheduled feeding (the traditional every four hours).

Studies attempting to resolve such issues face enormous difficulties. How do you gain access to sufficiently large and representative numbers of mothers and infants? How do you measure "personality" during the early years of life? How do you separate the piecemeal effects of feeding or weaning from the total constellation of childcare practices in a given family? It may come as no surprise, therefore, that such studies have not documented clear relationships between feeding and weaning and children's personality development (Caldwell, 1964; Orlansky, 1949). If important links exist, they have not yet been discovered. However, as one wag has put it, breast feeding can be ultimately beneficial for a father's mental health!

Attempts to establish causal relationships between early socialization factors and later development did not stop with the feeding issue. Important questions about toilet training or, more accurately, bowel and bladder training, also were raised. When does a mother or caregiver initiate it? How is training done? How do children react to training? And so on. Many of these questions reflect a concern for the critical-periods hypothesis discussed in Chapter 2. Early findings about variations in elimination training can be cited, but hold no clear long-term implications for personality development. For example, transitory or short-term disturbances in bowel and bladder functioning have been associated with punitive or premature training (Caldwell, 1964). Moreover, early elimination training based on coercion has been related to a mother's anxiety about sex and her compulsion for orderliness (McCandless, 1967). Yet different children respond differently to similar training techniques, whether benevolent or harsh, and techniques vary in impact de-

pending upon the more general nature of parent–child relationships. Thus it is nearly impossible to predict long-range effects of elimination training, particularly in isolation from other major socialization activities.

Feeding and elimination training are but two of the early experience factors that have captured the fancy of psychologists. Another is independence training. Questions about the onset and nature of parental attempts to influence children to do things on their own, using initiative and self-help, have been particularly popular in American society. Unfortunately, research about independence training in isolation from the total context of family experience is also ambiguous. One researcher, for example, has reported a strong positive relationship between early independence training—parental demands for autonomous problem-solving and task mastery—and later motivation to achieve standards of excellence (Winterbottom, 1958). Just the opposite relationship has been found by other researchers, who found early independence demands associated with low achievement striving (Bartlett & Smith, 1966). Some contradictory findings can be explained by differences in methodology, including the tools for measuring behavior and the samples of children and parents studied. However, fuzzy or weak relationships are a frequent outcome of attempts to extract simple, isolated cause–effect relations from dynamic, complex patterns of parent–child interaction. In any case, these data are correlational only.

Recognizing limitations in these single-variable data, psychologists have come to appreciate more fully the significance of overall patterns of socialization practice. Among other things, this has meant a consideration of the emotional climate in which socialization attempts are made, the scheduling of rewards and punishments, what behaviors are modeled by parents, the type and amount of cognitive and social stimulation parents provide, and how children's reactions to parental influence attempts may, in turn, affect parents themselves. Where possible it may involve a look at children's social cognitions (Chapter 2) and attempts to investigate how children actually perceive their parents' childrearing behavior (Armentrout & Burger, 1972; Burger, Lamp, & Rogers, 1975). This provides a more comprehensive picture of socialization practices and effects.

To incorporate all potentially significant components of childrearing practice into one study is a tall and perhaps impossible order. Time, money, and research methods are almost always limited. Important steps toward socialization pattern analysis can be cited, however. Consider the following example of increased sophistication in thinking about parenting.

Socialization for Competence: The Issue of Control

Diana Baumrind (1971) conducted a series of studies of childrearing practices and their relation to competence in young children. Specifically, she wanted to identify individual differences in *instrumental competence* among young children. Baumrind defined instrumental competence along two dimensions: *social responsibility* (achievement-oriented, friendly, and cooperative child behaviors) versus *irresponsibility* (not achievement-oriented, hostile, and resistive behavior toward peers and adults); and *independence* (dominant and purposive) versus *tractability* (submissive and aimless in behavior). She documented early in her series of studies a wide range of differences in instrumental competence among both boys and girls of nursery school age.

Baumrind reasoned that patterns of parental authority are major variables in the development of instrumental competence in children. Thus another of her research tasks was to determine if different patterns of parental authority could be observed and described. Using procedures too involved to describe here, three basic patterns were identified.

Authoritarian: characterized by a high degree of parental control, a stress on obedience, absolute standards, a tendency to utilize forceful, punitive disciplinary measures, and strong emphasis on respect for authority, tradition, and order, with little verbal give-and-take between parent and child. This pattern may or may not involve rejection of the child.

Authoritative: characterized by firm rational control. Both autonomy and disciplined conformity are valued for children, with a full recognition and respect for their interests. Encouragement and affirmation of present qualities prevail, but standards for future conduct are clearly communicated. Both reason and power are used as methods of parental control, but verbal give-and-take occur freely. Overrestrictiveness is avoided. This pattern may or may not include the explicit promotion of nonconformity in children.

Permissive: characterized by an attempt by parents to behave nonpunitively toward the child. Positive acceptance of the child's impulses, desires, and actions prevails. The parents consult the child about family policies and make few demands for order and household responsibility. The parents seek to be a resource for the child rather than a director of his activities. Self-regulation by the child is encouraged. Low control and emphasis on obedience to externally defined standards are preferred. The exercise of power over the child is avoided. This approach may or may not combine direct encouragement of nonconformity with laxity in discipline. Some permissive parents may stress high performance for the child in *some* areas, however.

Many specific findings have emerged from Baumrind's research, including a strong relationship between measured intelligence and instrumental competence. The results of her most recent study illustrate the relationship of parental authority to instrumental competence. In comparison to other patterns, *authoritative parental behavior* was most clearly associated with independent, purposive behavior in girls and with strong indications of social responsibility in boys. This pattern was also clearly associated with independence in boys when their parents were nonconforming, and with high achievement (but not with friendly, cooperative behavior) in girls.

Given these and similar findings, Baumrind argues for the following *general* idea: "A matrix of parental values that lay stress upon individuality, self expression, initiative, divergent thinking, and aggressiveness should promote independence *if* not accompanied by lax, inconsistent discipline and an unwillingness to place demands upon the child . . ." She stresses the general importance of "modeling desired behavior, firm control and enforcement policies, fairness, open verbal exchange, acceptance and positive reinforcement . . ." in relation to social responsibility.

The concept of instrumental competence embodies what many Americans mean by middle-class values. Baumrind derives her generalizations about the antecedents or correlates of this behavior from the study of literate, cooperative, "normal" parents and children, most of whom are reasonably secure financially. We would ask two questions. Is the goal of instrumental competence desirable for *all* children in *all* quarters of society? If so, should parents everywhere attempt to emulate the pattern of parental authority most clearly associated with this behavior in children?

Two Major Dimensions of Parenting Behavior

This and other pattern studies (for example, Clarke-Stewart, 1973; Thomas, Gecas, Weigart, & Rooney, 1974) indicate the importance of two, broad, interacting parental orientations toward child-rearing: *general affect* and *management style*. Consider first parental affect as described along a continuum from warmth and acceptance to coldness and hostility (Becker, 1964). Acceptance, encouragement, expression of affection, friendly joint activities, concern about and readiness to respond to children's needs, and general family harmony are among the indicators of warmth in parenting. Parents high in warmth, such as Juan's mother (Chapter 1), seem to enjoy their children, provide positive reinforcement for their accomplishments, and avoid running down their abilities. At the extreme, hostility takes the form of active rejection, insensitivity to children's needs, and denial of them as individuals of dignity and worth. Unfortunately, hostility may result in severe child abuse, as discussed in Chapter 12. The expression of parental hostility, or warmth for that matter, may vary according to situational factors. Thus, acts of hostility or love may be more evident in public or private settings (a restaurant or the family dining room) depending upon how parents perceive their immediate social context and how susceptible they are to social pressures from other adults.

Affect as a part of parenting style cannot be divorced from parents' general orientation to behavioral management. This orientation can be described along another related continuum, from freedom for autonomy to restrictive control (Schaefer, 1959). For example, warm parents who employ cooperative and democratic means to develop guidelines for their childrens' behavior are providing a laboratory for the practice of autonomy. In contrast, warm parents might exhibit protectiveness, overindulgence, or extreme possessiveness, establishing in each case a form of control that could limit the development of children's independence. Similarly, hostile parents who arbitrarily and punitively dictate and enforce a large number of rules may severely circumscribe their children's learning and decision-making opportunities. But hostile parents who are inaccessible to their children or who display indifference to or detachment from family activities, can provide a de facto setting for their children's autonomous behavior. (In this case, of course, parental encouragement, emotional support when problems arise, or benevolent guidance for autonomy would be absent.)

On the whole, conceptualizing parental behavior by affect and management style seems to account for many kinds of differences in children's development, including intellectual development, higher versus lower self-esteem, religiosity, conformity, and sociability. From this, it is plausible to argue that both dimensions of parent behavior are important sources of observational learning for children.

As children grow up and themselves become parents, their parenting behavior may reflect much imitation. Perhaps the most dramatic illustration is provided by studies of child abuse. Many, if not most, parents who physically abuse or neglect their children have themselves childhood histories of parental abuse or neglect (Chapter 12). Frightening patterns of child abuse cannot be explained simply or solely by imitation, but if in general parental role behaviors are sustained at least partly by observational learning processes, then we will tend to raise our children as we ourselves were raised. This can provide a certain continuity of family socialization practices across generations. In fact, cross-generation assessments of attitudes and beliefs about childrearing often show remarkable similarities, even though shifts in value priorities and socialization methods gradually occur (Cohler, Greenebaum, Weiss, & Moran, 1971).

Despite a degree of continuity in socialization practice from one generation to the next, there is strong evidence of changes over time in socialization goals and methods. The reasons for these changes are often obscure and subject to speculation. In America, the general trend has been toward a more liberal approach to childrearing. Advances in socialization research hold promise for a fuller understanding of how this trend, and basic patterns of parental influence, affect human development.

As changes, even improvements, in socialization practices may occur over time, we simultaneously observe basic differences in childrearing from family to family within the same generation. Some parents foster individuality; others obedience and conformity. Some parents routinely use coercive measures, including punishment, to control their children; others totally reject such measures. In terms of our three-cornered triangle of interaction (Chapter 1), some parents stress intellectual achievement, others place a higher value on sociality, and so on. These variations suggest caution before generalizing too broadly about trends in childrearing practice. They also provoke much curiosity among students of human socialization and development. What are the sources of differences in parenting? How can these differences be explained? What effects do such differences have on the development of children and youth? To answer these questions, we will examine some basic categories of family identity associated with differences in patterns of socialization practice.

VARIATIONS IN SOCIALIZATION PRACTICE

Culture

The broadest and most obvious level of comparison is the study of socialization practice across different cultures. Such studies have produced intriguing data about how adults approach the rearing of their young. Feeding and weaning practices, for example, vary widely among different cultural groups (Whiting & Child, 1953). In some cultures, children are nursed only briefly; in others, weaning may not occur until children are 5 or 6 years old. The weaning process itself may involve severe punishment or it may occur in a warmly permissive environment. Self-reliance training also differs considerably among cultures (Whiting, 1963). Children may be expected fully to dress and feed themselves by age 3 or earlier in one cultural setting, but not until age 5 or 6 in another.

We will have occasion to mention specific cultural differences in socialization at various points throughout this book. But the point of immediate interest is the powerful role cultural *values* have in shaping children's socialization environments (LeVine, 1974). In the Soviet Union, for example, these values include firm commitment to the welfare of the social group, internalized obedience and self-discipline, cooperation with others, and strict conformity to standards of good conduct. Presumably, a translation of these values into socialization effort is necessary to secure stability in the preferred form of government. The socialist system requires subordination of the individual to state service. According to one observer of the Soviet scene, systematically applied group pressure tactics figure heavily in the achievement of this goal. These tactics include peer evaluation, public criticism, group competition, social approval if work is well done, and swift punishment for deviant behavior (Bronfenbrenner, 1970).

We are led to believe that Soviet children and youth are effectively socialized according to the state interests. However, research data about intended (or unintended) outcomes of Soviet socialization practice are not available. Ample data do exist, however, to document a relationship between cultural belief systems and childrearing practices. Data from the study of preindustrial societies are perhaps most striking. In one study, for example, the approach to infant care has been linked to beliefs about the supernatural (Lambert, Triandis, & Wolf, 1959). Specifically, more punitive and less affectionate and nurturant infant care practices were found in societies with beliefs in aggressive or malevolent supernatural beings. In contrast, more positive and rewarding infant care was found among families holding beliefs in a benevolent deity. Apparently, religious beliefs can support childrearing practices. Perhaps the cumulative effects of childrearing practices also help sustain given religious beliefs. Such relationships are not easily interpreted, but do much to provoke our thinking about why humans behave as they do.

Socialization differences have also been related to a society's subsistence economy, or dominant method of accumulating food resources. One research team (Barry, Child, & Bacon, 1959) has reported contrasting goals and values between societies with a high-accumulation economy, whose food supplies require protection and gradual development throughout a year by crop growing, harvesting, and storage, and those that accumulate less and wrest food daily from nature by hunting or fishing. Pressures for obedience and responsibility mark the socialization practices in high-accumulation economies, while self-reliance and personal achievement are stressed in the low-accumulation economies. The researchers argue that each value system is best suited to survival within the respective societies.

Still another researcher (Berry, 1967) has used this subsistence-economy–socialization-practice hypothesis to assess personality differences among various cultural groups. Conformity was measured among representatives of Baf-

The Bettmann Arc

Kenneth Karp

Photograph by Arthur Sirdofsky

Photograph © 1975 by Arthur Sirdofsky

The Bettmann Archive

Kathryn Abbe

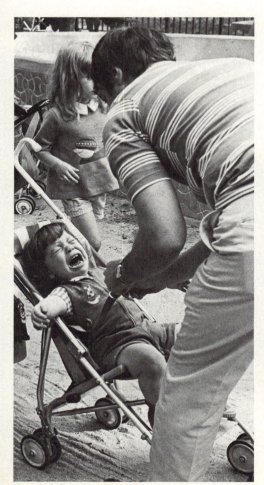

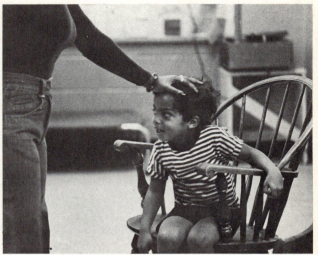

Kenneth Karp

Photo © Shelly Rusten 1973

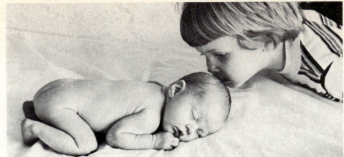

Photo by Suzanne Szasz

Photo by Suzanne Szasz

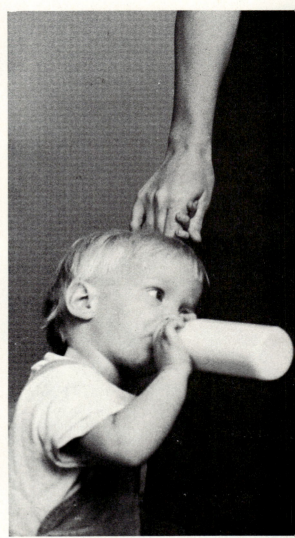

Leonard Speier

Photo by Suzanne Szasz

Photograph by Jean Shapiro

Michael Weisbrot

Kenneth Karp

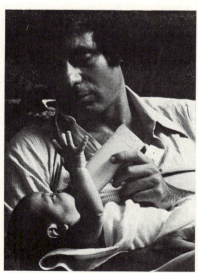

Kenneth Karp

TUNISIAN BEDOUINS

Photograph copyright © 1976 by Arthur Sirdofsky

HRW photo by Hella Hammid

CUNA INDIAN, PANAMA

Photograph by Arthur Sirdofsky

Photograph by Jean Shapiro

Photograph by Charles C

Kenneth Karp

Kathryn Abbe

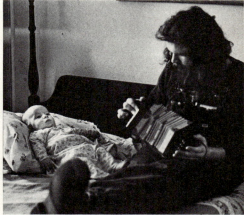

Michael Weisbrot

Photo © Mimi Cotter

Kenneth Karp

fin Island Eskimos and the Temne people of Sierra Leone. The results were compared with results from people of an industrialized Western society, the Scots. Conformity was measured in a way that has often been used. Confederates were recruited who agreed to make a false report about their judgment of the length of a line. Innocent subjects, who had already made independent judgments, were asked to judge again after hearing the false report from all others in the group. The more these innocents shifted their judgment in the direction of the false group judgment, the more conforming they were presumed to be.

To survive in their cold, austere, even hostile environment, Eskimos must rely heavily upon their own judgment and ingenuity. These tendencies, documented by previous anthropological evidence, suggested a prediction that Eskimo subjects would exercise their rugged independence to resist group pressure for conformity to the false report about the lengths of lines.

The Temne live on rice, harvesting only a single crop a year. The rice must be meted out to all members of the group in carefully planned, regular daily units until the next harvest. The welfare of each individual is thus directly related to the welfare of the entire group. This is so clearly recognized that nonconformity to the rules of Temne society is severely punished. It was predicted that the Temne would be relatively susceptible to group pressures to support false judgments. The only similarity between the Eskimo and the Temne is that both are subsistence cultures—there is never more than just enough food to go around.

Data obtained clearly support these predictions (Berry, 1967). The average traditional ("old line, un-Westernized") Temne changed their judgments to a considerable degree in the direction of the false group agreement, while the traditional Eskimo averaged a much smaller change in this direction. Rural and urban Scots were more individualistic than the Temne, but more conforming than the Eskimo. As might be expected from the stereotype of the ruggedly individualistic, proud Scot, the Scots were closer to the Eskimo than to the Temne, but nonetheless significantly more conforming than the Eskimo.

Studies such as these support the *adaptation hypothesis* about socialization (Weber, 1930) which suggests that a society strives through its methods of socialization to develop in its members the type of adult characteristics thought essential for the continued support and functioning of that society. Ideas such as "basic personality type" and "national character" are implicit in this hypothesis. Culturally patterned childrearing practices are seen as the primary factor in the development of socially appropriate adult behavior.

Research consistent with this viewpoint has not been limited to comparisons of nonindustrial or rural societies. For example, Miller and Swanson (1958) have examined the childrearing practices of American parents who differ in their occupational roles: bureaucratic versus entrepreneurial. Bureaucratic occupations are characterized by a direct salary and comparatively high job security. Generally speaking, public school teaching, civil service, the military, and many industrial or corporate jobs are bureaucratic, though the salaries vary widely. Occupations in which persons are self-employed or work on a direct commission basis are more entrepreneurial, because they involve a higher degree of risk-taking and competition. They also may range over a wide spectrum of personal income. Contrast, for example, the highly successful physician in private practice with a door-to-door broom salesman working on a commission.

Miller and Swanson report differing parental goals and methods of child-rearing in bureaucratic families and entrepreneurial families. The former tend to stress equalitarian practices and to emphasize social adjustment or "getting along." The latter emphasize independence training, mastery, and self-reliance. The entrepreneurial parents also depend heavily on psychological techniques of discipline. It is therefore likely that growing up in an entrepreneurial home or in a bureaucratic home represents quite a difference, in terms of the values reflected in family interaction.

Plausible as this seems, however, we have reason to believe that socialization is not simply a matter of adaptation. Adaptation first to ensure physical survival and health and then to foster development of children's capacity for economic self-maintenance at maturity are two goal structures basic to any culture (LeVine, 1974). A strict interpretation of the adaptation hypothesis might suggest that the socialization process ends there, but we disagree. There is more to human development than simply gaining a socially acceptable degree of self-sufficiency. There is, for example, the development of "children's behavioral capacities for maximizing cultural values—e.g., morality, prestige, wealth, religious piety, intellectual achievement, personal satisfaction, self-realization—as formulated and symbolically elaborated in cultural distinctive beliefs, norms, and ideologies" (LeVine, 1974, p. 230). In the United States personal satisfaction and self-realization have become increasingly valued as basic physical survival and economic security have been assured. In other words, the achievement of relative affluence among Western cultures provides a great majority of per-

sons, perhaps for the first time in history, the luxury of pursuing self-development values. One writer (Glasser, 1974) has coined the term "identity society" to describe this new level of consciousness and concern about life's personal meaning. In many ways, this can also be thought of as radical individualism. Liberationist movements, encounter groups, therapy to promote self-understanding and acceptance, intense concern with individual rights, the pursuit of racial-ethnic identity, and the like seem to mirror this value. The Miller and Swanson study described above provides a convenient transition from cross-cultural differences in parenting strategies to variations within the same culture.

Within-Culture Variations

People in the United States seem unified by their shared belief in and support of the American creed. Yet the "American experience" can also be likened to a kaleidoscope of diverse influences within the common culture. Social class, ethnic, and racial group differences in socialization practices are among the most pronounced and also the most studied. Other factors, more directly tied to variations in family structure, also merit consideration. We will examine briefly these sources of variation.

Social Class

Chapter 1 suggested social class or socioeconomic status as a shorthand description for a variety of economic, occupational, and educational factors that comprise an environment for human development and interaction. Differences in family income, place of residence, occupational prestige and educational level of parents, value placed upon self-improvement, preferences for leisure-time activities, and amount and kind of reading, are among the constellation of factors normally associated with social class differences (Deutsch, 1973; Hess, 1970).

Social class as such explains nothing about development. But comparisons of families from different socioeconomic levels usually reveal differences in values, skills, and general life styles, even though a considerable overlap or similarity in such qualities may exist within each level. For example, such comparisons show consistent class differences in the breadth and quality of early learning experiences provided for children, types of adult models available to children for patterning their behaviors, amount and quality of health care and nutrition, amount and kind of opportunity for cognitive-intellectual stimulation, and the kind of behavioral control exerted by parents over their children (Miller, 1970).

Between the advantaged and the poor, there are great average differences in family stability, job security, and marital satisfaction among women (all favoring the advantaged). It seems reasonable to infer that such differences can significantly affect parent–child relations. As a group the affluent, more than the poor, bring up their children to be achievement oriented, succeed in school, control their aggression, conceal their sexuality, and communicate expressively with their parents. Advantaged parents are more likely than the poor to be liberal in childrearing practices, perhaps because they have the time and the vocabulary required to practice liberality and also are less frustrated by crowded, uncomfortable living conditions.

Advantaged parents also have been found to use less physical discipline and show more affection toward their children. For better or worse, they seem to influence and control the behavior of their children even after these are grown more than do poor people. In advantaged families, joint activity and togetherness often are stressed more than they are in poor families. Attitudes (particularly moral attitudes) of advantaged parents and those of their children are more similar than in poor families. And, when circumstances dictate, advantaged parents seem to teach their children with greater clarity of purpose, encouragement, elaboration in language and presentation, and positive reinforcement (Hess, 1970). Generally speaking, less permissive and more punitive restrictive control by parents over their children have been observed among lower than among higher social class families.

Some authorities (such as Bronfenbrenner, 1961) maintain that social class differences in childrearing have decreased over the past several decades. This could be an outcome of a gradual extension of "middle class" life, of education, and of the sharing of similar attitudes and parenting skills among greater numbers of Americans. Direct cause–effect relationships among social class standing, preferred childrearing tactics, and children's development are not established. However, most recent research continues to indicate the extensive influence of social class on many aspects of development (Deutsch, 1973). Children from poorer families are more often born prematurely, are less healthy, and do and perform more poorly in school and on formal measures of intellectual ability than their more advantaged counterparts. Poorer children, as a group, also behave more impulsively and with less self-criticism than do children from more economically advantaged homes. They tend less often to plan ahead or to believe in their ability to master or control their personal destiny. Their language performance tends to be less elaborate in vocabulary and in style of expressing thoughts and feelings. They also begin premarital sexual intercourse at an earlier age and indulge in it more often, and are more likely to be repeatedly delinquent (or at least they get caught and booked more often).

These generalizations are perhaps too broad and sweeping, even though they are supported firmly by research evidence. However measured, social class is a matter of degree, rather than an either-or dichotomy. Within all classes there are also apt to be large differences in one or more areas of socialization. Even when cross-class differences are substantiated, value judgments can too easily creep into their analysis or interpretation. Rather than emphasizing the adaptive strengths of lower-class parents and their children, their problems are sometimes exaggerated, even to the point of sustaining myth over reality (Ginsburg, 1972). Psychologists, for example, searching to identify conditions that affect the development of human potential, have tended to focus on obstacles to growth and eventual fulfillment at maturity. The result is often deficit-oriented thinking about cultural or social class experiences (Chapter 12). It does not require a trained psychologist or social worker to recognize that poverty usually limits the positive growth experiences of many children and adolescents (although many of America's finest and most successful people have come from impoverished backgrounds). Poverty, especially when combined with racial discrimination, poor nutrition, segregated and inadequate schools, ghetto neighborhoods, and socially maladjusted adult models, is clearly detrimental to constructive behavioral development.

On the other hand, social-emotional poverty can and does occur in homes that on formal socioeconomic criteria are upper-middle class or upper class. Many children in the "best parts of town" and from the "finest" homes are neglected, or farmed out to inadequate caretakers, or openly rejected by their parents. Still

other children, well fed and materially rich, may come to believe that life is a "bowl of cherries" that requires little effort on their parts. Away from the security of home, they may experience confusion, fear, and even anger as they learn that life is, after all, a "do-it-yourself thing." Some psychologists see this attitude as a product of the "golden ghetto" (Grinker, 1977). At worst, they say, some children of the affluent run the risk of becoming emotional zombies, subject to frustration, hopelessness, boredom, low empathy, and a weak self-concept. Other affluent youth may suffer the materialist blues. Unlike their parents who have embraced the work ethic, such children of comfort have little incentive and may wile away their time in meaningless activities.

We cannot firmly document these ideas. We have observed intense conflicts in families where children are perceived as unappreciative and disrespectful of the material comforts and possessions provided by parents who work hard. On the whole, however, we do not dispute the strong positive, relationship between parental class (socioeconomic status) and early developmental advantages for children (Golden, Birns, Bridger, & Moss, 1971; Tulkin & Cohler, 1973).

Racial-Ethnic Differences

In American society, social class and racial-ethnic variables often overlap, making it difficult to establish or to separate independent relationships between either variable and parenting behavior. As Deutsch (1973) has observed, minority ethnic groups, especially blacks, are more often found at lower social-class levels. We believe, however, that trying to distinguish class and race has merit, especially in a multiethnic society such as the United States.

The terms *ethnic, ethnic group,* and *ethnicity* are often used in much the same way as the terms *race* and *racial group*. However, these two sets of terms are not synonymous. Ethnicity refers to a group of people who share cultural, religious, and language traditions, such as Italian-Americans or Jews. Race refers to a subdivision of the human species having distinguishable physical characteristics transmitted from one generation to another. Anthropologists generally distinguish three major racial groups: Caucasian or Caucasoid (most "white" persons, and many black or dark-skinned people in the subcontinent of India-Pakistan and elsewhere); Mongolian or Mongoloid (Chinese, Japanese, most Southeast Asians, American Indians); and Negro or Negroid (native Africans and most native Australians). Through crossbreeding, racial groups can become mixed over time, but obviously there are many more ethnic groups than racial groups. Indeed, every country with a common language can be considered an ethnic group without abusing the definition. Most often, race and ethnicity tend to work in combination.

This brings us to a major point. Parents with different racial-ethnic backgrounds, even though American born and bred, often exhibit different child-rearing orientations. In one study of parental attitudes, for example, mothers from Chinese backgrounds more strongly approved maternal control of children than did comparable groups of white Protestant and Jewish mothers (Kriger & Kroes, 1972). Ethnicity also affects parental *behavior,* as shown by an investigation of maternal teaching strategies. Anglo-, Mexican-, and Chinese-American mothers were observed as they taught a sorting and motor-skill game to their preschool children. Though all mothers seemed uniformly concerned about the quality of their children's learning, differences in preferred teaching styles were observed. Chinese-American mothers, for example, made greater use of positive reinforcement and Mexican-American mothers more use of criticism than did their Anglo-American counterparts. Differences in the pacing of instruction, extent of verbal interaction, nonverbal communication, and children's acceptance of their mothers' attempts to teach them were also observed (Steward & Steward, 1973). To cite a final example, Comer and Poussaint (1975) have documented a tendency for black parents to place highest importance upon control or discipline in their children, preferring docility to assertiveness. (They also observed, however, a trend among some modern black parents to deliberately instill antiwhite attitudes in their children, just as white parents may foster prejudicial attitudes in their offspring. To the extent such practices continue, argue Comer and Poussaint, positive interracial relationships are sure to suffer.)

Such results may reflect broader, more extensive patterns of parent–child interactions that contribute to differences in home learning environments and, in turn, to the skills and attitudes about learning that children bring with them to school. Taken together, these studies show that ethnic-racial identity is linked both to parent attitude toward and style of interaction with their children. Parent–child relationships so affected presumably will have different outcomes for individual child development and behavior. The value orientations and home teaching associated with ethnic-racial identity has, for example, been used to explain differences in developmental aspects of sexuality and aggression, patterns of drug use and abuse, competitiveness, and cooperation (Pollack & Valdez, 1973). They also affect the perceptions held by children of their parents. A recent study showed that French-Canadian children saw mother-father roles as more egalitarian than did their more traditionally oriented English-Canadian peers (Smith & Grenier, 1975).

Religiosity

Religion, though not part of racial identity, is usually a central force in defining ethnicity. Religious beliefs often provide guidelines for childrearing practices, educational experiences (for example, parochial versus secular schooling), social activity (for example, Christian Youth groups), intergroup relations (for example, anti-Catholicism), and ceremonies that denote the coming of age (for example, bar mitzvah in the Jewish faith).

It is easy to see how variations in religiously based human activity can contribute to differences in knowledge, attitudes, and ways of thinking. Marked differences in methods and goals of child training have been observed among families with different religious orientations and beliefs (Whiting, 1966). These differences range from the degree to which disciplinary practices are employed by parents to the relative emphasis they place on self-reliance. Differences in achievement motivation among children and youth are associated with their parents' religions (Elkind, 1968; Elder, 1974). Children from Jewish homes, for example, frequently rate higher in achievement motivation than their Catholic peers.

More broadly, the dominant racial-ethnic group in the United States—Caucasians of Anglo-Saxon and northern European extraction—has a value system based on religion. This value system, in turn, has been related to important American political and economic factors (Weber, 1930). Summarized by the term *Protestant ethic*, this religiously derived set of values serves to define the ideal person: individualistic, thrifty, self-sacrificing, an efficient user of time, strong in personal responsibility, and committed to personal productivity as the supreme value. In turn, the attainment and practice of independence, self-sufficiency, and accumulation of resources through productivity presumably are the means for increasing the chance of personal salvation. Since the Reformation, such religiously grounded beliefs have influenced family patterns. In turn, these patterns may have facilitated a strong orientation to personal achievement, competitiveness, and standards of excellence. It is this orientation that is seemingly vital to the success of capitalism (McClelland, 1961). If so, the achievement thrust in some modern societies may be traced, at least partly, to a religious base.

As our society becomes more bureaucratized, the classic Protestant ethic may diminish as a source of cues for childrearing and educational strategies. Some may even argue that ethnic-racial factors in general will lose power to produce variations in socialization practice. This argument is consistent with the familiar "melting pot" philosophy of Americanization. But this philosophy, if it ever was widespread, seems now to have given way to renewed pride in and efforts to preserve separate ethnic-racial heritages. The result is a greater consciousness of cultural pluralism and how it is translated into socialization practice as parents present models for their children and reinforce desired behaviors.

Family Organization and Structure

Virtually all the studies cited thus far have referred to intact families—children and both natural parents living together in a single family dwelling. In American society we have generally accepted this nuclear family unit as the preferred, if not ideal, setting for human development. Some writers (such as Aries,

1975) liken the nuclear family to a "prison of love" from which neither parents nor their children can escape even if they wish to. Parents and children are expected to extend mutual love and support the ethic of togetherness and may find no alternative but to grin and bear it. This notion questions whether the nuclear family is essential. Psychologically speaking, it also helps us to focus upon differences in family organization and structure and how they may affect socialization practice. We recall from Chapter 1, for example, that most of Juan's childhood and adolescence were in a fatherless home with five siblings. Rebecca, in contrast, lived continuously with both parents as an only child. Other persons known to the author illustrate still other circumstances. Todd, age 4, is the eldest of three children spaced only 3 years apart. He and his younger siblings live with their young mother, recently divorced, who maintains full employment outside the home. Early each working day Todd and his sibs are bundled off to a day-care home some five miles away, deposited there, usually not to see their mother again until about 6:30 that evening. Home at 7:00, there is time for little else but a snack, story, and then bedtime. Todd's situation is not uncommon in a society with rising divorce and maternal employment rates. Nor is an expert needed to see that the parenting available to him and his sibs is markedly different from, say, Rebecca. The issues raised by Todd's, Juan's, and Rebecca's examples are twofold. First, how do such variables as increased family size, spacing of children, father absence, and maternal employment affect parent–child interaction? Second, what are the short- and long-term effects of these interactions?

Answers to both questions are meagre and tentative not because interest is lacking, but because they present such serious problems of research method as locating and securing the extended participation of suitable families, applying appropriate measures of parent and child behavior, and separating crucial variables (such as maternal employment) from the total set of interacting family variables—value structures of the home, marital adjustment, and amount and quality of parent-child contact. Keeping these limitations in mind, we can briefly review some highlights of research about these two questions.

Family size.   Data are far from abundant, but what evidence has accumulated about family size can be summarized by two points (Johnson & Medinnus, 1974). First, as we might expect, increased family size usually means less parent contact for individual children. As contact decreases, there is the distinct possibility that parental influence wanes accordingly. Some researchers (for example, Douvan & Adelson, 1966) have reported greater similarity in values between adolescents and their parents in smaller, as compared to larger, family units. More recently, amount of adult contact has also been related to children's intellectual development. Only children, or children in small families whose spacing or birth order is several years apart, are reported to enjoy advantages in sharing parental knowledge and verbal give-and-take (Zajone & Markus, 1975).

A second point is that family size often seems to make a difference in the exercise of parental control. As the number of children increases, especially in families with limited living space and economic resources, authoritarian control strategies are more evident. Egalitarianism, or a democratic orientation to family decision-making, is apparently more feasible in smaller families. One could argue that democratically oriented parents prefer and plan for smaller families. This is a remote possibility, although, to our knowledge, no one has yet explored the relationship between parent personality and family size or how such factors as religion may account for the family-size–behavior-management relationship. Nor do we have good evidence about the manifest problems of sibling rivalry in large families.

We should not, however, overlook some potential benefits of larger family size. Children in large families can provide one another with much emotional security. Rich opportunities for responsibility training (as in the care of younger sibs) can exist. And there is perhaps a lesser risk of distortions in socialization patterning — parental overprotection or overindulgence, for instance. On balance, however, it does seem clear that in larger families a greater frustration load must be carried by both parents and their children. Increased parental economic liability with the addition of each child to a family is but one obvious source of this frustration. The sheer density of demands by children for parent time and energy is another. As Hurley and Hohn (1971) have reported, higher child production rates are often associated with increased maternal stress and shifts from initially positive to a more negative childrearing orientation. This again illustrates the role of family circumstance as a determinant or catalyst for parenting.

Birth order.   Still another aspect of family structure that may influence socialization practices is a child's birth order. It appears to make a difference in children's development if they are first-born or an only child, a later- or a last-born child. The idea that birth order contributes in some way to personality development has long intrigued psychologists. There have been an enormous number of studies of birth order, but the results are often inconclusive or even contradictory. One major survey of these studies, for example, has revealed only weak sup-

port for three modest generalizations (Warren, 1966): a higher proportion of first-borns (versus later-borns) than would be expected are found in America's colleges and universities; first-borns are generally more susceptible to social pressure than their later-born siblings; and first-born females seem especially attracted to the company of others in threatening or disturbing situations. These generalizations are based upon the study of large groups of first- and later-borns. Thus, they may not apply at all to a particular first-born person. And other authorities on the birth-order literature have expressed strong doubts about these generalizations (Schooler, 1972).

The quest to understand more about birth order continues, and the literature on this topic continues to grow. Several recent studies, for example, point to a strong relationship between children's birth order and their verbal ability (including reading) (Breland, 1974; Glass, Neulinger, & Brim, 1974). This relationship seems stronger, however, in smaller as compared to larger families. To discover possible reasons for this relationship, still other researchers have examined how parents interact with children of differing birth order. According to one such report (Cohen & Beckwith, 1977) first-borns receive more responsive care and general stimulation from their mothers than do later-borns. First-borns' social interactions with other persons (siblings and adults) also exceed those of later-borns. Possibly these "advantages" are in some way involved in the same first-born's higher scores on a measure of infant development. The data are correlational, however, and do not establish any causal relationship.

However, neither can we dismiss the possibility of causation. Two related hypotheses seem especially promising for further birth order research (Breland, 1974). One, the "isolation" hypothesis, suggests an achievement advantage to first-borns because they are not competing with other children for parental time and attention. In short, first-borns can receive more attention than laterborns. Parental interest and energy for childrearing may also be at a higher peak for a first-born child. The second hypothesis is based upon the first-born as "interlocuter." That is, first-borns can (and often are required to) serve as parent surrogates for their later-born siblings. This surrogate role demands the practice of verbal skills and also is an important form of responsibility training. As noted in Chapter 10, both verbal ability and responsibility are important factors in patterns of high achievement.

It is necessary to tread lightly with these ideas because they are not yet securely established by research evidence. Moreover, it is unlikely that birth order operates as a single factor to create differences in children's behavior. However, in relation to other factors we have mentioned (family size, spacing of children, parental values, and competence for socialization), it is likely that birth order can affect the context in which socialization occurs, thus accounting for some behavioral differences among children and youth. Debate among psychologists about the nature and extent of this influence is likely to continue for years to come (Breland, 1973; Mitchell & Schroers, 1973; Schooler, 1973).

Single-Parent Families. The potential strengths or limitations of a specific family's size may be exaggerated by the absence of one or another parent. Unfortunately, our knowledge about how the absence of one parent affects the remaining parent's approach to childrearing is limited. Researchers have been concerned mostly with the effects of parent absence on children's behavior and development. Furthermore, an overwhelming amount of attention has been

paid to the effects on children of father absence rather than mother absence. As a result, almost no research data are available about children reared only by fathers. Application of the "tender years" doctrine in America's divorce courts probably accounts for much of this lack. Our legal system almost invariably assumes that the needs of vulnerable young children are best met by the mother in all but the most bizarre circumstances.[1] Moreover, this doctrine usually extends beyond childhood to adolescence, especially where custody of female offspring is concerned. Consequently, few single-parent families headed by the father have been available for study.

Shortcomings aside, a few important points can be drawn from the literature on single-parenting. Examining the potential effects on the mother of father absence by divorce, some reports (for example, Burgess, 1970; Lerner, 1954; Tiller, 1958) indicate that formerly married women, compared to their married peers, profess greater unhappiness and fear of loneliness, have lower self-confidence and esteem, and display more hostility toward males and more guilt about wifely behavior. If so, a mother's childrearing stance may be affected. One research worker (Tiller, 1958) indicates that if changes occur, they are mainly towards greater restrictions on children or increased use of authoritarian control tactics. In the extreme, maternal depression may contribute to reduced mother–child contact or even suicide. As recently as a decade ago, for example, the suicide rate among divorced women was four times higher than among married women (Gould, 1968).

Intolerant cultural attitudes toward

---

[1] An alternative to the "tender years" hypothesis is that a masculine dominated society (and legal system) simply finds it more convenient to maintain childrearing as a feminine responsibility.

single parenthood and divorce may create a setting that complicates the adjustment of a formerly married female to a nonmarried status. Economic factors also figure heavily in such adjustment for many women. Especially when the custody of several children is involved, a divorced woman will face qualitatively different environmental circumstances than do her married peers. Some may be forced (or elect) to seek employment for monetary and other self-determined reasons and experience differing levels of success. Satisfactory post-divorce social relationships may or may not develop as well, depending on individual circumstances.

Thus, it would seem that individual personality differences of the single mother (versus single parenthood per se), interacting with post-divorce social and economic factors, will largely determine the course of future development for both mother and child(ren). Age of the child at the time of divorce is still another important variable; young preschool children, for example, may be especially vulnerable to family disruption by divorce (Wallerstein & Kelly, 1975). But much more knowledge about these various factors is needed.

There is a more abundant literature on the effects of father absence on children's development (Herzog & Sudia, 1970). Male children of preschool and early school age are most often studied. Collectively, the data indicate that the sex typing process (Chapter 9) is often (although not necessarily) affected by father absence. The probability of this is increased if father absence is prolonged and occurs prior to the child's school entry. Various forms of social "maladjustment" among male children and adolescents also are associated with a fatherless upbringing. Such deviations range from exaggerated masculinity through low self-control to disruptions in cognitive functioning and academic performance.

Father absence and the psychological development of young girls has been studied less often. Yet it is widely believed, and with good reason, that father–daughter contact is a strong force in shaping feminine sex role development (Biller & Weiss, 1970). Unlike the situation for males, however, the outcome of such contact is more apparent for females during adolescence. Two patterns of difficulties in heterosexual orientation among females have been tentatively suggested as possible results of father absence: general ineffectiveness complicated by sexual anxiety, shyness, and psychological discomfort around males; and aggressive promiscuity (Hetherington & Deur, 1970). Effects of father absence on other dimensions of behavior, such as cognition, have not been clearly documented for females.

Not all studies agree about the nature and extent of the results of father absence on child development (Herzog & Sudia, 1970). Other factors may significantly mediate the effects of father absence. For one thing, the reasons for father absence cannot be overlooked: heterosexual ineffectiveness, for example, is associated more clearly with father separation by death; aggressive promiscuity is the more likely result when either divorce or desertion causes the absence (Hetherington & Deur, 1970). Additionally, such variables as the age of the child at time of separation from father, the length of the period of father absence, the quality of the mother–father relationship prior to separation, the availability of appropriate substitute male models, and emotional stability and socioeconomic status of the mother may reduce any effects of father–child separation (Biller, 1971). To this should be added the nature and extent of the relationship between mother and father *subsequent* to separation where divorce is involved. This is yet another variable not much studied as this book is written.

Despite these general findings about father absence it should not be assumed that father presence necessarily prevents the occurrence of developmental deviations among children of either sex. Childhood socialization marked by maternal domination (including maternal overprotection) or rejection, even when the father is present, may impede desirable psychosexual development among males (Chapter 9). The attitude of a mother toward her spouse also appears important. For example, it is one thing for the mother to condemn all males and fail to reward masculine behaviors in her son; it is quite another for her to avoid allowing possible negativism to affect the way she treats her son. More information is needed to understand the relationship between these and other maternal characteristics on the total development of both male and female children. It is likely that, under certain conditions (such as intense marital conflict when father is present), father absence will not adversely affect a child's behavior.

In fact, father absence may even have beneficial effects, given the existence of positive substitute adult–child relations (Herzog & Sudia, 1970). This could be especially true if a father is abusive. For example, fathers are reported as the abuser in two-thirds of the incidents of child abuse in intact families; fathers also inflict the most severe injuries on their children (see Chapter 12).

The common implication throughout much of the literature on childrearing effects is that father absence is generally harmful. But when both parents are present, it is believed that the mother and her actions toward children do the most harm (or good). The weight of accumulated evidence about parent influence does seem to tip the scales in the mother's favor. Yet we can perhaps be misled about this simply because mother–child relationships have been so much more thoroughly studied. Much of this study has been motivated by the strong, but as yet unverified and often overstated belief that uninterrupted and gratifying maternal care during infancy and preschool years is essential for children's healthy personality development (Yarrow, 1964). Only recently have a sufficient number of studies begun to appear to give us a more balanced perspective on parental influence (see, for example, Lamb, 1977; Lynn, 1974).

Maternal employment. The growing number of single working mothers in America's work force has led to more studies about how maternal employment may affect parenting and the total context for children's development (Etaugh, 1974; Hoffman & Nye, 1974; Wallston, 1973). Most of these studies have used rather gross comparisons between the children of working and nonworking mothers. As with single-parent effects, it is clear that any effects of maternal employment are mediated by several important variables, including age and sex of child, socioeconomic status, whether employment is full or part time, the quality of the mother–child relationship and available substitute care, and prevailing maternal attitudes about and satisfaction with children and working (Etaugh, 1974; Hoffman & Nye, 1974). All told, maternal employment per se seems only weakly related to children's development and behavior. However, where disruptive home conditions are combined with prolonged maternal absence through employment and inadequate supervisory arrangements, problems may occur, especially among young males (Hoffman, 1961). Recent data also suggest that girls may be more often left unsupervised than boys and may, as a result, sometimes suffer some cognitive impoverishment (Woods, 1972).

Perhaps because of the human rights movement, a new interest in the positive effects of maternal employment has appeared. Hoffman and Nye (1974), for example, report that maternal employment can increase the power of the mother in a family, thus setting the conditions for her greater involvement in decision-making and increasing equity in marital role relationships. Similarly, some reduced marital conflict has been associated with maternal employment, possibly because of the increased economic contribution of the mother in combination with heightened self-fulfillment when her work itself is a gratifying experience. The implications for children's observational learning and positive mother–child interactions are evident. Finally, to the extent that maternal employment increases family income, possible advantages for children's growth environment may occur—less crowding, fewer and better spacing of children (presumably affected by work patterns), and qualitatively superior stimulation for learning (Cherry & Eaton, 1977).

To sum up, attributes of family structure and life style are a third broad category of variables that can alter the patterning of parent–child interactions. These attributes act together with the social class and racial-ethnic variables discussed earlier. Definitive statements about how attributes of family structure and circumstance affect an individual case or about how they specifically influence children's development can not be made in our present state of knowledge. Their potential power to create significant differences in a child's environ-ment is clear, but we must exercise caution in asserting relationships because our data are limited.

The reader has by this time noticed that our discussion about parenting has been confined to the nuclear family unit. There are, of course, other variations in "family" structure. Communal child-rearing in contemporary America is an example. A few reports about this approach have appeared (for example, Johnston & Deishar, 1973), but the research evidence seems to us insufficient for any meaningful comment. More extensive evidence can be drawn from other cultures. Israeli kibbutzim, for example, have been studied for their impact on children and youth. On the whole, life circumstances for kibbutz families seem quite satisfactory for normal child development (Gerson, 1974).

A still broader issue—home versus group care in institutional settings—transcends any specific culture. This issue has become increasingly important as industrial societies find it necessary to provide extensive day-care services for young children whose mothers work. Again, firm research data about the comparative effects of home versus group care are difficult to obtain and to interpret. There is some evidence that normal development can be, and usually is, maintained under "good" conditions of early group care as measured against home care (Goldman, 1971; Moyles & Wolins, 1971). However, extended longitudinal research about group care and its effects is rare, making it difficult to draw firm conclusions. The quality of group care and the length of time children spend in an institutional setting are critical variables, as is the nature of children's family situations. Alternatives to socialization in a single-dwelling nuclear family should not be considered inherently inferior. The conditions for healthy physical, personal-social, and intellectual development require analysis in *any* type of child-care setting. We discuss these conditions more specifically in Part III of this book.

ATTACHMENT: A CORNERSTONE FOR DEVELOPMENT AND SOCIALIZATION?

Thus far we have examined some but by no means all major sources of variation in socialization practice. Beyond the promising pattern-analysis studies discussed earlier in this chapter, we are intrigued by the meaning for parenting or caregiving of a phenomenon called *attachment*. This term refers to an "affectional tie that one person forms to another specific person, binding them together in space and enduring over time" (Ainsworth, 1973). For example, consider the commonly observed tendency for the young of a species to seek the proximity of certain other members of their species. Such a tendency is extremely functional for species whose young are born helpless. Human infants, for example, not only are born helpless, but are dependent for some time, requiring that the bond between the infant and caregiver remain intact. For human infants, the maintenance of this bond seems to be affected by the modifiability of their behavior, that is, an infant counters possible caregiver disinterest by consistently producing novel responses, behaviors showing developmental progress, and so on (Bell, 1974).

We have good reason to believe that attachment provides the groundwork for the socialization of children. Infants elicit not only physical caregiving from their parents, but also social interaction; they are talked to, held, and played with. It is through this interaction that differential parent responsiveness begins to mold the type of behavior the child will emit.

Interestingly, however, the attachment bond also provides for a detachment process. The attached caregiver provides an infant with a secure base from which to explore. To quell fears of a new environment, an infant initially requires direct physical contact with the attached individual. This gradually gives way to visual and auditory contact as the child matures, and eventually permits no contact when the child has achieved an inner certainty and trust through consistent interaction with the significant other. This development of trust corresponds to Erikson's (1963) first stage of psychosocial development, in which the child is said to resolve a conflict between trust and mistrust of the social environment.

Ways of Viewing Attachment

At this point we should distinguish between attachment as a concept and attachment as a behavior. Conceptually speaking, attachment is a bond between an infant and its caregiver, usually the mother, marked by enduring affectional qualities. Behaviorally speaking, attachment is indicated by actions by the infant that evoke a response from the caregiver, thus initiating a cycle of interaction which reinforces the affectional relationship (Ainsworth, 1964).

Several partially overlapping explanations for attachment have been advanced (Maccoby & Masters, 1970). One explanation is that attachment is instinctual. The infant's biological propensities for need satisfaction, including social interaction with other humans, are the instinctual basis for self-preservation. Thus, an external object attachment to a caregiver is thought to evolve from a self-centeredness to establish some sort of guarantee for security in growth.

A second view emphasizes learning more than instinctual needs. A nurturant mother capable of satisfying her infant's basic needs acts as a source of primary reinforcement. Because of a consistent association between the mother and infant need-satisfaction, her mere presence eventually becomes reinforcing. Attachment strength is thought to be influenced by the caregiver's "schedule" of reinforcement, that is, how much time or how many infant responses must occur before the caregiver responds to the infant's needs. It follows that the more responsively and consistently a mother ministers to her infant, the stronger the attachment.

A third view of attachment holds that an infant's level of cognitive development is the primary factor in attachment. Accordingly, specific attachment cannot occur until the child is able to recognize and discriminate the significant caregiver from others. Within a cognitive framework, the infant must also attain a concept of the object as something distinct from the self for a secure attachment to develop.

Still another—and perhaps the best-known—analysis of attachment comes from the study of ethology, or cross-species comparative study (Bowlby, 1958; 1960a,b) (see Chapter 2). Instinctual responses figure prominently in this analysis, but no assumptions about self-centeredness or ego needs are made. Rather, a maturation of responses occurs for which an infant is "pre-wired." This maturation mutually binds an infant and its mother. The species-specific responses that so mature include sucking, clinging, crying, smiling (which serves to activate maternal behavior), and following (in which the infant is a principal active partner). Collectively, these responses have both survival value and promote close proximity to the parent.

Representative ethological studies have involved both the Ghanda people of East Africa and American mothers and infants (Ainsworth, 1964). Thirteen behavior patterns were observed which, in concert, mediated infant–mother attachment: (1) differential crying, (2) differential smiling, (3) differential vocalization, (4) visual-motor orientation toward mother, (5) crying when mother leaves, (6) following, (7) "scrambling" over mother, (8) burying face in mother's lap, (9) exploration from mother as a secure base, (10) clinging, (11) lifting arms in greeting, (12) clapping hands in greeting, and (13) approaching through locomotion. (Responses such as rooting, sucking, and searching for the breast were not included because attachment to the mother as a person must be distinguished from attachment to the breast as a need-satisfying object.)

These and other data (such as Schaeffer & Emerson, 1964) suggest several important points about attachment. First, it seems clear that the infant is itself an active agent in the development of attachment. Second, attachment may not always require close physical infant–mother contact. Third, attachments to other persons are followed by attachment to the primary caregiver.

This last point suggests that attachment follows a sequence, or occurs in predictable stages. Ainsworth (1974) has more precisely described this probable sequence. Five phases of attachment are proposed. The initial phase, spanning roughly the first two or three months of life, is initially marked by the infant's apparent lack of discrimination and response to social advances by the caregiver; thereafter the infant will come to smile to adequate stimuli (a human face) though differential responses to such stimuli are not observed. The next three or four months encompass stages two and three in attachment. During phase two a differential responsiveness is observed. This means that the infant gives evidence of discriminating among others, especially between its caregiver and unfamiliar persons, by displaying differential smiling and crying. The third phase, differential responsiveness *at a distance*, follows. During this third phase, an infant can be observed to cry when its mother leaves the room and to greet her with a smile or coo when she returns. This phase is also marked by the appearance of separation anxiety, or signs of distress when an infant is removed from the caregiver and thrust into the company of strangers. Phase four in attachment, occurring at about age seven months, is termed active initiation. The infant now takes apparently deliberate action to establish and renew human contact and interaction, for example, by lifting or extending its arms to the nearby parent. The fifth, and final phase of attachment, at about 11 or 12 months of age, is defined by the onset of stranger anxiety, such as crying, clinging to the caregiver, and general avoidance responses when unfamiliar persons "intrude" into the infant's social world.

This ethological view of attachment is not without its critics. One authority (Gewirtz, 1969), for example, considers these species-specific behavior patterns relevant to attachment only as they establish context and limits within which social learning can occur. Beyond this, these behaviors do not themselves represent attachment. Moreover, it has become increasingly clear that factors in addition to the infant itself seemingly promote attachment and caregiving interaction (Bell, 1974). Among these are (1) the state of pregnancy itself, (2) an infant's appearance (presumably to affect the frequency and intensity of caregiver

approach or avoidance responses), (3) the infant's helpless thrashing movements (a cue for caregiver altruism), and (4) the extent to which an infant's sensory-motor system matches those of its parents. For example, an active, seeking infant born of lethargic, passive parents (or vice versa) may establish conditions that complicate the attachment process. This point is consistent with the idea of interaction stressed in Chapter 1.

In general, we believe that the ethological interpretation of attachment has much to commend it. We also agree with others that *maternal* or *caregiver responsiveness* is a key variable in determining attachment outcome. One important study (Robson & Moss, 1970), for example, has revealed that mothers who experience immediate and intense attachments to their infants demonstrate a strong investment in having a baby. That is, these mothers both highly desire and hold high expectations about giving birth and nurturing their offspring. Mothers who either develop late attachments, or who develop no attachment at all, tend not to want a baby in the first place, or give birth to infants whose early behavior is deviant or disturbing.

Mothers, like their offspring, may proceed through developmental stages in forming attachment bonds. The evidence suggests that during the first four to six weeks following birth, mothers tend to view their infants as nonsocial objects; feelings of affection may be only very general, even impersonal. Soon thereafter, however, infants are viewed more as unique persons. This changing maternal perception may occur as infants become more capable of visual fixation and social smiling in response to caregiving. As infants approach 4 months of age, maternal attachments can reach a high level of intensity. At this point, mothers will find the absence of their infants unpleasant. Any thought of losing them is intolerable.

On the basis of these and other data about attachment (for example, Lamb, 1974) we would expect stronger infant attachment to follow from greater amounts of positive maternal stimulation. To the extent that maternal stimulation depends upon an infant's responses, mothers who are sharply aware of and able to meet their infant's needs would seem to foster a strong affectional bond. As one authority observes (Martin, 1975), the same factors that foster attachment may also contribute in some way to the development of infants' intellectual and social competence. If so, the importance of attachment cannot be overemphasized.

Attachment provides us with a striking example of the nature-nurture interaction first discussed in Chapter 2. If the ethological view is correct, nature provides a genetic predisposition to "attach," but the object(s) and the quality of attachment seem more clearly a function of nurture. Thus, both nature and nurture must work in concert to produce attachment behavior.

Finally, a recent and extremely careful observation of attachment indicators in intact families (proximity, touching, approaching, seeking to be held, fussing, reaching) has revealed no preference by infants for either parent (Lamb, 1977). That is, the data support the idea that these infants were clearly attached to *both* mothers and fathers. In fact, somewhat more positive infant responses were observed for father–infant play than for the predominant caretaking activities of mothers. Though this specific division of activity need not be exclusive or inevitable across families, its broader implication is potentially significant. The two kinds of experiences for parent–infant interaction may set up

qualitatively different relationships, and thus possibly cause different parental influences from infancy onward (Lamb, 1977).

A FRAMEWORK FOR CONCEPTUALIZING THE PARENTAL ROLE

Having stressed the importance of a primary caregiving role for early human development we now turn to a more general but useful way to organize our thinking about parenting and the socialization process. This way of thinking summarizes much of what has been said in this chapter. We suggest a framework for conceptualizing four main components of the parental role (Emmerich, 1969).

The first is *goal values,* those positive (valued) and negative (disvalued) behaviors or traits of children and youth that shape parental selection of socialization outcomes. As we have indicated, goal-value priorities vary across cultures and often within the same culture, depending upon such aspects of parental identity as social class and ethnicity. Thus, white middle-class American parents of preschool children are reported to positively value trustingness, friendliness, obedience, and assertiveness; aggressiveness, submissiveness, and social withdrawal are devalued (Emmerich, 1969). Others (for example, Durrett, O'Bryant, & Pennebaker, 1975) report differences among low-income white, black, and Chicano parents in the extent to which they value achievement, individual responsibility, and emotional expressiveness. Goal values may shift with parental perceptions of their children's developmental stage or social maturity. As children move into adolescense, for example, autonomy and assertiveness may become more important, along with concerns about sexuality and personal liability. Some of these values may also present conflicts between parental needs and what they regard as important for life success. For example, obedience may be valued over independence, especially during early childhood. Continued into adolescence and beyond, however, this priority can create problems in family relationships, possibly even limiting opportunities for the practice of self-reliance among youth. This is an example of continuity–discontinuity in cultural role conditioning for children and youth discussed in Chapter 2.

A second component of the parental role is that set of beliefs about the strategies or techniques which will be effective for securing desired goal values and preventing undesired outcomes: ideas about what *means* will presumably accomplish desired *ends*. These *means–ends beliefs* actually represent the parents' theory, however informal or unstated, about how to train and control their children's development. According to Emmerich (1969), means-ends beliefs can be grouped into five distinct, though closely related categories. First, for some behavioral developments, parents may prefer deliberately to minimize or avoid any kind of intrusion into the child's situation. When parents believe that desired behavior will develop "naturally" as the child "matures," or that undesired behavior will dissipate of its own accord, we can speak of a belief in the practice of *nonintervention*.

Chances are, however, that parents are compelled to take a more active role in relationships with their children. Accordingly, they express approval and disapproval, provide and withdraw privileges, and even resort to spanking and other painful tactics. Parental beliefs about the potency of rewards for good

behavior and punishment for the bad usually can be associated with some variation of learning and reinforcement theory (Chapter 2). However crudely or naively applied in many homes, this second component of parents socialization theory concerns beliefs about how best to *modify observable behavior* quickly and directly.

A third category of means–ends beliefs concerns techniques to facilitate behavior change through reasoning, persuasion, and induction to modify children's *motivational patterns* (including the development of children's self-imposed standards of conduct). Induction is a method of generalizing from particular events to broader principles of human relations. Parents may attempt to promote altruism (acting to benefit others) by encouraging their children to share, help, or even sacrifice personal resources. Techniques that direct a child's attention to the plight of others, make explicit the harmful consequences of a child's actions on others (hitting, lying, or stealing), and encourage reparation or apology for misdeeds have, in fact, been associated to some degree with the development of altruism (Hoffman, 1975). The intent of such techniques is to foster children's sensitivity to others, including respect for other's rights and feelings, together with a more basic mental set that anticipates the consequences of behavior before acting. In sum, this third category includes parental beliefs about verbal instruction for motivational development.

A fourth category of means–ends beliefs concerns parental *modeling*. As discussed in Chapter 2, this involves attempts by parents to behave consistently with their goal values, thus establishing the condition for imitation learning. Such traditional grass roots phrases as, "He's a chip off the old block," "Like father, like son," and "The apple never falls far from the tree," seem to reflect beliefs about the power of modeling. Of more than passing interest, however, is the apparent belief of many parents in the adage, "Do as I say, not as I do." Effective modeling requires a consistency between word and deed, with deed usually the stronger source of children's imitation learning.

Finally, parents may concentrate primarily upon altering in some way the setting in which their children behave. Breakables are removed from the reach of crawling infants. Electric sockets are sealed. Stairways are blocked. Parental attempts to resolve conflicts among preschool playmates may mean the removal of contested toys. To prevent overstimulation of young children, parents may schedule changes in the amount and kind of play activity. Or, to promote creative activity, parents may provide their children with a wide variety of art and music materials. This category of means–ends beliefs about how best to structure the environment for learning is called *situational modification.* Parents who practice this approach to socialization believe in the power of the environment to determine behavior. Environmental structuring and restructuring may increase the probability for desired behavior to occur. Likewise, its effective use may prevent or decrease the rate of occurrence of undesirable behavior. According to Emmerich, parents generally view situational modification as an effective, if difficult and sometimes impractical, means for bringing children's behavior under control.

In summary, the five categories of means–ends beliefs are nonintervention, behavioral modification, motivational modification, modeling, and situational modification. These may not exhaust all variations in parental beliefs about behavior management, but most commonly observed control tactics fit into one or another category. Parents will, of course, differ in the strength of their beliefs across these five classes.

A third component of the parental role follows logically from the second: *means–ends capacities.* It refers to parents' abilities and desires to act upon their means–ends beliefs to achieve desirable and avoid undesirable socialization outcomes. Parents who can interpret their children's behaviors and motives perceptively and accurately and who command the necessary skills to maintain their beliefs rate high in this capacity. For most parents, however, there will be times when they are unable to act in ways they believe are effective. At other times they may find it easier to relinquish their beliefs in favor of a path of least resistance. For example, a parent might realize that giving in to an adolescent's persistent nagging demands for the family car will increase the likelihood of future nagging behavior. Yet, not wishing to alienate this adolescent (or needing momentary peace and quiet), the car keys are handed over.

Consistent with our earlier emphasis upon *patterns* of interaction, it is important to consider both parental competence and degree of flexibility in implementing means–ends actions. Some parents—because of ignorance, lack of interest, or for other reasons—may be ineffectual or self-defeating in means–ends capacities. Others may rely exclusively and in a limited way upon one or another approach, as do parents who constantly exhort their child to conform without providing reasons or rewards for compliance. Educational programs for parents are increasingly viewed as a good way to expand their repertoire of rational means–ends beliefs and skilled means–ends capacities (Chapter 12).

The fourth and final parental role

component concerns whether or to what extent the behavior of children and youth meets desired parental standards. These results of means–ends actions can be termed *goal achievements*. They can be short-term (responsibility for daily kitchen cleanup, apologizing for rudeness, promptness at bedtime) or long-term (responsible adult citizenship, mature moral decision-making, skills and attitudes for economic self-sufficiency). This distinction somewhat parallels the difference between control and training mentioned early in the chapter.

Two issues must be faced. First is the extent to which parental goal values and desired achievements are realistic. The second is how other influences intrude upon children's development (such as peers, schooling, and the mass media). Parents' spheres of influence may vary according to what aspect of development is involved, such as intellectual or social development. Their influence may also vary according to children's age and the range of outside learning experiences available to them. Parents may find it difficult to assess the extent of their influence and, occasionally, may even be deceived by it. In fact, both the strength of parent goal values and their perception of effectiveness in goal accomplishment may do much to affect their motivation for continuing or changing their socialization strategy. Children's behavior serves as feedback which can influence subsequent parent behavior. Alternatives may be considered, advice sought, discussions held, or whatever.

We must admit that parenting may not reflect rational, systematic thinking

Fig. 3.1. A scheme for thinking about important aspects of childhood socialization and development.

THE CHILD: Mainstreams of Development and Socialization	MAJOR COMPONENTS OF THE PARENTAL (CAREGIVER) ROLE			
	Goal values	Means–ends beliefs	Means–ends capacities	Goal achievement
Physical-motor development				
Language development				
Cognitive-intellectual development				
Development of sex role and sexual behavior				
Achievement & career development				
Moral development				

After Emmerich, 1969.

about goals, methods for achieving them, evaluating progress, and seeking improved ways for socializing children. At many times the process seems random, shortsighted, inconsistent, and even irrational. As the saying goes, some children may seem to "grow like Topsy." Yet conceptualizing the parental role in terms of these four components can assist in our thinking about socialization both as process and product. The question of goal achievements, in particular, is an impetus to much psychological research referred to throughout this book.

With this in mind, we invite you, the reader, to pause and consider your own goal values and means–ends beliefs about childhood socialization according to the diagram of Figure 3.1. We invite you also to assess your means–ends capacities and the specific goal achievements that you might seek as evidence of a "successful program" for human development and socialization. The aspects of development listed in this diagram provide the substance for Part III of this book. After a study of these chapters, it may be instructive to reconsider your responses to this task, with a view toward identifying both the known and unknown about development and socialization.

SUMMARY

In this chapter we have discussed major ideas about parenting or caregiving and their possible influences on human socialization and development. Concern about how best to raise children and what outcomes to seek have become increasingly acute and widespread during the twentieth century. These concerns are often intensely debated which itself provides some motivation for a scientific study of parent–child relationships and socialization practices. This study has taken a variety of forms over the past forty or fifty years as childrearing orientations themselves have changed. Throughout this period, the issue of the control of children's behavior has been prominent. Partly in response to questions about control, research psychologists have sought to identify general patterns or dimensions of behavior that are associated with children's behavior and personal-social adjustment. Two such interacting dimensions, *parental affect* and *management style,* have been described in several important studies. The observation of specific parent–child relationships within such dimensions has also seemed more productive for understanding interpersonal influence than were earlier attempts to link isolated parenting techniques (such as style of feeding or weaning) to children's long-term personality development.

The study of parental socialization practice is marked by considerable diversity. The most basic and pervasive source of this diversity is the general cultural context in which socialization occurs. Cross-cultural research emphasizes the impor-

tance of contrasting *values* and how they are translated into specific childrearing practices. Even within the same culture, however, important differences in childrearing orientation can be observed. Among the most thoroughly studied bases for those differences are social class status, racial-ethnic identity, religious beliefs, and the way in which families are organized and structured by size, children's birth order, presence or absence of one or the other parent, and so on. Because the research evidence about these within-culture variations is based largely on correlational studies, it is not possible to comment definitively about their effects on children's behavior. Ample evidence, however, indicates that these variations often do make a difference in the conditions under which children and youth are socialized.

To identify the most basic and critical socialization processes, psychologists have become increasingly interested in attachment, especially those affectional bond(s) that are or are not formed early in life as a foundation for socialization. Alternative conceptions of attachment were discussed, with special attention to the ethological view and the importance of caregiver responsiveness in the attachment process.

Finally, in anticipation of Part III of this book, we have examined a framework for organizing our thoughts about human socialization and development. This framework involves four interrelated components of a parental or caregiver role: goal values, means–ends beliefs, means–

ends capacities, and goal achievements. Each component has been defined and illustrated by example.

The broadest implication of Chapter 3 is that parents or primary caregivers exert the single most important social influence on children and youth. Of course, where the biological parents are also the primary socializing agents, this influence is even more profound because of heredity factors. It is commonly believed, and with good reason, that the social influence of parents is greatest during the formative years of infancy and early childhood. Thereafter, as a child's sphere of social interaction expands, other forces come into play. We now proceed to examine one such force, children's peers.

REFERENCES

Ainsworth, M. D. Patterns of attachment behavior shown by the infant in interaction with his mother. *Merrill-Palmer Quarterly,* 1964, *10,* 51–58.

Ainsworth, M. D. The development of infant-mother attachment. In B. M. Caldwell & H. N. Ricciuti (Eds.), *Review of child development research* (vol. 3). Chicago: University of Chicago Press, 1973.

Ainsworth, M. D. Phases of the development of infant-mother attachment. In R. A. LeVine (Ed.), *Culture and personality.* Chicago: Aldine, 1974.

Appleton, T., Clifton, R., & Goldberg, S. The development of behavioral competence in infancy. In F. D. Horowitz (Ed.), *Review of child development research* (vol. 4). Chicago: University of Chicago Press, 1975.

Aries, P. The family, prison of love. *Psychology Today,* 1975, *9*(3), 53–58.

Armentrout, J. A., & Burger, G. K. Children's reports of parental child-rearing behavior at five grade levels. *Developmental Psychology,* 1972, *7,* 44–48.

Ausubel, D. P. *Theory and problems of child development.* New York: Grune & Stratton, 1958.

Barry, H., Child, I. L., & Bacon, M. K. Relations of training to subsistence economy. *American Anthropologist,* 1959, *61,* 51–63.

Bartlett, E. W., & Smith, C. P. Child-rearing practices, birth order, and the development of achievement-related motives. *Psychological Reports,* 1966, *18,* 1207–1216.

Baumrind, D. Current patterns of parental authority. *Developmental Psychology Monograph,* 1971, *4*(1), Part 2.

Becker, H., & Hill, R. *Family, marriage and parenthood.* Boston: Heath, 1955.

Becker, W. C. Consequences of parental discipline. In M. L. Hoffman & L. W. Hoffman (Eds.), *Review of child development research* (vol. 1). New York: Russell Sage, 1964.

Bell, R. Q. Contributions of human infants to caregiving and social interaction. In M. Lewis & L. A. Rosenblum (Eds.), *The effect of the infant on its caregiver.* New York: Wiley, 1974.

Berry, J. W. Independence and conformity in subsistence-level societies. *Journal of Personality and Social Psychology,* 1967, *7,* 415–418.

Biller, H. The mother-child relationship and the father-absent boy's personality development. *Merrill-Palmer Quarterly,* 1971, *17,* 227–241.

Biller, H., & Weiss, S. D. The father-daughter relationship and the personality development of the female. *Journal of Genetic Psychology,* 1970, *114,* 79–93.

Bowlby, J. The nature of the child's tie to his mother. *International Journal of Psycho-analysis.* 1958, *39,* 350–373.

Bowlby, J. Ethology and the development of object relations. *International Journal of Psycho-analysis,* 1960, *41,* 313–317. (a)

Bowlby, J. Separation anxiety. *International Journal of Psycho-analysis,* 1960, *41,* 89–113. (b)

Breland, H. M. Birth order effects: A reply to Schooler. *Psychological Bulletin,* 1973, *80,* 210–212.

Breland, H. M. Birth order, family configuration, and verbal achievement. *Child Development,* 1974, *45,* 1011–1019.

Bronfenbrenner, U. The changing American child: A speculative analysis. *Journal of Social Issues,* 1961, *17,* 6–18.

Bronfenbrenner, U. *Two worlds of childhood.* New York: Russell Sage, 1970.

Burger, G. K., Lamp, E., & Rogers, D. Developmental trends in children's perceptions of parental child-rearing behavior. *Developmental Psychology,* 1975, *11,* 391.

Burgess, J. The single-parent family: A social and sociological problem. *Family Coordinator,* 1970, *19,* 137–144.

Caldwell, B. M. The effects of infant care. In M. L. Hoffman & L. W. Hoffman (Eds.), *Review of child development research* (vol. 1). New York: Russell Sage, 1964.

Campbell, A. The American way of mating. *Psychology Today,* 1975, *8*(12), 37–43.

Cherry, F., & Eaton, E. Physical and cognitive development in children of low-income mothers working in the child's early years. *Child Development,* 1977, *48,* 158–166.

Clarke-Stewart, K. A. Interactions between mothers and their young children: Characteristics and consequences. *Monographs of the Society for Research in Child Development,* 1973, *38*(153).

Cohen, S. E., & Beckwith, L. Caregiving behavior and early cognitive development as related to ordinal position in preterm infants. *Child Development,* 1977, *48,* 152–157.

Cohler, B., Greenebaum, H., Weiss, J., & Moran, D. The childcare attitudes of two generations of mothers. *Merrill Palmer Quarterly,* 1971, *17,* 3–18.

Comer, J. P., & Poussaint, A. F. *Black child care.* New York: Simon and Schuster, 1975.

Deutsch, C. P. Social class and child development. In B. M. Caldwell & H. N. Ricciuti (Eds.), *Review of child development research* (vol. 3). Chicago: University of Chicago Press, 1973.

Douvan, E., & Adelson, J. *The adolescent experience.* New York: Wiley, 1966.

Durrett, M. F., O'Bryant, F., & Pennebaker, J. W. Childrearing reports of white, black, and Mexican-American families. *Developmental Psychology,* 1975, *11,* 871.

Elder, G. H., Jr. Adolescent socialization and development. In E. F. Bagatta & W. W. Lambert (Eds.), *Handbook of personality theory and research.* Skokie, Ill.: Rand McNally, 1968.

Elder, G. H., Jr. *Children of the great depression: Social change in life experience.* Chicago: University of Chicago Press, 1974.

Elkind, D. The developmental psychology of religion. In O. H. Kidd & J. L. Rivoire (Eds.), *Handbook of personality theory and research.* Skokie, Ill.: Rand McNally, 1968.

Emmerich, W. The parental role: A functional-cognitive approach. *Monographs of the Society for Research in Child Development,* 1969, *34*(8).

Erikson, E. H. *Childhood and society* (2nd ed.). New York: Norton, 1963.

Etaugh, C. Effects of maternal employment on children: A review of recent research. *Merrill-Palmer Quarterly,* 1974, *20,* 71–98.

Frank, G. H. The role of the family in the development of psychopathology. *Psychological Bulletin,* 1965, *64,* 191–205.

Gerson, M. The family in the kibbutz. *Journal of Child Psychology and Psychiatry,* 1974, *15,* 47–57.

Gewirtz, J. L. Mechanisms of social learning: Some roles of stimulation and behavior in early human development. In D. A. Goslin (Ed.), *Handbook of socialization theory and research.* Skokie, Ill.: Rand McNally, 1969.

Ginsburg, H. *The myth of the deprived child.* Englewood Cliffs, N.J.: Prentice-Hall, 1972.

Glass, D. C., Neulinger, J., & Brim, O. G., Jr. Birth order, verbal intelligence, and educational aspiration. *Child Development,* 1974, *45,* 807–811.

Glasser, W. *The identity society.* New York: Basic Books, 1974.

Golden, M., Birns, B., Bridger, W., & Moss, A. Social class differentiation in cognitive development among black preschool children. *Child Development,* 1971, *42,* 37–45.

Goldman, R. Psychosocial development in cross-cultural perspectives: A new look at an old issue. *Developmental Psychology,* 1971, *5,* 411–419.

Gordon, T. *Parent effectiveness training.* New York: Wyden, 1970.

Gould, E. P. Special report: The single parent family benefits in Parents Without Partners, Inc. *Journal of Marriage and the Family,* 1968, *30,* 669–671.

Grinker, R. R., Jr. Being rich can be a handicap. *The Seattle Times,* Seattle, Washington, May, 16, 1977.

Herzog, E., & Sudia, C. E. *Boys in fatherless families.* Washington, D. C.: U.S. Department of Health, Education and Welfare, Office of Child Development, 1970.

Hess, R. D. Social class and ethnic influences on socialization. In P. Mussen (Ed.), *Carmichael's manual of child psychology* (3rd ed.) (vol. 2). New York: Wiley, 1970.

Hetherington, E. M., & Deur, J. L. The effects of father absence on personality development in daughters. Unpublished manuscript, 1970.

Hetherington, E. M., & Deur, J. L. The effects of father absence on child development. *Young Children,* 1971, *26,* 233–244.

Hoffman, L. W. Effects of maternal employment on the child. *Child Development,* 1961, *32,* 187–197.

Hoffman, L. W., & Nye, F. *Working mothers.* San Francisco: Jossey-Bass, 1974.

Hoffman, M. L. Altruistic behavior and the parent-child relationship. *Journal of Personality and Social Psychology,* 1975, *31,* 937–943.

Hurley, J. R., & Hohn, R. L. Shifts in child-rearing attitudes linked with parenthood and occupation. *Developmental Psychology,* 1971, *4,* 324–328.

Johnson, R. C., & Medinnus, G. R. *Child psychology: Behavior and development* (3rd ed.). New York: Wiley, 1974.

Johnston, C. M., & Deishar, R. W. Contemporary communal child rearing: A first analysis. *Pediatrics,* 1973, *52,* 319–376.

Kriger, S. F., & Kroes, W. H. Child-rearing attitudes of Chinese, Jewish, and Protestant mothers. *Journal of Social Psychology,* 1972, *86,* 205–210.

Lamb, M. E. A defense of the concept of attachment. *Human Development,* 1974, *17,* 376–385.

Lamb, M. E. Father-infant and mother-infant interaction in the first year of life. *Child Development,* 1977, *48,* 167–181.

Lambert, W. W., Triandis, L. M., & Wolf, M. Some correlates of beliefs in the malevolence and benevolence of supernatural being: A cross-societal study. *Journal of Abnormal and Social Psychology,* 1959.

LeMasters, E. E. *Parents in modern America* (3rd ed.). Homewood, Ill.: Dorsey, 1977.

Lerner, S. H. Effects of desertion in family life. *Social Casework,* 1954, *35,* 3–8.

LeVine, R. A. Parental goals: A cross-cultural view. *Teachers College Record,* 1974, *76,* 226–239.

Lynn, D. B. *The father: His role in child development.* Monterey, Calif.: Brooks/Cole, 1974.

Maccoby, E., & Masters, J. C. Attachment and dependency. In P. H. Mussen (Ed.), *Carmichael's manual of child psychology* (3rd ed.). New York: Wiley, 1970.

Martin, B. Parent-child relations. In F. D. Horowitz (Ed.), *Review of child development research.* Chicago: University of Chicago Press, 1975.

McCandless, B. R. *Children: Behavior and development* (2nd ed.). New York: Holt, Rinehart and Winston, 1967.

McClelland, D. *The achieving society.* Princeton, N.J.: Van Nostrand, 1961.

Meade, R. D., & Singh, L. Motives for child-bearing in America and in India. *Journal of Cross-Cultural Psychology,* 1973, *4,* 89–110.

Miller, D. R., & Swanson, G. E. *The changing American parent.* New York: Wiley, 1958.

Miller, G. W. Factors in school achievement and social class. *Journal of Educational Psychology,* 1970, *61,* 260–269.

Mitchell, G., & Schroers, L. Birth order and parental experience in monkeys and man. In H. W. Reese (Ed.), *Advances in child development and behavior* (vol. 8). New York: Academic, 1973.

Moyles, E., & Wolins, M. Group care and intellectual development. *Developmental Psychology,* 1971, *4,* 370–380.

Orlansky, H. Infant care and personality. *Psychological Bulletin,* 1949, *46,* 1–48.

Pollack, D., & Valdez, H. Developmental aspects of sexuality and aggression. *Journal of Genetic Psychology,* 1973, *123,* 179–184.

Rabin, A. I. Motivation for parenthood. *Journal of Projective Techniques and Personality Assessment,* 1965, *29,* 405–411.

Robson, K. S., & Moss, H. A. Patterns and determinants of maternal attachment. *Journal of Pediatrics,* 1970, *77,* 976–985.

Rutter, M. Parent-child separation: Psychological effects on the children. *Journal of Child Psychology and Psychiatry,* 1971, *12,* 233–260.

Sameroff, A. J. Early influences on development: Fact or fancy? *Merrill-Palmer Quarterly,* 1975, *21,* 267–294.

Schaefer, E. S. A circumplex model for maternal behavior. *Journal of Abnormal and Social Psychology,* 1959, *59,* 226–235.

Schaeffer, H. R., & Emerson, P. E. The development of social attachments in infancy. *Monographs of the Society for Research in Child Development,* 1964, *29*(3).

Schooler, C. Birth order effects: A reply to Breland. *Psychological Bulletin,* 1973, 161–175.

Schooler, C. "Birth order effects: A reply to Breland." *Psychological Bulletin,* 1973, *80,* 213–214.

Sears, R. R. Your ancients revisited: A history of child development. In E. M. Hetherington (Ed.), *Review of child development research* (vol. 5). Chicago: University of Chicago Press, 1975.

Sears, R. R., Maccoby, E. E., & Levin, A. *Patterns of child rearing.* New York: Harper & Row, 1956.

Senn, M. J. E. Insights on the child development movement in the United States. *Monographs of the Society for Research in Child Development,* 1975, *40,* Nos. 3-4.

Smith, N., & Grenier, M. English- and French-Canadian children's views of parents. *Canadian Journal of Behavioral Science,* 1975, *7,* 40–53.

Spitz, R. Hospitalism: An inquiry into the genesis of psychiatric conditions in early childhood. *Psycho-analytic Study of the Child,* 1945, *1,* 53–74.

Steward, M., & Steward, D. The observation of Anglo-, Mexican- and Chinese-American mothers teaching their young sons. *Child Development,* 1973, *44*(2), 329–337.

Sunley, R. Early nineteenth-century American literature on child rearing. In E. D. Evans (Ed.), *Children: Readings in behavior and development.* New York: Holt, Rinehart and Winston, 1968.

Thomas, D., Gecas, V., Weigart, A., & Rooney, E. *Family socialization and the adolescent.* Lexington, Mass.: Heath, 1974.

Tiller, P. O. Father absence and personality development of children in sailor families. *Nordish Psychologic Monograph Series,* 1958, *9,* 1–48.

Tulkin, S. R., & Cohler, B. J. Childrearing attitudes and mother-child interaction in the first year of life. *Merrill-Palmer Quarterly,* 1973, *19,* 95–106.

Wallerstein, J. S., & Kelly, J. B. The effects of parental divorce: Experiences of the preschool child. *Journal of the American Academy of Child Psychiatry,* 1975, *14,* 600–616.

Wallston, B. The effects of maternal employment on children. *Journal of Child Psychology and Psychiatry,* 1973, *14,* 81–95.

Warren, J. Birth order and social behavior. *Psychological Bulletin,* 1966, *65,* 38–49.

Weber, M. *The Protestant ethic and the spirit of capitalism.* London: Allen, 1930.

Whiting, B. B. (Ed.). *Six cultures: Studies of child rearing.* New York: Wiley, 1963.

Whiting, J. W. M. The learning of values. In E. Vogt & E. Albert (Eds.), *Peoples of Rimrock.* Cambridge, Mass.: Harvard University Press, 1966.

Whiting, J. W. M., & Child, I. L. *Child training and personality.* New Haven, Conn.: Yale University Press, 1953.

Winterbottom, M. The relation of need for achievement in learning experiences in independence and mastery. In J. Atkinson (Ed.), *Motives in fantasy, action, and society.* Princeton, N.J.: Van Nostrand, 1958.

Wolfenstein, M. The emergence of fun morality. *Journal of Social Issues,* 1951, *7,* 15-25.

Wollins, M. Young children in institutions: Some additional evidence. *Developmental Psychology,* 1970, *2,* 99–109.

Woods, M. B. The unsupervised child of the working mother. *Developmental Psychology,* 1972, *6,* 14–25.

Yarrow, L. J. Separation from parents during early childhood. In M. L. Hoffman & L. W. Hoffman (Eds.), *Review of child development research* (vol. 1). New York: Russell Sage, 1964.

Yarrow, M. R. Research on child-rearing as a basis for practice. *Child Welfare,* 1973, *52,* 209–219.

Zajone, R. B., & Markus, G. B. Birth order and intellectual development. *Psychological Review,* 1975, *82,* 74–88.

chapter 4

Peer group relations

Consider the following exchanges as an introduction to the complex topic of peer-group relations among children and youth. Each exchange is a segment from an interview held independently between one of the authors and three young people: Joanie, Roger, and Pat.

Joanie (10 years old; grade five; suburban, middle-class elementary school)
Interviewer: "How do you feel about kids who cheat in class?"
Joanie: "It's wrong, I guess."
Interviewer: "What if one of your classmates copied from your paper? Would you tell the teacher?"
Joanie: "It depends on who copies... I mean, if it was Barby or someone I like I wouldn't tell. Nobody rats on a friend. But if it was Randall or somebody like that I might tell."
Interviewer: "Why?"
Joanie: "Well, Randall is such a fink... nobody likes him!"
Interviewer: "Why?"
Joanie: "I dunno... he's just dumb... weird!"
Interviewer: "How does Randall feel about not being liked?"

Joanie: "How should I know? Anyway, who cares!"

Roger (12 years old; grade seven; large, urban, racially mixed junior high school)

Interviewer: "Are there any kids here at school that the other kids especially look up to?"

Roger: "Yeah, a few . . . let's see . . . there's Ken Craft, Bud Mance . . . and Sparkie Betz. Especially Bud, though . . . he's a ninth-grader, ya' know."

Interviewer: "Besides being a ninth-grader, what's special about Bud?"

Roger: "Well . . . he really knows where it's at, ya' know, and . . . uh . . . well he ain't afraid of tellin' a teacher to go stick it in his ear ya'know? Uh . . . I mean, Bud's cool . . . he makes it with the girls, too . . . I mean, uh . . . he'd just as soon rub 'em up as look at 'em!"

Pat (15 years old; grade ten all-male parochial high school)

Interviewer: "Is there a class in school that you like least?"

Pat: "Yeah . . . English!"

Interviewer: "What do you find unpleasant about English class?"

Pat: "Mainly the teacher . . . he plays favorites and treats a lot of us unfair."

Interviewer: "Have you ever talked to the teacher about this?"

Pat: "Well . . . no."

Interviewer: "Do you think it might help?"

Pat: "Maybe."

Interviewer: "Will you do it?"

Pat: "I may . . . but I'd want to check with the other guys first to see whether they'd do it, too."

These interview segments, the authors believe, illustrate some typical social attitudes anchored in the peer group relationships of many children and youth. In each case, peer influence is reflected in these attitudes. For Joanie, we see the power of a group code ("Nobody rats on a friend.") common to most social groups, along with a callous indifference to, if not outright rejection of, a peer perceived as "dumb" and "weird." For Roger, there is awe and near-idolization of the older, "cool swinger" on whom Roger and his friends may model themselves in their quest for social recognition. Finally, we see in Pat a peer consciousness that will likely affect the degree to which he acts autonomously or exercises independent judgment in social situations.

These and the many other facets of peer-group experience and influences on development are discussed in this chapter. First, we consider the cumulative layers of peer interaction typical for most children and youth. Developmental trends in peer interaction are then discussed, followed by an examination of popularity and leadership. Ideas about the relationship of parental to peer influence are then presented, with emphasis upon some matters of debate about social control and social values.

Layers of Peer Interaction

Strictly defined, peer-group behavior consists of children and youth interacting freely among each other unmonitored by adults (Ausubel & Sullivan, 1970). The resulting immediate, face-to-face, close association is perhaps second only to the family in its potential for cumulative influence. Our comments about peer influence, however, are not restricted to spontaneous, informal settings free from direct adult control. Organized and supervised group activity, so widespread among American children and youth, is also viewed as a significant medium for influence. For increasing numbers of children such activity begins with day-care or nursery-school experience. Initial school entry is another landmark in peer-group relationships. Thereafter, a mix of peer interaction in both formal and informal group settings does much to determine overall social development.

Specifically, we envision several layers of children's interaction with peers. Each layer has its own potential for supporting and reshaping past learnings and introducing new ones (Schmuck, 1971). At the base, of course, is the *family* itself. Quality of the initial maternal–infant relationship is the foundation from which broader social relations develop. Moreover, most children have siblings close enough to themselves in age so that they have played, confided, plotted, fought, and competed with one another. By-products of this sibling interaction can be profound, as illustrated in the case of Lyle (Chapter 1).

A second layer of interaction occurs in children's immediate *neighborhoods*. All but the most isolated children have living nearby playmates with whom they interact from their preschool years onward. Earliest friendship patterns tend to be based upon this together with children's preferences for the toys or other possessions of peers. Later friendship patterns are, of course, built around more sophisticated mutual perceptions of similarities in interests, competencies, and values. With increasing age, the basic ingredient for stable friendships seems to be personal qualities that serve as means for mutually satisfying, or positively reinforcing, interaction. Overwhelming evidence from research about children's friendships supports the idea that "Birds of a feather flock together" (Hartup, 1970).

Many friendships are built and maintained in school. But we can discuss children's regular school attendance in terms of a third layer of peer interaction. In *American schools*, children and youth are usually enrolled in classes with others of about the same age. Not all will be friends; in fact, some will be avoided or even rejected. But in any case, they will come to know much about each other both in the classroom and on the playground. Their interactions, both positive and negative, can affect them deeply. As in all informal groups, the norms for classroom behavior will determine what behavior is accepted, frowned upon, or forbidden. For children who value group acceptance, conformity to these unwritten but powerful guidelines for behavior will prevail, as we saw in Joanie's adherence to the code of silence and mutual support.

Fourth, children are influenced by children and youth in classes other than their own. "The big kids"—those in the higher grades—are likely to exert more influence than those who are younger and in lower grades. Peer influence from school segregation has not been thoroughly studied, but it seems likely that schools that are integrated by race, class, and sex (both boys and girls) provide significantly different peer influences from those schools that are segregated by one or another of these variables (Chapter 12). Even school size seems related to the nature of peer influence; students in smaller schools report a greater "sense of obligation" to their peer group to participate in school activities (Grabe, 1976).

Finally, there are generalized social expectancies about what children of different ages do. Such expectancies are likely to provide a form of peer-group influence, albeit at a high level of abstraction. For example, we are given to saying within earshot of the young such things as: "Two-year-olds are negative;" "Thirteen-year-olds are moody;" "Fifth-graders are a delightful age," and "Boys are noisier than girls." Such general social expectations are bound to influence behavior, although perhaps not profoundly.

Factors Affecting Peer Interaction

As we might expect, the extent of peer influence and group relations upon children's psychosocial development depends on a number of factors, including the quality and duration of interactions through time in different groups. Among the most important of these factors are degree of peer acceptance or rejection and the extent to which group experience reinforces or runs contrary to values practiced in the home. Neither is it surprising to learn that sharp cross-cultural differences in peer-group behavior exist. A study comparing Danish and American high school students, for example, has revealed that the U.S. adolescents value more highly the achievement of leadership positions within their peer groups; failure to accomplish some feat of leadership is seen more negatively by them than by the Danish students (Kandel & Lesser, 1972). Danes also profess to form fewer but more intense and deeper friendships than do Americans. The U.S. sample seemed more concerned with many broad, if not somewhat superficial, social relationships. Presumably cultural values and contrasting school settings contribute to these differences. Danish high schools, for instance, are limited in size to fewer than 300 students; in America, high school enrollments over 3,000 are commonplace.

Within cultures, ethnic and social class differences in peer interactions can also be observed. Two recent studies suggest the influence of modeling, reinforcement, and perhaps modes of social thinking. One study documented ethnic variations in the frequency of physical touch interactions. There were more touch contacts, both affectionate and aggressive, between blacks (especially girls) than whites (Willis & Reeves, 1976). Social class differences were clear in a second study, in which upper class privileged adolescents expressed significantly more coherent and internally consistent sociopolitical attitudes (for example, equality of opportunity, civil liberties, humanitarianism) than did their lower class, less economically privileged peers (Berg & Mussen, 1976).

We suggest that peers, like the family, constitute a primary social group. Within this primary group, the customs and values of a given community are translated into behavior that can be imitated and practiced, into patterns of reward and punishment, and into opportunities for discovery. While community customs and values may not always be consistent, or may even be at odds with family values, they have potential for sustained influence on the developing person. From kindergarten and for several years thereafter, influence is exerted mostly by children of one's own age, sex, and, by reason of family residence, social class. Of course, young boys and girls also interact and learn from each other, but a considerable amount of segregation by sex occurs until adolescence when, for most young persons, the peer group becomes more significantly heterosexual.

DEVELOPMENTAL TRENDS IN PEER INTERACTION

Given these general points about peer influences and interaction, we can now discuss specifically some important developmental trends in social behavior. It is reasonable to consider the maternal attachment process (Chapter 3) as a cornerstone of human social development. Moreover, we have sufficient evidence to view the development of infant social behavior in terms of four interrelated principles as follows (Rheingold, 1966).

Infant Social Behavior

First, infants are responsive to stimuli that arise from such social "objects" as human voices and faces, tactile and kinesthetic stimulation from contact with parents and siblings, and the like. Second, infants themselves initiate social behavior. They often look at other people before being looked at, smile before being smiled at, babble and coo before they are spoken to, and cry. Consequently, they draw attention from other people and receive social stimulation in return. Third, infant social behavior is modifiable. Possibly through conditioned learning, for example, infants come to discriminate among familiar and unfamiliar persons, show alternations in their rate or frequency of smiling, and develop general approach or withdrawal tendencies in given social circumstances (Fein, 1975). Perhaps the most dramatic illustration of modifiableness comes from animal study where infant monkeys raised on inanimate surrogate mothers failed to develop normal social behavior (Harlow, 1963). Finally, it seems clear that through their appearance and behavior, infants modify the behavior of other people, as the example of Susan (Chapter 2) so aptly illustrates. Infants will contribute much to the overall pattern of caretaking and nurturance they receive through their responsiveness to stimulation.

With these principles in mind, we observe that infants' "peer interaction" seems to take on a genuinely social character at about 18 months. Before this, infants usually seem to regard other, same-aged children as objects and things to manipulate rather than as playmates. From 6 to 12 months, for example, infants seem to react to other babies as playthings. At about 1 year, two infants together often engage in conflict over toys. At about 1½ years, true social interest seems to arise. Mutual social involvement begins to take on greater importance in playthings that are available to both infants (Maudry & Nekula, 1939).

Reasons for this kind of development seem clear. Very young children, especially infants, are egocentric (Piaget, 1970). They think of themselves, not of others, and find it difficult or impossible to take the points of view of others. Mature social relations depend, in part, upon the ability of one person to take the point of view of another. Certainly this ability seems important for genuine empathy with other human beings. Social relations also depend heavily on communication with other people by gesture and speech, more on the latter than the former. Children do not have the representational tools (language and gesture) to communicate very fully with others before the ages of 2 or 2 1/2 at the earliest. Socialization also demands foresight, and young children usually are not effective planners, because they have neither the tools nor the experience necessary for mapping their behavior far in advance. Thus very young children have trouble anticipating the actions of others and equal trouble in delaying their own gratification, which must frequently be achieved at the expense of other people. Moreover, young children do not tolerate frustration easily, and social interactions are full of frustrations.

In sum, because mature social interactions demand full communication, planning and anticipation, sacrifice of immediate personal gratification to preserve the social interaction, and substantial frustration tolerance, children during their early preschool years are not well socialized in the adolescent or adult sense of the word.

Social Behavior after Infancy

From about age 2 onward, developmental trends in peer-related behavior are about what is to be expected of children who gain in age, experience, impulse control, cognitive complexity, ability to play roles and see the point of view of others, and who acquire language and other forms of communication. For example, children become steadily more dependent on their peers for approval and acceptance, often to the dismay of parents and teachers. Physical aggression declines, particularly among girls, and is replaced to some degree by verbal aggression (see Chapter 12). Prosocial aggression, often rigidly moralistic, appears and children typically take the role of a moral authority to correct or reprimand those who deviate from the norm. Children become more altruistic (able to share with others), but at the same time also become more competitive.

Not surprisingly, sharp cultural differences exist in cooperative and competitive behavior among children. United States children, for example, are more competitive and less cooperative in structured strategy-demanding situations than are children from Mexican villages or Israeli kibbutzim (where the children have been reared in groups). Israeli urban children are more competitive and less cooperative than kibbutzim-reared children; and children of Mexican national origin living in the United States in urban communities are less cooperative and more competitive than Mexican village children (Kagan & Madsen, 1971; 1972; Madsen & Shapira, 1970; Shapira & Madsen, 1974).

In those studies, no ethnic differences among black, Hispanic, and white children living in urban areas were found. However, related research on the development of children's adaptive assertiveness, or strength of initiative in rational problem solving with peers, reveals an ethnic difference depending upon social class and rural or urban residence. Urban, middle-class, Anglo-American children of both sexes were stronger in assertiveness than semi-rural, poor, Anglo- and Mexican-American children of the same age. The latter children, in turn, were substantially more assertive than rural, poor Mexican children (Kagan & Carlson, 1975). As does competitiveness, however, adaptive assertiveness increases with age across these various groups, although at different rates.

Competitiveness and assertiveness can be expressed in many ways, but we have good evidence that social interactions for most children become increasingly more sophisticated with age. We would expect this as children learn socially appropriate skills and are able to select their own friendship groups. Both the nature of the situation and the way in which groups of children are handled by adults affect this phenomenon. For example, when reinforcements are given to children for social participation, constructive reactions to frustration, and cooperative and other high-level social play, these types of behavior increase in the group (Harris, Wolf, & Baer, 1967). It seems logical that the opposite can also occur and, indeed, to some degree such behavior has been repeatedly demonstrated. Classes where teachers are sharply critical, for example, are relatively high in disruptive social behavior at all age levels from first through eighth grades (Evans, 1976).

Play As a Context for Peer Interaction

Perhaps the most revealing context for peer relationships and mutual influence is play. Play is behavior that is enjoyed for its own sake. In this sense, work, to the extent that it is not drudgery, could also be play. Accordingly, some authorities make no distinction between children's work and play because of the seriousness and sense of purpose that characterizes most children's play (Dewey & Dewey, 1962). We now examine some developmental aspects of play to highlight their importance for peer relations and social learning.

Types of play behavior. Classically, the social interactions that transpire among children at play are divided into six categories of qualitatively different activity (Parten, 1932; Parten & Newhall, 1943). The first category, *unoccupied behavior,* represents the smallest extent of social involvement. It is also the least frequent sort of behavior that occurs among children in most preschool groups and beyond. In strict terms, unoccupied behavior is not play in the usual sense of the word. Instead, the child is occupied with watching anything that may be of interest at the time. Random movement may also be present—getting on and off chairs, crawling under a table, following the teacher, or just standing around fidgeting.

A second category, *solitary play*, refers to play in which children act alone, independently of others. They may play with toys different from those used by children nearby. No effort is made to initiate conversation or enter into association with others. Children seem simply to concentrate on their own activity; play occurs without involvement with or reference to what other children are doing. This form of play is usually more frequent among younger children (ages 2–3). As children grow older, they normally spend less and less time in this form of play, as opposed to more social forms. Recent evidence, however, points to an important distinction between mature, independent solitary play and similar play of a less mature, dependent nature. In fact, it is convenient to view such play along a continuum. At one end, we find active and goal-directed play—constructive work with blocks, arts and crafts, large muscle play, and challenging puzzles and workbooks. The other end of the continuum is defined by social withdrawal, pouting, sulking, and inactivity. The difference is critical, because mature solitary play among children as late as kindergarten and beyond can be a rich source of discovery learning (Moore, Evertson, & Brophy, 1974).

A third form of play, *onlooker behavior*, consists largely of observing the play of others. Conversations with other children may be initiated, including question-asking and advice-giving. Typically, children will station themselves close to a play activity so that things going on can be clearly seen and heard. Though there is no actual engagement in the play being observed, onlooker behavior usually represents a sustained interest in other children. Communication channels are often established as well, thus distinguishing onlooker behavior from unoccupied behavior.

Much more common among preschoolers is *parallel play*. Like solitary play, parallel play is independent, but the activity chosen by a child brings him or her naturally among other children. Children in parallel play will use toys similar or identical to those used by children nearby, but play with them individually. Such children do not try to get other children to participate; they play compatibly alongside others, yet do not play *with* the others. Parallel play can be readily observed among children ages 2 and 3. It continues with some frequency during the later preschool years but associative and cooperative play becomes increasingly dominant as children reach school age.

Associative play includes a variety of social interactions based upon play activity: "borrowing" and "lending" of playthings, leading and following one another with trains and wagons, and moderate efforts to control which children will or will not be "allowed" to participate. Children engage in basically the same activity; no attempt is made to divide play tasks or organize the activity. Children play as they wish and do not surrender their interests to the group. This form of play is perhaps most common among 3- and 4-year-olds, although 2-year-olds will often join in such fun. In fact, one report (Eckerman, Whatley, & Kutz, 1975) indicates that, given an opportunity, 2-year-old children will apparently prefer associative to solitary play with peers. In this study, even unfamiliar peers were quickly taken as playmates, resulting in much mutual imitation and friendly communication.

In contrast, 2-year-olds are seldom observed in a still more advanced form of play, *cooperative play*. In this form, common among older preschoolers, play is in a group organized for a purpose: making something material, competing to reach a goal, dramatizing adult or group life situations, or playing formal games. Children sense that they either do or do not "belong" to the group. Group control is in the hands of one or two members, who direct the activities of participants. Specific tasks are usually assigned to children, either individually or in subgroups. Activities are organized so that children do not work at cross-purposes or duplicate the activity of others. When cooperative play involves the acceptance of and adjustment to prearranged rules, we can speak of a highly advanced form of play that figures heavily in children's moral development (Chapter 11).

Clearly, children's play becomes more complex and interactive with age. The increasing social nature of play structures obviously requires a combination of physical-motor and interpersonal skills and involves certain basic cognitive skills. According to one authority (Gervey, 1974), three cognitive competencies are especially important. First, children must grasp what is and is not play. This means a clear distinction between fantasy or a state of pretending and absolute reality into which children can move easily and communicatively. Second, basic rules for organizing and guiding play activity must be recognized and adhered to. "Taking turns," for example, illustrates the rule of reciprocity. Third, children must together be able to construct the theme of their play activity and develop it consistently with their shared image of any play episode. Two girls playing house, for example, must be able to take on appropriate role behaviors and develop an interaction that

successfully sustains their relationship. We should note that the rate at which children develop these and other skills for advanced play differs with their social backgrounds. For example, cultural factors, especially social class, are associated with differences in the quality and extent of cooperative, or sociodramatic forms of play. Advantaged children have consistently been observed at more advanced play compared to less advantaged age mates (Rubin, Maioni, & Hornung, 1976). Sources of this difference are not well understood, but seem linked to general home stimulation. It is interesting to note that several researchers (for example, Rosen, 1974), have reported success in "teaching" disadvantaged children more competent social problem-solving and role-taking skills through cooperative play.

Thus far we have focused mainly on types of children's play through the preschool and into the early years of school. Many varieties of solitary and cooperative play extend beyond this stage into preadolescence and adolescence. Some are educational, such as board games, others are mainly social, such as "spin the bottle." Hobbies and leisure-time activity eventually take on the flavor of play. As one wag has put it, "The main difference between men and boys is mostly in the cost of their toys!" Organized sports for both sexes can even be thought of as play, as long as the activities are enjoyed for their own sake and not performed simply to gain approval, prove superiority to others, or achieve standards of excellence imposed by others.

Basic Patterns of Early Social Participation

Continuing our emphasis upon the social nature of play, we have reason to believe that basic peer orientations, or responses to group activity, develop early and remain fairly stable. Children first observed in play at age 2 1/2, then at age 7 1/2, show a strong consistency over time in friendly, active, socially-at-ease peer involvement (Waldrop & Halverson, 1975). Vigorous social participation at the earlier age is also positively correlated with cognitive-intellectual performance in later childhood, suggesting in part the constructive cumulative effects of rewarding peer relations (Halverson & Waldrop, 1976).

A successful involvement in early group settings (nursery schools or organized play groups) seems to call for the development of adaptive skills as patterns of group orientation (Kohn & Rosman, 1973). One broad pattern can be phrased in terms of a continuum, *interest-participation vs. apathy-withdrawal*. This pattern indicates how new learning opportunities will be used constructively and pleasurably. Positive adaptation can be observed among children who demonstrate initiative and curiosity, express their ideas to others, display interest across racial groups and in different individual activities, and are successful in getting others interested in what they do. Less positive are children who withdraw socially or respond apathetically to novel, stimulating tasks. They seem consistently uninvolved in or unattracted to social learning activities—"out of the swim" of social group affairs.

A second pattern of adaptive behavior in social groups is described by another continuum: *cooperation–compliance vs anger–defiance*. This pattern refers to how children learn to abide by rules or guidelines for conduct that are necessary for orderly group process. Such learning can be inferred from the extent to which children cooperate with others, accept group routines, and generally comply with reasonable adult requests and suggestions. Children who persistently show anger, defy authority, resist attempts by others to enlist their help, and act out in ways that disrupt group activity, usually will fare poorly in social relations with both adults and peers. Patterns of social behavior similar

to these two continua have been observed elsewhere (Labouvie & Schaie, 1974). Both patterns are apparent by observation in group settings with children as young as age 4. These patterns remind us of children's instrumental competence as discussed in Chapter 3: independence, social responsibility, and the like. These basic social tendencies appear to be important early indicators of subsequent patterns of acceptance or rejection by peers, popularity, and even the emergence of leadership behavior in group settings.

Forms of Group Participation

A final aspect of group participation is the trend from comparatively loose-knit neighborhood play groups during early and middle childhood to more organized and cohesive social groups during preadolescence and beyond. Many writers (for example, Ausubel & Sullivan, 1970) have observed that during preadolescence (ages 9 or 10 to 11 or 12) children's social group behavior usually takes two forms. One is participation in relatively formal, organized, and adult-sponsored group activities, such as Scouts and Little League sports. The second is the more informal, spontaneously organized, and member-controlled preadolescent *"social gang."* The social gang is usually unisex and is closely bound by strong interpersonal friendships and group loyalties. Its identity is formed and maintained by ritualistic procedures (such as initiation ceremonies), code names for members and for the group as a whole, passwords, special meeting times and places, and so on. Secrecy and isolation from adult influence sustain group cohesiveness. The basic orientation of such a gang is mutual peer support away from adult authority.

When gangs persist into adolescence, their identities are often determined by the collective delinquent behavior of their members (Chapter 12). This is more likely in densely populated, economically-de-prived urban communities than else-where. With these exceptions, social gangs usually dissipate during early ado-lescence (ages 12–14) to be replaced by smaller and more intimate *cliques*. Like gangs, cliques initially are unisexual and composed of members who are similar in age, interests, and family backgrounds. These cliques, which range from roughly 3 to 9 members, are also associated together in a broader way to form the *crowd*. A crowd, then, is an association of mutually attracted young persons that may include 30 or more members, representing a half-dozen or so cliques. This makes a crowd the largest unit of informal social organi-zation found in most adolescent popu-lations.

Like cliques, crowds usually are differ-entiated by their members' ages and social backgrounds. Crowds seem to provide a preferred medium for movement toward heterosexuality in group structure. Uni-sexual cliques gradually come together for the purpose of heterosexual interaction among adolescents. According to one analysis (Dunphy, 1963) the resulting *het-erosexual cliques* are a natural outgrowth of crowd behavior; they provide a rela-tively secure pathway for adolescents to learn appropriate and desirable ways to relate to members of the opposite sex (see Figure 4.1).

Social group participation seems to follow a predictable course for most nor-mally developing children and youth. This course becomes more highly orga-nized and differentiated as children achieve greater freedom from adult con-trol and expand their sphere of social in-volvements. Most children and youth seem to actively seek group involvements; a majority of them place a high value on clique membership, especially as it affects social life in school (Youthpoll America, 1977). Though group participation ranges widely from formal to informal contexts, all group structures share common ele-

ments. Among the most important is the hierarchy of interpersonal influence that exists in any group to affect the devel-opment of group relations over time. This interpersonal influence, in turn, can be thought about in terms of two important aspects of social life: *popularity* and *lead-ership-followership*. We now examine these aspects and their meaning for peer-group relationships.

POPULARITY AND LEADERSHIP

Popularity means being liked by others—having a positive appeal for other people who then seek to establish

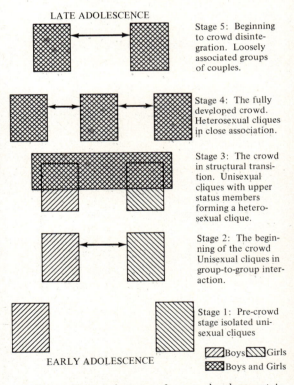

LATE ADOLESCENCE

Stage 5: Beginning to crowd disinte-gration. Loosely associated groups of couples.

Stage 4: The fully developed crowd. Heterosexual cliques in close association.

Stage 3: The crowd in structural transi-tion. Unisexual cliques with upper status members forming a hetero-sexual clique.

Stage 2: The begin-ning of the crowd Unisexual cliques in group-to-group inter-action.

Stage 1: Pre-crowd stage isolated uni-sexual cliques

EARLY ADOLESCENCE

Boys   Girls
Boys and Girls

Fig. 4.1 Proposed stages of group development in adolescence. Reproduced from D. C. Dunphy. The social structures of urban adolescent peer groups. *Sociometry,* 1963, 26, 230–246, by permission.

and maintain some form and extent of personal-social interaction with the liked person. Leadership means influencing the goal setting and goal-achievement activities of other people, usually an organized group situation. Popularity and leadership may appear together as characteristics of the same person, but they are not necessarily correlated. Most of us, for example, know popular persons who either avoid or are unable to exercise leadership. Similarly, most of us also know strongly capable and effective leaders who are not highly popular, or even much liked. In fact, one wonders if strong leadership can emerge without some cost to popularity (or vice versa).

As we will see, this popularity-leadership distinction is very important for psychological research about the development of both characteristics. Data about popularity and leadership among children and youth are gathered in several ways. One way requires the systematic observation and analysis of their social interactions for evidence of *social power*. Social power refers to an individual's ability to influence other people to do his or her bidding or, to say it another way, to evoke submissive responses from others. Children can be observed regularly in their attempts to influence their peers or associates. One telling index of social power is the ratio of successful to unsuccessful influence attempts. Thus, in a given social context and time span Lucy and Sally both may show a comparable number of influence attempts (asking others to do something, placing demands on others, making suggestions for activities, and so on). But if Sally's success rate is 90 percent and Lucy's is only 20 percent, Sally would be considered socially more powerful. Of course, both the nature or kind of influence attempts and the source(s) of Sally's apparent social power must be examined. Successful leaders, for example, often are noted for their effective use of suggestion and indirect requests for voluntary help rather than for heavy use of threats and coercive demands. As for sources of social power, there is an important difference between doing something for others because we like and respect them and submitting to their demands out of fear of punishment. Children who are competent in activities valued by their peers, and who are well liked because of their social acumen, are usually candidates for high social power in most peer groups. The playground bully may also be socially powerful, but for quite different reasons. It is unlikely that the bully will have more than transient influence; and in the long run bullies are not much liked.

This leads us to a second major way to gather data about popularity and leadership: *sociometrics*. Sociometric methods refer literally to the measurement of social relationships—friendship patterns, networks of peer influence, peer perceptions of role behaviors, and hierarchies of social power or the "pecking order" in groups. In some cases, this social measurement is made by asking children to choose, then list, their most liked or admired peers, or their most disliked peers. Peer ratings can also be used by having children provide estimates about the extent to which they like or have confidence in the leadership abilities of various age mates. This is often done on a scale, for example, ratings from "strongly like" or "superior leader" to "not my friend" or "does not make a good leader."

The "Guess Who" technique is still another sociometric tool. In this technique, two questions useful for revealing leadership are "Guess who is always willing to take the job as head of a committee?" or, "Guess who always seems to get other people organized and help them feel good about the work they are doing together?" Each child is asked to list three names. The peers most

Kenneth Karp

Kenneth K

Kenneth Karp

Kenneth Karp

Kenneth Karp

Michael Weisbrot

Michael Weisbrot

Photo © Shelly Rusten 1972

Michael Weis

Michael Weisbrot

Photograph by Arthur Sirdofsky

Michael Weisbrot

Photo © Shelly Rusten 1973

Michael Weisbrot

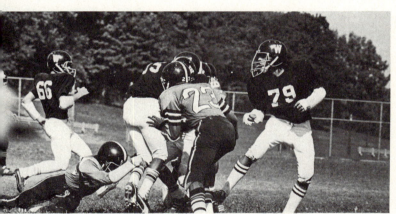

ichael Weisbrot

Photograph © 1975 by Arthur Sirdofsky

© George W. Gardner

Michael Weisbrot

Authenticated News International

Photo © Shelly Rusten 1970

Michael Weisbrot

hotograph by Arthur Sirdofsky

Photograph by Arthur Sirdofsky

HRW photo by Bob Adelman

frequently nominated are assumed to be the class leaders. This same technique can identify whom children perceive as aggressive, mischief makers, good followers, or almost any other social role one wishes to determine in a given group.

Another way to measure leadership from the primary grades of elementary school on is simply to count the number of offices held among the different organizations to which children and youth belong. With permission, this information can be obtained from school records, parents, or the children themselves.

Additional ways to measure social relationships, popularity, and leadership are described in detail elsewhere (Gronlund, 1959; Moreno, 1953 Mussen, 1960). These include ranking and rating methods by adults and sophisticated observational systems. In general, however, it is plausible to think that the best sources of information about peer relations, peer acceptance and rejection, social power, and leadership are children themselves. Any use of data about social relations, must be governed by ethical principles to guarantee children's rights: the right to privacy, participation by consent, protection of confidentiality of information, and so on. (The same principles apply, of course, to all research data.)

Popularity

Beginning in the late preschool years and continuing thereafter, several factors reliably distinguish popular from less popular peers. These factors fit nicely into the three-corner model of interaction presented in Chapter 1. Connie, a highly popular 11-year-old, illustrates the picture that has developed through formal research activity (Cavior & Dokecki, 1973; Deutsch, 1974; Gottman, Gonso, & Rasmussen, 1975; Jennings,

1975; Kleck, Richardson, & Ronald, 1974). For corner A, physical-motor, everyone agrees that Connie is physically attractive. She is also skilled in gymnastics, swimming, and other motor activities of high interest to her peer group. For corner B, personal-social, Connie is alert and cheerful, open and honest in her contacts with others, distributes much positive reinforcement within her peer group, and is seen as a person upon whom others can depend. For corner C, cognitive-intellectual, she is able to communicate effectively, taking into account and often viewing situations from her friends' point of view (role-taking). Moreover, she clearly understands the reasons underlying social conventions, is skilled in perceiving other's emotional states, shows mature moral judgment for her age, and achieves well in school. But Connie is perhaps more socially conforming than independent. Nor is she known for her assertiveness and ability to organize experiences in group settings. Perhaps this accounts in part for her comparatively low leadership profile, although, as we will see, popularity and leadership are not mutually exclusive.

Were Connie a boy, or of a different age, her traits might combine to establish for her a different popularity status. Adolescent boys, for example, seem to value peers whom others, especially adults, cannot intimidate. Yet it is remarkable how similar are the personal characteristics associated with peer popularity across age and sex groups (Ausubel & Sullivan, 1970). In sum, Connie is both socially responsive and responsible. She has the good fortune of having "good looks" as well. Physical attractiveness, of course, does not guarantee popularity. It simply helps.

Social Rejection

A general picture of social rejection by

peers can be obtained by reversing Connie's trait cluster. However, problems of social acceptance are diverse, and we should be aware of the difference between being ignored and being actively rejected by one's peers. Some children, for example, seem little motivated for vigorous group life although well suited for it. They may simply pursue their own interests independently and thus carry low social profiles. But avoidance by peers, the "cold shoulder" treatment, or even hostile disrespect can be the consequence of other patterns of social behavior (Ausubel & Sullivan, 1970). For example, children who are persistently self-centered, arrogant, rebellious, and demanding are disliked, although they may be feared. What influence they exert is usually based upon coercion or sheer domination. They usually know it, but seem unwilling or unable to change. Consequently, their peer interactions are largely negative. Neither do shy, withdrawn, and dependent children enjoy high esteem from their peers. But these children, like those who are apathetic and disinterested, often remain on the fringe of peer group life. The resulting insecurity may intensify their tendency to conform to group norms. Failure to do so may destroy even the thinnest thread of social recognition.

Leadership-Followership

Developing leadership qualities and learning leadership roles require at least two people. And the more common conception of leadership is that it occurs in groups of three or more. Leadership emerges when the group has a common task, which may range from playing a game in a sandbox or a doll corner among preschoolers through managing a class outing or plotting a delinquent act for the group among older children and adolescents. The qualities of leadership demanded may vary greatly from one kind of activity to another. The leader in sports or social activities may not be the leader in academically related activities, such as the French Club. This suggests that leadership status is often situationally specific, although some talented individuals demonstrate general leadership potential across a wide variety of situations. A final requirement before leadership emerges is some differentiation of roles and responsibilities within the group (Hartup, 1970). However, there is some evidence that, even among preschool children, leadership qualities are consistent from one situation to another and from one group to another (Gellert, 1961).

Qualities most important among leaders (as rated by male adolescents) are helpfulness, fairness, sociability, and expertness (Rosen, Levinger, & Lippitt, 1961). Not surprisingly, in some crisis situations fearlessness and physical strength are also considered important leader qualifications by many children and youth. As noted below, the attributes of leaders are not very different from those of popular children and youth, although the differences are sufficient to justify the distinction between popularity and leadership. However, followership is distinctly different from unpopularity or isolation from the group. Unlike popularity, leadership is more likely to fluctuate according to the nature of the situation. An inarticulate football leader may be popular among both his teammates and his fellow members of the French Club, but it is likely he will be a leader only in the football crowd.

Leaders are commonly and correctly considered to be socially powerful children and youth, just as is true for adult leaders. Power in this sense may be extended to include having something someone wants (or fears), coupled with the willingness to share it (or the ability to dispense it). Leaders, in other words, have within their repertoire reinforcers that are important to other members of the group in one way or another, and are known to be capable of administering them.

Core Characteristics of Leaders

The core leadership descriptions encountered in the research literature have mostly been provided by a group of professional people who are interested in both developmental psychology and group formation and function and who have long been centered at the University of Michigan. Their work is summarized (and has been referenced) in the following paragraphs (Hartup, 1970).

Intelligence is related to leadership, but not strongly. Intelligence is presumably more important for leadership in academic undertakings. Socially powerful children are also usually popular. Competence in the central task of the group is also a powerful determinant of leadership, and initiative—aptitude for starting an action—is also an important determiner of leadership. This finding underlines the importance of developing autonomy and independence. Leaders typically enjoy heavy social interaction and are more sociable (and well adjusted) than the average child or youth. They seem able to pick out central issues and argue them, or at least convince the group to follow their ideas about how to proceed on a course of action. This may be related more to social sensitivity than to high intellectual power. Among boys, but not among girls, aggressiveness (usually, but not necessarily, prosocial) is positively related to leadership. Apparently, this aggressive component in male leadership is less important among bright children and youth.

Leaders seem to be realistic about themselves (as are children who are popular and who have positive self concepts). As might be expected, leaders "believe in themselves" and possess higher self-esteem than the average child or the chronic follower. Good leaders are also good followers under appropriate circumstances. This follows logically if, indeed, leaders are realistic, socially sensitive, and high in self-esteem.

This cluster of behaviors (intellectually able, sociable in an active and appropriate way, and reasonably assertive and aggressive, at least for boys) seems to hold for leaders in a wide range of situations and socioeconomic levels. As one reviewer cautions (Burlingame, 1970), however, all the relations reported above are modest; they are tendencies for groups, not rules for individual children. Thus, some shy and somewhat withdrawn children and youth may be leaders, but most are not some ill-adjusted children may be leaders, but most are not; and so on. An important variable is the extent to which children have succeeded in a leadership role sufficiently to perceive themselves as capable of it. A recent study demonstrates that boys whose regular group status involves leadership will function well and with increased thrust in experimental leadership situations. Boys whose normal group status does not include leadership experience have responded with decreased pleasure, even though the performance of the group they are leading was equal to that of groups led by regular leaders (Klinger & McNelly, 1976).

Relationship of Popularity and Leadership

As hinted earlier, the relationship of popularity and leadership varies widely as a function of the situation. For a group on a desert island, among whom only one person is a carpenter who is heartily disliked, the relationship may be strongly negative. The most disliked individual becomes the leader because of his special skills. Where the group is homogeneous, where the climate is benevolently authoritarian, and where the goals of the group are all the same (and when most of them are set by the authorities), the relationship between popularity and leadership may be exceptionally high. In one study of freshmen in a Roman Catholic girls' school, for example, the correlation between leadership and popularity ranged from a high of .91, when the girls were just coming to know each other, to .72, after eight months' association together (Nemac, 1971) [1]

On the whole, the overlap between leadership and popularity is great. In the University of Michigan studies mentioned earlier relationships as expressed by correlation coefficients ranged in various situations from about .50 to about .80, with most in the low .70s (Hartup, 1970). It seems certain that leadership choices also will vary more according to the situation than will friendship choices.

In summary, about the same personal characteristics go into choosing a leader as go into choosing a friend, with one important addition: competence at the task in which leadership is to be shown. Assertiveness seems to be more important in leadership among boys than among girls. The competency dimension leads to variation in leadership choice depending on the situation. A different leader—stronger, braver—may be chosen for dangerous situations than for safe situations, for academics and athletics, for social occasions, or for political action. However, one's friend is likely to remain one's friend whatever the situation.

Uses of Friendship and Leadership Information

Many uses may be made of information about the popularity and leadership status of children and youth. We have stressed the usefulness of research for

understanding development. In addition to its research value, however, knowledge of friendship and leadership status adds much precision to our practical dealings with children and youth.

First, this information is useful in guidance. Common sense as well as scientific knowledge suggest that, within limits, almost everyone likes to be liked. If we know who in a group is liked—a star or a well-accepted member—and who is disliked—an isolate or a reject—we may be able to work with children and young people who find no place in a group and help them develop social and leadership skills that will give them a chance to operate more effectively within the group. By so doing, they may gain greater personal happiness and security. The group may also be guided toward tolerance and acceptance of "different" children who, despite or because of their differences, possess potential for contributing to the group *if* they can be accepted within it.

Information about friendship and leadership roles, if we are careful to employ ethical safeguards, can also be used to increase group morale and cohesiveness. In a rather dramatic case, sociometric information of the kind described earlier was gathered from delinquent adolescent boys. These boys lived in a particularly disrupted, out-of-control cottage in an institution for troubled youth. The two stars—boys who accumulated a plurality of votes for both best friends and leaders—were deeply antisocial even by the most tolerant standards. It seemed doubtful that any form of guidance could bring the boys in this cottage back within the accepted limits of behavior in the institution without taking special measures with the two stars. Thus, they were removed from the cottage situation for individual counseling and residence in a different cottage, while cottage staff sought to develop new and better socialized leaders. The morale of the cottage improved quickly,

[1] Once again, readers unfamiliar with the statistical values of correlation coefficients should consult Appendix B for an explanation.

the atmosphere of chaos and anarchy diminished, and within a few weeks, the two former stars were able to return to the cottage, more understanding of themselves and less disruptive (as well as less influential) leaders and associates.

While this story has a pleasant ending, sociometrics cannot claim magic solutions to problems of group conflict or social rejection. Patterns of social isolation or rejection translated into classroom group behavior, for example, can show strong resistance to change (Bonney, 1971). Effective group work requires thorough knowledge of social dynamics. Sociometrics provide one valuable source of this knowledge. Together with thoroughgoing knowledge of learning principles, especially reinforcement strategies, both antisocial and socially ineffective children may be helped to better social adjustment (Allen, Safer, Heaton, Ward, & Barrell, 1975).

PEERS "VERSUS" PARENTS

The above heading is deliberately provocative. It identifies an issue that often exists for individuals and perhaps for most children and their parents at one time or another. For American parents and their children, however, the issue is more properly stated as the "coexistence of peers and parents." In many ways this coexistence suggests a paradox in socialization. American parents as a whole seem to place a high priority on their children learning to "get along with others." Peer-group involvement is actively encouraged in schools and activity clubs of various kinds (e.g., Scouts, 4-H, Junior Achievement, church fellowship groups, Little League sports). In our experience, parents often seem more concerned with their children's social acceptance than with their school achievement. Yet on the other hand parents may simultaneously express concern that peer-group

involvement will undermine their "good influence." At the extreme, fear is expressed that the peer group can be a corrupting influence and act as a medium for antisocial (delinquent) or personally destructive (drug abuse) behavior.

How valid are these concerns? The question cannot be answered simply. Several relevant ideas deserve an airing. First, and partially to allay parental fears of corrupting influence, *most children and youth choose as their friends other children and youth of whom their parents approve*. This is often assured by where parents elect to live to raise their children. Moreover, to the extent that personal values affect friendship choices and group involvement, parental influence seems to make its mark well before most children spend large amounts of free and unsupervised time in peer-group activity. A typical study, for example, reported considerable stability in the way children express their value systems from the elementary school period and beyond (Beech & Schoeppe, 1974). Of course, neglectful or rejecting parents may forfeit their influence early, perhaps increasing their children's vulnerability to undesirable forces outside the home.

A second closely related point is that *peer-group influence is mediated in large part by salient personal characteristics of individual children*. As indicated earlier, children vary in the degree to which peer recognition and social acceptance are strong reinforcers. Children who express a generalized pattern of dependency, for example, and receive little support at home, are among the strongest candidates for deep and prolonged peer-group participation. This can be for better or worse, depending upon what group activities are available to the child.

Third, developmentally speaking, *a strong element of secrecy or concealment is typical of preadolescent and adolescent groups everywhere.* This is seen as a breaking from adult control. If viewed as a step toward autonomy or independence, it is both desirable and psychologically healthy. Parental apprehensiveness, however, is understandable because adolescents will find "kicks" in just about any activity, whether socially desirable or not, when they are able to act together on their own (Sherif & Sherif, 1965). Looking at this in a different way, group-based behavior is often less predictable and easy to understand than individual behavior because of the many situational dynamics that are created by numbers.

For example, consider an incident involving usually self-controlled pre-adolescent boys. Hiking together through a summer resort area in a group of six, a contest was begun to see who was most accurate in hitting fence posts with a rock. Shortly, the target became birds. Soon a poorly thrown rock struck a resident's mailbox. Rushing to inspect the damage, one lad asked, "I wonder what's in that mailbox?" The chain of events continued to the point where all mailboxes along the road were rifled. Eventually, group guilt took its toll, but instead of returning the mail, these boys buried their contraband in a ditch. The story came out and restitution was made. But our object lesson is that this incident could not have been easily predicted. Additionally, it is extremely unlikely that the incident would have occurred had any one of these boys been hiking alone on that day. In brief, group interaction can sometimes go afoul of parental or societal norms, but at the same time it is a powerful factor in fostering such developmental achievements as the stimulation of advances in moral judgment (Chapter 11). Similarly, the peer group can provide a degree of emotional support for its members. Agemates often understand the processes and the crises of development better than parents. As one authority suggests (Madison, 1969), peers can be their own best therapists.

A final point concerns the *peer group as a leveler.* For most children, the peer group supplements and reinforces what has been learned at home, but usually in a more tolerant and a less emotional way. However, when customs and practices in the home differ sharply from the community norm, the peer group gives the child the chance to learn "how most people do it." This may be for the better or the worse. Peers, of course, serve as models for each other's behavior. Where peer-modeled behavior is consistent with that modeled by parents, we can expect consistent behavior from those children and youth who are doing the observing. But, from social-learning studies (Bandura, 1969; Hoffman, 1970), we learn that observing behavior contrary to that formerly learned and practiced elsewhere can remove inhibitions. For example, merely observing a peer model's aggressive behavior may increase the likelihood of the observing peer's behaving more aggressively, even though this observer learned that aggression is "wrong" or has been consistently punished for it in the past.

The disinhibiting effect of modeling is perhaps most pronounced in studies of "resistance to temptation" behavior (Chapter 11). But, especially when accompanied by reinforcement, modeling can also have an inhibiting effect. That is, modeling can provide a stimulus condition for controlling or checking impulsive or antisocial behavior. Speaking more broadly, then, peer modeling and reinforcement may be a key mechanism in the *leveling* function of peer-group relationships. For example, if parents are extremely conservative, the peer group is likely to liberalize the children, and vice versa. A degree of parent-child conflict is thus almost inevitable except for the few completely middle-of-the-road parents. Peer influence on high school achievement and progression into college can be very strong (McCandless, 1970). By the end of high school, the plans of youths' best friends seem as likely to shape their own plans as do their parents' standards and aspirations. Standards held by teachers, on the other hand, are not very influential at all. On the whole, however, the influence of peers is clearest in such relatively superficial matters as current musical tastes, dress fashions, and recreation preferences. Parental influence usually prevails for more important life issues, such as marriage and work. Much superficial conflict may result between parents and children, but the old adage about the tree growing the way the twig is bent holds true for most children. There are still enough exceptions, both fortunate and unfortunate, to avoid taking this adage as automatic truth for any *individual* child or youth.

The influence of the peer group deserves serious attention from both theoretical and applied workers in human development. In individual cases, the peer group can dilute and distort influences of good home environments, or reduce the damage from harmful home environments, or assure that middle-of-the-road children generally remain in the middle of the road.

A Youth Culture?

Perhaps the most general question relevant to parents versus peers is whether adolescents in American society are a cultural group distinct from the broader adult culture (Penn, 1974; Smith, 1976). This question of cultural separation is hotly debated among students of adolescence. For example, some authorities argue that genuine cultural distinctions exist (Burlingame, 1970; Coleman, 1961; Spindler, 1970). Others argue that adolescent behavior more accurately reflects the prevailing adult culture, although frequently in exaggerated form (Bealer & Willits, 1961; Elkin & Westley, 1955; Offer, 1969). Evidence can be gathered to support both positions, a fact that has led still others (for example, Jahoda & Warren, 1965) to declare the entire question a "pseudo-issue."

Typical of advocates of the distinctive culture idea is Brown (1973), who has coined the phrase *expressive student subculture.* Its values may change with time; but are currently said to include greater commitments to love, peace, equality, individuality, freedom, and democracy. Behavioral norms to support these values include various kinds of *experimentation* (sexual, linguistic, religious, esthetic, drug use, political dissent, and pacifism). These value-behavioral norm relationships are claimed to differentiate the younger from the older generation and create a nearly unbridgeable chasm between the two.

In contrast, much evidence indicates a substantial overlap in values across generation, thus indicating greater continuity than discontinuity. Representative of this genre of research is a study by Fengler and Wood (1973), who examined the value orientations of college students and their parents toward major social issues: distribution of political and economic power, role of the military, patriotism and protest, sanctity of marriage, sexual norms and boundaries, religious values, marijuana use, and minority group acceptance. Degree of similarity in these value orientations was taken as a measure of parental influences on generational continuity. Results indicated more support for generational continuity than for conflict or rebellion. Strikingly similar findings are reported by Gallagher (1974), although a progressive liberalization across generations from grandparents to parents to youth was evident, especially about childrearing practices (Chapter 3). The greatest difference in this study was the greater acceptance of sexual freedom among the younger subjects.

Still another study revealed the younger generation to be more positively oriented toward leisure, with parents more strongly committed to the work ethic (Goudy, 1973). As in many studies of this type, a considerable range of value endorsement was observed within both generational groups as well.

On balance, it seems clear that studies of large groups of youth and their parents, pooled by generation for broad comparison, rarely fail to reveal differences. But within these groups, comparisons of individual parents and their biological offspring usually show considerable similarity. This observation has led one research team to declare that at any one point in time, there are far more children and youth like their parents than unlike them (Kandel & Lesser, 1972). Thus it seems reasonable to acknowledge similarities, as well as differences, rather than dramatize a wide generation gap, the extent and sources of which remain unknown. Some forms of undesirable or conflicting relationships between people in differing age categories seem inevitable, just as they are among people of the same or similar ages.

Lauer's (1973) research identified at least three groups of youth: those who prefer peers, those who prefer adults, and those who prefer both, depending upon the subject or value activity. In this study, all youth were communicating by preference with parents in some areas (such as career and family problems), and with peers in others (such as sex and dating). No evidence was found for a rejection of adults by youth or of a gap as manifested in a conspiracy of silence.

It is not uncommon to think about different subcultural groupings within the general adolescent population. Descriptions such as "straights," "elites," "hoodies," "jocks," and "leftouts" are often used. Any one of these groups can be studied from the perspective of what it does or does not share with the larger community of adult culture.

The study of values shared by youth and adults indicates substantial overlap. Although value changes can be noted from one generation to the next, one does not see much evidence of value reversals and dramatic discontinuities among successive generations. In final analysis, then, what is at issue is perhaps the degree of generational continuity (or the absence of it).

Areas of Distinctiveness in Youth Culture

A principal criterion by which to consider cultural overlap or distinctiveness is whether adolescent communication systems and behavior patterns truly distinguish youth from both the children they were and the adults they will become (Grinder, 1969). Given this criterion, a strong argument can be advanced that youth culture has distinctive qualities. Such things as clothing styles, musical preferences, unique slang, and dance forms come to mind. These seemingly mark a trend during adolescence toward increasingly idiosyncratic tastes. Collectively, these tastes create a distinct image for adolescents; one which, moreover, may strongly influence the "adult culture." Witness, for example, the impact that youth's preferences for clothing styles (denim) have had on the clothing industry in recent years. However, this distinctiveness is perhaps most significant in relation to the task of clarifying both personal and peer group identity during adolescence (Burlingame, 1970).

In viewing youth culture we can observe that the locus of interpersonal influence rapidly shifts from adults to the peer group during preadolescence. This possibly indicates that many young people prefer to base guidelines for their behavior on value and belief systems that they themselves generate. True, for many adolescents these values and beliefs may simply be extensions of those held by their parents. But the peer group seems to operate as a testing ground for individual adolescents to examine the validity of various values, ethics, and morals. Ultimately, and ideally, a commitment to a set of values, ethics, and guidelines for morality will occur. For many adolescents, however, the teen years serve as a psychological moratorium when differing degrees of conformity to peer group customs, alienation, insecurity, conflicts about life style, and self-awareness may be experienced. This perhaps serves to accentuate the distinctiveness of youth culture, although there are vast differences in the degree to which individual adolescents identify with their peers.

For most parents and teachers, the question of youth culture is perhaps most crucial in relation to whether its values support or run contrary to the educational and intellectual goals of the school. Much evidence has accumulated in the past decade or so to suggest that the value system of adolescents is non-intellectual, if not anti-intellectual (Kandel, Lesser, Roberts, & Weiss, 1970). The exact effects of this, if real, are difficult to determine. However, the consensus among researchers is that faced with this value system, many adolescents somehow mask or disguise strong intellectual attainment goals for the sake of peer acceptance (Kandel et al., 1970).

Yet the question remains whether youth groups collectively and deliberately conspire against academic excellence. To be sure, intellectual achievement may connote deference to the adult establishment and may therefore create a source of conflict for an adolescent striving for emancipation (McDill & Coleman, 1965). However, this need not result in persistent underachievement or a rejection of the value of intellectual competence. Rather than accept uncritically the idea that adolescents generally are non-intellectual or anti-intellectual, both the system of rewards and recognition and the existing avenues for development of personal competence in the schools should be scrutinized. In some cases, for example, it may be found that adults, as well as adolescents, reward more quickly and strongly achievement in athletics and social activities than in academics.

In sum, if youth culture is a reality, it may be more accurate to speak of youth *cultures* instead of a single unifying youth culture (Kandel et al., 1970). And, the effects of such "cultural" membership can be powerful and diverse, extending to moral and religious beliefs, esthetics, and educational plans and aspirations. At the extreme, we must acknowledge the much-discussed counterculture movement in the United States. Together with active protest, counterculture activity is viewed as a major way by which youth flaunt society's established values (Cross & Kleinhesselink, 1976). The values being flouted are those associated with what might be called an Apollonian life style: intellectual reason over emotion, self-reliance, personal responsibility, deferred gratification, and advance planning (Benedict, 1950). The leaders of this movement are said to be white, upper-middle-class youth who have reacted against the inauthenticity or hypocrisy of adult-controlled social institutions. These youth are said to be joined in many instances by articulate black youth who seek a liberation from oppressive social conditions. It is tempting to suggest that these youth have come to champion elements of the Dionysian life style, including a focus on immediate sensory experience, the cultivation of deep interpersonal relationships, and a general "back to nature" calling. The present appeal to many youth of communal group life, drug use, organic food, and the occult might be taken as evidence of their alleged anti-rational, pleasure-seeking orientation.

We cannot say how deep and widespread the undercurrents of this movement are, nor how persistent this form of counterculture will be. If this movement is a genuine manifestation of value conflict in United States culture, however, educators and others who foster the dominant, more conventional values of hard work, rationality, and future orientation may find their work increasingly difficult. At the very least, this conflict may necessitate workable educational alternatives to a degree heretofore unknown in American society.

The Conformity Mystique

The issue of peer influence leads naturally enough to the topic of conformity. Though we can herald the supportive function of peer-group experience for autonomy or emancipation from parents, widespread conformity among many youth (and adults!) cannot be overlooked. Conformity—yielding to group pressure—seems to be viewed negatively by many American parents, who strongly value independent judgment and personal autonomy. College students, many of whom are still in late adolescence, also more often than not decry the ills of conformity. Yet both parents and college students can be observed to conform, some slavishly, to various groups with which they are identified.

A certain degree of conformity, of course, is necessary for any group to maintain its distinctiveness. It is the collective support of shared norms that provides a group with its identity and often increases its effectiveness, whatever the group's specific goals. Without some degree of conformity to shared values, ac-

tivities, and goals, it is unlikely that the cohesiveness necessary for effective goal accomplishment will be developed and maintained. Conformity as such is not necessarily the ugly force that some persons might have us believe. The problem seems more a matter of degree. Conformity to others at the expense of one's individuality and sense of self-direction, or conformity for the sake of social acceptance even when conformity means behaving contrary to one's beliefs, moral-ethical standards, or sense of truth, can be problematical.

Developmentally speaking, peer-group conformity increases in intensity with age and reaches a peak during pre-adolescence, after which it decreases (Costanzo & Shaw, 1966; Landsbaum & Willis, 1971). In part, this reflects an age-related shift in the locus of children's dependency from parents and other adults to peers. Children gradually become more dependent upon (and seem to prefer) peer recognition and approval. In fact, during preadolescence and beyond, it is the peer group that seemingly has the greatest influence on children. Experimental studies with children and youth have revealed a high degree of going along with majority opinion among age mates, even when the majority is known to be wrong (Berenda, 1950). Such conformity is most apparent in ambiguous situations where children are unsure about what they should do or are supposed to do (Cohen, Bornstein, & Sherman, 1973).

Moreover, these same studies show that, in matters of opinion changes, a teacher is usually less influential than the peer group. Specifically, when teachers attempt to persuade individual children to change their opinions contrary to the majority, some success is noted with children under age 10, but almost none with older children. Sex differences are also apparent. Girls are more likely than boys to take their cues for behavior from the peer group as early as the elementary school years (Iscoe, Williams, & Harvey, 1963; Cantor, 1975). Moreover, adult, as opposed to peer, pressures to conform can be self-defeating, if we take to heart the results of one recent study of over 1700 adolescents ages 15–18. It found that the stronger the parental pressures on their offspring for educational achievement, the greater was the adolescents' dissatisfaction with school. In other words, negative attitudes toward school increased as parental demands for high achievement increased. This effect was explained by the "noncompliant hypothesis," that is, adolescents' strong desire to work free from parental restraints (Tec, 1973).

Peer group conformity is not always complete and permanent, nor is it always sincere (Krech, Crutchfield, & Ballachey, 1962). Occasionally, to conform is simply to do the easiest thing; at other times, it represents a calculated way to avoid unpleasant and unnecessary conflict. Some individuals are more general and persistent conformers than others. Compared to more independent and self-assertive persons, chronic conformers tend to be less intelligent, less able to cope with stress, higher in anxiety, more prone toward feelings of inadequacy, more passive, stronger in their desire for affiliation and social approval, more dogmatic, and less tolerant of ambiguity (Krech, Crutchfield, & Ballachey, 1962). It is tempting, therefore, to postulate a conformity-prone personality. But, in addition to personal attributes, many variables affect conformity behavior. The apparent influence of age and sex role identification has been noted. To these factors can be added others, including a variety of situational variables.

Situational factors that influence degree of yielding to group pressure include group size and composition, degree of group consensus, the nature of pressure techniques applied by group members, and the extent to which a situation evokes fear or apprehension about what may happen to group members (Asch, 1951; 1956; Crutchfield, 1959; Darley, 1966; Rosen, Levinger, & Lippitt, 1961). For example, near-maximum levels of yielding occur in small groups where at least three or four persons oppose an individual; but some individuals seem to yield even to one opponent. Yielding is also extremely high in groups where individuals find themselves in a minority—the only stranger in a group of comrades or a member of a racial-ethnic minority group. Typically, yielding is also influenced by the social power or status of those who exert pressure. For example, a high-status member of a group, a friend, or a person perceived as highly competent is more likely to effect yielding than are persons lower in a group's social power hierarchy (Landsbaum & Willis, 1971). Finally, group consensus is an important factor. Unanimity tends to produce greater yielding. Where an individual can elicit the support of at least one other person in the group (such as a partner with whom mutual agreement is recognized), yielding usually is lower. This bit of evidence has a profound social implication, well expressed in the following quotation: "A dissident opinion, if expressed loudly and clearly, can have a tremendous effect in strengthening the independence of like-minded people. The expression of a dissident opinion may not *change* the majority's beliefs, but it can conserve the minority view" (Krech, Crutchfield, & Ballachey, 1962, pp. 514–515).

However puzzling and frustrating peer-group conformity may be to adults, it is a fact of life from middle childhood through adolescence. Certainly statistically, much peer conformity is "normal." That is, if normalcy is defined by what a majority in numbers does and we observe that a majority of adolescents conform in some way to peer pressures, then we consider the conformity "normal." Conformity to peer-group norms that are generally consistent with accepted social values probably helps the socialization process. However, a problem can arise when conformity interferes with the development of autonomy or if it occurs in antisocial groups which collectively undermine constructive pathways of socialization.

Finally, our recent observations of adolescent behavior lead us to suggest that peer conformity can in many instances be illusory. That is, deference to peers may not be so much a matter of conviction that peers know best, but more a matter of distrusting or having been disillusioned by the inadequate or faulty behavior of adults. One study of delinquent gang activity in a large midwestern metropolis is consistent with this idea. Gang members, when interviewed about the persons of influence in their lives, attributed less importance to their friendships with peers than to their beliefs that their contact with adult models whom they could respect was virtually nil (Rivera & Short, 1967). A loss in favorableness toward adults also has been observed in a second study where as children got older they were found to increase their readiness to affirm peer-sponsored antisocial behavior, less out of loyalty or regard for peers than from a loss of confidence in the wisdom of adult judgments (Bixenstine, DeCorte, & Bixenstine, 1976).

Two Persistent Issues in Social Development

Our comments about parents versus peers and conformity suggest two matters of dispute about socialization and peer influence. These are issues of social control and goals for personal-social development. Let us consider each.

The Issue of Social Control

This first issue can be stated as a question. How desirable is it for parents and other adults to exert close, even tight, control over children's peer association, or is it more desirable to leave children largely free to explore the peer group for themselves? Some degree of adult control is inevitable. It occurs as a by-product of residential living. In many cases this segregation is intentional, based upon class, racial, and ethnic factors. We know that many city parents—of all races, but mostly white—move to the suburbs or to the country. Their reasons can be sincere: "It will be good for our children to provide a better place for them to grow up." Thus, a trade-off occurs: the diversity of urban life for the sameness and tighter control of suburban or country life. Greater physical safety and academically stronger schools may be gained. But it may also bring isolation, narrow-mindedness, and superficiality—which add to a peculiar, economically advantaged form of cultural deprivation. On the other hand, such a move may provide children with an opportunity to be alone so they can cultivate their inner resources. (One of the authors, who was born and reared on a farm, does not wish to undersell the virtues of space, isolation, and the need to combat one's own boredom and loneliness by developing these inner resources.)

The choice of residence, then, is for many a part of the socialization *process.* Growing up under certain physical conditions, some caregivers believe, is likely to result in their children's becoming the kind of person they desire: a good *product,* at least by their standards.

Whether in the suburbs, in the country, or in the inner city, caregivers of children make many day-to-day choices about their children's companions: "I do not want you to play with ——." The safeguards range from such explicit commands to more subtle running down of the kinds of children with whom caregivers do not want their children to associate. Either technique comes under the heading of exercising control over peer associations. Oddly, the principle of age grading so ingrained in school life seems also to influence parental preferences for their children's playmates. We know many parents who do not like their children to play with older or younger associates, especially of the opposite sex.

Other caregivers exercise little control over their children's playmates. Their children play with whom they wish (which, of course, they are likely to do anyway, because caregivers have only the indirect "psychological" control over their charges' associations during the important hours of the day when children are in school).

Tightly supervising caregivers (typically parents) attempt to reduce the margin of risk for children by keeping them from the influence of those who will "lure them" from the caregiver's way of doing things. The loosely supervising caregiver trusts more to the child's or the youth's inner controls. We know of no data bearing on the question of which policy is most suitable for children, in general or as individuals. Possibly some sort of golden mean is most defensible, as in so many complex human affairs. Responsible caregivers will know where and with whom their children are, but provide a wide range for the expression of individual tastes after providing firm, but benevolent guidance.

The Dilemma of Socialization Goals and Group Involvement

A second issue faced by those who guide the course of human development is the extent to which they emphasize for the young becoming "good members of the group" or autonomous, independent individuals who think for themselves. As we will note in Chapter 11, the highest level of moral judgment is basically individual; it is the autonomous formulation of and acting on our choices according to our own conscience, *after* considering the welfare and the interests of the group, but *sometimes directly counter* to that welfare and interest. Such an exercise of moral judgment can be lonely and difficult. This issue of good group member versus independent and autonomous person is reminiscent of the issue of goal values discussed in Chapter 3 about whether to rear children to be creative or to conform. This issue has been posed in many forms by many people for many years. For instance, we have heard it expressed as "organization man versus free soul"; group member versus loner; outer-directed versus inner-directed; introverted versus extroverted; and field-dependent versus field-independent. Henry Thoreau is said to have posed it to Ralph Waldo Emerson in a famous exchange. Thoreau, a man who valued his solitude but who also valued social justice, had been jailed for civil disobedience. When Emerson saw Thoreau in jail, he asked with concern, "What, my dear friend, are you doing in there?" Thoreau countered, "And what, my dear friend, are you doing out there?"

Over the long span of years, there seems to be little doubt that a rich inner life, a strong and reasonably self-sufficient ego, and a powerful but realistic conscience and sense of justice are the best ingredients to reach eventually the integrity aspect of what Erikson (1963) has called the eighth and final stage of human personality development: *integrity versus despair*. But such personal self-sufficiency and strength can almost certainly not be reached without deep respect and presumably affection for one's fellow humans. Such respect and affection are likely to be gained as the result of intense and continuing social interaction that can be experienced only if an individual is willing to conform to a sensible degree. The total nonconformist is simply cast out. As a loner, he or she has little opportunity to experience the delightful and good aspects of social groups, and can only watch their follies from a distance.

Another important related issue is the degree to which peer acceptance or rejection harms children. Teachers, for example, frequently express concern for socially rejected children, arguing that it interferes with classroom learning and mental health. Moreover, most parents seem to care deeply about the quality of their child's social relationships. One authority (Moore, 1967) believes that at least two patterns of social behavior warrant home and classroom concerns. These occur with the child who persistently and strongly avoids peer relationships and rejects or ignores all friendly overtures from others; or who is highly motivated to establish friendships with peers but goes about this in a way that distresses or alienates others. Concern for such children and youth may be reinforced by the many studies (for example, Schwartz, & Baden, 1973) indicating that peers and adults make important and independent impacts on a developing individual's self-esteem.

Obviously, one must make some basic value judgments to intervene in the lives of such children. Further, certain procedural problems must be solved, including the valid identification of such children, interpreting the meaning that social rejection or isolation has for the child, and selecting appropriate intervention strategies (see the earlier discussion of sociometrics). The persistent dilemma of establishing the goal(s) of intervention cannot be escaped. For example, should a parent or a teacher be content simply with reducing active rejection of a child by his or her peers? Or should an effort be made to promote genuine acceptance and peer preference? In any case, what skills must rejected or isolated children develop to ease their own social acceptance? These are but a few of the nagging questions that face adults who act as agents in children's social development. Answers do not come easily and, according to some, may too often be influenced by the "cult of extroversion" that seems to pervade American society (Ausubel, 1965). According to this cultist thinking, the ideal child should be socially outgoing, always in command of social relations, and eager to assume leadership tasks. Is this a desirable goal state, even if it were possible to mold all children accordingly?

To raise this question calls our attention once again to the goal-values dimension of our socialization paradigm discussed in Chapter 3. One panel of experts, for example, has proposed at least five social development priorities for which peer-group experience is important: sensitivity and understanding in social relationships, positively affectionate friendships and associations, understanding and appreciation of different role relationships, the appropriate regulation of antisocial behavior, and a strong sense of morality and prosocial action (Anderson & Mesnick, 1974).

Similar goal values are stated elsewhere (Havighurst, 1975). They draw our attention once again to important and related developmental functions of the peer-group experience (Ausubel & Sullivan, 1970; Schmuck, 1971). One concerns the peer group as a medium for the development of *primary status*. This means a personal identity as an individual in one's own right; to become known for personal achievements, competencies, attitudes, idiosyncratic tastes, and the like. This stands in contrast to status defined by whose child one is, or what family one represents. Primary status is viewed as a central component of the identity achievement crucial for gaining independence from parents and the self-understanding necessary for mature personal development.

Second, the peer group obviously provides a rich opportunity for learning the give-and-take of social relations. This can include the development of conflict-resolution strategies, the practice of social skills, and the establishment of appropriate controls over aggressive tendencies, to name a few. Additional developments fostered by peer-group involvement include the exercise of autonomous judgment or independent thinking. Moral-ethical views are tested within the peer group as well as the techniques of cooperation and competition. Simultaneously, the peer group can serve as a laboratory for the development and practice of deviant or delinquent behavior. For example, it is

no secret that patterns of drug abuse and crimes of aggression are instigated, practiced, and often reinforced through peer-group action. Especially threatening to the broader social order in America is the violent gang, usually composed of teenagers in urban communities whose activities include unpremeditated or spontaneous assault on strangers and even "killing for kicks" (Yablonski, 1970). To date, such behavior is neither well understood nor effectively coped with by adults who seek to help the young prosper in rational and moral social interaction.

We will reflect upon various aspects of peer relationships and peer group functions throughout this book. Because much of children's peer group involvement occurs within schools, we turn next to a consideration of formal schooling and its role in human development.

SUMMARY

Peer-group relations generally are considered as second only to parent-child relations as major social influences on child development and behavior. Several layers of social interaction combine to exert this influence, beginning with the family and sibling relations and building to neighborhood peer groups and the school. Developmental study of peer interaction begins with primary social relationships, such as parent or caregiver social behavior, and extends to the identification of broad patterns of social participation, such as interest-and-cooperation versus apathy-and-defiance.

For most children, peer involvement increases both in frequency and intensity as they become more mobile and skilled in language communication. These competencies are expressed clearly in children's play. And such children's behavior as solitary, parallel, and cooperative play provides a rich source of information about overall social development. Developmental trends in play during the preschool years were examined and certain cultural differences in cooperativeness–competitiveness among young children were noted. Advanced forms of social group participation beyond middle childhood

have also been examined, the preadolescent social gang and the cliques and crowds of early adolescence and beyond. The function of cliques in providing a transition from unisexual to heterosexual social relationships was highlighted, as was the importance of social group behavior as a medium for the development and practice of leadership.

Leadership–followership has been conceptualized in terms both of the personal qualities that are characteristic of group leaders and of the relationship of leadership to popularity. Sociometric techniques have been used for a better understanding of these phenomena. The research and educational values of such techniques were stressed, especially for gaining knowledge about the structure of groups and patterns of social power that develop among children and youth. However, the many ethical implications of using sociometry make it necessary for those in a position to influence children's social development to make certain that basic human rights are protected.

The widely discussed idea of a "generation gap" in American society was examined in the context of parents "versus" peers. Studies have revealed that both generational continuity and discontinuity occur in our society. It is also apparent that parent–child value differences, as well as similarities, exist. In general, parents seem to exert the single most powerful influence in determining what social values are adopted by youth, but peer group influences are extremely potent during adolescence. The impact of the peer group has been explored in relation to the concept of youth culture. The utility of a youth culture as a basis for identity-seeking and general emancipation from adults is supported by many authorities on adolescent development. Patterns of conformity, however, are also firmly imbedded in the youth culture, especially during early adolescence. Both personal and situational factors seem to affect conformity, including an individual's sense of personal competence, the nature of a task, group size and composition, and unanimity of group consensus.

Finally, two persistent issues in social development and interpersonal relations were identified. These both involve the "shoulds" and the "hows" of exerting social control over children and youth and imposing upon them predetermined socialization goals.

REFERENCES

Allen, R. P., Safer, D. J., Heaton, R., Ward, A., & Barrell, M. Behavior therapy for socially ineffective children. *Journal of the American Academy of Child Psychiatry,* 1975, *14,* 500–509.

Anderson, S., & Mesnick, S. Social competency in young children. *Developmental Psychology,* 1974, *10,* 282–293.

Asch, S. E. Effects of group pressure upon the modification and distortion of judgment. In H. Guetzkow (Ed.), *Groups, leadership, and men.* Pittsburgh, Pa.: Carnegie Press, 1951.

Asch, S. E. Studies of independence and conformity: A minority of one against a unanimous majority. *Psychological Monographs,* 1956, *70,* Whole No. 416.

Ausubel, D. P. Some misconceptions regarding mental health functions and practices in the school. *Psychology in the Schools,* 1965, *2,* 99–105.

Ausubel, D. P., & Sullivan, E. V. *Theory and problems of child development* (2nd ed.). New York: Grune & Stratton, 1970.

Bandura, A. *Principles of behavior modification.* New York: Holt, Rinehart and Winston, 1969.

Bealer, R. C., & Willits, F. K. Rural youth: A case study in the rebelliousness of adolescents. *Annals of the American Academy of Political and Social Science,* 1961, *338,* 63–69.

Beech, R. P., & Schoeppe, A. Development of value systems in adolescents. *Developmental Psychology,* 1974, *10,* 644–656.

Benedict, R. *Patterns of culture.* New York: New American Library, 1950.

Berenda, R. *The influence of the group on the judgments of children.* New York: King's Crown Press, 1950.

Berg, N., & Mussen, P. Social class differences in adolescents' sociopolitical opinions. *Youth and Society,* 1976, *7,* 259–270.

Bixenstine, V. E., DeCorte, M. S., & Bixenstine, B. A. Conformity to peer-sponsored misconduct at four grade levels. *Developmental Psychology,* 1976, *12,* 226–236.

Bonney, M. E. Assessment of efforts to aid socially isolated elementary school pupils. *Journal of Educational Research,* 1971, *64,* 359–364.

Brown, J. W. The values and norms of the expressive student subculture. *Youth and Society,* 1973, *4,* 483–498.

Burlingame, W. V. The youth culture. In E. D. Evans (Ed.), *Adolescents: Readings in behavior and development.* Hinsdale, Ill.: Dryden, 1970.

Cantor, G. N. Sex and race effects in the conformity behavior of upper-elementary school-aged children. *Developmental Psychology,* 1975, *11,* 661–662.

Cavior, N., & Dokecki, P. R. Physical attractiveness, perceived attitude similarity, and academic achievement as contributors to interpersonal attraction among adolescents. *Developmental Psychology,* 1973, *9,* 44–54.

Cohen, R., Bornstein, R., & Sherman, R. C. Conformity behavior of children as a function of group make-up and task ambiguity. *Developmental Psychology,* 1973, *9,* 124–131.

Coleman, J. C. *The adolescent society.* New York: Free Press, 1961.

Costanzo, P. R., & Shaw, M. E. Conformity as a function of age level. *Child Development,* 1966, *37,* 967–975.

Cross, H., & Kleinhesselink, R. *Youth and the counter culture.* In J. F. Adams (Ed.), *Understanding adolescence* (3rd ed.). Boston: Allyn and Bacon, 1976.

Crutchfield, R. S. Personal and situational factors in conformity to group pressure. *Acta Psychologica,* 1959, *15,* 386–388.

Darley, J. M. Fear and social comparison as determinants of conformity behavior. *Journal of Personality and Social Psychology,* 1966, *4,* 73–78.

Deutsch, F. Observational and sociometric measures of peer popularity and their relationship to egocentric communication in female preschoolers. *Developmental Psychology,* 1974, *10,* 745–747.

Dewey, J., & Dewey, E. *Schools of tomorrow.* New York: Dutton, 1962.

Dunphy, D. C. The social structure of urban adolescent peer groups. *Sociometry,* 1963, *26,* 230–246.

Eckerman, C. O., Whatley, J. L., & Kutz, S. L. Growth of social play with peers during the second year of life. *Developmental Psychology,* 1975, *11,* 42–49.

Elkin, F., & Westley, W. A. The myth of adolescent culture. *American Sociological Review,* 1955, *20,* 680–684.

Erikson, E. H. *Childhood and society* (2nd ed.). New York: Norton, 1963.

Evans, E. D. *The transition to teaching.* New York: Holt, Rinehart and Winston, 1976.

Fein, G. G. Children's sensitivity to social contexts at 18 months of age. *Developmental Psychology,* 1975, *11,* 853–854.

Fengler, A. P., Wood, V. Continuity between the generations: differential influence of mothers and fathers. *Youth and Society,* 1973, *4,* 359–372.

Gallagher, B. J. An empirical analysis of attitude differences between three kin-related generations. *Youth and Society,* 1974, *5,* 327–349.

Gellert, E. Stability and fluctuation in the power relationship of young children. *Journal of Abnormal and Social Psychology,* 1961, *62,* 8–15.

Gervey, C. Some properties of social play. *Merrill-Palmer Quarterly,* 1974, *20,* 163–180.

Gottman, J., Gonso, J., & Rasmussen, B. Social interaction, social competence, and friendship in children. *Child Development,* 1975, *46,* 709–719.

Goudy, W. J. The magical mystery tour: An encounter with the generation gap. *Youth and Society,* 1973, *5,* 212–226.

Grabe, M. Big school, small school: Impact of the high school environment. *Contemporary Educational Psychology,* 1976, *1,* 20–25.

Grinder, R. E. Distinctiveness and thrust in the American youth culture. *Journal of Social Issues,* 1969, *25,* 7–20.

Gronlund, N. *Sociometry in the classroom.* New York: Macmillan, 1959.

Halverson, C. F., Jr., & Waldrop, M. F. Relations between preschool activity and aspects of intellectual and social behavior at age 7 1/2. *Developmental Psychology,* 1976, *12,* 107–112.

Harlow, H. F. The maternal affectional system. In B. M. Foss (Ed.), *Determinants of infant behavior* (vol. 2). New York: Wiley, 1963.

Harris, F. R., Wolf, M. M., & Baer, D. M. Effects of adult social reinforcement on child behavior. In W. W. Hartup & N. L. Smothergill (Eds.), *The young child.* Washington, D. C.: National Association for Education of Young Children, 1967.

Hartup, W. W. Peer interaction and social organization. In P. H. Mussen (Ed.), *Carmichael's manual of child psychology.* New York: Wiley, 1970.

Havighurst, R. H. Objectives for youth development. In R. J. Havighurst & P. H. Dreyer (Eds.), *Youth.* Chicago: University of Chicago Press, 1975.

Hoffman, M. L. Word development. In P. H. Mussen (Ed.), *Carmichael's manual of child psychology* (vol. 2). New York: Wiley, 1970.

Iscoe, I. M., Williams, M., & Harvey, J. Modification of children's judgments by simulated group techniques: A normative developmental study. *Child Development,* 1963, *34,* 963–978.

Jahoda, M., & Warren, N. The myths of youth. *Sociology of Education,* 1965, *38,* 138–149.

Jennings, K. D. People versus object orientation, social behavior, and intellectual abilities in preschool children. *Developmental Psychology,* 1975, *11,* 511–519.

Kagan, S., & Carlson, H. Development of adaptive assertiveness in Mexican and United States children. *Developmental Psychology,* 1975, *11,* 71–78.

Kagan, S., & Madsen, M. C. Cooperation and competition of Mexican, Mexican-American, and Anglo-American children of two ages under four instructional sets. *Developmental Psychology,* 1971, *5,* 32–39.

Kagan, S., & Madsen, M. C. Experimental analyses of cooperation and competition of Anglo-American and Mexican children. *Developmental Psychology,* 1972, *6,* 49–59.

Kandel, D. B., Lesser, G. S., Roberts, G. C., & Weiss, R. The concept of adolescent subculture. In R. F. Purnell (Ed.), *Adolescents and the American high school.* New York: Holt, Rinehart and Winston, 1970.

Kandel, D., & Lesser, G. *Youth in two worlds.* San Francisco: Jossey-Bass, 1972.

Kleck, R. E., Richardson, S. A., & Ronald, L. Physical appearance cues and interpersonal attraction in children. *Child Development,* 1974, *45,* 305–310.

Klinger, E., & McNelly, F. W., Jr. Self states and performances of preadolescent boys carrying out leadership roles inconsistent with their social status. *Child Development,* 1976, *47,* 126–137.

Kohn, M., & Rosman, B. L. Cross situational and longitudinal stability of social-emotional functioning in young children. *Child Development,* 1973, *44,* 721–727.

Krech, D., Crutchfield, R. S., & Ballachey, E. L. *Individual in society.* New York: McGraw-Hill, 1962.

Labouvie, E. W., & Schaie, K. W. Personality structure as a function of behavioral stability in children. *Child Development,* 1974, *45,* 252–255.

Landsbaum, J. B., & Willis, R. H. Conformity in early and late adolescence. *Developmental Psychology,* 1971, *4,* 334–337.

Lauer, R. H. The generation gap as sociometric choice. *Youth and Society,* 1973, *5,* 227–241.

Madison, P. *Personality development in college.* Reading, Mass.: Addison-Wesley, 1969.

Madsen, M. C., & Shapira, A. Cooperative and competitive behaviors of urban Afro-American, Anglo-American, Mexican-American, and Mexican village children. *Developmental Psychology,* 1970, *3,* 16–20.

Maudry, M., & Nekula, M. Social relations between children of the same age during the first two years of life. *Journal of Genetic Psychology,* 1939, *54,* 193–215.

McCandless, B. R. *Adolescents: Behavior and development.* Hinsdale, Ill.: Dryden, 1970.

McDill, E. L., & Coleman, J. S. Family and peer influence in college plans of high school students. *Sociology of Education,* 1965, *38,* 112–126.

Moore, N. V., Evertson, C. M., & Brophy, J. E. Solitary play: Some functional reconsiderations. *Developmental Psychology,* 1974, *10,* 830–834.

Moore, S. Correlates of peer acceptance in nursery school children. In W. W. Hartup & N. L. Smothergill (Eds.), *The young child.* Washington, D.C.: National Association for the Education of Young Children, 1967.

Moreno, J. L. *Who shall survive?* New York: Beacon House, 1953.

Mussen, P. H. *Methods of study in child development.* New York: Wiley, 1960.

Nemac, A. M. A study of the determinants of interpersonal attraction among females. Unpublished M. A. thesis, Emory University, 1971.

Offer, D. G. *The psychological world of the teenager.* New York: Basic Books, 1969.

Parten, M. B. Social participation among preschool children. *Journal of Abnormal and Social Psychology,* 1932, *27,* 243–269.

Parten, M. B., & Newhall, S. Social behavior of preschool children. In R. Barker (Ed.), *Child behavior and development.* New York: McGraw-Hill, 1943.

Penn, J. R. Intergenerational differences: Scientific fact or scholarly opinion. *Youth and Society,* 1974, *5*(3), 350–359.

Piaget, J. Piaget's theory. In P. H. Mussen (Ed.), *Carmichael's manual of child psychology* (3rd ed.). New York: Wiley, 1970.

Radloff, R. Affiliation and social comparison. In E. F. Borgatta & W. W. Lambert (Eds.), *Handbook of personality theory and research.* Skokie, Ill.: Rand McNally, 1968.

Rheingold, H. The development of social behavior in the human infant. *Monograph of the Society for Research in Child Development,* 1966, *31,* Serial No. 107.

Rivera, R., & Short, J. Significant adults, caretakers, and structures of opportunity: An exploratory study. *Journal of Research in Crime and Delinquency,* 1967, *4,* 76–69.

Rosen, C. E. The effects of sociodramatic play on problem solving behavior among culturally disadvantaged preschool children. *Child Development,* 1974, *45,* 920–927.

Rosen, S., Levinger, G., & Lippitt, R. Perceived sources of social power. *Journal of Abnormal and Social Psychology,* 1961, *62,* 439–441.

Rubin, K. H., Maioni, T. L., & Hornung, M. Free play behaviors in middle- and lower-class preschoolers: Parten and Piaget revisited. *Child Development,* 1976, *47,* 414–419.

Schmuck, R. A. Influence of the peer group. In G. S. Lesser (Ed.), *Psychology and educational practice.* Glenview, Ill.: Scott, Foresman, 1971.

Schwartz, M., & Baden, M. A. Female adolescent self-concept: An examination of the relative influence of peers and adults. *Youth and Society,* 1973, *5,* 115–128.

Shapira, A., & Madsen, M. C. Between- and within-group cooperation and competition among kibbutz and non-kibbutz children. *Developmental Psychology,* 1974, *10,* 140–146.

Sherif, M., & Sherif, C. *Problems of youth.* Chicago: Aldine, 1965.

Smith, D. M. The concept of youth culture: A reevaluation. *Youth and Society,* 1976, *7,* 347–366.

Spindler, G. D. The education of adolescents: An anthropological perspective. In E. D. Evans (Ed.), *Adolescents: Readings in behavior and development.* Hinsdale, Ill.: Dryden, 1970.

Tec, N. Parental educational pressure, adolescent educational conformity, and marijuana use. *Youth and Society,* 1973, *4,* 291–312.

Waldrop, M. F., and Halverson, C. F., Jr. Intensive and extensive peer behavior: Longitudinal and cross-sectional analysis. *Child Development,* 1975, *46,* 19–26.

Willis, F. N., & Reeves, D. L. Touch interactions in junior high students in relation to sex and race. *Developmental Psychology,* 1976, *12,* 91–92.

Yablonski, L. *The violent gang* (Rev. ed.). Baltimore, Md.: Penguin, 1970.

Youthpoll America. Washington, D. C.: National Association of Secondary School Principals, 1977.

chapter 5

Schools and the mass media

America's schools are its most ambitious institutions for the young. The stage for a child's life is set in the home, but for most children the play is acted out in school for a crucial formative period in their lives, from age 5 to at least age 16, and often much longer. Even more than in the family, school is where children and youth test their formal competencies.

The paramount traditional function of schooling is to develop a youngster's unknown potential for intellectual achievement. During some twelve years of organized educational effort competencies presumably are developed to make young people capable of economic self-sufficiency, able to contribute constructively to society, and enjoy and appreciate the process.

As American society has become more complex over the last forty or fifty years, however, much more than academic achievement and intellectual skill development has been expected of the schools. Urban and technical schools have been expected to carry additional responsibilities for mental hygiene, and for social, moral, vocational, and even sexual development. These expectations have rarely been totally agreed on by everyone, nor have teachers been well equipped to respond to such diverse demands. Clearly, schooling has become an increasingly important part of the socialization of American children.

We may question how realistic are these expectations about socialization through schooling. Any hope for their fulfillment depends upon regular school attendance by America's children and youth. Despite compulsory attendance laws, however, a staggering number of children who should be in some kind of school program are not. A conservative estimate is that nearly 2 million children and youth ages 7–17 years, amounting to some 5 percent of those eligible for schooling, were unaccounted for by educators in the early 1970s (Edelman et al., 1974). This figure includes a disproportionate number of children from low income or unemployed households, ethnic minority families, and rural communities. Because of race, income, physical, mental, or emotional "handicap" and age, these out-of-school children are bound together by their differentness. And for the most part they are out of school less by choice than by exclusion.

Even among children and youth who regularly attend school, we see evidence of psychological insulation or outright alienation from educators' attempts to promote learning. Physical presence in school and teacher presentation of school lessons (however skillful) are no guarantees of effective learning of school objectives. Elaborate research studies are not necessary to document the widespread disinterest in school shown by great numbers of children and youth. They submit and endure, but may grow only feebly in the direction hoped for by parents and teachers.

However, the picture is not all dismal. Many children seem happy in school because their friends are there. Others respond with zest and personal gain to the array of curricular and extracurricular activities most schools provide. Patterns of pupil response are far from uniform because of the profound variations in school quality across America. Though schools often seem to fall short of accomplishing such traditional objectives as transmitting the culture and teaching skills, there is evidence that a counterbalance of successes contributes to more satisfaction than dissatisfaction with schooling among American children and their parents (Evans, 1976).

In this chapter we discuss a range of ideas about the influence of schooling on children's development, stressing the context of schooling and its general socialization effects more than specific patterns of achievement and vocational development, which are discussed later in the book. We begin by examining some general questions about the nature and purposes of American schooling. Recent ideas about the school as socializer and about the overall impact of schooling are then presented. Finally, the human factor in schooling, teacher–pupil relationships, is discussed. The chapter concludes with comments about a second, less directly controlled and well-understood socialization influence, the mass media.

GENERAL PURPOSES AND OUTCOMES OF SCHOOLING

Any full discussion of the purposes and outcomes of American schools demands attention to three interrelated questions. The first concerns the intended goals and objectives, or *functions*, of schooling and asks, "What are the schools for?" The second question concerns how the desired outcomes of schooling are sought, both in school organization and in curriculum and methods. What is intended and what actually happens in schools are not necessarily one and the same. The second question asks, "What actually goes on in schools?" (Goodlad, 1977). The third question follows logically from the first and second by asking about schooling impact: "What are the effects of schooling?" or "How effective is schooling in terms of its stated purposes?"

Issues about school functions and outcomes are tied to our theme of major social influences throughout this entire book. Accordingly, we discuss questions one and three in this chapter. Question two, about school organization and curriculum, is more clearly suited to textbooks on educational administration, educational psychology, and curriculum development. We will, however, have occasion later on in this chapter to mention some aspects of the school environment important for children's positive growth and development.

What Are Schools For?

Two Basic Functions of Schooling

Almost everyone seems to agree on at least two broad functions of today's schools for American children and youth (though the degree of emphasis placed on them is debated). First, we agree that schools should teach the skills necessary to survive in American life, such as clear speech, fluent reading, correct writing, and arithmetic facility. We also agree that children should emerge from their school years with knowledge of United States and world history, English literature, and so on. This function can be termed *skills training–cultural transmission*. It is a basic part of all curricula. Although there is disagreement about the specifics of curriculum content, there is no serious argument about whether the curriculum should develop skills in communication and mathematics and increase general cultural knowledge.

The second major function of schools is more disputed than the first. We refer to the *actualization* function. No school, say those who support this function, should provide children with anything less than the very best or better than they can obtain in their own homes. For example, proponents of actualization argue that schools should enhance students' self-esteem and social development, help them find joy in life, teach them to enjoy play, and strengthen their critical thinking and esthetic abilities. A child or a youth should end each day, week, or term of school more self-fulfilled than when he or she began it. Critics of this aspect of education often call actualization activities "frills." In rebuttal, advocates of actualization usually maintain that unless it is present, formal skills training is unlikely to succeed and, while a degree of cultural transmission may occur, cultural appreciation will not.

Although there is general agreement throughout American society that both skills-training and actualization are important functions of schooling, some authorities (for example, Bereiter, 1972) suggest that skills training should be the exclusive goal in our schools. They argue that explicit teaching for values development, moral judgment, and personal-social adjustment neither can nor should be performed effectively in the public schools. Teachers should recognize this and concentrate upon what the schools can and should do: basic skills training. Other institutional and cultural experiences are more appropriate for actualization.

Other authorities (such as Smith & Schumacher, 1973) argue for a balance between skills training and actualization, because they see socialization and education as intertwined in basic ways. And still others, especially those attracted by humanistic psychology (see Appendix A), champion self-actualization. These advocates of actualization believe that basic academic skills, for example, can and will develop in their own time. Such training should not become the "tail that wags the educational dog."

Developmental Psychology and Schooling

Within the discipline of developmental psychology there exists a parallel debate between advocates of "naturalistic, indigenous growth" theories and advocates of "cultural competence" or "environmental determination" theories (Evans, 1975). Supporters of the "natural growth" view of development claim that maximum socialization benefits can be achieved by giving children and youth an enriched, benign, accepting, permissive, and informal educational environment. Highest value is placed upon a need for children to freely express their creativity (Chapter 8). In this way, a positive sense of competent selfhood can be developed. Maturational processes and sequences provide the bases for nurturing complete and integrated growth patterns for all three corners of human development: physical-motor, personal-social, and cognitive-intellectual.

In contrast, supporters of the "cultural competence" school place greater emphasis upon the shaping power of learning experiences. Systematic, orga-

nized teaching is therefore given a high priority. Skill development and active teacher guidance toward mastery of cognitive-intellectual tasks are the means for children to achieve positive self-growth. The development of human potential cannot be left to chance. A careful analysis of cultural requirements for school success precedes a patterned approach to schooling. School success presumably is the best predictor of a successful life beyond school walls.

The difference in these two views of schooling is a matter of degree. As broad orientations to schooling, however, they underlie many educational issues, including the extent to which specific subject matter content and structured teaching methods are stressed in the classroom. Within early childhood education circles, for example, most traditional nursery-kindergarten practices have mirrored the "natural development" position, while many of the "new wave" intervention programs of the 1960s (associated with the compensatory education movement) took a stronger cultural competence approach.

Which of these positions is most correct or valid for answering the question about what schools are for? Neither, according to some developmental psychologists (such as Kohlberg & Mayer, 1972). The romantic, natural growth tradition is faulty because it is a "bag-of-virtues" ethic, based on arbitrary goal statements that represent vague personality traits and an opinionated philosophy of mental health without validity beyond our own culture. Thus, goals such as "spontaneity," "curiosity," "self-discipline," "positive social adjustment," "independent learning styles," and "esthetic responsiveness" suffer on two counts. First, such goals are difficult, if not impossible, to define clearly. Second, they represent arbitrary value judgments about what is good, based on conventional social standards. Such goals create puzzling paradoxes for the educator. What is self-discipline for one teacher may be compulsiveness or inhibition for another. What is an independent style for one teacher is stubbornness or nonconformity for another. Goal statements based upon a bag of virtues can also show inconsistency or conflict. For example, is it logical or even possible to arrange learning experiences for the development of both spontaneity *and* self-discipline? Or, for independence *and* getting along with others? Finally, the strong emphasis by natural growth advocates upon personal-social outcomes for children is criticized for implicitly creating a role for teachers as untrained amateur psychiatrists or mental health specialists. Critics maintain that this is a role for which teachers are not (nor should be) trained.

The cultural transmission viewpoint is also rejected by some developmental psychologists as a basis for educational planning (Kohlberg & Mayer, 1972). These psychologists believe that this approach is based upon faulty concepts of learning and motivation from "narrow and mechanistic" S-R psychologies (Chapter 2). They also claim that the cultural training view is as arbitrary as the bag of virtues tradition; the only difference is emphasis. For example, the rationale for determining academic content among those who take the cultural competence approach is said to be highly biased in favor of the majority white middle-class value system and therefore is discriminatory. Finally, this academic content emphasis is criticized for its inevitable and widespread use of inadequate achievement tests which, in turn, are used inappropriately to determine the worth of children and their educational development.

Development as the aim of education.
What, then, are the alternatives to these criticized approaches to educational plan-

ning? There is but one genuine option (Kohlberg & Mayer, 1972). Educational aims must be framed in terms of both *intellectual* and *moral* development: the attainment of successively higher stages of development (Chapters 8 and 11) that give the individual an understanding of logical and ethical principles that transcend culture and time. In short, the "true course" of human development should be the source of educational goals. Education is a matter of providing stimulation through stages of development believed to be universal for all children. Cognitive-developmental psychology (Chapter 8), then, is claimed as the theoretical basis of education. A "free and powerful character" is the ultimate educational aim.

Similar views have been advanced by others. Sigel (1973), for example, argues that before any proper decision about educational planning can be made, a more basic problem must be solved: how to achieve a clear understanding of human nature and development. Educators and psychologists are challenged to study more carefully children's self-regulatory behavior, their adaptive mechanisms, and other basic human behaviors. In this way, better cues should emerge to determine what contributions education can make to the course of human development. Of course, achieving a clear understanding of human nature and development is a formidable task, one that has occupied serious students of the human condition for centuries. It seems fair to say that progress toward this understanding has been at best modest.

Commentary on the Issue of School Purpose

What, then, is the final truth about a happy marriage between developmental psychology and education? We cannot say. Truth cannot be determined short of a full array of pertinent, observed facts about human development. To us, this array of facts is still incomplete. We support both continued study and debate among scholars about human development and about what the goals of schools are. Meanwhile, it is instructive to consider what the lay public has to say. According to Gallup Poll data over the past several years, for example, the public is more directly concerned with the practical, rather than theoretical, outcomes of schooling. A majority of adults indicate that the primary purpose of education should be "to get a better job." Personal intellectual and esthetic fulfillments are seen as secondary goals, though not incompatible with the primary goal. The weight of public opinion seems to stress that schools should function to prepare children and youth for the social and economic realities they will face as adults. It is this function for which the public holds school accountable (Postman & Weingartner, 1973). This ties schooling directly to the goal of improving an individual's socioeconomic circumstances. This, in turn, should improve the general quality of life and family circumstances for the development of successive generations of children.

Or so goes the logic. We consider the matter more fully in the next section of this chapter. To conclude, we note that neither the lay public nor developmental psychologists seem to give much explicit attention to still another significant schooling function: as general *custodian* for the young. Compulsory attendance laws, combined with the movement to restrict child labor in the United States, accentuate this broad social function (Bakan, 1971). Parents have come to expect and even depend upon the schools to limit children's mobility and guarantee their safekeeping during working days. Certification or credentialing policies control access by the young to jobs and higher education. Few, if any, alternatives to schooling exist for most chil-

dren and adolescents until age 16 at the earliest. Thus, they must bide their time, even if they are poorly served by the schools. Educators deal with a captive, if not always willing, audience. Many predict that utter chaos would result in American society if the young were not monitored and regulated by authority delegated to the schools. Apart from schools, alternative social institutions or programs to accommodate even relatively small numbers of children and youth simply do not exist in America.[1]

Perhaps because of this strong custodial function, Americans have created certain socialization problems in their very attempts to promote cultural or, more accurately, academic competence. We refer to the socioeconomic problems of early school leaving, delinquency and violence in the schools, underachievement, and the like (see Chapters 10 and 12). Educators often find themselves caught between "a rock and a hard place" in attempting both to control and to promote the attainment of satisfying and productive educational goals among children and youth.

To sum up, Americans seem consistently agitated about their schools. Yet general agreement about the importance of certain broad functions of schooling can be noted: skills training, actualization, and (by implication) custodial. Agreement lessens over certain specifics, such as how and the extent to which skills training and actualization are stressed. Fundamentally, there is deep

---

[1] Alternatives to *public* education, of course, are available to American parents, but usually at considerable cost. According to one recent report (Fantini, 1975), about 15 percent of all American families seek alternative schooling for their children. This includes parochial, academic prep, progressive, independent, and Montessori schools of one kind or another. The total enrollment in alternative schools is estimated at better than half a million students, only about 1 percent of the total elementary and secondary school population in America.

concern for how schooling helps people improve their socioeconomic status. Psychologists tend to look at schooling functions in broad theoretical terms. That is, they prefer to generate their ideas about education from the more basic study of human development and learning. And we have seen that contrary views of educational planning also inhere in the psychological study of children and youth. To this ferment comes the reality of the custodial function for schools and its implications for social order.

The Broad Outcomes of Schooling

Specifying what schools should accomplish, as reviewed in the previous section, is but one basic issue about education and human development. A second is the success of these hoped-for accomplishments. It is comforting to think, as people have for centuries, that education is a prime method for improving one's lot in life (Levin et al., 1971). Further, is it not logical to think that school experience can exert profound effects upon the quality of human development in general? Academic accomplishment and social experience should be particularly affected by school. Yet there is a considerable debate about evidence over whether or not formal schooling makes a real difference in the lives of thousands of American children and youth.

Interpretation of studies designed to assess home and school effects on learning is marked by a dazzling and confusing trail of methodological critiques. It is not uncommon for a researcher to draw conclusions from data about, say, pupil achievement gains over time attributable to one set of "causes," only to have another researcher reanalyze the same data and arrive at different, even contradictory, conclusions. A case in point is the continuing reanalysis of crossnational achievement in reading

comprehension, literature, and science among children of different ages (Coleman, 1975). The crux of this difficulty is whether and how accurately one can distinguish the relative or independent influences of home background, type of school and academic program, and specific instructional practices (including teaching styles), upon the growth of achievement in specific subject matter areas. This task is made even more difficult, because most studies about schooling "effects" are based upon complex *correlational* methods.

We have neither the space nor license to explore such complexities, but we do wish to emphasize that research about school impact is difficult, frustrating, and controversial. In this section we outline a few major general concerns about school influence on human development. In Chapter 10 we look specifically at patterns of achievement, achievement motivation, and vocational development.

The Popular View

For the most part, parents and educators have believed that education is the road to "success" for the great majority of individuals in American society, defining success as economic security, if not affluence. In other words, mass public education has been conceived as an economic leveling mechanism. We have been made poignantly aware in recent years that equal educational opportunity as conceived by our forebears has not in fact existed in America, but their basic idea that those who navigate successfully the course of formal education will reap socioeconomic rewards has been the cornerstone of our thinking about public education. It follows that those who apply themselves and achieve well in school should, under most circumstances, become more successful than those who do not. In theory, therefore, the higher the school achievement, the greater the postschool opportunities and benefits.

This idea is so deeply ingrained in our thinking about schooling in America that it seems beyond question. But scientists demand evidence, even for beliefs that seem self-evident. Do individuals who both complete more years of schooling (quantity) and excel in school achievement (quality) enhance their total life circumstances?

A comforting review of a vast number of correlational studies concludes with a definitive "yes" (Levin et al., 1971; Walberg & Rasher, 1977). Data are presented to indicate that as more formal education is completed lifetime earnings are greater and chances for upward social mobility increase. Occupational alternatives and options for further education are broadened. Active political participation occurs and less criminal activity is observed. Because of increased freedom of choice in determining life work and the privileges made possible by high income, educational attainment is positively if indirectly related to mental health as well. Of course, exceptions abound. In general, however, Americans have continued to bank upon schooling as the most direct route to occupational and personal fulfillment. Among the more specific aspects of education that seem to "allow" or make the difference, then, are amount of schooling, opportunity to learn, the psychological environment for learning, and possibly even class size (Walberg & Rasher, 1977).

This line of thinking has been extended to argue that the better are the schools we provide for children and youth, the greater will be their achievement and subsequent personal development. Efforts to hire superior teachers, provide varied and challenging curricula, create smaller classes, and "modernize" school facilities, are based on the idea that the quality of school experience is directly related to student achievement. In brief, to equalize educational opportunity and thus enhance the educational development of children from any socioeconomic or ethnic-racial background, school resources must be equalized. This requires money and may require school reorganization and desegregation. Improved teacher training and the delivery of educational services better suited to the developmental status of children and youth may be needed. Currently the question about the relation between education and postschool attainment takes a somewhat different form: what effect will equalizing educational opportunity through equality in school resources have on postschool socioeconomic inequalities among American youth and young adults?

The Dissenting View

Not much, if any at all, say a group of Harvard scholars after analyzing the relationship between massive amounts of school achievement test data and school quality (Jencks et al., 1972). They found little hard evidence to substantiate the idea that school reform, or improving school practices, contributes directly to increased educational attainment. Most telling, they claim that school quality has little relationship to postschool earning power. The relationship is better accounted for by the socioeconomic background of children when they enter school in the first place. Beyond this, these scholars make the overriding political argument that education is not an efficient or effective way to achieve socioeconomic equality in the United States.

Vast differences in school quality do exist, and the achievement level of student groups as measured by standardized achievement tests often varies with school quality. But the Harvard group argues that the critical factor is not school quality, but rather the "raw material" of students who happen to attend particular schools. They have attempted to "demythologize" our deep-seated belief that improving schools to equalize educational opportunity will foster high student achievement and, ultimately, greater earning power and social equality among Americans.

This argument is not intended to criticize any effort to improve schools. Rather, the issue is the purpose for which schools are improved. The Harvard group maintains that realistic grounds for educational improvement should be the general enrichment of children's lives and in providing more avenues for personal development. Effective schooling, therefore, will be more a matter of student motivation and sense of purpose than the magnitude of their achievement test scores.

For these researchers, changing to a socialistic design of government, not school reform, is the route to socioeconomic equality in America. The following conveys the essence of this position:

[Our] findings imply that school reform is never likely to have any significant effect on the degree of inequality among adults. This suggests that the prevalent "factory" model, in which schools are seen as places that produce alumni, probably ought to be abandoned. It is true that schools have "inputs" and "outputs," and that one of their nominal purposes is to take human "raw material" (i.e., children) and convert it into something more "useful" (i.e., employable adults).... Our research suggests, however, that the character of a school's output depends largely on a single input, the characteristics of the entering children. Everything else—the school budget, its policies, the characteristics of the teacher—is either secondary or completely irrelevant, at least so long as the range of variation among schools is as narrow as it seems to be in America (Bane & Jencks, 1973, p. 9).

Interpreting the Debate

At first glance, this argument appears to directly contradict the research mentioned earlier about education and postschool opportunity. In fact, it is more a matter of how the data about schooling and its "effects" are interpreted. Levin and his colleagues look more favorably upon the importance of high achievement while in school, and especially on accumulating additional formal schooling. No one can deny that the elaborate credentialing system for entry into high status and high-paying occupations (especially the professions) *requires* extended years of schooling. Jencks and his colleagues argue that those children best equipped by parental and home background influences are exactly those individuals who are likely to congregate together in similar schools, persist in meeting difficult and sometimes silly educational demands, and thus succeed despite the educational system. Such may be the power of social class factors to perpetuate levels of achievement, status, and adult earning capacity.

Still, many parents and educators seem unwilling to relinquish their belief that quality in individual educational development is directly affected by differences in school resources. Other analyses (for example, Spady, 1973) and our own observations lead us to suggest that factors of school quality influence pupils from diverse home backgrounds differently, thus masking potentially strong school effects for some children and youth. Two points about the pessimistic Jencks position are pertinent (Spady, 1973). First, the further children progress in school the more difficult it is to separate the complex linkages among school resources, family support, and attitude toward schooling. Because of this, any school-quality–student-achievement relationship will probably be clearest during the elementary years of schooling. Further, poor children seem more vulnerable to the influence of elementary schools (for better or worse) than are children from more affluent families (Coleman et. al., 1966). Data are more ambiguous at the high school level. A recent study by Jencks and Brown (1975), for example, has disclosed few relationships between high school characteristics and any measure of school effectiveness. At best, changes in such characteristics as amount of teacher experience, class size, and social composition are usually weakly associated with measures of high school effectiveness (usually standardized achievement test scores). On the other hand, high school student bodies differ in amount of aggression or internal violence, esprit de corps, involvement in extracurricular school activities, and expressed motivation for academic achievement (Stephens & Evans, 1973). Though school characteristics that may affect these differences are themselves obscure, it seems reasonable to examine faculty quality, the form of control exercised by school authorities, and peer-group factors that contribute to classroom atmosphere. We return to this idea below.

The second point about the Jencks position is that the strength of any relationship between student development and school-resource quality apparently varies by geographic region and ethnic-racial composition of schools (Spady, 1973). Partly because of different per pupil annual expenditures and community–peer-group factors, wide variations in student body achievement can be noted from one section of our country to another. But where clear-cut differences are observed, the association between school resources (facilities, programs, staff characteristics, expenditures, student body characteristics) and, say, verbal achievement by sixth grade is stronger for black than for white children. This association is further confounded by socioeconomic status factors mentioned earlier. In fact, analyses along both ethnic and socioeconomic lines have suggested that higher socioeconomic pupils, mostly white, achieve more as a function of greater home assistance and stimulation; lower socioeconomic pupils, more often black or from other ethnic-racial minorities, seem to depend more upon the school for support. Exceptions exist and much work is being done to strengthen home-support resources for poor children (Chilman, 1973). But overall, "the achievement of lower SES and black students varies more consistently with measured characteristics of their schools and teachers than does the achievement of higher status whites" (Spady, 1973, p. 144).

Human factors in school impact.   The implications of inequities in school financial support and staffing for future school-resource allocation are obvious, but politically controversial. They call our attention directly to the idea of compensatory education (Chapter 10). However, we have come to believe that the single most important school resource that can influence all students' achievement is the able teacher (Veldman & Brophy, 1974). Able teachers are not necessarily the most experienced, but they are committed to their work and provide positive models with which their pupils can identify. Oddly, formal teacher credentials (certificates, degrees), experience, and even salary frequently show no positive relationship (and sometimes even a negative one) to student academic achievement. Teacher enthusiasm, continued efforts for self-improvement in teaching, and skill in human relationships seem to far outweigh the mere attainment of an official teaching license (Evans, 1976).

A human-factor emphasis in school effectiveness studies is echoed by recent attempts to examine individual educational progress in relation to the student body or pupil peer group. This requires a broadening of the narrow focus upon financial expenditures for schools to include the attitudes, values, and other characteristics of classroom and school groups. In other words, group-process variables—norms, interaction styles, status hierarchies, conformity pressures, and the like—become research targets (Spady, 1973).

A brief mention of reference group theory is pertinent here. Reference groups are those social groups with whom any given person affiliates and looks to as a source of guidance and reinforcement. Students, perhaps because of the positive reinforcement of group acceptance and security, often adjust or conform their attitudes and performance standards for consistency within the peer group. Sometimes this can prompt stronger school achievement strivings than might otherwise occur. Rob, age 16, is tentatively established socially in the junior class of a moderately sized Great Lakes area high school. This school is noted for a strong tradition of academic excellence; intramural scholastic competition ("quiz owl" activities) is a high-status activity. Laggards are put down within this student group; best efforts are expected and clearly rewarded by social recognition. Rob has been observed to work hard to meet these peer expectations. Failure to do so will do little for his tentative social status in his class.

In contrast, Judd's classmates in an affluent suburban west coast school seemingly support their own version of the "keep cool" ethic common among American youth. Most broadly, this ethic calls for unflappable responses to adult demands, a casual approach to group activities, and, above all, no visible displays of emotion, including fear or excitement. To be "cool" in Judd's group, students *never* carry school books, give no evidence of having done homework, and never discuss academic problems within earshot of their fellows. This norm for behavior also excludes the wearing of a jacket (only sweaters are "in") or carrying a brown bag lunch to school.

These contrasting examples show that reference-group norms can variously facilitate, suppress, or have no effect at all upon school achievement behavior. These examples also remind us that peers can serve as role models, exhibiting highly visible patterns of behavior for observational learning. Similarly, friendship associations may establish direct links between broader group norms and individual students. Through friendship patterns, interpersonal influence can be exerted on achievement values and school attitudes, again for better or worse.

The racial-ethnic distribution of students among and within schools affects minority group achievement differences, especially for blacks (St. John, 1975). Where a goodly number of white, middle-class or otherwise achievement-oriented students exist within a given school, and where friendship patterns among blacks and whites can easily be established, the likelihood of educational gains and higher educational aspirations among blacks may be increased. Role models and friendship patterns do not account for all the variations in such gains. It also seems likely that teachers can be more influential in school settings favorable to formal school learning.

Parental and broad community support for intellectual achievement is also a factor not to be underestimated. Active concern among parents about the quality of their children's education, especially when clearly perceived by teachers as support for instructional efforts, has been identified as a pivotal factor for creating climates supporting educational achievement (McDill, Rigsby, & Meyers, 1969).

The issue of teacher influence. What form of influence, apart from direct academic instruction, should teachers (or other group specialists) attempt in their work with student or peer groups? This issue is implicit in our earlier discussion about the use of sociometrics (Chapter 4). At this point, however, we are directly concerned with the role that a teacher or a group worker may take during long-term interaction with the young.

Teacher influence on peer-group norms and structure is much more likely to occur at the elementary school level than the secondary school level, probably because elementary school teachers spend greater amounts of time than their secondary counterparts with more intact groups of children generally more amenable to adult directives (Evans, 1976). Furthermore, adult social influence is usually best achieved by modeling desired behavior than by exhortations or by social or authoritarian control. As the highly successful college basketball coach, John Wooden, has noted: "Young people need models much more than they do criticism." The issues center around the human values that one chooses to model "desirable" behavior. We agree with others (for example, Besell, 1972) that certain qualities of interpersonal relations are desirable in almost any group setting. These include acceptance of and respect for individual differences, equitable treatment of students (versus favoritism), enthusiastic involvement in group activities, forthright and constructive communication with children and youth, competence in facilitating group problem solving, and authenticity (versus masking one's true self). Group workers who wish to exert a positive influence on attitude development and change within a group setting must be perceived as trustworthy by their charges. Finally, it is important to provide ample opportunity for group involvement in setting desired goals, in establishing rules for group conduct, and in arranging activities appropriate to such guidelines.

Other forces at work. We cannot claim that conditions of positive interpersonal influence will result in problem-free classrooms or other social groups. Many forces oppose harmonious group relations and the pursuit of academic development in the schools. Such forces often compete for the attention and energy of children and youth.

One carefully executed study, for example, shows clearly that adolescents' strong social-sexual interests can detract from, and even interfere with, involvement in educational activities (Grinder, 1966). This study analyzed social dating patterns among adolescents of both sexes in terms of four incentive categories: *sexual gratification* (dating as a sanctioned opportunity for heterosexual physical contact); *independence assertion* (dating as a context for autonomous behavior and deviating from accepted parental or societal standards); *status seeking* (dating as a vehicle for upward social mobility or widespread social recognition); and *participative eagerness* (intrinsic social rewards and the avoidance of loneliness, boredom, work responsibilities, and activities with parents or same-sex peers).

A questionnaire to measure adolescents' social-dating interest for each of these four incentive categories was administered to 393 boys and 346 girls from the tenth, eleventh, and twelfth grades of a large, urban high school. Also obtained from each subject was a set of personal data; actual dating activity; academic status and aspirations; peer relationships; and participation in high school activities. Anonymity and confidentiality were guaranteed for all subjects.

Three sets of findings emerged. First, boys showed a negative relationship between interest in all four aspects of dating and academic performance in school; that is, the higher the expressed interest in dating, the lower a boy's academic achievement. A similar negative relationship was noted for girls, but only between academics and two aspects of social-dating, sexual gratification and independence assertion. Second, a negative relationship also was observed between participation in adult-sponsored extracurricular activities and certain social-dating attractions (social status and participative eagerness for boys; independence assertion for girls). Finally, dating interest and peer relations were significantly associated. Interest in all four dating aspects was related to extensive involvement with numerous close friends (boys only); and clique membership was reliably associated with the status seeking (both sexes) and the sexual (girls only) aspects of dating.

These findings held for adolescents in all three high school grades, indicating a widespread pattern of social and academic activity. The data also suggest that the reinforcements of social dating may draw many adolescents away from school-based educational activities; in effect, reinforcements for school achievement compete with peer reinforcements for dating. It is also likely that various frustrating and unpleasant aspects of school life repel still other adolescents, who then seek compensation in social-sexual activity. For whatever reasons, perhaps the most telling finding of this study is that a strong interest in sexual gratification and independence assertion is consistently related to lowered academic performance during the high school years.

This is but one study that exemplifies the vast array of features of school life which combines to affect both social and academic development among the young. Among other things, it reminds us of a basic issue in school organization: the relative advantages and disadvantages of unisexual versus coeducational schools. This issue is less pronounced in America today than in other countries such as the United Kingdom, but it remains a concern for some who wish to keep their children or youth from situations where early boy–girl attractions, steady dating, and the other joys and hazards of adolescent courtship behavior are likely to present themselves. Few United States public schools are now segregated by sex, but there remain many girls' and boys' boarding schools. Some are denominational, some nondenominational, and some (for boys) are military. Proponents of coeducation argue that life is full of associations among men and women and that the school years should be a preparation for the social system as it exists. Others worry that unisexual education is likely to lead to social naiveté, ineptness, or even sexual impulsiveness when young people are eventually exposed to the opposite sex. They are also concerned that unisexual schools may be dangerous to proper sex role development because crushes on those of the same sex may occur and possible homosexual ways of managing sex outlets may be learned.

Proponents of unisexual schools argue that boys and girls should be separated not merely for reasons of sexuality, but because boys mature later than girls and are thus at a disadvantage when placed in classes with girls of the same age. The argument has also been made that boys are more restless, active, and aggressive than girls. Thus, when boys are placed in classes with the girls, their behavior looks relatively "bad." Because of the contrast effect, boys are given more punishment and rejection and receive less praise and approval than girls. In other words, in coeducational classes, boys may become a "prejudiced-against minority group." Much evidence supports this, and shows it begins as early as the preschool years (Fagot & Patterson, 1969; Yarrow, Waxler, & Scott, 1971). The much higher incidence of reading, speech, and disciplinary problems among boys compared with girls may be further supporting evidence for the charge that boys are not fairly treated in school. In a unique study of a situation where demonstrably equal treatment (both negative and positive) was given by teachers to first-grade boys and girls, there were no differences in reading level between the sexes at the end of first grade, although such a difference (favoring girls) is commonly found (Davis & Slobodian, 1967).

It is unlikely, however, that a policy of coeducation in American schools will ever be changed in favor of unisexual education; the overwhelming majority of American children attend coeducational schools and will continue to do so. In fact, equal opportunity legislation has reinforced the policy of coeducation by extending it into athletics, home economics, manual arts, and other school activities formerly segregated by sex.

Coeducation provides a qualitatively distinct context for schooling and may influence scholastic development. One of the few carefully conducted studies on this topic, for example, suggests that students in coeducational schools are more socially and less academically oriented than their peers in unisex schools (Jones, Shallcrass, & Dennis, 1972). Popularity was seen as more important for status than was scholarship. Unlike single-sex schools, "rating and dating" and social acceptance were the preferred values in coeducational schools. Accordingly, students reported spending considerably less time on scholastic activities, including homework, than did their unisex school counterparts.

A later study (Feather, 1974) disclosed few differences in the value orientations of students from either type of school. In fact, boys from coeducational schools reported somewhat greater satisfaction with their teachers and classmates compared to boys from unisex schools. No differences in school satisfaction were reported by girls. These and other data from the Feather (1974) study were interpreted as limited support for the notion that single-sex schools may be more concerned with discipline and control.

On balance, then, such school enrollment factors as the coeducational or single-sex composition of a student body represent a "trade off." Certain advantages, such as more "natural" social development with coeducation, are traded off against the possible disadvantage of weaker scholarship. It is possible, of course, to work toward the "best of all worlds" in any school setting. With such widespread public support for coeducation, any questions about its suitability are academic. We believe, however, that it is important to recognize how coeducation may work for or against desired outcomes of schooling. This issue illustrates again how closely linked are peer and school influences on human development and socialization.

A Model for Understanding School Impact

Many of the features of school life we have thus far discussed are summarized in a thoroughgoing longitudinal investigation in England about how schools affect children (Himmelweit & Swift, 1969). This study asked two questions. (1) How do different kinds of schools affect children who come from much the same background? (2) How does the same school affect children who differ sharply in ability and/or who come from different social backgrounds? The powerful effects that schools can have emerge from this study. One striking finding is that more accurate predictions can be made about children's behavior, outlook, values, and achievements by knowing about their schools than can be made from information about socioeconomic status or intelligence.

Such findings led the authors of this study to construct a model of childhood socialization based on their belief that school is the most important variable. In their model, they isolate several specific aspects of the school environment. Furthermore, they believe these specific aspects, when combined, may determine the degree to which students are affected by their schools.

First, it is important whether the *values* held by school administrators are actually integrated and consistently put into educational practice. Second is the degree to which these values contradict or support other values to which the students are or have been exposed. For example, if the values favor college preparation, but the community influences lead most students to think that college is an impossibility, the effectiveness of the school is likely to be impaired. Third is the nature of the long-term and immediate rewards offered by the school in return for the students' cooperation in keeping the school going smoothly. Fourth is how the school administration deals with students who do not cooperate or who reject the objectives of the school. Finally, the student's status within the school is important. This includes the degree to which the student is actively engaged in working out or adapting to such school-defined roles as "good algebra student," "obedient student," "good athlete," and "competent class officer."

As indicated, the effectiveness of school depends on many things—the nature of the school, the nature of the community, parental values, the degree to which parents participate (Christopher, 1967; Gordon, 1971), and the student's sex. There is evidence that our schools are more consistent with our cultural stereotypes of girls and women than with what our society expects of boys and men (McCandless, 1970). Schools seem to reinforce the feminine stereotype of social sensitivity, obedience, and "don't rock the boat" conservatism. Thus, in a sense, the prevailing United States school atmosphere supports the idea that girls are "sugar and spice and

everything nice." Conversely, boys are more often expelled, punished, criticized, and graded lower for achievement that is in fact the same as that of girls. The competence aspect of the male role in this culture seems to have been discouraged by typical United States schools in the past. It is hoped that improvements will quickly occur in the years ahead.

There is also some evidence (McCandless, Roberts, & Starnes, 1972) that current school practices are such that teachers grade advantaged children, whether black or white, according to a fairly even mix of the student's intelligence and degree of social conformity. This is particularly true for advantaged white boys. On the other hand, poor students may be graded according to a more or less even mix of intelligence and objective achievement of the sort that shows up on standardized achievement tests. This is particularly true for black girls. Thus, the schools seem to be somewhat unfair in grading practices for all sorts of children. If advantaged children are not "good" (nice socially), they are graded down. If disadvantaged children are "good," they receive little credit for it. On the other hand, sensitive teachers may overcompensate to award grades higher than those actually earned by disadvantaged children (Potter, 1971). Either way, distortions in evaluation can occur—a serious ethical problem in American education.

Even friendly critics agree that few American schools achieve their constructive potential for affecting children's and youths' lives. Many schools produce negative attitudes among students, even to the point of alienating them. Certainly, many of the one-third of American students who drop out of high school before graduating could have stayed in school and have graduated creditably if they had been happier in school. Thus many schools and their students seem to be caught up in a self-defeating cycle.

In sum, the human factor is probably the critical one in schools (Hoy & Applebury, 1970). Teacher-student and student-student relationships collectively may be more important than all other aspects of the school experience. This reminds us again of teachers as models for behavior and as agents in promoting positive human relations in school settings. We emphasize the human factor not only to promote the traditional function of skills training or academic achievement but because it is intimately involved in the more ambiguous actualizing function of schooling.

THE SCHOOL AS SOCIALIZER

American parents, as we noted, have increasingly looked to the schools to provide social, athletic, moral-ethical, and citizenship training experiences. Whether by necessity or deliberate choice, many parents and educators have gradually come to think differently and more comprehensively about the role of collective school experiences in shaping attitudes, values, and concepts of moral-political life. Critics of the schools go further and decry the allegedly widespread blunting of potential human development in the schools. Ideas about the form and functions of schooling thus undergo periodic, if often uncoordinated reorganization. There remains, however, an undercurrent of belief in the power of formal schooling to provide a common, positive ground for socializing America's children and youth. This does not mean that schools are necessarily more important than parents for this purpose. Rather, the purposes of schooling are planned and systematically broadened to leave less to chance the personal-social learnings that

inevitably occur wherever children congregate in group settings. The schooling process thus in theory complements the role of the parents.

Dimensions of School Socialization Influence

An analysis by Smith and Schumacher (1973) illustrates the concept of school as socializer and integrates some of the diverse views about the aims of education discussed earlier. According to this view, schools should provide the principal means for promoting basic unity within American society. While freedom for expression of individual and group values should exist in America, so must a common tie exist to permit a basic order and continuity in social life. For Smith and Schumacher, this common tie is the ultimate value of human dignity. On this value is built the process of rational consent by which individual differences can be examined and, where necessary or desirable, compromised in the collective interest. Subvalues intertwined throughout this process are manifest in the American Creed: justice; freedom of speech, religion and assembly; equality of opportunity; general welfare; and domestic peace. The procedures established to guarantee these values are the rule of law, equal protection, due process, consent and representation, and so on. For Smith and Schumacher, any school can and should be a miniature society in which children gain early firsthand experience in these values and processes. In a real sense, then, one can envision schools as active agents for political socialization and development as well as teaching respect for human rights and individual dignity.

This is only part of the story. The school as a miniature society will (must) encompass three other interrelated domains of development. First is moral development, or growth in the self-management of behavior based upon values and standards of conduct encouraged by and essential for harmonious inter-dependence. Earlier in this century much was said but little done by educators about the importance of these values and standards, called by them "character education." Only recently has serious thought been given to models or blueprints for moral education in the schools (Chapter 11). And it must be said that considerable debate rages about the wisdom or possibility of organized approaches for this purpose.

A second dimension of the school as socializer involves a set of principles or normative outcomes believed well suited to school life and to broader adult social life. Two such normative outcomes are familiar: independence, or personal responsibility, which includes the acceptance of legitimate obligations and accountability for one's actions; and achievement, or the performance of tasks to mastery or to acceptable levels of excellence. Other normative outcomes include developing give-and-take in social relations, recognizing the right of others to respond to one as a member of an identity group (boy or girl, third or eighth grader, basketball team or debate club member), and becoming aware of the necessarily limited scope of personal interest in children and youth that adults may have because of their specialized functions (art teacher, coach, school principal, counselor, and so on). These learnings are also related to the first dimension, moral development, because they suggest a change from egocentrism and self-interest to perspectivism and concern for others.

The third major dimension of the school as socializer concerns the actualization function of schools. Smith and Schumacher prefer the term *personal meaningfulness*, which refers to a process of achieving individual satisfaction and significance from an accumulation of day-to-day experiences in school. This process contributes to an "enduring sense of self-awareness and self-direction" that continues beyond the school years into adulthood and family, work, and community life. Personal meaningfulness, satisfaction, and self-identity are basic to the development of human potential; therefore this theme calls for more than a passing nod. It reminds us of how Jencks preferred to determine the worth of schools: degree of pupil satisfaction with themselves and their school activities.

A disproportionate, nearly exclusive emphasis has been placed upon academic achievement, seemingly at any cost, for determining the worth both of children and schools. Until recently, few researchers systematically explored the bases for positive attitudes about school, except as those attitudes might influence school achievement (a relationship which, incidentally, is poorly understood and often negligible).

The Study of Quality in School Life

Researchers have been shortsighted in concentrating upon achievement gains among school children without fully considering the quality of life in American schools. In fairness, a major obstacle to good research has been the inadequate arsenal of techniques to measure student satisfaction and perceptions of quality in school life. Progress has been made, however, as shown in a revealing study by Epstein and McPartland (1976). We share their assumption that school satisfaction is an important factor in the degree of personal meaningfulness found by children and youth within their respective school settings.

Epstein and McPartland carefully developed a promising method for measuring student reactions to the quality of school life, suitable for both elementary and secondary schools. This method as-

Arthur Sirdofsky

HRW photo library

Arthur Sirdofsky

Kenneth Karp

Arthur Sirdofsky

HRW photo library

Charles Gatewood

photo library

Joseph Sza

Arthur Sirdofsky

Joseph Sza

Suzanne

Arthur Sirdofsky

ael Weisbrot

Arthur Sirdofsky

Arthur Sirdofsky

sesses the extent of three relatively independent dimensions of school work, and measures attitudes toward teachers. Their extensive investigation of students in the sixth to the twelfth grades disclosed, first, that *general school satisfaction* is heavily determined by a student's social well-being with peers and teachers, involvement in extracurricular activities, and the importance of the school as the locus of the student's social, as opposed to intellectual, life. A second dimension, *commitment to classwork*, specifically involves the student's academic behavior and career plans and indicates the importance a student attaches to the character and consequences of school work. The third component, *reactions to teachers*, reflects student–teacher relationships and reactions to the overall authority structure of the school. Included are student perceptions of teacher's decision-making style, fairness of grading practices, disciplinary practices, opportunity for classroom discussion, and general "we-feeling" in classroom groups. The researchers consider all three dimensions of school satisfaction critical in attempting both to account for student affect and to assess any changes in school organization, teaching faculty, or curriculum designed to improve student attitudes toward school.

Unfortunately, we do not learn from this study the proportion of students who express various degrees of satisfaction or dissatisfaction with their schooling. Estimates provided elsewhere (for example, Bereiter, 1972) suggest that nationwide as many as 20 percent of high school students are deeply dissatisfied with their school situations. A majority seems at best neutral or blase, while a smaller number of students seem to genuinely like school throughout the entire K–12 grade span. In general, however, the data suggest that school satisfaction both decreases with age and varies with genuine differences in the quality of school life throughout American urban and rural communities. With age, for example, students do seem to become more critical about the relevance of much schoolwork. School curricula also become less able to meet the growing diversity of student needs and interests, more in academic than in social activities. And certainly authoritarian teaching styles, combined with poorly designed rule structures for student conduct, can provoke anger and even hostility among adolescents seeking autonomy and personal freedom (Evans, 1976).

Even if school conditions maximize satisfaction, some disenchantment or impatience with formal school demands is inevitable. But student reactions across the three dimensions of general school satisfaction, work commitment, and teacher–student relationships seem valid indicators of the quality of school life. As positive reaction to school increases, students are more likely to remain in school, become more work-oriented for personal benefit, and simply enjoy more the reality of compulsory school attendance. Consequently, consistent with the argument of Jencks et al. (1972), educators are advised to consider alternatives which can increase the general level of student satisfaction with school.

Plausible hypotheses about how the organization and authority structures of schools may be associated with variations in student satisfaction or personal meaningfulness are not difficult to create. One authority (Grannis, 1967), for example, contrasts several school organizational patterns, two of which can illustrate several hypotheses. One pattern, the *factory school* model, displays standardization and set routines. Classrooms are self-contained or departmentalized along age or grade level or ability grouping. Knowledge is structured for presentation by traditional subject matter access, with a heavy emphasis upon textbooks, workbooks, and meeting uniform standards of achievement. In contrast, other schools are based upon a *family* model with flexible multi-age grouping, informal task structures, small-group or individualized lesson activity, using space for creative study centers (science, art, language activities, mathematics), and spontaneous, child-centered interpersonal relations. Ideal types are easily portrayed on paper, but such differences in school organization actually exist. Will they not make a difference in level of school satisfaction or personal meaningfulness among participating children? A more productive question may be, "Under what conditions, at what points in the developmental sequence, and for what kinds of pupil personalities will one or another school organizational pattern (or rule structure) be most effective for what purposes?" Because the question is rarely so asked, and because only gross comparisons of "factory" and "family" type schools have been made, the answers are ambiguous. In general, open, informed approaches to education seem to favor higher levels of school satisfaction, but not necessarily of school achievement (Evans, 1976).

Even this modest finding increases the difficulty of deciding how to best organize schools for desired priority outcomes. More broadly, we still are faced with significant questions about school impact on moral development and on generalized normative outcomes (independence, achievement) associated with the school as socializer. We have touched on these matters, especially achievement, in general terms, but we defer more specific comments to Chapter 10, which also fully examines cultural and parenting influences on such developments.

THE MASS MEDIA

Social Concern and the Mass Media

Few will deny that the mass media—radio, television, motion pictures, books, newspapers, magazines, periodicals, phonograph and tape recordings—not only spread but also to some extent shape American culture. Many benefits flow from these techniques for mass communication but we can also observe growing social concern about the role of them in our lives and, especially, the lives of our children. This social concern has at least three sources (Golding, 1974). First, and most basic, all rapid technological advances bring in their wake a diffuse anxiety about their effects on the human condition. Advances in broadcasting, for example, have created changes in the sleep habits, meal arrangements, use of leisure time, and conversation patterns of millions of American families (Liebert, Neale, & Davidson, 1973). Though the social effects of such changes are unclear, there is a general unease about and criticism of them.

A second source of concern about the media is its potential power to influence or manipulate human thought and action. An example is the long-standing and intense debate about the depiction of sex and violence in motion pictures and television. Golding points out that these media have been accused of breaking down necessary inhibitions and encouraging both imitative antisocial and libertarian behavior to the disadvantage of organized, lawful, and moral community life. Similarly some advertising is condemned for materialism, false glamour, promoting excessive consumption, and exploiting children (Melody, 1973). Recent evidence about the persuasive role of television advertising on children's attempts to influence their parents' purchasing habits in such places as the supermarket is a case in point (Galst & White, 1976).

The third, broader, social concern is that mass communications result in a diffusion of culture that inevitably produces a downward leveling of the "best." There is, for example, fear that economic or commercial interests will overwhelm any commitment to public education and welfare in the form and content of publishing and broadcasting. In other words, the trivia of mass entertainment is seen as harming the more finely tuned intellectual, social, and esthetic interests of civilized living. For many observers of the American social scene, the consistent trend toward raw violence and sex in the cinema justifies this concern.

Collectively, these concerns emphasize the negative impact of mass media upon adults and children. Two questions immediately come to mind. First, are the concerns valid? Can we generate unequivocal evidence to support such claims about mass media effects? Second, are there not also existing or potential positive benefits of mass media for human welfare and social development? These questions are not easily answered scientifically, because of the lack of convincing research about mass media effects, either pro or con. Except for research about television, subjective analysis has dominated most scholarly discussions about mass media impact. In fact, not until the years immediately prior to and during the Second World War did the effects of propaganda receive scientific study. Limited subsequent experiments in social and educational psychology have demonstrated that filmed communications can significantly affect adult viewer beliefs and attitudes about such things as war, race relations, and capital punishment (Leifert, Gordon & Graves, 1974). Other than box office figures and occasional viewer opinion studies, research about the mov-

ies' impact on American culture is infinitesimal. Nonetheless, strong beliefs about the influence of filmed communications persist among students of the mass media.

Even research on the effects of book and newspaper reading is notoriously scarce. The bulk of research about printed communications has been content analysis (values and social roles portrayed), reading difficulty level, and the evaluation of college textbooks by students and their professors. As Carroll (1974) states, "Beyond any doubt, students can and do learn from print" (p. 176), though precise, unequivocal data about how and about the long-term effects of print as a medium of instruction are lacking.

Moreover, apart from required school textbook reading, the print media seem less likely to influence concept and attitude formation among the young than do television and motion pictures. Newspaper reading and information-seeking about public affairs and political topics are relatively uncommon even among young adults (Liebert & Schwartzberg, 1977). Comic books probably are more widely read by children, but nothing substantial is known about either their incidence or possible influence among the young.

Despite limitations in mass media research, the ever-present eye of television has jolted social scientists to unparalleled efforts in an attempt to understand its effects on human cognition, attitudes, and behavior. Accordingly, and consistent with our point in Chapter 1 about its role in the "unmaking of American children," we shall concentrate upon television as a socialization influence.

The Peculiar Influence of Television

We begin by citing two important realities about television as a source of observational learning for its viewers (Atkin,

Murray, & Nayman, 1972). First, there is at least one television set in nearly 97 percent of all American homes. Mere presence, of course, does not mean a set is used. But the second reality is that television viewing rates are exceedingly high for the average American child. As early as age 3, a majority of children watch television at least two hours daily. Older, or elementary school age children continue and often increase this high average viewing rate, though at the extremes some children view rarely and others as much as 5 hours per day (Lyle & Hoffman, 1972). Even more dramatically demonstrating the early impact of television on children's lives is a report that a typical preschooler's watching hours exceed the time he or she will spend in the classroom for the first five years of schooling (Cooney, 1970).

This high viewing rate is not unselective. Individual preferences for programs are clearly evident by age 6: situation comedies and cartoons are most popular among younger children, while older children prefer adventure and variety shows. Viewing rate declines steadily for a majority of teenagers. Adolescents, especially males, seem to prefer the more violent programs. Other group differences in viewing habits are associated with social class, ethnicity, and intelligence. In general, children from lower socioeconomic circumstances maintain a higher frequency of viewing than do their high-status peers. Black children watch more than do white children, regardless of social class, and, compared to their brighter age-mates, children with lower measured intelligence often spend more time with television. Perhaps most significantly, a strongly positive relationship exists between amount of television viewing by parents and their children (Leifert et al., 1974).

These findings from correlational studies say nothing about the impact of viewing on children and youth. However, even from the early days of television research there seemed little doubt about exposure influence (Maccoby, 1964). Efforts were quickly marshalled to examine both the indirect and more direct nature of such influence. Indirect influence refers to how television may divert children's interests and participation away from other activities. It has been shown, for example, that television viewing limits children's play activity, although less for structured play (such as team sports) than for casual, spontaneous free play. Yet to be determined is at what point television viewing may interfere with or even compensate for play's functions in normal cognitive, personal-social, and physical-motor development. The root issue is how time is best used. Children passively watching television, for example, are not reading. Therefore, the more time consumed by television, the less time available for practicing this important skill. Several of our colleagues have expressed a conviction that television viewing is contributing to successive generations of inept readers. As yet, however, there is little firm evidence to document such a specific relationship. Some evidence has been reported, however, in the direction of a modest negative relationship between heavy viewing and school achievement (Stein & Friedrich, 1975).

Televised Violence and Children's Aggression

Turning to more direct exposure influence, we confront both the immediate and long-term reactions or learnings of children to televised content. Easily the dominant issue about direct influence is televised violence or aggressive content. No single, precise definition of aggression is universally accepted by social scientists, but the main idea involves acting-out behavior (verbal, but especially physical action) that causes injury or discomfort to others or damage to property (Leifert et al., 1974). Such acting-out behavior is very prominent in programs produced for and viewed by children, especially cartoons. Considerable evidence has accumulated to show that children are capable of imitating filmed aggression, although several factors may influence the extent of actual imitation (Atkin et al., 1972; Leifert et al., 1974). For example, the total amount of aggression seems significant, especially for younger children; that is, the higher the saturation level of violence in, say, a cartoon, the more likely young children are to imitate the aggression they have seen. A second factor is the degree of similarity between the filmed situation in which violence occurs and the circumstances in which a child actually lives. This involves the well-known "transfer" or generalization effect in learning: the greater the stimulus similarity across situations to which responses have been learned (by performance or observation), the greater will be the transfer of responses.

To reiterate, we have ample evidence that viewing violence on television increases the probability of subsequent aggressive behavior, both in laboratory and natural life contexts. The data are perhaps clearest for short- compared to long-term effects (Atkin et al., 1972). By and large, the findings hold up across age groups from preschool through adolescence. Studies of adolescents, however, have been narrowly confined to males, often predelinquent, or institutionalized delinquent boys. Thus we hasten to add the qualification that the influence of filmed violence does not seem uniformly adverse nor does it necessarily affect a majority of children and adolescents. In fact, children who appear most responsive to TV violence are those who are already angered, or who are more than "normally" aggressive in their social relationships, or who show little anxiety about thinking or behaving aggressively. Significantly, anxiety reactions to violence seem to decline with increased viewing of violence (Stein & Friedrich, 1975). To the extent that anxiety about aggression inhibits aggressive behavior, but is reduced by a heavy diet of violence viewing, the likelihood of acting-out behavior may be increased even among normally nonaggressive children.

In sum, we suggest that televised violence can and often does have a direct influence on later aggression. There remains room for argument about a cause–effect relationship. A popular competing hypothesis, for example, holds that both aggression and violence viewing are products or outcomes of a third set of "precausal" factors such as a child's dominant personality traits and parental attitudes toward aggression (see Chapter 12). Certainly we must accept a rather long chain of assumptions about how observational learning becomes manifest in behavior before speaking confidently about television *effects* (see Chapter 2). To review, we must assume that children pay sufficient attention to televised behavior, remember what they see, have an opportunity to imitate this behavior, are able to perform the behavior(s), and are motivated to do so. In any case, experts seem to agree that the violence-viewing–aggressive-behavior relationship is sufficiently valid to call for swift reductions in violence in television programming. To our knowledge, however, no one has yet answered satisfactorily the question of why watching violent action is apparently such an engrossing and entertaining activity for children and youth, to say nothing of adults!

For concerned parents who wish to minimize the appeal and possible adverse effects of TV violence, limiting viewing during early childhood is the most effective approach (Stein & Friedrich, 1975). Modeling a value system in the home that disapproves of aggression may also help. Beyond this, it seems mainly a matter of pressures, perhaps even legislation, to reduce the amount of violence in network television programming (see, for example, Liebert, Neale, & Davidson, 1973). Researchers also increasingly believe that using television to promote children's social cognition (Chapter 2) and teach prosocial behaviors (sharing, helping, giving, cooperating) may do much to counteract violence (Chapter 11). More generally, a strong case can be made for increasing the variety of programming to include these as well as other communication services. We suggest more educational programs for children. Children's Television Workshop, for example, has been a source of such successful instructional programs as Sesame Street and the Electric Company. The potential of television to foster children's cognitive-intellectual development has been only minutely tapped. Careful attention to the role of television in the development of general social attitudes or values, such as patriotism, altruism, male–female role relationships, and racial integration, also seems important. We agree with those (such as Leifert et al., 1974) who believe that television is more than entertainment. We respect its capacity to contribute to overall socialization. As one team of scholars has written:

Television, whether or not it accurately reflects our social system, does contribute to forming this social system. At the very least it helps to socialize a new generation of children into an already existing pattern. To the extent that television does not reflect reality, it socializes children into a fictitious social system, where criminals are always caught, minorities and the elderly are rarely seen, guilty people always break down under a good lawyer's barrage of questions, problems are solved in an hour, and things usually work out for the best (Leifert, Gordon, & Graves, 1974, p. 221).

To this we would add that violence is often portrayed on television as a routine method of solving problems. Rampant hucksterism exploits the economic potential of child and adolescent consumers for toys, candy, cereals, cosmetics, and clothing styles. Some will argue that children and youth should be free to take what they will from the medium as it exists in our political-economic system. The extreme counterargument calls for systematic censorship. Somewhere in between is an attitude of conscious and effective use of the medium as a constructive tool for human development and learning. The same can be said for other aspects of the mass media used by children and youth—tape-recorded material and local broadcasting received by the transistor radios so much in evidence among the young.

Some Psychological Functions of Mass Communications

Thus far we have stressed the information factor in mass communications and limitations in our knowledge about it. Much also remains to be learned about how the mass media fit into the total socialization pattern created for children by parents, peers, and schools. A noteworthy question is how patterns of media use are learned and what psychological functions they serve (Clarke, 1971). For example, much media use is collective behavior, such as joint involvement in music listening, movie attendance, and so on. In this sense, media go beyond communication to provide an occasion for social contact and integration. Cues for social status and peer acceptance, such as knowledge about "in" fashions, music, show business, personalities, cars, and sports activities, can be gleaned from the media and reinforced within peer groups. In a different sense, media use for some will be a form of compensation for desired, but unfulfilled or frustrated human interaction. Still other dynamics of media use may be at work, such as escapism into fantasy by disfranchised, alienated, or even emotionally disturbed persons. Or, much media behavior may represent simply a "wall paper experience"—a convenience for passing time until something more exciting occurs. Information seeking is but one of many possible motives for media use (Clarke, 1971).

Even when information seeking is a dominant motive, we have indications of individual differences in media content preferences and in ability to decode or process the form of communication involved. To quote: "Some youngsters may enjoy television because it engages two sense modalities and is undemanding. Others may avoid books because of modest reading skills" (Clarke, 1971, p. 16).

We cannot overlook the important role of parents in socializing children to media use. The home typically introduces children to the media. Parents differ in the opportunities they provide their children for media use, media use behavior they themselves model, and the communication patterns they establish about media orientation and use. One study of parents and their adolescent offspring, for example, has shown differences along two dimensions of family interaction (Chaffee, McLeod, & Atkin, 1971). One is the extent to which adoles-

cents are encouraged to express their personal ideas and join their parents in controversial discussions. A second pattern places greater emphasis upon the maintenance of interpersonal harmony and conflict-avoidance, even to the point of subordinating one's personal feelings and beliefs in deference to others. Differences in both amount (time) and content (news vs. entertainment) of television watching were associated with these patterns. Similarly, parent–child interaction patterns have been linked to differences in adolescents' knowledge and decision-making about advertising and consumer goods purchasing (Ward & Wackman, 1971). From a related study we learn that adolescents high in creativity (Chapter 8) watch less TV and engage in a greater diversity of leisure activities (Wade, 1971). This includes variety in media use as well. Thus, to the extent that such behaviors as critical thinking, social conformity, and creativity are influenced by the home, we place importance upon early socialization experiences for shaping individual response to and use of the media.

We have stressed social concerns about mass media influence, representative slices of mass media research pertinent to psychological development, and individual differences in media use. We leave this important topic to address specific streams of physical-motor, cognitive-intellectual, and personal-social development in Part III. We will refer again to the media, as well as such other social influences as parenting and schooling, which have comprised Part II of this book.

SUMMARY

In Chapter 5 we completed our introduction to major social influences on human development and behavior by discussing schooling and the mass media. An analysis of possible school influences on children and youth calls attention to

at least two important issues: the intended purposes or functions of schooling and evidence about the broad outcomes of the educational process. Broadly speaking, it is generally agreed that the schools should fulfill two major functions—*skills training*—*cultural transmission* and *actualization*. As one result, everyone who experiences schooling should be happier, more secure, and better suited for emotional as well as task-oriented living. We have noted some public disagreement about the emphasis that should be placed upon these two functions, a debate also apparent among psychologists, who may see theories of development and learning as an important basis for educational planning. We also noted another important function of schooling, the school as *custodian* of the young, a matter more of social convenience than of facilitating pupil growth.

Evidence about the effects of education is generally limited to findings from correlational studies. These show that a number of socioeconomic advantages are associated with the amount and, presumably, the quality of formal education that Americans obtain. Many authorities attribute these advantages directly to the educational process. Others challenge this interpretation and say that the *quality* of education seems irrelevant to success in adult life. Rather, children's socioeconomic status at school entry, together with a dash of good (or bad) luck, are seen as the factors that make the real difference in long-range development. Disagreement about the role of schooling in improving the individual's life circumstances has been examined in the light of additional evidence. Our conclusions are two: that schooling effects often *vary* according to children's ability and social background, and that quality of schooling *is* important for educational development, particularly if it involves able, humane teachers. A model for understanding school impact was discussed. Its important components are school–community values, a school's reward system, the management of individual differences, and the individual student's social status within the school itself.

Consideration of this model alerts us to the broader issue of the school as socializer. Schooling effects have most often been examined in terms of academic achievement levels and adult earning power. More recently there has been much ado about how schooling may influence personal-social development, including morality and independence. An organized way of thinking about how the schools may contribute to the overall socialization process has been presented, and the notion of the *personal meaningfulness* of schooling was emphasized in relation to the study of quality in school life.

Admittedly, answers to questions about school impact or effectiveness are tentative and often ambiguous. Yet most Americans continue to believe in the power of their schools to improve their individual and collective social conditions. Americans also believe in, and often express concern and even fear about, the power of the mass media to influence behavior. We noted a general lack of firm cause–effect evidence about socialization through the mass media. Possible television influences, however, have been studied. We reviewed some important evidence about the relationship of televised violence and children's aggression. We are inclined to accept a direct link between these two variables, but in so doing we must also make certain assumptions about children's observational learning. Moreover, the evidence is clear that any presumed influences of television, whether "good" or "bad," are not uniform for all children and youth.

Chapter 5 concluded by discussing some psychological functions of mass communication, including information-seeking, social affiliation, compensation for frustrated needs, and escapism. Stress has been placed upon the parental role in socializing children to media use and the potential of gaining positive social benefits from the mass media.

REFERENCES

Atkin, C., Murray, J., & Nayman, O. The Surgeon General's research program on television and social behavior: A review of empirical findings. *Journal of Broadcasting,* 1972, *16,* 21–35.

Bakan, D. Adolescence in America: From idea to social fact. *Daedalus,* 1971, *Fall,* 979–995.

Bane, M. J., & Jencks, C. The schools and equal opportunity. In P. Salmon (Ed.), *Christopher Jencks in perspective.* Arlington, Va.: American Association of School Administrators, 1973.

Bereiter, C. Schools without education. *Harvard Educational Review,* 1972, *42,* 390–413.

Besell, H. Human development in the elementary school classroom. In D. Solomon & J. Bergen (Eds.), *New perspectives in encounter groups.* San Francisco: Jossey-Bass, 1972.

Carroll, J. B. The potentials and limitations of print as a medium of instruction. In D. R. Olson (Ed.), *Media and symbols: The forms of expression, communication, and education.* Chicago: University of Chicago Press, 1974.

Chaffee, S., McLeod, J., & Atkin, C. Parental influences on adolescent media use. In F. Kline & P. Clarke (Eds.), *Mass communication and youth: Some current perspectives.* Beverly Hills, Calif.: Sage Publications, 1971.

Chilman, C. S. Program for disadvantaged parents. In B. M. Caldwell & H. N. Ricciuti (Eds.), *Review of child development research* (vol. 3). Chicago: University of Chicago Press, 1973.

Christopher, S. A. Parental relationship and value orientation as factors in academic achievement. *Personnel and Guidance Journal,* 1967, *May,* 921–925.

Clarke, P. Some proposals for continuing research on youth and the mass media. In F. Kline & P. Clarke (Eds.), *Mass communication and youth: Some current perspectives.* Beverly Hills, Calif.: Sage Publications, 1971.

Coleman, J. S. Methods and results in the IEA studies of effects of school on learning. *Review of Educational Research,* 1975, *45,* 335–386.

Coleman, J. S., et al. *Equality of educational opportunity.* Washington, D.C.: U.S. Office of Education, 1966.

Cooney, J. Sesame Street. *PTA Magazine,* 1970, *64,* 25–26.

Davis, O. L., Jr., & Slobodian, J. J. Teacher behavior toward boys and girls during first grade reading instruction. *American Educational Research Journal,* 1967, *4,* 261–269.

Edelman, M. W., et al. *Children out of school in America.* Cambridge, Mass.: Children's Defense Fund of the Washington Research Project, Inc., 1974.

Elliot, D. S. Delinquency, school attendance, and dropout. *Social Problems,* 1966, *8,* 307–314.

Epstein, J. L., & McPartland, J. M. The concept and measurement of the quality of school life. *American Educational Research Journal,* 1976, *13,* 15–30.

Evans, E. D. *Contemporary influences in early childhood education* (2nd ed). New York: Holt, Rinehart and Winston, 1975.

Evans, E. D. *The transition to teaching.* New York: Holt, Rinehart and Winston, 1976.

Fagot, B. I., and Patterson, G. R. An "in vivo" analysis of reinforcing contingencies for sex role behavior in the preschool child. *Developmental Psychology,* 1969, *1,* 563–568.

Fantini, M. D. Alternative educational experiences: The demand for change. In S. Weinstein & D. Mitchell (Eds.), *Public testimony on public schools.* Berkeley, Calif.: McCutcheon, 1975.

Feather, N. T. Coeducation, values, and satisfaction with school. *Journal of Educational Psychology,* 1974, *66,* 9–15.

Galst, J., & White, M. The unhealthy persuader: The reinforcing value of television and children's purchase-influencing attempts at the supermarket. *Child Development,* 1976, *47,* 1089–1096.

Golding, P. *The mass media.* London: Longman, 1974.

Goodlad, J. I. What goes on in our schools? *Educational Researcher,* 1977, *6,* 3–6.

Gordon, I. J. *Parental involvement in compensatory education.* Urbana, Ill.: Research Press, 1971.

Grannis, J. C. The school as a model of society. *Harvard Graduate School of Education Association Bulletin,* 1967.

Grinder, R. E. Relations of social dating attractions to academic orientation and peer relations. *Journal of Educational Psychology,* 1966, *57,* 27–34.

Himmelweit, H. T., & Swift, B. A model for the understanding of school as a socializing agent. In P. H. Mussen, J. Langer, & M. Covington (Eds.), *Trends and issues in developmental psychology.* New York: Holt, Rinehart and Winston, 1969.

Hoy, W. K., & Applebury, J. B. Teacher–principal relationships in "humanistic" and "custodial" elementary schools. *Journal of Experimental Education,* 1970, *39,* 27-31.

Jencks, C., et al. *Inequality: A reassessment of the effect of family and schooling in America.* New York: Basic Books, 1972.

Jencks, C. S., & Brown, M. D. Effects of high schools on their students. *Harvard Educational Review,* 1975, *45,* 273–324.

Jones, J. C., Shallcrass, J., & Dennis, C. Coeducation and adolescent values. *Journal of Educational Psychology,* 1972, *63,* 334–341.

Kohlberg, L., & Mayer, R. Development as the aim of education. *Harvard Educational Review,* 1972, *42,* 449–496.

Leifert, A. D., Gordon, N. J., & Graves, S. B. Children's television: More than mere entertainment. *Harvard Educational Review,* 1974, *44,* 213–245.

Levin, H. M., et al. School achievement and post-school success: A review. *Review of Educational Research,* 1971, *41,* 1–16.

Liebert, R. M., Neale, J. M. & Davidson, E. S. *The early window: Effects of television on children and youth.* New York: Pergamon, 1973.

Liebert, R. M., & Schwartzberg, N. S. Effects of mass media. *Annual Review of Psychology,* 1977, *28,* 141–174.

Lyle, J., & Hoffman, H. R. Children's use of television and other media. In E. Rubenstein, G. Comstock, & J. Murray (Eds.), *Television and social behavior* (vol. 4). Washington, D. C.: U.S. Government Printing Office, 1972.

Maccoby, E. The effects of mass media. In M. L. Hoffman & L. W. Hoffman (Eds.), *Review of Child Development Research* (vol. 1). New York: Russell Sage, 1964.

McCandless, B. R. *Adolescents: Behavior and development.* Hinsdale, Ill.: Dryden, 1970.

McCandless, B. R. *Adolescents: Behavior and development.* Hinsdale, Ill.: Dryden, teacher marks variation by sex, race, and social class. *Journal of Educational Psychology,* 1972, *63,* 153–159.

McDill, E. L., Rigsby, L. C., & Meyers, E., Jr. Educational climates of high schools: Their effects and sources. *American Journal of Sociology,* 1969, *74,* 567–586.

Melody, W. *Children's television: The economics of exploitation.* New Haven: Yale University Press, 1973.

Postman, N., & Weingartner, C. *How to recognize a good school.* Bloomington, Ind.: Phi Delta Kappa, 1973.

Potter, T. H. *Intellectual achievement responsibility as a variable influencing prospective teacher grading practices.* Unpublished Doctoral Dissertation, University of Washington, Seattle, 1971.

St. John, N. *School desegregation: Outcomes for children.* New York: Wiley, 1975.

Sigel, I. *Contributions of psychoeducational intervention programs in understanding of children.* Unpublished manuscript, State University at Buffalo, New York, 1973.

Smith, L. M., & Schumacher, S. The school as socializer. In J. Goodlad & H. Shane (Eds.), *The elementary school in the United States.* Chicago: University of Chicago Press, 1973.

Spady, W. G. The impact of school resources on students. In F. N. Kerlinger (Ed.), *Review of research in education* (vol. 1). Itasca, Ill.: Peacock, 1973.

Stein, A., & Friedrich, L. Impact of television on children and youth. In E. M. Hetherington (Ed.), *Review of child development research* (vol. 5). Chicago: University of Chicago Press, 1975.

Stephens, J. M., & Evans, E. D. *Development and classroom learning.* New York: Holt, Rinehart and Winston, 1973.

Veldman, D. J., & Brophy, J. E. Measuring teacher effects on pupil achievement. *Journal of Educational Psychology,* 1974, *66,* 319–324.

Wade, S. E. Adolescents, creativity, and media. In F. Kline & P. Clarke (Eds.), *Mass communication and youth: Some current perspectives.* Beverly Hills, Calif.: Sage Publications, 1971.

Walberg, H. J., & Rasher, S. P. The ways schooling makes a difference. *Phi Delta Kappa,* 1977, *58,* 703–707.

Ward, S. E., & Wackman, D. Family and media influences on adolescent consumer learning. In F. Kline & P. Clarke (Eds.), *Mass communications and youth: Some current perspectives.* Beverly Hills, Calif.: Sage Publications, 1971.

Yarrow, M. R., Waxler, C. A., & Scott, P. M. Child effects on adult behavior. *Developmental Psychology,* 1971, *5,* 300–311.

PART III

MAINSTREAMS OF HUMAN DEVELOPMENT

In the first chapter of this book three major and interrelated components of human development were explained and illustrated by a three-corner schematic diagram: physical-motor, cognitive-intellectual, and personal-social development. In Chapter 2, interacting genetic and learning processes important for human development were explained. We then took up the topic of major social influences on development by examining parenting, peer-group relations, schools, and the mass media. Having set this stage of facts, concepts, and principles for the study of human development in general, we now turn to specific mainstreams of development consistent with the three-corner model of interaction.

Part III begins with an overview of major aspects of physical-motor development, including the study of health and illness and related perceptual-motor developments such as body image. This provides an explicit link to our discussion of basic cognitive factors in development. Among all species, human beings are most advanced in their use of symbols and reasoning in attacking the problems they face as they and their societies evolve. Chapters 7 and 8, therefore, are devoted to the symbolic nature of humans: their use of language, the acuity with which they manage problems, and other important aspects of cognitive processing, including creative thinking.

However fundamental cognitive factors are to overall development, they cannot be taken as the full story. All human beings must accommodate in some way to their gender, their sexual needs, and their sexual identification as they move from infancy through childhood to maturity. Especially in complex technological societies such as the United States, they must also accommodate to pressures or needs for personal achievement and economic self-sufficiency. And all humans must eventually assume a moral-ethical stance, both as autonomous persons and in relation to the larger social order of which they are a part. Hence, we consider streams of development in psychosexuality, achievement and career preparation, and morality, to include prosocial ways of behaving. Throughout these chapters certain challenges for improving conditions for human development will be noted, such as better nutrition and health care, parent education, equal educational opportunities, and career guidance. We conclude this book with Chapter 12, in which further social challenges are discussed in some detail: aggression, racial prejudice, and exceptionality in development. These aspects of human development are notable both for their relations with social policy and the need for further research. Throughout each chapter in Part III we attempt to maintain our emphasis upon developmental trends and issues, and especially the research literature about major social influences on human development

chapter 6

Physical-motor development

Our model of interaction (Chapter 1) suggests that every facet of social and personal development is affected by the body. The first, though not necessarily the most important, impression individuals make on others in ordinary social interaction is usually based upon their physiognomy and the manner in which the body is handled. Typically, our first comments in attempting to describe strangers are about their physical characteristics and age. Features common in such descriptions are height, weight, general body build, coloring, and attractiveness. Unusual or striking attributes of grace or awkwardness, thinness or obesity, apparent strength or weakness, and voice pitch are also likely to be mentioned.

Our perception of our own bodies is an important aspect of our more general self-concept. Chances are that if we think well of ourselves, we are likely to be tolerant and accepting of our physical make-up; self-rejection usually involves dissatisfaction with our bodies (Johnson, 1956; Secord & Jourard, 1953). Self-rejection has been associated with parental rejection, which may include notions of being seen by one's parents as unattractive, weak, or sickly (McCandless, 1967).

Moreover, the nature of our body and its functioning may have much significance for the development of interest patterns, even in selecting a vocation. Weak, ill-coordinated males seldom, if ever, become professional athletes. Their sturdy, graceful age-mates may have before them a wider range of avenues for work and leisure activities that require physical prowess. Unwritten cultural standards can also create problems of social life for those of us who "deviate" from preferred facial and body configurations.

Additional relationships between physical and other dimensions of growth can be cited. A large group of children selected because they are far above average in measured intelligence, will also likely be heavier, healthier, stronger, and more agile compared to another large group of the same age and sex distribution who are considerably below average in intelligence. This generalization will not hold for each and every member of either group, but the idea that "good things cluster together" for total development is generally valid. Of course, many of these relations are not the result of intelligence. Instead, growth-enhancing social conditions may provide a setting for a better all-around development of human potential.

A final general point about physical development is the extremely wide range of individual differences in body size, shape, and general appearance among developing children and youth. Largely because of different rates of physical maturation, this range increases with age and peaks from age 11 or 12 to about age 16. During this time,

children typically undergo their pubertal growth spurt, generative organs become capable of mature functioning, and "secondary" sex characteristics (facial hair and voice change in males, breast development in females) appear. But even though individual differences in physical development are marked, the *sequence* of this development is normally the same for all children and youth. In addition, this development seems governed by a set of common principles that help us to describe and understand developmental processes.

In the next section we present information about these matters. We begin with development before birth. Aspects of physical development from birth onward are then discussed, including major growth trends and threats to normal, healthy development. Consistent with the theme of *psychosocial* development, we refer to some important social influences upon physical growth, emphasizing implications for psychological and social behavior. We should note at the outset that development before (prenatal) and after (postnatal) birth differs little in basic mechanisms or processes. Three specific processes are (Hamilton & Mossman, 1972): (1) *growth*, or increases in size and weight; (2) *differentiation*, or increases in complexity and organization; and (3) *metabolism*, or changes in biochemical activity. The final outcome of physical development, as of other aspects of human functioning, will depend upon both genetic make-up and the environment in which development occurs. Environmental influences are not restricted to development after birth, however, as will become increasingly clear in the first section of this chapter.

PRENATAL DEVELOPMENT

The duration of human pregnancy, commonly called the gestation period, ranges from 250 to 310 days, with an average of about 280 days. During this time period, a single, nearly imperceptible cell divides, grows, and differentiates. The process culminates with the birth of a full-term infant, weighing, usually, from 6 1/2 to 7 pounds (2.92 to 3.15 kg), containing literally millions of cells (Hamilton & Mossman, 1972).

Phases in Prenatal Development

The gestational, or prenatal period has three phases, each defined by landmarks of developmental process. The first phase (0–3 weeks) begins with fertilization and ends with the embryo completely embedded in the uterine wall before the intraembryonic blood system has been established. The second phase (4–8 weeks) is the embryonic phase during which the main organ systems are established. The final phase (the third month to the end of intrauterine life) is the fetal period, during which there is rapid body growth and little further differentiation (Langman, 1975).

Phase 1

Of the 200 to 300 million sperm deposited in a female's genital tract, only about 300 to 500 survive the arduous journey to the site of fertilization in her fallopian tube. Normally, only one of these will penetrate and fertilize the egg. The fertilization process results in restoring the full number of chromosomes and in determining the sex of the new individual (see Chapter 2).

The fertilized egg begins to divide as it moves down the fallopian tube, and it is thought to be composed of 12 to 16 cells by the time it reaches the uterus. Implantation within the uterus occurs approximately six days after fertilization; a specific area of the cells penetrates the surface cells of the uterine wall which has already been prepared by the hor-

mone, progesterone. During the next two weeks complete imbedding occurs, the amniotic cavity is formed, and the embryo becomes attached to its shell of cells by a connecting stalk which will become the umbilical cord.

Phase 2

The embryonic period spans the time for organogenesis, the time when the major organ systems are developed. This stage in development is very important for increased cellular complexity and organization. It is also when the embryo is most susceptible to "outside" factors that may interfere with development. Most congenital malformations originate during this phase.

By the end of the second month the formation of limbs, face, ears, nose, and eyes has greatly influenced the appearance of the embryo; its "humanness" is becoming evident. Amazingly, the embryo—now in transition to fetal form—is only 1 to 2 inches (2.5 to 5.0 cm) long, yet it contains all the major organs and organ systems. Little more than growth and differentiation are now required to properly complete its prenatal life. Fetal motor activity is first noted during this phase.

Phase 3

This fetal period is marked by a slow-down in head growth in relation to body growth. To illustrate, early in the third month the head is approximately one half the sitting height of the fetus; by the beginning of the fifth month the head is approximately one third the standing height; and at birth the head is approximately one fourth the standing height (Langman, 1975).

During the important third month, the eyes and ears become located in the general vicinity of their final positions, to provide a more human face. The first rudiments of hair appear, to be replaced by true hair during the following month. The limbs reach their relative proportional length in comparison to the rest of the body, although the lower limbs tend to lag behind the upper in growth and development. Additionally, the external genitalia are sufficiently developed so that fetal sex can be determined by external examination.

During the fourth and fifth months the fetus lengthens rapidly (fetal standing height at 5 months is about 50 percent of neonatal height), but little weight gain is apparent (the fetus is only about 10 to 12 percent of its newborn weight at month 5). The myelinization process has now begun and appears to coincide with the beginnings of specific neural functions. (Myelin provides a sheath around some nerve fibers and promotes efficient electrical transmission along those fibers.) Fetal movements (quickening) may now be felt by the mother.

The sixth month finds the fetus red in color and wrinkled in appearance. However, during the last few months subcutaneous fat will be deposited. The fetus takes on the more rounded, soft look characteristic of a newborn infant (neonate).

Prenatal Developmental Problems

As we have said, prenatal development is an especially vulnerable stage of life. Only about 50 percent of fertilized human eggs survive long enough for pregnancy to be recognized in the mother. Of these recognized pregnancies, 10 to 25 percent are aborted spontaneously, mostly during the first 5 to 8 weeks (Smith & Der Yuen, 1973). It is estimated that among liveborn infants, 2 to 3 percent will show one or more significant birth defects. This figure may double by the end of the first year as defects not apparent at birth are discovered (Langman, 1975).

It is estimated that, of all human malformations, about 10 percent are caused by environmental factors, 10 percent more are caused by genetic and chromosomal factors, and the remaining 80 percent result from the interaction of genetic and environmental influences (Langman, 1975). Specific causal factors are myriad. They include bacterial infections, radiation, hazardous drugs, vitamin deficiencies, allergies, and sex chromosomal abnormalities. However, the importance of quality in genetic material provided by parents cannot be overemphasized. One authority reports the occurrence of roughly 2500 genetically distinct defects in human development (Kugelmass, 1975).

Factors affecting prenatal development originating in the mother's social environment are discussed later in this chapter. We note here, however, that observers of prenatal life have been interested in environmental influences on development, because medical intervention prior to birth may have the greatest impact in avoiding or countering adverse forces. To date, three main ideas about the impact of noxious environmental forces have been formulated (Langman, 1975).

First, and consistent with the critical-periods concept (Chapter 2), the amount of influence that a particular force may exert will depend upon the phase of embryonic development (Table 6.1). It will be recalled that the first phase of prenatal life involves rapid multiplication of cells with little, if any, differentiation. Contact with a noxious force or agent at this time can be so profound as to cause death or, if only a few cells are damaged, some form of cellular adjustment or "compensation." From animal studies, for example, we have learned that high doses of vitamin A administered during the first phase have no apparent effect on newborns, thus suggesting some sort of adjustment; high doses in later pregnancy can cause many abnormalities (Langman, 1975). The second phase in embryonic development—a period of intense differentiation—is a particularly vulnerable time, as shown by the heart defects and eye abnormalities of many infants whose mothers contract rubella (German measles) during the fifth to tenth week of pregnancy. This indicates marked susceptibility to infection among organs in their early stages of differentiation. Lessened susceptibility to environmental intrusions may accompany the third phase in embryonic development, except for areas of the brain. For example, certain viral infections during this period of pregnancy have been associated with distorted central nervous system development.

The second idea about prenatal environmental influences is that malformations are most likely to occur from adverse forces where underlying genetic instabilities exist. Again, the idea is best documented from animal studies. Litters of mice genetically "predisposed" to skeletal abnormalities and whose parents were starved for certain short periods of time during pregnancy, have shown a greater incidence of actual skeletal maldevelopment than comparable litters whose parents enjoyed uninterrupted nutrition (Runner, 1959).

The third related principle of prenatal environmental impact is that

noxious agents act in specific ways on specific aspects of cell life processes. From the tragic thalidomide story, for instance, we know that this chemical substance irreversibly altered prenatal limb development among infants carried by mothers ingesting the drug early in their pregnancy. In contrast, infants whose prenatal environment is marred by maternal syphilis infection frequently are affected by congenital deafness, mental retardation, and even blindness. Hence, if different environmental agents cause different abnormalities, they are thought to act upon different biochemical aspects of prenatal metabolism.

Fetal monitoring. Management of the pregnancy is not limited to observation and care of the mother. There are numerous ways to monitor the condition of the fetus (Spellacy, 1976). Sampling the mother's blood and urine to assess the level of hormones and enzymes can provide information on the status of the placenta and fetus. Amniocentesis (the withdrawing of a sample of the amniotic fluid surrounding the fetus) also provides much information. For example, studying the circulating protein from the fetus can be helpful in diagnosing congenital abnormalities. Under some conditions, blood samples from the fetus itself may be taken.

Except for urine sampling, these techniques require radical intrusions into the mother's body. Some fetal monitoring techniques have been developed that do not require such intrusions. Ultrasound, for instance, can be used to assess fetal size, age, and organ development. This involves directing sound waves to the fetus and analyzing the returning echoes. An amnioscope can also be inserted into a mother's partially dilated cervix to visualize the amniotic membranes and fluid which it contains. Still another example is monitoring fetal heart rate through such special equipment as

TABLE 6.1 Critical Time Periods for Specific Malformations in the Human Fetus

Central nervous system	3.0 to 6.0 weeks
Heart	3.5 to 6.5 weeks
Arms	4.5 to 6.5 weeks
Eyes	4.5 to 8.0 weeks
Legs	4.0 to 7.0 weeks
Teeth	6.75 to 8.0 weeks
Palate	6.75 to 9.0 weeks
External genitalia	7.25 to 11.5 weeks
Ears	4.25 to 10.0 weeks

Adapted from Blair and Salerno, 1976.

stethoscopes, microphones, and ul-trasound.

Labor and Delivery

There is no period in human development, from conception to death, when adaptive requirements are so compressed in time and so critical to the continued survival of the individual as the birth process. During prenatal development the placenta, not a part of the fetus itself, shares or totally controls the functions of nearly every major organ in the body. At birth this regulation is abruptly cut off, and body organs must suddenly assume the functions for which they were programmed (Wennberg, Woodrum, & Hodson, 1973). The process of labor and delivery, then, is a crucial time of developmental transition.

Labor is that time in the birth process when the uterine muscles begin to contract at diminishing intervals until the baby is expelled. The exact cause of this muscle action is unknown. One explanation is that the onset of labor results from extreme stretching of the uterus; another suggests that the onset is based upon a change in hormonal level. The duration of labor varies, but usually is longer for the first pregnancy than for subsequent ones. It is convenient to think about labor in terms of stages. The longest — the preparatory stage — lasts from the first sign of labor (pains or contractions at regular intervals) until the opening from the uterus is completely dilated. During the second stage, the baby leaves the uterus, passes through the birth canal, and enters the outside world. The third stage consists of a period of uterine contractions until the placenta is expelled (Breckenridge & Murphy, 1969).

The labor and delivery process is important because the problems or hazards encountered during this transition may adversely affect subsequent growth and development. For example, such complications as improper positioning of the fetus, premature closure of the umbilical cord, and infant size disproportionate to the maternal pelvis through which it must pass, may reduce or cut off the infant's oxygen supply, resulting in brain damage, or even in death. A lack of oxygen or physical trauma to the brain are widely cited as antecedents to mental and physical handicaps among children (Oxorn & Foote, 1975).

Although the data are sparse, it is reasonable to think that the labor and delivery process may also have implications for the personal-social development of the child. In a method of childbirth such as the Lamaze (Karmel, 1959), in which the mother is an alert and active participant and in which the husband is often permitted to take an active part, parental role behaviors will begin earlier than in circumstances where the first parental–offspring contact follows the mother's recovery from anesthesia. We can speculate that such earlier participation may be helpful in promoting the parent–child attachment process (see Chapter 3). Perhaps the future will bring scientifically acceptable data about this and other possible consequents of the Lamaze method.

Another way to view the personal-social effects of labor and delivery requires us to take the newborn infant's perspective. As an example, one authority (LeBoyer, 1975) maintains that birth is a terrifying process for infants, largely because of unnecessarily harsh medical practices. Thus, we can ask how must it feel to be suddenly wrenched from a dark, quiet, warm secure resting place and thrust into a dazzling bright, noisy, relatively cold and austere delivery room. Will such an experience have lasting detrimental effects on personality development? Certain early theorists (such as Rank, 1929) claimed that birth trauma — a bombardment of noxious stimuli from the outside world to which the infant is unprepared to adapt—is the prototype of all anxiety or tension. The greater the trauma, the greater the anxiety, and the greater the anxiety the more miserable is one's psychological existence. As indicated in Chapter 3, no convincing evidence of a birth trauma—general personality development relationship has yet been offered. But champions of the nonviolent, benevolent birth process can build their argument on moral, if not empirical grounds. They prefer soft lights, gentle handling, and the use of warm water for immersing the infant as conditions for delivery. Only time will tell how extensively such modified birth techniques will become part of accepted medical practice.

POSTNATAL DEVELOPMENT

We now attend to important aspects of physical and motor development from point of birth onward. Our discussion is selective, but provides a reasonably broad and detailed picture of such development. We begin with an overview of the newborn infant's—the neonate's—developmental status. Changes in height, weight, and shape are then discussed, followed by comments about physiological change, perceptual-motor developments, and health and illness during childhood and adolescence.

The State of the Newborn

Approximately two-thirds of all normally developed newborns weigh between 6 and 8½ pounds (2722 to 3856 g) and are between 19 and 21 inches (48.3 and 53.3 cm) in length (Wenner & VanderVeer, 1973). These normative data, however, vary across race, socioeconomic status, and so on. For example, the above figures were derived from white infants; black infants generally are

slightly smaller. These differences are not well understood, but we can say with confidence that any infant's size at birth is not a reliable indicator of eventual adult size. Rather, birth size tends to reflect the uterine environment more than it does heredity. Thus, children born of small mothers but genetically "programmed" to be large, will go through a "catching up" period in their growth. Another interesting point is that except for cases of severe maternal malnutrition, a newborn's size is independent of maternal diet. The fetus will be supplied directly from the mother's tissues, if need be, to meet its own nutritional needs.

Neither is size by itself an indication of general reactivity among infants. They normally will display a variety of reflexes, or involuntary movements, given appropriate external stimulation. Some seventy different reflexes have thus far been described (Illingworth, 1975a). Some are present at birth and disappear within a few weeks, while others appear shortly following birth and disappear some weeks later. The presence, absence, and timing may all have diagnostic significance; however, the value of many reflex behaviors has not yet been determined (See Table 6.2).

In any case, these reflexes vary greatly. They include oral reflexes, such as sucking and rooting (a search reflex helpful in locating the mother's nipple); eye reflexes, such as blinking and pupillary response; hand and foot reflexes, such as the palmer and planter grasps; placing and walking reflexes; righting reflexes which function to restore the normal position of the head in space; and so on.

Beyond these involuntary reflexes, human infants are intricate and well-organized beings at birth. Their visual power includes the ability to discriminate among patterns. In one study (Frantz, 1963), for instance, infants gave

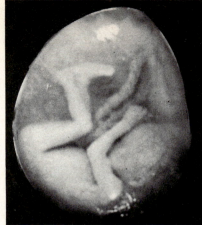

12 WEEK FETUS   Landrum B. Shettles, M.D.

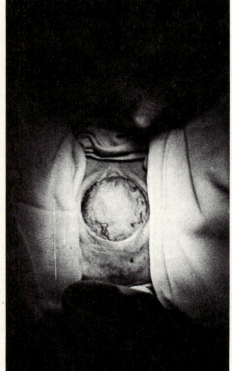

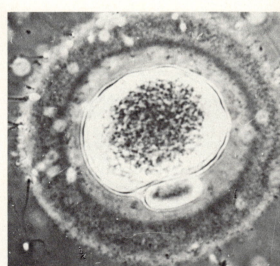

THE MOMENT OF CONCEPTION   Landrum B. Shettles, M.

Landrum B. Shettles, M.D.   THE MOMENT OF BIRTH

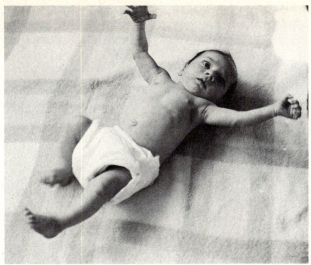

Kathryn Abbe

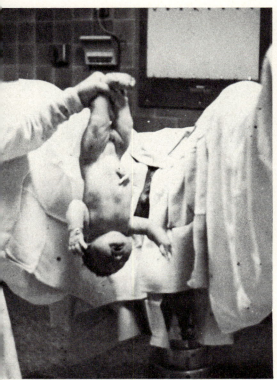

drum B. Shettles, M.D.

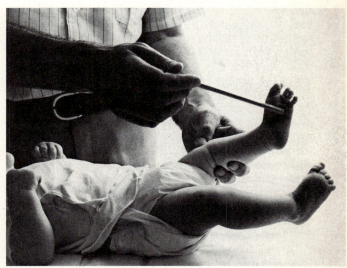

Suzanne Szasz

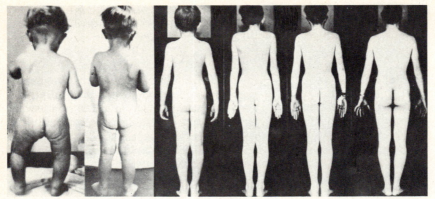

BODY PROPORTIONS FROM BIRTH TO MATURITY   Bayley (1956), p. 48, by permission

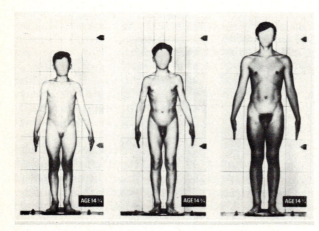

J. M. Tanner, "Different degrees of development at the same chronological age," in *Genetic and Endocrine Diseases of Childhood*, Lytt L. Gardner, ed., courtesy W. B. Saunders Co.

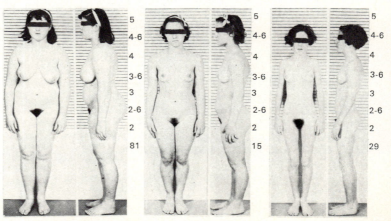

16-YEAR-OLD ENDOMORPH, MESOMORPH AND ECTOMORPH   G. H. Lowrey

Kenneth Karp

Kenneth Karp

Kenneth Karp

twice as much visual attention to patterns as they did to plainly colored surfaces. Moreover, pattern *preferences* were observed; these newborns preferred faces to concentric circles and concentric circles to newsprint. Still other studies (such as Bridger, 1961) indicate that newborns not only can hear, but quickly discriminate between sounds. Newborns can also discriminate between odors, as shown by a study (Lipsitt, 1966) in which infants were continually

TABLE 6.2   Early Reflex Behaviors in the Human Infant

Reflex	Description	Diagnostic Significance
Babinski	Upon scratching sole of foot from toes to heel, the toes will flare out.	Absent in defects of the lower spinal cord
Plantar	Upon pressing balls of feet, toes will "grasp"	Absent in defects of the lower spinal cord
Standing	Weight bearing in a supported standing position	Degree of weight bearing indicates muscle strength and tone
Walking	Stepping movements in standing position	May be absent in infants delivered with an incorrect presentation.
Placing	Upon stroking top of the foot with an edge, e.g., of a table, foot will be raised and placed on the surface of the table	Absent in slight or partial paralysis of lower limbs
Palmar	Upon pressing palm of hand, hand will grasp	Too little or too much pressure indicates some neurological dysfunction (Cratty, 1970)
Tonic neck reflex (TNR)	Upon turning head and neck, an arm and leg will extend into a "fencer's pose"	Persistence beyond a couple of weeks after birth may indicate neurological dysfunction
Moro	Upon a quick shake of head, e.g., a controlled striking of the pillow, arms, fingers, and legs will spread and then return to a flexed position against the body	An absent or weak response indicates a serious disturbance of the central nervous system
Glabella	Upon tapping area between the eyebrows, the eyes will close tightly for a moment	Low threshold for hyperexcitable infants

Adapted from Prechtl and Beintema, 1964.

exposed to an odor until they provided little reaction—that is, they habituated to the odor. Following habituation to the first odor, a second odor was introduced. The newborns reacted quite strongly. Further studies clearly demonstrated that newborns are capable of tactile sensations and can experience pain (Gullickson & Crowell, 1964).

Perhaps more impressive than these sensory abilities is the newborn's ability to coordinate them into a single activity. A newborn, for instance, can focus its eyes on a visual target and then "track" its movement by turning the eyes and head back and forth. A more involved skill is a newborn's ability to locate a sound source. Upon hearing a noise to the side, an infant will turn its head toward the sound source and focus on it with its eyes. A coordination of motor, visual, and auditory responses is evident. Such intricate coordination has been observed in infants as early as 3 minutes following birth (Wertheimer, 1961). The habituation, discrimination, and coordination of newborns reveal that even at this early age they are not simply passive receivers of external stimuli. Instead, they are actively involved with the world, although what portion of the brain they use is not completely understood. This further reinforces the idea of interactionism, even in the earliest stage of postnatal learning and development.

The early development of newborn infants is a marvel to behold. And the promise of a full and normal life ahead for an infant can be a major source of gratification for parents. Tragically, however, even normal and healthy appearing infants may not survive beyond the early months of life. We refer specifically to a perplexing phenomenon of infancy known as the Sudden Infant Death Syndrome (SID), or Crib Death, where apparently normal, healthy babies suddenly and unexpectedly die in their sleep. The SID incidence reports range from 10,000 to 15,000 deaths per year, with the peak incidence occurring in infants 2 to 4 months of age. This syndrome is considered the leading cause of death among infants in the first year (Marx, 1975). Infants with low birth weight, especially if premature, and siblings of victims are at higher risk for SID than the normal population.

Although the actual cause of SID is unknown, more than a hundred theories have been proposed to account for it (Beckwith, 1975). Possibilities range from inadequate respiratory control with a central nervous system origin (Naeye, Messmer, Specht, & Merritt, 1976) to respiratory blockage in the infant's anatomically vulnerable airway (Tonkin, 1975). Most theories focus upon infant respiratory activity. These infants seem prone to abnormally long periods of not breathing while sleeping; and as many as half of them may have mild, undetected upper respiratory infections at time of death. Thus a general picture of infection among infants with initial respiratory control inadequacies has emerged (Marx, 1975).

Another aspect of SID is its psychological effect on parents. A sudden and unexpected loss can produce intense shock and grief. Feelings of guilt and self-doubt can also occur as parents agonize about the extent to which they were responsible for the death (Salk, 1971). There are no easy answers to these unfortunate consequences of SID; however, positive steps are being taken by organizations of parents of SID infants to counsel and support parents of recent victims until emotional stability has been reestablished.

Changes in Height, Weight, and Shape

A most impressive feature of early postnatal life is the rapidity of growth. From their 19- to 20-inch (47.5 to 50.0 cm) birth length, infants typically grow in body length by 50 percent to about 30 inches (75.0 cm) in one year. During the second year, an additional 5 inches (12.5 cm) will be added. As a rule, children will grow approximately 2 to 2 1/2 inches (5.0 to 6.2 cm) per year from their third year until adolescence. Growth during adolescence is characterized by a marked increase in rate, or a growth "spurt," which begins at around 10 to 11 years for girls and 12 to 13 years for boys. During this time boys will add an average of about 8 inches (20.0 cm) to their height, and girls will add an average of about 6 1/2 inches (16.25 cm) to theirs. The "spurt" peaks at approximately age 14 years for males, 12 years for females. Following the peak, the rate slows until there is no noticeable growth, at about 18 years for females, 20 years for males. Another way to characterize growth in height is by comparing earlier age-level status with mature height: by age 2 years among girls and 2 to 3 years among boys, most children will have grown to 50 percent of their eventual adult height; girls by age 7 to 8 and boys by age 9 will have reached 75 percent of their adult height (Bayley, 1956). As remarkable as this trend may be, however, the period of fastest growth rate in height still is the prenatal period.

Rate of weight gain among children, in contrast, reaches its peak shortly *after* birth. In the first 4 to 6 months following birth infants double their birth weights; by the end of the first year, birth weight has tripled; and by the end of the second year it has quadrupled. From the third year until adolescence there is a steady increase of about 5 to 6 pounds (2.25 to 2.70 kg) per year. Similar to height, the rate of weight gain during the "adolescent spurt" increases tremendously, with boys gaining as much as 45 pounds (20.25 kg) and girls as much as 35 pounds (15.75 kg). Adult weight, however, is not reached until a number of years after adult height has been attained.

The shape and proportions of the infant differ substantially from those of the adult, and it is these differences that provide the "cute baby look" associated with the infant and young child. That this difference in appearance is not simply because of size can be demonstrated by imagining an adult shrunken down to 2 to 3 feet (60 to 90 cm) in height, yet retaining adult proportions in head and limbs. Such an individual would not likely be considered "cute" by the same standards used in judging babies. An infant's head is far larger and its legs far shorter in proportion to its body than an adult's. In fact, the head to body length ratio will change from 1:4 at infancy to 1:7 1/2 at adulthood; lower limbs change from 1:3 for the infants to 1:2 for adults. Skeletal structure, musculature, and distribution of fat also change markedly during the growth and maturation process. This is especially striking during adolescence, when for males the shoulders grow more than the pelvis, while for girls the reverse pattern occurs. Among females, fat deposits accumulate in the hips and breasts to provide the curved shape characteristic of adult women.

The "adolescent spurt" also affects other body proportions. Hand and foot growth accelerates first, followed by increases in growth rate for calf and forearm, hips and chest, shoulders, and trunk and depth of chest, in that order. As much as a year's time may separate growth peaks for lower limb and trunk lengths. This discrepancy may contribute to the embarrassing ungainliness reported by many adolescents and their watchful parents.

Physical growth in general can be summarized graphically by an S curve depicting rapid rates of growth and maturation during infancy and adolescence.

This is illustrated in Figure 6.1. This representation reminds us that development is a continuous process even though spurts and periods of consolidation may give the illusion of sporadic or cyclical growth.

Cultural Variations in Body Size

Cross-cultural research has revealed considerable variation in the body size of children and youth. In one massive comparison (Meredith, 1969a), for example, the average standing height for children from different cultural groups ranged a full 9 inches (from 106 to 129 cm). Shorter groups were found in such areas as Southeast Asia and Oceania; taller children were observed in northern and central Europe, eastern Australia, and the United States. A broad range in these children's weight was also recorded, with a mean (average) of less than 29 pounds (13.05 kg) to more than 45 pounds (20.25 kg). This remarkable range of group differences continues into early and middle adolescence (Meredith, 1969b). Girls, age 13, have shown an average range in height of from 52.8 to 60.5 inches (132 to 151.25 cm); group averages for boys, age 15, were 56.3 to 66.9 inches (140.75 to 167.25 cm). Similarly, weight averages for the two sexes differed across cultures by as much as

44 pounds (19.80 kg) for girls, 57 pounds (25.65 kg) for boys. These studies indicate that, on the average, United States children are among the tallest and heaviest in the world.

Yet even within the same culture, racial differences in growth rate and physical size are apparent. As a group, white American males tend to surpass their black age mates in both height and weight during early adolescence, while white and black females are roughly equal (Krogman, 1970). Body proportions also vary by race, with whites exceeding blacks in trunk length. Black children, however, surpass their white peers in total arm and leg length. We can surmise that such patterns may be largely influenced by genetic factors and nutrition, although these generalizations about United States race differences have been based on children with adequate diets.

Physiological Changes

Physical growth, of course, is but one facet of postnatal development. Maturation of many structures and systems also occurs, with corresponding development of interaction networks among organ systems (Hammar & Owens, 1973; Holm & Wiltz, 1973; Wenner & VanderVeer, 1973). Infants, for example, become better able to handle increasing quantities of mother's milk as the kidneys develop their function of concentrating urine output. Furthermore, infants at birth, though fortunate to have some immunities acquired through the placenta during prenatal development, have little protection against health hazards through their own immunity systems. And these "borrowed" immunity substances provide only initial and decreasing protection. Thus infants must compensate for this liability by producing their own substances after vaccinations and exposure to infections. Infants' ner-

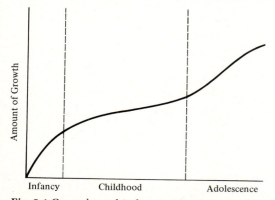

Fig. 6-1 General trend in human physical growth

vous systems also undergo extensive development. Great increases in interneuronal connections and reduction in conduction time for neural impulses occur. (This impulse velocity increase is partially due to a layering of the myelin sheath mentioned earlier.)

By the preschool years (age 3 and beyond) most body systems are well on their way to functional maturity. Components of the central nervous system continue to mature throughout ensuing years, a process that is revealed by the increasingly complex fine and gross motor tasks children undertake as they grow older. An interesting example of sensory change involves young children's hyperopic status, a state where a visual image "falls behind" the retina of the eye. Although young children's lens function easily to accommodate to this condition, sight vision normally improves to about age 5 when this accommodation is no longer necessary. But if children continue to have deficient sight they are unlikely to complain about it. They have no baseline from which to recognize any impairment. Hence, close monitoring of children's visual behavior is advised.

General clues to visual problems, for instance, may include squinting, persistent eye-watering, frequent shutting of one eye, complaints of headache, and eye-rubbing (Charles, 1964). Similarly, hearing difficulties—a further sensory problem for which children may have no frame of reference for determining deficiency—may be indicated by head turning to favor one ear, cupping the hand behind the ear, frequent requests to adults for verbal messages to be repeated, and general listlessness. The early identification and treatment of sensory function disorders are critical; not only is healthy functioning important for children's general welfare, but it is essential for normal educational progress.

Changes at Adolescence

Understanding physiologic changes is also useful for discussing normal adolescence in modern society. Among the important developments are increased blood pressure (because of change in the ratio of heart size to blood vessel size), vital lung capacity (a threefold increase from about age 6 to age 16), perspiration activity, stomach acidity, and the like. A gradual decrease in basal metabolism (especially among girls), respiration rate, and rate of recovery to physiological balance after exercise can also be noted. The latter trend seems to continue throughout life. As one wit has remarked: "You're not old until it takes you longer to rest up than it does to get tired!"

Easily the most talked about change of adolescence is the sexual development in puberty (ages 9–14 for girls, 10–15 for boys). Among boys, the first signs of puberty include increased size of penis and testes, with parallel growth in the scrotum. By mid-adolescence (11–18), their pubic hair and voice changes are apparent. And by late adolescence (14–20), facial and body hair will have developed along with the full capacity for reproduction. Though rate of pubertal change varies considerably, most of the basic developments are complete within two or three years after onset of the process. Body shape changes often take somewhat longer to complete.

Among girls, the appearance and elevation of breast buds generally coincide with the onset of height spurt. By mid-adolescence (10–16), pubic hair has appeared along with physiological changes necessary for menstruation. Although average age of menarche among U.S. girls is about 12.8 years, their bodies are not yet prepared for full reproductive capacity. Within 12–18 months following the menarche, ovulation will have become a regular pact of the menstrual cycle. Pubic hair and breast development usually are complete by late adolescence (13–18). For both sexes, pubertal changes and the achievement of fertility are direct outcomes of hormonal activity—testosterone in males, estrogen in females.

Three other genetically controlled reflexive functions of the neuromuscular system accompany maleness and femaleness (Kinsey, Pomeroy, & Martin, 1948). The first is the capacity for tumescence. For example, complete male genital erection is possible during the neonatal period. This reaction may accompany bladder distention or may result from penile manipulation.

A second reflex component in sexual behavior is orgasm and ejaculation. According to the Kinsey data, orgasm (sexual climax) can be produced in human infants of either sex. However, ejaculatory power in the male is not acquired until puberty, and the production of normal sperm for males and eggs for females occurs somewhat later in the cycle of pubescence. For the sexually mature male, orgasm and ejaculation occur together; for females, orgasm is not accompanied by the ejaculation of any sort of fluid.

Third, the capacity for rhythmic, pelvic thrusts is a neuromuscular component of sexual behavior that facilitates the mating act.

If we consider the total cluster of biological components of sexuality, it is apparent that different segments of sexual behavior mature at different rates. Apart from these biological underpinnings of sexual behavior, an individual's form or style of sexual expression is heavily, if not completely, determined by learning. Learning the forms of sexual expression is inseparably linked to learning sex roles and sexual identity (see Chapter 9). Further details about the endocrinology of puberty can be found in Root (1973a, b).

Some Related Perceptual-Motor Developments

Among the most important developments of purposeful behavior in growing children is their coordination of different maturing systems: for example, the visual with the auditory and the motor with the cognitive. Without such coordination, a simple act like picking up a pencil would occur only as a random event because it requires control of motor movement based on visual feedback. A living example of troublesome perceptual-motor control is Charles, an adolescent with severe cerebral palsy. Because of brain damage he is unable to perform even the basic of self-help skills. Although Charles seemingly is able to think the entire activity through, his body responds poorly to his thought directed actions; little or no motor function control is possible for him.

Technically speaking, perceptual motor development can be described as a progressive diffusion and integration of behavioral patterns (Cratty, 1970). This means that specific cognitive, perceptual, and motor abilities or skills overlap in time in their development, even though the emergence and rate of development may differ across skills. As maturation proceeds, the number of skills (such as vision and motor movement), so that integrated purposeful ac-walking will branch off into running, jumping, and such variations of walking as skipping. Maturation also facilitates bonding among initially independent skills, such as vision and motoric movement, so that integrated purposeful activity is possible. Examples are jumping over a fence, dodging a thrown rock, catching a ball, and playing marbles. All require coordinated action. These and hundreds of other behaviors requiring bonding become both more effective and efficient with maturation and practice.

One way to depict the essence of perceptual-motor development is the "tree" diagram in Figure 6.2. Initially, many of an infant's sensory-system behaviors are predominantly reflexive. With time, however, system integration occurs as stimulation from the environment or simple exploratory behaviors result in fewer random, nonreflexive motor activities. With maturation, modes of passive responding give way to purposiveness, or deliberate attempts to act upon and change the environment. As purposive perceptual-motor activity evolves, feedback from the environment provides a basis for more activity. In short, a cycle of continuous interaction is built.

Branching, bonding, and interaction cycles are abstractions. It is instructive to illustrate perceptual-motor development more concretely. For this, we refer to observational data about Robbie, a normal, energetic five-year-old at the time of this writing. Our focus is Robbie's early, general manipulative behavior and, more specifically, his drawing behavior. Robbie's development fits well within the more carefully charted, normative data in this area (Cratty, 1970; Gesell & Amatruda, 1947).

Manipulative Behavior

At birth, Robbie's grasp, like that of all normal infants, was controlled by the palmar reflex (see Table 6.2) which continued for the first few months of his life. At 4 weeks of age, his predominant hand state was a closed fist. By 8 weeks, however, he briefly retained small objects placed in his hand; and by 16 weeks, he was actively holding and attending to such objects—small blocks, a plastic rattle, and other crib playthings. Around 20 weeks, Robbie was routinely grasping objects placed near his hand, although in a primitive manner using the side of the palm opposite his thumb. Not until some 8 weeks later was he using the side of the palm closest to his thumb for grasping. A major "breakthrough" in Robbie's manipulative behavior development occurred at about 40 weeks: he demonstrated the ability to oppose his finger and thumb for use in picking up small items. A crude ability to release objects also began to emerge, but several weeks lapsed before this movement became efficient. By 1 year, Robbie still was unable to perform skills like inserting pellets in a bottle and stacking small cubes to build a tower, even when shown how by his parents. A short 6 months later, however, Robbie performed these tasks with ease. Both involve an integration of perceptual-motor skills for voluntary action, with the trend illustrating increased efficiency

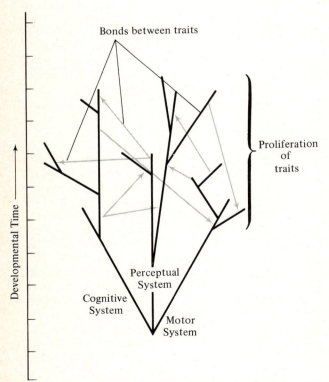

Fig. 6-2 A model of perceptual-motor development. (Adapted from Cratty, 1970.)

and accuracy. The total process was heavily governed by sensory system maturation, but we cannot discount the importance of general sensory stimulation and opportunities for practice. Finally, it is clear that Robbie's manipulative development was predictably sequential, beginning with gross, comparatively simple coordinations and progressing to successively finer, more complex ones. Perceptual-motor tasks such as cube-stacking and bead-stringing are among the first used to measure the development of very young children's "intelligence" (Chapter 8).

Drawing Behavior

Sequential, progressively complex differentiation and coordination are further shown in Robbie's development in using crayons or pencils to draw on paper. Given the availability of these tools, spontaneous scribbling can usually be first observed between 15 and 20 months, as it was for Robbie. Perhaps because of increased confidence and familiarity with drawing activity, his random marking was gradually replaced by repetitive strokes in horizontal, vertical, and radiating patterns. As motor control increased during his second year, Robbie showed attempts to enclose space by using shaky circular and spiral shaped patterns. During his third and fourth years, circles of single circumference were formed; he also began his attempts to copy squares when asked. Later during this period he drew rough geometric shapes to resemble familiar objects, such as his house, together with simple stick figures to represent people. Now, at the age of 5, his buildings are more recognizable and he often adds his pet dog and trees to his pictures. Knowing the normal sequence of drawing skills, we can predict that Robbie will not master such difficult geometric shapes as triangles and diamonds until age 6 or 7

years. By age 9 or 10, he probably will be able to produce three-dimensional figures with ease. A year or two later, Robbie will be able to draw with a linear perspective.

We have reason to believe that Robbie's present human figure drawings indicate certain limitations in the amount of information that he can process as well as the locus of his perception. For children generally, the developmental process is: (1) circles with marks in or around them; (2) circles containing marks resembling facial features; (3) circular faces with stick arms and legs projecting directly out from them; (4) fingers and a trunk are added; (5) increased definition of features and facial expression; and (6) limbs and body are given width. Developmental progression occurs, in how children perceive the human figure, in how they store an image in memory, or in how they represent cognitive images in their motor movements for drawing. Possibly all three progressions exist, and some form of interaction occurs among them in perceptual-motor development.

Body Image

As a final illustration of interaction between physical and perceptual development, we refer to body image development. Robbie, active runabout that he is, shows considerable awareness of his body and its movement through space. In a general way, he can describe his size and shape and seems clear about his physical capabilities. Robbie is firmly on his way toward full development of a body image, that is, how he perceives himself as a physical being.

Body image is thought to consist of three, related components (Corbin, 1973). One, the sensorimotor component, is described from research and theory such as Piaget's (see Chapter 8). A newborn infant is said to have no concept of self as separate from the environment. Through constant feedback from bodily actions, including exploration of its own and its mother's body, an infant becomes aware of the "me–not me" difference—the body is recognized as separate from its physical surroundings.

A second component of body image involves the conceptualization of, and eventual vocal expression about, spatial features of the body. This includes the ability to recognize oneself and to identify and name parts of the body. Eventually, this second component will also include a concept of laterality (right–left discrimination) and directionality (projection of left–right into objective space). Robbie is quite proficient with body part identification and naming, but unable yet to reliably differentiate right and left. Apart from highly systematic, and debatable, special training (see Chapter 2), children generally do not accurately and regularly distinguish right and left until around age 7.

The third component of body image concerns affect, or emotion. This includes the feeling and opinions that children have about their physical make-up and capabilities. In later childhood, it includes perceptions about how other people view and evaluate one's physical being. Together, those developments are significant aspects of any child's broader *self-concept* and *self-esteem*, as discussed in Chapter 1. Robbie is fortunate enough to have a healthy, strong, and well-structured body that is suited to play activity and social interaction. He is more successful than not with new, more complex motor activities such as swimming and roller skating. Indications are that he feels positively about his body and what it can do. As such, he provides a stark contrast with Charles, our adolescent with cerebral palsy.

To conclude, it seems fair to say that body image is an important factor in overall personality development. The process of body-image formation begins early, perhaps even with fetal movements before birth. A recognition of early origin has more than theoretical significance, as indicated by clinicians who work with handicapped infants and young children. An example of promising medical practice is attaching material of specific sizes and weights to stumps of infants without limbs. This is done to prepare them better to accept and utilize forthcoming prosthetic devices (Cratty, 1970). Finally, we should mention the task of reorganizing body image as children move into puberty. The appearance of primary and secondary sex characteristics, in particular, requires rapid readjustment. What mixture of pride, confusion, and dissatisfaction accompanies the reorganization process will depend on several factors, including cultural attitudes toward the body and how early or late these changes for given individuals occur relative to their circles of peers (Muuss, 1975). This point is again considered in our discussion of social influences. The implications of negative body image, for example, are far-reaching for counseling adolescents and youth toward greater self-understanding and acceptance.

Principles of Motor Skill Development

We conclude this section by referring to three important ideas about motor skill development. First, development in motor control and motor skills generally manifests a *direction* in growth. Two major directions can be observed—from head to foot (cephalocaudal) and from the center of the body outward (proximodistal). The first is shown by infants who are initially capable of head lifting, then of sitting up, and finally of standing up. The second direction is revealed by children's ability to move their arms and shoulders effectively before they gain the control over fine muscles necessary for writing with a pencil.

One important implication of growth direction is that motor activities are best coordinated with children's developmental capacities. A good day-care environment for younger children, for instance, should contain ample equipment for large muscle activity (mats for tumbling, tricycles, balance boards, and gym sets for both indoor and outdoor use) because they are well suited to such children's motor competencies.

A second and related idea about motor development is that maturation is a primary factor in the appearance of various motor skills. This cautions us against making premature demands for motor activities, especially having children practice certain skills before they are sufficiently equipped to learn them efficiently. An average 3-year-old is not usually "ready" to learn shoe-tying skills satisfactorily because of the fine, complex motor movements required. In fact, pressuring the child to do so may have negative side effects, such as creating unnecessary failure-frustration and negative sentiment about self-help behaviors. But the same child, a year or two later, typically will learn shoe-tying both quickly and happily.

Our third point is the comparatively low relationship between gross and fine motor skills. Children who are adept in large muscle activities may not necessarily demonstrate equal competence in small-muscle activities. The reverse is also true. Greater or less skill in one area of motor behavior cannot be taken to indicate an advantage or disadvantage in some other, different area (Charles, 1964). This variation reflects differences in maturation rate, experience, and basic physical equipment. Increased skill in motor abilities among preschoolers reflects increased speed in reaction time, increased strength, and a specific factor that involves the manipulation of small objects (Munsinger, 1971). Children should not be expected to demonstrate equal levels of motor competence, but it is desirable to provide them with opportunities to experiment with as many skills as possible.

HEALTH DISORDERS IN CHILDREN AND YOUTH

Conventional textbook discussions of human physical-motor development often are confined to a review of growth trends from infancy through adolescence or beyond. We believe that general health problems among children and adolescents are also significant and should not be overlooked. Depending upon their duration and severity, illnesses can seriously limit the learning opportunities and peer relationships of afflicted children and youth. Health problems can also harm parent–child relationships, for example, by sustaining dependency, contributing to parental rejection of a sickly child, or creating general psychological stress. Certain health problems are themselves life-threatening; it is difficult to exaggerate the importance of early diagnosis and proper medical therapy in such cases. In this section we present an overview of major ideas about health disorders from a developmental perspective.

Some Generalizations about Health Disorders

Four general points about the development of health disorders in the young are important. First, and perhaps basic, is that many of the more serious health disorders seem governed by genetic forces whose workings are not very clear; still others are reactions to certain environmental conditions favoring their development in a constitutionally predisposed person (Shiller, 1972). Genetically linked disorders vary in their incidence. Most are severely handicapping. Some of the more life-threatening are listed in Table 6.3.[1]

Second, many illnesses and growth disorders correspond with successive stages in the life cycle—infancy, early and middle childhood, adolescence, young adulthood, and so on. Certain threats to normal prenatal development have already been reviewed. Infancy is notorious for its incidence of "colic," whose principal symptom is excessive crying during the first several months following birth. Whatever the cause, colic usually wanes quickly thereafter for most afflicted infants and seems no longer distressful. During middle childhood we see further evidence of "normal" illness patterns. For example, children most frequently contract measles sometime between 6 and 8 years, although it can occur earlier depending upon circumstances of first exposure (Krogman, 1970). Other common illnesses during the elementary school years are chicken pox, mumps, and whooping cough, in descending order of frequency. Ear and streptococcal infections ("strep throat") are also common. Statistics about the total range of childhood infections often seem overwhelming. For example, the average for school-age children is from 3 to 5 infections during any given year, accounting for over 70 percent of school absences (Holm & Wiltz, 1973).

As a further example of developmental-stage–related illnesses or disorders, consider the familiar acne condition first seen during adolescence. Uncommon, but also distinctive in adolescence, is a mysterious illness marked by self-inflicted starvation. Known as *anorexia nervosa*, this illness is thought to originate with a psychological disturbance, possibly a morbid fear of fatness. Whatever its cause, the dynamics of anorexia nervosa are neither well understood nor easily treated. In fact, the condition occasionally results in death from malnutrition (Kugelmass, 1975). Finally, during middle and late adolescence we see the appearance of venereal disease as a major health problem (Hammar & Owens, 1973). The incidence of both syphilis and gonorrhea, for example, is higher among 15-to-24-year-olds than among any other age group.

A third generalization about health disorders is that many are influenced by or strongly associated with such variables as gender and race. Most obvious are functional disorders of the male and female reproductive systems, as in undescended testes and menstrual disorders. For unknown reasons, anorexia nervosa occurs mostly among adolescent females as does scoliosis, the major spine deformity of adolescence. On the other hand, the most common form of muscular dystrophy affects males almost exclusively. We see from Table 6.3 that black children are primarily affected by sickle cell anemia, while cystic fibrosis occurs most often among whites. Moreover, alcoholism—a growing health problem among adolescents—occurs considerably more often among native Americans than among other ethnic minorities and the white majority. It is believed that genetically different enzyme functions for metabolizing alcohol may be implicated in this disease, although such sociological forces as frustration from prolonged oppression cannot be dismissed as contributing factors.

Threats to normal development from disease are legion, but our fourth and final point takes us from illness to the single greatest cause of death and disability among both children and youth: accidents. Each year, about 15,000 American children die and some 45,000 are permanently disabled because

[1] This table is illustrative only and does not begin to exhaust the variety of diseases characteristic of childhood and adolescence. Medical textbooks can be consulted for full details.

TABLE 6.3   A Sampling of Major Threats to Normal Human Development

Disease	Onset	Incidence	Symptoms	Cause	Treatment
Acute leukemia	Sudden, with peak incidence between 2 and 7.	Exact statistics not available, but is easily the commonest childhood malignancy.	Pallidity, fever, headache, vomiting, pain in extremities, hemorrhages often appearing as skin bruises, kidney failure, and general anemia.	Chromosomal abnormalities are suspected, created by an unknown heredity mechanism or possibly mutation. Maternal irradiation during pregnancy has been implicated. The malignancy affects bone marrow and the balance and quality of blood cells.	Drug therapy and blood transfusion to relieve symptoms and attempt remission. Successful remission implies a relatively normal, but short-termed life; the condition is terminal in all but the rarest cases. A primary focus of treatment is to facilitate parental adjustment to the child's condition.
Asthma	At any age from infancy. More common in males during childhood; more common in females after puberty.	Roughly 2.5% of childhood population; one of commonest diseases encountered by classroom teachers and one that results in excessive school absence.	Labored, wheezing breathing with pronounced noise at exhalation; shortness of breath; cough often present. Frequency, duration, and severity of attacks vary with the individual. Can be fatal.	Poorly understood. Constitutional predisposition with a strong hereditary component. Distinguishing feature is allergic reaction involving an over-abundance of allergy antibodies to certain substances. Asthma attacks are triggered by contact with these substances (ingestants, inhalants). Pollen, house dust, drugs, and common foods are primary culprits.	Preventive measures to reduce or eliminate allergies; respiratory therapy often for long-range treatment; drug therapy to treat acute attacks.

TABLE 6.3 (cont.)

Disease	Onset	Incidence	Symptoms	Cause	Treatment
Cerebral palsy	Some 85–90% of cases are congenital and present at birth. Postnatal complications account for the remainder, with most occurring during infancy and the preschool years.	Exact statistics unavailable. Earlier estimates had some 7 children per 100,000 with some form. Advances in medical technique, including preventive medicine, have apparently helped reduce the incidence.	Disordered movement and posture that may involve from one limb to all four, depending upon severity. Exaggerated reflexes are characteristic. Equilibrium and coordination are adversely affected. Tremor of afflicted limbs is common, as are associated handicaps in speech and other oral functions such as swallowing. Can also involve some degree of mental retardation, although some 25% have average or above-average intelligence.	Brain malfunction or damage due to prenatal, perinatal, or postnatal insults. These can range from maternal infection, Rh incompatibility and fetal anoxia (impaired oxygen supply), through premature birth or birth trauma, to brain infection and hemorrhages. Some cases are due less to insult than to brain maldevelopment during the early weeks of pregnancy from unknown causes.	Some cases are so severe that death ensues during infancy; others so mild that little if any special treatment is required. A majority, however, require institutional or special home care. Physical therapy, speech and hearing therapy, occupational therapy, orthopedic surgery, bracing, and slings are common. Prognosis varies according to severity of the disorder. Generally, individuals have a life expectancy below average. Many, however, are capable of self-sufficiency and can anticipate a fairly long life. The diagnostic category of cerebral palsy is gross. Careful individual assessment and therapeutic care are required to maximize their potential.

TABLE 6.3 (cont.)

Disease	Onset	Incidence	Symptoms	Cause	Treatment
Cystic fibrosis	Congenital, although an early diagnosis is not always made. The disease is progressive and may initially mimic other diseases such as pneumonia, bronchitis, or asthma. Recent advances make possible a diagnosis during the neonatal period or early infancy.	Estimated at 1 in 1,500. Most frequently among white children, infrequently among blacks, and rarely among children of Asian extraction.	Abnormal feces, respiratory difficulty, often accompanied by chronic coughing, high salt level in perspiration, lung hyperinflation, and large volume of fecal matter and gas in the abdominal cavity often affect the child's appearance, giving a rounded chest and distended abdomen.	A recessive gene disorder that is manifest in abnormal protein in the blood and abnormal secretions of calcium. The underlying cause is unknown. Much of the symptomatology is due to loss of pancreatic function and accumulation of mucus in the lungs.	No known cure. Drug therapy and methods of cleansing the lungs of mucus can slow the rate of progression. When successful, life can be prolonged to adulthood. The disease usually proves fatal, however, with the average life expectancy roughly 14–15 years. Massive lung infection and secondary heart failure are common direct causes of death.
Diabetes mellitus	Can occur any time between early infancy and several decades thereafter. Usually not apparent at birth.	Precise statistics not available. Prior to age 17, the incidence is approximately 1.3 per 1,000 (slightly higher among females). Increased incidence is associated with aging.	Abnormal quantity of urine with sugar and acetone usually followed by excessive drinking and eating accompanied by weight loss. General fatigue and loss of strength. If untreated, a child may become comatose and die.	An inherited disorder. The likelihood of being passed to a child increases greatly if one or both parents have the disease, but the method of inheritance is unknown. Whatever the genetic anomaly, its result is a failure of the pancreas to produce insulin (a protein hormone) which is essential for the proper metabolism of glucose.	Drug therapy, specifically insulin treatment, together with controlled diet and regular exercise. Successful treatment can result in a normal life, save for the continued monitoring of the diabetic condition.

TABLE 6.3 (cont.)

Disease	Onset	Incidence	Symptoms	Cause	Treatment
Muscular dystrophy	Usually by age 3 or shortly thereafter; progressive deterioration subsequently.	Estimated at about 2.8 cases per 10,000. A decreased incidence has been linked to increased genetic counseling.	Early signs of awkwardness, persistent tip-toeing when walking, "poor" posture. Later muscle weakness in the upper torso and face. (This progression may be reversed in some cases.) Eventually, the fat–muscle ratio and bone structure are affected. Children often are in wheelchairs by age 10. Mental development is frequently impaired, resulting in moderate intellectual retardation. The disease is usually terminal by late adolescence, caused by heart or respiratory failure created by muscle weakness.	Unknown, although most cases are genetically determined in the form of a sex-linked recessive gene. Males are mainly affected.	No known cure. Physical therapy, mechanical supports for the body, and surgery may assist in making afflicted children more comfortable.
Sickle cell disease	Usually within the first 4 or 5 years.	Commonest among blacks, although noted to some extent in India, southen European and Middle Eastern countries. Exact statistics are unavailable, but the potential for the disease is thought to exist in some 10% of American blacks and run as high as 40% in certain black societies along the	Several possible symptoms, which may not be present simultaneously. Include pain and swelling in the extremities and abdomen, abdominal distention, jaundice, nausea, sudden loss of arm or leg function, respiratory infection, general lethargy, and occasional fainting.	An inherited disorder transmitted by genes for sickle hemoglobin. The red blood cells are affected, specifically in terms of insufficient manufacture in bone marrow and in disruption of oxygen supply to vital tissues and organs.	Control of exercise, medical treatment of the symptoms, blood transfusion during periods of crises. Severe incapacitation is not unusual nor are secondary infections of a life-threatening nature. Typically results in a shortened life span.

of accidents (Holm & Wiltz, 1973). The death rate is higher between the ages of 10 and 19 (21,000 per year in the 1960s), partly because of the greater freedom of movement for older children and adolescents. During this time, violent deaths—especially from automobile accidents, but including drowning, homicide, suicide, and falls—comprise a substantial majority (60 percent) of all fatalities. Disease-related deaths are led by cancer, followed by a lesser incidence of fatalities caused by cardiovascular, renal (kidney), and congenital malformations in that order (Heald, 1976).

The Growing Problem of Obesity

The study of obesity and its development provides us with a particularly apt illustration of the relationship of physiology and psychology in human functioning. For this reason, and because the incidence of obesity among young people has been on the increase, we examine the topic in some detail. "Obesity" refers to the excessive accumulation of adipose (fatty) tissue, distinguished from "overweight" based upon large skeletal or muscle mass. Beyond this important physiological distinction, medical definitions of obesity differ. Consequently, reports of the incidence of obesity among children and youth vary considerably. Defining obesity as 40 percent or more above medium weight for height, one research team has suggested an incidence of 2 to 15 percent of all children (Bray et al., 1972). A less stringent definition—over 20 percent of ideal weight—may increase this figure (Hammar & Owens, 1973). Based upon adult obesity figures, a relatively higher incidence of obesity is expected among children of lower socioeconomic status and possibly also among girls than boys, particularly during adolescence. Medical experts generally agree that obesity has become a major health problem in the United States. The data unequivocally show that persistent obesity is associated with a shortened life span and sundry medical problems contrary to healthy functioning. And this says nothing about the possible psychological hazards of obesity, including social rejection, impaired ability to participate effectively in athletics, and so on. We may defend a person's right to be fat by choice, but in a culture that rewards trimness and physical fitness, obese persons seem more often unhappy and depressed.

The Development of Obesity

A tendency for obesity becomes established between birth and age 4 (Heald & Khan, 1976). Infants who are overfed, on formula instead of breast fed, then weaned early and introduced to solid food, may be particularly vulnerable to the development of an obese condition. Other "peaks" in the development of obesity have also been reported in the age period from 7 to 11 years and in early adolescence. Exact causes, however, are obscure. Most authorities point to a complex interaction of genetic and environmental factors. Certain body chemistry imbalances, for example, may result in defective fat utilization in metabolism, contributing to increased adiposity. Yet this is less likely to occur in a home or culture, where eating patterns are modest, where fat in the daily diet is low, and where physical activity is rewarded.

The combined influence of genetic and experiential factors has also been reported in an early study that found an incidence of obesity among children of normal weight parents of 8–9 percent. This incidence rocketed to 40 percent among children with one obese parent, and to 80 percent when both parents were obese. In short, fat parents tend to raise fat children (Johnson, Burke, &

Mayer, 1956). The availability of ample food, consistent opportunities for over-eating, observational learning, and positive reinforcement for eating undoubtedly contribute to this pattern.

Perhaps because of sheer amount of caloric intake, obese children often appear advanced in their height growth and sexual maturation. Consequently, such children are usually conspicuous among their more normally developing age mates. Their eating habits and physical activity also may differ from the norm, with more rapid eating of greater quantities of food combined with a lower level of daily exercise. Thus a cycle that sustains obesity can easily take effect; weight increase further reduces a child's desire and ability to remain active.

Treating Obesity

The medical treatment of obesity is very difficult during childhood and adolescence (Heald & Khan, 1976). Many dietary restrictions can be more harmful than helpful, especially during important phases of rapid growth such as the pubescent growth spurt. Drug therapy is of limited use, if not ill-advised, especially with younger children. Extreme measures, such as surgery to accomplish an intestinal bypass, can result in undesirable physiological side-effects. Furthermore, all these measures may be misguided if the basic cause of overeating is psychological. Even then, children who become accustomed to receiving much attention (even negative) from others because they are obese may not want to endanger their social recognition by reducing the reason for it. More powerful substitute reinforcements must be found to break the cycle of obesity and move children in new directions of self-control. In fact, strategies for modifying overeating and underexercise patterns based upon reinforcement principles

have shown some promise for dealing with obesity (Leon, 1976). On balance, however, the results are not very encouraging.

Given the pessimistic picture for helping obese individuals, even those who strongly desire to alter their condition, we can argue that the best offense is a good defense. To pun, an ounce of prevention is worth a pound of cure. Obesity prevention must begin in infancy. Parent education is critical. Recent data suggest that far too many infants are overweight because of overfeeding by parents (Skukla et al., 1972). In the schools, obese children need special understanding and acceptance, perhaps including sensitive peer supports. All too often, an obese child is taunted and ridiculed by other children. We know of two such children in a nearby school whose unwanted nicknames are "Lardtank" and "Pigbelly." Not all obese children may suffer social disadvantages. Nor are all necessarily doomed to poor health, or even lifelong obesity. Obesity and its negative correlates are a matter of degree, yet the general pattern is clear and must be coped with realistically.

SOCIAL FACTORS AND PHYSICAL DEVELOPMENT

As we have suggested, the state of children's health and physical development is not simply a product of maturation. Increases in both frequency and duration of illness among children, for example, are positively correlated with increases in social adjustment demands by such life events as changing schools, parental divorce, or death of a parent (Coddington, 1972a, b; Heisel, Ream, Raitz, Rappaport, & Coddington, 1973). Once again we are reminded of the complex interaction among developmental processes and environmental events. In some cases, this interaction involves social or environmental influences (such as nutrition) working in concert with biological development. In others, the interaction has a somewhat different basis, for example, in how we are limited or advantaged by physical appearance and motor skills for culturally approved activities. Our physical self will determine, at least in part, both our degree of success in accomplishing certain tasks and the social reactions of others to us.

In this final section we examine physical development more thoroughly from the perspective of social influences and their psychosocial accompaniments. We begin by some general comments about nutrition and growth, followed by further comment about social factors and prenatal development. The chapter concludes with a section about psychosocial implications of physical development.

The Importance of Nutrition

Perhaps the most basic "social" influence on physical growth and development is nutrition. Severe malnutrition can retard growth during childhood. Fortunately, malnutrition effects may not be irreversible for height and weight growth, depending on the duration and severity of the deficiency. Nutrition therapy can produce an acceleration in growth after malnutrition to "make up" for lost time. Some evidence suggests that compensation may be complete if the period of malnutrition has been short. Though reassuring, this evidence is tenuous and does not address other, more subtle, and long-term effects of malnutrition.

During adolescence, nutritional problems are most commonly revealed in obesity, dental caries, and a common iron-deficiency anemia (in females). In some cases, poverty limits the nutrition of children and youth. Children of higher socioeconomic status, for ex-

ample, tend to be taller than their lower-status peers. However, this difference cannot be accounted for completely by type of diet; it is likely that other factors—regularity of meals, sufficient sleep and exercise, and superior health habits—are also involved. Questionable food habits may develop, however, even among privileged children. Nutrition experts, for example, warn against omitting breakfast, snacking exclusively on "empty calorie" foods (such as potato chips and soft drinks), and other dietary imbalances (Young, 1976). Such food habits are established early in the home, but peer-group influences often are paramount during adolescence.

Despite the hazards of poverty and ill-advised food habits, better nutrition characterizes life among today's children and youth. This, together with improved disease control and advanced health habits, help to explain the pattern of accelerated growth in height and weight among children across successive generations during the past century. Since the mid-1800s, for both the sexes, the average height and weight of American and western European children have steadily increased. Some hundred years ago, for instance, the average 18-year-old American male stood a fraction over 5 feet 5 inches (162.5 cm) tall; by 1976 this average had increased to slightly over 5 feet 9 inches (172.5 cm). A parallel decrease of nearly two years in average age of menarche in girls has also been observed (Cone, 1976). Such changes may not be unlimited. The National Center for Health Statistics recently reported that growth in height, but not necessarily weight, for American children appears to have leveled off since the mid-1950s. To the extent that nutrition is a factor in promoting the achievement of full growth potential in height, any "leveling off" may indicate an upper limit to maximum dietary influence. In contrast, there is yet no evidence that the progressively earlier average age of menarche in girls is decelerating. One plausible hypothesis about this trend is that a critical body weight triggers menarche (Frish & Revelle, 1972). Thus, if girls continue to grow in average weight from one generation to the next we would expect an earlier menarche. Recall also that obese females tend to show early sexual maturation. Surely there is some lower limit, but the full potentialities of maturational processes remain something of a mystery.

Social Conditions and Prenatal Development

Earlier in this chapter certain developmental problems of prenatal development were reviewed. We now explore additional influences in more detail, although a comprehensive review of these varied conditions is beyond the scope of this chapter. Among the more significant influences that accentuate the importance of careful prenatal care are foreign substances ingested by the mother which can pass through the placenta into the fetal circulatory system and exert direct effects. Smoking mothers, for instance, consistently give birth to more growth-retarded and premature infants than do comparable nonsmoking mothers. Carbon monoxide and other products from the smoke apparently enter the fetal blood and harm the developing child. Inevitable long-term effects of maternal smoking are not yet established, but medical authorities generally advise pregnant women to cease smoking during the gestation period.

Less equivocal are the apparent long-term effects of chronic alcoholism among pregnant women on their infants' development. Maternal alcoholism is strongly linked to infant growth deficiencies, altered body features such as microcephaly (abnormally small head and brain), limb abnormalities, delayed gross and fine motor development, and mental retardation. This pattern of characteristics in newborns has been termed the *fetal alcohol syndrome* (Streissguth, 1976). Medical records show that some infants born to alcoholic mothers do not show this syndrome, yet do appear to suffer from alcoholic withdrawal symptoms (extreme irritability and tremor). Fortunately, these less-affected children can recover and develop normally during the first year (Nichols, 1967). Still other newborn infants show no adverse prenatal reactions to their mothers' alcoholism. We cannot say for sure what factors cause the difference in response to maternal alcoholism, but amount and frequency of alcohol consumption combined with qualitative differences in nutrition are suspected.

Alcohol is America's most widely abused "social" drug, but other drugs are also associated with prenatal complications. Narcotic addiction to heroin, is a case in point. Generally speaking, a social environment in which such addiction occurs is hostile to the stable support necessary for healthy pregnancy. Most addicts live in areas of major cities where physical care and nourishment are poor. Addicted mothers tend to be single or separated from their spouses. The mechanics of the drug habit itself tend to introduce infections, such as hepatitis, into the mother's system. These factors increase substantially the degree of risk to normal fetal development (Stevenson, 1973). The chemical effect on infants of narcotics such as heroin on the infant is twofold. First, these infants generally are small for their gestational age and many are born prematurely. Second, between 50 and 90 percent will manifest withdrawal symptoms, with the onset most frequently occurring within 24 hours following birth. Symptoms include tremors, hyperactivity, vomiting, diarrhea, and respiratory problems. Though our data are scant, infant mortality from complications associated with this addiction has been decreasing. Surprisingly, the few infants followed longitudinally appear to be developing in a normal way. It is possible, however, that prenatal contact with narcotics will predispose children to drug dependency should they experiment with them later in life (Baker, 1960).

The use and abuse of barbiturates (sedatives) know no socioeconomic boundaries. If barbiturate addiction occurs among pregnant women, their newborn infants may go through withdrawal symptoms similar to those associated with narcotics. Long-term effects of this kind of uterine environment have not been established; however, there may be increased risk of congenital malformations.

As mentioned earlier, severe malnutrition during pregnancy, often a consequence of socioeconomic factors, can also affect the quality of prenatal development. Depending on what maternal dietary deficiencies exist, a developing infant may be aborted, or it may be born with low birth weight and length and congenital malformations. Particularly when the malnutrition extends beyond birth into the first years of life, the developing infant may suffer some mental deficiencies. It is interesting to note that maternal overnutrition or obesity can also harm the developing child. Obese pregnant women tend to have greater fetal loss and suffer from preeclamptic toxemia (a metabolic disorder characterized by high blood pressure, swelling, and problems with protein excretion) more often than do women within the normal weight range. Associated with prenatal toxemia are fetal loss, low birth weight, and congenital malformations. Postnatal correlates of toxemia include higher incidence of disease and more behavior and reading disorders among the children (Ferreira, 1969). Obese women also tend to have more difficult labors and deliveries (Emerson, 1962), the possible effects of which have already been discussed (see section on labor and delivery).

Maternal age is another important variable in both prenatal and postnatal child development. Extremes in maternal age, adolescence and middle age, place the developing child at greater risk of developmental problems. For both periods, congenital malformations, prematurity, miscarriages, and stillbirths are more common than in the intervening years. An interplay of hazardous social factors can also complicate childbearing for mothers at the two age extremes. For example, young mothers are often unwed, emotionally unprepared for caregiving, and limited in their education and job skills. Although older mothers are usually better served by experience, they may show a decline in health and stamina with aging. Thus, both groups may be less well suited to provide the proper postnatal care and guidance required for successful childbearing and rearing (Stevenson, 1973).

Less directly related to physiological processes, as affected by maternal drugs, nutrition, and age, are characteristics of the social environment that may influence the emotional stability of pregnant women (Ferreira, 1969; MacDonald, 1968; Montagu, 1962; Roe & Chandler, 1976). Some women may experience emotional stress as they redefine their role to include motherhood. Other sources of maternal stress include financial strain, altered sexual relations with husbands, threat of loss of employment, and unwanted pregnancy. Whatever the source, prolonged fatigue and emotional stress or disturbance during pregnancy are correlated with a variety of infant characteristics: restlessness, excess crying, irritability, vomiting, and diarrhea. Extreme maternal stress has been associated with spontaneous abortion. Women who habitually abort before their infants reach full term are noted for their strong dependency motivation and uncertainty about husband support. Similarly, maternal anxiety and insecurity, and hostility and rejection of motherhood, are linked to premature birthgiving. These are but a few examples of the complex relationship between maternal emotional life and infant development. Presumably, certain alterations in body chemistry occur as a response to stress. These, in turn, may create conditions less favorable to desirable development. That broader cultural factors may also play some part in maternal response to pregnancy is indicated by cross-cultural differences in the appearance and extent of "morning sickness." Toxemia of pregnancy is observed primarily in industrially advanced cultures. Birth malformations have consistently been noted throughout history among countries at war, even in the absence of increased malnutrition.

Psychosocial Factors and Postnatal Physical Development

The influence of social forces, mediated by physical development, on psychological development probably begins as early as birth. Parents who desire their infants, regardless of sex or appearance, will accept and value them. Not all infants are so fortunate. One family well known to us illustrates the point. An orthopedically handicapped but otherwise normal son, Mark, was recently born into this family. The father, a robust, athletic, outdoorsman, has admitted his profound depression about this event. His hopes for vigorous recreation with his son were dashed. The father now speaks of "another try." We cannot say for sure how this father's attitude will influence his parenting behavior. Per-

haps an adjustment will be made. Chances are, however, that the cycle of father–son interaction would have been less threatening to Mark had he entered this family without physical handicap.

Thus we can identify as one important mediating factor in psychological development, the degree of "match" between parental expectations for child-rearing and the physical potentials of their children. Another source of interaction may be found in the family structure itself. A second or third child, for instance, will tend to be smaller than an older sibling simply by virtue of age. This child will be less likely to rely on his physical stature to secure a favorable social position among his brothers and sisters than would a larger, stronger sibling. Also important for a younger sibling is the early contact with physical values or characteristics of individuals from an older age group. For example, a young child with an athletically oriented older sister or brother may become prematurely concerned about muscle growth and development. A young girl with an older sister may become more sensitive to the development of her secondary sex characteristics than her age mates.

That sibling modeling influences on physical activity may occur within families is suggested by data from a recent study (Longstreth et al., 1975). Kindergarten through sixth grade teachers were asked to nominate their most and least physically active pupils of both sexes. Further comparison of these children led to the main finding that physically active pupils were much more likely to have an older brother than were their physically passive peers.

Beyond the family, we can expect that as children grow older, their peer group will exert increasing influence. Peer attitudes about "ideal" size, physique, and physical capabilities can influence children's self-concepts and self-esteem. It may even affect children's motivation to change aspects of their physical status, such as body-building exercises and lessons to improve athletic skills. As noted in Chapter 4, peer pressures are particularly strong during adolescence, when identity achievement becomes a central developmental task.

Constitutional Variables

Body type   One aspect of the relationship between psychosocial and physical development is the attempt to link body build, or somatotype, with personality. Interest in this relationship can be traced back some 2,500 years to Hippocrates. The most definitive American effort to associate body build and personality culminated in a theory of constitutional psychology several decades ago (Sheldon, 1940). Three general human body configurations were formulated, each having an associated temperament. Although the "pure types" are rarely found they serve as models. One basic body type, *endomorphy*, is predominantly soft and round or pear-shaped in appearance, with a tendency toward overweight. The associated temperament, called *visceratonia*, seeks creature comforts, is generally relaxed, and displays strong social motivation.

A second major somatotype, *mesomorphy*, is best described as an athletic configuration—upright, firm and muscular, with relatively broad shoulders and narrow hips. The associated temperament, *somatotonia*, displays vigorous bodily assertiveness, action, and a general power orientation.

The third and final basic somatotype is *ectomorphy*. An ectomorphic individual appears lean (a large external body surface in relation to weight), less muscular than the mesomorph and is generally "gangly." *Cerebrotonia* is the associated temperament, noted mainly for restraint, inhibition, and comparatively mild manner.

Most individuals are variations of these pure types. Whether or to what extent somatotype contributes directly to personality characteristics is a matter of unresolved debate. There is little doubt, however, that people respond differently to persons of different body types. One study, for example, has clearly demonstrated that children make discriminations about somatotype as early as 8 years (Johnson & Staffieri, 1971). These children reacted most favorably to mesomorphy, rated endomorphy as socially unfavorable, and associated ectomorphy with social submissiveness and low personal favor. Similarly, we have good reason to believe that children of different body types may also differ in self-concept. For example, preadolescent male children who tend toward endomorphy have reported less positive self-concepts than have their "balanced" and "linear-type" peers (Felker, 1968). The somatotype–self-concept relationship may not hold uniformly across age groups. For example, there is evidence to indicate that pubertal changes may attenuate this relationship (Felker & Kay, 1971). Furthermore, very little is known about girls in this area. It is plausible to think that somatotype will influence how children are perceived and responded to by others, the net effect being social feedback that can influence the way children perceive and feel about themselves.

Finally, there is some indication that physique is related to more than personal-social aspects of behavior. For example, to the extent body-build influences self-perception, it may provide an indirect link to children's cognitive strategies (see Chapter 8). One important study of this relationship among elementary school children has shown that boys of shorter stature were more impulsive in problem-solving tasks than were their taller age-mates (Kagan, 1966). The preferred interpretation for this relationship is that greater anxiety about growth and potency exists among short boys in a peer culture that values tallness and strength. This anxiety, in turn, can be further accentuated in ambiguous problem-solving situations for which these children have no ready responses. Consequently, the shorter boy may respond quickly, even unwittingly, in an attempt to reduce this unpleasant anxiety. This stature-impulsivity relationship was much weaker and less consistent among girls, who, presumably, are also less subject to sex-typed cultural-social norms about shortness. Shorter girls may experience less anxiety about their status and be less prone to react defensively or impulsively on difficult problem-solving tasks.

We cannot guarantee the accuracy of this interpretation. Possibly there are some more basic physiological factors that underly both body build and cognitive orientation. These data do, however, establish still another relationship between constitutional and behavioral variables.

Maturation rate A second constitutional variable important for self-development is the rate at which one approaches physical maturity. This is especially pertinent during adolescence. Several competently executed studies illustrate differences between adolescents who are extremely early (accelerated) in their physical development and age mates who are extremely late (retarded) (Jones & Bayley, 1950; Jones & Mussen, 1958; Mussen & Jones, 1957, 1958). Bone ossification status—the extent to which bone structure has hardened to its mature state—is generally used as the criterion to determine maturation in such studies. Their collective results indicate an apparent advantage in self-concept and peer status among early-maturing youth, especially males. Specifically, early-maturing males (as compared to their late-maturing counterparts) more consistently receive positive ratings from both peers and adults on attractiveness, composure, and social sophistication. They are also more frequently chosen for positions of school leadership and identified as prominent participants in extracurricular school activities. As a group early-maturing boys also seem to exhibit greater physical strength throughout adolescence than do their late-maturing counterparts (Carron & Bailey, 1974). This is attributed primarily to their superior body weight, especially that part contributed by musculature, rather than to any consistent advantage in overall height.

In contrast, later-maturing males, when compared to early-maturers, more often report feelings of inadequacy, low self-esteem, and the belief that they are rejected. Perhaps to compensate or overcome these feelings in some way, late maturers also often demonstrate a pattern of attention-seeking and rebellious autonomy. Such behavior could increase instead of reduce their social and personal difficulties.

Still other authors (such as Weatherly, 1964) indicate that late physical maturation is generally a handicap among males at the college level. Moreover, some of the psychological differences associated with maturation rate during adolescence, including those involving personal dominance, independence, and self-control, have been observed among males during the third decade of life. By mid-life, however, any clearcut social or self-concept advantages of early-maturing males seem to have disappeared (Jones, 1957). And we hasten to add that even during adolescence, the apparent disadvantages of late maturation need not be inevitable. Physical development status is by no means the only factor associated with self- and social development. For girls, at least at the time, extremely early maturation may even be somewhat handicapping (Jones & Mussen, 1958). Recent data also suggest that late-maturing adolescents of both sexes may excel their early-maturing peers in spatial abilities and brain hemispheric lateralization for speech perception (more accurate discrimination of speech sounds directed to the right or left ear) (Waber, 1977). The reasons for this advantage are not certain; possibly endocrinological functions are involved. Early maturation does not necessarily bring uniform advantages to adolescents. What advantages may occur concern primarily social and, indirectly, self-esteem development.

Physical handicap As for body build and maturation rate, physical handicap is at least indirectly involved in self-development. Parent and peer reactions to a physically handicapping condition provide social feedback that influences a person's view of himself as a more or a less adequate or worthy person. In one important study, for example, pre-adolescent children demonstrated a strong tendency to consider physical handicap in establishing their preferences for other children. Girls seem more frequently to focus on such cosmetic attributes as obesity and facial disfigurement; boys, in contrast, apparently respond more negatively to such functional impairments as amputation of an arm or a leg.

Despite such findings, it is likely that attitudes toward a given physical handicap or disability are not uniform among children and youth (Alessi & Anthony, 1969). However, the collective impact of social isolation or rejection of physically handicapped children and the reduced opportunities they may have for partici-

pation in socially valued activities surely will affect the self. Related problems, such as chronic illness, may also negatively influence a child's self-development, especially if chronic illness interferes with academic progress (Sheperd, 1969). And finally, physical handicap may interact adversely with cognitive developments among certain children. One authority (Kershner, 1974) reported that physically impaired children (bilateral amputees), normal in their verbal intelligence, were significantly poorer in their spatial ability than were comparable, but nonimpaired, children.

To summarize, body build, maturational status, and physical handicap all can influence both the degree of achieved competence in given activities and the social reactions one receives from other people. To the extent that success and positive social reinforcement are important to a child or a youth and serve to shape his self-evaluation, these three constitutional attributes are likely to be strongly involved in self-development. Attributes such as physical handicap or body build do not inevitably lead to maladjustment; nor is it always easy to demonstrate definite associations between specific physical attributes and the quality of behavior, including self-development (Pringle, 1964).

Some Thoughts About the Schools and Mass Media

Several examples will illustrate the mediating influence of physical status in the formal educational environment. Sensory handicaps, such as visual or auditory deficiencies, are important at school entry and beyond. Uncorrected, these handicaps can interfere with learning. We have known occasional children and youth who prefer to endure mild sensory deficits rather than to wear glasses or hearing aids in the presence of their peers. Children who are retained in grade because of unsatisfactory academic progress are automatically removed from their age mates and set among younger children where "advanced" physical size and maturity may become a stigma. One recent study indicates that teachers can easily express more favorable academic expectations for physically attractive than for less attractive pupils (Clifford, 1975). Still other studies (for example, Dion, 1974; Rich, 1975) suggest that adults, including teachers, rate attractive children as "more desirable" in personality; adult females, in particular, are more apt to behave more leniently with attractive children (especially boys) in task situations.

As school becomes the center for youth social activities, further dynamics of psychosocial development can occur. Athletically built and competent males are usually admired; well-endowed females are sought after for dating. "Pretty" girls may be more frequently chosen for prestigious positions, such as cheer leader and student council, regardless of ability. Though these outcomes are not inevitable, it seems that adolescents are constantly bombarded with the ideal physical person as a standard against which to measure their own appearance and motor competence. As an example, consider the illustrations commonly found in textbooks and other educational materials. Most, if not all, of the individuals pictured possess culturally valued physical characteristics or represent the stereotypic "ideals." Characters tend to be slim, well-built, and of clear complexion—as if no overweight children or adolescents with acne exist.

More generally, we can ask about the effects of curriculum and instructional practices upon physical development, especially physical education. Few parents or educators argue that exercise and organized games are important for physical well-being. School athletics, for ex-

ample, are promoted for their value in building cardiovascular fitness, although we cannot marshall much direct research evidence about the physical-education–physical-fitness relationship. But despite the educators' good intentions, physical fitness among many of today's children and youth may be lacking (Solomon, 1977). Dependence upon the automobile, the growth of spectator sports, and increased television viewing are but three factors that indicate a trend toward more sedentary living.

These points highlight the issue of what society really wants, will encourage, provide opportunity for, and reward in pursuit of physical fitness through school programs. Undeniably, athletics are strongly valued in American society. But, as one authority (Kniker, 1974) has observed, priorities at the public school level may be muddled and opportunities for physical education too selective. The presumed but rarely documented social benefits of physical education—developing skills of cooperation and competition, sportspersonship, self-discipline, and overall "good character" through athletics—may come to dominate the more basic concern for conditioning: physical exercise carefully tailored to the developmental status of children and youth. School playground equipment is often limited, unimaginative, and even unsafe. Provision for specific sports differences in agility, flexibility, speed, and strength are often lacking. Interscholastic athletics, success in which is limited to a comparatively small percentage of able students, can easily undermine the prestige and enjoyment of less sensational intramural sports participation. Though progress has been noted in the past several years, sex role stereotyping has limited children's freedom to experiment with and develop competence in school sports activities. And adult pressures on children and youth to excel in athletics may too easily blind us to the hazard of sports injuries.

In sum, the philosophy and practice of physical education seem as much if not more determined by social values and attitudes as by knowledge and concern about biological development. Much more needs to be learned about both the intended (and possibly unintended) effects of physical-education programs, including athletics, upon human development. Parents and educators should evaluate both the goals and methods of physical education periodically in light of research evidence. In the past, winning at any cost seemed all too often the athletic tail that wagged the physical-fitness dog. This is not to deny the many potentially positive social contributions of competitive games and organized sports. Proficiency in athletic skills can provide children and youth with a variety of powerful social sanctions. Unfortunately, physical educators themselves admit that an "unacceptably large number of children who attend physical education classes are not able to acquire the sanctioned skills in sports and games satisfactorily" (Nixon & Locke, 1973, p. 1210). Research has not yet disclosed to physical educators how to teach athletic skills effectively.

Similarly ambiguous, if not pessimistic, findings come from other school program activities concerned with health and safety education. For example, the rapid spread of nonmedical drug use (and abuse), including alcohol abuse, among America's young is a potential and often real threat to physical health (McGlothlin, 1975). If drug dependency occurs, especially to the point where children or youth organize their lives around acquiring and ingesting drugs, a threat to psychological health or social well-being can also exist. These concerns underlie in part the frantic implementation of "drug education" programs in the schools. Such programs generally are considered to have three purposes: to increase knowledge about drugs, to promote "healthy attitudes" toward drug use, and to prevent or decrease drug-abuse behavior (Horan, 1974). These goals, however worthy, and the instructional tactics used to achieve them, have been notoriously difficult to evaluate. In fact, many drug education programs reportedly are followed by increased, rather than decreased, drug use (Horan, 1974). Peer influence about drugs, either pro or con, seems considerably more potent in determining drug-related attitudes and behavior than do formal attempts at drug education (Wong, 1976). In short, drug-education research presents a confusing and frustrating picture. It seems unrealistic to expect that the schools can "solve" problems of drug use, even though they are a logical place to give students accurate information about drug effects on health.

These thoughts have a parallel in safety education, especially that designed to promote "good" driving habits among adolescent automobile users. The need for this education is easily justified given our earlier statistic about automobile-related accidents as the leading cause of death and disfigurement during adolescence. For reasons yet undetermined, driver-education programs seem generally to have made little difference in youths' actual driving habits (Griffeth & Rogers, 1976). As in drug use, perhaps peer influences in combination with certain characteristics of youth—the wish to experiment, the desire for autonomy or independence, an attitude of omnipotence, and general fearlessness—establish a sort of "immunity" against appeals to rationality and self-discipline. Human beings are not easily changed.

Our final thoughts about social influences and psychological correlates of physical development concern the mass media, especially television. Advertising strategy, for example, typically involves portrayals of ideal physical stereotypes (handsome, beautiful, trim, well-dressed and groomed). The products themselves are heralded to produce or perpetuate these ideal characteristics. Toothpaste, hair spray, soap, cologne, and other personal hygiene products often have the not-so-hidden message that their use is the road to social success.

Television stars also seem to exert influence as models through their physical appearance and status, however fanciful. In fact, a role played by actors or actresses may even affect public opinion about the physical appearance of characters they play. One popular television program, for example, has as its main character an overweight private detective who enacts his duties with much masculine flair. A television critic has maintained that this role has shown a skeptical public that fat can be sexy.

As styles of living, dress, and grooming are pictured by the mass media, we can see that it is not just attitudes about physical appearance that are affected. The media may also trigger efforts by individuals to alter their physical characteristics. Consider, for example, the changing ways in which the female breast is emphasized by clothing styles. At one time, styles centered on clothes to accentuate the fullness and curvature of female breasts. Women, and men, were very breast-conscious. Well-endowed females were "in," the less well-endowed often resorting to padding and even physical exercise to increase their bustlines. Later, a flatter style became chic, as in the "Twiggy" look, with breast size far less important.

Because so little clear-cut research about media effects is available, we must consider these points tentative, even speculative. Few can deny, however, the presence everywhere of the mass media and the ability of Madison Avenue techniques to create consumer wants, influence buying habits, and condition attitudes about what is socially desirable. Perhaps media input will have (or has had) some positive effect on public attitudes about exercise and general health care. The potential seems huge for informing the public, including children and youth, about such matters as nutrition, medical care, and physical fitness.

SUMMARY

Physical-motor development has been discussed in terms of four major categories of related ideas. The first category was prenatal development. Three phases in normal prenatal development were described, along with recent gains in the understanding of prenatal developmental problems. The critical-periods hypothesis first discussed in Chapter 2 is particularly well suited to analysis of these problems. The first section of the chapter concluded with reference to the crucial processes of labor and delivery and to a controversy about the possible long-range consequences of birth trauma.

A variety of data about postnatal development comprised the second major category of ideas. Important reflex behaviors and sensorimotor capacities of the newborn were discussed. Though the human infant seems remarkably sturdy and adaptive, it is also vulnerable to certain early hazards, for example, the sudden infant death syndrome. After early stabilization of life-sustaining processes, we can observe extremely rapid growth in both height and weight during infancy. Cultural variations in both body size and growth rate can also be observed during the preschool years; differences that become progressively apparent with advancing age. Aging calls our attention to further sources of individual differences in physical-motor development. Especially important are sex-related differences in the onset of puberty, with girls generally achieving their physiological maturity a year or two earlier than boys. Sequential development of primary and secondary sex characteristics was discussed along with genetically controlled reflexive functions of the neuromuscular system. Selected perceptual-motor developments were examined to emphasize two general principles of development: age related differentiation and integration of motor movements, and the interaction of perceptual-motor with cognitive developments. These principles are exemplified by early manipulative behaviors, the normal course of development in using tools for drawing, and the development of body image. Still further principles of motor control and skill development include *directionality* in growth and the primary role of *maturation* in the appearance of various motor skills.

The third major category of ideas involved health disorders in children and youth. General points about health disorders include the role of genetics in establishing constitutional predisposition to disease, characteristic age-related health problems, and sex and racial differences in disease. We cannot minimize disease as a threat to normal growth and development, yet accidents, not illnesses, are the leading cause of death and disability among children and youth. Even so, the study of health problems once more reveals important interrelationships between physiological

and psychological functioning. We have discussed the obesity phenomenon in some detail to reinforce this notion.

The chapter 6 concluded by a return to our theme of major social influences on human development. This fourth category of ideas included data about nutrition and growth, with an explanation of the nutrition-related *secular trend* in growth among children and youth in western cultures. Further social conditions and prenatal development were documented by reference to the usually adverse relationships of maternal variables (malnutrition, drug use, and emotional stress) and fetal development. From birth onward, certain psychosocial factors and physical development have undergone systematic study. Noteworthy relationships between constitutional variables (body type, maturation rate, physical handicap) and personal-social development were discussed. Finally, some implications of physical-motor development for health and safety education in the schools and possible mass media influences on personal hygiene habits and social attitudes toward the body were proposed.

REFERENCES

Alessi, D. F., & Anthony, W. A. Uniformity of children's attitudes toward physical disabilities. *Exceptional Children,* 1969, *35,* 543–545.

Baker, J. B. E. The effects of drugs on the foetus. *Pharmacological Review,* 1960, *12,* 37–90.

Bayley, N. Growth curves of height and weight by age for boys and girls, scaled according to physical maturity. *Journal of Pediatrics,* 1956, *48,* 187–194.

Beckwith, J. B. The Sudden Infant Death Syndrome: A new theory. *Pediatrics,* 1975, *55,* 583–584.

Blair, C. L., & Salerno, E. M. *The expanding family: Childbearing.* Boston: Little, Brown, 1976.

Bray, G. A., et al. Obesity: A serious symptom. *Annual Internal Medicine,* 1972, *77,* 797.

Breckenridge, M. E., & Murphy, M. N. *Growth and development of the young child* (8th ed.). Philadelphia: Saunders, 1969.

Bridger, W. H. Sensory habituation and discrimination in the human neonate. *American Journal of Psychiatry,* 1961, *117,* 991–996.

Carron, A. V., & Bailey, D. A. Strength development in boys from 10 through 16 years. *Monographs of the Society for Research in Child Development,* 1974, *39*(4), Serial No. 157.

Charles, D. C. *Psychology of the child in the classroom.* New York: Macmillan, 1964.

Clifford, M. M. Physical attractiveness and academic performance. *Child Study Journal,* 1975,5,201–209.

Coddington, R. D. The significance of life events as etiologic factors in the diseases of children: I. A survey of professional workers. *Journal of Psychosomatic Research,* 1972, *16,* 7–18. (a)

Coddington, R. D. The significance of life events as etiologic factors in the diseases of children: II. A study of a normal population. *Journal of Psychosomatic Research,* 1972, *16,* 205–213. (b)

Cone, T. E., Jr. Secular acceleration of height and biologic maturation. In J. R. Gallagher, F. P. Heald, & D. C. Garell (Eds.), *Medical care of the adolescent* (3rd ed.). New York: Appleton-Century-Crofts, 1976.

Corbin, C. B. *A textbook of motor development.* Dubuque, Iowa: William C. Brown, 1973.

Cratty, B. J. *Perceptual and motor development in infants and children.* New York: Macmillan, 1970.

Dion, K. K. Children's physical attractiveness and sex as determinants of adult punitiveness. *Developmental Psychology,* 1974, *10,* 772–778.

Emerson, R. G. Obesity and its association with the complications of pregnancy. *British Medical Journal,* 1962, *2,* 516–518.

Felker, D. W. Relationship between self-concept, body build, and perception of father's interest in sports in boys. *Research Quarterly,* 1968, *39,* 513–517.

Felker, D. W., & Kay, R. S. Self-concept, sports interests, sports participation, and body type of seventh- and eighth-grade boys. *Journal of Psychology,* 1971, *78,* 223–228.

Ferreira, A. J. *Prenatal environment.* Springfield, Ill.: Charles C Thomas, 1969.

Frantz, R. L. Pattern vision in newborn infants. *Science,* 1963, *140,* 296–297.

Frish, R., & Revelle, R. Height and weight at menarche and a hypothesis of initial body weights and adolescent events. *Science,* 1972, *169,* 397.

Gesell, A., & Amatruda, C. S. *Developmental diagnosis: Normal and abnormal child development: Clinical methods and pediatric applications.* New York: Hoeber, 1947.

Griffeth, R. W., & Rogers, R. W. Effects of fear-arousing components of driver education on students' safety attitudes and simulator performance. *Journal of Educational Psychology,* 1976, *68,* 501–506.

Gullickson, G. R., & Crowell, D. H. Neonatal habituation to electrotactual stimulation. *Journal of Experimental Child Psychology,* 1964, *1,* 388–396.

Hamilton, W. J., & Mossman, H. W. *Hamilton, Boyd and Mossman's human embryology* (4th ed.). Cambridge: Heffer, 1972.

Hammar, S. L., & Owens, J. W. M. Adolescence. In D. W. Smith & E. L. Bierman (Eds.),*The biologic ages of man.* Philadelphia: Saunders, 1973.

Heald, F. P. Morbidity and mortality. In J. R. Gallagher, F. P. Heald, & D. C. Garell (Eds.), *Medical care of the adolescent* (3rd ed.). New York: Appleton-Century-Crofts, 1976.

Heald, F. P., & Khan, M. A. Obesity. In J. R. Gallagher, F. P. Heald, & D. C. Garell (Eds.), *Medical care of the adolescent* (3rd ed.). New York: Appleton-Century-Crofts, 1976.

Heisel, J. S., Ream, S., Raitz, R., Rappaport, M., & Coddington, R. D. The significance of life events as contributing factors in the diseases of children: III. A study of pediatric patients. *Journal of Pediatrics,* 1973, *83,* 119–123.

Holm, V. A., & Wiltz, N. A. Childhood. In D. W. Smith & E. L. Bierman (Eds.), *The biologic ages of man.* Philadelphia: Saunders, 1973.

Horan, J. J. Outcome difficulties in drug education. *Review of Educational Research,* 1974, *44,* 203–211.

Johnson, L. C. Body cathexis as a factor in somatic complaints. *Journal of Consulting Psychology,* 1956, *20,* 145–149.

Johnson, M. L., Burke, B. S., & Mayer, J. Relative importance of inactivity and over-eating in the energy balance of obese high school girls. *American Journal of Clinical Nutrition,* 1956, *4,* 37.

Johnson, P. A., & Staffieri, J.R. Stereotypic affective properties of personal names and somatotypes in children. *Developmental Psychology,* 1971, *5,* 176.

Jones, M.C. The later careers of boys who were early- or late-maturing. *Child Development,* 1957, *28,* 113–128.

Jones, M. C., & Bayley, N. Physical maturing among boys as related to behavior. *Journal of Educational Psychology,* 1950, *41,* 129–148.

Jones, M. C., & Mussen, P. H. Self-conception, maturation, and interpersonal attitudes of early- and late-maturing girls. *Child Development,* 1958, *29,* 491–501.

Kagan, J. Body-build and conceptual impulsivity in children. *Journal of Personality,* 1966, *34,* 118–128.

Karmel, M. *Thank you, Dr. Lamaze.* Philadelphia: Lippincott, 1959.

Kershner, J. R. Relationship of motor development to visual-spatial cognitive growth. *Journal of Special Education,* 1974, *8,* 91–102.

Kinsey, A. C., Pomeroy, W. B., & Martin, C. E. *Sexual behavior in the human male.* Philadelphia: Saunders, 1948.

Kniker, C. R. The values of athletics in schools: A continuing debate. *Phi Delta Kappan,* 1974, *56,* 116–120.

Krogman, W. M. Growth of head, face, trunk, and limbs in Philadelphia white and Negro children of elementary and high school age. *Monographs of the Society for Research in Child Development,* 1970, *35*(3), Serial No. 136.

Kugelmass, I. N. *Adolescent medicine: Principles and practice.* Springfield, Ill.: Charles C Thomas, 1975.

Langman, J. *Medical embryology* (3rd ed.). Baltimore: Williams & Wilkins, 1975.

LeBoyer, F. *Birth without violence.* New York: Knopf, 1975.

Leon, G. R. Current directions in the treatment of obesity. *Psychological Bulletin,* 1976, *83,* 557–578.

Lipsitt, L. P. Learning processes of human newborns. *Merrill-Palmer Quarterly,* 1966, *12,* 45–71.

Longstreth, L. E., et al. The ubiquity of big brother. *Child Development,* 1975, *46,* 769–772.

MacDonald, R. L. The role of emotional factors in obstetric complications: A review. *Psychosomatic Medicine,* 1968, *30,* 222–237.

Marx, J. L. Crib death: Some promising leads but no solution yet. *Science,* 1975, *189,* 367–369.

McCandless, B. R. *Children: Behavior and development* (2nd ed.). New York: Holt, Rinehart and Winston, 1967.

McGlothlin, W. H. Drug use and abuse. *Annual Review of Psychology,* 1975, *26,* 45–63.

Meredith, H. V. Body size of contemporary groups of eight-year-old children studied in different parts of the world. *Monographs of the Society for Research in Child Development,* 1969, *34*(1), Serial No. 125. (a)

Meredith, H. V. Body size of contemporary youth in different parts of the world. *Monographs of the Society for Research in Child Development,* 1969, *34*(7), Serial No. 131. (b)

Montagu, M. F. A. *Prenatal influences.* Springfield, Ill.: Charles C Thomas, 1962.

Munsinger, H. *Fundamentals of child development.* New York: Holt, Rinehart and Winston, 1971.

Mussen, P. H., & Jones, M. C. Self-conception, maturation, and interpersonal attitudes of early- and late-maturing boys. *Child Development,* 1957, *28,* 243–256.

Mussen, P. H., & Jones, M. C. The behavior-inferred motivations of late- and early-maturing boys. *Child Development,* 1958, *29,* 61–67.

Muuss, R. *Theories of adolescence* (3rd ed.). New York: Random House, 1975.

Naeye, R. L., Messmer, J. III, Specht, T., & Merritt, T. A. Sudden infant death syndrome: Temperament before death. *Journal of Pediatrics,* 1976, *88*(3), 511–515.

Nichols, M. M. Acute alcohol withdrawal syndrome in a newborn. *American Journal of Diseases of Childhood,* 1967, *113,* 714.

Nixon, J. E., & Locke, L. F. Research on teaching physical education. In R. M. W. Travers (Ed.), *Second handbook of research on teaching.* Skokie, Ill.: Rand McNally, 1973.

Oxorn, H., & Foote, W. R. *Human labor and birth* (3rd ed.). New York: Appleton-Century-Crofts, 1975.

Pilowsky, I., & Sharp, J. Psychological aspects of pre-eclamptic toxaemia: A prospective study. *Journal of Psychosomatic Research,* 1971, *15,* 193–197.

Prechtl, H., & Beintema, D. *The neurological examination of the full-term newborn infant.* London: Heinemann, 1964.

Pringle, M. The emotional and social adjustment of physically handicapped children: A review of the literature published between 1928 and 1962. *Educational Research,* 1964, *6,* 207–215.

Rank, O. *The trauma of birth.* New York: Harcourt, 1929.

Rich, J. Effects of children's physical attractiveness on teachers' evaluations. *Journal of Educational Psychology,* 1975, *67,* 599–609.

Roe, M. D., & Chandler, L. *Behavioral problems: Prenatal implications.* Paper presented at the Fourth Annual Pacific Northwest Educational Research and Evaluation Conference. Seattle, May 1976.

Root, A. W. Endocrinology of puberty: I. Normal sexual maturation. *Journal of Pediatrics,* 1973, *83,* 1. (a)

Root, A. W. Endocrinology of puberty: II. Aberrations of sexual maturation. *Journal of Pediatrics,* 1973, *83,* 187. (b)

Runner, M. N. Inheritance of susceptibility to congenital deformity: Metabolic clues provided by experiments with teratogenic agents. *Pediatrics,* 1959, *23,* 245.

Salk, L. Sudden infant death: Impact on family and physician. *Clinical Pediatrics,* 1971, *10,* 248–249.

Secord, P. F., & Jourard, S. M. The appraisal of body-cathexis: Body cathexis and the self. *Journal of Consulting Psychology,* 1953, *17,* 343–347.

Sheldon, W. H. *The varieties of human physique: An introduction to constitutional psychology.* New York: Harper & Row, 1940.

Sheperd, C. W., Jr. Childhood chronic illness and visual motor perceptual development. *Exceptional Children,* 1969, *36,* 39–42.

Shiller, J. G. *Childhood illness.* New York: Stein and Day, 1972.

Skukla, A., et al. Infantile overnutrition in the first year of life: A field study in Dudley, Worcestershire. *British Medical Journal,* 1972, *4,* 507.

Smith, D. W., & Der Yuen, D. Prenatal life and the pregnant woman. In D. W. Smith & E. L. Bierman (Eds.), *The biologic ages of man.* Philadelphia: Saunders, 1973.

Solomon, N. Youth have not made progress in fitness. Seattle, Washington: *The Seattle Times,* January 30, 1977.

Sontag, L. W. The significance of fetal environmental differences. *American Journal of Obstetrics and Gynecology,* 1941, *42,* 996–1003.

Spellacy, W. N. (Ed.), *Management of the high risk pregnancy.* Baltimore: University Park Press, 1976.

Stevenson, R. E. *The fetus and newly born infant.* St. Louis, Mo.: Mosby, 1973.

Streissguth, A. P. Maternal alcoholism and the outcome of pregnancy. In M. Greenblatt (Ed.), *Alcohol problems in women and children.* New York: Grune & Stratton, 1976.

Tonkin, S. Sudden infant death syndrome: Hypothesis of causation. *Pediatrics,* 1975, *55,* 650.

Turner, E. K. The syndrome in the infant resulting from maternal emotional tension during pregnancy. *Medical Journal of Australia,* 1956, *1,* 221–222.

Waber, D. P. Sex differences in mental abilities, hemispheric lateralization, and rate of physical growth at adolescence. *Developmental Psychology,* 1977, *13,* 29–38.

Weatherly, D. Self-perceived rate of physical maturation and personality in late adolescence. *Child Development,* 1964, *35,* 1197–1210.

Wennberg, R. P., Woodrum, D. E., & Hodson, W. A. The perinate. In D. W. Smith & E. L. Bierman (Eds.), *The biologic ages of man.* Philadelphia: Saunders, 1973.

Wenner, W. H., & VanderVeer, B. Infancy: The first two years. In D. W. Smith & E. L. Bierman (Eds.), *The biologic ages of man.* Philadelphia: Saunders, 1973.

Wertheimer, M. Psychomotor coordination of auditory and visual space at birth. *Science,* 1961, *134,* 1962.

Wong, M. R. Different strokes: Models of drug abuse prevention education. *Contemporary Educational Psychology,* 1976, *1,* 285–303.

Young, C. M. Adolescents and their nutrition. In J. R. Gallagher, F. P. Heald, & D.C. Garell (Eds.), *Medical care of the adolescent* (3rd ed.). New York: Appleton-Century-Crofts, 1976.

chapter 7

Language development

No matter how skilled an obstetrician or midwife is, there is always some anxiety upon delivering an infant. This quite natural anxiety shows concern for the health and general well-being of the newborn person and usually persists at least until pediatric evaluation reveals that a neonate has passed its "well baby" test. But a newborn infant's robust birth cry can do much to reassure us that the basic life functions are operative. Beginning with this primitive

though significant bellow, normal infants will a short year later be saying their first meaningful words. By 18 to 24 months, they will be communicating by putting words together to produce a variety of two- or three-word "sentences" that express emotions, personal desires, and possession rights ("That's mine!"); that name objects, and that report about the self (Schacter et al., 1974).

Patterned speech develops rapidly thereafter. Three- or four-year olds, for example, will generally be able to understand and use most of the basic sentence structures of their native language. Four-year-olds may also be able to adjust their speech to their listeners, for example, by talking differently and more simply to younger children than to their age-mates or adults (Shatz & Gelman, 1973). By school age, children in all cultures are close to mastery of their native language for communication, although much remains to be learned about its further symbolic aspects, as in reading and writing. Normally speaking, full competence with one's native language is fully achieved by age 10 or 12 (Bloom, 1975).

These are remarkable achievements, not yet completely or thoroughly understood. In fact, adult explanations about how children come to master their language (including what exactly it is that children master!) are marked by confusion and debate. Even so, much has been learned from the study of children's language behavior. The importance of language within the broader context of human development is beyond question. Most activities that occur in daily life require language communication of one sort or another. There is little reason to doubt that communication skill is a significant factor in one's cognitive, emotional, and social dealings with others. Also, the role of language in almost all forms of learning can hardly be overemphasized. For example, learning self-governance, the exercise of foresight, the ability to profit from experience, and complex memory functions all depend heavily on language.

In this chapter we examine selected aspects of language development, including some influences on such development. We begin with some necessary definitions and conceptual distinctions about the formal study of language. Developmental trends in language and the relationship of parenting and school practices to language behavior are then discussed. We conclude with a brief explanation of two major issues important for the study of language: the rationalist–empiricist debate and the controversy about the relationship between language and thought.

CONCEPTUAL DISTINCTIONS FOR LANGUAGE DEVELOPMENT

Strictly defined, human language is a learned code or system of symbols (spoken or written) that is used for purposes of *verbal* communication (Kleffner, 1973). Human beings, of course, do not limit their communication to verbal behavior. They also communicate nonverbally, for example, with gestures or "body language." Thus we can think more broadly about human language as a *coordinated system* of verbal and gestural communication. Language *development* refers to the increasing differentiation and complexity of this communication system over time. The formal study of language explores the sequence, rate, and factors that may affect language acquisition from infancy onward throughout life.

To this general definition three important distinctions about language should be added.

First, as implied in our introductory passage, a distinction can be made between language and speech. Language is generally viewed as a complex system of grammatical and semantic properties; speech refers to actual utterances. Language and speech are closely related, but they should not be considered the same, for reasons that will become apparent below.

A second related distinction can be made between *receptive* (understanding) and *expressive* (producing) language. The ability of children to understand and act on the language communications they *receive* is not equivalent to the language communications they are able to *express.* For example, a 3-year-old child may be able to follow a simple story line and give every indication that he or she understands generally what is going on; yet the same child may be unable to repeat the story events clearly, in sequence, and with the constructions used in it. At any given point after infancy, children are usually able to understand words and sentence forms that they have not yet incorporated into their own expressive repertoire. Adults can be easily deceived about children's language development if their expressive language is taken as the sole indication of competence with words and sentences.

Similarly, as indicated in Chapter 2, the mere mouthing of words cannot be taken as evidence of conceptual understanding. Jimmy, a four-year-old, once waxed enthusiastic throughout our neighborhood about his mother's "delicate condition." A probing soon revealed that he had not the vaguest idea about the meaning of this "condition." Unfortunately for his mother, Jimmy inadvertently was a courier for a premature and public announcement of her pregnancy. Such "empty verbalisms" are important for adults to recognize, lest we misjudge the depth of meaning with which a child may speak, however fluent the utterance may be.

Third, a distinction between expressive language and the "self-communication" or "inner speech" aspect of language must be noted. This involves the use we make of language "inside the head," for example, in daydreaming, planning how to solve problems, or giving direction and organization to our movements. This aspect of language is important because during the early years learning becomes increasingly controlled by language, especially formal classroom learning. In fact, many early childhood education programs focus on the principle that language-skill development is a necessary part of the foundation for academic success. The "inner language" function is also well illustrated by reflective thinking during adolescence and beyond based on *formal operations* (see Chapter 8). More broadly, it calls our attention to the ambiguous language–thought relationship discussed below.

APPROACHES TO THE STUDY OF LANGUAGE DEVELOPMENT

Among the most popular approaches to the psychological study of language development have been the *normative-descriptive* and *correlational* approaches. By normative-descriptive, we mean study that charts language behaviors as they relate to age changes. Such charts include the age of onset of speech, age of first spoken word with meaning, vocabulary size at successive ages, and the number of words per sentence used by children as they grow older.

In contrast, the correlational approach describes relationships between various aspects of language behavior, both with themselves (vocabulary size and average sentence length, for example) and with other factors (vocabulary size of children correlated with that of their mothers; age of onset of speech with later measured intelligence; or level of language skills with social status among peers, for example).

These two approaches to the study of language development have been augmented by the study of factors associated with individual differences in language development. For example, generally faster rates of development during the early years have been observed for girls than for boys, children from smaller versus larger families, singletons as opposed to twins, and higher-social-class children compared to lower-social-class children (McCarthy, 1954). As a vast storehouse of descriptive information about this aspect of development began to take shape, it gradually became apparent that better ways to organize and interpret such information were needed. The storehouse rated high on factual data, but low on explanation and analysis.

A broader range of approaches to the study of language has gradually appeared. Among the more promising for generating new insights into language development are those inclined toward *linguistics*. Psychologists have been particularly stimulated by the insights of linguist Noam Chomsky. Chomsky has argued persuasively that language is structured by a generative grammar that permits individuals to create and understand sentences they have never heard before.

Linguistics, according to Chomsky (1957; 1968) and others, is the study of the structure and content of language, including grammar, sound combinations, and meaning. Linguists studying child language will typically record a variety of language samples along with a description of the context in which the language occurs, and proceed to analyze these productions for underlying patterns (Dale, 1976). Linguists are largely limited to observed speech but subfields of linguistics have even more specialized interests. One is *biolinguistics*, the study of maturational factors (anatomical and physiological) that set the stage for language development (Lenneberg, 1967). A second is *psycholinguistics*, or the study of the relationship between language and the characteristics of the language user. Psycholinguistics also studies how individuals use their capacity for language acquisition and their knowledge of the language to understand and produce utterances (Menyuk, 1970). Most psycholinguists are interested in discovering the rules that govern language behavior and how these rules are developed. The third major subfield is *sociolinguistics*.

A relatively new field, sociolinguistics studies the language or dialect differences associated with ethnic, geographic, and social-class variables. Sociolinguists, to a greater extent than their biolinguist and psycholinguist peers, focus upon the social origins of linguistic codes, attitudes toward language, and social implications of language use (Gumperz & Hymes, 1972).

Within psychology, social learning theory has exerted much influence on the study of language. As emphasized in Chapter 2, social learning is basically concerned with conditions in the environment that affect development. This has led specifically to an examination of the role of imitation learning, stimulus and response generalization, and selective reinforcement in language acquisition. For example, it has been demonstrated that such nonlanguage users as autistic or mentally retarded children can be helped to talk, and that speech can be improved through a systematic application of reinforcement contingencies (Reynolds & Risley, 1968; Schiefelbusch, 1967). Such demonstrations do not necessarily say anything about normal language development, but many psychologists believe that reinforcement is an important influence on both the frequency and quality of expressive language.

Some Important Insights from Linguistic Studies

Collectively, the points of view explained above have provided us with many insights, most of which have had an impact in shaping both the formal study of language and current thinking about the social aspects of language behavior. However, before we proceed to discuss specifics about language development, five insights from various aspects of linguistic study should be mentioned (Dale, 1976; DiVesta, 1974;

Edmonds, 1976). First, students of language development now realize that children do not simply speak a "garbled version" of the adult language in their surroundings. Formerly, it was widely believed that children's language was essentially a form of adult language that was erroneous because of children's "handicaps" in memory span, attention, and thinking. Today, most authorities believe that children speak their own language with its unique structural characteristics and patterns. This language changes during the course of development, and the sequence of these changes has captured the interest of many scholars (particularly psycholinguists).

A second insight involves an analogy between the child and the linguist. A child's task of language acquisition has a direct parallel to a linguist's task of analyzing a language. Both must discover underlying rules for creative language production from a morass of utterances provided by people. One of the most striking things about language development in children is that they quickly become proficient in generating novel sentences to communicate their thoughts and feelings, sentences that have not been "learned" or even been heard before in that exact form. Through exposure to verbal stimulation from others, children apparently develop a rule system for grammar, sound, and measuring production. This is precisely the goal of linguists interested in the formal analysis of language. Most linguists assume that a code or set of rules which permit children to understand and speak their language can eventually be discovered. It is just one step further to the psycholinguistic goal of understanding the *processes* by which children inductively accomplish their own analysis of language.

Third, all human languages are structurally complex and no one language is structurally superior to any other (Williams, 1970). This is important because prejudice often manifests itself in the belief that one language, or one form of a language, is "better." We have observed adults, including teachers of young children, express a belief that if one speaks ghetto English or the dialect of *any* language, one is not as good a thinker or as cultured as if one speaks the formal "standard" language. Worse, we have seen non-English-speaking children actually punished for speaking their native, presumed inferior, language in schools that were intolerant of deviations from standard English. Even if all languages are roughly equivalent in the structural complexity, however, this does not mean that all speakers of a given language are equally proficient in their language comprehension and use. In other words, within any language community there are individual differences in language abilities.

This leads directly to a fourth important insight about language: the distinction between linguistic *competence* and linguistic *performance*. Linguistic competence refers to children's grasp of the abstract properties of language, including their knowledge about how to interpret and to generate language. Linguistic performance is the actual production of language—directly observable language communication. This distinction can be illustrated by a child, Jerry, who remarks on Saturday, "I go to school and see teacher," when referring to something that occurred Friday. If Jerry understands and knows how to discuss past experiences but neglects to use the past tense, his performance is at issue, not his competence. If, however, he is unable to translate verb tense from present to past to describe a previous experience, or otherwise indicates that he does not understand the difference, both performance and competence are at issue (Cazden, 1967). From this distinction it is clear that performance, but not competence, can be precisely measured or described; competence can only be inferred on the basis of performance (Kleffner, 1973).

Fifth, psychologists and psycholinguists place increasing significance upon the relationship between children's language and cognitive development. Children speak of what they know. What children know is, among other things, a function of their capacity for attention, perceptual ability, curiosity, and reasoning. And language becomes a means of symbolizing the meanings derived from experience. Thus the aspect of language most clearly linked to children's general cognitive development is *semantics*—knowledge needed to understand sentences and connect them with past experience (Dale, 1976). Semantics goes beyond word meaning as such to inquire how sentence meaning is determined both by word meaning and by how words are organized in sentence form (syntax). Consider, for example, the difference in meanings among the following sentences: (1) "The dog will bite you"; (2) "The dog may bite you"; (3) "The dog may bite, but not if handled gently"; and (4) "You may bite the dog." None of these sentences will have any meaning for a child with no experiential base for knowing about such things as dog, bite, and so on. But even with the pertinent experience there is a considerable difference between "will bite" and "may bite," with the latter introducing the element of probability. The third sentence contains an important qualifier with a concept of the negative (not) and a still further idea about "gentle handling." More dramatically, sentence (4), though composed of the same words as sentence (2), has a totally different meaning because of the reversed subject–verb relationship.

Our broader point concerns the extent to which children's semantic no-

tions are governed by their general cognitive development. Recent evidence suggests both a broad universality in stages of cognitive development (Chapter 8) and a predictable acquisition of semantic notions correlated with such stages (Ferguson & Slobin, 1973). The apparent inseparability of cognitive and language behavior, especially semantics, requires us to always be mindful of this relationship in interpreting or analyzing children's language behavior. We emphasize this point because of strong evidence that children's word and sentence meanings are not always consistent or in conformity with adult meanings. For example, children ages 3 or 4 may commonly take *less* to mean the same thing as *more* and interpret *after* to mean *before* (Clark, 1971; Palermo, 1974). These meanings are eventually clarified. Unaware of such tendencies, however, adults may too easily jump to unwarranted conclusions about a child's intelligence or learning ability.

THE DEVELOPMENT OF LANGUAGE

With the above insights in mind, we now explore more deeply some developmental aspects of children's growing mastery of their language. These include children's skill in *articulating* or *pronouncing* the words they use, their understanding and use of *grammar*, and their comprehension and use of word *meanings*, or the semantic properties of their language. Together with a child's *rate* and *frequency* of language expression (how often and rapidly a child chooses to talk), the pronunciation, grammatical, and semantic features of expressive language make up a child's characteristic *communication style*. This style is associated with important social experiences in the home and school, raising again the topic of social influences on development.

Articulation

To dramatize the difference between "immature" and "mature" articulation, consider the following contrasts between the normal speech of a very young child and the adult forms:

Child's Utterance	Mature Version
"I eiling thoup"	"I am eating my soup"
"Shuwer poon, pease Daddy"	"(Give me a) sugar spoon, please. Daddy."
"Wash for the kwirls and bunny wabbits!"	"Watch for the squirrels and bunny rabbits"

These commonly observed "mispronunciations" are colorful testimony to the approximations through which children go en route to mature articulation. To become competent native-language speakers, children must learn to produce each of the sounds that are considered distinctive in that language. In English, for instance, there are some 44 sounds that people perceive as being significantly different from one another. The sound of *a* in "fat" is different from its sound in "fate." The proficient speaker of English must be able to utter both sounds. True enough, the sound of *a* in "fat" is far from uniform. If we had a dozen different people each utter the word "fat" several times, we would find a wide range of sounds for the letter *a*. But, in the English language, most of these differences are ignored, and this whole cluster of sounds is treated as a single unit or *phoneme*. Similarly, the English-speaking person will ignore the many different ways of pronouncing the *a* in "fate." This whole cluster of pronunciations will also be treated as a single phoneme. In other languages the differences that are ignored in English may be very important. In Chinese, for instance, the *a* uttered with a high pitch would have one effect, whereas the effect of the same *a* emitted in a lower pitch would be entirely different. In English these two sounds would belong to the same phoneme. In Chinese they would be different phonemes. Children begin to show progress in the task of being able to utter the separate phonemes that matter in their language at an early age. Some phonemes appear at the age of 2 months or so. These, of course, are not heard in formal conversation, but in the more primitive process of crying or complaining. These outbursts, however unlike language they may sound, may include as many as seven or eight different phonemes that play a part in the English language. In these seven or eight phonemes, the explosive consonants predominate. By 4 months infants will have given utterance to many vowel sounds. By the age of 8 months, or so, they play endlessly with these speech sounds, and in the next few months they will produce most of the sounds possible in speech, even some that may not be used in their native language.

It is one thing, of course, to emit speech sounds in the course of random babbling, and quite another thing to produce distinctive sounds in voluntary fashion as part of systematic speech. This comes later. In striving for deliberate or systematic use of language, the child probably first succeeds with the broad sound distinctions (Jakobson & Halle, 1956). There is most difference, for instance, between vowels as a group and consonants as a group, and this distinction is achieved fairly soon. Among the consonants, the most clear-cut differences are probably found between the "stop" consonants (*p* or *t*), on the one hand, and "nonstop" consonants (*m* or *f*), on the other. This distinction is often the next achievement. At this state, however, the child may still confuse a "stop" that is "voiced" (*b*), on the one hand, and a "stop" that is not "voiced" (*p*), on the other. Success with this more difficult discrimination will come later.

In sum, articulation development includes learning three interrelated tasks: (1) the contrasting speech sounds of one's language; (2) how to produce these sounds; and (3) the rules of sound usage. We use the term articulation without differentiating the complexities of these various tasks, partly because the processes by which they develop are poorly understood. There does appear to be a system of rule governance at work as children form their speech sounds. To date, however, no agreement has been reached about the contribution of learning theory (for example, selective reinforcement and modeling) and genetic factors to this process (Dale, 1976).

However, it is obvious that complete articulation skills development requires a healthy vocal apparatus and facility in coordinating the various tools for speech production (for example, the tongue and lower jaw). *Auditory discrimination,* or the ability to tell the difference between sounds, is also an important element in such development. For example, it is necessary for children to discriminate classes of sound (phonemes) that are paralleled by different meanings, as in the case of "pin" and "tin" or "lake" and "rake" (Templin, 1967). Such a skill begins to develop very early in life. At 1–5 months of age, for example, infants seem differentially sensitive to speech and are often able to discriminate speech from other sounds, and can distinguish contrasting speech sounds (Trehub, 1973). Sound imitation and simple word production—other important developments during later infancy—provide still another portion of the foundation for progress in articulation.

Some Implications of Articulation Development

Several features of articulation development are important for parents and teachers. The receptive ability of speech sound discrimination, as with that for grammar, develops ahead of speech sound production. For instance, children generally recognize correctly articulated sounds even though they may not be able to produce the sounds themselves. This is illustrated by the following exchange between Jeff, a 2 1/2-year-old, and his baby-sitter:

Jeff:	"Les play idensee!"
Baby-sitter:	"Play what?"
Jeff:	"Idensee"
Baby-sitter:	"Idensee?"
Jeff:	"No! Idensee!"
Baby-sitter:	"Hide and seek?"
Jeff:	"Yah! Idensee!"

Misarticulation among children in the late preschool years is not necessarily a cause for alarm. Young children often have difficulty with various sounds, and substitute one for another, as in *"wabbit"* for *rabbit,* or *"soos"* for *shoes.* Difficult consonant blends such as *st, str, dr,* and *fl* are often among the last to be mastered. Pronunciation difficulties with these and other sounds may persist until age 7 or 8.

A related point concerns the mild stuttering frequently observed among children between the ages of 3 and 4. Stuttering at this time is not usually a danger signal. It is typically a "phasic" problem (if, indeed, one chooses to call it a "problem" at all). Stuttering during the later preschool years apparently reflects a wide gap between what children are able to understand and what they want to talk about. They may not yet have the words under their command for satisfactory self-expression. Excitement brought about by new experiences may also affect a child's speech at this time. Thus, a 3- or 4-year-old at the circus may stutter and stammer for some time before he or she is able to communicate intelligibly any thoughts about the lion tamer or the aerial performers.

Fortunately, most children's articulation difficulties indicate no serious pathology. More often, they reflect faulty speech habits or incomplete learning. By age 5, most children are speaking clearly, although they may still mispronounce some sounds. For the more severe problems, of course, referral to a speech specialist or a medical expert is advisable.

There is an interesting longitudinal study about diagnosing children's articulation difficulties early in their school experience in order to make decisions about special services (Van Riper, 1966). Nearly 300 first-grade pupils were identified as having articulation difficulties of one kind or another. These children were given a specially constructed diagnostic test that asked them to repeat words and syllables illustrating typical articulation problems (such as *zipper*, tee*th*, *matches*, *jar*, *spider*, *tree*, *puhtuh-kuh*, *lalala*). They were also required to repeat short sentences and produce individual letter sounds. As the children entered third grade two years later, they were again tested with this phonetic skills inventory. Samples of their spontaneous speech were also taken. Together, these data were used to determine their articulation status at age 8.

This longitudinal investigation indicated that the earlier predictive test of articulation ability could discriminate among children who do and do not eliminate their articulation problems after one or two years without speech therapy. Specifically, 25 percent of the misarticulating first-grade children were error-free by the second grade, and 47 percent were error-free by the start of the third grade. In short, nearly one-half of the children initially identified for speech therapy by language specialists had spontaneously mastered normal articulation within two years. Moreover, it was discovered that the most effective predictors of self-mastery in articulation were the tested articulation skills themselves (versus motor skills, phonetic discrimination ability, auditory memory span, and the like). In other words, this study indicates that the best predictors of articulation mastery are to be found in speech itself.

Grammatical Development

Grammar is a complex system of rules for organizing sentence and word form. The internal structures and forms for sentence or phrase construction are known as *syntax*; the internal structures and forms for words are known as *morphology*. To illustrate, consider this sentence: "Mary bought ripe cherries." Syntactically, this is a simple declarative sentence, including a subject noun (Mary), a verb (bought), and a predicate noun (cherries), which is modified by an adjective (ripe). Morphologically *Mary* is a proper noun (a given name), *bought* is the past tense of *buy*, and *cherries* is the plural of *cherry*.

Compare this with the syntactic and morphological complexity of, "Not understanding her mother's order, Mary had bought cherries instead of bananas, all the while planning how she would spend the money so saved the next time she went to the toy store." Very young children grasp both sentences amazingly well. Children develop and use this complex rule system with impressive facility. The sequence of its acquisition shows characteristics that clearly differentiate "early" from "mature" language production. For example, compare the following common expressions of infants and preschool children with their mature adult versions:

Child's Utterance	*Mature Version*
(a) "Allgone cookie."	"The cookie is all gone."
(b) "That a nice kitty was."	"That was a nice kitty."
(c) "I'm are here, Daddy!"	"I am here, Daddy!"
(d) "Lookit mine feets in the water!"	"Look at my feet in the water!"

The child's utterance examples represent a mix of normal grammatical construction related to sentence and word form. Examples (a) and (b) involve sentence form (syntax), while examples (c) and (d) involve word form (morphology). By adult standards these utterances represent grammatical "errors," but such constructions are normal and typical of the young child's system of expressive language.

Perhaps the most impressive feature of grammatical language development is the rapidity with which children incorporate grammatical rules into their language systems during the early years of life. Generally speaking, a child's grammatical development is well advanced by school age and closely resembles full adult form by the middle elementary grades. With some exceptions, advances in the control of syntax are more apparent in writing than in speaking for children in the higher grades (grade five and beyond) (O'Donnell, Griffin, & Norris, 1967). Yet recent evidence suggests that the complete story of syntactical development may not be told until early adolescence (DiVesta & Palermo, 1974). Older children (ages 9–12), for example, may experience comprehension difficulty with sentence constructions involving verbs such as *ask/tell/promise*, certain connectives (*because, but, although*) and even the tiny word *or*. However, it is during the preschool period that the most rapid acceleration of grammatical development occurs, both in comprehension and speech.

A Sequential View of Grammatical Development

This rapid acceleration of grammatical development can be described sequentially (Brown, 1973; McNeil, 1970). A broad and general description takes the form of major periods, the first marked by the onset of one-word utterances around 1 year. These one-word utter-ances constitute *holophrastic* speech because a single word is taken to infer more complete phrases or meanings. For example, 1-year-olds may say "Dink" ("drink") to mean a number of things—their act of drinking, their desire for a drink, or their reference to someone else's drinking. Awareness of the context in which such utterances occur is necessary to understand an infant's communication. Holophrastic utterances are typically related to sensory motor actions performed by infants or actions that they desire of other people or objects.

In general, two-word "sentences" begin to appear around age 1 1/2. For example, the child now will say "Baby drink," "Want drink," or "Doggie drink," to communicate needs or observations. This use of two- and three-word sentences marks the period of *telegraphic* speech, so called because utterances typically contain only the necessary nouns, verbs, and adjectives for communicating ideas. Gradually, function words such as prepositions, conjunctions, and articles (*up, to, on, in, an, the, and*) are added to form complete sentences. By age 4, most children demonstrate competence with fairly complex sentences, including the appropriate application of tenses (Clifton, 1970).

It is convenient, then, to think of this more mature level of development as the *sentence* period. In truth, this third period may be observed as early as age three when children's sentences are functionally complete, that is, contain a clear idea in sentence form even though they may be grammatically incomplete. An example is, "This one riding horse" (DiVesta, 1974). Thereafter, over the next few years, children will use all types of sentences. Sentence complexity is directly associated with age. Beyond age 5, increases in sentence complexity, variety, and length are common.

A more specific and somewhat more complicated description of sequential grammatical development is based upon increments in the average length of children's utterances in morphemes (Brown, 1973). Morphemes are the smallest meaningful elements of a language. They may be words, as in *hear*, but they also include units of language smaller than words. For example, the word *chairs* contains two such units, or morphemes—chair and the plural indicator *s*. The *s* cannot stand alone, but is an independent unit in the sense that it combines with many other words to affect meaning.

A series of stages has been postulated for grammatical development, each stage defined by *increases* in mean (average) length of utterance or *MLU* (Brown, 1973). Stage I in grammatical development is said to begin when children's MLU increases beyond 1.0 (a time when word or morpheme combinations initially occur) to a MLU of 2.0, when some utterances may include as many as 7 morphemes. Beyond Stage I, four successive stages have been identified, each defined by increases of .50 to the MLU.

To date, detail about the characteristics of speech progression is greatest for Stages I and II (Brown, 1973). As mentioned above, Stage I children produce sentences from one to seven morphemes long, generally restricted to two-term relations. Examples of such relations are the *nominative* ("That milk"), *possessive* ("Mommy milk"), and *locative* ("Ball floor" and "Go store"). Subsequently, expansions of two-term relations appear in spontaneous utterances (from "Hit ball" to "Hit Daddy ball"), as well as various three-term relations. These more complex relations typically involve statements constructed by references to *agent-action-object* ("Daddy drive car"), *agent-action-locative* ("Daddy drive store"), and *action-object-locative* ("Daddy car store").

Missing from Stage I speech, however, are such functional morphemes as prepositions, articles, and case endings.

(In this sense, Stage I speech is roughly synonymous with telegraphic speech.) These functional morphemes are not observed until Stage II, when MLU reaches 2.0–2.5. Thereafter, successively greater complexity of word order marks children's speech. For example, noun phrases, verb phrases, and complex adverbial clauses are evident by age 5. By this time, and throughout the early school years, word classes are subject to categorization rules: nouns become either singular or plural, verbs are transitive or intransitive, prepositions are categorized by time or place, and so on.

The specifics and nuances of syntactical development are described elsewhere (Cairns & Cairns, 1976; Dale, 1976; Wood, 1976). The important point is the remarkably ordered way in which syntactical development progresses. We repeat: syntactical acquisition among English-speaking children, including the accompanying semantic relations, is said to follow an invariant sequence, although the *rate* of development will vary among them (Brown, 1973). And, as with articulation development, no one knows exactly how this development occurs. Because children routinely construct novel sentences they have never before heard (for example, no adult says "Allgone horsie," or "Bobby winned us," but children commonly do), their native language syntactical development cannot be adequately explained strictly by imitation learning.

Perhaps more significantly, preliminary data from the study of sign-language development among deaf children indicate that their linguistic milestones are similar to those of hearing children (Dale, 1976). This is striking testimony to the generality and strength of children's language learning ability, an ability that apparently functions independently of sense modality. Such information also raises the question of exactly how language is acquired.

One of the most popular answers to this puzzling question is based upon the idea of a generalized "master plan" for language learning (McNeil, 1970). Children are thought to work out their rules for speech (or sign language) from simple to complex, according to some innate program for acting upon linguistic input. For deaf children, this program may provide a basis for the creation of an orderly language system, at least in the initial stages of development. For the normal course of language development, however, the idea of a "program" takes the explicit form of a hypothetical *language acquisition device* (LAD). Presumably, humans are somehow "wired" for LAD by their genetic makeup. LAD is said to be composed of certain assumed mechanisms, or innate capabilities for language processing. And LAD is active during an early critical period for native language learning. It is thought to enable children to scan, detect, sift out, and tie together pertinent features or properties of language and aspects of concrete experience related to them. A cycle of analysis and synthesis of language rules and learning experiences is thus created, eventually resulting in full language competence.

Not all agree with this interpretation. There is much debate about children's competencies in bringing structure to their language, and scholars persist in their attempts to make good sense out of the language development puzzle (Braine, 1976; Edmonds, 1976; Lieberman, 1973). LAD, of course, cannot be verified empirically; it is the product of reasoned inference. But, as we have indicated, such learning principles as imitation and reinforcement by themselves are inadequate to explain language acquisition. We therefore have little recourse but to live with considerable ambiguity about this acquisition process at least for the present.

We can feel secure, however, in concluding with four points about grammatical development. First, children's recognition of grammatically correct language forms generally occurs before they produce such forms on their own. This is important for distinguishing between language *competence* and language *performance,* as discussed in the introduction to this chapter.

Second, although children's ability to understand grammatically correct language forms generally precedes their spontaneous use of such forms, their ability to imitate complex grammatical contrasts often exceeds their understanding of them. For example, a young child may be perfectly able to imitate the sentences "My bonny lies over the ocean," and "The ocean lies over my bonny," yet may show no understanding of the profound difference in meaning between these two constructions.

Third, the application of sentence form rules (syntax) in expressive language generally precedes the application of word form rules (morphology), at least in English-speaking populations (Rebelsky, Starr, & Luria, 1967). For example, a child may say "two mouses" instead of "two mice," and almost everyone will understand; the child's meaning would be most unclear, however, if "mouses two" were said.

Fourth, despite commonalities in the sequential development of grammar, widespread individual differences in rate of grammatical development continue to be observed. For example, girls surpass boys in their rate of advancement in the use of complex grammatical structures (Koenigsknecht & Friedman, 1976). Social class differences in the spontaneous production, but not necessarily the comprehension, of advanced syntax are also reliably observed by school age (Bruck & Tucker, 1974). More obviously, children who are retarded in their general intellectual development usually give evidence of comparatively immature syntax and morphology in their expressive language (see Chapter 12). All told, children show both substantial regularity and significant variation in their grammatical development.

Vocabulary Development

Technically speaking, children's compilation of their "word dictionaries" is best described by the term previously introduced, *semantic development*. It includes the development of word meaning, the influence of meaning on syntax, and the relationship of meaning to action (McNeil, 1970). We use a less technical term, vocabulary development, to refer in the simplest way to major trends and some practical aspects of this phase of language. We do so because an increasingly familiar theme in the research literature about semantic development is that: "There is no single framework that covers all children, all word meanings, and all patterns of [such] development—semantic development is as varied as the concepts that language encodes" (Dale, 1976, p. 189).

It is generally agreed that by age 10 or 12 months, infants will normally respond to simple commands like "No," "Come here," and "Give," especially when such commands are accompanied by gestures. By the end of the first year of life, infants usually utter their first word with meaning. Vocabulary development then proceeds rather slowly until about 18 to 24 months, when a rapid acceleration in word acquisition begins. For example, while the recognition vocabulary (words children understand but may not use regularly in their own speech) of a typical 2-year-old contains about 300 words, the average first-grader knows thousands of words (McCarthy, 1954). As with grammatical development, the period of most dramatic vocabulary development typically occurs

between ages 18 and 36 months. In fact, some authorities (Lenneberg, 1967) refer to this period as the "naming explosion." Encouraging children to learn labels useful in describing their actions and objects in their environment is probably especially important during this period.

Vocabulary skills are important for children's general development. For instance, children who are adept at describing their needs, feelings, and experiences richly are likely to receive more positive environmental feedback than will their less verbal peers. Moreover, the range and complexity of one's vocabulary has long been considered a good, if not the best, single indicator of general intelligence (see Chapter 8). Although the process of vocabulary development is poorly understood, the growth and stimulation of vocabulary differs clearly from syntactical and articulation development in at least two basic ways.

First, while development in syntax and articulation is nearly complete by the primary grade years, vocabulary development continues throughout life. This includes some predictable variations, among the most notable being the special role of nonstandard language—slang or argot—among adolescents and youth who identify themselves with gangs or other "subcultural" interest groups. Slang vocabularies vary by age, across time, among group settings such as schools, and from one sex to another (Nelson & Rosenbaum, 1972). Notable examples include use of the words "bread" (for money), "short" (for car), "crib" (for place of residence), "joint" (for marijuana cigarette), and so on. Attempts to explain why adolescent argot is so widespread are speculative at best. One popular interpretation, however, holds that adolescent slang provides an identity distinct from adult culture, a means for transmitting values and norms, and an expression of dominant social attitudes (Lewis, 1963). Knowledge of "street" argot has even been strongly associated with such antisocial behavior as delinquency (Kulik, Sarbin, & Stein, 1971). More broadly, the existence of slang colorfully highlights the important social functions of language.

The second way vocabulary development differs from grammatical and articulation developments is that it seems more affected by informal and formal educational experiences. For parents and teachers, this means that thoughtful assistance may profitably be given to children to acquire new words and to sharpen the meaning of words they have already learned. Certainly the availability and quality of a child's language models (parents, older siblings, teachers) seem more important for vocabulary than, say, syntactical development. This importance can be illustrated in several ways. According to one study the best single indicator of preschool children's vocabulary is the vocabulary test score obtained by their mothers on an adult test (Stodolsky, 1965). Other important early aspects of vocabulary development include the extent to which: (1) children are rewarded responsively for their naming behavior and question asking ("What's that, Mommy?"); and (2) adults use verbal description to specify actions and events that occur in the child's presence ("This is the way we *brush* our teeth," "See the *kettle* on the *stove?*," The *water* in the *kettle* is *boiling* over!").

Rate of Talking

Still another important part of language behavior is the rate or frequency with which children express their thoughts and feelings, ask questions, and begin conversations with others (word fluency). This dimension is especially important for children who do not express themselves when it is appropriate or desirable for them to do so. At the extreme, one may encounter a nontalking or a mute child who, because of physical or emotional insult, is unable or unwilling to talk. We focus, however, on children, otherwise not handicapped, whose rate of talking is so low that it may interfere with normal progress in social development based on language interactions with others. In the absence of talking, it is often difficult for an interested adult to determine what a child may or may not have learned.

There are many possible reasons why children may not choose, or are unable, to speak or express themselves frequently. These reasons range from a sincere belief that what they have to say is unimportant to severe emotional disturbance. Causation, diagnosis, and remedial techniques are matters for specialized professionals. We focus on an aspect of the language environment associated with individual differences in talking rate that is directly under the control of adults concerned about such rates: positive reinforcement.

The discussion of positive reinforcement in Chapter 2 stressed the satisfying consequences for behavior that one wishes to maintain or increase in frequency. Thus, we are interested in the extent to which a child or a youth generally associates pleasant consequences with talking. Some pleasant consequences are "natural"—for example, most children like to hear themselves talk. A sort of esthetic pleasure is involved. Other consequences include the sense of self-importance that children may experience by using language to influence others. Adult recognition, acceptance, and praise of children's talking are also important. Perhaps the most effective and natural reinforcement is simply showing an interest in what children have to say.

Fortunately, there is ample evidence from the literature that positive reinforcement makes a difference in rate and frequency aspects of language behavior. For example, it has been demonstrated that both vocalization rate during infancy and continuous speech during early childhood are influenced by positive reinforcement (Rheingold, 1959; Salzinger, 1962). Psychologists also report a beneficial effect of reinforcement on verbal fluency, vocabulary usage, the nature of topics one discusses with others, and verbal meditation, or the "inner speech" that serves to coordinate motor behavior (Ervin-Tripp, 1966). Moreover, the reinforcing consequences of higher talking rates apparently "spill over" into other facets of a child's existence. For example a positive relationship between popularity with peers (social acceptance) and rate of talking in play interactions has been reported (Marshall, 1961).

While such information is encouraging, the influence of reinforcement on the quality of children's expressive language and on the adequacy with which they respond verbally to requests by others is by no means clear. Nor has the influence of reinforcement on sound production and grammatical development been demonstrated decisively (Ervin-Tripp, 1966). But striking results of carefully scheduled reinforcement upon frequency or rate increases in children's use of meaningful adjective-noun combinations and similar contentives, for example, have been reported (for example, Hart & Risley, 1968).

Nonverbal Communication

Early in this chapter we defined human language broadly as a coordinated system of verbal and gestural communication. Most of our discussion thus far has been about verbal production, or expressive language. But expressivity obviously is not confined to verbal output. Gestures, body position, facial movements, and eye contact are among the principal sources of nonverbal communication—cues that we send out to others to emphasize what is being said verbally, transmit a signal that cannot be formulated in words, or that may even conflict with what is verbalized. For many psychologists (for example, Beier & Gill, 1975), such communication also includes *paralinguistics*—the study of intonation in speech, or *how* something is said versus *what* is being said. Manner of speaking, including the volume and stress upon spoken words, can alter the meaning of one's verbal communications. For example, a criticism delivered harshly and with a frown will usually convey greater displeasure or anger than the same criticism voiced softly with raised eyebrows. In fact, young children, and even adolescents, may object less to the content of adult criticism than to the *way* in which adult criticism is communicated. On the other hand, the believability of expressions of love and approval can be altered by nonverbal cues, even to the point of communicating phoniness. And, of course, certain gestures (such as finger signs) often communicate ideas and feelings more effectively, and certainly more quickly, than well-articulated speech.

Unfortunately, little is known about the development of nonverbal language. This topic presents a wealth of research needs and opportunities. We can point to cross-cultural, sex, social class, racial, and ethnic differences in the extent to which and how people maintain eye contact while talking, posture themselves while speaking, attempt to touch others during communication, and so on (Wood, 1976). While the reasons for these differences are obscure, nonverbal language patterns contribute in important ways to any individual's general *communication style*. The characteristic manner in which we attempt to get our ideas across to others, relate to them socially, express our feelings, and describe our experiences can be thought of as a style of communication that may facilitate or impede our effectiveness in dealing with the social environment.

What little data are available indicate that the nonverbal aspects of communication style develop sequentially (Wood, 1976). From early studies of emotional development (Bridges, 1932), for example, it appears that body language becomes increasingly differentiated during infancy. Emotions are first expressed during early infancy by random, uncoordinated movements of the entire body. These movements soon become more patterned or rhythmic. As early as five or six months of age, expressions of affection, fear, and joy may be communicated by "making faces" and by such specific movements as poking and head turning. During the second year of life, body language extends to contact movements and includes touching, caressing, and hitting, all of which can serve as nonverbal communication, or as accents to primitive verbal expressions. By two years of age, children usually are capable of communicating a dozen or so different emotions through gestures and facial expressions (Wood, 1976).

Children by this age will also be using prosodic features of expressive language, that is, varying the pitch, volume, and tempo of speech. This is especially evident in their use of questions, exclamations, and negatives. During the third year of life, children's sentences begin to sound very much like adult prosodic forms. In contrast, their ability to identify emotions communicated vocally by others develops more slowly. Not until the late elementary years, for example, may children accurately process the prosodic aspects of sarcasm and joking,

or be able to resolve messages in which vocal prosody, content and body language are not "matched." Consider Tony, age 9, who accounts for his missing and overdue arithmetic paper by truthfully reporting its destruction by an 11-year-old playground bully. Tony's unsympathetic teacher, in response, smiles and says sarcastically, "That just breaks my heart!" In this example, the prosodic, semantic, and nonverbal aspects of the teacher's communication are contradictory. The subtle discrimination necessary for understanding such conflict messages may not be fully developed until about age 12 or thereafter (Bugenthal, 1970). This again illustrates the important relationship between cognitive and language development.

To summarize, five principal features of language development during infancy and childhood have been reviewed: articulation, syntax, vocabulary, talking rate, and nonverbal language. We emphasized major developmental trends in these areas. Although these areas were discussed separately, in fact they all interact in complex ways with each other and with other aspects of development, including the intellectual and academic (McCarthy, 1954). For example, children who do not demonstrate early satisfactory progress in reading are often also children whose linguistic behavior is marked by the absence of elaborated sentences, a high proportion of short sentences (three to four words), an absence of connectives, and redundancy in vocabulary. A strong interrelationship between (1) the length, elaboration, and complexity of children's speech units and (2) the accuracy of children's speech sounds has also been observed. Moreover, normal progress in vocabulary development and both oral and silent reading is less likely among children having functional articulation defects. Although the causal factors involved are not clear, such findings further illustrate *correlated development.* Table 7.1 presents a summary of some major norma-

---

TABLE 7.1   Some normative highlights in the early development of expressive language

By 12 weeks	Much less crying than at 8 weeks; vowel-like cooing [squealing-gurgling sounds]
By 20 weeks	Consonant sounds, as well as vowel sounds, produced in cooing.
By 6 months	Cooing replaced by babbling [Resembles one-syllable utterances]
By 8 months	Continuous repetitions with distinct intonations become frequent, e.g., *mamamamama*
By 10 months	Sound-play, such as gurgling or bubble blowing, interspersed among utterances. Receptive comprehension becomes manifested through differential response to different words.
By 12 months	Single words produced.
By 18 months	Word repertoire of approximately 3 to 50. Little ability to join words into two-item phrases.
By 24 months	Word repertoire over 50; two-word phrases spontaneously formed.
By 30 months	Tremendous increase in vocabulary, with utterances typically at least two words; some three-, four-, and even five-word phrases.
By 3 years	Vocabulary of approximately 1000 or more words; about 80% of utterances are intelligible.
By 4 years	Language firmly established; differs little from adult form. What deviations occur are more often stylistic than grammatical.

Adapted from Lenneberg, 1967.

---

tive developments in expressive language.

MAJOR SOCIAL INFLUENCES

We have already acknowledged some ambiguity, if not ignorance, about the extent to which environmental factors affect the course of language development. Some authorities (such as Brown, 1973) claim that no compelling evidence yet exists to indicate that selective social pressures operate to bring children's speech into conformity with adult models. This claim is perhaps most applicable to syntactical development. It cannot be taken to mean, however, that parents or caregivers take their role as language models lightly. For example, recent data from the observation of specific mother–child verbal interactions clearly show that mothers actively teach all aspects of language, including grammar (Moerk, 1975). That is, mothers act as informal tutors of their children by introducing new language forms, reinforcing children's language skills, providing corrective feedback, and so on.

The widespread individual differences that exist in children's rate (as opposed to order or sequence) of language development and in their speech content, especially as children approach school age, prompt serious thought about the quality and impact of such informal tutoring. To most of us, it seems logical that children's overall language development depends to some extent on such things as the quality of their language models (parents, older siblings, teachers), amount of general language stimulation (conversation at mealtime, stories read to the child, extended conversations on walks), and the extent to which their language is effective for obtaining desired goals (reinforcement). Ample encouragement and opportunity for self-expression would seem also to make a difference, at least in the general attitude that children develop about their language communications with others. That these aspects may influence the style, if not structure, of language is further suggested by the work of sociolinguists.

Thus it can be instructive to at least consider influential aspects of the language environment under parental, caregiver, or teacher control by sampling freely from the correlational and experimental literature about home and school influences. These two sources of possible influence are by far the most often studied. Possible peer-model influence on young children's language acquisition has rarely been studied in the past. Some data suggest that vocabulary development, in particular, may be enhanced by children imitating their peer's language (Hamilton & Stewart, 1977). The research literature on peers and language learning, however, is minuscule. Nor can much be said at this time about any effect(s) of television and other media upon native-language development. Therefore, we shall concentrate mainly on parents and the schools.

Parental Influence

Most research about general parental influences on children's language, including that on parent–child interaction patterns, has involved mothers. Representative in both method and results is a longitudinal study of language acquisition among 1- and 2-year-old middle-class children of both sexes (Nelson, 1973). Intensive observation and analysis of the children's early language revealed several differences associated with their language environments. For example, some children progressed faster than others. In general, a faster rate occurred in homes where mothers were high in acceptance of their children's behavior

(verbal and nonverbal) and used nondirective management strategies. More outings, exposure to many adults, and relatively little television were other environmental factors associated with children's language progress. These children also differed in the functional aspects of their speech, possibly because of language emphasized by their mothers. Language for some children, for example, became more self-oriented, while for others it was largely object-oriented or referential. Referential speakers showed a more rapid increase in vocabulary size.

Such studies, while not the last word in documenting home influence or in sophisticated causal analysis, do sensitize us to subtle differences in language communication from home to home, even among similarly educated and economically advantaged parents. Furthermore, these studies tend to be more relevant to communication style, including extent of vocabulary, than to syntax (for another example, see Schacter et al., 1974). Even if children "work out" their own rules, however, the process can be facilitated by good modeling procedures or by the type of response adults make to children (Cazden, 1972). This raises the issue of language interaction techniques.

Language Interaction Techniques

The observation of parent–child communication has revealed several tactical aspects of language interaction. The precise effects of these tactics cannot be specified, but they seem to influence the quality of interaction in a general way. We refer to the parental use of expansions, extensions, occasional questions, and selective modeling.

Expansions and extensions. One tactic of language interaction is the adult use of expanding and extending a child's expressive language. On hearing a child's

Suzanne Szasz

Michael Weisbrot

Suzanne Szasz

Kenneth Karp

Michael Weisbrot

Michael Weisbrot

Photograph copyright © 1976 by Arthur Sirdofsky

Michael Weisbrot

telegraphic utterance, we might expand or extend his or her statement as follows.

Child's Utterance	Expansion (Adult Response)
(a) "Mommy wash"	"Mommy is washing the dishes."
(b) "Daddy no work"	"Daddy is not working now."

In both examples, the adult (parent) provides a more complete, grammatically correct version of the child's presumed ideas. For expansion, no modification or addition to the idea is made, nor is any new grammatical twist introduced.

In contrast, *extensions* are more likely to have the effect of maintaining a conversation with a child. The adult's contribution carries the presumed idea into a wider related context, and in so doing presents additional grammatical patterns. Examples are:

Child's Utterance	Extension (Adult Response)
(a) "Mommy wash"	Yes, I am washing the dishes now. But we can play again after the dishes are washed. What shall we play?"
(b) "Daddy no work"	Daddy is not working, but he is hungry and tired. Let's fix our dinner now."

We are not sure about the actual power of expansions and extensions to promote children's language development. However, both techniques are probably superior to such limited adult responses as the commonplace simple yes-or-no answer. Such techniques are also probably preferable to the practice of correcting children's language unnecessarily. Adults, especially teachers, often seem compelled to immediately label a young child's ungrammatical utterance as wrong, and then to correct it. This may discourage children from expressing themselves spontaneously and even provoke feelings of insecurity and incompetence. In fact, the pains taken by adults to "correct" children prematurely (before children have had sufficient opportunity to incorporate a new grammatical form) often have little, if any, constructive effect. Consider the following exchange between a 4-year-old girl and her nursery school teacher.

Child: "That man digged some hole."
Teacher: "No, say, 'That man *dug* some *holes*'!"
Child: "That man digged some hole."
(Four repetitions of this exchange)
Teacher: "Now listen *very* carefully! Say, 'That man dug some holes'!"
Child: "Okay! That man digged some holes."

Occasional questions. Still another kind of informal adult-child interaction or exchange, the use of occasional questions, may be of some help to very young children as they go about the discovery of grammatical rules. At least two kinds of occasional questions have been identified (Brown, Cazden, & Bellugi, 1968). One kind, the "say again" type, can be illustrated by example. Child: "I like canny!" Mother: "You like what?" Child: "Canny." Mother: "You like candy!" Child (nodding his head): "I like canny!" In this example, we see that the mother's questioning actually amounts to a request for the child to "say again" the main subject of his utterance. It is possible that such exchanges help the child to understand the relationship between grammatical forms used in declarative statements and those used in *wh*-questions (where, who, what, when). Moreover, such responses on the part of a parent are good indications to children that someone important to them is interested in what they say.

A second kind of occasional question is a means of both *prompting* a child to respond and *demonstrating* that differently worded *wh*-questions can be used for achieving the same purpose. These two contributions can also be illustrated by example. Mother: "Which cookie will you choose?" Child (no response). Mother: "You will choose which cookie?" Or, Mother: "Where should we hide it?" Child (no response). Mother: "We should hide it where?" Again the examples show how a parent continues to show interest in a child while modeling different grammatical forms and prompting a meaningful response.

Selective modeling. Closely related to the use of "natural interaction" techniques such as expansions, extensions, and occasional questions, are basic grammatical structures that may be modeled for children routinely, but in a planned way, by parents and other adults during the day as part of special informal educational activities. Selective modeling is an integral part of some contemporary approaches to early childhood education (Lavatelli, 1970), but the question of what grammatical structures should be emphasized is preeminent.

Research provides some extremely interesting clues to grammatical structures that are simultaneously important for good interpersonal communication and difficult for many children, especially those from ethnic backgrounds limiting their experience with formal English (Bellugi-Klima, 1969). Some examples of these important grammatical structures are provided in Table 7.2. It is perhaps most crucial that children understand the differences involved in these grammatical contrasts, but their ability to use them appropriately in expressive language is also important.

The constructions presented in Table 7.2 are only a few important grammatical forms many of us assume children

will understand. Careful observation reveals that young children often behave as though they do not comprehend such forms. Consequently, it may be helpful to model these forms selectively as needed or desired. To illustrate, a caregiver who says in the presence of the child, "I am picking up the toy(s)" and "I picked up the toy(s)" as the corresponding actions are performed is modeling the forms in (b) and (g) of Table 7.2. By pointing or verbal description, this caregiver can also check on the child's ability to distinguish between pictures that show objects and events. Suitable for this purpose, for example, are items such as the mother–baby situation in (a), brother–sister in (c), footwear and nonfootwear in (d), or similar occurrences. There are countless opportunities for such informal interactions in the normal course of a child's day.

Thus, parent- or caregiver–child interactions as a flow of verbal communication can embody a number of informal "language-teaching" devices: imitation through expansion, extensions, occasional questions, and modeled interrogations. From observing mother–child interactions, we have learned that mothers apparently teach increasingly complex extensions and modeled constructions as their children grow older (Reichle, Longhurst, & Stepanich, 1976). Other more formal and intentional tactics can also be observed in many families—question and answer games, playing out nursery rhymes, structuring language concepts through the use of picture books, and so on (Moerk, 1972). Parental skill in language communication is not uniform across families. In turn, the parent-skill variable, and other general contextual factors commonly associated with social-class differences, are correlated with children's language proficiency (Milgram, Shore, & Malasky, 1971; Jones, 1972; Bruck & Tucker,

TABLE 7.2   Some Important Grammatical Contrasts for Early Language Development

(a) Basic noun-verb relationships, such as in active and passive sentences.

(Active)

The mother kisses the baby.
The baby kisses the mother.

(Passive)

The baby is kissed by the mother.
The mother is kissed by the baby.

(b) Singular and plural forms.

(Singular)

"Pick up the toy."
"The dog runs."
"The block is wooden."
"This is a shovel."

(Plural)

"Pick up the toys."
"The dogs run."
"The blocks are wooden."
"These are shovels."

(c) Possessives.

(Positive form)

"This is the brother's sister."
"This is the sister's brother."

(Negative form)

"This is not the brother's sister."
"This is not the sister's brother."

(d) Affirmative and negative statements and questions.

(Affirmative)

"This dog has a collar."
"What can you wear on your feet?"

(Negative)

"This dog doesn't have a collar."
"What can't you wear on your feet?"

(e) Adjective-noun relationships with prepositions involved.

"Find a green car in the red box."
"Find a red car in the green box."
"Put the little triangle under the big tray."
"Put the big triangle under the little tray."

(Other important prepositions include
"over," "next," "behind," "on," "above," "below," and the like.)

(f) Prefix and multiple negation.

(Prefix)

"Which shoe is untied?"
"The children are unhappy."

(Multiple negation)

"Which shoe is *not* untied?"
"The children are *not* unhappy."

(g) Various embedded sentences (Two or more ideas in the same sentence)

"A boy jumps and another boy climbs."
"The dog sees the cat running."
"The girl who is sitting there laughs."
"Mother does her sweeping with a broom."

TABLE 7.2   (cont.)

(h) Use of tense

(Present)

"The ice cream is melting."
"Johnny is crawling."

(Past)

"The ice cream melted."
"Johnny has crawled over the chair."

(Future)

"The ice cream will melt."
"Johnny will crawl over the chair."

Adapted from Bellugi-Klima, 1969, and Lavatelli, 1970

1974). Social-class differences in nonverbal communication have also been reported (Schmidt & Hore, 1970).

These observations call specific attention to the development of *communication styles* within different language environments. Communication style, as noted earlier, refers to the characteristic way in which language is used to express thoughts and feelings, exchange ideas with others and relate socially to them, respond to questioning, describe experiences, clarify word meanings, and so on. Sociolinguists have learned that families can differ markedly in their communication styles, based in unknown proportions upon such variables as racial-ethnic identity, social-class status, and geographical residence. More often than not, these same variables are also associated with *dialect* differences. We consider first the more general notion of communication style and then examine dialect differences.

Communication Style

Children will show a typical progression in communication style from infantile speech toward the pattern used by the adults with whom they associate. The style of an 18-month Vermonter, for example, will not be greatly different from an 18-month Georgian. By age 6, however, if legend is accepted, the New England child may express himself chiefly in laconic phrases, whereas his Georgian cousin may use an elaborate, rhetorical flourish for the simplest greeting.

For students of language development, including teachers, the important question is not, "How far has this child progressed in approaching the adult model?" but "Which style has been adopted?" or "How many styles are in the repertoire?" In brief, it is the type of style or number of styles that is significant. For instance, many families use mainly one style of communication, often a *restricted* style (Bernstein, 1961). Allegedly, this restricted language consists largely of exclamations or incomplete sentences. These are often stereotyped repetitions of expressions popular in local small talk or in the current slang. In these exchanges, repetition and redundancy are the rule. "Those kids don't know where to stop." "Sure don't." "Can't figure it out." "Beats me." The same point may be made over and over again with only slight variations in phrasing. This restricted language serves fairly well to underscore action, or support a mood, but turns out to be awkward and inefficient when it must be used to convey precise information.

Other families, particularly those with middle-class backgrounds, may command at least two "languages." Within the family itself, or with intimates, there can be much use of a restricted language, or stereotyped phrases repeated over and over again. These provide acceptable social noise, or indicate a mood. On more formal occasions, however, for example, when strangers are present or when there is a need to convey precise or important information, these families switch to an elaborated language. This resembles the formal written language. Sentences tend to be complete and grammatical. There is relatively little repetition or redundancy. Like the written language, this spoken, elaborated language can stand on its own feet and convey meaning even without the help of action or gestures. Children who grow up in such homes thus learn two languages, and also learn when to use one and when to use the other. They know when words mean what they say in no-nonsense fashion, and they also know when they are mere pleasantries.

Children with only a restricted language at their command cannot easily switch from one style to another or readily move into the world where words can have serious meanings of their own, irrespective of the action being carried on. For them, "Yes" is chiefly something that goes with a smile and means "I like you!" or "You can't have it." Within the goes with a frown and means "Damn you! You can't have it." Within the classroom they may face problems whenever these familiar words no longer serve their accustomed, informal functions. In the grim business of conveying precise information, "Yes" may not be the answer that pleases. In this bewildering new world, this placating word may, unaccountably, give offense, and may lead a powerful adult to act in a critical and rejecting manner.

Families not only differ in the type of sentences constructed. They may differ also in the part that verbal language plays in the communication within the group. In some American homes, for example, the language of words often carries little significance. In this noisy world, the hunger for general auditory stimulation is met, and more than met. To survive at all, some of this overabundant noise must be tuned out or ignored while sounds that mean something must be noticed. The slowing down of the police car or the drunken lurch on the stairs may demand unquestioned attention. Within the home, however, the language of words can often safely be ignored. As children accept the invitation offered by the smile and the opened arms, they need not listen carefully to the words of endearment. In drawing back from the threatening gesture, it is not so important that they also listen to the verbal exclamation of anger. They may seldom be required to deal with words when more primitive stimuli are lacking. With this type of experience, the ghetto child may come to school as an accomplished master in disregarding the unique communicative function of words and symbols standing alone.

In the contrasting middle-class home, there may be less meaningless noise to be tuned out. In this often more subdued auditory environment, the sounds that do occur may receive eager attention. Quieter sounds are more ordered and fit more easily into a pattern. In such a world, moreover, language plays a unique and important part. In attending closely to different words that really count, the child is reinforced by many interesting and important experiences. Here language is not only a supportive or intensifying background for actions that would be self-sufficient in any case, but is often the substitute for the more primitive act or signal. Ignore it, and you miss out entirely. There is no temptation to tune it out, and there are many rewards for giving it a high priority. For children from this background, the classroom is simply one of the places to use the elaborated, formal language with which they are already familiar.

We must, of course, avoid generalizing too widely about possible social-class differences. While many studies have revealed social-class differences, many others have not (Higgins, 1976). The gross variable of social class may mask other more pertinent social processes that affect communication style. At issue is the individual child's language proficiencies regardless of such gross familial classifications as socioeconomic status.

The significance of communication style can be phrased in terms of a relative continuity or discontinuity from home to school and eventually to work that facilitates or interferes with learning and interpersonal communication (Getzels, 1974). Schools generally require the use of an elaborated code or style. Children unable to function comfortably and skillfully with such a code can be and often are severely handicapped for academic learning (Kirk & Hunt, 1975). Dialect differences, if they deviate markedly from the standard English form preferred in schools and most professional business operations, can also pose potential communication difficulties.

The overwhelming bulk of research about social influences and children's language development has centered upon parents or adults. This bias has come at the expense of our knowledge about direct peer influences. Little can be said about peer models and language development, particularly among very young children. There are some data to indicate that, in adult-organized group settings such as day care centers, young children do imitate the language of their peers with some frequency (Hamil-ton & Stewart, 1977). Children can also acquire new words rapidly from their playmates. In terms of relative influence, however, adults seem to carry the day by a substantial margin.

Dialect Differences

At any time beyond the first months of life, children will differ in several important aspects of language: verbal knowledge (words and grammar), fluency with words and ideas, oral speech ability, and overall communication style. They will also differ in their abstract reasoning ability involving the use of language (Carroll, 1964). But children and youth in American society also differ among themselves in dialect and native language (Cazden et al., 1971). For example, many children from rural New England, Appalachia, and parts of the south (Creole and black English) speak dialects with grammars that differ in striking ways from standard formal English grammar. Yet all these children may have achieved comparable levels of language competence in their respective dialects. The following examples illustrate some common differences in standard and nonstandard English forms. These examples represent a variety of grammatically different additions, deletions, and word combinations as compared to their "grammatically correct" standard English versions.

Standard Construction	Nonstandard Dialect
"We were sitting and talking."	"We was sittin', an' talkin'."
"Jeff needs those clothes."	"Jeff, he need them clothes."
"I went to the kitchen to get an orange."	"I done went to kitchen to get a orange."
"Lisa's brother lives upstairs."	"Lisa, she brother live upstairs."

"Do you have a match? I don't have any."

"Do you got a match? I don't got none."

In addition to dialects, many Americans speak some language other than English, and incorporate many of the rules of that language into their English. Examples include the English spoken by children and youth who come from Indian tribes, areas near French-speaking Quebec, and communities close to Spanish-speaking Mexico. Children of migrant workers often learn and speak a different language as their mother tongue, as do some children of immigrants who settle in our large cities.

The significance of group language differences is clear: if one's native dialect or language is accompanied by a limited command of standard English, academic tasks that require facility with the standard form may pose difficulties. It seems equally clear that the language of the American classroom *is* and will probably remain standard English. Unfortunately, there is a danger that language-based learning difficulties will be taken by teachers as indications of social or intellectual inferiority, language retardation, or a primitive linguistic system. Such a position is at best uninformed; at worst, it is destructive for children and youth. No language system, whether it be French, Spanish, Creole, or Black English, is superior to any other in terms of indicating more sophisticated thinking skills. A recognition of this, however, does not eliminate the basic problem of children or youth whose natural language is different from Standard English—learning to negotiate successfully in an educational environment and (as adults) in a society based on the standard English form. How best to solve this problem? No single answer to this question has yet gained acceptance in American society, but we can look briefly at contemporary school practices in search of reasoned alternatives.

The Schools and Language Development

Traditionally, the schools have been regarded as a place for formal activities to facilitate the skills of language comprehension and use, including the symbolic functions of reading and writing. Uniform procedures have been established for this purpose, generally based upon normative aspects of children's development. For example, reading "readiness" activities are prescribed for kindergarten. Formal reading instruction is usually begun during the first grade. By the end of the third grade children are generally expected to be sufficiently proficient with the language activities of classrooms, especially reading, to learn in an increasingly independent manner.

The harsh realities of experience, however, show us that not all children are equally "ready" for uniform language activities at school entry and beyond. Nor is their progress uniform once they embark upon early school learning (Stephens & Evans, 1973). In other words, there exist vast individual differences in language development, communication style, and preparedness for formal instruction even among children of the same chronological age. Consequently, many school activities may be unsuited for some of them. Not surprisingly, psychologists and educators differ in their beliefs about how best to conduct language training, especially for children who are "at risk" academically. Debate about the best approaches to language programming, including the teaching of reading, extends also to privileged children in good command of standard English (Chall, 1967). Space limitations prevent a full discourse about the language-reading relationship. Nor do we have space here to review in any detail the interesting problem of bilingual education, or teaching children who enter school speaking a non-English mother tongue. (For sources see DiVesta & Palermo, 1974; Schumack, 1975.) Instead, we focus briefly upon some major educational approaches to language training in the preschool and early school years when children's language is still undergoing important developmental changes and serves as a foundation upon which almost all subsequent school learning is built.

Some Major Approaches to Language Training in Early Childhood

It is reasonable to assume that the larger a child's vocabulary, the better—especially to the extent that word knowledge facilitates learning. In fact, this assumption has long been reflected in the enrichment practices of nursery schools and kindergartens, many of which are expressly designed to increase vocabulary. Vocabulary building is attempted through relatively unstructured activities such as "show and tell," field trips, and story-telling. But it can also be a fairly systematic strategy. An example is the famous Montessori three-period sequence for vocabulary development (Montessori, 1914). Period one, *naming*, is initiated by the adult, generally during a demonstration phase of learning. For example, children manipulating color chips may be shown (by pointing) which ones are green, blue, yellow, or red ("This is red," "This is blue."). During period two, the *recognition* period, children are required to respond to identity statements that take the form of a request. The teacher may say, for example, "Give me the red," or "Give me the blue." Subsequently, children enter phase three, the *pronunciation* period, and respond to such questions as "What

is this?" (caregiver pointing to a red or a blue chip). A basic purpose of this strategy is to help children become more precise in describing their environment and experiences.

However important vocabulary-building may be, word knowledge is only one aspect of language competence. Moreover, some argument exists over the limitations of vocabulary training per se as a way to foster language growth and thinking in children. In the past, most approaches to language improvement have involved mainly vocabulary enlargement, presumably because vocabulary is viewed as the principal unit of language. The question is whether "mere exposure to the basic unit [of language] will 'lubricate' the entire language system" (Blank & Solomon, 1968).

This question is especially important for children whose language may be undeveloped as a tool for structuring or guiding thought, a purpose perhaps ill-served by adding more words to a child's vocabulary. For example, simply teaching Johnny words like "apple, "orange," "grapefruit," "bean," "potato," and "parsley" is no guarantee that he will classify these objects into their appropriate categories (fruit, vegetable), further group them as all belonging to the class concept *food,* and then be able on command to name objects that are food but *not* fruits or vegetables. In other words, many authorities believe that language training should be designed specifically to help children develop their "inner speech" or their self-communicative language so that greater use of language in problem solving and logical thinking tasks is achieved. This belief is reflected in the use of specially designed tutorial activities and feedback strategies for working systematically with children on a one-to-one basis (Blank, 1974; Blank & Solomon, 1968).

A more radical approach is pattern

drill, a highly structured system for instructing children in small groups during which they are drilled on basic language patterns of syntax and semantic relations (DISTAR, 1972). Organized according to principles of behavior modification (Stolz, Weinckowski, & Brown, 1975), first the imitation, then a reinforcement of these language patterns, occur for children in a simple-to-complex sequence similar to the way in which Spanish or French is formally taught to adults. Thus, children who are considered "language deprived" are taught standard English *as a foreign language*. The tutorial approach is much more flexible or adaptable than patterned drill, but both directly emphasize the development of more abstract functions of language.

Educators who champion informal education often do not take kindly to highly structured, teacher-centered language training. For them, a more appropriate alternative is to emphasize "natural language learning" (Hughes, Wetzel, & Henderson, 1969). Two assumptions are made (Lavatelli, 1970): first, that children's normal biological capacity for language is best activated by general language stimulation and opportunities for language expression; and second, that while language impoverishment may contribute to children's *expressive* language handicaps, it does not retard their basic capacity for and *competence* with language. In short, language production difficulties can be overcome by exposure to appropriate syntactic structures.

Successful exposure requires several conditions. One is that language communications be directed toward children, to which they can respond in turn. Another is that teachers selectively model a variety of basic sentence structures in suitable circumstances so that children's language practice can be "raised" to increasingly higher levels. Thus, we can think of this informal, yet organized

method as a *language lift* approach to language education. A teacher's skilled use of questioning techniques with children is also important. Children must hear, process, and be helped to derive language rules or generalizations in a medium of natural conversation. These conversations must be two-way, with teachers consciously attempting to develop children's awareness of their language and opportunities for the satisfying practice of syntactical discoveries. From this it follows that teachers must be aware of themselves as modelers of language and in firm command of knowledge about the syntactic structure of the language being modeled.

General vocabulary training, tutorial methods, pattern drill, and the language lift approach are but four of many frameworks for planning and implementing language education for young children. Prepackaged language curricula based upon still other theoretical premises (such as the Peabody Language Development Kits) have come increasingly into use with both normal and retarded children. In general, proponents seek evidence, empirical or otherwise, to argue the merits of their preferred approaches. Perhaps the most basic generalization along these lines is that children often can be helped by instruction to become more skilled users of their language (Evans, 1975). Some children seem to advance in their development despite educators' attempts to influence the process or rate; other children seem not to respond positively to even the most concerted instructional efforts.

All things considered, language education is enormously complex and still in a relatively elementary stage of development. Above all, it cannot be well understood apart from the social context in which it occurs (Cazden, John, & Hymes, 1972). Readers interested in the role and effects of education on language development beyond the primary grades, including writing and foreign languages, can consult Blount (1973) and Birkmaier (1973).

One's attitude and general philosophy about the form and functions of language in classroom learning are crucial factors. Earlier, for example, we pointed to the issue of discontinuity in the communication style from home to school, particularly if the *dialect* deviated from standard English. At least three philosophical stances about this issue are possible. First, although the idea seems impractical in the long run, all formal schooling for children and youth could be conducted in their native dialect or language. This approach has its advantages but would be very expensive for schools already underfinanced. There is also the danger that American society would become even further fractionated by such an educational approach. An equally problematic approach would involve absolute conformity to the standard English model, including, if possible, the elimination of variant dialects or languages. This is now common practice in many, if not most, United States schools. The danger here, of course, is that rigid and intolerant insistence on standard formal English probably has done harm to countless children: immigrant children from non-English-speaking countries and Chicano, Appalachian, American-Indian, and poor black children, among others.

We prefer a third approach: helping all children and youth to use standard English competently when appropriate or necessary for their own welfare. This should include a policy of helping children learn to discriminate when and where the use of either native dialect or standard English is more or less functional. Nor does this exclude conducting the early years of school in the child's own dialect (or mother tongue), then shifting gradually to standard English.

This indicates greater acceptance of children "as they are" during the crucial first years of formal schooling and also represents an explicit commitment to the value of linguistic and cultural pluralism.

To date, no compelling evidence has been marshalled to document the effects, beneficial or otherwise, of bidialectical instruction for young school children. There is reason to believe that children whose natural dialect is nonstandard English are (or can be) equally competent in their receptive language for both the standard and nonstandard forms. For example, several studies (Quay, 1972; 1974) have revealed no significant differences in the intelligence test performance of black preschool and school-age children when the test was administered either in black or standard English dialect. Still other studies of children who speak black dialect (for example, Nolan, 1972) indicate that reading comprehension is not increased by providing materials in dialect form. We do not take such data to argue against the classroom use of spoken and written dialects, but the value of such practices for improving children's achievement has yet to be firmly substantiated by research evidence.

The story is different, however, for bilingual children. *Bilingualism* means the ability to comprehend and express two languages. Developmentally, one or another language usually, if not always, comes "first." Thus we can speak of first-language *dominance*. Children who are bilingual in Spanish and English, but whose dominant language is Spanish, perform better on intelligence measures administered in Spanish (Dale, 1976). We could expect the same finding to apply to other dominant–subordinate language combinations. It is but one short step to the position that bilingual children whose dominant language is other than English and, especially, those children who are monolingual with a non-English language, should receive school instruction appropriate to their language competencies. This means *bilingual education* (Paulston, 1974). Bilingual education requires the concurrent use of two languages of instruction for children in any part or all of the school curriculum (Andersson & Boyer, 1969). Its aims generally are twofold: to facilitate full literacy in two languages and to give a full appreciation of the cultures in which those languages have evolved. (This is sometimes referred to as bilingual-bicultural education.)

Impressive and constructive applications of bilingual education have been made, both in America and elsewhere (Lambert & Tucker, 1972; Nedler, 1973). Success in such education, however, seems to demand that educators and others reject the idea that language differences somehow fall along a continuum of inferior-to-superior language and thinking abilities. This implies a genuine respect for the cultural heritage of different language communities. We can note in passing that political forces have also recently come into play around the bilingual education issue. Pursuant to the Bilingual Education Act of 1975 and a whole series of federal and state court decisions and administrative guidelines, American public school districts benefitting from any federal financial support *must* provide bilingual education to pupils whose native language is not English and who are incapable of profiting from instruction in English. Otherwise, federal funding can be withdrawn.

TWO PERSISTENT ISSUES ABOUT LANGUAGE DEVELOPMENT

An issue can be defined as a matter of dispute, debate, or puzzlement, often accompanied by questions of value. As a crusty old sage from West Virginia mountain country once observed, "No matter how thin the pancake, it always has two sides." And so it is with issues in the study of language development. Space limits our discussion of such issues, but two are both significant and illustrative: the rationalist–empiricist debate and the dispute about the relationship of language and thought.

The Rationalist–Empiricist Debate

In Chapter 2, we explored the nature–nurture controversy and suggested that in various forms it would be encountered throughout this book. Its parallel for language development, the rationalist–empiricist debate (or nativist–environmentalist controversy), is summarized here.

At one end are the rationalists or nativists, who maintain that language development depends upon some important biological givens. These include certain innate structures or capacities, such as the concept of a sentence. Children are prepared by their biological makeup to develop language in a sequential fashion; prelinguistic and early linguistic behavior are determined primarily by maturation processes. For example, one spokesman for this position says: "Children everywhere begin [their language development] with the same initial hypothesis: Sentences consist of single words . . ." (McNeil, 1970, p. 2). The rationalist finds too many linguistic universals—commonalities in language development from culture to culture—to believe that experience has very much to do with native language development during the early years. Additionally, the rationalists make much of the rapid native language development among infants and preschool children, with a cessation of such development around puberty or about age 12 or 13 (except for vocabulary increase). Because this period of "maximum ability" to acquire language apparently tapers off dramatically about the time the normal brain reaches full weight, rationalists point to species-specific biological factors as critical determinants of language development (Lenneberg, 1967).

Obviously, *some* experience is necessary. A child must hear a language to speak it. But this only "activates" the child's innate capacity (Dale, 1976). Once activation has occurred, language is developed rapidly and rather effortlessly despite the enormous complexity of the task. Rationalists are most interested in marshalling evidence for this position, including identifying language universals. At the very least, they question the adequacy of concepts such as imitation and reinforcement for "explaining" basic language development (Chomsky, 1968). The rationalist position also prompts sophisticated research about the heritability of language abilities. In one study, for example, the language comprehension and syntactic skills of identical twins, fraternal twins, and siblings of identical twins were compared (Munsinger & Douglass, 1976). After adjusting the language measure scores appropriately for differences in the children's ages and measured intelligence, the researchers concluded that genetic factors account for up to 80 percent of language ability. If true, this obviously leaves little room for environmental factors to make much difference in language skill and development. More research is needed, of course, to confirm this estimate, as well as to validate the assumptions about language measurement and statistical analysis underlying this nature–nurture question in language study.

In contrast, environmentalists assume that experiential factors are powerful determinants of language development and that such factors, once thoroughly analyzed in terms of learning principles (Chapter 2), will account for much of the mystery surrounding language acquisition. The idea of innate linguistic structures is not taken as seriously as the notion that social forces shape the course of language development in much the same way that they shape other aspects of development. A species-unique highly specialized ability to learn language is challenged. Psychologists with a strong environmentalist bent have attempted to buttress this challenge, among other ways, by intriguing work in teaching language communication skills to chimpanzees (for example, Premack, 1972). It is easy to paint a portrait in extremes. The truth is that the conflict between nativists and environmentalists is more a matter of degree than of irreconcilable difference (Dale, 1976). Some points of convergence between the two positions even exist. For example, representatives of both groups agree that language is acquired in a social context, that individual and group differences in linguistic performance exist, and that certain methods of studying language development are more appropriate than others (Osser, 1970). But a dilemma remains. No one really knows the extent to which either point of view is more correct, and proponents of neither position can account satisfactorily for all aspects of language development.

Our pragmatic environmental orientation leads us to consider first how experiential factors are involved in language phenomena. Biology is fixed for every child, but the environment need not be. To the extent that early experience, even to the point of planned education, can facilitate language, our recommendation is to capitalize on learning. Yet as theoreticians we also commend the pursuit of understanding for the sake of understanding, and cannot close our eyes to either the rationalist or the environmentalist position.

The Language-Thought Dilemma

Based to some extent in the rationalist-empiricist distinction and certainly in the specifics of contemporary psychological theory, is the dilemma of the language–thought relationship. With few exceptions, psychologists agree that language plays a crucial role in thinking, but the exact contribution of language to thought is a matter of debate. Can one think without language? In what way does language control thought? Exactly how and for what purposes are language and thought associated? Our personal, subjective experience can validate certain links between language and cognition. Earlier in this chapter, for example, we referred to the "inner speech" or self-communication aspect of language. We "talk" to ourselves, guide many of our physical actions by some sort of language processing, and recall past events primarily with the use of words. We learn from verbal instruction and usually find that many such learnings can be better remembered if they are coded symbolically (for example, mnemonic devices). On the other hand, not all thinking requires language. For example, we may think in terms of both images (graphic art) and sounds and their relationships (music). Some people report that they think in terms of still other vivid sensory experiences, such as odors and colors.

Because verbal language may be more or less necessary for different kinds of thinking, psychologists have proposed different explanations of the language–thought relationship (McCandless & Trotter, 1977). It is convenient to refer to extremes in discussing these differences. One extreme view is based upon the linguistic-relativity hypothesis, which suggests that thought is shaped by the particular language through which it is processed (Whorf, 1956). That is, language shapes ideas and serves to guide mental behavior. Both the pattern and the direction of thought are functions of the linguistic structure of a given language. If one takes this view, language is obviously much more than simply a servant of communication. For example, if

a particular jungle people have a dozen or more words to describe subtle shades of green, they will be able to think more precisely about foliage color than, say, desert people who have only one or two words for green color differences.

Conversely, if these desert people whose experience with vegetation was limited were suddenly thrust into the deep jungle, they would likely begin to think carefully about foliage, with or without a suitable vocabulary. This brings us to the opposite extreme in viewing the language-thought relationship. According to Piaget (1970), cognitive processing does not depend upon language. Rather, thought exists independently of language, most obviously in the early years of life when cognitive development begins prior to the emergence of language. Nor is language considered a necessary medium for the development of more advanced logical thought operations, those mental mechanisms by which physical reality is ordered and classified (see Chapter 8). Instead, it is argued that language is structured by logic and serves primarily to express, not govern thought.

We must admit that verbal language does not seem to be a sufficient condition for thinking processes to emerge. This insufficiency is perhaps best illustrated by the ability of deaf children to think logically even though they have never heard spoken words (Furth, 1966). But are language and thought really independent? Even if they are, we cannot dismiss the importance of language as a tool for many kinds of cognitive activity. This conclusion is supported by recent brain research (McCandless & Trotter, 1977). It has become increasingly clear that verbal language abilities are mainly controlled in the brain's left hemisphere; spatial abilities, in contrast, are more controlled by the right hemisphere. Thus language may be variously important for thinking, depending upon the nature of the cognitions involved. Of course, both hemispheres and types of cognitions—verbal and spatial—are extremely important and should not be neglected.

We have deliberately couched the language–thought issue in its extremes. Most psychologists probably fall somewhere between these two extreme positions. The issue is much debated, however, and may deceive us if we fail to realize that language has multiple functions. Language is used not only to communicate, but also to reason, memorize, and symbolically represent concrete experience. And we must also distinguish between the *structural* and *functional* aspects of language: mastering the linguistic structure—a prime task of early childhood—is not the same as utilizing it efficiently (Dale, 1976). The functional use of language seems related to advances in cognitive development. Taken together, these ideas suggest that language and thought emerge early in life from relatively independent wellsprings of development. Thereafter, they become inextricably fused. Perhaps the real question, then, is how this occurs.

The language-thought dilemma is a classic case of the search for truth. Even a cursory overview of all pertinent evidence about this search far exceeds the scope of this discussion. We can, however, reflect upon some immediate practical implications for early language training and intellectual development.

If we lean toward the linguistic-relativity hypothesis, we might argue that systematic language training must be an integral if not a central feature of any attempt to improve children's intellectual functioning. This would be particularly true for children from impoverished backgrounds whose qualitative language development has been affected adversely. Various "compensatory" early-education programs based on such an argument have in fact been devised and implemented. One such program, men-

tioned earlier, focuses on refining the structural features of language to improve reasoning ability (Bereiter & Engelmann, 1966). Another involves the training of functional language; that is, ways in which existing language can be better used to promote improved abstract thought (Blank, 1974; Blank & Solomon, 1968).

On the other hand, those who lean toward the opposite end of the language-thought dilemma argue that formal didactic and tutorial language-training approaches are misguided, if not potentially harmful. They argue that there is no substitute for self-initiated and self-arranged experiences for developing reasoning ability. Children must be allowed to construct their own reality out of their sensory experience. During this period, language may gradually be introduced as means to abstract such experience, but not to determine thought.

We caution against the either–or trap implicit in such discussions. Advocates of contrasting persuasions are usually able to provide some kind of support for their arguments. Concerning the matter of early educational strategies, it is most accurate to say that the jury is still out. What evidence is available seems to indicate fairly strong support for organized, systematic approaches, to facilitate both language and intellectual skill development. However, we know of nothing to indicate incontrovertible support for either extreme view of the language–thought relationship. And the contribution of organized experience may well be more apparent in some aspects of intellectual behavior than in others, an idea further explored in the next chapter. Readers interested in deeper discussions of the language-thought relationship can consult Edmonds (1976) and Olson (1970).

Broadly speaking, language development refers to the increasingly complex elaboration of receptive (understanding) and expressive (production) language through time. Much psychological research describes age changes in language behavior and relationships between language production and demographic variables. The discipline known as linguistics has become a major influence in guiding the psychological study of language development. Drawing on data from the total range of language study, we have discussed several basic components of children's language development: grammar, pronunciation, vocabulary, and rate factors in talking. Though most psychologists limit their definition of language to a system of verbal communication, some now include paralinguistics and nonverbal communication in this system. Accordingly, we have touched upon these aspects to emphasize how they become coordinated with verbal language as children grow older.

Development in pronunciation skills, technically grouped under the concept *articulation,* consists of learning the speech sounds within one's native language, the way these sounds are produced, and the rules for their usage. Children's ability to recognize correctly articulated sounds generally precedes their ability to produce them; misarticulation of the more difficult consonant blends is common, even as late as the year children enter school, and does not necessarily indicate any pathology in speech production. Even so, it is important for language specialists in the school setting to be alert to exceptional cases that may warrant remediation. Normally, the full range of articulation skills is mastered by the middle childhood years.

Grammatical development involves the generation and application of rules for both sentence formation (syntax) and word form (morphology). Such development is very rapid during the early years. By school age most children comprehend and speak "adult" sentence and word forms; the developmental sequence involves a simple-to-complex progression of *holophrastic* (one-word) utterances about age 1, *telegraphic* speech (cryptic sentences void of prepositions, conjunctions, and other "fillers"), and, finally, elaborated speech consisting of full, grammatically correct *sentences.* Syntactic development generally precedes morphological development, with major advances in overall grammatical development af-

SUMMARY

ter the early school years occurring primarily in written language.

In general, the development of vocabulary—the child's word dictionary—proceeds slowly until about age 18–24 months, when a rapid acceleration in word acquisition begins and continues throughout the preschool years. Unlike grammatical and articulatory development, growth in vocabulary continues throughout life and presumably is influenced by educational experiences, including direct instruction, much more extensively than many other aspects of growth.

Rate factors in language (including the frequency with which a child expresses himself, asks questions, initiates conversations, and makes ample use of adjectives in describing objects and events) have captured the interest of behaviorists, who believe that reinforcement is a crucial variable in language development. Little is known, however, about the relevancy of reinforcement for an understanding of nonverbal communication. We have learned that by age 2 or so children are capable of communicating their basic emotions with body language. By age 3, children's expressive language is quite similar in prosody—variations in pitch, volume, and the tempo of speech—to the adult form.

In its broadest sense, communication style encompasses all dimensions of language development—grammar, pronunciation, vocabulary, rate factors, and nonverbal communication. Most research studies, however, have focused on the verbal aspects of communication style. One way of thinking about style in speech is *elaborative* (full, rich, grammatically formal, and descriptively varied) versus *restrictive* (often including nonstandard grammar, and more elliptical and stereotyped).

We have examined language development in relation to major social influences, notably parents and the school. There is much disagreement about the extent to which biological and social factors contribute to specific aspects of language development. One widely held opinion is that language is a function of "preprogramming" by genetic factors. Universality in certain sequential aspects of language is taken to support this idea. But given the widespread individual differences in the rate and quality of language development, environmental aspects cannot be dismissed. Total communication skill development seems strongly influenced by the nature and quality of children's language models. In this connection, several processes and techniques involved in native language acquisition have been identified. Strategies for language training in the schools have also been discussed, with attention to alternative views on how this may best be accomplished to benefit young children. In addition to the issue of valid strategies for sharpening children's native language skills, educators also face the problems of bidialectical and bilingual education. As yet there is little evidence to indicate any real value for bidialectical approaches. Bilingual education seems both more necessary and encouraging, considering the role of language in formal school learning.

Chapter 7 concluded with a discussion of two persistent issues or dilemmas in the study of language development. One, the nativist versus environmentalist (or rationalist versus empiricist) interpretation of language development, is akin to the broader nature–nurture controversy discussed in Chapter 2. For language, the dilemma concerns the degree to which one views language as affected more by biological than by experiential variables; the ultimate issue is perhaps the origin of language itself. A second related dilemma concerns the relationship of language to thought. Again, this dilemma involves arriving at a clear understanding of the degree to which a given language form will shape, or become shaped by, thought. The dilemma is more than academic, since it is associated with opposing schools of thought about the appropriate methods for language training in early childhood education programs.

REFERENCES

Andersson, T., & Boyer, M. *Bilingual schooling in the United States*. Austin, Texas: Southwest Educational Development Laboratory, 1969.

Baratz, J. C. Teaching reading in an urban Negro school system. In F. Williams (Ed.), *Language and poverty*. Chicago: Markham, 1970.

Beier, E., & Gill, J. D. *Non-verbal communication: A library cassette*. New York: Ziff-Davis, Tape No. 24, 1975.

Bellugi-Klima, U. *Evaluating the child's language competence*. Urbana, Ill.: National Laboratory on Early Childhood Education, 1969.

Bereiter, C., & Engelmann, S. *Teaching the disadvantaged child in the preschool*. Englewood Cliffs, N.J.: Prentice-Hall, 1966.

Bernstein, B. Social structure, language, and learning. *Educational Research,* 1961, *3,* 163–176.

Birkmaier, E. M. Research on teaching foreign languages. In R. M. W. Travers (Ed.), *Second handbook of research on teaching*. Skokie, Ill.: Rand McNally, 1973.

Blank, M. *Teaching learning in the preschool*. Columbus, Ohio: Merrill, 1974.

Blank, M., & Solomon, F. A tutorial language program to develop abstract thinking in socially disadvantaged preschool children. *Child Development,* 1968, *39,* 379–390.

Bloom, L. Language development review. In F. D. Horowitz (Ed.), *Review of child development research* (Vol. 4). Chicago: University of Chicago Press, 1975.

Blount, N. S. Research on teaching literature, language, and composition. In R. M. W. Travers (Ed.), *Second handbook of research on teaching*. Skokie, Ill.: Rand McNally, 1973.

Braine, M. D. S. Children's first word combinations, *Monographs of the Society for Research in Child Development,* 1976, *41,* Ser. No. 164.

Bridges, K. M. B. Emotional development in early infancy. *Child Development,* 1932, *3,* 324–341.

Brown, R. Development of the first language in the human species. *American Psychologist,* 1973, *28,* 97–106.

Brown, R., Cazden, C. B., & Bellugi, U. The child's grammar from I to III. In J. P. Hill (Ed.), *The 1967 Minnesota symposium on child psychology*. Minneapolis: University of Minnesota Press, 1968.

Bruck, M., & Tucker, G. R. Social class differences in the acquisition of school language. *Merrill-Palmer Quarterly,* 1974, *20,* 205–220.

Bugenthal, D. Perception of contradictory meanings conveyed by verbal and nonverbal channels. *Journal of Personality and Social Psychology,* 1970, *16,* 617–625.

Cairns, H. S., & Cairns, C. E. *Psycholinguistics: A cognitive view of language.* New York: Holt, Rinehart and Winston, 1976.

Carroll, J. B. *Language and thought.* Englewood Cliffs, N.J.: Prentice-Hall, 1964.

Cazden, C. B. On individual differences in language competence and performance. *Journal of Special Education,* 1967, *1,* 135–150.

Cazden, C. B. *Child language and education.* New York: Holt, Rinehart and Winston, 1972.

Casden, C. B. et al. Language development in day-care programs. In E. Grotberg (Ed.), *Young child in America.* Washington, D.C.: U.S. Government Printing Office, 1971.

Cazden, C. B., John, V. P., & Hymes, D. (Eds.), *Functions of language in the classroom.* New York: Teachers College Press, 1972.

Chall, J. *Learning to read: The great debate.* New York: McGraw-Hill, 1967.

Chomsky, N. *Syntactic structures.* The Hague, Holland: Mouton, 1957.

Chomsky, N. *Language and mind.* New York: Harcourt, 1968.

Clark, E. V. On the acquisition of the meaning of "before" and "after." *Journal of Verbal Learning and Verbal Behavior,* 1971, *10,* 266–275.

Clifton, C., Jr. Language acquisition. In T. D. Spencer & N. Kass (Eds.), *Perspectives in child psychology.* New York: McGraw-Hill, 1970.

Dale, P. S. *Language development: Structure and functions* (2nd ed.). New York: Holt, Rinehart and Winston, 1976.

DISTAR. Chicago: Science Research Associates, 1972.

DiVesta, F. J. *Language, learning, and cognitive processes.* Monterey, Calif.: Brooks/Cole, 1974.

DiVesta, F. J., & Palermo, D. S. Language development. In F. N. Kerlinger (Ed.), *Review of research in education* (vol. 2). Itasca, Ill.: Peacock, 1974.

Edmonds, M. H. New directions in theories of language acquisition. *Harvard Educational Review,* 1976, *46,* 175–198.

Ervin-Tripp, S. Language development. In L. W. Hoffman & M. L. Hoffman (Eds.), *Review of child development research* (vol. 2). New York: Russell Sage, 1966.

Evans, E. D. *Contemporary influences in early childhood education* (2nd ed.) New York: Holt, Rinehart and Winston, 1975.

Ferguson, C. A., & Slobin, D. I. *Studies of child language development.* New York: Holt, Rinehart and Winston, 1973.

Furth, H. *Thinking without language.* New York: Free Press, 1966.

Getzels, J. W. Socialization and education: A note on discontinuities. *Teachers College Record,* 1974, *76,* 218–225.

Gumperz, J. J., & Hymes, D. *Directions in sociolinguistics.* New York: Holt, Rinehart and Winston, 1972.

Hamilton, M. L., & Stewart, D. M. Peer models and language acquisition. *Merrill-Palmer Quarterly,* 1977, *23,* 45–55.

Hart, B. M., & Risley, T. R. Establishing use of descriptive adjectives in the spontaneous speech of disadvantaged preschool children. *Journal of Applied Behavior Analysis,* 1968, *1,* 109–120.

Higgins, E. T. Social class differences in verbal communicative accuracy: A question of which question? *Psychological Bulletin,* 1976, *83,* 695–714.

Hughes, M. R., Wetzel, R., & Henderson, R. *The Tucson early education model.* Tucson: University of Arizona, 1969.

Jakobson, R., & Halle, M. *Fundamentals of language.* The Hague: Mouton, 1956.

Jones, P. A. Home environment and the development of verbal ability. *Child Development,* 1972, *43,* 1081–1086.

Kirk, G. E., & Hunt, J. McV. Social class and preschool language skill: I. Introduction. *Genetic Psychology Monographs,* 1975, *91,* 281–298.

Kleffner, F. R. *Language disorders in children.* Indianapolis: Bobbs-Merrill, 1973.

Koenigsknecht, R., & Friedman, P. Syntax development in boys and girls. *Child Development,* 1976, *47,* 1109–1115.

Kulik, J., Sarbin, T., & Stein, K. Language, socialization, and delinquency. *Developmental Psychology,* 1971, *4,* 434–439.

Labov, W. The logic of nonstandard English. In F. Williams (Ed.), *Language and poverty.* Chicago: Markham, 1970.

Lambert, W. E., & Tucker, G. R. *Bilingual education of children: The St. Lambert experiment.* Rowley, Mass.: Newbury House, 1972.

Lavatelli, C. S. *A Piaget-oriented approach to early education.* Boston: American Science and Engineering, 1970.

Lenneberg, E. H. *Biological foundations of language.* New York: Wiley, 1967.

Lewis, M. *Language, thought, and personality in infancy and childhood.* New York: Basic Books, 1963.

Lieberman, P. On the evolution of language: A unified view. *Cognition,* 1973, *2,* 59–94.

McCandless, B. R., & Trotter, R. *Children: Behavior and development* (3rd ed.). New York: Holt, Rinehart and Winston, 1977.

McCarthy, D. Language development in children. In L. Carmichael (Ed.), *Manual of child psychology* (2nd ed.. New York: Wiley, 1954.

McNeil, D. The development of language. In P. H. Mussen (Ed.), *Carmichael's manual of child psychology* (vol. 1) (3rd ed.). New York: Wiley, 1970.

Marshall, H. R. Relations between home experiences and children's use of language in play interactions with peers. *Psychological Monographs,* 1961, *75,* No. 5.

Menyuk, P. Language theories and educational practices. In F. Williams (Ed.), *Language and poverty.* Chicago: Markham, 1970.

Milgram, N. A., Shore, M. F., & Malasky, C. Linguistic and thematic variables in recall of a story by disadvantaged children. *Child Development,* 1971, *42,* 637–640.

Moerk, E. Principles of interaction in language learning. *Merrill-Palmer Quarterly,* 1972, *18,* 229–257.

Moerk, E. L. Processes of language teaching and training in the interactions of mother-child dyads. *Child Development,* 1975, *47,* 1064–1078.

Montessori, M. *Dr. Montessori's own handbook.* New York: Stokes, 1914.

Munsinger, H., & Douglass, II, A. The syntactic abilities of identical twins, fraternal twins, and their siblings. *Child Development,* 1976, *47,* 40–50.

Nedler, S. *A bilingual early childhood program.* Austin, Texas: Southwest Educational Development Laboratory, 1973.

Nelson, E., & Rosenbaum, E. Language patterns within the youth subculture: Development of slang vocabularies. *Merrill-Palmer Quarterly,* 1972, *18,* 273–285.

Nelson, K. Structure and strategy in learning to talk. *Monographs of the Society for Research in Child Development,* 1973, *38,* Serial No. 149.

Nolan, P. S. Reading nonstandard dialect materials: A study at grades two and four. *Child Development,* 1972, *43,* 1092–1097.

O'Donnell, R. C., Griffin, W. J., & Norris, R. C. *Syntax of kindergarten and elementary school children: A transformational analysis.* Urbana, Ill.: National Council for Teachers of English, English Research Report No. 8, 1967.

Olson, D. R. Language and thought: Aspects of a cognitive theory of semantics. *Psychological Review,* 1970, *77,* 257–273.

Osser, H. Biological and social factors in language development. In F. Williams (Ed.), *Language and poverty.* Chicago: Markham, 1970.

Palermo, D. S. Still more about the comprehension of "less." *Developmental Psychology,* 1974, *10,* 827–829.

Paulston, C. B. *Implications of language learning theory for language planning: Concerns in bilingual education. (Papers in Applied Linguistics, Bilingual Education Series: I.)* Washington, D.C.: Center for Applied Linguistics, 1974.

Piaget, J. Piaget's theory. In P. H. Mussen (Ed.), *Carmichael's manual of child psychology (vol. 2)* (3rd ed.). New York: Wiley, 1970.

Premack, D. Teaching language to an ape. *Scientific American*, 1972, *227*, 92–99.

Quay, L. C. Negro dialect and Binet performance in severely disadvantaged black four-year-olds. *Child Development*, 1972, *43*, 245–250.

Quay, L. C. Language dialect, age, and intelligence-test performance in disadvantaged black children. *Child Development*, 1974, *45*, 463–468.

Rebelsky, F. G., Starr, R. H., Jr., & Luria, Z. Language development in the first four years. In Y. Brackbill (Ed.), *Infancy and early childhood*. New York: Free Press, 1967.

Reichle, J. E., Longhurst, T. M., & Stepanich, L. Verbal interaction in mother–child dyads. *Developmental Psychology*, 1976, *12*, 273–277.

Reynolds, N. J., & Risley, T. R. The role of social and material reinforcers in increasing talking of a disadvantaged preschool child. *Journal of Applied Behavior Analysis*, 1968, *1*, 253–262.

Rheingold, H. L. Social conditioning of vocalizations in the infant. *Journal of Comparative and Physiological Psychology*, 1959, *52*, 68–73.

Salzinger, S. Operant conditioning of continuous speech in young children. *Child Development*, 1962, *33*, 683–695.

Schacter, F. F., et. al. Everyday preschool interpersonal speech usage: Methodological, developmental, and sociolinguistic studies. *Monographs of the Society for Research in Child Development*, 1974, *39*, Serial No. 156.

Schiefelbusch, R. L. (Ed.) *Language and mental retardation*. New York: Holt, Rinehart and Winston, 1967.

Schmidt, W. H. O., & Hore, T. Some nonverbal aspects of communication between mother and preschool child. *Child Development*, 1970, *41*, 889–896.

Schumack, S. (Ed.) Bilingual/bicultural education. In *Inequality in Education*, No. 19, Center for Law and Education, Harvard University, February, 1975.

Shatz, M., & Gelman, R. The development of communication skills: Modification in the speech of young children as a function of listener. *Monographs of the Society for Research in Child Development*, 1973, *88*, Serial No. 152.

Stephens, J. M., & Evans, E. D. *Development and classroom learning*. New York: Holt, Rinehart and Winston, 1973.

Stodolsky, S. *Maternal behavior and language and concept formation in Negro preschool children: An inquiry into process*. Unpublished Doctoral Dissertation, University of Chicago, 1965.

Stolz, S. B., Weinckowski, L. A., & Brown, B. S. Behavior modification: A perspective on critical issues. *American Psychologist*, 1975, *30*, 1027–1048.

Templin, M. C. Research on articulation development. In W. W. Hartup & N. L. Smothergill (Eds.), *The young child*. Washington, D.C.: National Association for the Education of Young Children, 1967,

Trehub, S. E. Infants' sensitivity to vowel and tonal contrasts. *Developmental Psychology*, 1973, *9*, 91–96.

Van Riper, C. *A predictive screening device for children with articulatory speech defects*. Washington, D.C.: U.S. Office of Education, Cooperative Research Report Project, No. 1538, 1966.

Whorf, B. L. *Language, thought, and reality*. New York: Wiley; and Cambridge, Mass.: MIT Press, 1956.

Williams, F. (Ed.) *Language and poverty*, Chicago: Markham, 1970.

Wood, B. S. *Children and communication: Verbal and nonverbal language development*. Englewood Cliffs, N.J.: Prentice-Hall, 1976.

chapter 8

Cognitive-intellectual development

Throughout this book we have empha-sized the point that all of us, as individual human beings, are significant factors in our own development. What we do and what we say determine much of how we are viewed and treated by others. The treatment we receive from others and the environmental consequences of our actions in turn influence our future behavior.

An extremely important aspect of this interaction pattern is how we come to know, comprehend, and strive for mas-tery over the environment. Much of this knowing, comprehending, and striving can be summarized by the term *in-telligence*. Recall, for example, the life sketches of Lyle, Juan, and Rebecca pre-sented in Chapter 1. That each of them made satisfactory life adjustments and had unique individual accomplishments is at least partial evidence of their general intelligence. All three demonstrated a level of competence important for adaptation to and even mastery of our increasingly complex social-technological environment. Whether they are equally intelligence. A third section describes there is anything about which psychologists agree, it is that human beings differ among themselves in intelligence, both at the general level and in how intelligence is manifest in behavior. The question of why or how these differences come to exist is much more hotly debated, as is the exact nature of intelligence itself.

Two of the four major sections in this chapter discuss different conceptual approaches to the psychological study of intelligence. A third section describes the major social factors that may influence intellectual development or performance. The fourth section explores two related, yet somewhat different, aspects of human cognitive functioning known as cognitive style and creativity. As a preliminary to all four sections, however, we must examine some definitions of intelligence and make explicit some general points about individual differences and cognitive essentials in intellectual development.

Some Definitions of Intelligence

Many different definitions of intelligence can be cited. They range from the "biologically inherited potentiality for the development of mental abilities" through "central mental operations for the processing of information" to the dryly operational "Intelligence is what intelligence tests measure (that is, a score on an intelligence test—the 'IQ')." Our preferred definition is that intelligence is learning aptitude, coupled with abstract thinking and problem-solv-

ing skills. We think about intelligence as both a means to gather and process information and the ability to use this information to solve the problems of life circumstances. Such problem solving means dealing successfully with the demands of our environment. It also takes the form of active efforts to exercise control over that environment—whether it be the bush country of Australia, the arctic tundra of Alaska, the steppes of Russia, or the sidewalks of New York.

We must admit at the outset that much dissatisfaction has been expressed about viewing intelligence as a general learning or problem-solving ability (Labouvie-Vief, 1976). Learning theorists, in particular, seek to achieve greater specificity about the concept of "ability" by studying learning processes thought to provide a basis for the development of various intellectual skills with which different children become more or less proficient. This kind of analysis appeared as early as the 1930s, when progressive increases in intellectual "capacity" were viewed as the accumulation of associative connections between stimulus–response (S–R) events (Estes, 1970). Greater or lesser "intelligence" was seen basically as differences in the quantity and variety of S–R connections available to children. More sophisticated analyses have since appeared, especially of intellectual processes and the hierarchic organization of successively more complex associative relationships (Gagné, 1968). But the basic idea has remained the same, the application of learning theory to account for mental development.

Work along these lines, while encouraging, has not yet advanced to a point where definitive statements about the relationship of learning processes to intellectual abilities can be made (Labouvie-Vief, 1976). Our general orientation to cognitive-intellectual development is based on the idea that intelligence is an integrated, generalized set of problem-solving abilities. Some children and youth can be considered more intelligent than others to the extent they solve more varied and more difficult problems more rapidly. In other words, intelligence is revealed in the accuracy, and often speed, with which persons react to a broad range of complex problem situations. Some of these problems may require the manipulation of physical objects, others the exercise of deductive logic, and still others the creation of something novel or original.

Eventually, most of us become somewhat specialized in the performance of intellectual activities—because of opportunity, motivation, and practice—even if we are roughly comparable in "general intelligence." Thus Roger, at age 29, is a highly productive architect who deals in a world of space configurations, building materials, and rules of structural design. Ann, age 36, is an enterprising salesperson whose clear knowledge of business principles and human behavior has made her a respected and financially comfortable sales director of a large American corporation. Frank, age 45, is a widely published writer of science fiction whose creative plots and literary style are crafted to the point of excellence. These individuals are diverse in their knowledge and preferred ways of thinking. Yet all perform at roughly the same level on a general measure of adult intelligence, that is, they seem about equal at solving mental problems which they do not ordinarily encounter in day-to-day living or have not been specifically "trained" to answer. Coming from similar home and school backgrounds, they apparently have profited in comparable ways from broad, general cultural experiences.

For these individuals, as for most of us, problem-solving ability extends far beyond that measured by tests. But such ability will normally have profound implications for the quality of developmental experience, including relationships with parents and peers, schooling, employment, and countless other aspects of human existence.

The Fact of Individual Differences

Though we can find a variety of life-styles represented at any one level of measured intelligence—low, average, or high—it is the idea of individual differences in intelligence that has intrigued psychologists since the earliest days of scientific study. Differences in intelligence appear as early as infancy, and increase in magnitude through childhood and adolescence. Among some of the more pronounced relationships between measured intelligence and other areas of development and behavior are age of talking, general language ability, memory, rate at which new concepts are learned, and general resourcefulness. Intelligence is also a determinant or source of individual differences for a broad range of behaviors, including such varied characteristics as sense of humor, leadership, popularity, fear, assertiveness, emotional maturity, and creativity (Ausubel & Sullivan, 1970; Brannigan, 1975; Dorman, 1973).

Until the last several decades many psychologists believed that intelligence was so heavily determined by hereditary factors that experience made little difference. One's intelligence quotient (IQ) was viewed as fixed at birth, something that would not change appreciably because of learning. Accordingly, the effects of early experience during infancy and preschool or, for that matter, during adolescence, were not considered very important in intellectual development. Today, most psychologists believe that experience plays a critical role in intellectual development.

Of course, we cannot dismiss the importance of genetics. The level and quality of intelligence are perhaps determined within broad limits by the structure of the nervous system. The human nervous system differs from the nervous system of the goldfinch or the white rat in the level of intelligent behavior it permits, for instance. In this sense, intelligence is "native ability" and "unfolds." And many psychologists continue their attempts to isolate the hereditary component of human intelligence. One psychologist, Arthur Jensen (1969), seems convinced that human intelligence is mostly inherited. He goes even further and suggests racial differences in the inheritance of intelligence. Among other things, doubters fault both Jensen's theory of intelligence and his interpretation of statistics used to determine its hereditary component. And the idea of racial differences, of course, is volatile, especially in societies valuing individual equality and human rights.

Whatever data and theory about human intelligence may some day prove correct, we must be prepared to accept them accordingly. For truth-seeking, basic research about the inheritance of intelligence is no less important than the study of social influences. We prefer in this chapter to strongly emphasize environmental factors in human intellectual development for two reasons. First, practically speaking, little or nothing can be done about influencing intellectual development through heredity. In other words, if intelligence is fixed by the genes, we cannot be very optimistic about increasing human intellectual power, assuming we value this objective. Second, we believe that intelligence develops as a function of the interaction of persons and their environments—very rich environments will nurture more intelligent people than will very poor environments. In this sense, intelligence can be viewed as "achievement," or as a "learned" constellation of skills and abilities. For students of human development, the important problem is how

cultural experience is translated into cognitive-intellectual behavior. In other words, the question is not *whether,* but *how* (Ausubel & Sullivan, 1970).

Cognitive Essentials in Intellectual Development

Normal cognitive-intellectual development presupposes an adequate system for receiving and processing information from the environment. First, children must be capable of *attention,* or "tuning in" to sensory information (visual, auditory, and tactile sensations). Attention can be thought of as having two phases (Reese & Lipsitt, 1970). Phase 1 is the *orientation reaction,* as if children are asking, "What is it?" An orientation reaction suggests alertness and vigilance; it is a stance or a behavior designed to help one identify something. Orientation reactions include such things as turning our eyes to the stimulus, or sniffing, or staying very still so as to "hear it again—or hear it better." These reactions have the effect of preparing us for additional stimulation and response, they comprise attention span. A logical definition of attention span is the range of stimuli our orientation reactions can encompass, either in number or time (such as remembering digits spoken slowly and monotonously). Phase 2 of attention is the scanning, or searching, or selective process that makes up attention when we pick out a specific stimulus to "study," when we are learning new things, doing abstract thinking, or solving problems.

However basic attention is for eventual problem solving, it cannot tell the whole story. We must also *perceive.* Perception differs from attention because when perceiving we go a step further to organize, interpret, and codify the raw sensory experience to which we attend. Perceptual skills, themselves learned, are essential for the learning that contributes to intellectual development. For example, learning the identity of such things as salt and sugar, gasoline and water, toothpaste and clay, and alarm clock and whistle depends upon one's ability to (1) perceive the basic qualities and (2) determine the differences and similarities between these substances and objects. Sensory attributes relevant to the learning of these identities include color, texture, odor and sound. Perceptual skills such as form perception and symbol recognition are also basic to many academic tasks, notably reading. The successful pursuit of artistic activities also requires the development of refined perceptual skills. Consider, for example, the subtle pitch, intensity, and rhythm matching by members of a choral ensemble, or the subtle shading of color hues and forms by a professional oil painter.

Finally, we must emphasize the importance of memory for any understanding of cognitive-intellectual development. Without memory, it would not be possible to profit from past experience. Through memory our experiences become more meaningful. We also recreate or reconstruct events and past learnings by using images and language, both verbal and nonverbal. It is convenient to think about memory processing in three stages (Kumar, 1972). First, data from the environment are attended to and perceived—they impact our *sensory register*. Depending upon the amount, type, and organization of data, a temporary storage mechanism—*short-term memory*—is activated. Again, depending upon the nature of the input and our manipulation of it, data may be committed to *long-term memory*. If so, a relatively permanent storage of information is achieved. From this store can be drawn information of value or utility for future learning and problem solving. Full discussions of attention, perception, and memory can easily require separate

chapters, if not complete books. Interested readers may consult pertinent references for details (e.g., Brown, 1975; Farnham-Diggory, 1972; Gibson, 1969; Reese & Lipsitt, 1970; Wright & Vlietstra, 1975).

Having introduced the cognitive-intellectual stream of development, we now proceed to an overview of two major bodies of thought about intelligence. The first focuses on the number of correct or incorrect responses that people of successive ages give in carefully controlled and specialized testing conditions. It establishes a numerical value for human intellectual abilities both across and within specific populations, often subdivided by gender, social class, and race. Along with classifying individual differences in intelligence, this approach has practical objectives—predicting school or job success, diagnosing limitations in mental functioning, measuring the impact of intellectual stimulation strategies, and the like. We refer to this approach as the *psychometric* tradition (Cliff, 1973).

Within psychometrics, a number of competing "theories" of intelligence have been constructed. Many seem less concerned with intellectual development than with the more basic nature or structure of intelligence. Some theories are based upon the idea of a general or unitary ability, others postulate two or more separate factors of intelligence, for example, verbal and psychomotor performance. At one extreme is a theory of 120 separate mental abilities, based upon combinations and permutations of intellectual processes, the content of thought, and the products of thought (behavior) (Guilford, 1967). We choose not to review these theories, which are available for detailed inspection elsewhere (Brody & Brody, 1976; Rohwer, Ammon, & Cramer, 1974). Instead, we take the psychometric perspective in general to illustrate developmental aspects of intelligence test performance. This requires a look at IQ variations across populations of children and youth and over time.

The second major body of thought about intelligence focuses on how persons come to organize and use their understanding of physical and social reality. It tries to identify the development of universal logical thought structures in the mind through a series of fixed or invariant stages (Piaget, 1970). Individual differences in intelligence are subordinate to common, unifying aspects of qualitative intellectual behavior at successive age levels. We call this the *cognitive-developmental* approach to intelligence. The essential difference between the two approaches is a matter of emphasis. The psychometric perspective envisions quantitative, linear intellectual growth; its focus is what and how much an individual knows. Qualitative changes in thought processes and organization of new mental structures are the substance of the cognitive-developmental position; its focus is how an individual thinks.

THE PSYCHOMETRIC APPROACH

American psychologists, influenced by their British and French mentors, adopted early the psychometric tradition for the study of intelligence and intellectual development. Information about human intellectual functioning has been derived from measures, usually tests, specifically constructed to describe individual differences in mental performance. In practice, any distinction between general intelligence and the measurements we call intelligence often becomes blurred. Thus, a test score, usually represented by the IQ (Intelligence Quotient), can too easily become synonymous with intelligence. No serious student of human intelligence will claim

that the IQ is a totally comprehensive summary of human intelligence. Thus we advise restricting ourselves to the term *measured* intelligence when discussing this psychometric approach.

The first step in this approach to intelligence must be to formulate test items, or tasks, thought to sample the unique mental functions that are basic to "intelligent" behavior across different content areas at various age levels. The bulk of such tasks involves the use of language and reasoning skills to solve certain kinds of problems that are presented verbally by an examiner, or in writing for the paper and pencil test. To assess mental functioning fairly among children and youth, test makers have attempted to take into account (or control) as much as possible extreme variations in the quality of past experience. By so doing, they hope to extract reasonably "pure" indicators of problem-solving ability. Control generally has been exercised by applying one or both of two principles (Thompson, 1961). The first is to build into a test a combination of relatively *novel* problems that are not tied directly to children's planned learning experiences, such as school, or for which children have not been specifically prepared. The second principle of test construction is that if acquired knowledge and understandings are to be measured, the items must be developed in light of general age-related learning opportunities that have been both ample and roughly equal for most children. Obviously, if the assumptions about learning experiences represented by these two principles cannot be met in any given testing situation, the test results may be distorted and produce inaccurate estimates of measured intelligence.

Types of Intelligence Tests

There are many different types of intelligence tests and many versions of each type. One authoritative source (Buros, 1965) reviews some 130 different intelligence tests or similar measures. These tests range from those designed for infants to those which give pause to the most superior and well-educated adult. Most favored are individual intelligence tests administered by a trained examiner. This type is essential to test infants and young children who cannot read. Once basic literacy is achieved, group-administered paper-and-pencil tests often are used. They can yield useful, but not always fair scores.

A typical test—individual or group—will include verbal reasoning analogies ("*Good* is to *bad* as *love* is to _____") and items to measure vocabulary (from simple words like *orange* to more complex ones like *pejorative*). It will also include items to measure the ability to match or discriminate abstract symbols, detect hidden figures within complex designs, and the like. If it is an individual test, certain motor performances may also be required, such as maze-tracing, fitting puzzles together, building a design with blocks to match an abstract picture, or selecting from a set of choices the one that fits with what has been "cut out" of a whole picture or pattern.

There are tests and individual items within tests that are based on speed. The faster one works, the higher the score. Other items tap such powers as the ability to solve increasingly difficult verbal reasoning problems, with no time limit imposed. Some kinds of items stress a mixture of breadth and depth or power, such as the range of vocabulary or information. And still other tests measure simple reactivity, for example, infant items that require infants to follow a moving object with their eyes or to turn their heads in the direction of a sound. For older children, youth, and adults, number facility tests (Q for quantitative) are widely used. In all tests, however, the meaning of respondents' score is de-

rived from how well or poorly they perform on the tests in comparison to others of the same age.

Infant Intelligence Tests

Some researchers think that the term "intelligence" has no place in the psychology of infancy, because the items used to test infant intelligence have little in common with items in intelligence tests for older children and adults. But infant tests (tests for children under 2 years) can be useful if the scores from them are not confused with the IQ scores that are quite good predictors of a number of useful things for individuals of age 5 or 6 years and older. Some infant tests, such as the visual tracking test mentioned, seem to have no relation to intelligence as a problem-solving ability—learning aptitude. Other items, such as learning to use the string to pull the object to which it is tied within the baby's reach, seem more likely to tap general problem-solving ability.

The following are the principal things we now know about infant intelligence testing (Bayley, 1970; Lewis, 1976).

1. Seriously mentally defective babies can be distinguished from normals.

2. Babies who live in institutions similar to the old-line orphanages score lower than children living in homes with either their true parents or their foster parents.

3. Scores from intelligence tests given to children less than 18 months old are often quite unrelated to scores they earn when they are 3 or 4 years old and older. This lack of a strong correlation between infant and older child intelligence test scores may stem from either or both of the following:

(a) The items used to measure infant intelligence do not measure ability to solve problems. Many of them, for example, are essentially sensorimotor tasks.

(b) The rate of development varies widely, so that infants who are well ahead of their age mates may move more slowly through the developmental tasks of later childhood. Consequently, they may compare less favorably with others of their age during the elementary school period or beyond.

4. Studies of cross-cultural and racial differences in infant test performance indicate patterns of comparatively early acceleration among nonwestern infants (traditional African, Asian, and South American), and black infants within western societies. This is thought to reflect some combination of genetic and environmental factors that produces a rapid initial development in psychomotor capacity. These differences generally disappear during the second year of life. Subsequently, western children usually move ahead of their nonwestern counterparts, although the advantages may be mostly an artifact of testing.

5. Only with very severe deprivation, including malnutrition, does socioeconomic status seem to affect infant intelligence test scores below the age of about 18 months. The children of the poor and the ill-educated score about the same as the children of the affluent and the well-educated up to about 1 1/2 years. (Some authors place this age level higher, and say that social class level exerts little effect up to perhaps 3 1/2 years [Palmer, 1970].)

6. A sensitive, well-trained tester can detect such infant difficulties as defects in social responsiveness, vision, or hearing. Like a good physical examination, an infant intelligence test provides a fairly good picture at that particular point in time.

7. When infants are tested who are well fed, comfortable, and of good disposition, their performance is a better predictor of later test scores than if tested during a bad mood (as judged by the tester).

8. Different tests of infant intelligence often provide quite different results for the same baby. Apparently, not all infant tests measure the same behaviors to a similar extent. It can be deceiving, therefore, to place too much confidence in any one test performance.

Tests for Preschool-aged Children

Intelligence tests for children up to about age 5 must be given individually. Both verbal and performance tests exist for these children and are fairly widely given for both research and clinical reasons. Goal directedness seems to play an important part in success with test items designed for the preschool years, whereas sensory alertness is more involved in items designed for infants.

As children grow older, their intelligence test score performances are more reliable or consistent from one time to the next and the more similar the items or processes included in tests are to those used for adolescents or adults. In one of the most ambitious studies of the predictive powers of IQ, California children were given many intelligence tests from birth to age 18 (young adulthood was taken as 18 years) (Bayley, 1949). Test scores for the 6-month-olds actually showed a slight *negative* relationship to young adult IQ, although the correlation was not statistically significant. Tests given at age 1 year had a low positive, but not very useful, correlation (+.25) with tests for 18-year-olds. For tests given at ages 2 and 3, the correlation increased to about .50 (respectable and modestly useful as a predictor, but at a low level of confidence). By age 4, the correlation was in the high .60s and moved to the middle .70s for tests given at ages 5, 6, and 7.[1]

In other words, some prediction of young adult intellectual status is provided by preschool tests, but the prediction is still a long way from perfect and there is much individual variation. We should therefore be very cautious and tentative in making judgments about future intellectual status and labeling children as dull if they happen to score low on a given test. However, extremes in brightness or dullness—especially to the point of retardation—provide a more confident basis for prediction than scores in the wide range of "average" performance.

The topic of testing preschool-aged children is particularly important. Such testing, carefully done, holds promise for useful guidance of young children, particularly if they have developed in circumstances unfavorable for learning and practicing their intellectual skills. If factors that will interfere with later school and life success can be identified during the preschool ages, when, it is presumed and hoped, the child is malleable, it may be possible to correct them.

Tests for Older Children, Adolescents, and Adults

As soon as children reach the age when they can follow instructions, are not too easily distracted, and can use a pencil, group intelligence tests can be given. As a rule of thumb, individuals do about as well on group intelligence tests as on individual tests. However, children with reading problems will obviously do very poorly on a group test, as will those who do not understand English well. Individuals high in anxiety often go to pieces and do badly in the group intelligence-

[1] See the Appendix B for interpretation of the magnitude and direction of correlation coefficients.

testing situation, but do better in an individual testing situation where a skilled examiner can put them at ease. People who have trouble working against time typically do better on individual tests, because many group tests are timed for those who work at an "average speed."

To summarize briefly, different intelligence tests clearly measure somewhat different specific behaviors. A given test must be examined closely if the tester wishes to know what specific aspects of "intelligent behavior" are being tapped. It is equally clear that intelligence tests measure somewhat different behaviors at different ages; the contents of an infant intelligence scale and that of a scale to measure intelligence in early adolescence are simply not the same. It is also true that at successively higher age levels, intelligence test content becomes more homogeneous. Most tests at these levels are heavily loaded with verbal items. Finally, intelligence tests are designed for either individual or group administration. Ordinarily, the individual test is more comprehensive and relies very little on reading ability for performance. Generally speaking, however, the relationship between a person's individual and group test performance is remarkably close.

Some Developmental Aspects of Intelligence Test Performance

Turning to the question of intellectual development, we note that any understanding of the growth and patterning of intelligence is based primarily upon the analysis of test performance data from longitudinal and cross-sectional studies of children. Taken collectively, the results of these studies have been interpreted to formulate several generalizations about developmental changes through time. We will discuss six of the

most firmly supported of these generalizations (Bayley, 1970; Honzik, 1973).

Rapid Early Growth

First, in relation to eventual maximum
intellectual performance in adulthood, a
disproportionately large amount of
growth occurs during the prepubertal
years of life. Using Figure 8.1 as a rough
approximation of the growth curve for
intelligence, we can see that growth is
especially rapid during infancy and the
preschool years. Though difficult to depict graphically, growth rate seems to
decelerate during the elementary school
years. By preadolescence, a strong semblance of the organizational pattern of
adult intelligence can be detected (Fitzgerald, Nesselroade, & Baltes, 1973).
Growth thereafter is considerably slower.

Traditionally, it was believed that
growth in intellectual power peaked during the mid-20s, subsequently declining
with age. More recent evidence suggests
continued growth through midlife, perhaps not peaking until ages 50 to 60 (Kangas & Bradway, 1971; Schaie & Strother,
1968). There is some evidence that *some*
age decline occurs in the speed with
which older persons deal with complex

cognitive tasks; actual intellectual power
or accuracy seems less affected (Cunningham & Birren, 1976). The idea of rapid
early growth, however, remains significant, especially if the goal is to facilitate
maximum development by environmental
design. From studies of intellectual and
other aspects of development we infer
that the effects of environmental intrusions on a growth variable (positive *or*
negative) will be greatest during the period of greatest change for that growth
variable (Bloom, 1964). It follows that appropriate environmental stimulation will
have its most potent impact on intellectual development during infancy
and the preschool years of life. This notion is implicit in organized attempts at
infant and preschool ''education'' that
have become so popular in recent years
(Evans, 1975).

Increased Range of Individual Differences

Second, the degree of individual differences in test performance increases with
age, especially after about age 2 or 3.
This means that the range in absolute
amount and quality of intellectual performance by same-aged children will
widen as they grow older. Differences in
growth rate are surely influenced to
some extent by genetic factors, but differences in the amount and variety of
learning experiences also affect this pattern. Differences are most striking, of
course, when we compare grossly retarded children with, say, exceptionally
able children, who by age 4 may be self-
taught readers and who behave intellectually in ways more similar to 6- or
7-year-olds than to their own age mates.

Even discounting the extremes in
growth retardation and acceleration, the
extent of individual differences in measured intelligence becomes increasingly
apparent throughout the elementary
school years and into adolescence. In a

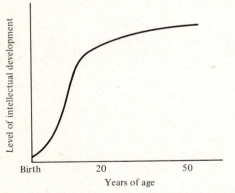

Fig. 8-1 A hypothetical composite age curve representing the growth of measured intelligence from
birth to the middle years.

relatively "normal," unselected population of 6-year-olds, for example, the range in "mental age" may extend from 4 1/2 to 7 1/2 years. Some 6-year-olds may perform more like an average 4 1/2-year-old; others will show a similarity to the average 8-year-old. By the time this group of 6-year-olds reaches later adolescence, the age range in mental functioning may have increased from 4 to 6, or even 8 years (Symonds, 1961). (These figures are only approximate.) The fact of such heterogeneity in groups of children makes it increasingly difficult for educators to appropriately implement their instructional practices. Thus, one form or another of ability grouping, or "tracking," is often used. By reducing heterogeneity, it is thought that more effective instruction can take place, "meeting individual differences." More extreme differences are often met by providing "special" classes where children are segregated by ability. As the reader might suspect, ability grouping and special classes are controversial and there are contradictory findings about the impact of these practices on children (Stephens & Evans, 1973).

Stability–Lability in Test Performance

Third, longitudinal studies of intellectual development have disclosed some rather marked fluctuations among children in their performances on repeated testing over time. As noted earlier, this variability in test performance is greatest during infancy and is somewhat less during preschool years. With age, test performances tend to stabilize, especially for verbal abilities. For reasons still unclear, verbal scores stabilize somewhat earlier among girls. But once scores are firmly established, boys often score with greater consistency on verbal tasks than girls.

An illustration of the general fluctua-tions is shown in a major longitudinal study (McCall, 1973) in which normal middle-class children varied as much as 28.5 IQ points on test performances between ages 2 1/2 and 17 years. More striking, one of every seven children in this study displayed shifts of over 40 points! It is difficult to explain such wide fluctuation satisfactorily. For some children, growth rate may be less continuous or more sporadic because of transitory developmental problems, such as illness or unstable home conditions. For others, the immediate testing conditions, including motivation for a test, may account for the variability. Differences in a genetically influenced patterning of abilities may also be involved.

The occurrences of such fluctuation even under relatively normal growth conditions remind us again of the hazard of attaching too much significance to any one test score, especially during the early years. If intelligence test data are to be used for educational decision making or diagnosis, children should be tested frequently during the early years of school. Otherwise a distorted view of their abilities could prevail. One recent study, for example, has shown that for children below age 10, IQ scores from the more commonly administered group verbal tests are considerably less stable than individual test IQs (Hopkins & Bracht, 1975).

Factors in IQ Change over Time

A fourth related point about intellectual growth over time concerns individual differences in the overall trend in development. Some children show consistent gains in IQ as they grow older; others display a relatively stable pattern, neither increasing nor decreasing their intellectual stature compared to age-mates; and still others seem to show consistent decrease in intellectual power with age in relation to their peers. Apart from possible hereditary influences, these overall growth trends seem largely affected by learning experiences and certain personality factors.

A common interpretation of learning-experience differences is the cumulative-deficit hypothesis (see Chapter 2) which argues that experiential lacks or deficiencies contribute to growth deficits that interfere progressively with subsequent growth processes, learning, and motivational development. A vicious cycle thus occurs; inadequate learning leads to inadequate coping as successively more complex intellectual demands confront a child. Gradually, failure breeds more failure. With age, the cumulative effects become more pronounced, even to the point of environmentally induced intellectual retardation.

Data about the cumulative-deficit hypothesis show that age losses are more pronounced on verbal than on performance ("nonverbal") tasks (Jensen, 1974). Still, there is a serious question about the absolute nature of deficit. Perhaps much of this is explained by selective biases in test content (Schulz & Aurbach, 1971).

Problems of psychological adjustment can also interfere with children's test performances and cause a deceptively low performance. Highly anxious children may perform poorly on tests. To the extent that curiosity affects the scope and depth of children's learning, a child low in curiosity (or a child who is fearful, passive, and withdrawn) may increasingly be at a disadvantage in test-taking. There is even some tantalizing but inconclusive evidence that individuals with rigid race-prejudices are less likely to gain in (or perhaps even to hold) their intellectual level over time (McCandless, 1970). Possibly this is because prejudiced persons are less open to new experience and expend more intellectual energy maintaining their prejudice than in accomplishing constructive learnings that may contribute to intellectual gains.

On the other hand, consistent gains in IQ from early childhood through adolescence have been associated with personality traits generally considered more positive (Bayley, 1970; Kagan & Moss, 1962). Active assertiveness is one such trait, and high achievement motivation—a generalized predisposition to compete successfully using self-defined standards of excellence—is another. Positive self-regard, high curiosity, and wide-ranging interests also are associated with IQ increments. Much remains to be learned, however, about the relationship between children's behavioral and affective characteristics and their growth in mental ability (Damarin & Cattell, 1968). Research thus far suggests that these interrelationships are stronger, both positively and negatively, for boys than for girls (Bayley, 1970). Again, the principle that all aspects of development interact stands clear.

Differentiation of Intellectual Abilities

The fifth point about intellectual development concerns the differentiation of patterns of mental abilities over time. Our comments thus far about mental development have been based upon the global IQ score as derived from repeated measurements of children and youth as they mature. As noted earlier, the IQ score itself is a composite of items that require the use of many different mental abilities. Some authorities (Thurstone & Thurstone, 1962) have preferred to build their concept of intelligence using a set of relatively independent "primary mental abilities." If separate abilities can be reliably measured and individual differences in them observed, we can then build a *factor* theory rather than a *unitary* theory of intelligence. This implies that children will develop more or less proficiency with verbal, number, space, reasoning, memory, and perceptual-motor abilities. Gradually, differential ability development will result in a profile of relative strengths, and perhaps limitations, in mental functioning. Children become increasingly similar to their parents in general IQ over time (Scarr-Salapatek, 1975). This may reflect both extended genetic influence and, of course, home stimulation. But different kinds of home stimulation or environmental processes will likely affect ability potentialities selectively. For example, one study has shown that father's occupational level and parental encouragement of children's language and general activity are related to higher reasoning and verbal, but lower number ability (Walberg & Marjoribanks, 1973).

Some of our clearest data about differential pattern development comes from the study of verbal and quantitative abilities (McCarthy, 1975). These data show that differences in these two abilities appear early. By college age, many youth possess significantly greater facility with one or the other. Sex differences in pattern differentiation are also reported (Maccoby & Jacklin, 1974). On the average, males, starting at about puberty, exceed females in numerical reasoning and visual-spatial ability, while females generally continue to excel in verbal ability. Other studies (such as Backman, 1972) indicate sex differences in perceptual speed, perceptual accuracy, and memory, with the advantage again going to females. (These differences, of course, are based upon group performances, and will not hold for all individuals.) Under some circumstances, sex differences in patterned abilities may be important for educational and vocational decisions, but sex differences in

general ability (IQ) are inconsequential.

Finally, racial and ethnic variables apparently contribute in some way to the differential patterning of mental abilities. For example, careful testing of a large number of children (N=320) from four cultural groups—Chinese, Jewish, black American, and Puerto Rican—has revealed both group and individual differences as early as ages 6–7 years in verbal, reasoning, number, and space abilities (Lesser, Fifer, & Clark, 1965). These differences, if reliable, may be important for educational planning to maximize intellectual development. As yet, however, little can be said about the practical implications of racial and ethnic factors in patterned abilities. And though racial differences continue to appear on selected cognitive measures, there are strong indications that social class may be more significant than race (Hall & Kaye, 1977).

The Secular Trend in IQ

Sixth, a considerable body of evidence suggests that average measured intelligence among humans has increased over the past several generations (Koppen-Thulesius & Teichman, 1972). That is, an accelerative tendency for both verbal and nonverbal intelligence test performance, including infant and preschool motor-mental tests, can be observed when we compare children and youth of today with their counterparts in generations past. This trend, though not dramatic, is reminiscent of the secular trend to increased height and earlier sexual maturation across generations noted in Chapter 6. The trend is not easily explained. Some hypothesize as causes increased learning opportunities through mass education and access to the mass media. Others (Walberg & Marjoribanks, 1976) propose that this IQ rise may also reflect better nutrition, immigrants' mastery of English, and smaller families enabling parents to concentrate their efforts at stimulation on fewer children. Thus the trend may reflect less an absolute increase in intellectual capacity from one generation to the next than a broader base of accumulated learnings and greater cultural emphasis on intellectual achievement within families. Or, more simply, the trend may reflect increases in "test-wiseness," especially among older children and youth. The net effect for students of human intellectual development is a need for continued monitoring of the content of intelligence tests and the basis from which the meaning of scores is determined. To achieve valid measurements, tests require periodic revision better to portray genuine individual differences in intellectual performance.

To sum up, we have fairly firm documentation for six general trends in intellectual growth: rapid early growth; an increasing range of individual differences in IQ; stability and fluctuation in intelligence test performance; increments and decrements in IQ over time; increased differentiation in the pattern of mental abilities; and accelerative development across generations. All these data are products of psychometrics applied to the study of intelligence. To the extent that our measures of intelligence are faulty, our understanding of intellectual growth suffers. It is entirely possible that important developmental aspects of human intelligence are not measured at all by existing tests. In fact, the long-standing and somewhat narrow emphasis upon *product* in intelligence testing—whether or not test items are answered "correctly"—has led some authorities to believe that we should expand our study to include *process* variables in intellectual functioning (Sigel, 1963). By this is meant the developmental study of changes in how children and youth go about solving in-

tellectual tasks. This shift results partly from the influence of a theory of intellectual development established independently of conventional psychometrics. We refer specifically to the renowned work of a Swiss scholar, Jean Piaget, whose cognitive-developmental view of intelligence is now examined. Our decision to concentrate on Piaget's work means we neglect other influential and respected cognitive psychologists who have provided rich data about intellectual functioning. Notable for their contributions, for example, are Jerome Bruner (1964) and Heinz Werner (1948). But since Piagetian thought has become such a dominant and pervasive force in the psychological study of intelligence, we present Piaget to illustrate the cognitive-developmental perspective.

A COGNITIVE-DEVELOPMENTAL VIEW OF INTELLIGENCE

Throughout a long and productive scientific career, Piaget has sought to understand the origins, nature, and scope of human thought. His views are especially interesting because they consist of a theory in the making and are focused on certain aspects of human development that in the past have not been examined extensively by American psychologists, whatever their theoretical persuasion. Piaget's way of viewing human development has rapidly attracted many followers, both in the United States and abroad, and is one of the most influential perspectives on children and youth in contemporary psychology.

Piaget's theory has been developed through the careful clinical observation of children, including a questioning procedure designed to discover the reasons used by children and youth to solve mental problems the way they do. The problems themselves have little resemblance to conventional intelligence test items. Rather, they involve questions, and even demonstrations, about physical reality and causality similar to laboratory experiments in science. They also involve the use of objects for counting, measuring, pouring, and constructing. All problem tasks are arranged to tap mental operations thought to comprise logical analysis, not specific verbal or mathematical skills.

Applied to measurement, this emphasis highlights the quantitative-qualitative distinction mentioned earlier. Psychometricians, for example, usually assign equivalent point scores for different test items, even though the mental processes required to answer them are markedly different. Recalling an item of general knowledge from memory, for instance, may be weighted the same as an item that demands the use of deductive or inductive reasoning. The Piagetian approach, in contrast, looks specifically at mental processing as inferred from explanation and prediction offered by a given child; theoretically, a "wrong" answer can reveal as much information about mental functioning as can a "right" one. Moreover, Piagetians explore the basis for children's understanding of a phenomenon more thoroughly than the psychometricians. It is one thing to calculate the area of a paper rectangle, for example, by using the standard formula of length times width. It is quite another to understand that, if this same rectangle were divided into eight or ten smaller "chunks" and spread out on a table, the area would remain constant (conservation of area despite transformation in appearance). Children may be adept at calculation, yet believe that the "chunking" transformation results in more area, "because there are more pieces" or "because the pieces cover more territory." If so, a genuine understanding of area—the more basic and important achievement—is lacking (Elkind, 1969). Table 8.1 presents some representative Piagetian tasks that are often used to assess certain aspects of concrete and formal reasoning.

Characteristics of Cognitive-Developmental Psychology

For Piaget, mature intelligent behavior is the ability to reason and think critically in objective, abstract, and hypothetical terms. When youth or adults attain this level of thought they are said to have reached the "peak" in a developmental pyramid or hierarchy the lower levels of which have emerged sequentially and in progressively more complex form. In infancy, these subordinate hierarchic elements (literally the foundations of abstract thought) are *sensorimotor coordinations* (pulling, pushing, twisting, sorting, manipulating, and so on). In a cumulative fashion, thought forms then move through a concrete level to the abstract level we associate with formal logic.

Four factors act in concert to produce this progression of thought development: *biological maturation,* experience with the *physical world* (including knowledge about the sensory attributes of objects and the effects of actions on objects, such as cutting, throwing, burning, and freezing), *social experience* (including interacting with others and learning social customs), and *equilibration.* Equilibration means the achievement of greater cognitive balance or stability at successively higher levels as new experience and past experience are reconciled.

The active reconciliation that defines successful equilibration actually requires the operation of two subsidiary interacting mechanisms of behavior change: *assimilation* and *accommodation.*

Assimilation refers to our comprehension of a new experience and "tucking it away" in our existing repertoire of meanings. Any new experience must be so tucked away to fit it with previous

Suzanne Szasz

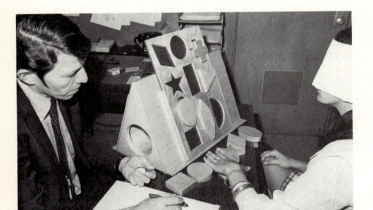

© Van Bucher 1972 from Photo Researchers

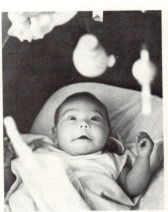

Michael Weis

Michael Weisbrot

© Van Bucher 1972 from Photo Researchers

Ann Zane Shanks from Photo Researchers

Suzanne Szasz

© Van Bucher 1971 from Photo Researchers

iriam Reinhart 1975 from Photo Researchers

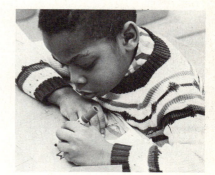
Suzanne Szasz

Michael Weisbrot

Kenneth Karp

knowledge and understanding. For example, Lance, a 3-year-old, behaves as though anything that moves is alive. His concept of life has been built primarily upon the characteristic of movement. For Lance, then, a new windup toy will have life. So may a cloud moving quickly across the sky. This is the logical best he can do given his current level of comprehension. He *assimilates*. Maturation and experience, however, will move him along. Eventually he will experience disequilibrium about life and movement. He will learn that moving things are not necessarily alive and that things alive do not necessarily move. He will be forced to revise his idea about life, to reconcile new and old experience. In short, he will *accommodate* to discrepancies that reveal incomplete or inaccurate information. Accommodation involves the removal of disequilibrium in the direction of ever-more-accurate perception and tucking away of new experiences. Accurate accommodations will mark developmental progress in thinking. However, major conceptual learnings will occur only when the child is "ready." Both experience and maturation are equally important for the development of cognitive structures to process and find meaning in information about the physical social worlds.

Learning in this way, of course, takes time. Countless interactions are necessary for us to accurately represent physical and social reality. For Piaget, these interactions make up the core of age-re-

TABLE 8.1   Some Piagetian Tasks to Measure Concrete and Formal Reasoning.

Concrete Reasoning Tasks	Task Description	Subject's Problem
1. Matrix task (to measure multiple classification)	Eight cards are used. One card depicts 5 geometric figures; the remaining 7 cards depict 1 figure each. A subject is shown the 8 cards with their circle, triangle, and square figures. (See below.)	Explain which 1 of the 7 single card figures best fits the blank space (both horizontally and vertically) on the larger card.
2. Tactile seriation task (to measure seriation)	Subject is invited to examine by touch 5 pencils that are hidden from sight behind a screen.	Order the pencils from longest to shortest, then represent the resulting scheme by drawing the pencils on paper so that bases of all 5 pencil figures are on the same horizontal line in order from longest to shortest.
3. Animal classification task (to measure conceptual class inclusion and hierarchical or additive classification)	Twelve cards are shown, each showing a picture of a different animal: 4 ducks, 3 other birds, (chicken, sparrow, and parrot), and 5 animals that are not birds (mouse, fish, horse, poodle, and snake).	Group the animal cards "like each other" into separate piles thereafter explain their answers to several questions: "Are there more ducks or more birds?" "Are there more birds or more animals?" "If a fox ate all the birds, would there be any ducks left?" "What if all the animals were to die, would there be any birds left?"

TABLE 8.1   (cont.)

Formal Reasoning Tasks

4. Projections of shadows test (to measure the scheme of proportionality)	Materials include a screen, electric light, a baseboard with a sequence of holes set at 1-inch distance, and 4 rings with diameters of 1, 2, 3, and 4 inches, respectively. These are arranged for the subject's inspection and response.	Indicate what distance from the light a given ring should be placed to bring its shadow on the screen into comformity to a shadow produced by a second ring placed at a certain distance.
5. Oscillations of the pendulum task (to measure combinatorial reasoning)	A pendulum is constructed, consisting of a string that can be lengthened or shortened, a wooden apparatus from which to hang the string, and a set of weights.	Identify and explain what determines the pendulum's oscillation velocity.
6. Conservation of motion in a horizontal plane task (to measure combinatorial reasoning)	A slide apparatus is constructed from a long board with a central groove, a thick plastic pendulum hammer fixed at one end of the board, and 6 balls, each of which can be propelled down the groove when struck with a given force by the hammer.	Identify and explain the factors that regulate the distances traveled by the balls along their path when a constant force is applied.

Cards for the Matrix Task

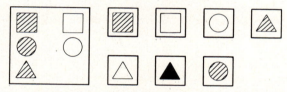

Adapted from W. M. Bart and P. W. Airasian, Determination of the ordering among seven Piagetian tasks by an ordering-theoretic method. *Journal of Educational Psychology,* 1974 *66*, 277–284. By permission. Derived from Inhelder and Piaget, 1958; 1969a.

lated experience that, as it accumulates, eventually culminates in comprehensive logical thought. The important interactions are those that occur in the "natural environment," that is, in the relatively informal, unarranged learning experiences common to children and youth in all cultures. "Good" developmental learning means to actively explore, discover, experiment, and order our concrete experience. Out of this springs the essence of abstract thought that will be organized into specific mental processes and structures for logical reasoning.

A Sequence of Development

For Piaget, the evolution of logical thought structures begins with a state or stage of egocentrism and, ideally, terminates in a state or stage of perspectivism (Langer, 1969). Young, egocentric children are unable to conceive that other people may view the world differently. Theirs is the only view that can exist.

They behave as though the world exists for their sake and that their feelings and desires are shared and known by everyone. Milne's (1926) Winnie-the-Pooh exemplifies egocentric thinking when he reasons that if something buzzes it must be a bee, that the only reason for being a bee is to make honey, and that the only reason for making honey is so that he, Winnie, can eat it! Kindergarten-age children typically go to school for the first time fully expecting their teacher to know all about them, their pets, their friends, and their toys. They further expect that the teacher will share their feelings about these things. Changes in this orientation gradually occur, however, and children come to distinguish between their own and others' viewpoints. Thought becomes more reflective. With normal development, children eventually reach objectivity; that is, they become capable of both recognizing and accepting multiple viewpoints and feelings. They are able to examine ideas and problems from many different perspectives.

Piaget's major efforts have been directed toward describing the successive steps taken by children in their movement to perspectivism. The result is a broad, general, though somewhat loose *sequence-concept* of development (Chapter 2). But, as we will see, Piaget's sequence is also tied to general age periods. Finally, the sequence is claimed to be *invariant*. This means that development occurs in a fixed order of stage progressions for all children, even though individual differences in the rate of development can and do exist.

Piaget's invariant, hierarchic sequence of intellectual development is grouped into four qualitatively distinct periods: the *sensorimotor stage* (birth to 18 months or 2 years); *preoperational thought* (about 2–7 years); *concrete operations* (ages 7–11); and *formal operations* (11 years and beyond). (See Table 8.2.) Convenient labels have been provided which perhaps point more clearly to the central characteristics of these stages than do Piaget's terms (Elkind, 1967). During the sensorimotor stage, the *conquest of the object* is made. In the preoperational stage, the task is the *conquest of the symbol*. The task within the concrete operations stage is *mastering classes, relations,* and *quantities*. Finally, in the formal operations (most mature) stage of thought, the central task is *conquest of abstract thought*. Although these periods are age-linked, the ages assigned are approximations and should not be regarded as rigidly correct or absolute.

Sensorimotor period. Sensorimotor behavior (looking at things heard and felt, grasping things seen and felt) provides the action basis for eventual symbolic thought. Infants initially bring meaning into their world through perception and motor movement organization called *action schemes*. The primitive, reflexive, passive characteristics of very young infants are quickly followed by goal-seeking behaviors and rudimentary concepts of causality, time, space, and matter. For example, infants learn that by shaking themselves in their cribs, they can make a mobile which is beyond reach move, thus establishing a cause-effect relationship. This extends also to the important notion that certain actions result in reliable effects on the environment. When brushed aside, knick-knacks fall from the table to the floor; water spilled from a cup creates wetness; kitty howls when its tail is pulled. Such experiences provide the sensorimotor basis for predicting or anticipating the consequences of one's actions.

Closely related to the genesis of causality and prediction is the concept of probability. Piaget illustrates this by an infant coming to expect that footsteps heard advancing down the hall are likely to be mother's. The origin of time concepts is more difficult to trace, although by the time infants are toddling about they seem able to retain something about the order or sequence of events. When asked, "Where is Mother?" for example, the infant can point in the direction mother has gone (Lavatelli, 1964).

The most important learning about space and matter during the sensorimotor period is *object permanence*. Infants have the sense of object permanence when they understand that things continue to exist whether or not these things can be seen. The very young infant, Piaget argues, behaves as though objects no longer exist when they disappear from view. A toy can be presented, then taken away, and the young infant makes no attempt to look for it. Toward the end of the first year, however, the maturing infant realizes that objects seen, then removed or hidden, still exist in their full form. All subsequent logical thought obviously depends upon this basic information.

Another important development during the sensorimotor stage is that the infant comes to realize *invariance despite change*. This means that while objects or people may appear in different contexts or circumstances, their basic identity stays the same. Father is father whether dressed in work clothes, pajamas, or

TABLE 8.2 Piaget's Stages of Intellectual Development

Stage	Approximate Ages	Characterization
I. *Sensorimotor period*	Birth to 2 years	Infant differentiates himself from objects; seeks stimulation, and makes interesting spectacles last; prior to language, meanings defined by manipulations, so that object remains "the same object" with changes in location and point of view.
II. *Preoperational thought period* Preoperational phase	2–4	Child egocentric, unable to take viewpoint of other people; classifies by single salient features: if A is like B in one respect, must be like B in other respects.
Intuitive phase	4–7	Is now able to think in terms of classes, to see relationships, to handle number concepts, but is "intuitive" because he may be unaware of his classification.
III. *Period of concrete operations*	7–11	Able now to use logical operations such as *reversibility* (in arithmetic), *classification* (organizing objects into hierarchies of classes), and *seriation* (organizing objects into ordered series, such as increasing size).
IV. *Period of formal operations*	11–15	Final steps toward abstract thinking and conceptualization; capable of hypothesis-testing.

From "Piaget's stages of intellectual development" in *Review of Child Development Research*, Volume 1, edited by Martin L. Hoffman and Lois Wladis Hoffman, © 1964 by Russell Sage Foundation, New York.

bathing suit, before or after he shaves his beard, and so on. Similarly, milk is the same whether in a bottle, cup, dish, or spilled on the floor.

Still further sensorimotor stage developments can be cited. Through manipulative action, infants distinguish between the "me" and "not me." A primitive sense of the self as independent from the environment thus emerges. As the end of the sensorimotor period approaches, repetitive manipulations of self and objects are replaced by a greater variety of novel manipulations—as if the infant was beginning to develop a characteristic style of problem solving on a motoric action level. Improved memory capacity is increasingly demonstrated, particularly by evidence of *deferred imitation*. This means that the infant will perform imitative behavior at more extended points in time *after* observing a model's performance. This is also taken as evidence of an important advance in thinking, because deferred imitation requires a mental representation of a model's behavior. This representational ability is further apparent in more complex searching behaviors, such as looking for toys and other objects displaced both in space and time. In short, the infant makes a transition from an existence based on sensorimotor action and reactions to one increasingly marked by symbolic thought.

Piaget has actually described six sequential substages for the development of sensorimotor intelligence, beginning with the practice and modification of reflex schemes (such as sucking, recognizing the nipple or bottle, then searching for the source of food) and ending with an impressive repertoire of action schemes that provide the basis for symbolic activity (developing mental solutions to problems). Interested readers may wish to consult Flavell (1963), Hunt (1961), and Piaget (1952) for further details.

Preoperational thought.   During the second year of life for many children, and by age 2 for almost all children, sensorimotor interactions with the environment are strengthened and made more powerful and complex by the child's growing ability to use and to understand language. Language mushrooms in the third year of life. During this period, the child learns the difference between the *signifier* (the word, usually nouns at first) and the *signified* (the object, event, or characteristic for which the word stands); that is, the word *chair* is not itself what one sits on. Language, then, becomes a vehicle for symbolic mental activity (the beginning of thought as we know it).

However, children's thought is limited during this developmental phase, probably because of maturational level and limited experience (Flavell, 1963). Preoperational thought is apparently dominated by "before the eye reality." This means that perceptions dominate conceptions. A preoperational child who sees six marbles closely grouped and another six marbles widely spread will say there are more marbles in the dispersed than in the tight grouping: "This pile has more because it is bigger." The same behavior is likely among preoperational children even when the piles are at first identical and close together and later one pile is altered and spread out *while the child watches*. It is as though the child does not comprehend that contextual appearance can change with no effect on quantity. This, in Piaget's terms, means that the preoperational child cannot *conserve number through irrelevant transformations*. The same failure to conserve occurs for weight, length, volume, and other general characteristics of objects, things, and classes.

A second limitation in thought characteristic of preoperational children is their apparent inability to categorize objects and events along more than one dimension or according to more than one criterion. A drinking cup must be tall *or* wide, but does not possess *both* height *and* width at the same time. A balloon may be big or red, or blue or small; but a cluster of balloons will not be conceived along the multiple dimensions of big, red, small, blue balloons. This sort of multiple classification seems beyond the preoperational child's power of combinatory thought—objects are attended to one at a time. Children also have problems with "superordinate conceptual classification." For instance, 4-year-old Brenda correctly acknowledges that a doll is a toy. But she reasons that if all dolls in the world were burned, there would be no more toys. In other words, she deals with the subordinate class, *doll,* and the superordinate (more general and abstract) class, *toy,* as if they were equivalent.

Despite such limitations in their thought, preoperational children move rapidly through this stage of the "conquest of the symbol" in the direction of more sophisticated symbolic functioning. Growth is particularly rapid in the last two years of the preoperational stage, from about 5 to 7. Basic classification rules, concept integration, and elementary quantitative thinking can be inferred from the behavior that accompanies children's thinking. However, preoperational children rarely verbalize their rules and strategies. For this reason, Piaget envisions preoperational thought as *intuitive.*

Concrete operations. The intuitive thought of the 5- or 6-year-old is a transition to the next higher rung in the developmental ladder. Typically, the transition is achieved around age 7, which roughly marks the beginning of the period of concrete operations. The distinctive features of thought during the period of concrete operations are that logic and objectivity progressively characterize the child's thought. As suggested earlier, this stage involves the conquest of classes, relations, and quantities. Children become able to think deductively: If 1 foot equals 12 inches, then 12 inches put together equal 1 foot. If *all* dolls are toys, then *this* doll is a toy. In other words, logical operations—acts of reasoning—are performed in relation to real, or concrete, events and objects. Hence, the name of this stage, *concrete operations.*

Among the capabilities developed throughout this stage are multiple classification and conservation. Unlike the preoperational child, the concrete operational children will develop a capacity to think about concept classes in equivalent and hierarchic forms: Apples and pears are both fruit, fruit is food, but all food is not fruit. Similarly, a house is a house, but it is also a building, though not all buildings are houses. The child also comes to *conserve,* as in understanding that a given amount of water can be frozen, then thawed, with no loss of volume. Underlying these capabilities is an understanding of *equivalence.* Objects of varying size and texture can be equal in weight. Changes in one dimension, such as height, do not necessarily mean that other dimensions, such as weight, must change (the child learns to *covary*). The child also becomes capable of *reversibility.* Transformational sequences can be traced back to their point of origin to account for changes in appearance; actions can be canceled by counteractions. One of the simplest cases of reversibility is learning that the number of fingers on a hand, counted sequentially from thumb to little finger, is the same as the number counted from little finger to thumb. Another instance: When poured back into a tall, thin glass, the liquid that was judged less in quantity by the preoperational child when it was poured into a short, wide [...] be seen to hav[...] spite its appar[...] went from one [...]

Transitivity [...] come to be und[...] crete operations [...] opment. Transit[...] underlies *seriat*[...] series of events [...] such as "greater than," "less than," "more than," "fewer than." Understanding of this operation is essential if children are to understand number and size relationships.

Children may demonstrate an understanding of associativity by showing that parts of a whole may be combined in different ways without effecting a change in the whole. To produce a given shade of brown paint, for example, requires only that constant quantities of red, yellow, and black paint be combined. It makes no difference whether one puts the black paint in first, second, or third, as long as all three shades are mixed in the prescribed amounts.

However, the abstract derivations from such processes are not yet understood. Concerning transitivity, for example, concrete operational children can correctly order physical objects such as building blocks of different sizes and weights, then show that one or another is larger, heavier, smaller, or lighter. But they do not yet solve the problem: "If A>B, and B>C, and C>D, which is heavier, A or D?" Only as the stage of formal operations is entered can the abstractions from principles be formulated and employed in thought. Then, the child or the youth becomes able to generate hypotheses and to arrive at logical deductions performed symbolically without assistance from concrete props.

In summary, during the concrete-operational period, children gradually become capable of logical seriation, class inclusion, the recognition of equivalence (for example, that objects of varying size and color can be of equal weight and height does not necessarily denote increased weight), the exercise of reversibility in thought (for example, tracing a transformational sequence back to its point of origin to account for change in appearance), conservation, and associativity. Another way to view this stage is that the child gradually comes to master *classes*, *relations*, and *quantities* (Elkind, 1967). These achievements occur neither rapidly nor simultaneously. Only when all have been achieved do we say that children are fully concrete-operational. Piaget stresses that although this period is governed by these principles of thought, the child is not consciously aware of them. It is the next and final stage of development when "explainer thinking" emerges.

Formal operations. Operations prior to age 10 or 11 are oriented toward concrete phenomena in the immediate present; in the final stage, they encompass the potential or hypothetical and the nonpresent. Operational thought systems become integrated to form structures from which hypotheses can be generated and logical conclusions deduced purely symbolically. The ability to perform *combinatorial analysis* (combine in thought several rules, operations, or variables to solve problems) becomes apparent, as does the ability to formulate and execute symbolic plans of action. Logical form can be examined apart from the content of a situation or statement, and potential relations among objects can be imagined, hence the term *formal* operations. To illustrate, consider a child's ability to deal effectively with syllogisms involving a major premise, a minor premise, and a conclusion:

> Every virtue is laudable.
> Kindness is a virtue.
> Therefore, kindness is laudable.

In the formal operational stage, the child is capable of reasoning and explaining that where a conclusion necessarily follows the premises and the premises are true, the conclusion must also be true. The child also becomes able to detect logical incongruities in hypothetical contexts. For example, consider what is wrong with the following: "The five-year-old shell of a three-tailed turtle who lived for over a hundred years was found on a mountain top." Before the stage of formal operations, a child would likely respond by saying, "Turtles don't live on mountain tops," "Turtles have only one tail." In contrast, the formal operational child would be capable of ferreting out the logical contradiction and answering accordingly.

Piaget suggests that adolescents' proclivity for criticizing and theorizing arises from new cognitive powers. They can now envision alternatives to how things are done (child-rearing, education, government) and advance hypotheses for improvements. This newly acquired power in turn feeds the idealism of youth. The combination of idealism and neatly packaged solutions to complex problems, without consideration for the practical limitations of such solutions, represents the last "high-water" mark in egocentrism (Elkind, 1967; Flavell, 1963).

Finally, during this period adolescents become capable of evaluating the quality (logic) of their own thought (termed *second-order*, or *reflective*, *thinking*). Equally important, human beings of this age can reflect upon and evaluate themselves as persons. They are gradually able to see themselves as others see them. This, we may presume, indicates the emergence of a mature concept of self and the beginning of the time when *logical* (not emotional) egocentrism recedes, eventually to disappear. At best, young persons will further refine their reflective thought to develop standards for self-criticism and evaluate the quality of their own thinking. Further details about formal operational thought can be found in Gallagher and Noppe (1976) and Neimark (1975a; b).

To summarize Piaget's views, cognitive-intellectual development consists of four stages. The first stage is the period of sensorimotor intelligence, when infants learn about the world by exploring and experimenting with the physical environment. Action schemes for manipulative movement are gradually integrated and coordinated to facilitate self-directed interaction with objects and occurrences that can be seen, felt, smelled, tasted, and heard. Motoric action schemes are internalized in thought during the second stage, or preoperational period, of intellectual development. Language and other symbols are acquired which enable children to represent and operate on their experience in symbolic form. Thought remains rather disorganized, however, because symbolic mental schemes are not yet fitted together according to a master plan. Evidence for an overall plan of thought organization comes around age 6 or 7. This marks the beginning of the third, or concrete-operational, stage of development. Behavior is now guided by mental acts that involve logical reasoning. The basis for such reasoning however, remains concrete physical reality, or what actually exists in the child's sphere of perceived experience. Around age 11 or 12, this limitation to concrete reality gives way to still further advancements in thought. Children now are able to reason logically about things not present in concrete form. From this single accomplishment develops a more fully elaborate thought system for analyzing, deducing, and predicting logical relations on a purely hypothetical level. The fourth and final stage of cognitive development, formal-operational thought, has now emerged, although it may take several more years before the system of abstract logical competencies is fully integrated. For Piaget, then, native intelligence is not a "content," but a means by which the individual constructs and reasons about the world (Furth, 1973).

COMPARING THE TWO PERSPECTIVES

Having sketched the major developmental aspects of the psychometric and Piagetian perspectives on intelligence, we may wonder about their major similarities and differences. Three points can be made about similarities (Elkind, 1967). Both perspectives share the assumption that mental development is governed in some way by genetic forces. Their interpretations of genetic action, however, differ as we will soon discuss. These perspectives are also similar in that both are essentially descriptive accounts of age changes in mental functioning. But as compared to psychometrics, the cognitive-developmental approach seems richer in detail about both the qualitative nature of change and the mechanisms important for this change. Finally, both perspectives agree that the fundamental nature of human intelligence is rational thought.

Beyond these general similarities, comparison poses a challenging question: Which of these perspectives gives the best accounting of human intellectual development and functioning? Correlational studies show that each represents somewhat different aspects of human intelligence (Stephens, McLaughlin, Miller, & Miller, 1972). That is, the extent of commonality or overlap in intellectual performance as assessed from these two perspectives is only modestly positive. Correlations between conventional IQ and Piagetian task performance seldom run higher than .50, and are often

quite low (DeVries, 1974; DeVries & Kohlberg, 1977). The magnitude of correlation varies with age, stage, and the skills measured. It would take much stronger correlations, .80–.90, before we could seriously challenge the notion that these conceptions of intelligence are too similar to discuss separately in any meaningful way. Yet if we proceed with the idea that psychometric and Piagetian intelligence, though positively correlated, are in many respects independent, we cannot escape the question, "Which approach is most accurate and useful?"

An answer to this question requires a comparison of these perspectives on some criterion of fundamental truth about human intelligence. Such a criterion, to our knowledge, does not yet exist. Rather than ask which conception is more accurate and useful, it may be more instructive to ask, "Accurate and useful for what?" The psychometric and Piagetian perspectives have been established for particular and essentially different purposes. With this in mind we will consider the usefulness issue.

The Usefulness Issue

An examination of the usefulness of these two approaches to intelligence requires that we examine the specific purposes for which they were conceived. The psychometric view, for example, developed largely from such practical concerns as the prediction of behavior in situations that call for the use of conceptual abilities, especially the school. Psychometric intelligence testing has an impressive record in meeting such needs. The IQ, for example, is useful for making "quite good predictions of performance in school, job, and similar situations which call for conceptual skills" (Scarr-Salapatek, 1975, p. 5). We might add that the efficiency of the predictions is a matter of degree varying somewhat from individual to individual and depending upon the conditions of a given test performance and the similarity between tested abilities and those generally required for successful school or job performance.

In contrast, prediction of school or job success has never figured heavily in the work of cognitive-developmentalists. Instead, they emphasize understanding the interrelationship of mental functioning or thought processes at successive levels of development for the same person.

To the pragmatics of prediction can be added a second difference of emphasis between the psychometric and Piagetian perspectives. Psychometrics has long been oriented toward the description of individual and group differences in intellectual performance. Thus a "normal range" of intelligence is proposed (see Table 8.3), based in part upon certain assumptions about the distribution of genetic traits in a given population. Individuals are ranked on a scale of "brightness." From this distribution designations are made from "severely retarded" through "average" to "genius," all based upon the IQ. Group differences are also closely examined in the attempt to "explain" sources of variation in intelligence. The result is a massive amount of data (Bayley, 1970). Studies of sex, race, and social class differences have been especially popular. Other illustrative differences are those associated with family size, birth order, father absence, and maternal deprivation. Any differences found are straightforwardly empirical. If reliable, they must be acknowledged to exist. Thus, we can say that psychologists who take a psychometric approach to intelligence have factually demonstrated widespread individual differences. In this sense, the approach is useful for research. Always haunting, however, are the questions of the fairness and representativeness of test content. We agree with others (such

as Tulkin & Konner, 1973), that psychometric intelligence is limited because it emphasizes almost exclusively the mastery of abstract conceptual skills. It is very heavily weighted to the use of formal language, including the printed word, within a particular framework of cultural values. Cross-cultural study reveals other behaviors important for environmental adaptation that may help us expand the range of our thinking about group and individual differences in intellectual development (Glick, 1975; Kleinfeld, 1973).

The classical Piagetian approach pays little attention to individual differences in intelligence. Its focus is species-specific commonalities in development. A hypothesis about stage-sequence universality has been the guiding research light. To query the validity or truth of the cognitive-developmental view is to ask for verification of such universality. In general, research has supported this universality hypothesis, although the story is neither complete nor without discrepancies (Evans, 1975). Most convincing are the data about the distinctiveness of Piagetian stages. The broad sequence of development seems to hold up well, although differences in the *rate* of developmental progress among culturally different but same-age children have been documented (Gaudia, 1972; Wasik & Wasik, 1971). The culturally based rate difference seems to favor children from more technologically advanced societies. Within the same culture, city children are often ahead of their rural counterparts. Even the ultimate level of development attained by children may be affected by background circumstances (Dasen, 1972). And some researchers (for example, Webb, 1974) maintain that the rate or speed with which tasks are mastered within the concrete and formal operational stages is largely a function of psychometric intelligence. On the whole, however, the human intellectual capacities examined from the Piagetian perspective seem less culture-bound and more "pure" across different cultural experiences than do the intellectual skills commonly measured by "conventional" intelligence tests.

Discrepancies in the validating evidence for Piagetian theory may partially result from methodological problems too complex to discuss here. Whatever the complexities, cross-cultural study shows the strongest support for Piaget's ideas about sensorimotor intelligence; somewhat less strong is the evidence for the transition from preoperational to concrete operational thought. Much study remains before moving from cautious skepticism to comforting tentativeness about universality in formal operational thought. There are relatively few independent studies about this allegedly "final" stage in intellectual development. Piagetian theory holds that any development beyond adolescence is largely a matter of progressive refinement in the raw cognitive material of early adolescence. In recent years, still further qualitative changes have been hypothesized in the form of a "fifth stage" involving still more complex abilities for "problem-finding" or the development of dialectic operations (Arlin, 1975; Riegel, 1973).[2] Persuasive rebuttals to these arguments show how Piagetian theory can account for these purported "advances" (Fakouri, 1976; Youniss, 1974). As yet, the issue is still open

Finally, and perhaps most important, many researchers have observed qualitatively different cognitive performance

among elderly persons. These are usually at a more primitive level than performances exhibited by adolescents and middle-aged persons (Denny & Wright, 1976). Performances by the elderly on Piagetian conservation and classification tasks, for example, seem more to approximate those of young children. The reasons for this apparent change are unclear. Regressive changes in cognitive functioning may occur. Tasks themselves may have different meanings at different life stages. Perhaps the changes simply reflect cross-generational discrepancies in learning experiences. In any case, the fact of developmental change during later life periods calls for a more comprehensive theory of lifespan cognitive development (Huston-Stein & Baltes, 1976). The Piagetian perspective is neither final nor are all its premises conclusively verified. In time, the theory may be extended and perfected to "accommodate" these discrepancies. Meanwhile, we find the perspective admirable, both as a model of theory and method and for the comparative specificity with which it defines mental operations.

For the final point of comparison between psychometric and Piagetian conceptions of intelligence we return to the contribution of genetics to human intellectual ability. The psychometric perspective has long been at the center of the nature–nurture controversy discussed in Chapter 2. Nature and nurture have each been thought to contribute a certain proportion of the variation in intelligence among different individuals and groups. Estimates of the "heritability" of intelligence have been sought. Data have largely come from two sources: extent of correlation in the measured intelligence of (1) identical twins, fraternal twins, and siblings, raised in the same or different environments; and (2) parents and their children, both biological and adopted. From these data a

---

[2] Dialectics refers to a method of logic involving the contradiction of opposites (thesis and antithesis) and their continual resolution (synthesis). Unlike Piaget's emphasis upon the social verification of world events in accordance with a presumed and absolute truth, dialectics involves only partial or relative truths at never-ending, but always more-encompassing, levels of experience.

general rule of thumb has developed that the closer the genetic tie between people, the stronger are the correlations between their measured intelligence. Estimates of "heritability," calculated statistically, have ranged as high as 80 percent for nature, 20 percent for nurture. From these estimates it has often been claimed that the major proportion of intelligence is genotypic and directly inherited (Chapter 2). This genotype for intelligence will be only modestly influenced by nurture. Even more specifically, for IQ, the contribution of nurture has been expressed as 20 points one way or the other, depending upon the quality of environmental experience.

Unfortunately, "heritability" estimates are often translated into the idea of genetic determination. It is one thing to suggest nature as a source of *variation* in intellectual development, quite another to say that intelligence is largely fixed or determined by inheritance. At this point in our understanding of psychometric intelligence it seems most ac-

curate to concede that about half of the variation of intelligence test performance can be explained by individual genetic differences (Scarr-Salapatek, 1975). This means that the remaining variations are probably produced by environmental factors, or nurture. Even this notion is based primarily on the study of white children and their parents in modern industrial society; little is known about different populations raised in contrasting environments. Many students of psychometric intelligence, with their emphasis upon sources of individual differences, have from the beginning sought to pinpoint direct estimates of the extent of genetic influence on intellectual functioning. Genetic traits have been assumed to underlie to a large degree the so-called "normal distribution" of measured influence. This thrust in research has not yielded satisfying results but it has led to heated social and political conflicts, especially when inferences about racial differences in intelligence are drawn.

TABLE 8.3   A Classification of Intelligence Based upon Children's Performance on the Wechsler Intelligence Scale for Children (Wechsler, 1974).

	Intelligence Classifications		
		Percent Included	
IQ	*Classification*	*Theoretical normal curve*	*Actual sample*[a]
130 and above	Very Superior	2.2	2.3
120–129	Superior	6.7	7.4
110–119	High Average (Bright)[b]	16.1	16.5
90–109	Average	50.0	49.4
80–89	Low Average (Dull)[b]	16.1	16.2
70–79	Borderline	6.7	6.0
69 and below	Mentally Deficient[b]	2.2	2.2

[a] The percents shown are for Full Scale IQ, and are based on the total standardization sample ($N = 2200$). The percents obtained for Verbal IQ and Performance IQ are essentially the same.
[b] The terms *High Average (Bright)*, *Low Average (Dull)*, and *Mentally Deficient* correspond to the terms *Bright Normal*, *Dull Normal*, and *Mental Defective*, respectively, used in the *WPPSI*, *WAIS*, and 1949 *WISC* manuals.

(Reproduced from the Wechsler Intelligence Scale for Children—Revised Manual by permission. Copyright 1974, by The Psychological Corporation, New York, N.Y. All rights reserved)

For a variety of reasons, many psychologists have found the Piagetian conception of genetic influence more compatible with the presumed truth about human intellectual functioning. To Piaget, genetic influences bear mostly upon how the individual is "wired" to seek interaction with the environment—to assimilate and accommodate. Genetics provides the basis for a definite direction in development, as exemplified in stage invariance. "Heritability" as a factor in individual differences is not at issue within this perspective. Given a normal, healthy biological makeup, all children will progress in the same direction, although at different rates. Biochemical action in concert with equilibration contributes to the organization of systems of mental operations. Unless something is grossly amiss in biological equipment or age-related cultural experience, all persons will (according to the theory) develop their common potentiality for formal operational thought. "Heredity" and learning are so intertwined that they cannot be separated statistically. For Piagetians, therefore, the nature–nurture question is irrelevant (Furth, 1973).

In fact, however, there are questions about the universality of formal operations. Studies (such as Dulit, 1972) indicate that not all youth fully achieve this stage, even in literate, technological societies. No one knows whether or how genetic factors may be implicated in this apparent deficiency, thus pointing up again how much we still have to learn about all aspects of human intellectual development.

MAJOR SOCIAL INFLUENCES

The uncertainties that envelop the idea of genetic determination of intelligence or intellectual potential give us pause when attempting to assess the power of social influences in this area of human development. Strong arguments can be made to show that, relatively speaking, genetics is the single most powerful factor, followed by family background and school, in that order (Nichols, 1976). This statement holds up best for psychometric intelligence. To our knowledge, comparable analyses of variation in Piagetian intelligence are not available. Whatever the relative power of genetics, there are ample data to suggest that social factors make some difference in mental growth over time. Our comments below apply largely to psychometric intelligence. Specific reference to Piagetian intelligence will be made when the data warrant.

Parenting and Caregiving

Chapter 7 stressed the importance of early verbal stimulation and enriched learning experiences for language development. Much the same applies to intellectual development, although the two aspects of development are not identical. As we noted, verbal fluency does not guarantee skill in conceptualizing, problem solving, and critical thinking. Yet language does play an extremely important role in intelligence.

Socioeconomic Factors, Nutrition, and Family Structure

Technicalities aside, we are concerned with nutritional and experiential factors based in the home that seem to affect intellectual growth. Perhaps the most thoroughly documented correlate of both psychometric and Piagetian intelligence is socioeconomic status. Children and youth from the lower social class or from economically handicapped populations are reliably associated with "poor nutrition, high incidence of disease, slow growth and small size" (Bayley, 1970, p. 1189). Accompanying such conditions we find diminished intellectual performance.

Health and nutrition are especially important variables. They come into play as early as the prenatal period. As one authority summarizes the evidence: "Maternal malnutrition during the period of gestation is associated with offspring deficits in body weight and maturation, brain cell number at birth and later in life, and learning ability as measured in adulthood" (Vore, 1973, p. 256).

Of course, malnutrition is a matter of degree and most data involve severe nutritional deficiency. A "threshold hypothesis" has been proposed along these lines, namely, that normal mental sufficiency growth will require a certain minimum level of balanced nutrition, especially protein calories (Read, 1972). Beyond this level, nutritional enrichment may have little, if any, bearing on intellectual growth. Below the threshold level, chronic malnutrition may have permanent or irreversible effects on neurological structures that contribute to the expression of human intelligence.

Thus, to the extent that low socioeconomic status is revealed by poor maternal or subsequent infant nutritional deficiencies, we can identify an apparent link between social class and mental development. Other apparent links include maternal educational and occupational levels and paternal occupation. As these levels rise, so does the level of children's intellectual performance (Honzik, 1973; Marjoribanks, 1972; Rees & Palmer, 1970). Certain family structure variables—often associated with social class—can also account for differences in intellectual performance over time. For example, recent studies of family size (for example, Cicirelli, 1976) report a decrease in IQ among children as the number of siblings in a family increases from 2 to 7 or more. The "effect" has been generally interpreted in terms of the amount of parental attention and stimulation available to each child—the more children, the less attention per child. An alternative hypothesis to account for this relationship brings genetics more strongly into the picture; namely, that it is the less intelligent parents who tend to have larger families. Both interpretations seem more speculative than otherwise.

Father absence is another aspect of family structure that may affect mental growth. Boys, especially, may suffer competence retardation when they have no fathers in the home (Blanchard & Biller, 1971). Even when fathers are present, the quality of the father-son interaction seemingly is important. One study of 4-year-old boys and their fathers showed a positive correlation between parental nurturance and children's IQ; parental restrictiveness was negatively correlated with the boys' intellectual performance (Radin, 1972). We also have evidence that fathers are important factors in girls' cognitive development as early as age 2 (Repucci, 1971).

Home Interaction and Climate

The most often studied home factor is mother–child interaction and the general home climate for children's learning. One study has shown a strong relationship between several early home factors and the mental test performance of preschool-aged children. Home factors were the general emotional and verbal responsiveness of mothers, overall maternal involvement with children, and the provision of appropriate play materials. These factors may be important for the development of children's trust in and enjoyment of their environment which, in turn, facilitates the expression of competence and curiosity motivation (Bradley & Caldwell, 1976). A second related study found increasing correlations in children's test performances with evidence of parental concern for achievement, parental competence, and maternal energy and worrisomeness (Honzik,

1967). This suggests the possibility of strong modeling effects in combination with encouragement, if not demands, for intellectual achievement. Still another study has pointed to the importance for cognitive (and social) competence of sheer amount of language directed at children, opportunities for the exploration and manipulation of objects in the home, practicing simple skills such as block-building and scissor-cutting, and so on (White, 1975). These variables are associated with individual differences in competence among children as early as age 6. They also fit compatibly with the antecedents of instrumental competence discussed in Chapter 3.

The role of play. Many authorities have emphasized *play* as a medium for early cognitive-intellectual stimulation and development. Strictly speaking, of course, play is not a social influence per se. But since children's play occurs mostly in a social context and opportunities for play vary from family to family, we discuss it under the topic of home factors. The reader will recall that different *forms* of children's play were first discussed in Chapter 4, but we reserved our comments about a special form of play — *symbolic play* — until now, because it figures strongly in the Piagetian account of intelligence (Piaget, 1951). Symbolic play, at its zenith between about ages 3 and 6, has a special make-believe or pretend quality. Children use their imaginations to elaborate upon and even modify their immediate concrete reality so as to reenact symbolically things that have happened to them or that they would like to have happen to them. Consider 4-year-old Jennifer, for example, who after hearing a story about her Daddy's airplane trip to the east coast, spent several hours over the next few days playing airline stewardess. The plane was represented symbolically in the child's mind by a certain area of the kitchen. The oven was the

cockpit and a towel drawer was the service area from which all kinds of exotic meals were served to imaginary passengers.

Symbolic play includes play situations that are created by children to express ideas and feelings that either cannot be expressed satisfactorily through language or that represent their best attempts to make sense out of the world they perceive. For example, one father tried to make it clear to his 3-year-old daughter that under no circumstances would their family be able to bring a baby kitten into the household. Various reasons for this were "explained" with no apparent effect on the child's desire for a "meow-cat." Subsequently, the child's play was dominated in a number of ways by the kitty theme. Several times, for instance, elaborate play episodes were organized around the idea of finding and bringing home a kitty to care for. A fuzzy, yellow toy duck was assigned the role of kitty. Daddy's chair was the kitty's bed. The supply of loving attention to this new household addition seemed limitless. Occasionally, the 3-year-old would take on for herself the role of "kitty-cat," complete with a halter of twine fashioned by her 5-year-old sister. Symbolic play is how preschool children incorporate reality into the self in their own way, on their own terms, and without pressures from adults to conform or learn things they cannot fully understand. In short, symbolic play represents children's best means for dealing with life at this unique stage of development.

With age, children's symbolic play gradually gives way to more advanced play forms, including *games with rules* (marbles, hopscotch, hide-and-seek) and *games of construction* (mechanical constructions, adult-like problem-solving activities). These play forms indicate both the expanding sphere of children's social involvement and maturing intellectual skills. But the preschooler's symbolic play has its own important by-products: joy or pleasure gained from self-determined activity, and cementing and practicing newly developing abilities and concepts that are essential for normal growth. In brief, for Piaget symbolic play is required for basic intellectual preparations that facilitate later logical and social development. There is some preliminary evidence that young children who are disadvantaged in their play opportunities can even be "trained" in the ways of imaginative play thereafter to show more advanced cognitive skills, as well as spontaneous fantasy play behaviors (Saltz & Johnson, 1974).

These are but a few of the many important ways home background factors may contribute to, and even accelerate cognitive-intellectual development. Many studies show strikingly similar findings (for example, Hanson, 1975; Yarrow et al., 1972). From these and earlier studies, a general pattern of home environment factors conducive to mental growth has taken form. Though it remains tentative and cannot be taken as *guaranteeing* maximum, positive development, we believe this pattern is a reasonable basis for thinking about humane and facilitative parent–child interaction. One respected student of intellectual development summarizes the pattern as follows:

In essence, given the undamaged genetic potential, mental growth is best facilitated by a supportive "warm" emotional climate, together with ample opportunities for the positive reinforcement of specific cognitive efforts and successes (Bayley, 1970, p. 1203).

This brief but significant statement would seem to hold for any conception of intelligence, both the conventional psychometric and the Piagetian. To this we would add the importance of the general, overall "press" for achievement established by adults within the young child's environment (Harris & McArthur, 1974). The extent to which parents actually *model* intellectual interests, activi-

ties, and verbal reasoning also seems important (Hanson, 1975).

Yet some readers may prefer a more conservative stance, arguing that we can marshall more convincing evidence about producing a "poor" phenotype for intelligence, than creating a "good" one. Extremely poor environments that may include such things as malnutrition and disease, extreme parental abuse, and deprived learning opportunities can radically lower IQ scores (Scarr-Salapatek, 1975). These factors also seem to interfere with the normal progression of operational thinking. But can the provision of a "positive" growth environment do anything more than allow genetically governed growth processes to flourish? That is, can human intelligence be "stretched" or extended to a level of superiority for all children?

This question is purposely exaggerated to prompt speculation. Those persons who believe in the power of environmental forces and the mutability of human intelligence would argue affirmatively. One noted learning theorist (Staats, 1971), for example, views intelligence as simply a cluster of many different specific behavioral skills. The better and more varied are the opportunities and conditions for learning, the better our "intelligence." At the extreme, parents may be led or misled by the promise of giving their children a "superior mind" through environmental design (Engelmann & Engelmann, 1966). In contrast, those who believe in genetic determinism will place little stock in such ideas, especially for the development of abstract conceptual and reasoning skills (Jensen, 1969).

Organized Interventions To Foster Early Intellectual Development

A majority of Americans are an optimistic lot and believe that much can be done to stimulate intellectual development. At the minimum, this means efforts to offset the potentially detrimental effects of environmental deprivation. Such thinking is reflected in the many intervention programs—home-based, group day care, and educational—for infants and young children developed over the past decade (Evans, 1975). Most of these programs involve infants and children from economically deprived backgrounds or families with a history of mental retardation (see Chapter 12). One type of program, for example, focuses on home-based intervention to promote or prevent deficiencies in cognitive functioning. Trained child welfare and education specialists work with mothers of young children in the home environment to arrange growth-enhancing learning activities. Modestly encouraging results from such sustained interventions have been reported. A program, for example, that emphasized mother–child verbal interaction based upon selected play activities, especially educational toys and books (Malden, Levenstein, & Levenstein, 1976), had an impact measured by improved intellectual performance among participating children as compared to nonparticipating children.

Comprehensive day care for infants in group settings outside the home is another type of program (Robinson & Robinson, 1971). If they are of high quality and sufficient duration, these programs are often associated with better mental functioning, especially for verbal tasks, than might be expected among children who do not receive special treatment. We quickly add that the impact seems greater for initially deprived than for privileged children. And there is considerable question about how "permanent" the beneficial effects are. As noted elsewhere (Horowitz & Paden, 1973), both the extent and maintenance of success are associated with two important variables. First is the nature of a program itself, especially the consistency and intensity with which learning activities are provided. Second is the age when infants begin to participate in a program. In general, the earlier and more intensely infants are subjected to intervention techniques, the more likely is success.

The goals of home-based and of comprehensive day-care programs are usually stimulation and enrichment for overall growth. Extraordinary efforts to promote cognitive development are also found among the many experimental preschool education programs for young children. Again, the "most successful" programs share certain common characteristics (Evans, 1975), including clearly established objectives, sequential learning activities with active involvement and ample reinforcement, a strong intellectual-academic curriculum and, of course, able teachers. Even given these program characteristics home support and parental involvement remain important. In fact, they may be necessary to sustain any genuine gains in the children's mental growth.

This leads us to favor long-range programming for positive development rather than the simplistic view that children can be quickly and conveniently "inoculated" against the hazards of environmental deprivation. Until more complete, or possibly contradictory data appear, a long-range "program" for enhancing cognitive-intellectual development can be conceptualized as involving five continuous stages (Bronfenbrenner, 1974). This assumes, of course, a set of value judgments about the importance of goals for socialization and development. It also requires the joint exercise of societal and personal responsibilities for total human welfare.

1. Experiences to prepare youth and young adults for parenthood, including the best available information about child care, nutrition, and home management.

2. Provision of adequate housing and

basic economic security for parents before children are born.

3. During the first three years of life, a parent–child relationship should be established on the principle of reciprocal interaction. This will include joint family activities that are stimulating and challenging for children, home visits by health and education personnel where desirable, and community meetings to reinforce the competence of parents as the primary agents of socialization.

4. From ages 4 to formal school entry (age 5 or 6), an opportunity for children to participate in organized preschool programs should be provided. Together with continued parental involvement, this experience should occur in a benevolent environment rich in cognitive and language activities.

5. From school entrance through the elementary years, parental support of children's educational activities at school (and at home) should be uninterrupted; parents retain the principal responsibility for children's total welfare.

There is room for argument about this blueprint for action. Some persons will maintain that not all children need or want preschool education. Others may object to the socialistic overtones of such a plan, even though it stresses individual parental responsibility. Still others will argue that the great majority of American children and youth already have such experience. The reader is encouraged to ponder these ideas and perhaps formulate alternatives. We think these five guidelines are a reasonable translation of behavioral science research findings into social action prescriptions for children's cognitive-intellectual development.

A Word about Formal Schooling

This brings us directly to consider the influence of traditional public schooling upon the development of intellect. Once children have entered school, however ill or well-prepared by their home backgrounds, can we observe any reliable impact of formal education on their cognitive-intellectual development? Our preliminary discussion in Chapter 5 showed that the impact of schooling has generally been measured by academic achievement, not IQ performance gains. In other words, we have firm evidence that children and youth who perform at higher levels on intelligence measures do better in school. They are also much more likely to stay in school through the secondary school and into college. Indeed, measures of intelligence, or "scholastic aptitude," are often used as a basis for admitting or denying admission to educational programs in many private schools and colleges. But what, exactly, is the effect of education as such on human intelligence?

Our answer cannot be definitive. Intelligence tests are often used in schools to classify, sort, group, and predict the academic success of children and youth but they rarely seem routinely used as a criterion to assess the impact of general schooling. To the extent that success breeds success, and failure breeds frustration and more failure, we can argue for a continuous cycle of positive (or negative) interactions between children's mental abilities and their academic experiences. Where measured intellectual skills have been examined, however, it appears that a comparatively small proportion of the individual differences in IQ stems from formal education (Nichols, 1976). Special educational efforts to "compensate" for educational disadvantages among older children and youth have seldom resulted in substantial and lasting IQ gains. Even carefully designed curricula that cultivate specific skills of problem solving and critical thinking have neither impressive nor uniform effects among groups of children and youth (Hudgins, 1973).

To some extent the lack of firm evidence can be traced to problems of measurement and research methodology. It is very difficult, for example, to clearly separate any effects(s) of schooling from home stimulation or from the general cultural experiences of children and youth. To the extent that (a) schooling provides experience pertinent to children's intelligence test taking and (b) children are capable and motivated to profit from that experience, we would expect that schooling contributes modestly to psychometric intelligence. At least *length* of schooling and IQ are positively correlated (Goulet, Williams, & Hay, 1974). This, of course, does not exclude the possible influence of within-school factors not directly related to instruction, such as peer interactions and extracurricular activities. Perhaps it is more fruitful to ask about the impact on intelligence of different *types* of school experiences, rather than asking about formal education as such. Intensive tutoring programs or school programs built upon a low teacher–pupil ratio, for example, are heralded as more influential for intellectual development than the more typical larger and more loosely organized classrooms (Evans, 1975).

Still another important variable in the schooling-intelligence relationship is the developmental status of the learner. Our most pertinent evidence on this point comes from the study of schooling effects on Piagetian intelligence. In general, for Piagetians, there is no substitute for general, massed, age-related experience (Kohlberg, 1968). Specific "training" for intellectual development is considered relatively futile, although appropriately arranged training may facilitate rapid stage transition. That is, young children in the intuitive period of transition from preoperational to operational thinking can often be accelerated, though the educational advantage of this has not been clearly demonstrated (Bearison, 1975). Apart from highly specific training procedures, formal schooling does not seem to affect in any profound way the achievement of concrete operational thinking. In other words, this stage in intellectual development seems more closely tied to the spontaneous and unarranged learning experiences common to most children everywhere, and not as much to their structured and largely verbal classroom experiences.

There is, however, a suggestion that advanced education may have greater influence in the achievement of formal operational thinking (Dasen, 1972; Gallagher & Noppe, 1976). Perhaps this is because advanced levels of education call for the practice of, or may even activate, the mental operations required for formal logic and scientific analysis. This point is speculative and further research is needed to illuminate the relationship between schooling and formal operational thinking.

We will touch again upon issues about human intellectual ability and schooling in Chapter 10. Now we emphasize that, in general, formal education has a limited influence on cognitive-intellectual development, perhaps because much of the constellation of skills, abilities, and motives important for continued development has already taken shape by the time children come to school. Quality of schooling may thus be more important for general cognitive development among children from initially disadvantaged circumstances (Chapter 5). But we can too easily forget that measured intelligence is a rather narrow sampling of intellectual functions within a distinct framework of cultural values about verbal knowledge, language proficiency, and abstract reasoning. It is comforting to think that many worthy outcomes of education are not suitably measured by intelligence tests. There is ample evidence that exposure to formal instruction is followed by gains in academic achievement (Wiley & Harnischfeger, 1974). And certainly academic progress will require the use of various intellectual skills. Perhaps schooling can be viewed constructively as an important context in which intelligence can flourish.

As for such other possible social influences on intellectual development as the mass media, we reserve comment until Chapter 10. The media, especially educational television, seem more clearly geared to inform and promote academic achievement, than to improve intellectual problem solving. There remain, however, at least two important aspects of human cognitive-intellectual development about which nothing has yet been said: cognitive-style and creativity. Both of these aspects also seem important for illustrating the interaction of cognitive and personal-social attributes in overall development. Thus, Chapter 8 concludes with an overview of these related areas of human functioning.

SOME FURTHER ASPECTS OF COGNITIVE DEVELOPMENT

Cognitive Style

Our discussion of cognitive-intellectual development has emphasized problem-solving ability. Problem solving can also be thought about as a process during which information is gathered, organized, and applied to the solution of various tasks. It is instructive to consider at least five major components of this process: *encoding* (selective attention to and preferential perceptual analysis of an event), *memory* (information storage and retrieval), *hypothesis formulation* (producing alternative hunches), *evaluation* (examining the quality or validity of these hunches), and *deduction* (implementing a hypothesis or arriving at conclusions) (Kagan & Kogan, 1970). It is the

encoding, hypothesis formulation, and *evaluation* phases of information processing for problem solving that reveal particularly intriguing individual differences among children and youth—differences that seem more a matter of preference for perceiving, categorizing, and reflecting upon information than the actual intellectual ability or power to do so. For example, we may ask a group of children to tell us how they would group or "put together" in some way certain objects like (1) *dog* and *sheep* and (2) *pitcher* and *glass*. Some children may show a distinct preference for *categorical* grouping: "They are both *animals;* they are both *containers.*" Each object serves as an independent instance of a broader, more abstract concept. Other children may group these objects on a *descriptive* basis: "They both have four legs;" "They are both made of glass." In this case, classification occurs by objectively common parts of the whole stimulus. And still other children may group by functional *relationship:* "Dogs are used to herd sheep;" "A pitcher is used to pour milk into a glass." Here the meaning of the items or objects depends largely upon their relationship to one another in a particular contextual relationship. We might agree that all three grouping preferences are essentially "correct," although the first indicates a greater sensitivity to abstract conceptual classes. The point is that grouping occurs on a distinctive basis, apparently a reflection of personal preference for *form* or *manner* in cognition.

Individual differences in form and manner of cognition—distinctive ways of apprehending, transforming, and utilizing information—have been summarized by the term *cognitive style* (Kogan, 1971). Many variations on the theme of cognitive style have been proposed. Indeed, one authority (Messick, 1970) has pointed to nine dimensions of cognitive style, though it is possible that many of these are more differences in *labels* than genuinely different aspects of cognitive style. (See Table 8.4.)

Among the more widely studied of these cognitive styles is a difference in the extent to which individuals analyze a stimuli field in terms of part–whole relationships and smaller elements imbedded within the total configuration of objects or properties (see Number 1 in Table 8.4). Looking skyward on a dark, clear night some children may view a constellation of stars both in terms of its total pattern and subpatterns within the larger whole. Or when confronted with line drawings of a forest in which small birds are "hidden" among tree branches, they easily detect these subelements without being distracted by the overall complexity of the picture. Such children are said to be *field independent* in their cognitive style. They effectively abstract patterns, designs, or configurations independently from the total perceptual field. Other children are more undifferentiated in their perceptual responses. They attend more to the global pattern presented by objects in the environment. Children whose responses rely upon the totality of given sensory information to organize their perceptions can be described as *field dependent* (Witkin et al., 1962).

This distinction does not mean that there are two kinds of people, field-dependent or field-independent. Cognitive style is more like many other human characteristics that, when measured, show a continuum of scores. In other words, people are more or less field-dependent or -independent. Even so, individual differences in field dependence–independence are correlated with a variety of other cognitive-intellectual and personal-social behaviors (Messick, 1970; Witkin, 1976). Most of these behavioral differences have been discovered by comparing persons at the relative extremes in field-dependence and

-independence. From these comparisons we have learned that field-independent persons usually do better on analytical intelligence tasks (mathematics, spatial relations, mechanical aptitude) though they are not superior to field-dependent individuals in general intelligence. Field-independent persons also show more articulated, differentiated body concepts and autonomous personal identities. Field-dependent persons, on the other hand, seem more sensitive to social cues and show a stronger preference for activities that feature interpersonal relations. Further differences extend into such domains as creativity, reading achievement, assertiveness, pain reactivity, persistence, educational and vocational planning, and even forms of psychological disturbance (Witkin, 1965). As a characteristic way of perceiving the world and oneself in relation to it, field dependence–independence seems to function across a wide variety of human experiences.

TABLE 8.4   Varieties of Cognitive Style

Nine Cognitive Styles
1. *Field independence versus field dependence.* An analytical, in contrast to a global, way of perceiving (which) consists of a tendency to experience items as discrete from their backgrounds, and reflects ability to overcome the influence of an embedding context.
2. *Scanning.* A dimension of individual differences in the extensiveness and the intensity of attention deployment, leading to individual variations in the vividness of experience and the span of awareness.
3. *Breadth of categorizing.* Consistent preferences for broad inclusiveness, as opposed to narrow exclusiveness, in establishing the acceptable range for specified categories.
4. *Conceptualizing styles.* Individual differences in the tendency to categorize perceived similarities and differences among stimuli in terms of many differentiated concepts, which is a dimension called conceptual differentiation, as well as consistencies in the utilization of particular con-

ceptualizing approaches as bases for forming concepts (such as the routine use in concept formation of thematic or functional relations among stimuli as opposed to the analysis of descriptive attributes or the inference of class membership).

5. *Cognitive complexity versus simplicity.* Individual differences in the tendency to construe the world, particularly the world of social behavior, in a multidimensional and discriminating way.

6. *Reflectivity versus impulsivity.* Individual consistencies in the speed with which hypotheses are selected and information is processed, with impulsive subjects tending to offer the first answer that occurs to them, even though it is frequently incorrect, and with reflective subjects tending to ponder various possibilities before deciding.

7. *Leveling versus sharpening.* Reliable individual variations in assimilation in memory. Subjects at the leveling extreme tend to blur similar memories and to merge perceived objects or events with similar but not identical events recalled from previous experience. Sharpeners, at the other extreme, are less prone to confuse similar objects and, by contrast, may even judge the present to be less similar to the past than is actually the case.

8. *Constricted versus flexible control.* Individual differences in susceptibility to distraction and cognitive interference.

9. *Tolerance for incongruous or unrealistic experiences.* A dimension of differential willingness to accept perceptions at variance with conventional experience.

From S. Messick, The criterion problem in the evaluation of instruction: Assessing possible, not just intended, outcomes. In M. C. Wittrock and D. E. Wiley (Eds.), *The evaluation of instruction.* New York: Holt, Rinehart and Winston. Copyright 1970. Reproduced by permission.

Further research has resulted in even more specific and consistent findings about cognitive style as an important source of individual differences in problem-solving behavior (Hall & Russell, 1974). One of the most reliable of these differences is individual consistency in the speed and efficiency with which hypotheses are selected, evaluated, and tested in problem-solving situations. This dimension of cognitive style is referred to as *conceptual tempo* (Kagan, 1965).

Conceptual Tempo

Conceptual tempo involves the extent to which children or youth ponder and reflect on the adequacy or correctness of ideas for problem solving before they actually volunteer a specific answer. Thus tempo seems most apparent in problem situations that contain an element of uncertainty or ambiguity. Some individuals are characteristically deliberate and reflective about their problem-solving activities, including the way they approach new tasks. They examine new information or materials carefully and systematically. Others respond impulsively, quickly, and thoughtlessly in new situations. They do not take sufficient time to think carefully about the nature of the information and the materials or the alternative responses that they might make. On the other hand, style of approach to problem solving cannot simply be measured by time lapse in response, or response latency. There is some indication that efficiency in information processing is also involved. That is, even when response time differences in problem solving among children become more equal, some children seem to make better use of the time they have. Because of more efficient processing (solving matrix problems, matching patterns, playing the game of 20 questions, thinking in terms of class inclusion, abstracting common properties) those children apparently have more adequate information upon which to base a response. As a consequence, they are less prone to error in their final response selection (Egelund & Higgins, 1976; Haskins & McKinney, 1976; McKinney, 1975; Weiner, 1975; Weiner & Berzonsky, 1975).

Children and youth who are efficient and deliberate in their style and tempo and conceptual processing have been called *reflective*; children who respond less efficiently, even though often more quickly, are referred to as *impulsive*.

Figure 8.2 presents an example of items for the formal measurement of conceptual tempo. A behavioral example can illustrate how reflectivity or impulsivity may be observed as early as the late preschool years. Suppose two 3-year-old male children enter for the first time a room full of unfamiliar toys and games. One child pauses to look about the entire room, taking note of the various alternatives for activity. He then selects a marble game, which occupies his attention for the next 10 or 15 minutes. After looking about still further, he next chooses to play a block-building game, and so on. In contrast, the second child does not look over the many possibilities for play. Rather, he runs immediately to a jack-in-the-box, which, in a few seconds, he discards in favor of a set of toy train cars. After a minute or two this child picks up some nesting blocks, only to drop them in favor of a 10-piece wooden puzzle. Then, instead of completing the puzzle, he moves to still another toy. This example suggests a basic difference in the way these two children survey, approach, and engage in various activities.

An important result of this difference for learning is that children prone to respond impulsively are more likely to make unnecessary mistakes than are children who first reflect on the quality of their tentative answers. The greater number of mistakes made by impulsive children does not necessarily mean that such children are less bright or knowledgeable about their world (Kagan, 1965), but this difference in timing or tempo does show up in behavior. Most of us have observed that some children engaged in group recitation or discussion activities raise their hands to answer questions, apparently without thinking about whether their responses are right or wrong. Some children volunteer answers even before they hear the entire question. In some situations, such as pretend quiz shows and guessing games, such behavior may be appropriate. In others, such as working independently on a perceptual matching task (matching pairs of pictures of letterlike forms on the printed page) or responding to a test where one must choose from among many different answers, impulsive behavior may be harmful. In fact, one authority reports that male children who are retained in the first grade are more often impulsive than their promoted peers, even though the two groups of children are not different in measured intelligence (Messer, 1970a).

Developmental aspects of reflectivity-impulsivity. Long-term studies of children's problem-solving tempo or style have led to two important findings: (1) that individual differences in this aspect of cognitive style may appear as early as age 2; and (2) that children generally become more reflective with age through adolescence and beyond (Kagan & Kagan, 1970). It is also possible that some children change little in impulsivity with age. Some may even become more impulsive. Constitutional factors such as general activity level may be involved, although developmental changes in tempo are undoubtedly also affected by children's social and academic experiences. For example, some teachers and parents may place a greater value on speed than on accuracy of response in task situations and may reinforce behavior accordingly. Various links between problem-solving tempo and several important academic-related behaviors have been made. Reflective children, for example, seem to demonstrate more sustained attention spans, greater frustration tolerance, fewer errors in beginning reading (especially girls), stronger coordination of attention-perceptual skills in analyzing problems, less fidgety or easily distracted behavior in formal learning situations, greater flexibility and resourcefulness in method of attacking problems, and generally stronger aca-

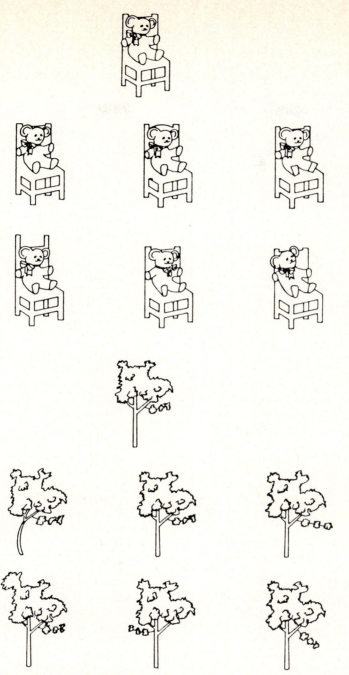

Fig. 8-2 Sample items from a test to measure conceptual tempo, or reflectivity–impulsivity. A child's task is to match the familiar figure at the top of each stimulus array with its duplicate among the six alternatives provided in each case. Only *one* figure is correct in each item. Scoring is determined by accuracy and amount of time consumed for a given response. (From J. Kagan, Impulsive and reflective children: Significance of conceptual tempo. In J. Krumboltz (Ed.), Learning and the educational process. Skokie, Ill.: Rand McNally. Copyright 1965. By permission.)

demic performance in school (Block, Block, & Harrington, 1974; Bush & Dweck, 1975; Feij, 1976; Grant, 1976; Kagan, 1965; Siegelman, 1969).

With such data in mind, we might easily make a value judgment to the effect that reflectivity is good and impulsivity is bad. Impulsive children, however, have been observed to be more often active socially, more likely to interact spontaneously with peers and adults, and to enjoy such interaction more (Kagan, 1965). In certain stages of the creative process (see next section) it is also possible that some degree of impulsivity may be valuable. It has been further suggested that reflective children may be more anxious about making errors or displaying incompetence (Messer, 1970b). Actually, the role of anxiety in conceptual tempo is not too clear. Anxiety about self-perceived incompetence to master a task could underlie the tendency to be impulsive, but anxiety about making mistakes on tasks that one believes can be solved or mastered may prompt reflectivity (Kagan & Messer, 1975). Whatever the relationship of anxiety to conceptual tempo, it is the impulsive child who is probably most often handicapped in formal learning situations, especially those where making mistakes results in faulty learning or disapproval and criticism from others.

Some implications of reflectivity–impulsivity. Consider first some tentative implications of conceptual tempo for everyday adult–child interaction. Adults rarely attend to a child's style for approaching conceptual problems. Children are more often categorized by adults as bright–dull, responsible–irresponsible, outgoing–shy, and the like, rather than as being careful in their work (reflective) or hair-trigger (impulsive) (Kagan, 1965). Accordingly, adults may be deceived into looking upon impulsive, quick children as "brighter"

than their equally intelligent peers who take more time to examine data and organize their responses. Quickness does not necessarily indicate brightness, although it seems good (adaptive) to be alert. By the same token, deliberating and pondering do not necessarily indicate slowness or indecisiveness. Moreover, in some learning situations (for example, reading-readiness activities), a child's errors may result less from "slow maturation," "sensory impediments," or "low intelligence" than from conceptual tempo. If tempo is important for success in a certain activity, helping a child to adopt the most appropriate tempo for the circumstances may be desirable.

Modifying conceptual tempo.   It follows that, where appropriate and desirable, deliberate efforts to modify or change an impulsive or reflective tendency may be called for. This need may be clearest where one or the other response style interferes with educational progress. Such a task is more easily written about than done. Though reflectivity may increase with age for children in general, some children—especially impulsives—may become habitual in their cognitive style. Hence most attempts or strategies for modifying conceptual tempo have occurred with these more impulsive children. Such attempts range from general to specific and vary in the extent to which they incorporate such learning principles as imitation and reinforcement. In one study, for example, a direct tutoring procedure for impulsive first-grade children was implemented to help them learn how and when to inhibit fast responses to problems. The tutoring procedure was generally effective, although little improvement in the quality of these children's intellectual performance was noted (Kagan, Pearson, & Welch, 1966).

Other studies suggest the value of

several other conditions: explicit advance explanations about an appropriate task strategy, prompting or cueing during problem-solving activities, planned positive reinforcement for desired conceptual tempo and analytic behavior, and prolonged exposure to adults who model a given conceptual style (Baird & Bee, 1969; Brodzinsky, Feuer, & Owens, 1977; Denney, 1972; Heider, 1971; Yando & Kagan, 1968). For parents and teachers the modeling procedure is particularly important. Anyone who has observed extensively in classrooms has probably noted differences in conceptual tempo among teachers themselves. Some teachers proceed rapidly with the presentation of activities, are constantly mindful of time limitations, encourage children to respond quickly, verbalize instructions and ideas rapidly, and generally operate at a high rate of speed. Others are more concerned with deliberations and alternatives and move at a moderate pace. We should be alert to the possible effects of teacher tempo on the conceptual tempos of children in a given classroom, in addition to the pattern of reinforcement for impulsive or reflective behavior and explicit, relevant task-appropriate instructions for performance. In some instances, simply a reminder or caution to consider alternative meanings or possible solutions may be sufficient.

We close this brief discussion of conceptual style and tempo with two reservations. First, there is always some element of risk in expressing optimism about the modifiability of any habit pattern for human beings. As one recent study has shown, successful impulse-control training can be extremely difficult, especially for very young children who show some evidence of inheriting the trait (Plomin & Willerman, 1975). Second, there is much argument about the exact nature, measurement, and generality of conceptual style and tempo. Much time and effort are required to achieve even the most rudimentary understanding of cognitive style, even though a large body of information has accumulated. Our generalizations must be considered tentative and acknowledging the lack of agreement about measurement and research methodology suitable for a valid picture of cognitive style (Ault, Mitchell, & Hartmann, 1976; Block et al., 1974; Egelund & Weinberg, 1976; Harrison & Nadelman, 1972).

Creativity

The first and most basic issue in discussing human creativity is the nature of creativity itself. Taking our cues from the major theoretical approaches to this issue, we prefer to think about creativity as behavior that represents both a *process* and a *product* (Golann, 1963; Wallach, 1970). As a *process*, creativity can be considered complex thinking that requires as yet unknown proportions of knowledge, the ability to see new relationships among objects or events, radar-like attention to the environment, a willingness to engage in fantasy in thought, the formulation and testing of alternative hypotheses, skill in communicating one's thoughts to others, and a concern for both complexity and esthetics in problem finding and solving.

Creativity can also be discussed as a *novel* or an *original product* that is satisfying, meaningful, and valuable, to the creator, to his or her culture, or to both. Usually, such a product is a modification or a rejection of previously accepted ideas, represents large amounts of motivation and intellectual energy, and is prompted by an initially ambiguous and ill-defined problem (Newell, Shaw, & Simon, 1962). Consider, for example, the remarkable Polaroid camera developed by Edwin Land. He has expressed a strong belief that, "If a problem can be defined, it can be solved."

Creativity has been a subject for armchair analysis and speculation for centuries, but a major upsurge in the scientific study of creativity can be traced to an important distinction made several decades ago between *convergent* and *divergent* thinking (Guilford, 1959). Convergent thinking can take many forms, but its core is the production of information from given information where the goal is one best or most acceptable answer or solution. Thus, in the following word pattern, only one answer logically follows: Pot-Top, Nip-Pin, Keep-*(Peek)*. Syllogistic reasoning also calls for convergent production, for example: All magpies are noisy—This bird is a magpie—Therefore, this bird is noisy. Many intelligence-test items require convergent production.

In contrast, divergent thinking calls for the production of information from given information where the emphasis is upon more than one answer—a variety of solutions, often with attention to uniqueness or cleverness. Actually there are many different components of divergent production. We will mention here only three of the most important for illustrative purposes. One is *associational fluency*, or the ability to produce information from a restricted area of meaning: "How many things can you think of that (are round) (have wheels) (move in water) (sparkle)?" A second important aspect of divergent thinking is *ideational fluency*, or the number (and novelty) of different ideas that can be generated in response to a task or problem: "How many different ways could we find to use a (coat hanger) (string) (brick) (old light bulb)?" Fluency need not be limited to verbal tasks. "Nonverbal" responses can also be called for, as in drawings, pattern construction, body movements, and sound configurations. Finally, related to fluency, is *originality* in responding. Originality is determined by the relative infrequency with which certain responses occur within some

general and meaningful context. The task of providing plot titles to stories, or writing stories to plot titles, can illustrate. In the first case, one might ask for three (or more) endings (humorous, moralistic, sad) to a familiar story, such as "The Tortoise and the Hare." In the second case, we might ask for a story about "The Teacher Who Couldn't Talk," or "The Pencil That Couldn't Write." These examples pertain more to younger children than, say, to adults, but nevertheless convey the spirit of measuring divergency in thought.

By no means should divergent thinking be equated to or considered synonymously with creativity. We consider creativity a much broader concept of human ability. But as will be seen, divergent thinking has come to dominate much of the recent research about creativity and its development.

Assumptions about Creativity

We can usefully discuss creativity in the light of five basic assumptions. First, it is generally assumed that creativity is an aspect of intelligent behavior that can be expressed in a variety of ways at a number of levels. For example, just as a nuclear physicist or a jazz composer can be creative in the laboratory or the music room, so can a cook in the kitchen and a kindergartner during "Show and Tell."

Second, it is assumed that all children and youth possess creative abilities to some degree. One person may demonstrate creative abilities more often than another, but no one completely lacks them.

A third assumption is that creative abilities can be developed under the "right" conditions. The exact nature of these facilitating conditions may not be the same for any two children or adolescents, but it seems clear that some general conditions apply to most people.

Fourth, we assume with Piaget that

development of creative abilities is (or at least should be) a prime educational goal. This assumption raises some sticky issues, including how to achieve a balance between the intellectual conformity necessary in a society and individual tendencies toward the unconventional. This assumption also requires that one have clearly in mind the specific behavioral components of creative expression so that independence or meditation is not confused with destructive rebelliousness or indecision. Nevertheless, we believe that creativity is a valuable part of human development that must be nourished and encouraged within the schools.

Finally, and perhaps most important given the foregoing discussion of intelligence, we assume that creativity (with its central component of divergent thinking) and measured intelligence (with its central component of convergent thinking) are not one and the same. There is no consensus among psychologists on this point. Intelligence and creativity certainly overlap to some degree. But there is simply too much evidence to deny at least a moderate distinction between these two aspects of human functioning (Getzels & Jackson, 1962; Wallach & Kogan 1965; Welsh, 1975). In fact, some children and youth who score high on conventional intelligence tests do not show as much creativity as children and youth who score lower on such tests (Stein, 1968). This may mean that certain abilities important for creative expression are different from those important for intelligence-test performance. The point is threefold (Piers, 1976). First, while creativity is surely an aspect of man's intelligence, high scores on intelligence tests and elevated levels of creativity do not necessarily go hand in hand. Second, performance on tests of intelligence is not a reliable predictor of creative achievement across life's many path-

ways. And third, higher levels of creativity probably involve factors over and above learning aptitude and problem-solving skills, and are likely to include curiosity and other personality characteristics.

Research Orientations to Creativity

Psychometric methods. Psychologists have blazed a network of related trails of inquiry in their effort to understand more about creativity. One basic and extensively explored trail has involved psychometric efforts to devise instruments that measure creativity or, more accurately, *divergent thinking abilities,* in a reliable and valid manner. A persistent problem for this line of research work has been to find measures that are truly distinct from traditional measures of general intelligence and achievement. Nevertheless, much success has been achieved, particularly in the measurement of fluency in generating a variety of original ideas in situations involving only moderate amounts of structure (Wallach, 1970). A wide range of individual differences during childhood and adolescence has been revealed by psychometric instruments. It has also been discovered that test conditions sometimes make a difference in creative performance. Indices of creativity for some children and youth are often higher when time limits are removed, a gamelike atmosphere is established, and people are allowed to share ideas (Torrance, 1969; 1971). This suggests that creativity is more likely to flourish in situations where stress, anxiety, and social isolation do not prevail, though the evidence is far from consistent on this point (Channon, 1974; Milgram & Milgram, 1976).

Perhaps the most serious challenge to the psychometric study of creativity is that, oddly enough, many researchers find little or no relationship between children's tested performance of divergent thinking abilities and their later creative achievements in high school years and beyond (Kogan & Pankove, 1974). In other words, straightforward cognitive testing, even of abilities thought important for creativity, has rather limited value for predicting "real life" attainments. This seems especially true in fields such as art, drama, literature, and music for children and youth who are at least average or above in measured intelligence (Jordan, 1975). Such low predictability leads us quickly to speculate that other "noncognitive" factors may be more crucial in accounting for creative achievement, including leadership, writing, and independent scientific work. Some researchers stress the usefulness of autobiographical information to study this (Torrance, Bruch, & Morse, 1973). A growing number of investigators emphasize the importance of *personality differences*.

Personality differences   This second related approach to creativity study has most often involved a comparison of attitudes, values, motivations, and temperament between extremely creative and less creative children and youth. Results of these investigations are difficult to summarize for at least two reasons. First, the sheer number of such studies is virtually overwhelming. Second, results are often conflicting, perhaps because of different ways of defining and measuring creativity. For example, some psychologists use ratings of children and youth by teachers or other "experts" to identify more and less creative individuals. Others use psychometric devices of the Guilford type (Guilford, 1959). Still others infer creativity level by less direct means, such as the analysis of children's fantasies obtained through interviews.

Despite these obstacles, it is fair to say that some commonalities run through the studies of the creative person. Creative children or youth are often highly self-confident and accepting, intellectually curious, independent in judgment and behavior, less concerned than most with social convention, genial (although not necessarily intimate with their parents), favorably disposed toward complex and novel activities, tolerant of ambiguity, persistent, sensitive to problems, neither dogmatic nor authoritarian, express strong esthetic interests, are strong in disciplined effectiveness, and are prone to value and cultivate a strong sense of humor (Berelson & Steiner, 1964; Piers, 1976).

These findings suggest that creativity and characteristics normally associated with positive development and adjustment go together. Yet no cause–effect relationship is indicated by these data. "Good" personality adjustment does not necessarily guarantee creativity, nor can it be said that creativity does not occur in the absence of such characteristics. We believe, however, that these data contraindicate the popular myth that equates creativity with maladjustment and emotional disturbance or undisciplined thinking and social alienation (Garfield, Cohen, & Roth, 1969). There is also some preliminary evidence to indicate that, to the extent that creative performance calls for deliberate and systematic analysis in the early stages of a problem or task situation, a *reflective* (versus impulsive) conceptual style would seem advantageous (Fuqua, Bartsch, & Phye, 1975). But a *readiness* to express impulses and imaginative thoughts through conscious thought or in active, assertive ways also seems important (Elton & Rose, 1974). Thus highly creative persons may be generally more adept at both reflection and deliberate introspection on the one hand, and free-wheeling impulsivity on the other, depending upon the point in the creative process where each is useful.

Background factors   A third line of creativity research involves the search for background factors in creative development, including cultural and family influences that may contribute to individual differences in creativity. For example, in one of the few cross-cultural studies of creativity among elementary and junior high school children, creative expression was judged more frequent in cultures characterized by less authoritarian attitudes toward childrearing and social relationships (Anderson & Anderson, 1965). It is argued that the dominant pattern in some cultures is one of restrictiveness, conditional acceptance, and failure to stimulate free interplay of differences among children and youth. An individual who grows up under the influence of such a pattern is less likely to become creative, especially because creativity implies communicating the truth as one sees it.

As the reader might suspect, the relationship between creativity and social class factors has also been explored. Among the most provocative findings are those that point to the stronger relationship between social class factors and creative output during the preschool and early school years than during the later school years (Lichtenwalner & Maxwell, 1969; Solomon, 1967). In contrast to developmental data about intelligence, creative performance apparently is not affected as much by socioeconomic background, especially in later childhood and adolescence. A related finding is that youth who drop out of high school, many of whom come from lower socioeconomic backgrounds, often score higher on creativity tests than their stay-in counterparts (Janssen, 1968). Still another intriguing study has shown that bright, but economically disadvantaged children can excel their gifted and more advantaged peers in competitive creative problem-solving performance (Torrance, 1974).

We do not suggest that social class factors are irrelevant to the study of creativity—more work is needed to understand the workings of these factors. But we can suggest that creativity is not much restricted by social class boundaries, perhaps much less so than is conventional measured intelligence.

Studies of childrearing practices comprise a third cluster of reports about background factors in creativity. Most frequently, these studies have involved a comparison of parents whose offspring are high in creativity (or creative potential) with parents whose offspring show less creative promise. In an early study of adolescent creativity, for example, parents of high creatives were found to be less critical of their adolescent offspring and their schools; more liberal and tolerant in general outlook, tending to focus on their child's values; and open to experience, interests, and enthusiasms (Getzels & Jackson, 1962). These findings suggest that child-centered orientation, along with creative parental models, facilitate creative development. This interpretation is reinforced by still other data. Parental characteristics associated with higher rates of divergent production in children are: (1) low degree of punishment in the home, (2) low pressure for conformity, (3) absence of intrusiveness, (4) emotional support of and satisfaction with the child, and (5) self-acceptance. Opportunities for and parental encouragement of social make-believe or pretend play may also partly account for individual differences in divergent thinking abilities as early as the late preschool years (Johnson, 1976).

As with cultural and social class factors, data about child-rearing practices do not prove causation. The establishment of conditions such as those described cannot guarantee high creativity in children. It is possible that such parental behaviors occur after a child's creative potential becomes apparent rather than before; indeed, the child's very creativity may lead to such behavior. No one knows for sure what conditions in the home facilitate creativity for a given child. As for developmental trends in creativity, individual differences in behaviors considered important for creative expression are apparent by age 4 or 5. These include differences in impersonal and social conformity, a willingness to try difficult tasks, and originality (Starkweather, 1971). Thereafter, these differences become more pronounced with age. As we would expect, however, most (if not all) children show a rather steady increase in divergent-thinking abilities with age through the high school years. Perhaps the most basic issue, then, is how best to encourage or enhance this development.

How can creativity be encouraged? The question of what conditions best facilitate creativity is central to the fourth and last avenue for creativity research to be discussed. Psychologists concerned with facilitating conditions have concentrated largely on studying specific environmental factors that are subject to manipulation in the laboratory or the classroom. Because this is so directly relevant to educating for creativity, a virtual explosion of research into facilitative conditions has occurred in recent years. Some authorities began by attempting to identify characteristics of teachers and classrooms where low rates of creative production among students prevailed (Torrance, 1963). As the reader might predict, classrooms characterized by low creative output are often those where challenging activities are rarely pursued, sanctions are established against questioning and exploring, a strong division is made between work and play (for example, "The fun's over now children; it's time for arithmetic."), and pressures for absolute intellectual and social conformity are applied (for example, "Johnny, only girls write love stories in English composition. Why don't you write about football or deep-sea diving?") or ("Whoever heard of a

green Santa Claus? Do your picture again and color Santa *red!*").

Subsequent research has revealed that teachers who are rated by their superiors as resourceful and pupil-centered increase creative behavior among their charges (Turner & Denny, 1967). Another research worker found that a consistently indirect teaching style (accepting and clarifying student feelings, praising and encouraging student ideas, using student ideas to build and develop classroom discussion) was associated with growth in verbal and figural creative expression over a four-year period (Weber, 1968).

Gradually, however, more focused attempts to "train" for creativity have evolved. Though not mutually exclusive, training strategies can be grouped by certain emphases (Meichanbaum, 1975). One strategy emphasizes systematic cognitive skill training with particular attention to fluency and originality in responding; abilities to manipulate information are given highest priority. Behavioral principles such as modeling and reinforcement figure strongly in this approach. A second strategy is concerned more with the provision of a secure and supportive emotional climate for the expression of imaginative and fanciful ideas. In this way, it is hoped that any mental blocks to creativity, including defensiveness and self-critical tendencies, can be removed to free a flow of creative ideas. A third strategy goes still further to promote the development of certain attitudes such as a willingness to take risks, heightened self-understanding and acceptance, and a belief in oneself as a creative person. Training strategies are usually based upon a particular belief, or theory, about the nature and development of creativity.

Two prominent scholars (Torrance & Torrance, 1976) have recently surveyed over 140 "experiments" designed to influence creativity among school age children and youth, including many that fit the above emphases. Generally speaking, these experiments have shared some basic and common objectives: increasing the extent of originality, associational and ideational fluency, flexibility in creative problem solving, and the ability to elaborate upon simple ideas. Two main conclusions can be drawn from this survey. First, the ability to perform creatively or, better, to exercise divergent thinking, *can* be influenced to some extent by environmental manipulations feasible in the classroom. Not all children and youth show gains, nor is the gain always impressive. But change can occur. Second, in general, the more "disciplined" or organized and systematic strategies are the most effective. Yet no one strategy yet studied can be said to guarantee gains in creative thinking. It is clearly a matter of increasing the *probability* of success.

Having made these two points we hasten to qualify them by raising three related issues about teaching for creativity. First, most studies have dealt with relatively short-term effects of training. It is difficult to marshall evidence about the longer-term or more permanent effects of training strategies. Second, the intriguing question of why training "works" has not yet been answered satisfactorily. Especially puzzling is why some children and youth respond positively to one or another training strategy while others do not. Third, the important issue of *transfer* or generalizability of training effects beyond the classroom and into nonacademic life looms across the broad horizon of creativity education. It is one thing to promote skill development in contrived settings. Demonstrating that children and youth need or subsequently utilize these skills to build creativity into their lives out of school is another. To date, the evidence about transfer is minuscule.

This need not be taken to refute the possible values of creativity education. It does, however, present a challenge to psychologists and educators who seek to expand the form and function of education to include explicit creativity objectives and methods for achieving them. Taking a strongly optimistic stance, we can argue that nothing yet contraindicates the potential worth of a cluster of teaching techniques for encouraging creativity. This cluster represents neither a prescription nor a substitute for genuinely humane and competent teaching. We offer the following suggestions, however, for our readers' consideration: (1) leading the student to question, (2) using analogy, metaphor, and the free association of ideas, (3) permitting logical analysis to come late in the discovery process, (4) encouraging skepticism, (5) permitting moderate disorder, (6) leaving blocks of time free for thought, (7) furnishing esthetic experiences, (8) reinforcing creative expression, and (9) relating material that is studied to other subjects or to broader concepts and problems of relevance to learners (Zahn, 1966). Specific activities relevant to this cluster of techniques are described elsewhere (for example, Davis, 1976). Perhaps the most important factors underlying any success in the use of such techniques will be positive teacher (or parent) attitudes toward human development and creativity, together with skill in modeling abilities important for creative thinking (Belcher, 1975; Frederickson & Evans, 1974).

To summarize, we have considered the nature of creativity in terms of both processes and product, have made explicit some basic assumptions that underlie contemporary thinking about creativity, and have examined several lines of research into creativity and its development. Many dilemmas are associated with the psychological study of creativity. These dilemmas range from the definition and measurement of creativity to procedures for promoting creative development within the formal academic setting. Some of our own students maintain that creativity is such a personal and individual matter that it either cannot or should not be studied scientifically. We respect this view, but believe that a

search for understanding human development and behavior is incomplete without paying serious attention to creativity, a unique characteristic of humankind. Also, the potential value is vast of the insights reaped from discovering conditions that maximize rather than minimize or subvert the creative potential of children and youth.

Most generally, intelligence has been discussed as learning aptitude, coupled with abstract thinking and problem-solving abilities. Intelligence is genetic or inherited, at least to the degree that the human species' nervous system is genetically determined and possibly genetically limited. But intelligence is environmentally determined to the extent that learning opportunities strongly facilitate or retard the development of cognitive skills. More specifically, we approached the topic of intelligence from two perspectives, the psychometric and the cognitive-developmental. In so doing, the concept of intelligence can be differentiated somewhat according to what aspects of intelligent behavior we seek to understand.

From the psychometric perspective we have seen that the study of intellectual development is essentially the study of age changes and individual differences in how individuals perform on intelligence tests and what they know in response to specially constructed problems or test items. Applied to infants, intelligence testing is useful as a "here-and-now" description of their developmental strengths and weaknesses. After infancy—from about ages 2 to 3 years onward—intelligence-test results can be moderately useful in planning educational programs for children and youth. In such planning, the emphasis should be on *promotion and facilitation,* and certainly not on limitation of opportunity.

The common types of intelligence tests are *individual* (for infants and preschool children, or for careful assessment procedures at any age) and *group.* Another classification is by verbal intelligence and performance intelligence. In performance tests, expressive language is not required for responses. Quantitative (number) ability is often measured apart from either verbal or performance intelligence.

SUMMARY

Intellectual growth is very rapid and positively accelerated during infancy and the preschool years. It slows, and the curve to represent it becomes negatively accelerated thereafter. Evidence has now accumulated that, except for items requiring speed of response, intelligence may continue to grow well into and beyond the middle years of life, or at least may hold its level until much later than has traditionally been thought.

Even so, the range of individual differences in psychometric intelligence increases predictably through the formative years of life. This is presumably a result of nature–nurture interaction. Various factors in the stability of IQ scores, changes in intellectual status over time, and the differentiation of verbal, quantitative, and spatial abilities have been discussed. We have also noted the secular trend in IQ, analogous to that observed for growth in height discussed in Chapter 6. Intelligence test scores are moderately useful in predicting school (and perhaps life) achievement, but they are only one factor in such predictions. Extreme caution should be exercised in using them to help others to plan, and dogmatic predictions from IQ scores should never be made.

In contrast to the psychometric emphasis upon estimating intelligence from what individuals know, cognitive-developmentalists focus more sharply on the development of structures for processing information—how individuals think. The developmental psychology of Jean Piaget was reviewed to illustrate this perspective on human intelligence. Rational thinking processes are seen as evolving through a sequence of fixed invariant stages. The first stage, called the period of *sensorimotor intelligence,* provides the concrete sensory and motoric action basis for later conceptual thought. It is roughly equivalent to the age period of infancy, or from birth to about age 2. Intuitive symbolic thinking dominates the second stage, *preoperational thought,* from about age 2 to age 5 or 6, when children normally make a transition to the concrete-operational period. Thereafter, until about age 11 or 12 in a normative sense, children develop and come to master various thinking operations important for classifying their experience and reasoning about the physical world. The emergence of mature, abstract thought about hypothetical as well as real world events, however, is not apparent until the period of formal operations during early adolescence, and even later for some individuals.

A comparison of psychometric and cognitive-developmental conceptions of human intelligence revealed several major similarities and differences. We suggested that both conceptions are useful and, in many ways, complementary views of intellectual development. The psychometric tradition has involved primarily the study of individual differences and the accuracy with which measured intelligence can be used to predict subsequent life status. Cognitive-developmentalists have been concerned mostly with verifying species-specific commonalities in development and the structure and processes of logical thinking.

However intelligence is viewed, certain environmental factors are correlated with the rate, and to some extent the quality, of intellectual development. These environmental factors have been discussed as possible social influences on development. Social influences are perhaps more pronounced for data about psychometric intelligence, perhaps because such influences have been more widely and thoroughly studied from the psychometric perspective. Recent research evidence about nutrition, family structure, and general home stimulation was reviewed to stress the apparent importance of quality care during the early years of life. This evidence, coupled with that from the study of organized intervention programs to facilitate maximum intellectual growth, clearly suggests a basic principle: the earlier, more sustained and comprehensive are efforts to influence intelligence positively, the better. If this is true, we can perhaps better understand why formal school experience may contribute in a comparatively minor way to intellectual development. Again, however, school impact typically has not been analyzed in terms of intelligence test performance. Rather, aca-

demic achievement—a relatively narrow form of intellectual expression—is the common criterion for assessing school influence. Academic achievement and exposure to schooling are positively correlated, as confirmed by many studies, but if there is a critical period in intellectual development, it is both a practical and a moral necessity to provide all children with an environment in their preschool years, from infancy onward, that will assure optimal growth.

Intelligence, however measured, cannot tell the complete story about cognitive-intellectual development. To illustrate this point, we reviewed additional related aspects of individual differences: cognitive style and creativity. Many cognitive-style dimensions have been studied, all of which concern the manner or form of cognition in one way or another. But we chose to discuss mainly reflectivity–impulsivity to illustrate the role of cognitive style in human development. Reflectivity in cognitive style seems to increase with age, although a wide range of individual differences in reflective or impulsive behavior is apparent throughout the course of development. In general, reflectivity is associated with more successful accomplishments, especially in the formal academic setting. However, cognitive impulsivity may be important for many valued activities, including the early stages of creative production. There is some question about how general reflectivity–impulsivity is across various activities or situations. Recent evidence suggests that procedures can be employed successfully to modify conceptual tempo when it is desirable to do so.

Finally, issues and research strategies involved in the psychological study of creativity were discussed. The treatment was built around the notion of creativity as both process and product. We recognize that controversy about the meaning of creativity is the rule rather than the exception in American society. A number of assumptions that underlie most conceptualizations of creativity were identified. They range from the idea that creativity can occur at different levels in different forms to the notion that creative development is a desirable educational goal. Several different pathways of creativity research were also discussed, including those involving mental measurement, personality differences in more and less creative individuals, background factors in creativity, and the dilemma of promoting creative growth and expression.

REFERENCES

Anderson, H. H., & Anderson, G. L. A cross-national study of children: A study in creativity and mental health. In I. J. Gordon (Ed.), *Human development: Readings in research.* Glenview, Ill.: Scott, Foresman, 1965.

Arlin, P. K. Cognitive development in adulthood: A fifth stage? *Developmental Psychology,* 1975, *11,* 602–606.

Ault, R., Mitchell, C., & Hartmann, D. Some methodological problems in reflection–impulsivity research. *Child Development,* 1976, *47,* 227–231.

Ausubel, D. P., & Sullivan, E. V. *Theory and problems of child development* (2nd ed.). New York: Grune & Stratton, 1970.

Backman, M. E. Patterns of mental abilities: Ethnic, socioeconomic, and sex difference. *American Educational Research Journal,* 1972, *9,* 1–12.

Baird, R. R., & Bee, H. L. Modification of conceptual style preference by differential reinforcements. *Child Development,* 1969, *40,* 903–910.

Bart, W. M., & Airasian, P. W. Determination of the ordering among seven Piagetian tasks by an ordering-theoretic method. *Journal of Educational Psychology,* 1974, *66,* 277–284.

Bayley, N. Consistency and variability in the growth of intelligence from birth to eighteen years. *Journal of Genetic Psychology,* 1949, *75,* 165–196.

Bayley, N. Development of mental abilities. In P. Mussen (Ed.), *Carmichael's manual of child psychology* (3rd ed.). New York: Wiley, 1970.

Bearison, D. Induced versus spontaneous attainment of concrete operations and their relationship to school achievement. *Journal of Educational Psychology,* 1975, *67,* 576–580.

Belcher, T. L. Modeling original divergent responses: An initial investigation. *Journal of Educational Psychology,* 1975, *67,* 351–358.

Berelson, B., & Steiner, G. *Human behavior.* New York: Harcourt, 1964.

Blanchard, R. W., & Biller, H. B. Father availability and academic performance among third-grade boys. *Developmental Psychology,* 1971, *4,* 301–305.

Block, J., Block, J. H., & Harrington, D. M. Some misgivings about the Matching Familiar Figures test as a measure of reflection-impulsivity. *Developmental Psychology,* 1974, *10,* 611–632.

Bloom, B. J. *Stability and change in human characteristics.* New York: Wiley, 1964.

Bradley, R. H., & Caldwell, B. M. The relation of infants' home environments to mental test performance at 54 months: A follow-up study. *Child Development,* 1976, *47,* 1172–1174.

Brannigan, G. Wechsler picture arrangement and comprehension scores as measures of social maturity. *Journal of Psychology,* 1975, *89,* 133–135.

Brody, E. B., & Brody, N. *Intelligence: Nature, determinants, and consequences.* New York: Academic Press, 1976.

Brodzinsky, D. M., Feuer, V., & Owens, J. Detection of linguistic ambiguity by reflective, impulsive, fast-accurate, and slow-inaccurate children. *Journal of Educational Psychology,* 1977, *69,* 237–243.

Bronfenbrenner, U. Is early intervention effective? *Teachers College Record,* 1974, *76,* 279–303.

Brown, A. L. The development of memory: Knowing, knowing about knowing, and knowing how to know. In H. W. Reese (Ed.), *Advances in child development and behavior* (vol. 10). New York: Academic Press, 1975.

Bruner, J. S. The course of cognitive growth. *American Psychologist,* 1964, *19,* 1–15.

Buros, O. K. (Ed.) *The sixth mental measurements yearbook.* Highland Park, N.J.: Gryphon Press, 1965.

Bush, E., & Dweck, C. Reflections on conceptual tempo: Relationship between cognitive style and performance as a function of task characteristics. *Developmental Psychology,* 1975, *11, 567*–574.

Channon, C. E. The effect of regime on divergent thinking scores. *British Journal of Educational Psychology,* 1974, *44,* 89–91.

Cicirelli, V. G. Sibling structure and intellectual ability. *Developmental Psychology,* 1976, *12,* 369–370.

Cliff, N. Psychometrics. In B. B. Wolman (Ed.), *Handbook of general psychology.* Englewood Cliffs, N.J.: Prentice-Hall, 1973.

Cunningham, W. R., & Birren, J. E. Age changes in human abilities: A 28-year longitudinal study. *Developmental Psychology,* 1976, *12,* 81–82.

Damarin, F. L., Jr., & Cattell, R. B. Personality factors in early childhood and their relation to intelligence. *Monographs of the Society for Research in Child Development,* 1968, *33* (6) Serial No. 127.

Dasen, P. R. Cross-cultural Piagetian research: A summary. *Journal of Cross-Cultural Psychology,* 1972, *3,* 23–40.

Davis, G. A. Research and development in training creative thinking. In J. R. Levin & V. L. Allen (Eds.), *Cognitive learning in children.* New York: Academic Press, 1976.

Denney, D. R. Modeling effects upon conceptual style and cognitive tempo. *Child Development,* 1972, *43,* 105–119.

Denny, N. W., & Wright, J. C. Cognitive changes during the adult years. In H. W. Reese (Ed.), *Advances in child development research,* (vol. 2). New York: Academic Press, 1976.

DeVries, R. Relationships among Piagetian, IQ, and achievement assessments. *Child Development,* 1974, *45,* 746–756.

DeVries, R., & Kohlberg, L. Relations between Piagetian and psychometric assessments. In L. G. Katz (Ed.), *Current topics in early childhood education.* Norwood, N.J.: Ablex, 1977.

Dorman, L. Assertive behavior and cognitive performance in preschool children. *Journal of Genetic Psychology,* 1973, *123,* 155–162.

Dulit, E. Adolescent thinking á la Piaget: The formal stage. *Journal of Youth and Adolescence,* 1972, *1,* 281–301.

Egelund, B., & Higgins, A. Selective attention of impulsive and reflective children. *Contemporary Educational Psychology,* 1976, *1,* 213–220.

Egelund, B., & Weinberg, R. The MFFT: A look at its psychometric credibility. *Child Development,* 1976, *47,* 483–491.

Elkind, D. Egocentrism in adolescence. *Child Development,* 1967, *38,* 1025–1034.

Elkind, D. Piagetian and psychometric conceptions of intelligence. *Harvard Educational Review,* 1969, *39,* 319–337.

Elton, C., & Rose, H. Prediction of productivity from personality test scores. *Journal of Educational Psychology,* 1974, *66,* 424–431.

Engelmann, S., & Engelmann, T. *Give your child a superior mind.* New York: Simon and Schuster, 1966.

Estes, W. K. *Learning theory and mental development.* New York: Academic Press, 1970.

Evans, E. D. *Contemporary influences in early childhood education* (2nd ed.). New York: Holt, Rinehart and Winston, 1975.

Fakouri, M. E. Cognitive development in adulthood: A fifth stage? A critique. *Developmental Psychology,* 1976, *12,* 472.

Farnham-Diggory, S. (Ed.) *Information-processing in children.* New York: Academic Press, 1972.

Feij, J. Field independence, impulsiveness, high school training, and academic achievement. *Journal of Educational Psychology,* 1976, *68,* 793–799.

Fitzgerald, J. M., Nesselroade, J., & Baltes, P. Emergence of adult intellectual structure: Prior to or during adolescence? *Developmental Psychology,* 1973, *9,* 114–119.

Flavell, J. *Developmental psychology of Jean Piaget.* Princeton, N.J.: Van Nostrand, 1963.

Frederickson, N., & Evans, F. Effects of models of creative performance on ability to formulate hypotheses. *Journal of Educational Psychology,* 1974, *66,* 67–82.

Fuqua, R., Bartsch, T., & Phye, G. An investigation of the relationship between cognitive tempo and creativity in preschool-age children. *Child Development,* 1975, *46,* 779–782.

Furth, H. G. Piaget, IQ, and the nature–nurture controversy. *Human Development,* 1973, *16,* 61–73.

Gagné, R. M. Contributions of learning to human development. *Psychological Review,* 1968, *75,* 177–191.

Gallagher, J. M., & Noppe, I. C. Cognitive development and learning. In J. Adams (Ed.), *Understanding adolescence* (3rd ed.). Boston: Allyn and Bacon, 1976.

Garfield, S., Cohen, H., & Roth, R. Creativity and mental health. *Journal of Educational Research,* 1969, *63,* 147–149.

Gaudia, G. Race, social class, and age of achievement of conservation on Piaget's tasks. *Developmental Psychology,* 1972, *6,* 158–165.

Getzels, J. W., & Jackson, P. W. *Creativity and intelligence.* New York: Wiley, 1962.

Gibson, E. *Principles of perceptual learning and development.* New York: Appleton, 1969.

Glick, J. Cognitive development in cross-cultural perspective. In F. D. Horowitz (Ed.), *Review of child development research* (vol. 4). Chicago: University of Chicago Press, 1975.

Golann, S. The psychological study of creativity. *Psychological Bulletin,* 1963, *60,* 548–563.

Goulet, L. R., Williams, K. C., & Hay, C. M. Longitudinal changes in intellectual functioning in preschool children: Schooling- and age-related effects. *Journal of Educational Psychology,* 1974, *66,* 657–662.

Grant, R. A. The relation of perceptual activity to matching familiar figures test accuracy. *Developmental Psychology,* 1976, *12,* 534–539.

Guilford, J. P. Three faces of intellect. *American Psychologist,* 1959, *14,* 469–479.

Guilford, J. P. *The nature of human intelligence.* New York: McGraw-Hill, 1967.

Hall, V. C., & Kaye, D. B. Patterns of early cognitive development among boys in four subcultural groups. *Journal of Educational Psychology,* 1977, *69,* 66–87.

Hall, V. C., & Russell, W. J. Multitrait-multimethod analysis of conceptual tempo. *Journal of Educational Psychology,* 1974, *66,* 932–939.

Hanson, R. Consistency and stability of home environmental measures related to IQ. *Child Development,* 1975, *46,* 470–480.

Harris, C., & McArthur, D. Another view of the relation of environment to mental abilities. *Journal of Educational Psychology,* 1974, *66,* 457–459.

Harrison, A., & Nadelman, L. Conceptual tempo and inhibition of movement in black preschool children. *Child Development,* 1972, *43,* 657–668.

Haskins, R., & McKinney, J. Relative effects of response tempo and accuracy on problem solving and academic achievement. *Child Development,* 1976, *47,* 690–696.

Heider, E. R. Information processing and the modification of an "impulsive conceptual tempo." *Child Development,* 1971, *42,* 1276–1281.

Honzik, M. P. Environmental correlates of mental growth: Prediction from the family setting at 21 months. *Child Development,* 1967, *38,* 337–364.

Honzik, M. P. The development of intelligence. In B. B. Wolman (Ed.), *Handbook of general psychology.* Englewood Cliffs, N.J.: Prentice-Hall, 1973.

Hopkins, K. D., & Bracht, G. H. Ten year stability of verbal and nonverbal IQ scores.

American Educational Research Journal, 1975, *12,* 469–477.

Horowitz, F. D., & Paden, L. Y. The effectiveness of environmental intervention programs. In B. M. Caldwell & H. N. Ricciuti (Eds.), *Review of child development research* (vol. 3). Chicago: University of Chicago Press, 1973.

Hudgins, B. B. *The improvement of children's thinking.* St. Louis: CEMREL, Inc., 1973.

Hunt, J. McV. *Intelligence and experience.* New York: Ronald, 1961.

Huston-Stein, A., & Baltes, P. B. Theory and method in life-span developmental psychology: Implications for child development. In H. W. Reese (Ed.), *Advances in child development and behavior* (vol. 11). New York: Academic Press, 1976.

Inhelder, B., & Piaget, J. *The growth of logical thinking from childhood to adolescence.* New York: Basic Books, 1958.

Inhelder, B., & Piaget, J. *The early growth of logic in the child.* New York: Norton, 1969.

Jackson, N., Robinson, H., & Dale, P. *Cognitive development in young children.* Washington, D.C.: U.S. Department of Health, Education and Welfare, 1976.

Janssen, C. Comparative creativity scores of socioeconomic dropouts and non-dropouts. *Psychology in the Schools,* 1968, *5,* 183–185.

Jensen, A. R. How much can we boost IQ and scholastic achievement? *Harvard Educational Review,* 1969, *39,* 1–123.

Jensen, A. R. Cumulative deficit: A testable hypothesis? *Developmental Psychology,* 1974, *10,* 996–1019.

Johnson, J. Relations of divergent thinking and intelligence test scores with social and nonsocial make-believe play of preschool children. *Child Development,* 1976, *47,* 1200–1203.

Jordan, L. Use of canonical analysis in Cropley's "A five year longitudinal study of the validity of creativity tests." *Developmental Psychology,* 1975, *11,* 1–3.

Kagan, J. Impulsive and reflective children: Significance of conceptual tempo. In J. Krumboltz (Ed.), *Learning and the educational process.* Skokie, Ill.: Rand McNally, 1965.

Kagan, J., & Kogan, N. Individual variation in cognitive processes. In P. Mussen (Ed.), *Carmichael's manual of child psychology.* New York: Wiley, 1970.

Kagan, J., & Messer, S. A reply to "Some misgivings about the MFFT as a measure of reflection-impulsivity." *Developmental Psychology,* 1975, *11,* 244–288.

Kagan, J., & Moss, H. *From birth to maturity.* New York: Wiley, 1962.

Kagan, J., Pearson, L., & Welch, L. Modifiability of an impulsive tempo. *Journal of Educational Psychology,* 1966, *57,* 359–365.

Kangas, J., & Bradway, K. Intelligence at middle age: A 38-year follow-up. *Developmental Psychology,* 1971, *5,* 333–337.

Kleinfeld, J. S. Intellectual strength in culturally different groups. *Review of Educational Research,* 1973, *43,* 341–360.

Kogan, N. Educational implications of cognitive styles. In G. Lesser (Ed.), *Psychology and educational practice.* Glenview, Ill.: Scott, Foresman, 1971.

Kogan, N., & Pankove, E. Long-term predictive validity of divergent-thinking tests: Some negative evidence. *Journal of Educational Psychology,* 1974, *66,* 802–810.

Kohlberg, L. Early education: A cognitive-developmental view. *Child Development,* 1968, *39,* 1013–1062.

Kohlberg, L., & Mayer, R. Development as the aim of education. *Harvard Educational Review,* 1972, *42,* 449–496.

Koppen-Thulesius, L. K., & Teichman, H. Accelerative trends in intellectual development. *British Journal of Social and Clinical Psychology,* 1972, *11,* 284–294.

Kumar, V. K. The structure of human memory and some educational implications. *Review of Educational Research,* 1972.

Labouvie-Vief, G. Intellectual abilities and learning: Retrospect and prospect. In J. R. Levin & V. L. Allen (Eds.), *Cognitive learning in children.* New York: Academic Press, 1976.

Langer, J. *Theories of development.* New York: Holt, Rinehart and Winston, 1969.

Lavatelli, C. B. *Readings in child behavior and development* (2nd ed.). New York: Harcourt, 1964.

Lesser, G. S., Fifer, G., & Clark, D. H. Mental abilities of children from different social-class and cultural groups. *Monographs of the Society for Research in Child Development,* 1965, *30,* Serial No. 102.

Lewis, M. (Ed.) *Origins of intelligence.* New York: Plenum Press, 1976.

Lichtenwalner, J. S., & Maxwell, J. W. The relationship of birth order and socioeconomic status to the creativity of preschool children. *Child Development,* 1969, *40,* 1241–1247.

Maccoby, E., & Jacklin, C. N. *Psychology of sex differences.* Stanford, Calif.: Stanford University Press, 1974.

Malden, J., Levenstein, P., & Levenstein, S. Longitudinal IQ outcomes of the mother-child home program. *Child Development,* 1976, *47,* 1015–1025.

Marjoribanks, K. Environment, social class, and mental abilities. *Journal of Educational Psychology,* 1972, *63,* 103–109.

McCall, R. B. Developmental changes in mental performance. *Monographs of the Society for Research in Child Development,* 1973, *38,* Serial No. 150.

McCandless, B. R. *Adolescents: Behavior and development.* Hinsdale, Ill.: Dryden, 1970.

McCarthy, S. V. Differential V-Q ability: Twenty years later. *Review of Educational Research,* 1975, *45,* 263–282.

McKinney, J. Problem-solving strategies in reflective and impulsive children. *Journal of Educational Psychology,* 1975, *67,* 807–820.

Meichanbaum, D. Enhancing creativity by modifying what subjects say to themselves. *American Educational Research Journal,* 1975, *12,* 129–146.

Messer, S. Reflection-impulsivity: Stability and school failure. *Journal of Educational Psychology,* 1970, *61,* 487–490. (a)

Messer, S. The effect of anxiety over intellectual performance on reflection–impulsivity in children. *Child Development,* 1970, *41,* 723–735. (b)

Messick, S. The criterion problem in the evaluation of instruction: Assessing possible, not just intended, outcomes. In M. C. Wittrock & D. E. Wiley (Eds.), *The evaluation of instruction.* New York: Holt, Rinehart and Winston, 1970.

Milgram, R., & Milgram, N. Group vs individual administration in the measurement of creative thinking in gifted and nongifted children. *Child Development,* 1976, *47,* 563–565.

Milne, A. A. *Winnie-the-Pooh.* New York: Dutton, 1926.

Neimark, E. D. Intellectual development during adolescence. In F. D. Horowitz (Ed.), *Review of child development research* (vol. 4). Chicago: University of Chicago Press, 1975. (a)

Neimark, E. D. Longitudinal development of formal operations thought. *Genetic Psychology Monographs,* 1975, *91,* 174–225. (b)

Newell, A., Shaw, J. C., & Simon, H. A. The processes of creative thinking. In H. E. Gruber, G. Terrell, & M. Werthermer (Eds.), *Contemporary approaches to creative thinking.* New York: Atherton, 1962.

Nichols, R. C. Nature and nurture. In J. Adams (Ed.), *Understanding adolescence* (3rd ed.). Boston: Allyn and Bacon, 1976.

Palmer, F. H. Socioeconomic status and intellective performance among Negro preschool boys. *Developmental Psychology,* 1970, *3,* 1–9.

Piaget, J. *Play, dreams, and imitation in childhood.* New York: Norton, 1951.

Piaget, J. *The origins of intelligence.* London: Routledge, 1952.

Piaget, J. Piaget's theory. In P. Mussen (Ed.), *Carmichael's manual of child psychology* (3rd ed.). New York: Wiley, 1970.

Piers, E. V. Creativity. In J. Adams (Ed.), *Understanding adolescence* (3rd ed.). Boston: Allyn and Bacon, 1976.

Plomin, R., & Willerman, L. A co-twin control study and a twin study of reflection–impulsivity in children. *Journal of Educational Psychology,* 1975, *67,* 537–543.

Radin, N. Father–child interaction and the intellectual functioning of four-year-old boys. *Developmental Psychology,* 1972, *6,* 353–361.

Read, M. S. The biological bases: Malnutrition and behavioral development. In I. J. Gordon (Ed.), *Early childhood education.* Chicago: University of Chicago Press, 1972.

Rees, A. H., & Palmer, F. H. Factors related to change in mental test performance. *Developmental Psychology Monograph,* 1970, *3,* No. 2, Part 2.

Reese, H. W., & Lipsitt, L. P. *Experimental child psychology.* New York: Academic Press, 1970.

Repucci, N. D. Parental education, sex differences, and performance on cognitive tasks among two-year-old children. *Developmental Psychology,* 1971, *4,* 248–253.

Riegel, K. F. Dialectic operations: The final period of cognitive development. *Human Development,* 1973, *16,* 346–370.

Robinson, H. B., & Robinson, N. M. Longitudinal development of very young children in a comprehensive day care program: The first two years. *Child Development,* 1971, *42,* 1673–1683.

Rohwer, W. D., Jr., Ammon, P. R., & Cramer, P. *Understanding intellectual development.* Hinsdale, Ill.: Dryden, 1974.

Saltz, E., & Johnson, J. Training for thematic-fantasy play in culturally disadvantaged children: Preliminary results. *Journal of Educational Psychology,* 1974, *66,* 623–630.

Scarr-Salapatek, S. Genetics and the development of intelligence. In F. D. Horowitz (Ed.), *Review of child development research* (vol. 4). Chicago: University of Chicago Press, 1975.

Schaie, K. W., & Strother, C. K. A cross-sequential study of age changes in cognitive behavior. *Psychological Bulletin,* 1968, *70,* 671–680.

Schulz, C. B., & Aurbach, H. A. The usefulness of cumulative deprivation as an explanation of educational deficiencies. *Merrill-Palmer Quarterly,* 1971, *17,* 27–40.

Siegelman, E. Reflective and impulsive observing behavior. *Child Development,* 1969, *40,* 1213–1222.

Sigel, I. How intelligence tests limit understanding of intelligence. *Merrill-Palmer Quarterly,* 1963, *9,* 39–56.

Solomon, A. D. A comparative analysis of creative and intelligence behavior of elementary school children with different socio-economic backgrounds. ERIC: *ED 017 022,* 1967.

Staats, A. W. *Child learning, intelligence, and personality.* New York: Harper & Row, 1971.

Starkweather, E. K. Creativity research instruments designed for use with preschool children. *Journal of Creative Behavior,* 1971, *4,* 245–255.

Stein, M. I. Creativity. In E. F. Borgatta & W. W. Lambert (Eds.), *Handbook of personality theory and research.* Skokie, Ill.: Rand McNally, 1968.

Stephens, B., McLaughlin, J., Miller, C., & Miller, G. Factorial structure of selected psycho-educational measures and Piagetian reasoning assessment. *Developmental Psychology,* 1972, *6,* 343–348.

Stephens, J. M., & Evans, E. D. *Development and classroom learning.* New York:

Holt, Rinehart and Winston, 1973.

Symonds, P. *What education has to learn from psychology.* New York: Columbia University, Teachers College Press, 1961.

Thompson, G. G. *Child psychology.* Boston: Houghton Mifflin, 1961.

Thurstone, L. L., & Thurstone, T. G. *SRA Primary Mental Abilities.* Chicago: Science Research Associates, 1962.

Torrance, E. P. *Education and the creative potential.* Minneapolis: University of Minnesota Press, 1963.

Torrance, E. P. Curiosity of gifted children and performance on timed and untimed tests of creativity. *Gifted Child Quarterly,* 1969, *13,* 155–158.

Torrance, E. P. Stimulation, enjoyment, and originality in dyadic creativity. *Journal of Educational Psychology,* 1971, *62,* 45–48.

Torrance, E. P. Interscholastic brainstorming and creative problem solving competition for the creatively gifted. *Gifted Child Quarterly,* 1974, *18,* 3–7.

Torrance, E. P., Bruch, C. B., & Morse, J. A. Improving predictions of the adult creative achievement of gifted girls by using autobiographical information. *Gifted Child Quarterly,* 1973, *17,* 91–95.

Torrance, E. P., & Torrance, J. P. *Is creativity teachable?* Bloomington, Ind.: Phi Delta Kappa Educational Foundation, 1976.

Tulkin, S. R., & Konner, M. J. Alternative conceptions of intellectual functioning. *Human Development,* 1973, *16,* 33–52.

Turner, R. L., & Denny, D. Teacher characteristics, classroom behavior, and growth in pupil creativity. ERIC: *ED 011 257,* 1967.

Vore, D. A. Prenatal nutrition and postnatal intellectual development. *Merrill-Palmer Quarterly,* 1973, *19,* 258–260.

Walberg, H. J., & Marjoribanks, K. Differential mental abilities and home environment: A canonical analysis. *Developmental Psychology,* 1973, *9,* 363–368.

Walberg, H., & Marjoribanks, K. Family environment and cognitive development: Twelve analytic models. *Review of Educational Research,* 1976, *46,* 527–552.

Wallach, M. A. Creativity. In P. Mussen (Ed.), *Carmichael's manual of child psychology.* New York: Wiley, 1970.

Wallach, M. A., & Kogan, N. *Modes of thinking in young children.* New York: Holt, Rinehart and Winston, 1965.

Wasik, B., & Wasik, J. Performance of culturally deprived children on the concept assessment kit: Conservation. *Child Development,* 1971, *42,* 1586–1590.

Webb, R. A. Concrete and formal operations in very bright 6-to-11-year-olds. *Human Development,* 1974, *17,* 292–300.

Weber, W. A. Relationships between teacher behavior and pupil creativity in the elementary school. ERIC: *ED 026 113,* 1968.

Wechsler, D. *Manual for the Wechsler intelligence scale for children* (Rev. ed.). New York: The Psychological Corporation, 1974.

Weiner, A. S. Visual information-processing speed in reflective and impulsive children. *Child Development,* 1975, *46,* 998–1000.

Weiner, A., & Berzonsky, M. Development of selective attention in reflective and impulsive children. *Child Development,* 1975, *46,* 545–549.

Welsh, G. S. *Creativity and intelligence: A personality approach.* Chapel Hill: University of North Carolina Institute for Research in Social Science, 1975.

Werner, H. *Comparative psychology of mental development.* New York: International Universities, 1948.

White, B. L. Critical influences in the origins of competence. *Merrill-Palmer Quarterly,* 1975, *21,* 243–266.

Wiley, D. E., & Harnischfeger, A. Explosion of a myth: Quantity of schooling and exposure to instruction, major educational vehicles. *Educational Researcher,* 1974, *3,* 7–12.

Witkin, H. A., et al. *Psychological differentiation.* New York: Wiley, 1962.

Witkin, H. A. Psychological differentiation and forms of pathology. *Journal of Abnormal Psychology,* 1965, *70,* 317–336.

Witkin, H. A. Cognitive style in academic performance and in teacher-student relations. In S. Messick (Ed.), *Individuality in learning.* San Francisco, Calif.: Jossey-Bass, 1976.

Wright, J. C., & Vlietstra, A. G. The development of selective attention: From perceptual exploration to logical search. In H. W. Reese (Ed.), *Advances in child development and behavior* (vol. 10). New York: Academic Press, 1975.

Yando, R., & Kagan, J. The effect of teacher tempo on the child. *Child Development,* 1968, *39,* 27–34.

Yarrow, L. J., et al. Dimensions of early stimulation and their differential effects on infant development. *Merrill-Palmer Quarterly,* 1972, *18,* 205–218.

Youniss, J. Operations and everyday thinking: A commentary on "dialectical operations." Human Development, 1974, *17,* 386–391.

Zahn, J. C. Creativity research and its implications for adult education. *ERIC: ED 011 362,* 1966.

chapter 9

Psychosexual development

Diane (age 7) home at the snack table after school: "Daddy, you know what?" ("What?") "Girls are lots luckier than boys." ("Why?") "Cause, girls get to wear both jeans and pants *and* skirts if they want—boys only can wear pants!"

Alicia (age 5) addressing her sister and two neighbor girls near the front door of her home: "Be careful and don't let the cat (Shadow) out. Mommy says Shadow's on the prowl for a daddy cat." *Carrie* (age 10): "Oh, she's in heat?" *Alicia:* "No, she's a she!" *Tina* (age 10): "Is she pregnant?" Alicia's sister, *Jennifer* (age 8): "No, but she's going to have babies!"

Stephen (age 9) driving with his parents through an "adult" entertainment section of a large city: "Hey, that sign says nude dancing!" *Stephen's father:* "Yes, you can go in that place to watch people dance nude." *Stephen:* "You mean *naked*?" *Father:* "Yes." *Stephen:* "Why do people do that?" *Father:* "Some people just like to see naked men or women." *Stephen:* "Weird. You mean people just take their clothes off and dance around in front of other people?" *Father:* "Yes." *Stephen:* "That's dumb. Won't they get cold? I think that's just dumb!"

Sarah (age 7) on a walk with her mother along a wooded suburban street: "Mommy?" ("What?") "Why don't we see boys on horses around here, just girls?"

("I wonder? What do you think?") "I don't know. I guess they like motorcycles better." ("Maybe so. I wonder why?") "Well, boys race around everywhere. I guess they just want to go fast and make noise. I think girls are better at taking care of things like horses."

Natasha (age 12) coming out of a grocery store with milk and bread for her father: "That's the last time I ever get my hair cut this short!" ("Why, what's wrong.") "I was standing in line and the check-out lady pointed to me and said, 'I'll take *him* next.' She thought I was a *boy!*" (begins to cry).

These are but a few of countless exchanges involving psychosexual concepts that we have observed among parents and children of our acquaintance. They range from astute observations about sex differences ("Boys can only wear pants") through uninhibited though incomplete ideas about sexuality ("Is she pregnant?" "No, but she's going to have babies") to incredulous reactions to adult sexual behaviors (nude dancing) and deep anxiety about sex-role identity ("She thought I was a boy!"). Broadly speaking, these exchanges pertain to *psychosexual development*, the topic of this chapter.[1] Like all other aspects of human socialization, psychosexual development can be seen as both a product and a process. In the product sense, certain terms about people—heterosexual, homosexual, manly, feminine, promiscuous, and frigid—are used freely in our society. These terms generally refer to behavioral patterns that characterize a person's social and sexual relationships with others. As a *process*, psychosexual development can be discussed as the way in which sex-related behavioral patterns are

[1] We use the broad term, *psychosexual* development, without implying a specific theoretical framework such as psychoanalysis (discussed in Appendix A), as the basis of our discussion.

acquired, including how we adjust to our biologically defined gender. This again raises the issue of nature and nurture, with special focus on any major social influences on how children and youth develop their full sexuality.

We begin our discussion of psychosexual development with some comments about sex differences. Then we consider the concepts of sex typing and sex-role identification, emphasizing some developmental trends in sex role acquisition. Next, research findings about major social influences are discussed. The second major section of Chapter 9 specifically discusses sexual and reproductive behavior. We distinguish in this chapter between the *social* and the *sexual* aspects of gender. Chapter 9 concludes with a discussion of possible family and school influences on children's sexual knowledge and behavior.

A LOOK AT SEX DIFFERENCES

One's biological sex (gender), which includes the social role prescribed for people according to sex, is perhaps the single most important aspect of human existence for overall psychological development. Initially, of course, our gender is established genetically (Chapter 2). From birth onward, our sex affects how we are treated by others, the nature of expectations for behavior they have of us, the opportunities made available within our culture, and how we view and govern our behavior throughout life (Payne, 1970). These factors seem important in accounting for sex differences observed early in life. For example, even casual observation of groups of children as young as 2 years old shows that most boys play differently from most girls. Boys seem to gravitate more toward wheeled toys, big blocks, and rougher play equipment. They often seem to manipulate toys and play materials more vigorously than girls. Girls, in contrast, are often quieter, engage more in "dress up" games, and more often play with the doll and playhouse facilities present in most day-care or nursery-school settings. Such sex differences in play preferences and behavior are also recorded in the research literature (Fagot, 1974; Pederson & Bell, 1970). Since there is little, if any, difference in size, strength, or motor skill between preschool boys and girls, it is plausible to argue that play preferences are more strongly influenced by social learning experience than biology.

The Issue of Sex Differences

But are play preferences learned? During the past several years the issue of sex differences and their origins has become increasingly controversial among psychologists. The beginning point of this debate is usually the research literature documenting reliable differences in psychological or behavioral characteristics between the two sexes from infancy onward.

During infancy and childhood sex differences have been reported (though not always consistently) across a wide spectrum of behavior (Birns, 1976; Mischel, 1970). These include greater mouth sensitization, attentiveness, and imitativeness among females. Males show greater irritability, aggressive play, field independence, susceptibility to disease, and learning disabilities, especially reading problems. Sex-linked differences also continue to appear through puberty and beyond. During adolescence, these differences appear in vocational skills and aspirations, social interests, conformity, specific cognitive abilities, forms of delinquency, and so on (see Chapters 4, 10, 12).

But the descriptive research about sex differences has come under careful scrutiny. For example, one pair of psychologists (Maccoby & Jacklin, 1974) maintain that very few basic psychological differences between the sexes actually hold up under a critical analysis of the research. In fact, they reject as "myths" such popular beliefs as girls being more sociable and suggestible and less positive in self-esteem and achievement motivation than boys. Certain other areas of possible sex difference—tactile sensitivity, anxiety, activity level, competitiveness, dominance, compliance, and nurturance—are reportedly "too close to call." The available data about these characteristics are presently too weak to reveal any pattern in sex differences one way or the other. Only four sex differences are accepted as "fairly well established." Girls reportedly excel in verbal ability, while boys excel in both mathematical and visual-spatial ability and are also more aggressive than girls.

Even such a rigorous analysis and accounting of sex differences should not be accepted blindly or uncritically (Block, 1976). What is firm evidence to one person may be weak to another. Individual studies can be misinterpreted or overlooked. Research settings and methods, samples of children, standards for comparing behavior, and statistical procedures for analyzing data can vary so widely across studies that it is risky to draw conclusions by lumping them together. The study of sex differences is much disputed. The results of research about them seem more equivocal than not, thus limiting our confidence in descriptions of sex differences.

Indeed, simply describing sex differences is a difficult task, even if there are more similarities than differences between males and females. Explaining any differences is even more difficult, as we will soon show. Undeniable, however, is a strong social emphasis on gender that begins at the moment of birth. A physician or nurse will commonly introduce the new baby to its parents by saying, "It's a fine baby girl (boy)." For many American infants a sex-role distinction literally begins with the color of swaddling clothes at birth: pink for girls and blue for boys. Infants' early personal-social behaviors may also be interpreted differently by the adults around them, depending upon whether the infants are known as boys or girls.

This point is well illustrated by a recent study in which over 200 college students were first shown a videotape of a 9-month-old infant, then asked to rate the infant's emotional responses to several different arousing stimuli—a loud buzzer, teddy bear, jack-in-the-box, and so on (Condry & Condry, 1976). For half of this student group, the infant was introduced as a male; for the remaining half, the same infant was identified as a female. The *same* infant was seen as displaying different emotions and, significantly, even different levels of emotional arousal, depending upon the infant's "sex identity" and the observer's own sex role identity. For example, the infant's agitation and crying were seen as *anger* by both male and female raters if they thought the infant was male. In contrast, observers who were led to believe the infant was female interpreted this same agitation and crying as *fear*. Similarly, the "male" infant was rated generally more *active and potent*. And female observers, but not their male counterparts, consistently ascribed greater *intensity* of emotion to the infant whether identified as male or female.

These findings cannot be automatically generalized to real-life settings involving parents and their children. But the results do suggest that we are somehow socialized to view behavior differently, depending upon our ideas about maleness and femaleness. Traditionally in American culture, many of these ideas have provided a generalized basis for determining the social acceptability of "male" and "female" behavior.

Sex-Role Stereotyping

Relatively fixed ideas about how males and females should or can be expected to behave are often called *sex-role stereotypes*. They seem heavily determined by cultural values about masculinity and femininity. As recently as a decade ago, there was wide agreement among both youth and adults about what is valued for masculine and feminine sex roles in American society. A study involving college students provides us with a good example of this consensus (Rosenkrantz et al., 1968). Asked to specify and evaluate masculine and feminine characteristics, students of both sexes expressed nearly perfect agreement both about what is *feminine* and *valued* and what is *masculine* and *valued*.

Traits Valued and Masculine
Aggressive
Unemotional, hides emotions, never cries
Independent, not easily influenced
Adventurous, ambitious
Objective, logical
Dominant, acts as a leader
Likes mathematics and science
Not excitable in a minor crisis
Active, worldly
Competitive, self-confident
Direct, makes decisions easily
Skilled in business
Able to separate feelings from ideas
Talks freely about sex with men
Not conceited about appearance
Thinks men are superior to women

Traits Valued and Feminine
Does not use harsh language
Tactful
Gentle

Aware of others' feelings
Religious
Interested in own appearance
Neat in habits
Quiet
Strong need for security
Appreciates art and literature
Expresses tender feelings

These data suggest that the "ideal" man was, at the time of this study, seen as having the most fun and freedom, and possessing most of the competence and strength in our culture. In contrast, women were perceived as gentle, mild, aware of social relations, and somewhat self-centered. On the whole, the "esteemed woman," as described above, will probably seem to many readers as a bit less than exciting and perhaps may not represent total self-development and fulfillment. The "esteemed man," on the other hand, emerges as a rather intriguing and active person.

These stereotypes leave little room for individuality in behavior. They have also been much maligned in recent years by liberationist thinkers who with good reason believe that stereotypes may inhibit or restrict the development of human potential (including egalitarian relationships between the sexes) and general mental health, especially among females.

The results of the above study and of others (for example, Broverman et al., 1970) enable us to make three related points. First, perceptions of and values associated with sex-role stereotypes apparently reflect a rich history of cultural conditioning, or social learning, which strongly emphasizes children and youth behaving consistently with prevailing ideas about sex-appropriate behavior. The power of these ideas is further illustrated by the common tendency of many people to view departures from such expectancies as showing weakness in males or psychological disturbance in females. Second, as sex-role values come to in-

fluence our behavior, including our responses to others, we would expect them eventually to affect how we raise our own children. A somewhat rigid socialization cycle can result, thus sustaining certain beliefs about sex differences that are more illusory than real.

Finally, despite the sex-role stereotypes, wide individual differences in "masculine" or "feminine" behavior exist among members of both sexes. Few women are "totally feminine"; few men are "totally masculine." In short, the development of sex-role characteristics seems largely a matter of degree, especially in complex, industrial societies such as the United States. In fact, an overlapping in sex roles is not uncommon, particularly in middle and upper social class groups.

Possibly this reflects the liberalizing effect of education among more advantaged segments of American society. It is plausible to think that the overlapping has provided impetus for some recent and important changes in how we think about traditional sex roles. Among the most important of these is the emergence of a new value termed psychological *androgyny* (Bem, 1975; Stein, 1976). Psychological androgyny refers to the valuing, adoption, and integration of both "masculine" and "feminine" characteristics by the same individual. To say it more formally, psychological androgyny is the "capacity of a single person of either sex to embody the full range of human character traits, despite cultural attempts to render some exclusively feminine and some exclusively masculine" (Hefner et al., 1975, p. 152).

It is argued that androgynous persons, capable and free to act flexibly in terms of sex-role attributes, will benefit from a widened range of occupational choices, interpersonal relationships, and life styles. They may also be generally more adaptive than a rigidly stereotyped person, finding it easier to modify their social behavior according to particular situations. Such "masculine" traits as autonomy and assertiveness, for example, are adaptive in some situations. Other situations may call more strongly for the expression of such "feminine" traits as nurturance and empathy. Does it follow, then, that androgyny should be a preferred goal of socialization? If so, what methods will be most suitable for this purpose? What will be the effects of this orientation on society as a whole? Does androgyny imply bisexuality?

These questions about androgyny cannot yet be answered from a coldly objective and empirical point of view. They require deep philosophical thought and more than a little speculation. We must also distinguish psychological androgyny from physical androgyny, a condition of development associated with endocrine function. Physically androgynous males and females will show greater than normal proportions of female and male hormones, respectively. As yet, there is no conclusive evidence to link physical and psychological androgyny, though there is some preliminary work in this area (Peterson, 1976). Neither is there much reason to expect a necessary causal relationship between endocrine function and psychological characteristics—unless we take a strongly biological view of psychosexual development. Some authorities (for example, Diamond, 1965; 1976) strongly favor the idea that chromosomal and hormonal make-up provide the direction for gender development, sexual behavior, and, possibly, psychological differentiation.

We mention this to suggest the possibility that sex-role stereotypes themselves represent social implementations designed to accommodate male–female biological differences. Cross-cultural study reveals that in an overwhelming number of societies boys are more likely to be involved in overt aggression and conflict with others. Males in almost all cultures have greater authority and execute more physically demanding and risky tasks (D'Andrade, 1966). In a phrase, the *instrumental* role of males is almost universal in cultures. Activity, assertiveness, independence, initiative, and psychological toughness characterize this role, traits that are instrumental for achieving goals of security, recognition, and material success. Similarly, females in most cultures are more likely to be nurturant, sociable, and responsive to others—a strong human-relations orientation for maintaining social and family harmony. This is described as an *expressive* role (Parsons, 1955). Of course, these cultural regularities in role behaviors tell us what *is*, not what *should be*. If we embrace the value of androgyny, it would follow that all persons may become competent *and* comfortable with both instrumental and expressive role behaviors, given suitable learning experiences. Taking an extreme biological view, however, the extent of this achievement may be governed somehow by our genotype (Chapter 2).

Despite these cultural regularities, we find it difficult to argue that sex role differences arise directly from biological givens (Mussen, 1968). Striking exceptions to these presumed cultural universals have been observed often enough to show the strong influence of cultural training (Mead, 1961). In some cultures, for example, adult males have assumed female roles (and vice versa), including transvestism (dressing as the opposite sex). This is most common in cultures where specific careers are open only to one or the other sex, for example, actors in early Greek society. It is unrealistic to deny biological factors in sex-role development, but the weight of the evidence seems clearly on the side of nurture in shaping sex-differentiated behavior (Birns, 1976). As will be seen, however, a question remains about the *timing* of environmental events that may shape the course of sex- or gender-role development. Keeping this question in mind, we now sample the work of psychologists and other scientists who have guided us toward an improved understanding of this important stream of human development.

SEX ROLE DEVELOPMENT

Sex Typing and Sex-Role Identification

Two psychological concepts have provided a basis for studying sex-role development: sex typing and sex-role identification. Sex typing is a shorthand term for describing the acquisition of behavior associated with the male and female sex roles at various ages during the course of development. Sex typing can be consistent or inconsistent with a person's biological gender. Either way, it is defined as a *process* by which individuals acquire, value, and adopt for themselves cultural patterns of sex-typed behavior (Mischel, 1970).

Most individuals manifest sexual behavior that is directed toward persons of the opposite sex. This, too, reflects a degree of sex typing. However, many individuals find both sexes appealing sexually, and some come to restrict their sexual interests and behavior exclusively (or almost exclusively) to their own sex. Individual differences in sexual preference aside, it is one's sexual orientation (object choice) toward the opposite sex that is the most essential and (in the reproductive sense of normalcy) biologically the normal aspect of adequate sex typing (Mussen, 1968).

A second major concept from the literature about psychosexual development is *identification*. This concept is less easily defined because its meaning has changed through the years with the formulation and modification of personality theories (Mischel, 1970). In one sense,

identification can be thought of as behavior. If we say one person identifies with another, we mean that person behaves like the other person in many significant ways—which may include mannerisms, language habits, value orientation, interests and even ways of thinking. In another sense, however, identification cannot be defined simply by behavioral similarity. An emotional relationship of some kind must also exist to motivate efforts to model oneself after another person. In other words, one person must desire to emulate another person and, as emulation occurs, develop a stronger emotional tie with that person. Identification is thus defined by a close empathic relationship. In still another sense, identification can be thought about as a process, or the mechanisms through which children or youth come to emulate a model (Mischel, 1970). At first glance, this third sense of the term identification seems synonymous with the idea of sex typing. As will be seen, however, the actual mechanisms involved in this process of sex typing and identification are defined differently by psychologists of alternative theoretical persuasions. If we allow ourselves considerable liberty with the technical vocabulary of psychology, it is convenient to use the terms sex typing and sex-role identification interchangeably. But many psychologists will object strenuously on the grounds that certain unique premises or assumptions about identification would thus be violated. Before moving ahead, then, it seems appropriate to briefly examine three different, but extremely important, interpretations of sex typing and identification: psychoanalytic, cognitive-developmental, and social learning.

Interpreting Sex Typing and Sex-Role Identification

The reader will recognize that only gradually and incidentally have we given explicit attention to "theory" about human development. In fact, our first extended sortie into psychological theory came in Chapter 8 when we presented the Piagetian interpretation of intellectual development. Because the role of theory is so pronounced in the study of human psychosexual development we now begin to lay some theoretical groundwork.

Psychoanalytic theory The first and, for many, the most influential explanation of psychosexual development has come from the work of Sigmund Freud and his close followers, notably his daughter, Anna (Appendix A). Their approach, *psychoanalysis*, is both a theory of personality development and a method for analyzing and treating psychological disturbances. Psychoanalysis suggests that identification is critical for total personality development (Freud, 1949). At some risk of oversimplification, we can specify two processes of identification important for psychosexual development. One involves a strong dependency and love relation with the mother that begins in infancy and occurs for both boys and girls. This process, called *anaclitic identification*, is said to be the only process, or at least the major one, for girls. With age, the mother's attention is diverted to some degree from her growing child. The girl develops her conscience or superego to please her mother and not lose her love.

Boys are thought to seek to recapture the mother and to have sexual fantasies about her. Boy's demands for mother love and attention reach a peak during the preschool years and in effect provide the basis of competition with father for maternal favors. But father is strong and powerful, capable of dismissing his young competitor, even to the point of physical force. Or so it seems to the son. Realizing father's power leads to a general fear reaction in the normal boy. This fear becomes, about age 5 or 6, the basis

for a defensive identification with the father. This identification marks the end of alternately fearful and hostile competition with the father for mother's charms. The boy *identifies with the aggressor,* a process aptly described by the phrase, "If you can't lick them, join them." Because the anxiety or fear aroused by this hopeless competition has been so painful, the young male is said to repress, or push into his unconscious mind, the intensely sexual and aggressive impulses that mark the competition. Successful repression resolves the boy's dilemma, he becomes like his father and is presumably well on his way to an appropriate masculinity. Some reference is also made to an analogous, though milder, competition for paternal affection between mothers and daughters. This conflict, however, does not figure as strongly in psychosexual development for young females.

Cognitive developmental theory Piaget's ideas about cognitive intellectual development have been extended to offer an alternative account of sex role development. The central premise is that commonly held social stereotypes define what is masculine and what is feminine for almost all members of a culture (Kagan, 1964). These stereotypes provide cues for children, who actively select and organize their experience by such sex-role "definitions." Sex typing begins when the child is labeled "boy" or "girl." This label, presumably associated with positive interactions in the home, provides the gender-identity basis of an "abstract self-concept" and is also used to label others (Kohlberg, 1966). Gender identity or sex self-concept thereafter serves as both an organizer and a determinant of social attitudes and values. Masculine or feminine values arise from the need to assimilate things that are consistent with gender identity. Hence, as the reader would anticipate, cognitive consistency or equilibration is a prominent explanatory concept for the cognitive-developmental approach to sex typing.

According to cognitive developmentalists, sex self-concept stabilizes around the beginning of the concrete-operational period (see Chapter 8), when genuine identification usually takes place. Just as children then understand that physical properties such as quantity, volume, and weight are invariant, they also understand that their gender identity is invariant. Subsequently, children assimilate and accommodate important cross-cultural stereotypes of sex-appropriate behavior (stereotypes) that reflect perceptible sex differences in biological structure and function (Kohlberg, 1966).

In sum, for cognitive-developmentalists, sex typing is an accompaniment of maturation and cognitive development, independent of specific training or organized teaching. Some degree of observational learning is, of course, essential for sex-role acquisition. But the critical factor is the child's own cognitive role in the process—a "motivated adaptation" to physical and social reality combined with the need to maintain a positive stable self-image. Unlike the psychoanalytic approach, cognitive developmentalists see sex typing as the forerunner, rather than the product, of identification.

Social learning theory According to social learning theory, children very early learn their gender and what is expected of, and valued for, people of that gender. This learning is influenced largely by imitation, direct reinforcement, vicarious reinforcement, and the organization of social cognitions (Chapter 2). Parents, or primary caregivers, are viewed both as potent role models and as agents of direct reinforcement for culturally sex typed behaviors. No dynamic process of identification is needed to explain sex typing. Children of *either* gender who come to display a masculine

typing will have been exposed to and interacted with parents who model and reinforce *instrumental* role behaviors: active involvement, dominance, assertiveness, cognitive independence, and patterned goal-directed behaviors. Similarly, children—again, of either sex—who come to behave in a feminine way will have been influenced by parents who are more *expressive* in their role behaviors: sensitive, warm, affectionate, supportive, and noncompetitive behaviors. It follows that where children are exposed to parents who themselves model *both* instrumental and expressive role behaviors, and who are reinforced for both classes of role behaviors, psychological androgyny can be the outcome of the sex-role learning process. Or children who demonstrate few sex-typed behaviors of either class will have developed in homes where one or both parents are indeterminate in their sex-role behavior (Kelley & Worrell, 1976). From a social-learning perspective then, masculinity and femininity need not be seen as opposite ends of a bipolar continuum of sex-typed behaviors. Rather, they are basically independent behavioral domains and most certainly not mutually exclusive.

Concluding comment There is no absolute proof for any one of these views of sex-role development. Nor are these the only views (see, for example, Lynn, 1969; Rosenberg & Sutton-Smith, 1972). Perhaps the issue is less a matter of which theory is "proven" and more one of how useful any of them is for explaining and predicting behavior. For this purpose, social-learning principles are potent. But we cannot discount the strong role of selective perception and cognitive consistency about which the cognitive-developmentalists have much to say. And, as suggested earlier, we cannot deny important physical or biological factors that influence sexual identity.

All things considered, then, an interpretation based upon nature–nurture interaction, with due attention to cognition and social learning, seems reasonable. Some authorities (Money & Ehrhardt, 1972) begin by stressing the role of nature at point of conception. Gender-role development thereafter is analogous to a relay race. The first leg of the race is the responsibility of the x or y chromosome, establishing an individual's genetic gender. The gender "program" is then passed to the undifferentiated sex glands (gonads). With the gender program, the gonads can differentiate and secrete hormones appropriate to the genetic sex. These sex hormones affect anatomical development and, it is thought, a certain neural organization in the brain. But it is the prenatal sex-hormone *mix* that is said to establish thresholds for the different behaviors associated with sex typing (Money & Tucker, 1975). Thresholds are minimum limits that must be surpassed before activity is triggered. For example, a mix favoring the female sex hormones would affect brain organization in such a way that a slight stimulus would set off nurturant behavior, while an intense stimulus would be required to set off aggressive behavior. Neither behavior excludes the other; both are present. However, one is elicited with less effort. Masculinity and femininity need not be considered opposites, but independent dimensions.

Prenatal hormone mix thus carries a potential for influencing postnatal behavior. But according to this view, postnatal socialization (nurture) remains the primary force in gender-role development. In the cognitive-developmental interpretation, identifying the infant as male or female at birth is the significant first step in determining the course of socialization and development. Sex assignment at birth, on the basis of external genitals, creates a further extension of the gender development program.

Sex-role acquisition is then completely determined by reinforcement of maleness or femaleness during the earliest years of life.

Intriguing evidence for this view has come from the study of hermaphrodites, individuals who are born with genitals so ambiguous that their sex cannot be clearly defined by external examination. Some hermaphroditic children have been mistakenly labeled as male or female at birth, that is, counter to their chromosomal sex. Thereafter, they have been raised as males or females in the absence of knowledge about their true gender.

Investigators have learned two dramatic lessons from these cases, though we must state them tentatively until more data come in (Money, 1976). First, male and female hermaphrodites, when labeled and raised as opposite sexed individuals, show a sex-role development congruent with their *assigned* sex, not their genetic sex. The second lesson relates to our earlier question about *timing* in sex-role development. Where mistaken sex assignments have been discovered and the children's sex-role programs are changed to "conform" to their genetic sex before about age 2 or 2 1/2, no apparent difficulties in gender development are observed. If a change occurs after this time, however, considerable adjustment problems have been noted among the children involved. This suggests a "critical" period in sex-role development, with the first 2 years or so representing a maximum susceptibility to learning. A widely publicized case history further reinforces this point (Money, 1975). It involves a normal male identical twin whose penis was destroyed by a circumcision accident. A decision was made to "reassign" this twin as a female at about age 17 months. After 9 years, this genetically male child reportedly has successfully acquired a "normal" female gender role.

Thus far, our knowledge about critical periods and gender shifts is based upon comparatively few cases. Accordingly, any definitive statements about undifferentiated sex at birth and critical periods are premature. Most people agree, however, that this is a fascinating area of study and may provide strong support for suggestions about the flexible nature of something as basic as human sex-role development.

Some Generalizations about Sex Role Development

Having familiarized ourselves with some major explanations of the process of sex-role development, we now examine some developmental trends and other generalizations based on the descriptive research in this area. The measurement of sex-role behavior and development is difficult, especially in young children. Psychologists usually use relatively subjective approaches to this measurement, inferring sex typing or sex-role identification from children's drawings of human figures, toy preferences, fantasy play with dolls, or various interview methods. Tests and scales of various kinds are used extensively with older children and youth. However varied and complex the measurement problems and procedures, there is some consistency in the general pattern of research findings. Interested readers can consult an extensive literature for details (Biller & Borstelmann, 1967; Flerx, Fidler, & Rogers, 1976; Green, Fuller, & Rutley, 1972; Heilbrun, 1970; Hetherington, 1970; Johnson, 1963; Mischel, 1970; Stein, 1976).

First, both an awareness and a manifestation of "sex-appropriate" behavior are apparent among children as early as age 3, and among nearly all children by age 5. Thereafter, sex-role behaviors are consistently enacted with age by chil-

dren and youth of both sexes. One recent study, for example, has shown that 3-year-old children consistently use accurate gender labels (boy, girl, lady, man), are certain of their own gender, and show a budding awareness of sex-role stereotyping, independent of their parents' socioeconomic status or sex-role attitudes (Thompson, 1975). Similarly, children's knowledge about adult sex stereotypes, especially the male stereotype, has grown substantially by kindergarten age and apparently influences play preferences and general social relationships (Williams, Bennett, & Best, 1975).

There is some evidence that these early developments occur in a stage like progression, beginning with gender *awareness* (Slaby & Frey, 1975). As children's concepts of their own gender become more firmly established (boyness, girlness), we can speak of gender *identity*. Thereafter, children's behavior is consistent with this identity concept. Children seem to learn quickly that the fact of biological maleness or femaleness does not change; that is, gender remains *constant* in the face of superficial changes in appearance (dressing differently) and even behavior (playing with "boys'" or "girls'" toys). As gender constancy develops, usually by school age or earlier, children's preferences for watching same-sex models can be observed, especially among boys. From such data, we may infer that children's normal gender development will include a *preference* for being male or female consistent with their biological makeup. Eventually, a sexual partner orientation also develops, with preference given to partners of one or the other sex (or both, as in bisexuality) (Green, 1975).

A second important generalization is that children (and youth) with biologically appropriate sex-role typing or identification seem on the whole to have stronger self-concepts than those with less appropriate sex typing. This is not surprising, given strong adult and peer approval and reinforcement for behaving in accordance with accepted notions about gender-role prescriptions. There is mixed evidence about the self-concepts and personal-social adjustment of young men and young women who are openly homosexual in their sexual preferences. Apparently, those who function reasonably successfully vocationally in the open society (that is, who are self-supporting and not in psychiatric care) are neither better nor worse adjusted than comparison heterosexual groups. In any case, the relationship between self-concept and sex typing seems stronger for males than females, possibly because males who behave "girlishly" are less tolerated in a masculine-oriented society such as the United States. This does not rule out a strong possibility that psychological androgyny is also related to strength in self-concept. Few data are as yet available on this question, but we are intrigued by the apparent links between positive self-concept and creativity on the one hand, and creativity and psychological androgyny on the other. As noted in Chapter 8, for example, high creatives of both sexes are noted for relatively strong masculine characteristics such as assertiveness and autonomous judgment *and* strong feminine characteristics such as sensitivity and introspectiveness. Background factors in creativity also seem to involve parents whose sex-role orientation is less conventional (Grant & Domino, 1976). We look forward with interest to more data about the hypothesis that psychological androgyny can provide satisfying personal fulfillment which extends to values of creative expressiveness.

A third generalization concerns the differentiation by sex of general behavior patterns. As suggested earlier, much re-search about such sex differences has centered on aggressive and dependent behavior. The former is considered to characterize males, the latter females. No solid evidence has accumulated, however, to indicate that there are general traits of aggressiveness or dependency. Girls, for example, usually express their aggression differently than boys. That is, they generally show less *physical* aggression, although they may resort to verbal aggression in the form of rebukes, criticism, and moralizing. According to one study, however, when anonymity is guaranteed, these differences partially disappear; girls seem as capable as boys of meting out aggressive consequences or punishment for disapproved behavior (Mallick & McCandless, 1966). Also, boys, girls, young men, and young women are more reluctant to behave aggressively toward females than toward males. But, in general, aggressiveness is perhaps the clearest behavior pattern that distinguishes males and females throughout the life span.

In addition to aggression, however, investigators continue to observe certain *group* differences between males and females on selected traits consistent with ideas presented in the first section of this chapter (Hakstian & Cattell, 1975). Many of these seem directly related to sex-role stereotyping, especially during adolescence and beyond. One pair of researchers, for example, has reported that high school students of both sexes (but especially males) tend to evaluate more positively the contributions of male as compared to female authors (Etaugh & Rose, 1975). Similarly, college students have been observed to rate a masculine mode of teaching (self-confidence, independence, aggressiveness, activity, logical-objective analysis) more highly than a more feminine mode (awareness of student needs, gentleness, tactfulness, passive facilitator of student learning) (Harris, 1975). Of course, it is possible that some integration of both teaching modes will represent a more powerful and preferred teaching style for most students than either one considered separately.

A fourth and final generalization about sex-role development concerns deviations from the "normal" or biologically appropriate pattern. We speak not of androgyny, but of atypical sex-role behavior—effeminacy for males, masculinity for females. The generalization about atypical gender development can be stated simply (though the factors that produce it are enormously complex).

As in "normal" gender development, the pattern of atypical gender development usually seems well established by the late preschool years—in some cases, even earlier (Green, 1974).

The behavior and psychological test data about strongly effeminate boys show them to be much more similar to "typical" girls of their own age than to their male age mates. Such boys are aware of their maleness, but often express a wish to be a girl. Effeminacy in young males does not, however, indicate eventual homosexuality or transsexuality, as we will show later in this chapter. A general portrait of feminine boys may include "cross-dressing" as early as age 3 or 4, a preference for female playmates and toys, difficulty in relating to male peers, avoidance of roughhouse games, taking a female role in fantasy play, and a tendency to prefer the company of mother. Such boys are often less successful in their peer group, especially during the late elementary and early high school years. They can be the subject of much ridicule and taunting ("Hey sissy, aren't you the sweetie pie, though!") and are often misperceived as "gay" or "queer" when, in fact, they more often develop a normal heterosexual orientation.

The antecedents of male effeminacy are not clearly documented. One authority, drawing largely on clinical data, reports that the most common home background factor among effeminate boys is simply a lack of parental discouragement of girlish behavior, perhaps based on an attitude that the child will "grow out of it" (Green, 1974). It is not unusual, however, for some parents actively and early to encourage or reinforce such behavior as "cute" or "funny." Some researchers (for example, Harrington, 1970) have gone further to suggest that many effeminate boys, through the identification process, will have developed *both* a primary feminine identity and a genuine preference for feminine role behavior.

Less is known about masculinized girls, though it can be said that "tomboyishness" in girls is considerably more common and socially accepted than is boys' effeminacy. Many authorities consider tomboyishness a transitory phase in female sex-role development, normally embracing ages 7–12. Such girls often express a male gender *preference,* but retain a basic female identity. With adolescence, of course, the circumstances of male–female social activity can rapidly change. Physically attractive girls, even if tomboyish, may quickly come to recognize the social advantages of femininity. Gender-role behaviors will be modified accordingly; masculine behaviors are simply dropped from the response repertoire. But if male gender *identity* has developed in combination with a masculine role preference, the tomboy pattern is likely to persist. We know of one such girl, now age 14, who literally refuses to accept or think about anything other than maleness. Her dress and grooming habits, manner of walking and speaking, and preferred activities are distinctly male. She is not well accepted in her school peer group, but seems not much affected by this. She does enjoy three extremely close friendships and is intensely loyal to these persons, one female and two males. On the whole, however, she prefers to be a "loner" and spends most of her leisure time in demanding, out-of-doors activity.

Because of the relative lack of studies about masculine, but otherwise heterosexual females, little can be said about any "causes" or predisposing factors. Preliminary hunches include parents who give their daughters a male derivative name (perhaps indicating their own preference for maleness), a warm, stable, and extremely affectionate father (thus establishing a reinforcing role model), a mother who is emotionally detached from and generally unavailable to her young daughter, and rewarding rough and tumble play with boys (Green, 1974). In some cases, we must again entertain the sex-hormone hypothesis. This hypothesis figures strongly in some preliminary comparisons of physically androgenized girls (girls affected prenatally by male sex hormones taken by their mothers to prevent miscarriage) and underandrogenized boys (boys who are partially insensitive to androgen and thus do not respond fully to its input). In both cases the gender identities of these boys and girls have been appropriately developed. Their behavior, however, is observed to be somewhat atypical for their biological sex. As compared to "normal" girls, androgenized girls are more involved in strenuous physical activity, more interested in future careers, and so on. Similarly, underandrogenized boys reportedly are quieter and less competitive than their "normal" male peers (Money & Tucker, 1975). Again, we stress that these hunches are tentative. Such environmental forces may work only in concert with certain as yet undetermined genetic predispositions.

To conclude, the early years of socialization and development are crucial for both typical and atypical sex-role orientation, preference, and adaption. Data that support this idea do not prove, but are generally consistent with, the critical-periods hypothesis discussed earlier in this chapter. Differentiations along the lines of sex-role stereotyping are easily observed by school age. Sex-role development and general psychological adjustment seem closely related (Bates, Bentley, & Thompson, 1973), although influenced by both cultural values and individual family constellations. A growing body of data points to certain advantages of psychological androgyny—greater flexibility and freedom of choice in social relationships and general life style. References to atypical gender development have drawn our attention to the importance of early social influences in this area of human functioning. We now broaden our attention to social factors, first considering parental influences in typical gender development, and then school and mass-media influences.

Major Social Influences

Family Background Factors

Predictably, there has been much research about the relationships between sex typing and identification and the emotional climate and family structure in intact and single-parent homes, with a modest look at more global factors such as social class. Among other things, social class influences are revealed by an apparently less rigid sex-role stereotyping by ages 5 and beyond among children from middle, as compared to lower socioeconomic backgrounds (Naddman, 1974). Even during the preschool years, however, we can see evidence of this class-related phenomenon. In a recent study of preschool children's story preferences, middle-class boys were more "accepting" of a story about a male dancer than were their working-class peers, even though their strongest preference was for stories involving same-sex characters (Jennings, 1975).

Such differences presumably reflect a more strongly differentiated and more traditional sex-role stereotyping among many parents of lower socioeconomic status. Obviously the exceptions are many. We know several fathers in professional occupations, for example, who refuse to let their young sons watch the children's television program, "Mister Roger's Neighborhood," because they think it is too feminine. Even if the social-class differences are widespread, in the final analysis it is specific parent characteristics and parent–child interactions that are important for sex typing. Little can be explained by using such gross variables as socioeconomic status.

Parent characteristics   Parental warmth and power, in particular, seem very important influences on sex typing or sex-role acquisition (Mischel, 1970). It seems best for children's psychosexual development if the parent of the same sex is both warm and powerful, although the evidence is clearer for boys than for girls. Boys pattern themselves most after fathers (and here the evidence is clear) who are loving toward them and who are also powerful in the sense that they exert leadership roles in their marriages and families.

Girls whose mothers identify with them by being informed about their daughters' interests imitate their mothers more closely than do girls whose mothers are unaware of their interests. Femininity in girls, like masculinity in boys, is strongly associated with maternal warmth and affection. But by college age, girls who identify more with their fathers seem to be at least as well and perhaps better adjusted than those who identify with their mothers. The most competent girls seem to be those who are moderately distant from their mothers, but reasonably close to their fathers. The most competent boys are moderately distant but by no means estranged, from their mothers and close to but also rather firmly disciplined by their fathers (who in turn show warmth toward them but are not overly nurturant or overprotective).

Reinforcement patterns   The pattern of rewards and punishments for sex-typed behavior also seems to operate a bit differently for boys and girls, at least within United States culture. Rewards and punishments seem to be given in about even mixture to boys who develop congruently with the male sex-role stereotype held within a given culture (sex-role stereotypes vary widely from one culture to another); that is, they are punished when they act girlishly, rewarded when they act boyishly. The nature of the punishments varies from severe parental and particularly paternal discipline or criticism for "sissy" behavior through self-correction: "This is how boys should behave. This is how I behaved. My behavior does not fit what is expected of, and valued in, boys. Thus, I should not behave this way again." (The reader will recall that this sort of "self-correction" is akin to the cognitive-consistency theory held by cognitive developmentalists.)

Rewards to boys for being masculine are plentiful, particularly (it seems) from their fathers and their masculine peers. However, the instrumental role for boys often leads to nonconformity, disobedience, and classroom discipline problems. Thus, it is often discouraged in schools, as early as the nursery school years (Fagot & Patterson, 1969).

Girls apparently learn feminine stereotypic "sex-role appropriate" behavior principally through rewards, perhaps from fathers even more than mothers, and certainly from girl peers, teachers, and, by adolescence, from male peers. The evidence is plentiful that girls are not punished for boyish behavior to the degree that boys are punished for girlish behavior. Thus, it can be predicted (and evidence supports the prediction) that girls do not identify with their gender role as early or, perhaps, as firmly as boys. As might be expected (and some evidence supports the expectation), they *do* identify with their sex role more congruently than boys, perhaps because their learning occurs more through reward and less through punishment. The main evidence for this is that there appear to be fewer women than men who misidentify in their sex role. That is, there are apparently fewer women homosexuals, transvestites, and transsexuals. On the other hand, this may result from the greater activity and tendency to explore among boys and men. Learning also seems to play a more important role in shaping the sexual behavior of males (Ford & Beach, 1951).

Father absence If the above interpretation of rewards and punishments is accurate, and again taking into consideration the major theories of sex typing and identification, it would follow that boys will be more clearly affected than girls by father absence. This indeed seems true as we noted in Chapter 3. In general, the earlier in a boy's life his father leaves the home, the more likely will the boy's development be affected adversely. Specifically, when there has been reasonably prolonged father absence, boys are less efficient in school and do not show as advanced moral judgment. Compared to father-present boys, there is greater evidence of unsatisfactory psychological adjustment among father-absent boys from elementary school through to college (LeCorgne & Laosa, 1976; Oshman & Manoservitz, 1976). Boys with fathers absent also more often demonstrate "feminine cognitive development" in that they score higher for verbal than quantitative intelligence (Carlsmith, 1964).

Girls with fathers present are more evenly balanced cognitively. Their quantitative intelligence scores are closer to the same level as their verbal intelligence scores than for father-absent girls. Father-absent girls are also reported to be either extremely shy heterosexually or inclined toward overeagerness in their courting behavior. When very young, father-absent boys seem to be rather feminine in their attitudes and behavior; but there is no clear evidence, for example, that being without a father is more likely to result in a boy's having a homosexual adjustment. On the whole, for both sexes but more clearly for boys, social adjustment is better when fathers are in the home. Of course, this may not be directly related to the father as such, but simply to the fact that life is likely to be more difficult in homes with only one parent. So few homes are without a mother or mother surrogate that we have no data about what mother absence does to the psychosexual and other social-development patterns of children. However, it appears that boys from fatherless homes whose mothers are competent and strong and who like men will develop normally psychosexually.

Sibling influence As noted in Chapter 3, any father-absence effects may be mediated or even obliterated given the presence of a strong paternal surrogate, such as an older brother or other close male relative or friend. Sibling influences are illustrated by a report that both father-absent boys and girls with an older brother in the home behaved more aggressively and less dependently than father-absent children without an older brother (Wohlford et al., 1971). Five- and six-year-old girls with brothers reportedly have more masculine characteristics than do girls with sisters. Yet these same girls with brothers had equally strong feminine characteristics (Brim, 1958). The same pattern does not seem to hold for boys. Greater femininity and lesser masculinity were found among boys with sisters compared to boys with brothers. Such studies badly need replication. But they do suggest an important difference in learning sex roles within the family context.

Schooling and Sex-Role Development

Not until the Civil Rights Movement of the 1960s was serious thought given to how schools are implicated in the sex-role development of children and youth. Prior to that time, it appears that educational practices perpetuated conventional sex-role stereotypes. Not all educators, however, necessarily supported or were happy about this. From the literature about adolescence came occasional lonely cries about excessive emphasis upon marriage and homemaking as the principal pathway to adulthood for females (Frank, 1944). By and large, however, the level of consciousness about schooling and sex-role stereotyping was rather low. An even worse problem was open sex discrimination in the public schools. Evidence has been marshalled to claim that females were actually second-class citizens in many, if not most, American school districts (Martinez, 1974). Some examples: excluding women from elite academic schools or programs even though they were more highly qualified than male applicants; unwitting counseling and tracking of female students into "appropriate" or "acceptable" vocational education programs (such as "homemaking" rather than industrial arts); and denying females the opportunity to participate in various school athletic programs.

These and other practices were correctly interpreted as a violation of the constitutional right to equal educational opportunity. But it was not until 1972 that any substantive federal legislative action was taken to correct this inequity. The key provision of this legislation, Title IX of the Education Amendment of 1972, is:

No person in the United States shall, on the basis of sex, be excluded from participation in, be denied the benefits of, or be subjected to discrimination under any education program or activity receiving Federal assistance.

This prohibition does not extend beyond programs subsidized wholly or partly by federal monies. It remains up to individual states and school districts to follow through on this movement to guarantee equal educational equality opportunities for the sexes. As the creaky wheels of change have moved slowly toward this end, perceptive accounts of sex-role stereotyping in the schools have also appeared (for example, Levy & Stacey, 1973; Saario, Jacklin, & Tittle, 1973; Trecker, 1973). Such accounts describe the presumably adverse effects of sex-role stereotyping on female pupils.

Sources of sex bias in schools. Four aspects of schooling have been condemned. One is leadership models for females. In the early 1970s, for example, 67 percent of public school teaching positions were held by women, yet they held only about 16 percent of school administrative positions. The argument is that girls have ample models for classroom teaching, but little else. We cannot overlook the possible implications for male children of a dominant female work force in schools. In fact, concerns about the feminizing influence of schooling on males, especially at the elementary school level where 85 percent of teachers are female, have long been expressed (Lee, 1973). Critics have called for more male elementary school teachers, especially in the early years of schooling, to better balance role modeling for young boys. This would seem particularly important for boys with limited father contact or from father-absent homes. Conceivably, young girls could also benefit from the availability of cross-sex models as well. Unfortunately, speculation far outweighs hard evidence about modeling effects in schools. Either way, the clarity of and consistency with which specific forms of behavior are modeled by male *or* female teachers strike us as the important issue.

A second aspect of sex-role stereotyping in schools about which much has been written is the content of pupils' textbooks. Analyses of basal readers, for example, have revealed that greater numbers of boys and men appear as main characters. These mainly male characters portray a wider range of vocational pursuits and behave more adventurously, autonomously, and with greater success in mastering the environment than female characters. Females are more often portrayed as passive-dependent and less intellectually active than young males. In addition, textbook writing style has clearly been dominated by the use of masculine pronouns and generic terms ("mankind," "forefathers"). The collective message for females is thought to work against positive self-image development.

A third, perhaps less obvious, source of sex bias in schools is educational testing (Tittle, 1973). Analyses of the language used in commercially published achievement tests have revealed a sexist orientation toward the use of male noun and pronoun references. A bias has occurred in test item content as well. As subjects in story problems, for example, doctors and lawyers may be identified specifically as males, secretaries and nurses as females. In activity-centered items, boys have been shown as hikers, campers, and class leaders; girls as kitchen helpers or in pursuit of hobbies such as gardening and sewing. And

items to measure reading comprehension typically have mirrored the same prejudiced view of women. The main function of testing—assessing pupil achievement status—may be strongly augmented by a teaching function, by conveying cultural mores (and prejudices), if in a relatively subtle way (Saario et al., 1973).

Fourth, we can view the school curriculum itself as a source of sex-role stereotyping. Ideas about the suitability of various avenues for study and vocational preparation have long been influenced by sex-role perspectives. Automotives, wood and sheet-metal working, and even science study have been encouraged for males, and often discouraged for females. The reverse pattern holds for home economics. We have already mentioned the long-standing differential treatment of the sexes in athletics. College enrollment data indicate still further stereotyping; police science and engineering for males, secretarial and beautician schools for females. These few school curriculum examples are only the tip of an iceberg of relationships among educational, vocational, and life-style differences set in motion by conventional notions about sex roles.

We, and perhaps many of our readers as well, have recently observed efforts to provide both greater equality of educational opportunity and more freedom to diverge from conventionally sex-typed educational activities for both sexes. Activist groups and educators committed to democratic philosophy as a basis for school programming have done much to pave the way. Such action is focused as early as the preschool period. The Women's Action Alliance (1973), for example, has worked to establish a teacher–parent "consciousness raising program" and develop nonsexist curricula for early childhood education. Perhaps the most visible change from traditional public school practice has been increased support, not unopposed, for women's interscholastic athletic competition. On balance, however, we are some distance away from the assumed ideal of androgyny in education. Altered conceptions about sex role and education may be more talked about than practiced, even among young persons themselves. One recent study, for example, has shown that adolescents generally still hold fairly traditional sex-role stereotypes, particularly about cross-sex ratings by males of females and vice versa (Urberg & Labouvie-Vief, 1976). In this study, the only evidence of "real" change from conventional thinking involved a "desexing" of two formerly sex-typed characteristics: affiliation for males and achievement for females.

We have a feeling that further changes will depend heavily upon several other aspects of school practice and general cultural experience for children and youth. Two factors seem especially important. One is the specific nature of teacher–pupil interaction. There is ample evidence to suggest, for example, that teachers (especially females) continue to encourage and strongly reinforce feminine (sedate, dependent, compliant, nonassertive) behaviors for *both* boys and girls in preschool and elementary school settings (Etaugh, Collins, & Gerson, 1975; Etaugh & Hughes, 1975; McCandless, Bush, & Carden, 1976). This is understandable given teachers' concerns with the preservation of order and achievement of academic objectives with learners whose attendance is compulsory (Lee, 1973). But to the extent that children "get the message" we would not expect drastic changes in their concepts about femininity and acceptable behavior.

The second important factor in any change in sex-role stereotyping is children's experience with television. Again, studies have indicated that television programming can be notoriously biased in favor of traditional sex-role behaviors. This is clearly shown in one analysis of ten popular, commercially produced programs for children's viewing (Sternglanz & Serbin, 1974). As in much of children's literature, there were both more male than female roles and a greater variety of male role behavior depicted in these programs. Males were shown as more involved in construction activities (planning, building), higher in aggression, but substantially less deferent to others than females. Females, in contrast, were seen as more admiring and complimentary of males and also more likely to follow the directions of others. Also, males received more positive reinforcement, whereas females more often received no consequences or were punished, especially for high levels of activity.

While this study is typical of many, we cannot leap to the conclusion that such programs directly affect children's concept formation about sex-role behavior. However, to the extent that such programs reinforce role behaviors modeled elsewhere (for example, in the home), we would infer some influence. This is especially likely in the event children witness few, if any, credible deviations from traditional stereotypic roles. But data about the television-viewing–sex-role behavior relationship are largely correlational and from them causation cannot be established. One pair of research workers, for example, has found much higher viewing rates among elementary-school-age children of both sexes with more, as compared to less, rigid sex-role orientations (25 or more hours per week compared to less than 10 hours per week of television watching). This finding leads us to question whether television contributes to stereotyping, or more rigidly stereotyped children are more attracted to television, or a little of both occurs, or that some further variables—pattern of parental authority or variations in family structure—may account for the relationship.

The reader is encouraged to examine for changes new television programs watched by children during peak hours (after school until about 8 or 9 P.M. and Saturday mornings). At this writing there is not much evidence that America's commercial network personnel are seriously reconstructing sex-role relationships in children's programs. Even educational programs for children, such as Sesame Street, have been justly criticized for narrow or unrepresentative sex role portrayals.

Of course, demands for change must be made in full view of the value judgments necessary for reorienting socialization goals in this important area of psychological development. In the past, we have assumed that adopting gender-appropriate sex roles was the healthy and desirable goal of socialization. Research activity was largely concerned with identifying conditions to promote masculinity in males, femininity in females. Among other things, a belief in the moral rightness of differentiated sex roles has prevailed, associated with deep concerns about preserving the nuclear family and a flourishing heterosexuality. The extent of changes in such values and beliefs throughout the whole of American society is not easily established. But it appears that we are in an important period of transition both to a reconceptualization of sex-role relationships and to a reordering of priorities about human values associated with psychosexual development. To date, the transition seems most apparent in the thinking of females, as early as adolescence, whose options for behaving have been most restricted by traditionalism in sex-role definition (Joesting & Joesting, 1975). Males, however, would also seem to benefit from greater freedom to de-

velop their emotional expressivity and full personal-social relations, qualities heretofore discouraged by a concept of rugged masculinity. It is not unusual, though, to hear more about male *problems* with readjusted sex roles than about *advantages*. As an example, the phenomenon of male psychological threat from female competence can be cited (Pleck, 1976). That is, male fears about females achieving success in their competitive achievement striving with men may result in defensiveness or even heightened aggressiveness in male–female relationships. Thus it appears that equality for the sexes, as with racial equality and the value of cultural pluralism, is not without its psychological risks. As optimists, however, we anticipate that conflict resolutions will occur and result in a higher synthesis of thought about human development and welfare among people regardless of their sex.

SEXUAL DEVELOPMENT AND BEHAVIOR

We now shift our discussion from the social aspects of sex roles to the more directly *sexual* aspects of psychosexual development. Biological definitions for male and female sexuality were given in Chapter 6. At that time we emphasized puberty and the development of primary and secondary sex characteristics. While puberty dramatizes an individual's sexuality and, for most persons in United States society, marks the beginning of mature sexual behavior, we view sexuality as a product of cumulative development. It is not something suddenly achieved with puberty, the first orgasm, or the first intercourse. Sexuality seems strongly determined by attitudes toward the self and others; it is part of an individual's total personality. With the possible exception of cases of sexual pathol-

© Margaret Durrance, from Photo Researchers

© Jan Lukas, from Photo Researchers

Dick Davis, from Photo Researchers, Inc.

© Jan Lukas, from Photo Researchers

Richard Frieman, from Photo Researchers, Inc.

© Jan Lukas, from Photo Researchers

Michael Weisbrot

ella Hammid, from Photo Researchers

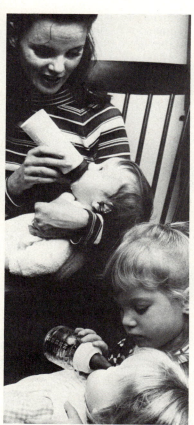

© 1972 Erika Stone, from Photo Researchers

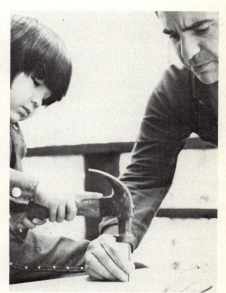

© Alice Kandell, from Photo Researchers

Michael Weisbrot

Gerald Holly, from Black

Michael Weisbrot

Michael Weisbrot

Kenneth Karp

Michael

Galyn, from Photo Researchers

Copyright by Chester Higgins, Jr., from Photo Researchers

Rhoda Galyn, from Photo Researchers

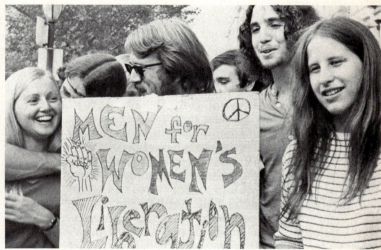

Betty Lane, from Photo Researchers

ry Suris, from Photo Researchers

ogy, sexual expression usually reflects an individual's prevailing personality characteristics. For example, a male who is generally aggressive, hostile, and inconsiderate toward others will probably be aggressive, hostile, and inconsiderate in his sexual relations. Similarly, a passive, dependent, and anxious male is likely to manifest this general social orientation when engaged in the sexual act. In short, sexuality is but one aspect of socialization.

Having said this, however, we must acknowledge the fundamental importance of sexuality and its functions in human relationships. Sexuality obviously functions to reproduce and thus maintain the development of our species, but human sexuality also serves important nonprocreative functions, such as profound physical pleasure and an intimate form of communication between persons who may commit themselves to a spiritual relationship. Traditionally in our society, this kind of relationship is symbolized by marriage between two opposite-sexed partners. Though sexual communication is but one dimension of this contractual relationship, sexual adjustment problems loom strongly as a factor in unhappy or unsuccessful marriages. During the mid-1970s, for example, it is estimated that some 40 percent of first-time marriages will eventually end in divorce (over 50 percent of marriages occur during the teen years) (Masters, 1976; Menninger, 1976). Of this number, about half will terminate because of sexual dysfunction and dissatisfaction. Moreover, it is believed that roughly half of those couples who stay married experience some degree of difficulty in sexual adjustment. In addition, sex guilt or anxiety, conflicts, and dysfunctions are seen as either causes or symptoms in a wide variety of psychological disturbances in both adult males and females.

How can we account for differences in adult sexuality? Only since the late 1940s has any semblance of scientific information accumulated in answer to this question. To be sure, cultural anthropologists for many years have been studying patterns of sexual behavior in selected primitive societies, and sexuality played a central role in Sigmund Freud's thinking about personality development. By and large, however, sexuality — like death and to some extent religion — has until recently tended to be a "taboo" subject for scientific research. A significant breakthrough occurred in 1948 with the publication of the first in a series of reports about adult sexual behavior by Alfred Kinsey and his colleagues at Indiana University. Since then, significant advances have been made toward an understanding of human sexual development. But our understanding remains incomplete, especially about children's sexuality.

We will first examine the importance of cultural context for sexual development. Then we review some highlights from research about sexual development in United States children and youth, including reference to several variations on the theme of normal heterosexual development. Finally, we comment briefly upon major social influences on sexual development, especially parenting and schooling.

Culture and Sexuality

Cultural Variations in Sexual Behaviors

No one seriously questions the universality of biological sex or the energizing power of sexual motivation for wide-ranging human behavior patterns. At puberty, regardless of culture, youth must make certain behavioral adjustments to increased size and strength, maturation of sexual characteristics, and accompanying biological rhythms and pressures (for example, the menstrual cycle for girls and insistent pressure for sexual outlet for boys, with attendant erections, nocturnal emissions or "wet dreams," masturbation, and various sexual encounters). But the form and the tempo of sexual development and behavior vary greatly within and between cultures. So do the style and frequency of sexual practices, marital or otherwise, and the degree of tolerance for sexual "deviation" (Ford & Beach, 1951; Marshall & Suggs, 1971). The wide cross-cultural variations in sexual practices indicate strikingly the influence of social factors or cultural learning on sexual behavior and attitudes. These variations illustrate both the malleability of human behavior and the power of social influences to mediate a basic human drive.

Illustrations may be drawn from anthropological studies of sexual behavior. One classic anthropological analysis of such behavior arranges societies along a continuum of restrictiveness-permissiveness about sexual practices and the socialization of sexual behavior (Ford & Beach, 1951). In extremely restrictive societies, for example, ultrasecretive and limited social contact usually occurs between adults; young children and adolescents are denied access to sexual knowledge and are prevented from expressing sexual interests in any form. Methods of enforcement for this restriction may include strict segregation of the sexes until marriage, continuous adult chaperonage of girls, and threats of severe disgrace, physical punishment, or even death. Active punitiveness or repression, however, is not always apparent in societies with low sexual involvement. The Dani Tribe of New Guinea, for example, seem simply to have given sex a low priority. The "first night" of a Dani marriage is always postponed for two years. When a child eventually is born, parents observe a five-year period of abstinence from sex. Sexual talk or anxiety does not seem to occur nor are the Dani observed to indulge in sexual deviations. All of this goes on without signs of social disorder or psychological disturbance.

In contrast, other societies take a permissive approach to sexuality. Sex play among children and adolescents may occur in public, apparently in the absence of adult sanctions. Children are not prevented from watching adult sexual activity in the home, and may even be sexually stimulated by their parents or caregivers through masturbation. The point is that, in addition to wide variation in sexual practices, widely different beliefs (even superstitions) usually underlie punitive or tolerant approaches to this aspect of human behavior. Belief in a malevolent god and fear of social retribution are often associated with restrictiveness. Where open sexuality among the young is encouraged, beliefs include the notion that children must exercise themselves sexually early in life to achieve fertility or that girls will not mature without benefit of sexual intercourse. In still other cultures (for example, the Turu in Tanzania) a system of adultery for adults, which has tenuous support by law, is supported to make romantic love possible without endangering the institution of marriage (Suggs & Marshall, 1971). Thus, one cannot overlook institutionalized legality in determining what facilitates or inhibits sexual behavior.

Cross-Cultural Regularities

While cross-cultural variations in sexual behavior obviously affect sexual attitudes and behavior, it is important also to note certain regularities surrounding sex and marriage from culture to culture. These regularities illustrate the controls that cultures find necessary for economic and ecological survival. No culture is without laws, whether written or "unwritten" or both (sometimes unenforceable and unenforced), that pertain to sexuality, regardless of how permissive or how restrictive the culture. For example, sanctions against incest, rape, and sexual relations between adults and children exist in virtually every organized society (Marshall & Suggs, 1971).

Values supporting preservation of the family unit, personal hygiene, and the control of property are other cross-cultural regularities. For example, one authority reports such universals as the general expectation (or at least preference) that mothers should be married; that marriage is not undertaken for a specified, short-term period; that mothers should live in the same domicile as their children; and that sexual intercourse should not occur during the menstrual period (Stephens, 1963). Such universals or near universals suggest that, even in the face of marked cultural diversity, there are some regularities in human existence that govern family life and sexual behavior. While every society must exercise control of sexual behavior that is disruptive, such control is achieved in a variety of ways (Mead, 1961).

American society has in the past been more restrictive than permissive in its approach to sexuality. Considerable data now exist, however, to indicate a trend toward greater permissiveness or liberality. This trend is perhaps most clear in attitudes about nudity and premarital sex. Gallup Opinion Poll data (1973), for example, have shown a consistent increase in the "acceptability" of nudity in films and magazines, masturbation, and justifications for premarital coitus, particularly if it occurs in the context of a love relationship. As we might expect, permissiveness about sex tends to be stronger among younger than among older Americans. A majority of adults, young and old, still disapprove or view negatively extramarital intercourse and homosexuality, though a sizeable minority of Americans is tolerant of both forms of sexual expression. It

seems fair to say that as a total society we are more conservative than liberal about sexuality, though it is risky to evaluate attitudes so globally. Perhaps more pertinent for students of human development are data about sexual knowledge and sexual *behavior* among children and youth.

Some Developmental Aspects of Sexuality

Sexual Knowledge

Gender awareness, as indicated earlier in this chapter, involves both knowledge of the body parts that distinguish one sex from the other and correct use of the corresponding vocabulary in reference to self and others. An important aspect of this awareness is discovery of the genitals through self-exploration during the first year of life. As gender identity begins to crystallize during the later preschool years we can observe children in the process of learning about and attempting to understand such things as excretory functions and where babies come from. Curiosity is piqued as children undergo their "toilet training" and perhaps view nudity in the home.

Unfortunately, there are very few systematic studies about the origin and development of children's concepts of sexuality. What data are available, however, suggest a stage-sequence evolution of such concepts generally consistent with the cognitive-developmental interpretation of intellectual development (Chapter 8). A recent cross-sectional study of children's concepts of the origin of human life (Bernstein & Cowan, 1975) and our own less-formal investigation will illustrate. From a total lack of comprehension, children seem first to assume that babies simply exist somewhere; parents must somehow find or buy their babies. From this point, ideas evolve about babies being in tummies and variations on the theme of "seed planting" to somewhat more advanced notions about the necessity of sperm and egg for successful "hatching."

By school age, fathers may correctly be seen as a necessary ingredient for the birth of babies. Penis function may also be recognized, with reference to terms like "baby making," "hunching," or other euphemisms for sexual intercourse. Slang or four-letter words may also be picked up early from older children and used freely, often as empty verbalisms without understanding their full meaning. Many children, however, may still believe that love is required for babies to be made. Still later, usually by ages 10–12, a more differentiated concept of fertilization is comprehended, even including approximate ideas about genes. By this time, a full awareness of the act of sexual intercourse will normally have emerged, though in the absence of first-hand observation children may have difficulty visualizing how it actually occurs. It is common for children to indicate a posture they observe among animals, with the male mounting the female from the rear. There is little understanding about such things as orgasm, impotence or venereal disease.

Obviously, children's knowledge about sexual matters depends upon the information available to them, and it seems fairly clear that an informal policy of sexual information-control is followed in many American homes. Surveys have shown consistently that a substantial majority of adolescents gain most of their knowledge about sex, however accurate or inaccurate, from peers and slick magazines rather than from their parents (Youth Poll America, 1976). Of course, adults may themselves be variously ignorant or misinformed about sexual matters. It strikes us that the amount and accuracy of knowledge about human sexuality are woefully inadequate in large segments of the youth population. For example, one recent study of 4,200 unmarried females, ages 15–19, showed that an overwhelming majority of these girls *disagreed* with the true statement that conception is most likely to occur midway between one menstrual period and the next (Zelnik & Kantner, 1972). These girls expressed a belief that conception is most likely either immediately before or after the menstrual period. We have also observed that many adolescent females and males believe conception cannot occur in the absence of female orgasm.

Such false ideas are probably the direct result of learned misinformation. But even in the absence of information, correct or otherwise, it seems that children (and youth) may actively construct their ideas about sexual intercourse, reproduction, birth, and the like. In fact, some elements of theory construction about creation and birth are apparent as early as age 4 or 5 (Kreitler & Kreitler, 1966). Some children, for example, reason that babies are created in the mother's belly from the food that she eats. Others seem convinced that the baby has always existed in the mother's tummy, even when she was a small girl, and that mothers must eat good things to help the baby grow. Still others argue that the baby was swallowed in tiny form, thereafter to grow and come out through the navel.

Such "theories" eventually are modified to fit the truth. But what we may view as misinformation or misunderstanding may instead represent the outcome of the assimilation process at work on data too complexly structured for children to comprehend (Bernstein & Cowan, 1975). Thus, after several discussions between Judy, age 4, and her mother about how baby kittens are made, daddy cat's semen became "glue" that sticks to the mommy cat's egg so that the baby kittens will be safe until big enough to "crawl out." In short, children seem to take only what they can comprehend, then transform and integrate it into existing structures, thus gradually accommodating to full reality.

Sexual Behavior

The sex drive and its psychological accompaniments (or the new state of the organism and its new reinforcers) unquestionably act as major forces on behavior during adolescence. However, sexual behavior is not unique to puberty and the years that follow it. Sex interest and sex play are common among preschoolers and preadolescents. Boys and girls exhibit to each other, within and across sexes. "Doctor-nurse" and "House" games often result in mutual genital inspection. "Peepee places," to use one version of the term, are much talked of and looked at. Preadolescents are fascinated with nudity and peeping. Males, especially, incorporate sex-related slang words and jokes into their repertoire within and often outside the peer group.

The motivational basis (or reinforcing basis) for prepubescent sexuality, however, seems to be curiosity rather than the mature reinforcer such as an orgasm or romantic love (Ausubel, 1954). To be sure, some preadolescents, probably more girls than boys, engage in sexual intercourse, usually initiated by adults, although their behavior is not typically a search for sexual gratification (Gagnon & Simon, 1970). There is also evidence that male children, usually runaways, can become involved in male prostitution as early as preadolescence (Lloyd, 1976). And a despicable trend in pornographic film-making as this book is written involves the recruitment of young children, both male and female, to perform oral sex on adults.

Age trends and sex differences in adolescent sexuality As they move into later adolescence, more young people engage in some form of sexual activity: masturbation, heterosexual petting, or intercourse. Although percentages vary with the sampling procedures, surveys indicate that most adolescent males masturbate at some time during adolescence, with a frequency of anywhere from once to over twenty times per month (Sorenson, 1973). Masturbation among adolescent females is apparently less frequent and widespread, although it may occasionally occur earlier among them than among their male age mates. From 40 to 60 percent of adolescent girls admit to masturbation, many of whom masturbate more frequently after having experienced orgasm in situations involving others. But it is not until the late 20s that the incidence of orgasm for females, through masturbation or other means, typically reaches the frequency that it does for males at age 16 (Simon & Gagnon, 1968). Regardless of percentages, masturbation during adolescence is generally considered both normal and harmless.

Sex differences in sexual outlets are also reflected in the incidence of premarital intercourse. Roughly 60–85 percent of adolescent males admit to intercourse before marriage with at least one partner, whereas about 45–50 percent of females so report. These percentage figures vary with social class. At least in the past, a greater incidence of premarital intercourse has been found among adolescents from lower socioeconomic backgrounds (Rainwater, 1966). Lower-class adolescents of both sexes reportedly experience intercourse at an earlier age than do their middle-class counterparts. For lower-class males, intercourse is more likely than masturbation as a major sex outlet. Intercourse for such males occurs more frequently and with more partners than for the average middle-class male. This difference is commonly explained by lesser inhibitions about sexual contact and greater value placed on "manliness" and the masculine status accorded by exploitative sexual conquests. A "cult of virility" seems especially pronounced among lower-class black youth, whose peer status may be largely determined by frequency, versatility, and endurance in sexual behavior (Staples, 1973).

Other sex differences in adolescent sexuality have also been reported (Sorenson, 1973). For example, in their sexual relations, males are more easily and frequently aroused solely for physical gratification as compared to love expression. In contrast, females are generally more concerned and satisfied with the romantic aspect of love-making and usually demonstrate a less erotic sexual orientation than males. Reactions to pornographic film content also vary by sex. In one study, for example, both males and females reported comparable arousal levels after viewing a film depicting sexual intercourse, but males were aroused more and females less by a film depicting oral-genital sex (Mann, 1970).

The consistency with which sex differences in attitudes and behavior concerning sexual expression have been found suggests a basic difference in male and female orientation during sexual development (Gagnon and Simon, 1970). In general, early sexual activity among males is organized primarily around masturbation. This private self-gratification may foster a detached kind of sexuality, even when self-gratification is accompanied by elaborate fantasies. Masturbatory activity's principal reinforcement is physical; the sexual commitment is almost entirely genital. The male must move from this private, physical commitment toward a broader sociosexual orientation in which a commitment to romantic love is made. Training is required in the language and actions of romantic love and the way to deal appropriately with the emotional aspects of a genuine heterosexual relationship.

For females, the pattern is usually reversed. Girls seem to be better and ear-

lier trained for a commitment to and capacity for romantic love and the subtleties of emotion that lead to strong heterosexual attachments. For females, sexual experience, including orgasm, is more likely to occur first as part of a relatively stable love relationship. For many, perhaps most, females, commitment to sexuality begins on a sociosexual foundation. The typical girl will often continue to seek the romantic qualities of heterosexual affiliation, whereas the male continues to seek the erotic and the physical. It is no wonder that heterosexual involvements, particularly those which occur early in adolescence, are often marked by conflicts, misunderstandings, and disappointment. But the importance of developing a healthy sociosexuality can hardly be overestimated given its importance for family formation, adult roles and obligations, and self-definition (Simon & Gagnon, 1968). It should be added that this clear sex difference in seeking physical sexual gratification may be disappearing; the data are not yet in. Even so, it is interesting to note that most adolescents at least *say* they do not believe in sex without love (Sorenson, 1973).

Teenage pregnancy There has been a substantial increase over time in the number of young unmarried females who each year become pregnant. Since 1945, the number of "illegitimate" births in America reportedly has increased at a rate of about 60 percent per decade. The Planned Parenthood Federation of America, for example, reports that in the 1970s pregnancies occurred in about one million teenage females in the 15–19 age group each year (Jaffe, 1977). (This means that from 10 to 15 percent of the adolescent female population becomes pregnant each year, varying with geographical location and assuming the accuracy of the statistics.)

Two-thirds of these pregnancies occur out of wedlock, and an overwhelming majority of them are unintended or unwanted. Successively earlier experimentation with sex is a major factor in producing these pregnancies. But in addition to more frequent sexual intercourse, today's young females seemingly are both fertile at an earlier age and have fewer spontaneous abortions than their counterparts from generations past (Cutright, 1972). This alerts us to the need for information about and availability of contraceptive measures for sexually active youth. Paradoxically, young females who become pregnant usually have only superficial knowledge of such measures and may use them only sporadically, if at all. This seems especially true among economically disadvantaged black females (Furstenberg, 1976). Undoubtedly, attitudinal or personality factors also affect to some extent the use or nonuse of contraceptive devices. And in some cases, deliberate nonuse may occur in the belief that "It can't happen to me" (omnipotence) or that contraceptive planning in advance conflicts with a preferred "moral" self-view: "I'm not *that* kind of girl!" (Wagner, 1970).

In fact, studying the personality characteristics of sexually active teenagers who become pregnant has become increasingly popular in recent years. One typical study reveals at least three "subgroups" among nearly 300 young unwed mothers (Horn & Turner, 1976). The largest group (44 percent) were rated as psychologically healthy females who were simply ignorant about the facts of life and usually unsupervised by their parents. A second nearly as large group (38 percent) reported a moderate-to-severe degree of adjustment problems (perhaps precipitated in part by their pregnancy). The third, and smaller group (18 percent) showed deeply disturbed patterns of interpersonal relationships, where sexuality apparently was a form of delinquent acting-out. A further comparison of these unwed mothers by whether or not they kept their babies revealed little except that, significantly, the deeply disturbed females were somewhat more likely to keep their babies.

Similar data suggest that social rejection, guilt about sexual activity, and a belief that one's destiny is more controlled by luck, fate, or chance than by exercising personal responsibility are correlated with adolescent illegitimate pregnancy (Kane & Lachenbruch, 1973; Meyerowitz & Malev, 1973). Generally speaking, the data are considerably more abundant for females than males. Very little about any differences, say, between teenage fathers and "nonfathers" can be found (Pauker, 1971). It is important, however, to note that the prevailing attitude in United States society (unfairly we think) holds the female more responsible for contraception than the male. Perhaps if females were more emphatic about denying sexual favors until their male partners exercised suitable precautions, the situation would change. This is a straightforward application of the reinforcement-contingency management principle (Chapter 2). Otherwise, only three alternatives are available to a female: abstinence, maximum personal contraceptive planning, or accepting the consequences of a pregnancy the probability of which increases greatly without preventive measures. Personal-social responsibility is clearly at issue. It can be argued, of course, that there is always abortion. Aside from the moral question, abortion for young females can be financially expensive, physiologically risky, and a threat to psychological well-being (Martin, 1973). On balance, it seems more advisable to argue for responsible planning. Yet the issue is divisive. While a majority (73 percent) of American adults agree that contraceptives should be offered to sexually active teenagers, this leaves a sizable opposing minority (Planned Parenthood Federation, 1972). And it is clear that access to or availability of contraceptives is no guarantee that they will be used, even among married couples who wish to restrict childbearing. Supercharged emotions, it would seem, dominate the human intellect when it comes to sexual relationships.

Some Variations on the Normal Course of Sexual Development

The interplay of constitutional and social forces creates a dazzling array of individual differences in human sexual behavior and development. In this section we refer to some of the more extreme variations in biological and social aspects of sexual development (Jolly, 1968; Shiller, 1972).

Sexual precocity Sexually precocious children show sexual development much earlier than is normal: before age 10 and sometimes as early as age 5 or 6. The condition is more common among females, who have the greatest incidence of *constitutional* precocity. Full sexual maturity, including a capacity for pregnancy, marks this development. Though growth in height also increases prematurely, such children are ultimately shorter than average. The same can be said for males. In addition to constitutional sexual precocity, selectively premature sexual development can occur among children with glandular anomalies. Adrenal-gland overactivity, for instance, is associated with precocity in males, manifested in an enlarged penis and appearance of pubic hair as early as age 5. In this condition, however, the testicles are not affected and remain infantile. Adrenal activity in girls results in the development of male secondary sex characteristics, a condition known as virilism.

Other hormonal conditions Other alterations in sexual development include eunuchoidism and gynecomastia in males. The former syndrome is indicated by a failure of testicular or pituitary function so that puberty does not occur. The male eunuch usually grows quite tall, with very long arms and legs. Voice change and secondary sex characteristics, especially facial hair, do not appear. The condition must be distinguished from delayed puberty, a diagnosis usually made by examining the testicles and bone structure of the individual.

Gynecomastia refers to a transitory enlargement of the breasts among pubescent males. In its most common form, gynecomastia occurs in about 30 percent of the adolescent population. For such cases, the suspected cause is a temporary hormonal imbalance; estrogens (female hormones) are more than usually active. When gynecomastia is so caused, breast size will normally recede within 12–18 months. If not, and when the breasts are unusually large, surgical intervention may be prescribed. Such was the procedure for Max, now a normal-appearing 18-year-old. But he experienced an unfair amount of psychological agony, much of which was brought on by his inconsiderate peers at school. Aware of his relatively large breasts, Max's peers quickly developed a nickname for him—"Mama Max"—and were responsible for such things as planting a baby doll in his school locker and placing lipstick in his lunch box. Fortunately, since his operation, Max has achieved a good psychosocial adjustment.

Chromosomal disorders Gynecomastia is but one outward sign of a much more serious growth disorder in males whose cause is chromosomal abnormality. Known as Klinefelter's syndrome, this condition is marked by a failure of testicular development. Growth in height may be normal, even above normal; secondary sex characteristics may also develop on schedule at puberty. But the testicles and penis remain underdeveloped. Unfortunately, diagnosis is very difficult prior to puberty without extensive chromosomal analysis. Such analysis typically will reveal the presence of an extra female chromosome (XXY) instead of the normal male pattern (XY). The syndrome is sometimes accompanied by moderate mental retardation.

A pattern similar to Klinefelter's syndrome for males can be observed for females. The parallel chromosomal aberration for females, however, is XO, instead of the normal XX. Thus a critical sex chromosome is missing. The ovaries are either missing entirely or fail to develop normally. Breast and genital development do not occur at puberty as expected, although pubic hair does appear. Problems associated with this condition, known as Turner's syndrome, include webbing of the neck, widely spaced nipples, congenital heart defects, and, occasionally, mental retardation. Hormonal therapy is recommended for both the Turner and Klinefelter syndromes, but at the usual age of puberty.

Possibly the most dramatic deviation from a pattern of normal biosexual development is hermaphroditism. This "intersex" condition appears in two forms. One form, genuine hermaphroditism, is extremely rare: the individual develops both ovarian and testicular tissue. More common is the condition known as pseudohermaphroditism, where the testes or ovaries are normal for the male or female involved but the external sex organs resemble to a varying degree those of the opposite sex. A female pseudohermaphrodite will have masculinized genitals; the reverse holds for her male counterpart. Little is known about the psychosexual relationships of hermaphroditic individuals. Appropriate medical treatment and psychological counseling can hopefully assist them toward satisfactory life adjustments.

Homosexuality A final difference in psychosexual development to be discussed here is homosexuality, meaning an exclusive preference for sexual relationships with persons of the same biological sex. No corresponding heterosexual interest is shown. Until recently, homosexuality was "officially" classified as a pathological condition according to the American Psychiatric Association. Recently, it has been removed from this classification, ostensibly to recognize it more accurately as a different, but not abnormal psychosexual adjustment. That the British counterpart to the APA has not so acted perhaps illustrates something of the controversial nature of homosexuality.

As in other patterns of sexual behavior, a homosexual orientation usually first becomes evident during late preadolescence or early adolescence. One recent study (Sorenson, 1973) has revealed that some 9 percent of adolescents report having one or more homosexual experiences (11 percent boys, 6 percent girls) by the age of 11 or 12. Other surveys (such as Kinsey, 1948) put this figure higher. Early experimentation with homosexual acts is not a reliable indication of preference for same-sex physical intimacies. A consistent homosexual preference, however, is usually in evidence by late adolescence though not always fully recognized, and even less frequently admitted by the individual involved. Social sanctions against homosexuality, of course, play a strong part in this situation. Never has homosexuality been a preferred sexual outlet among a majority of humans in any society; and it is still viewed with some apprehension, even hostility, by many people in these days of liberationist thought.

Homosexuality, however, has been a

subject of intense scientific curiosity. Nearly 1300 scientific articles and books on the subject were published in English between the years 1940 and 1968 (Weinberg & Bell, 1972). This interest has continued during the past decade and includes the appearance of a new periodical, the *Journal of Homosexuality*. But it is with some degree of frustration that we can report little in the way of consensus about the incidence or causes of homosexual behavior. Concerning incidence, it is "guesstimated" that somewhere between 1 and 2 percent of the male adolescent and adult population are basically homosexual (Bieber, 1976). Homosexuality among females is very poorly documented, perhaps because there actually are fewer girls and women with lesbian preferences or because they are subculturally less well organized and visible for study than male homosexuals (Weinberg & Bell, 1972). As for causation, the nature–nurture controversy is clearly in evidence throughout the literature about homosexuality. Impassioned arguments, with supportive evidence of varying credibility, exist on both sides of the ledger.

One scholar, for example, argues for a neurohormonal gender identification as the basis for homosexuality (Murphy, 1971). An equally vociferous argument is made for adverse socialization as the antecedent condition, especially that involving disturbed parent–child relationships. It does appear that fathers play a prominent role in the homosexual development of their children of either biological sex. Weak, but especially, hostile and detached fathers surface with regularity in home background studies of homosexuality (Thompson et al., 1973). The role of mothers is less clear. Ineffectual and dominant, affectionate mothers are associated with female and male homosexuality, respectively. In general, it is not uncommon to find that male and female homosexuals also report more

strongly cross-sexed socialization experiences as children, similar to those discussed in the earlier section on effeminacy-masculinity in sex-role development. But exceptions to this pattern abound; many children who become heterosexual may experience backgrounds similar to those in which homosexuality develops as well. Thus the picture is fuzzy and requires much more study.

This reference to home background factors in homosexuality anticipates our fuller discussion of major social influences on sexual behavior and development. From this point on, however, we will concentrate on the general normative aspects of human sexuality.

Major Social Influences

We have so far stressed some general cultural variables associated with differences in sexual development and behavior. In the remaining pages we again turn to the family and school, to examine further the socialization of sexuality. Particular emphasis is placed upon selected and widely discussed social issues involving sexuality.

Parenting

As the reader may appreciate, comparatively little is known about the specific nature, much less any effects, of child-rearing practices on sexual behavior and attitudes among the young. We noted earlier that only since the publication of the first Kinsey report in 1948 has much psychological research been done about human sexuality. Since then researchers have gradually improved our understanding of sexual behavior, mainly through studies of individuals of college age or beyond. This is understandable, of course, given the highly personal and emotional nature of sexual behavior, concern about the invasion of privacy, and difficult methodological problems in obtaining accurate sexual information from people, especially children. From clinical reports and correlational studies, however, one fairly clear and consistent finding has been reported: human sexual problems often accompany personal maladjustment during adolescence and beyond (McCandless, 1967). Whether sexual problems cause or even contribute to this maladjustment cannot be stated confidently. It is possible that sexual problems are more often symptoms than causes of maladjustment. But it is not unreasonable to suggest a relationship between childhood socialization experiences and later sexual beliefs and attitudes. For example, attitudes toward sexuality revealed in parental behavior toward nudity in the home, responsiveness to children's questions about sex and childbirth, children's masturbatory behavior, and the like, surely affect the sexual outlook of the growing child. As yet, however, we lack sufficient evidence to indicate how extensive the effects may be.

In one of the few studies of sex and modesty training in United States families, a large group of mothers from middle and low socioeconomic households indicated four basic concerns about their children's sexuality. Each of these suggests an avoidance orientation to socialization: (1) internalization of the incest taboo, (2) training to avoid masturbation, (3) training to avoid heterosexual sex play, and (4) information control (Sears, Maccoby, & Levin, 1956). In general, mothers strongly disapproved of sexuality in their children, but few indicated that they regularly punished to restrict sexual activity. Where punitive measures were taken, they were more often applied in lower-class homes than in middle-class homes.

No comparable study has been reported in more recent years. Thus we cannot be sure that these concerns persist among young parents in the 1970s. But if such sex-training practices are an indication of a general approach to sex and modesty training in United States culture, at least two points can be made. First, such disapproval of sexuality (however tacit it may be) and emphasis on limiting sexual activity in children suggest a generally restrictive approach to sexuality in our society. Second, such data highlight the discontinuity in sex socialization in this culture. Few parents seriously and consciously intend to deter their children from attaining the goal of a successful adult sex life. Yet in the early stages of socialization, most parents seem to expect their children to be asexual and discourage any overt sign of sexuality. This restrictiveness is replaced with the often subtle, yet powerful encouragement of heterosexual relations (short of intercourse) during adolescence as a preparation for marriage. Thus, an about-face in socialization occurs precisely at the time when sexual urges are intensifying.

The issue is whether such discontinuity interferes in any way with satisfaction in adult sexual relations. Again, the evidence is indirect and fuzzy. As an example, one authority reports that the reason most frequently given by men for unsatisfying marital sex relations is that their wives are too inhibited sexually. Women complain about dissatisfaction with sex in marriage because of their husbands' lack of sensitivity and concern for general romance and sexual foreplay (Kinsey, Pomeroy, & Martin, 1948; Kinsey, Pomeroy, Martin, & Gebhard, 1953).

It is possible that parental restrictiveness and discontinuities in socialization are somewhat implicated in such findings. But this does not mean that a permissive approach to the socialization of sexual behavior in United States culture is necessarily good or even possible. Tacit or active approval of childhood and adolescent heterosexual behavior can conceivably have profoundly harmful ramifications for individuals and for society. The easy availability of birth-control techniques has never prevented frequent paternity and maternity during adolescence; nor has access to prophylaxis had much impact on the incidence of venereal disease among adolescents. Any change in parental orientation toward premarital sexual activity should be examined carefully in the light of our unique cultural framework and the broader spectrum of values around which American life is organized. For example, does easy and early sex gratification reduce the need for fantasy and dreaming, and thus reduce the value of people of the opposite sex as *people?* What effect does early and easy sex gratification have on the achievement motive? Will the many people who work and achieve to be able to marry and support a family continue to do so under extremely permissive conditions?

Socialization and human sexuality We continue our emphasis on the parental role in the socialization of sexuality by asking a series of related questions. First, what do parents think *should be* the outcome of such socialization experience on the *goal values* for sexuality (Chapter 3)? Second, to what extent are parents committed and prepared to assist children and youth toward these goals? Third, what socialization practices are most likely to facilitate these goals? Fourth, to what extent do broader cultural influences and changes affect parental response to this important socialization task, possibly even creating conflict between parents and their offspring about sexual behavior? Answers to these questions are neither definitive nor agreed on, but we believe that airing them from the standpoint of mental health and social interdependence can be helpful in thinking through problems of socialization for human sexuality.

Consider first basic goals. Our own surveys of parental opinion, limited and largely informal, confirm the existence of a seemingly pervasive value throughout our society that its members display a certain degree of self-control or restraint in sexual expression. These survey data also support the value of developing a judgmental capacity and general respect for others in determining the appropriate circumstances for sexual communication. Personal responsibility is also widely endorsed. Although sexual intercourse is endorsed as a most intimate and enjoyable form of communication between two people, in our culture it also implies the necessity that one take responsibility for the consequences of that communion. Where the consequences may be unwanted pregnancy or venereal disease, it seems that appropriate precautions are imperative. Otherwise, both society and the parties involved are faced with problems that complicate, rather than facilitate, mental and physical health. Finally, an overwhelming majority of parents whom we have surveyed seem to agree that sexuality interlaced with shame and guilt about sexual urges, genital functions, and undue inhibitions is generally undesirable. Thus, for their children's socialization, parents are faced with how to define a "happy medium" between poorly controlled and overly controlled self-recriminating sexual expression. A person capable of both self-fulfillment and tender regard for others as part of an emotionally honest (as opposed to exploitative) sexual relationship may represent the most desirable outcome of socialization.

This idea is consistent with our comments about moral maturity in Chapter

11. Rarely are goals and guidelines for sexual behavior discussed without touching upon morality in one way or another. Much of United States morality and law refer to sexual behavior and the nuclear family. Ultimately, however, the choice of goals and guidelines for an individual's sexual life and the choice of childrearing practices about sexuality are matters of personal conscience.

As to the second question—whether or to what extent adults are committed to facilitating healthy sexual development among the young—we can only speculate. In our personal experience most adults seem to pay at least lip service to the value of healthy sexual attitudes for children and youth; attitudes that accept one's sexuality and the capacity for sexual communication that is satisfying both to oneself and to one's partner. Yet, if we examine carefully what many adults do and say (or fail to do and say) to their children, we cannot help questioning the validity of even this lip service. For example, it seems to us that accurate knowledge about one's body, its functions, and the dynamics of sex is an integral part of healthy sexuality. Survey after survey indicates, however, that as many as 50 percent of children and youth receive no information or instruction about sex in the home (Payne, 1970; Youth Poll America, 1976). In fact, one recent survey indicates that childrens' peer groups are the chief sources of information about sex, followed by books and pamphlets, school programs, and parents, in descending order (Forthman, 1974). Peer-group sources are rarely complete and are often inaccurate.

Students are interested in, but rarely get, information in schools about contraception, venereal disease symptomatology and prevention, alternative sexual life styles, and the like. The often violent opposition to organized sex education programs, either in the churches or in the schools, suggests that many adults are themselves fearful or are in conflict about the socialization of sexual behavior. What evidence is available on the second question, then, suggests that many American parents have a long way to go before they are both willing and able to serve as sources of accurate sexual knowledge for their children.

The third question—even if a consensus about a healthy sexuality is obtained, what socialization measures can be employed to promote its achievement?—is mainly a matter for reasoned speculation, because insufficient data are available about the socialization of sexual behavior. However, at least three general guidelines are helpful. First, it seems wise to avoid extremes in childrearing, such as harsh, punitive, and restrictive methods, a laissez-faire, or a direct overstimulation approach to socialization of sex. It is plausible to argue that the former extreme can result in inhibitions, anxieties, and negative attitudes about one's body and sexual functions. By the same token, overstimulation or no guidance, particularly during the formative years and adolescence, may result in distortions of attitude. For example, given the growing eroticism reflected by the mass media, an emphasis on the physical aspects of sex can possibly dominate an individual's sexual perspective at the expense of the interpersonal aspects.

A second guideline concerns the nature and quality of parent–child or parent–youth interactions (Hobbs & Townsend, 1974). We think that such interaction should from the outset be based on honesty, truth, and openness in communication. There seems no valid reason for adults intentionally to promote discontinuity in sexual information. Children who first learn untruths about sex may be at once confused and disillusioned when they confront reality. A willingness by parents to discuss sexuality when the need arises seems basic to a sound parent–child relationship.

Finally, we stress the value of modeling a healthy sexuality, in both attitude and behavior, just as we try to model other aspects of constructive personal–social and intellectual behavior. It is *not* suggested that parents should model the sex act for their children or flaunt their nudity to "prove" that no sexual inhibitions exist in the home. What is suggested are adult self-acceptance about sexuality, natural expressions of physical affection for members of one's family, and a nonfearful approach to sexual matters. Some authorities (for example, Miller & King, 1974) strongly urge sex education for parents to prepare them better for their constructive role in socializing their children.

Our fourth, and final, question about sexuality concerns impingement by further social influences upon parents' socialization attempts in this area of human development, notably by peer groups and the mass media. Peer influences are often cited in relation to recent increases in the rate of illegitimate births, abortions, and venereal disease. For example, unsupervised dating and social group experiences, especially in early adolescence when conformity pressures for social acceptance are at work, have been associated with greater adolescent sexual activity (Boyce & Benoit, 1975; Spanier, 1976). In later adolescence, however, still other personal–social variables are associated with premarital sexual activity, especially among females. These include a high value on independence, lower value on achievement, a tendency to criticize society,

strong tolerance of deviant behavior, and greater involvement with peers who model sexual activity (Jessor & Jessor, 1975).

Other manifestations of changing patterns of sexuality are often linked with the mass media (Gagnon & Simon, 1970; Liebert & Schwartzberg, 1977). Sexual representations in magazines, plays, and movies, formerly censored or not permitted, are now commonplace. They range from explicit, sex-related language to nudity and graphic depictions of sexual intercourse and male and female homosexuality. The remarkable sales of books about sex, including specific advice about how to become more sensuous and seductive, are also cited as evidence of a culture that is becoming successively more "obsessed" with sex. Research data about the possible influence of filmed, televised, and literary erotica are not yet plentiful. Our best evidence to date, however, is that exposure to erotica is associated with increased sexual arousal, conversation about sex, and in some cases, actual interpersonal sexual activity (Liebert & Schwartzberg, 1977). These "effects" of erotica are apparently more short- than long-term. The data indicate a diminished effect as individuals grow more accustomed to explicit depictions of sexual behavior.

Possibly more significant as a source of changing attitudes and patterns of sexual behavior is technological development. With advances in methods of contraception, the biological (procreative) and social (nonprocreative) functions of sexual intercourse can be separated. Through technology, individuals can now maintain a sexual relationship solely on social grounds, without fear of pregnancy or need to justify sex on procreative grounds. Moreover, as birth-control measures have become more reliable, many legal, economic, and social sanctions previously applied to discourage premarital sex have become irrelevant. Parents who seek to exert control over their offspring's sexual behavior now find themselves faced with determining a rational and moral basis for their attempted influence.

Apparently, some parents choose not to take on such a task, and even express little or no concern about their teenager's out-of-wedlock childbearing (Boyce & Benoit, 1975). Others may take a negative stance with their adolescents, thus creating a potential for conflict in settings where progressively liberal peer-group attitudes about sexual intercourse exist. This may be viewed as an example of the generational conflicts discussed in Chapter 4. For example, mothers and their daughters often hold opposite opinions about the value of premarital chastity and marriage as a condition for sexual intercourse, with mothers typically holding the more conservative view (Bell & Buerkle, 1961).

Compared to past generations, today's youth seem much more likely to discuss sex among themselves openly. At times, this openness may be falsely interpreted by parents as an indication of heightened sexual activity among youth. But this is not to underplay genuine value changes that may result in strong generational conflict. That youth themselves seek to minimize this conflict is indicated in several ways: by spending increased amounts of time away from home for social activities, by being secretive, and through reduced communication with parents about heterosexual involvements (Bell, 1966). This is tantamount to a "game" where parents can assume that their children are abiding by traditional values, while youth go about developing their own modified standards. The following quote aptly conveys this notion: "For many parents and

their children, the conflict about premarital sex will continue to be characterized by the parent's playing ostrich and burying his (her) head in the sand, and the youth's efforts to keep the sand from blowing away" (Bell, 1966, p. 44).

Schooling

To examine the development of sexuality and schooling brings our attention to one of the most complex and controversial aspects of American public schools: sex education. The most basic issue seems to be whether and for what reasons schools should attempt sex education at all. If the answer is "Yes, they should," and if it is soundly based, still further issues are encountered. As in parenting, for example, the goal values for sex education must be clarified. What should be the outcome of a given sex-education program? Some educators take a pragmatic approach to this question by suggesting that the success of a sex-education program is measured through lowered rates of illegitimate births, venereal disease, and sexual maladjustment. Other educators may stress idealistic, less tangible goals such as an increased capacity for spiritual union through heterosexual relations and positive attitudes toward childrearing. In either case, however, it is extremely difficult to link a public school sex-education program directly to such outcomes, because so many other out-of-school experiences impinge upon the individual to affect sexual behavior and attitudes. Still other educators may look at sex education more simply as a means for providing the young with answers to their most "burning" questions. For example, among the areas of greatest adolescent curiosity or desire for information are masturbation, homosexuality, sexual perversions, venereal disease, penis size, pornography, birth control, and abortion (Gordon, 1971).

Even when program goals and content areas are clearly specified and logically sound, strong objections to the whole concept of sex education in the public schools are usually raised by a vocal minority. Objections range from rational to irrational. For example, some opponents of sex education argue sincerely that schools should be devoted to academic and intellectual pursuits. Education for mental health, sociability, or sexuality is rejected entirely on philosophical grounds. Others express fear that sex education will lead to increased promiscuity. They argue that once the details of sexual anatomy and reproduction are revealed to children and youth, they will be tempted to experiment and sample the "forbidden fruit." We know of no evidence to support this belief.

Other opposition to sex education reflects religious and moral values, especially related to birth control. Many people apparently believe that instruction about contraception is inevitable in a sex-education program and that, once birth-control techniques are disclosed, youth can and will enjoy sex without marriage. This condition, in turn, may result in lowered marriage rates and eventually threaten the family as a social institution.

Again, we cannot cite any data to support this argument. But such viewpoints are reflected in stands against public school sex education. Educators and parents who want some form of sex education in the schools should be aware of and prepared for such opposition.

Some effects of sex education Unfortunately, existing sex-education programs have not been carefully studied. Moreover, their quality and scope are so variable that drawing secure generalizations about them is not easy. What few data exist, suggest that adolescents:

(1) are not receiving adequate sex education in the home; (2) desire sex education as part of their formal school experience; (3) show substantial increases in the amount of knowledge about sexual matters after participating in them; and (4) may change their attitudes about sex in the direction of their instructors, especially if nondirective instructional methods are used (Kirkendall & Miles, 1968; Mims, Brown, & Lubow, 1976; Olson & Gravatt, 1968; Reichelt & Wesley, 1974; Shipman, 1968). Evidence about the sex education–sexual behavior relationship is inconclusive. One study has revealed some increase in sexual behavior, including masturbation, among college male (but not female) students who took a course in sexuality (Zuckerman, Tushup, & Finner, 1976). On the whole, however, there are few data to indicate that formal instruction influences sexual practices much one way or the other (Rees & Zimmerman, 1974). The finding about attitudes, however, is significant because it highlights the potential influence of educational authorities who communicate with involved, interested adolescents in the classroom. It also relates directly to the idea about teachers as models for identification.

A psychologist's view of sex education It is possible, of course, that formal instruction makes little difference because it is poorly timed and out of tune with student needs and concerns. This prompts us to consider how developmental psychology might contribute constructively to the design of sex education. Consider, for example, a general framework for sex education advanced by David Ausubel (1954). Ausubel, who is both a psychologist and a physician, sees two fundamental purposes of public school sex education: the provision of accurate sex information and the opportunity to establish an ethical perspective on sexuality. We agree with Ausubel that the development of a capacity for intelligent self-direction in sexual expression is unlikely without these factors. Concerning sex information, Ausubel suggests that careful attention be given both to the physiology and the psychology of sex. One's personal-ethical perspective on sexuality, it is to be hoped, will develop through free and open discussions of the emotional and social goals of sex expression, where guiding principles of honesty, respect, and consideration for the feelings of others are highlighted. Specific problems about sex practices, however, should be left to individual guidance and counseling by trained personnel.

Ausubel's framework for sex education is not uniquely psychological, but a sound developmental orientation is reflected in his recommendations for designing a sequential program in relation to changing interest patterns. For example, during preadolescence the principal focus for program content would be the physiology and anatomy of sex, including reproduction, conception, and the birth process. Factual education, in other words, should be complete before puberty. During early adolescence, when adult heterosexual behavior patterns are becoming established, such matters as sex roles, courting problems and practices, any sex differences in sexual motivation, and moral-emotional aspects of sex would be emphasized. Finally, as the upper level of high school is reached, concepts and problems relating to marriage, family relations, parenthood, childrearing, homemaking, and even nonmarital sex could be addressed.

This general plan provides many helpful cues for the design of sex-education programs for the schools. However, even with elaborate and well-executed sex-education programs, it is unrealistic to believe that school experience alone will produce dramatic changes in adolescent sexual behavior. As one authority states:

Perhaps the most important contribution that secondary school sex education programs can make is to assist individuals to develop an explicit cognitive frame of reference within which they may view themselves. Those programs which are descriptive and allow individual adolescents to make their own judgments concerning the personal relevance or import of various sexual topics and questions are likely to be more helpful in this process than those which attempt to take over this function. Finally, while it is necessary to keep in mind that any program or curriculum will achieve this result to different degrees . . . those which include the most diversity of content and format are those most likely to succeed (Payne, 1970, p. 175).

We conclude this section on social influences by stressing more what remains to be learned about them than pointing confidently to what has been learned in the past. There is a pressing need for more varied and controlled socialization research in the area of human sexuality. To date, imprecise surveys, clinical data, and anecdotal reports have dominated the literature on this topic. While informative, they leave unanswered many important questions about social influences upon sexual attitudes and functioning.

SUMMARY

Psychosexual development has been examined in terms of both social and sexual aspects of biological gender. As can most areas of socialization, psychosexual development can be thought about as product and process. Terms such as "hetero-sexual," "homosexual," "bisexual," "masculine," "feminine," and "androgynous behavior" imply product or outcome of psychosexual development in the sexual and social components of gender role. As process, we are concerned with the ways a sexual orientation and social sex-role preference are acquired.

A study of both the sexual and social aspects of gender requires us to examine carefully the exact nature of sex differences and their origins. We noted the current dispute within psychology about the reliability and generality of sex differences in all but a few basic areas of cognitive and personal-social behavior. Whether and to what extent these differences are inherent or socialized remain open questions. Either way, the value of traditional sex-role stereotypes in United States society has been criticized as an obstacle to human potential development for both males and females. Psychological androgyny has been offered as a preferable standard for socialization by many writers, though little is yet known or understood about androgynous development and its implications for society.

The concepts of sex typing and identification have been used to discuss the *process* of sex-role development. Sex typing is learning gender behavior. Identification is taken further to mean learning attitudes and values that are held by one's sex model, usually involving socially approved masculine or feminine gender characteristics. Several alternative explanations of sex typing and identification have been reviewed, emphasizing nature–nurture interaction. Though any explanation of sex-role development is necessarily tentative at this time, certain generalizations seem firmly established by research. These include early sex role awareness and gender identity, the relationship between gender identity and psychological adjustment, sex-related differentiation of such behavior patterns as aggression, and conditions associated with deviations from normal sex-role behaviors. Such conditions relate directly to our theme of major social influences. Once again we examined a major aspect of human development in terms of family and school influences. The role of schooling was strongly emphasized because of sources of sex bias and discrimination in educational practice.

Against a background of the psychosocial aspects of sexuality, specific biological and cultural aspects of sexual behavior were examined. Variations and regularities in form, style, and tempo of sexual practices were linked to cultural learning. Having also noted certain cross-cultural regularities in sexual practices, a developmental view of sexual knowledge acquisition and sexual behavior was discussed. Age trends and sex differences in adolescent sexual behavior were emphasized. An overview of variations on the normal course of sexual development followed, with attention to sexual precocity, chromosomal disorders, and the ill-understood condition of homosexuality.

Although emergent aspects of sexuality serve as a powerful motivation during adolescence, we indicated that very little is known about socialization practices in the home or the school at this critical stage in life. There is good reason to believe that attitudes toward sexual functions are shaped during childhood, and that many are the result of incidental learning rather than direct tuition. The actual working out of psychosexual development occurs within the peer group and may also be affected to some extent by the mass media. In our United States culture, premarital sex is negatively sanctioned by adults, especially for girls. These sanctions generally have not been successful in limiting the sexual behavior of adolescents. Many problems can result, such as personal–social problems presented by venereal disease, out-of-wedlock births, and personal recrimination, that demand the attention of youth workers.

Any discussion of adolescent sexuality highlights many questions. Foremost among these is the question of what should be the goals of socialization for sexuality. This question extends also to school practice as an issue about formal sex education.

Sources of controversy about sex education were discussed, most of which have moral overtones that are unfounded in fact. We have taken the position that, in principle, sex education is a legitimate and essential aspect of formal schooling. Consistent with this orientation, we presented some guidelines for a developmental approach to sex education that is relevant for today's children and youth.

REFERENCES

Ausubel, D. P. *Theory and problems in adolescent development.* New York: Grune & Stratton, 1954.

Bates, J. E., Bentler, P. M., & Thompson, S. K. Measurement of deviant gender development in boys. *Child Development,* 1973, *44,* 591–598.

Bell, R. R. Parent child conflict in sexual values. *Journal of Social Issues,* 1966, *22,* 34–44.

Bell, R. R., & Buerkle, J. Mother and daughter attitudes to premarital sexual behavior. *Marriage and Family Living,* 1961, *23,* 390–392.

Bem, S. Sex role adaptability: One consequence of psychological androgyny. *Journal of Personality and Social Psychology,* 1975, *31,* 634–643.

Bernstein, A., & Cowan, P. Children's concepts of how people get babies. *Child Development,* 1975, *46,* 77–91.

Bieber, I. A discussion of "homosexuality": The ethical challenge. *Journal of Consulting and Clinical Psychology,* 1976, *44,* 157–162.

Biller, H. B., & Borstelmann, L. J. Masculine development: An integrative review. *Merrill-Palmer Quarterly,* 1967, *13,* 253–294.

Birns, B. The emergence and socialization of sex differences in the earliest years. *Merrill-Palmer Quarterly,* 1976, *22,* 229–254.

Block, J. H. Issues, problems, and pitfalls in assessing sex differences: A critical review of *The Psychology of Sex Differences. Merrill-Palmer Quarterly,* 1976, *22,* 283–308.

Boyce, J., & Benoit, C. Adolescent pregnancy. *New York State Journal of Medicine,* 1975, *75,* 872–874.

Brim, O. G. Family structure and sex role learning by children: A further analysis of Helen Koch's data. *Sociometry,* 1958, *21,* 1–16.

Broverman, I. K., et al. Sex role stereotypes and clinical judgments of mental health. *Journal of Consulting and Clinical Psychology,* 1970, *34,* 1–7.

Carlsmith, L. Effect of father absence on scholastic aptitude. *Harvard Educational Review,* 1964, *34,* 3–21.

Condry, J., & Condry, S. Sex differences: A study of the eye of the beholder. *Child Development,* 1976, *47,* 812–819.

Cutright, P. The teenage sexual revolution and the myth of an abstinent past. *Family Planning Perspectives,* 1972, *4,* 24–31.

D'Andrade, R. G. Sex differences and cultural institutions. In E. Maccoby (Ed.), *The development of sex differences.* Stanford, Calif.: Stanford University Press, 1966.

Diamond, M. A critical evaluation of the ontogeny of human sexual behavior. *Quarterly Review of Biology,* 1965, *40,* 147–175.

Diamond, M. Human sexual development: Biological foundations for social developments. In F. A. Beach (Ed.), *Human sexuality in four perspectives.* Baltimore: Johns Hopkins University Press, 1976.

Etaugh, C., Collins, G., & Gerson, A. Reinforcement of sex-typed behaviors of 2-year-old children in a nursery school setting. *Developmental Psychology,* 1975, *11,* 255.

Etaugh, C., & Hughes, V. Teachers' evaluations of sex-typed behaviors in children: The role of teacher sex and school setting. *Developmental Psychology,* 1975, *11,* 394–395.

Etaugh, C., & Rose, S. Adolescent's sex bias in the evaluation of performance. *Developmental Psychology,* 1975, *11,* 663–664.

Fagot, B. I. Sex differences in toddler's behavior and parental reaction. *Developmental Psychology,* 1974, *10,* 554–558.

Fagot, B. I., & Patterson, G. R. An in vivo analysis of reinforcing contingencies for sex-role behaviors in the preschool child. *Developmental Psychology,* 1969, *1,* 563–568.

Flerx, V., Fidler, D., & Rogers, R. Sex role stereotypes: Developmental aspects and early intervention. *Child Development,* 1976, *47,* 998–1007.

Ford, C. S., & Beach, F. A. *Patterns of sexual behavior.* New York: Harper & Row, 1951.

Forthman, S. Sex education: How effective are the high school programs? *Clearing House,* 1974, *48,* 369–371.

Frank, L. K. The adolescent and the family. In *Adolescence.* Forty-third Yearbook, National Society for the Study of Education. Chicago: University of Chicago Press, 1944.

Freud, S. *An outline of psychoanalysis* (1st ed., 1940). New York: Norton, 1949.

Frueh, T., & McGhee, P. Traditional sex role development and amount of time spent watching television. *Developmental Psychology,* 1945, *11,* 109.

Furstenberg, F. F. *Unplanned parenthood.* New York: Free Press, 1976.

Gagnon, J. H., & Simon, W. *The sexual scene.* Chicago: Aldine, 1970.

Gallup Opinion Poll. Sexual revolution in U.S. continues. Seattle, Wash.: *The Seattle Times,* August 12, 1973.

Gibbons, D. C. *Delinquent behavior.* Englewood Cliffs, N.J.: Prentice-Hall, 1970.

Gordon, S. *Ten heavy facts about sex.* Syracuse, N.Y.: Syracuse University, Institute for Family Research and Education, 1971.

Grant, T. N., & Domino, G. Masculinity-femininity in fathers of creative male adolescents. *Journal of Genetic Psychology,* 1976, *129,* 19–27.

Green, R. *Sexual identity conflict in children and adults.* New York Basic Books, 1974.

Green, R. *Sexual identity conflict in children and adults.* New York: Basic Books, 337–352.

Green, R., Fuller, M., & Rutley, B. It-Scale for children and Draw-a-Person Test. *Journal of Personality Assessment,* 1972, *36,* 349–352.

Hakstian, A. R., & Cattell, R. B. An examination of adolescent sex differences in some ability and personality traits. *Canadian Journal of Behavioral Science,* 1975, *7,* 295–312.

Harrington, C. *Errors in sex-role behavior in teenage boys.* New York: Teachers College Press, 1970.

Harris, M. Sex role stereotypes and teacher evaluations. *Journal of Educational Psychology,* 1975, *67,* 751–756.

Hefner, R., et al. Development of sex role transcendance. *Human Development,* 1975, *18,* 143–158.

Heilbrun, A. B., Jr. Identification and behavioral effectiveness during late adolescence. In E. D. Evans (Ed.), *Adolescents: Readings in behavior and development.* Hinsdale, Ill.: Dryden, 1970.

Hetherington, E. M. Sex typing, dependency, and aggression. In T. D. Spencer & N. Kass (Eds.), *Perspectives in child psychology: Research and review.* New York: McGraw-Hill, 1970.

Hobbs, D. F., Jr., & Townsend, L. P. B. Parent-adolescent relations, adolescent coital status, and contraceptive usage. ERIC: *ED 103 790,* 1974.

Hoffman, M. L. Father absence and conscience development. *Developmental Psychology,* 1971, *4,* 400–406.

Horn, J., & Turner, R. MMPI profiles among subgroups of unwed mothers. *Journal of Counseling and Clinical Psychology,* 1976, *44,* 25–33.

Jaffe, F. *Conference on early adolescent sexuality.* Seattle, Washington, March 2–4, 1977.

Jennings, S. A. Effects of sex typing in children's stories on preference and recall. *Child Development,* 1975, *46,* 220–223.

Jessor, S. L., & Jessor, R. Transition from virginity to nonvirginity among youth: A social-psychological study over time. *Developmental Psychology,* 1975, *11,* 473–484.

Joesting, J., & Joesting, R. Sex differences in equalitarianism and anxiety in ninth grade students. *Adolescence,* 1975, *10,* 59–61.

Johnson, M. M. Sex role learning in the nuclear family. *Child Development,* 1963, *34,* 319–333.

Jolly, H. *Diseases of children* (2nd ed.). Oxford: Blackwell, 1968.

Kagan, J. Acquisition and significance of sex typing and sex role identity. In M. L. Hoffman & L. W. Hoffman (Eds.), *Review of child development research* (vol. 1) New York: Russell Sage, 1964.

Kane, F. J., Jr., & Lachenbruch, P. A. Adolescent pregnancy: A study of aborters and non-aborters. *American Journal of Orthopsychiatry,* 1973, *43,* 796–803.

Kelley, J. A. & Worell, L. Parent behaviors relating to masculine, feminine, and androgynous sex role orientations. *Journal of Consulting and Clinical Psychology,* 1976, *44,* 843–851.

Kinsey, A. C., Pomeroy, W. B., & Martin, C. E. *Sexual behavior in the human male.* Philadelphia: Saunders, 1948.

Kinsey, A. C., Pomeroy, W. B., Martin, C. E., & Gebhard, P. H. *Sexual behavior in the human female.* Philadelphia: Saunders, 1953.

Kirkendall, L. A., & Miles, G. J. Sex education research. *Review of Educational Research,* 1968, *38,* 528–544.

Kohlberg, L. A cognitive-developmental analysis of children's sex-role concepts and attitudes. In E. E. Maccoby (Ed.), *The development of sex differences.* Stanford, Calif.: Stanford University Press, 1966.

Kreitler, H., & Kreitler, S. Children's concepts of sexuality and birth. *Child Development,* 1966, *37,* 363–378.

LeCorgne, L. L., & Laosa, L. M. Father absence in low-income Mexican-American families: Children's social adjustment and conceptual differentiation of sex role attitudes. *Developmental Psychology,* 1976, *12,* 470–471.

Lee, P. C. Male and female teachers in elementary schools: An ecological analysis. *Teachers College Record,* 1973, *75,* 79–98.

Levy, B., & Stacey, J. Sexism in the elementary school: A backward and forward look. *Phi Delta Kappan,* 1973, *55,* 105–109.

Liebert, R. M., & Schwartzberg, N. S. Effects of mass media. *Annual Review of Psychology,* 1977, *28,* 141–174.

Lloyd, R. *For love or money: Boy prostitution in America.* New York: Vanguard, 1976.

Lynn, D. B. *Parental and sex role identification: A theoretical formulation.* Berkeley, Calif.: McCutchan, 1969.

Maccoby, E. E. (Ed.) *The development of sex differences.* Stanford, Calif.: Stanford University Press, 1966.

Maccoby, E. E., & Jacklin, C. N. *The psychology of sex differences.* Stanford, Calif.: Stanford University Press, 1974.

Mallick, S. K. & McCandless, B. R. A study of catharsis of aggression. *Journal of Personality and Social Psychology,* 1966, *4,* 591–596.

Mann, J. Effects of erotic films on sexual behavior of married couples; sex guilt and reactions to pornographic films. Exposure to pornography, character, and sexual deviance: A retrospective survey. ERIC: *ED 043 076,* 1970.

Marshall, D. S., & Suggs, R. C. (Eds.) *Human sexual behavior: Variations in the ethnographic spectrum.* New York: Basic Books, 1971.

Martin, C. D. Psychological problems of abortion for the unwed teenage girl. *Genetic Psychology Monographs,* 1973, *88,* 23–110.

Martinez, S. Sexism in public education. *Inequality in Education,* 1974, No. 18, 5–11.

Masters, W. H. *Seminar on human sexuality.* King County Medical Society, Seattle, Washington, April 9–10, 1976.

McCandless, B. R. *Children: Behavior and development* (2nd ed.). New York: Holt, Rinehart and Winston, 1967.

McCandless, B. R., Bush, C., & Carden, A. Reinforcing contingencies for sex-role behavior in preschool children. *Contemporary Educational Psychology,* 1976, *1,* 241–246.

Mead, M. Cultural determinants of sexual behavior. In W. C. Young (Ed.), *Sex and the internal secretions* (3rd ed.) (Vol. II). Baltimore: Williams & Wilkins, 1961.

Menninger, W. In-sights. Universal Press Syndicate, 1976.

Meyerowitz, J. H., & Malev, J. S. Pubescent attitudinal correlates antecedent to adolescent illegitimate pregnancy. *Journal of Youth and Adolescence,* 1973, *2,* 251–257.

Miller, H. R., & King, E. M. Sex education for parents using behavioral rehearsal. *Journal of Family Counseling,* 1974, *2,* 28–31.

Mims, F., Brown, L., & Lubow, R. Human sexuality course evaluation. *Nursing Research,* 1976, *25,* 187–191.

Mischel, W. Sex typing and socialization. In P. H. Mussen (Ed.), *Carmichael's manual of child psychology.* New York: Wiley, 1970.

Money, J. Ablatio penis: Normal male infant sex reassigned as a girl. *Archives of Sexual Behavior,* 1975, *4,* 65–71.

Money, J. Human hermaphroditism. In F. A. Beach (Ed.), *Human sexuality in four perspectives.* Baltimore: Johns Hopkins University Press, 1976.

Money, J. B., & Ehrhardt, A. A. *Man and woman/boy and girl.* Baltimore: Johns Hopkins University Press, 1972.

Money, J., & Tucker, P. *Sexual signatures.* Boston: Little, Brown, 1975.

Murphy, N. Anxiety, homosexual attitude, duration of time since explicit sexual response, and number of explicitly sexual responses: Admitted homosexual and heterosexual samples. Seattle, Washington: Unpublished Doctoral Dissertation, University of Washington, 1971.

Mussen, P H. Early sex role development. In D. Goslin (Ed.), *Handbook of socialization theory and research.* Skokie, Ill.: Rand McNally, 1968.

Naddman, L. Sex identity in American children: Memory, knowledge, and preference tests. *Developmental Psychology,* 1974, *10,* 413–417.

Olson, D. H., & Gravatt, A. E. Attitude change in a functional marriage course. *Family Coordinator,* 1968, *17,* 99–104.

Oshman, H. P., & Manoservitz, M. Father absence: Effects of stepfathers upon psychosocial development in males. *Developmental Psychology,* 1976, *12,* 479–480.

Parsons, T. Family structures and the socialization of the child. In T. Parsons & R. F. Bales (Eds.), *Family, socialization, and interaction process.* New York: Free Press, 1955.

Pauker, J. D. Fathers of children conceived out of wedlock: Prepregnancy, high school, psychological test results. *Developmental Psychology,* 1971, *4,* 215–218.

Payne, D. C. Sex education and the sexual education of adolescents. IN. E. D. Evans (Ed.), *Adolescents: Readings in behavior and development.* Hinsdale, Ill.: Dryden, 1970.

Pederson, F. A., & Bell, R. Q. Sex differences in preschool children without histories of complications of pregnancy and delivery. *Developmental Psychology,* 1970, *3,* 10–15.

Peterson, A. Physical androgyny and cognitive functioning in adolescence. *Developmental Psychology,* 1976, *12,* 524–533.

Planned Parenthood Federation. *Report on adolescent sexuality and contraception.* Washington, D. C.: Planned Parenthood Federation, 1972.

Pleck, J. H. Male threat from female competence. *Journal of Consulting and Clinical Psychology,* 1976, *44,* 608–613.

Rainwater, L. Some aspects of lower class sexual behavior. *Journal of Social Issues,* 1966, *22,* 52–56.

Rees, B., & Zimmerman, S. The effects of formal sex education on the sexual behavior and attitude of college students. *Journal of the American College Health Association,* 1974, *22,* 370–371.

Reichelt, P. A., & Wesley, H. H. Evaluation of information imparted in a sexual-contraceptive educational program for teenagers. ERIC: *ED 098 478*, 1974.

Rosenberg, B. G., & Sutton-Smith, B. *Sex and identity*. New York: Holt, Rinehart and Winston, 1972.

Rosenkrantz, P., et al. Sex role stereotypes and self-concepts in college students. *Journal of Consulting and Clinical Psychology*, 1968, *32*, 287–295.

Saario, T. N., Jacklin, C. N., & Tittle, C. K. Sex role stereotyping in the public schools. *Harvard Educational Review*, 1973, *43*, 386–416.

Sears, R. R., Maccoby, E. E., & Levin, H. *Patterns of child rearing*. New York: Harper & Row, 1956.

Shiller, J. *Childhood illness*. New York: Stein and Day, 1972.

Shipman, G. The psychodynamics of sex education. *Family Coordinator*, 1968, *17*, 3–12.

Simon, W., & Gagnon, J. H. On psychosexual development. In D. Goslin (Ed.), *Handbook of socialization theory and research*. Skokie, Ill.: Rand McNally, 1968.

Slaby, R. G., & Frey, K. S. Development of gender constancy and selective attention to same sex models. *Child Development*, 1975, *46*, 849–856.

Sorenson, R. C. *Adolescent sexuality in contemporary America*. New York: World, 1973.

Spanier, G. B. Formal and informal sex education as determinants of premarital sexual behavior. *Archives of Sexual Behavior*, 1976, *5*, 39–67.

Staples, R. *The black woman in America*. Chicago: Nelson-Hall, 1973.

Stefic, E. C., & Lorr, M. Age and sex differences in personality during adolescence. *Psychological Reports*, 1974, *35*, 1123–1126.

Stein, A. H. Sex role development. In J. Adams (Ed.), *Understanding adolescence* (3rd ed.). Boston: Allyn and Bacon, 1976.

Stephens, W. N. *The family in cross-cultural perspective*. New York: Holt, Rinehart and Winston, 1963.

Sternglanz, S. H., & Serbin, L. A. Sex role stereotyping in children's television programs. *Developmental Psychology*, 1974, *10*, 710–715.

Suggs, R. C., & Marshall, D. S. Anthropological perspectives on human sexual behavior. In D. S. Marshall & R. C. Suggs (Eds.), *Human sexual behavior*. New York: Basic Books, 1971.

Thompson, N., et al. Parent-child relationships and sexual identity in male and female homosexuals and heterosexuals. *Journal of Consulting and Clinical Psychology*, 1973, *41*, 120–127.

Thompson, S. K. Gender labels and early sex role development. *Child Development*, 1975, *11*, 339–347.

Tittle, C. K. Women and educational testing. *Phi Delta Kappan*, 1973, *55*, 118–119.

Trecker, J. L. Sex stereotyping in the secondary school curriculum. *Phi Delta Kappan*, 1973, *55*, 110–112.

Urberg, K., & Labouvie-Vief, G. Conceptualizations of sex roles: A life span developmental study. *Developmental Psychology*, 1976, *12*, 15–23.

Wagner, N. W. Adolescent sexuality. In E. D. Evans (Ed.), *Adolescents: Readings in behavior and development*. Hinsdale, Ill.: Dryden, 1970.

Weinberg, M. S., & Bell, A. P. *Homosexuality: An annotated bibliography*. New York: Harper & Row, 1972.

Williams, J., Bennett, S., & Best, D. Awareness and expression of sex stereotypes in young children. *Developmental Psychology*, 1975, *11*, 635–642.

Wohlford, P., et al. Older brothers' influence on sex-typed, aggressive, and dependent behavior in father-absent children. *Developmental Psychology*, 1971, *4*, 124–134.

Women's Action Alliance. Sex-stereotyping in child care: Non-sexist Child Development Project. ERIC: *ED 093 476,* 1973.

Youth Poll America. National Association of Secondary School Principals, 1976.

Zelnik, M., & Kantner, J. Sexuality, contraception, and pregnancy among young unwed females in the United States. In C. Westoff & R. Parke, Jr. (Eds.), *Demographic and social aspects of population growth,* Vol. 1 of Commission Research Reports. Washington, D.C.: U.S. Government Printing Office, 1972.

Zuckerman, M., Tushup, R., & Finner, S. Sexual attitudes and experience: Attitude and personality correlates and changes produced by a course in sexuality. *Journal of Counseling and Clinical Psychology,* 1976, *44,* 7–19.

chapter 10

Achievement and career development

Clark and Neil, both age 17 and attending a moderately sized suburban high school, appear remarkably similar in appearance, health, and general developmental status. Both come from comfortable, middle-class, intact families. Each has an older sister in college. Their fathers are securely employed in white-collar occupations, Clark's as an accountant and Neil's as manager of the furniture department in a large department store. Each boy's mother is active in community volunteer work. Their family's residences, though separated by several miles, are in economically equivalent neighborhoods—generally well maintained and free from social problems such as crime or juvenile delinquency.

But at this point the life situations of Clark and Neil begin to differ. Clark is a top student in his senior class. His record of school achievement has been strong and consistent throughout his 12 years of formal education. He competes vigorously in the classroom and on the athletic field, having earned both National Honor Society membership and two letters in basketball and track. Well-liked by his peers, Clark is a leader in the cooperative school–community Junior Achievement Program, where high school youth are supported by local businessmen to learn first-hand about business. Clark had a paper route at age 10 and after that had odd jobs such as mowing lawns and shoveling snow for neighbors. Since the summer of his eighth grade in school, Clark has worked well at several part-time jobs: restaurant bus boy, service-station attendant, and most recently, salesperson for a suburban men's clothing store. Clark has firm plans to follow his sister to the state university and is currently exploring scholarship opportunities to help do so.

Clark's classmate, Neil, is very different. Though equally bright in measured intelligence, Neil's school history is marred by inconsistent and generally low academic performance. He seems to actively avoid his school responsibilities, is usually late with class assignments, and places little value on his examinations or relationships with teachers. Neither is Neil inclined toward sports or working outside the home. At the urging of friends, he once went out for football, but turned in his equipment after the first week of practice. Neil does little to help out in his own home, and shows even less interest in working for neighbors. Spurred by his desire for a motorbike, Neil agreed to take a modest "apprenticeship" as a furniture mover at his father's place of business. Soon after his father delivered the bike, however, Neil quit his job without notice. His preferred activities are watching television, shooting pool, and playing pinball at the local teen center, where he "hangs out" most evenings and weekends. Asked about his plans after high school, Neil makes vague references to working at a "stereo place" or maybe the "Navy." He has no interest in college. Deeply infatuated with a sophomore girl, Neil has begun to worry about what will happen to his romance when he leaves school. In general, however, his future orientation is weak. Immediate self-indulgence dominates any apparent concern for self-improvement and economic independence. Yet Neil is well liked by those peers with whom he "goes around." Moreover, adults with whom Neil relates believe that he has "strong potential for success."

The comparison of Clark and Neil is one of many illustrating individual differences in achievement striving and career orientation that we have observed over the years. Taken together, these differences arouse the curiosity of students of human development, especially in United States society where achievement has traditionally been viewed as the way to personal life success. Of course, valuing achievement can be overdone. Pressures for competitive achievement may be accompanied by certain psychological hazards, such as aggression and anxiety. On the whole, however, personal achievement is among the strongest values in United States culture. Moreover, according to some theorists (for example, White, 1959), achievement is closely linked to a more basic human need for competence through *effectance motivation*—being able to produce desired effects on the environment. Few will argue the strong positive relationship between achievement and self-esteem in our society.

With this in mind, we will examine the meaning of achievement in more detail, then discuss developmental trends in achievement, sources of achievement differences, and school underachievement among children and youth. A related issue is the national effort to establish equal educational opportunity for intellectual achievement and career preparation. We will examine both the rationale and initial outcomes of selected aspects of this effort. Finally, the psychology of career or vocational development itself is an increasingly important topic. Industrialization, advanced technology, population growth, inflation, and the extended period of adolescence in American society are but a few factors that call our attention to the individual and the work force.

ACHIEVEMENT

Conceptual Distinctions

We begin with a definition and clarification of terms. First, we can distinguish between achievement behavior and achievement motivation. Achievement behavior refers to the quantity and, especially, quality of one's actual accomplishments, whether performance on school achievement tests, mastery of athletic skills, creative artwork, scientific research, or other human endeavors. The hallmark of achievement behavior is doing something *well*. This implies that standards of excellence inevitably operate in achievement situations that call for a demonstration of skill and competence.

Achievement motivation refers to a learned and generalized predisposition to attain success in competition with these standards of excellence. The standards are taken by an individual as criteria to evaluate the adequacy of his or her performance. Such a predisposition is most pronounced when challenging tasks are confronted and we see ourselves as responsible for the outcome of the situation. Achievement motivation is also thought to involve an affective state where successful task accomplishment results in self-approval. We feel good for having done a job well. This amounts to

self-reward or self-reinforcement, an important sustaining factor for mastery behavior. Behavioral indicators of achievement motivation in our culture will normally include persistence, a moderate degree of risk-taking, advance planning and realistic goal setting, budgeting and efficient use of time, and seeking feedback from the environment that contributes to improved performance.

Some authorities (such as Atkinson & Raynor, 1974) further indicate that achievement situations may energize two somewhat conflicting motive states: a motive to achieve success *(Ms)* and a motive to avoid failure *(Maf)*. The relative strength of these two enduring predispositions is thought to vary both among individuals and among achievement tasks, depending upon difficulty level and a person's expectation about how likely it is that success can be achieved. Similar achievement behaviors may result from a success orientation or the threat of failure. Roland, for example, may strive for an "A" grade as a measure of success; Frank may work hard, and perhaps be satisfied with a lesser grade, primarily to avoid the consequences of failure. In any case, *Ms* would seem to be the critical ingredient for positive achievement motivation as commonly defined (Schultz & Pomerantz, 1974).

While achievement behavior and ability are strongly and positively related, ability and achievement motivation often are not (Maehr & Sjogren, 1971). Thus ability and motivation may make their own unique contributions to a given pattern of achievement behavior. Even high achievement motivation does not necessarily mean that a person will strive for excellence in all situations. We may desire to achieve in mathematics or creative writing, for example, yet be indifferent to our performance in less-valued tasks. Males may put forth strong effort to achieve in settings they judge to be masculine, but not in things they think of as feminine.

The situational nature of achievement motivation leads to a second point: cultural relativity is the basis for achievement striving. In United States society, achievement motivation and behavior are tied most clearly to the value of autonomous, independent, personal achievement. One indication of this is the many systems we have for recognizing individual achievement: Pulitzer Prizes, *Who's Who in America,* "All-American" athletic awards, "Oscars," "Emmys," National Merit Scholarships, Eagle Scout Awards, and the like. In fact, one authority (McClelland, 1961) has developed a theory about the United States as an "achieving society" based on individual achievement motivation emphasized in childrearing practices, schooling, and the corporate enterprise. But motives to achieve may take quite different concrete forms, depending upon cultural context (Maehr, 1974). In Japan, for example, success striving is reportedly motivated more by concern for the reaction, welfare, and approval of others than by what we may consider self-satisfaction and personal identity (DeVos, 1968). In other words, the affiliation motive seems strongly related to "success" in Japan (and other non-Western societies). Opportunities for achievement can also vary across culture and time. Consider, for example, how the achievement of so many Americans has been tied to relative freedom for upward social mobility (compared, for example, to the rigid caste system as in India), to easy access to education, and to the availability of vast natural resources (compared, for example, to the limited resources available to the Inuits in the frozen Arctic wastelands). Social pressures and restraints also can selectively limit the form and extent of achievement in various societies. Discrimination by race and sex are all-too familiar examples.

Even the privileged members of a society can be affected by social convention. British upper class youth during Winston Churchill's formative years (the late nineteenth century) seemingly had only four "acceptable" career achievement options: law, politics, the military, or the church. In short, achievement requires more than ability and motivation. There must be opportunity as well.

Two additional cautions are important. First, while the preferred way of thinking about achievement includes an element of independence (autonomy), achievement and independence are not necessarily related. Independence is doing things on one's own; achievement is doing things well. One could exercise independence without showing quality in performance. Training children and youth for independence thus will not guarantee high achievement. Conversely, high achievement may occur in a context of dependency (Zigler & Child, 1973) illustrated by siblings who achieve competitively for their parent's favors.

Second, too often the term achievement is equated with school achievement. School achievement has dominated the developmental study of achievement behavior, but we stress that achievement can take many forms: academic pursuits, engaging intellectual skills for creative problem solving, manual arts, social leadership, and so on. In a society oriented strongly to school performance, children's worth may be too quickly determined by a restricted concept of achievement.

Developmental Trends in Achievement

Possibly the closest things to achievement behaviors in the earliest years of life are those marked by persistence in sensorimotor activities (erecting things, stringing beads, playdough activity) or by the desire of young children to do things alone. Activity may be satisfying for its own sake as well as provide opportunities for children to observe the effects of their actions on the environment. This has been termed "function pleasure" by some authorities, and, together with a budding preference for challenging tasks and assertiveness (vs withdrawal), can be viewed as forerunners, but not necessarily causes of achievement motivation (Heckhausen, 1967). No one has yet demonstrated a conclusive relationship between infants' early mastery attempts and later achievement behavior. Rather, it is not until individual differences in responsiveness to social reinforcement (approval–disapproval) around age 3 or 4 that any sort of predictable pattern may begin. Cognition, of course, is a key factor in discriminating task difficulty, monitoring one's progress toward problem solving, and making elementary predictions about whether or how well one can do something.

From about age 4 or 4½ onward, children generally show increases in their concentration and persistence in accomplishing achievement goals. Failures also are tolerated better and there are more active attempts to remedy them (Heckhausen, 1967). According to one major longitudinal study (Kagan & Moss, 1962) there is general stability for individual levels of intellectual and competitive achievement from this point through adolescence, especially for boys. Intelligence plays an important part in the pattern, as does the ratio of success to failure and the consistency of achievement demands in the child's environment.

Remarkably strong relationships are found between preschool activity and short-term intellectual and social achievements into the primary grades. In Chapter 3, for example, we pointed to individual differences in interest-participation (vs apathy-withdrawal) and cooperation-compliance (vs anger-defiance) and the relationship of these behavioral tendencies to advances in early school achievement. Similar findings are revealed by still other data. One study, for example, has shown a strong, positive relationship between preschool children's vigorous social participation and play achievements and achievement on various cognitive-intellectual tasks at age 7 1/2 (Halverson & Waldrop, 1976). Intensity of activity as such—for example, in hyperactivity—does not show this relationship. Goal-directed or purposive activity is the important correlate.

The early school years, in turn, seem critical for the development of an even more generalized predisposition to respond with effort and concern for the quality of work, as well as deriving satisfaction from industriousness. Indeed, one prominent theorist (Erikson, 1963) views the elementary school years collectively as a critical period for the development of industry and a positive work orientation (vs work paralysis and a sense of inferiority). It follows that children's early school experiences and their home environments can be pivotal for such developments. As school curricula are presently structured, basic communication skills and literacy are perhaps most fundamental. In one longitudinal study of children's school careers, it was found that the single most important difference between those who did and did not graduate from high school was reading achievement by the third grade (Krauss, 1973).

The pattern of achievement behavior and motivation seems to emerge rather early in life and thereafter remains more stable than not. The strongest predictor of future achievement is past achievement. Children who are doing well with basic school work by about age 8 tend to continue to do so into junior high school and beyond. (Those in trouble academically may not, as we discuss below.) If we take scholastic achievement as our guide, then, the growth curve is similar to that of measured intelligence: rapid early development followed by a steady rate of growth from ages 9 to 18. To paraphrase one researcher, using the general achievement pattern at age 18 as our criterion, roughly 50 percent of this pattern will have developed by age 9, 75 percent by age 13, and the remainder in the ensuing 5 years (Bloom, 1964). Beyond this, the potency of high school grades and achievement-test performance for predicting success in college is among the most firmly documented facts in educational psychology. These data, of course, describe the general case and are derived from the study of large groups of children and youth. Exceptions to the general case do occur and we must avoid the hazards of overgeneralizing. "Late bloomers" seem rare, however, as we will note again below. All told, the principle that experiences have a cumulative effect seems to hold well for the development of achievement behavior and motivation.

There is also an age-related association between children's personality characteristics and their intellectual-academic achievement. Differences in self-esteem and self-concept of ability, for example, are associated with patterns of relative school success as early as the primary grades (Purkey, 1970). This relationship seems to grow stronger as children successively enter higher grade levels. As we might expect, aggressive, disruptive behavior shows an increasingly negative relationship to school achievement from the primary grades to the early high school years (Feldhusen, Thurston, & Benning, 1970). Effective study skills are also positively related to personality characteristics, especially among older students. A diligent, organized, and methodical approach to studies, for example, has been found among college students high in achievement motivation, intellectual efficiency, and social maturity and responsibility (Rutkowski & Domino, 1975). Within the classroom itself, low achieve-

ment patterns have been associated with a greater frequency of such behavior as inattentiveness, self-stimulation, daydreaming, random looking around, horseplay, and failure to follow teacher directions (King et al., 1976). Possibly such behaviors reflect a more basic condition of general anxiety and the resulting avoidance tendencies. Psychological journals are full of studies about the negative relationship between anxiety (an unpleasbnt emotional state characterized by diffuse, anticipatory fear) and various measures of cognitive-intellectual and achievement behavior. In contrast, measures of extraversion and achievement are usually positively correlated (Jensen, 1973).

Intellectual Achievement Responsibility

Achievement and numerous other personality states or traits such as intellectual achievement responsibility or *IAR* are also positively correlated (Kifer, 1975).[1] IAR involves the extent to which children or youth believe that they are responsible for the consequences of their behavior in achievement situations; that what happens to them is because of their behavior or personal characteristics, not because of luck, chance, fate, or the whim of others. Children and youth high in IAR will expect that their intellectual-achievement activities are under their personal control. They generally will assume credit for causing good things to happen and accept blame for unpleasant consequences because they perceive a causal relationship between their behavior and the occurrence of rewards and punishments. In short, they are *inter-*

[1] The "parent" concept of IAR is *locus of control*. This refers to the degree to which individuals perceive that they have control over their environment across a wide variety of situations, and especially their perceived control of reinforcements. See Rotter, 1966.

nally-controlled (Crandall, Katkovsky, & Crandall, 1965). Children low in IAR generally fail to perceive this causal relationship between behavior and its consequences. For them, rewards and punishments seem not much under their personal control. Instead they perceive themselves to be more controlled by environmental forces immune to strong personal action. Consequently, they may have difficulty predicting the likelihood of dealing successfully with achievement situations and they may be less active in their attempts to manipulate their learning environments effectively. Such children and youth are said to be more *externally-controlled* (Phares, 1973).

Although the origins or antecedents of IAR are not thoroughly understood, reliable differences in this characteristic are clearly observed as early as age 8, and possibly even earlier (Crandall et al., 1965). Moreover, IAR is associated with differences in achievement behavior (Phares, 1973). High, as compared to low, IAR children tend to get higher grades and achievement test scores. They also show greater preference for achievement situations where skill is clearly a factor in determining success. Such children are more likely to defer immediate rewards when larger ones can be gained in the future. And they seem to exercise more autonomy in decision-making; they are more resistant to persuasive attempts by others to induce conformity.

All told, the general picture of higher IAR children and youth is one of greater activity and seeking behavior. Especially alert to learning situations that hold information relevant to their future goals, they value reinforcements that are contingent upon personal skills. IAR shows no consistent relationship with measured intelligence, thus illustrating again that there is more to achievement than mental ability. Attitudes, beliefs, and expectancies about control of the environment may be important factors in an overall pattern of achievement (Nord, Connelly, & Daignault, 1974).

Some Sources of Variation in Achievement

Many complex factors contribute to individual differences in achievement behavior and motivation. Most obvious is general intelligence. Correlations between measured intelligence and school achievement (tests, grades), for example, are strongly positive, commonly reported in the range from .50 to .75 (Lavin, 1965). Verbal facility seems a particularly potent link between intelligence and early school achievement (Puser & McCandless, 1974). But this still leaves much of the achievement pattern to be accounted for by other factors. Biochemical correlates have recently come under scrutiny. For instance, one authority presents data to suggest a relationship between serum uric acid and achievement and also between negative stress reactions in achievement situations and higher blood cholesterol (Kasl, 1974). Much remains to be learned about such matters. Meanwhile, as implied above, the study of achievement more frequently has involved social and personality factors. Since the general impact of schooling has been previously discussed (Chapter 5), we concentrate on less global variables in this section of the chapter.

Family Background Factors

Perhaps because of value system differences and differential learning opportunities, we can observe reliable differences in school achievement patterns among children from contrasting socioeconomic backgrounds. Middle- and upper-class children and youth show a clear advantage. But, as one scholar has noted, social class is not very useful as an explanatory concept (Miller, 1970). We must look deeper for things that occur *within* differing social class environments to improve our understanding of why socioeconomic status is so important.

We have good reason to believe that much of what has been said about social class and language and about social class and intellectual development in Chapters 7 and 8 also holds for achievement. Peer influences on scholastic achievement were examined in Chapter 4. Differences in parental teaching style associated with children's later achievement can be observed within as well as between the social classes. As for between-class differences, middle-class mothers tend to excel as proactive teachers. That is, they are perhaps more skilled in planning in advance and implementing learning experiences for specific purposes, usually involving clearer directions and standards for their children's performances, elaborated language, and contingent reinforcements. For *reactive* teaching — informal responses to children's questions and concerns on their own initiative — there may be little difference in maternal style across social class lines (Brophy, 1970). This finding about proactive and reactive teaching probably holds also for fathers, but very little has been done to compare paternal teaching styles by social class. In any event, we can speculate that to the extent children's home experiences with proactive teaching are consistent with those received in school, a greater continuity in learning will prevail with an advantage to middle-class children. We also would hypothesize that the varied rich intellectual-academic stimulation possible in more economically advantaged homes may make a difference in the development of achievement behavior.

Differences within each class, however, may be as important, perhaps even more so, than those between the social classes. One study of black working-class mothers, for example, has shown variations in preparatory teaching behaviors that were predictive of their children's school achievements (Slaughter, 1970). In general, the more involved these mothers were with their children, the better. Achievement demands in the home are another factor that apparently varies among economically disadvantaged and minority-group families (Henderson, 1972). Just as in middle-class homes, such pressure includes consistency of parental demands and expectations for quality performance, encouragement and rewards for accomplishing difficult tasks, the use of hints and subtle guidance for problem solving rather than specific help in giving children answers to their problems, and parents' positive attitudes about their own achievements (Hermans, ter Laak, & Maes, 1972; Madsen & Kagan, 1973; Rosen & D'Andrade, 1959). Similarly, parental management style and affect are also antecedents of achievement differences, as noted in Chapter 3. Still another study shows a strong relationship between the achievement status of sixth and seventh grade children and these parenting dimensions (Barton, Dielman, & Cattell, 1974). Specifically, lower achievement among the children was associated with mothers who discipline their children more harshly and often without providing any reasons for their actions and with fathers who begin an early pattern of strict control over their children. Higher-achieving children had fathers who encouraged but did not necessarily praise academic success lavishly and mothers who displayed much warmth, affection, and acceptance in childrearing.

We cannot claim cause and effect from such data. Indeed, such differences may often indicate parental responses *to* rather than reasons *for* children's achievement status. But these findings are consistent with the more widely documented relationship between patterns of parental authority and children's early instrumental competence (Chapter 3).

However, a given family's achievement pressure may often include high levels of active parental involvement, especially of mothers, that "push" children to achieve and criticize unsatisfactory performances (Crandall, 1964). This seems particularly clear in the socialization of achievement for girls. In a phrase, all is not peaches and cream. Children who are relatively unresponsive to social approval and disapproval may rebel against such parental pressures. But children who value social reinforcement and are helped in other ways by their models for achievement seem to "get cracking," as the British would say. Once again, we see that findings about family background factors are often contradictory, making it difficult to develop clear and certain guidelines about childrearing and achievement.

Other family variables can be linked to academic achievement patterns for both boys and girls. Family size and birth order again appear important, for instance. A large-scale study of over 550 children of both sexes showed, after taking into account any IQ differences associated with school marks, that boys (but not girls) from smaller families tended to excel their larger family classmates (Nuttall et al., 1976). First-born girls (but not boys) had higher academic performance than later borns. These differences were explained by responsibility training and reference-group values. Whatever the family size, parents may be more likely to stress habits of responsibility and hard work for their first-born daughters as they help care for younger siblings. Such habits, in turn, help in school work. Parental expectations for sibling care, however, may be lower for boys, thus accounting for the sex difference in birth-order effects. To explain the importance of the family-size variable for boys it can be argued that greater emphasis upon and identification with adult values for achievement occur for boys in smaller families. But as families grow in

size, such influence may lessen and boys become more oriented toward a peer culture with values that run counter to school achievement. While similar peer involvement may occur for girls from large families, the peer culture for females is usually more in tune with the values stressed in the school.

Sex Differences

The preceding interpretation, of course, is a "best guess" at an explanation of the research findings. The sex-specific nature of these findings, however, draws our attention once again to children's sex or sex roles as a source of difference in behavior and development. As noted in Chapter 9, girls generally excel boys in measures of verbal ability, at least through the formal school years. With the exception of arithmetic achievement after about grade five or six, girls generally also show higher overall school achievement. This is especially clear when teachers grades (vs standardized achievement tests) are the measure of achievement, possibly reflecting teacher's preferences for the girls' school decorum as well (McCandless, 1967). Furthermore, the incidence of specific learning disorders, underachievement, and school dropout behavior is lower for girls than boys.

Thus it may seem paradoxical that much ado has been made about the development of a motive in females that may encumber their full achievement, especially in competitive situations where males are involved. This disposition has been termed *fear of success* or *success avoidance* (Horner, 1972). The analysis goes something like this. Traditionally for males, success in competitive achievement striving is congruent with sex-role concepts of autonomy, aggressiveness, self-esteem, and general masculinity. For women, however, striving to excel competitively (especially against men) is much less consistent with accepted feminine sex-role behavior. Successful achievement in activities considered masculine may be perceived as a lack of desirable femininity. This, in turn, may lead to disapproval or even social rejection by men, and perhaps other women who behave more in conformity with sex role stereotypes. Given the high value placed by females upon satisfactory interpersonal relations and acceptance and approval by others, successful achievement may cost too much, leading to de-emphasis on competitive achievement among females. To say it another way, men may be unsexed by failure, because achievement success is a defining characteristic of masculinity; women, in contrast, may be unsexed by success (Mead, 1949).

As recently as a decade ago, striking evidence (for example, Horner, 1968) was presented about widespread success fears among college women. Such a finding quickly drew the wrath of feminists advocating liberation. In the years since, a considerable amount of research about such success fears has taken place. Despite the women's liberation movement and the increased career orientation of college women, most available data do not indicate that success fear has decreased much among females. A representative study (Hoffman, 1974) has shown that the percentage of females indicating a fear of success has remained fairly stable (about 65 percent of those studied). A striking time change, however, was noted for males. Whereas during the 1960s, fewer than 10 percent of males studied had success fear, the percentage had increased to nearly 80 percent in the 1970s! An extremely important sex difference in the basis for high-achievement anxiety was noted. Whereas for females the most common theme was affiliative loss following success, for males it was questioning the value of achievement itself.

The results from any single study should never be taken as definitive. Some groups of American college females may, in fact, be in the process of redefining sex roles and achievement orientations. A cross-cultural comparison of American and Australian males and females shows a somewhat lowered proportion of success fears about competitive achievement among the females in the United States, especially in relation to earlier findings (Feather & Raphelson, 1974).

Careful analyses of these and other studies prompt us to appreciate more how situational factors may affect women's achievement motivation. It seems unwise to suggest a global generalized fear of success that inhibits either sex across all variations of achievement striving. But such fears, and even lower self-confidence about achievement, do more often characterize women than men. Several situational variables may affect such findings (Lenney, 1977). One is the specific ability required for successful task achievement. Females may too quickly underestimate their abilities in male sex-typed school subjects, thus reducing their performance expectancies. A second variable is the availability of feedback about the quality of one's performance. Females, it seems, express self-confidence and perform on a par with males (if not higher) when feedback is clear, structured, and immediate. For unknown reasons, females often seem more negative in their self-evaluation when there is scanty and ambiguous feedback or knowledge of results. A third variable affecting differences is how much the evaluation of self-worth and social comparison with others is stressed in achievement situations. Again in contrast with men, women's relative self-evaluations may depend more upon how they subjectively assess the competencies of others. If females are both more benevolent in ascribing competence to others and more sensitive to the impact on others of "winning out" over the competition, their goal expectancies may be affected. Consistent with this notion is a study of the motive to avoid success among children in grades 5–11 (Romer, 1975). Success-avoidance girls performed better in noncompetitive than in competitive situations, while their male classmates with motive to avoid success performed better under competitive conditions.

As social conditions continue to change, values are reordered. And, as socialization patterns become modified, we can expect to encounter increasingly complex findings about sex roles and achievement. In fact, an alternative hypothesis to explain female achievement problems has already emerged (Heilbrun, Piccola, & Kleemeier, 1975). Rather than emphasizing the anticipation of negative consequences for achieving success, a notion of vicarious reinforcement is preferred. Females whose sex-role identification tends toward maleness are said to develop an ability to obtain vicarious satisfaction from the accomplishments of males. The greater the satisfaction, the less the female's own need to achieve. Thus, a pattern of low competitiveness may result not out of fear, but because the rewards can be experienced anyway. Conceivably, both hypotheses—fear of success and vicarious reinforcement— are valid, but for different individuals. Other, as yet unformulated, explanations may be required for other individual cases.

The lack of complete information, however, does not prevent us from again arguing for the ideal of maximum opportunity for self-realization through freely chosen avenues for personal achievement. This is important in relation to sex as it is for race, color, and creed. From the viewpoint of this value, there is ample room for improved socialization practices for female achievement, as the following research conclusion indicates:

'During the early school years, females achieve well, particularly in school, by applying a pattern of careful, cautious work habits bolstered by a high sense of responsibility for any failure. They value achievement and set high standards for themselves, though they appear more anxious about failure than males. Many of these behaviors that help in school achievement are less adaptive for continued achievement striving outside the school setting or even within the school setting at advanced educational levels.

Reduced achievement efforts occur for many young women as they reach adolescence and adulthood partly because there is pressure to adhere to feminine role definitions and because females internalize the low expectations of the culture for their continued achievement. Attainment in the occupational world not only produces some negative sanctions but often requires the self-esteem and assertiveness that are contrary to traditional feminine personality attributes. Although achievement striving may simply drop out of some females' repertoires, it appears that it is often manifested in various channels that are at least partially congruent with the feminine sex role' (Stein & Bailey, 1973, pp. 362–363).

Issues about School Achievement

The considerable literature about school achievement among children and youth is an indication of the high value and importance most American parents place upon it. Most teachers also are strong advocates of an academic work ethic. Theoretically, at least, studies must come first before other school activities are encouraged, such as athletics and extracurricular social clubs. It is thus not surprising that school underachievement is a major source of worry for many adults. Perhaps even more alarming for many adults is the dropping-out from school by large numbers of youth prior to their high school graduation.

Not all adults, of course, and certainly not all children and youth, are bothered by these problems. Even some prospective teachers in our own classes express a belief that little, if any, relationship exists between school achievement and postschool success. Some persons have unquestionably achieved success in life without a background of formal schooling. However, the relationship is strong between educational attainment and eventual income, social mobility across generations, political participation, further school options, and so on. *Why* this relationship is strong and *how much* school expenditures actually increase youths' life chances for happiness are much debated questions. (Extended discussions of these issues were presented in Chapter 5.) Also arguable is whether a higher level of formal education is necessarily the best route to personal fulfillment. Some maintain that Americans are gradually becoming "overeducated" and thus are either overprepared or inappropriately prepared for the actual jobs that exist in American society (Freeman, 1975).

Such issues deserve deep thought. As for the near future, however, Americans are not likely to abandon their formal system of schooling, much less discourage their young from educational achievement. With this in mind, we examine some aspects of school underachievement, including discussion of compensatory education to promote children's scholastic development.

School Underachievement

Most parents and teachers think of underachievement as failure by pupils to "work up to their potential." Attempts by psychologists to operationally define underachievement also imply this view. The most widely used definition of underachievement is based on a discrepancy index: the degree of difference between predicted achievement based on a measure of scholastic aptitude and actual classroom achievement as measured by achievement tests or teachers' grades (Asbury, 1974). Accordingly, underachievers are typically defined as pupils who perform significantly less well in school than would be predicted from their performance on measures of learning ability, intelligence, or in some cases, past achievement. It is important to distinguish between selective and chronic underachievement. Selective underachievement may occur occasionally for relatively brief periods in a given class or with certain subject matter, while strong achievement is maintained in other school situations. In this sense everyone probably underachieves at one time or another. Chronic underachievement persists through time and is more widely generalized across school-achievement situations. Hereafter, our comments pertain mostly to chronic, not selective, underachievement.

Chronic underachievement occurs among children of both sexes, from all social classes, and in racial and ethnic groups. Many studies, however, have involved bright underachieving males. The reasons are at least four: (1) The discrepancy between high scholastic aptitude and low classroom achievement is more readily apparent among bright students. (2) The low utilization of intellectual resources by individuals whose potential for making contributions to society is high is especially disturbing to many adults. (3) A failure to utilize one's own potential is often implicated in mental-health problems, at least in theories based on the idea of self-actualization. (4) Male underachievers seem to outnumber female underachievers by at least 3 or 4 to 1 (Asbury, 1974).

Onset of underachievement. Longitudinal studies of underachievement are rare. Limited evidence suggests that the pattern can be detected as early as the third grade for boys and the fifth grade for girls—perhaps even earlier (Shaw & McCuen, 1960). If so, whatever problems underlie underachievement are likely brought to the secondary school, at least in budding form. Underachievement is often accentuated by certain characteristics of the high school environment: increased academic pressures, peer-group values contrary to intellectual and academic striving, necessity for greater independence in learning, and the like.

Data that suggest a fairly early onset of underachievement patterns fit well with our earlier comments about the stability of school achievement over time. Similarly, the idea of a "late bloomer"— one who starts slowly in school but later suddenly bursts forth with a remarkable improvement in school achievement— also seems to be more myth than reality (Stennet & Fienstra, 1970). The implication of these data is clear: if the problem of pupil underachievement is neglected at the elementary school level, the pattern may stabilize or worsen, and become increasingly difficult to change later. This, of course, assumes that the school (and home) environment is also stable and reinforces the pattern.

Coping with underachievement. If we judge underachievement as a problem about which something should be done, what is our choice of strategy? This choice will probably depend on our view of the causes of underachievement. There are at least two basic ways to think about causation. One is that underachievement is a function of *personal deficit*. That is, even under the "best" of school learning conditions, some pupils will seem ill-disposed or equipped to achieve because of personal deficiencies. Some clues to these deficiencies come from studies that compare achievers with underachievers who are otherwise similar in family background and intellectual ability. Among the commonly reported cognitive and personal-social "inadequacies" of underachievers are: low self-esteem, hostile attitudes toward authority, distractibility, lapses in attention, low regard for advance planning, social immaturity, general weak adaptability or personal adjustment, and a host of others (Asbury, 1974; O'Shea, 1970; Shaw, 1968). In some cases, a child's family situation may be the source of difficulty—low parental support for achievement, parental rejection, and so on. In other cases, peer-group conflicts and social isolation may be implicated. Some cases of underachievement may be symptomatic of deeper personal problems about which the school can do little.

A second way to think about the causes of underachievement involves the school much more directly: a mismatch between pupil learning styles and motives and the school learning environment. Certain school conditions, such as a lack of challenging materials, incompetent teachers, authoritarian or punitive pupil-control tactics, and low individualization of instruction, may contribute to underachievement (Kowitz & Armstrong, 1961; St. John, 1971; Yee, 1968). This problem of match can extend also to include home–school discontinuity in values, language use, and ways of thinking, especially common among children and youth from minority co-cultures or non-middle–class homes (Getzels, 1974). A cycle of progressive underachievement may result from such discontinuities.

In any given case, either one or both of these ways of thinking about underachievement may be useful. Each has its unique implications for addressing the underachievement "problem" (though they are by no means mutually exclusive). In taking a personal deficit approach, educators usually attempt to somehow change the individual pupil in ways that facilitate a better adjustment to the demands of schooling. Psychological counseling, often in combination with special programs to strengthen academic skills and study habits, is often provided. Because the quality, appropriateness, and duration of such counseling programs vary so widely, it is difficult to generalize about their effectiveness. Modest successes are reported, however, especially in helping students come to terms with their personal-social problems and develop more positive attitudes toward school (Bednar & Weinberg, 1970).

Interpreting underachievement as a problem of the match leads logically to an evaluation of school conditions that may inhibit or suppress students' achievement striving. Curriculum reform and faculty retraining may follow to reduce, if not eliminate, sources of failure and frustration. This may require innovative instructional strategies to promote mastery learning and increased pupil freedom to choose what, when, how, and with whom they will learn. This approach, of course, neither is nor should be restricted to so-called "underachievers." It is applicable to all children and youth.

Special problems can be encountered, however, if a culturally based home–school discontinuity is the source of achievement difficulties. Schooling for the majority of white, middle-class children is fairly uniform across America in its values and objectives. But to accommodate and meet the needs of nonwhite or non-middle–class children may require a deeper analysis of these values and objectives in relation to culturally different life styles. If the values that dominate our current educational system—industriousness, personal responsibility, self-regulation, skilled communications, punctuality, order, and convergent thinking, for example—are judged in-

appropriate or irrelevant for certain segments of American society, substitutions will have to be found. The problem is that the formulation of a value base for education that accommodates radically different orientations and functions for large subsegments of society apparently has not yet been developed, much less agreed upon. For some psychologists, however, the first step in dealing with this problem is clear: "When cultures are in competition for resources, as they are today, the psychologist's task is to analyze the source of cultural difference so that those of the minority, the less powerful group, may quickly acquire the intellectual instruments necessary for success of the dominant culture, *should they so choose*" (Cole & Bruner, 1971, p. 875; italics in original).

Compensatory Education

This task, taken seriously, calls for intense, comprehensive, long-range study and research. To date, however, the most visible attempt to facilitate improved educational achievement among children and youth subject to home–school discontinuity is *compensatory education*. Quite literally, this means education to compensate for disadvantages coming from poverty and cultural minority status that impede achievement and opportunity for full personal development. Since the mid-1960s, a considerable increase in federal and state financial support has occurred for such educational programming at two principal levels: organized preschool experience (especially for 4-year-olds prior to kindergarten entry) and assistance to school dropouts or potential dropouts. Gradually, other directions have been taken, including some dramatic curriculum innovations within the K–12 sequence itself, tutoring, expanded vocational development and manpower training programs, bilingual-bicultural education experiments, alternative schools, and greater access to institutions of higher learning. The large majority of programs, however, are directly related to schooling and aim to upgrade scholastic achievement, especially in "basic skills" such as reading, mathematics and communication skills (Passow, 1974). We shall discuss compensatory education primarily from this perspective, with an emphasis upon *early intervention* (preschool–primary grade years).

Compensatory education programs for academic achievement vary considerably in their details, but most share at least two related goals (Gordon, 1968). First, they are *remedial,* they attempt to fill gaps — social, cultural, or academic — in the individual's total education. Second, they are *preventive,* they try to forestall either initial or contributing failures in school and later life. The preventive aspect is most clearly associated with early childhood compensatory education. Several assumptions are common (Evans, 1975). The first is that specialized early (rather than late) intervention stands a better chance to capitalize on the modifiability and flexibility of the human organism. A second assumption is that potential learning disorders that interfere with scholastic development can be identified and treated early to prevent the cumulative school failure so typical of disadvantaged children. Both aspects — preventive and remedial — are based on a prediction that improved educational opportunity and status result in a number of gains: progress toward the ideal of fully realized civil rights, enhanced social mobility, more humane race relations, and a better opportunity to share in this nation's economic resources (Gordon, 1968). A tall order indeed for any educational system!

The impact of compensatory education. Since its inception, compensatory education has been alternately praised and condemned by commentators of all sorts, but criticisms have been especially heavy (Evans, 1975). For some, the very

term "compensatory education" is a misnomer, because it is illogical to speak about "compensation" when disfranchised children and youth have not been offered a suitable education in the first place. For others, compensatory education draws attention to the wrong dimension of the problem. We are distracted by presumed deficiencies of the poor and culturally different instead of making a critical evaluation of American school practices. The result of providing education to compensate for these alleged deficiencies, they say, implies an intolerable, institutionalized racism — a wrongheaded belief throughout the schools that children from poor homes or ethnic or racial minority heritage are basically inferior.

The need for social action programs to benefit disadvantaged children and youth is not denied by these critics. Rather, it is the way of thinking about program goals and methods that they find objectionable. The most serious criticism has been that compensatory education has failed to meet its most basic, immediate objective: helping disadvantaged children to succeed better in school at a level comparable to their more advantaged peers.

In fact, the first returns about the impact of compensatory early education were less than favorable. But the programs for young children, such as Project Head Start, were hastily and inconsistently implemented and evaluated. Initial gains in intellectual and achievement-test performance often were observed, only to dissipate as children left the special programs and moved into regular classrooms. Fortunately, however, this important educational movement retained its momentum. Experimentation began with even earlier intervention programs, for example the infant-stimulation programs described in Chapter 8. Innovations in kindergarten–primary grade practices, designed in concert with preschool programs for the disadvantaged, also were undertaken. These innovations, known as Project Follow Through, did much to establish alternatives in curricula for young children. Longer-term evaluation strategies were set in motion.

The results of these and related efforts at compensatory education give us reason to be more optimistic about facilitating the educational development of disadvantaged children. Achievement gains are not uniform in breadth and magnitude across all types of programs. Nor do these special programs guarantee progress for all children. But certain patterns are clear, as noted in a recent report to the American Association for the Advancement of Science (Palmer, 1977). Ten representative longitudinal studies involving over 2,000 children in various experimental programs of preschool education were taken as illustrations. Compared to control children (those not receiving some type of compensatory education), experimental-program children generally showed consistently higher IQ test performance, a durable increase in scholastic reading ability, and were more likely to advance normally through the elementary school grades. Program results were more consistently positive when parents were trained for home teaching roles. And, consistent with our remarks in Chapter 8, the earlier and longer the intervention, the better the results. Of course, program quality is another important variable. The conclusion is that well-designed and competently executed programs can benefit children's achievement. There is also some encouraging evidence about the impact of complementary educational television programming designed for disadvantaged children. Children who regularly view *Sesame Street* and related programs, for example, show an improved repertoire of academic readiness skills (Ball & Bogatz, 1973).

Additional benefits of compensatory programs, such as improved medical care and early identification of children likely to have problems with their mental and physical health, can be documented. Such benefits, as well as other effective educational programs for children (disadvantaged or not), are described in other sources (*Educational Programs That Work*, 1976; Evans, 1975; Nimnicht & Johnson, 1973). These benefits reaffirm our confidence in the potential of environmental influences, such as education and social services, to improve the life circumstances of the disadvantaged. Ultimately, and in theory, compensatory education will also create expanded adult career opportunities and training for today's disadvantaged children. There is already evidence that thousands of persons from low income and ethnic and racial minority backgrounds have received college training as a result of their involvement as compensatory education staff workers (Zigler, 1972). We now examine in broader perspective the important topic of career development.

CAREER DEVELOPMENT

Career development is a process occurring over the life span. It includes home, school, and community experiences as they affect our self-awareness, expectancies, choice of general life style, and—most important—means for earning a living (Pietrofesa & Splete, 1975). This involves coming to know one's strengths, limitations, values, and preferred reinforcements, and somehow integrating these into a satisfactory work experience that represents career choice. Socialization for career development involves at least two developmental tasks (Havighurst & Gottlieb, 1975). The first is mostly educational, heavily influenced by the family and school.

Michael Weisbrot

© 1974, Judy Gurovitz, from Photo Researchers

© Chester Higgins, Jr., from Photo Research

© 1977, Lynn McLaren, from Photo Researchers

seph Szabo

Myron Wood, from Photo Researchers

© 1976, Ray Ellis, from Photo Researchers, Inc.

Knowledge about occupational endeavor, opportunity, and requirements must be acquired. Self-assessment is also part and parcel of this task. Ideally, a variety of first-hand work experiences can be gained to establish a broad perspective from which to channel our energies to a long-term work commitment. The second developmental task is finding employment itself. This requires opportunities for youth to become integrated into the work force to provide for self-sufficiency and, hopefully, self-expression through meaningful work.

In this section we discuss aspects of socialization that highlight some of the more important research findings about career development in American society. This includes major psychological conceptions of career development and choice, psychological functions of work experience for children and youth, and major social influences on the occupational orientations of youth. Chapter 10 concludes with a brief discussion of some timely issues about work and career education.

Stories of Career Development

A formal discussion of career development can be enlivened by reference to real people. We saw in Chapter 1, for example, how Lyle seemed to "drift" into his life work, although he was well suited to be a salesperson given his strong personal-social orientation. Juan showed more strikingly how chance circumstances can jell at unique times in life-span development to facilitate career development. We now introduce the reader to still other individuals whose collective situations illustrate some general points about career development and guidance in America.

Thelma, age 32, is a black female. She left her high school in a large Great Lakes industrial community to marry at age 16. By age 24 she was the mother of five children, all of whom are living. Her marriage deteriorated during these years and ended in divorce when Thelma was 25. She was ill-prepared or trained for economic self-sufficiency. As a teenager, she had no vocational plans other than doing domestic chores if opportunity and need arose. Shortly after her divorce, a federally sponsored program of early childhood education was established in her neighborhood. It seemed suitable for her younger children, so she enrolled them, and agreed to participate in the related parent-education program. Thelma did not like the parts of her training that involved child care, and offered to act instead as a receptionist. She had a warm and skillful way with people who visited the project and who telephoned for appointments or information. As her self-confidence grew, Thelma enrolled in a night secretarial course and was a superior student. After further night study, Thelma passed a high school equivalency examination and left her initial position to become head receptionist in a large insurance company office. She earns an adequate salary, likes the work, and now feels secure and optimistic about the future.

Gerald, age 24 and an only child, grew up in a bustling Rocky Mountain resort community. His parents had managed a ski lift there since before Gerald was born. The family income grew along with the increased popularity of recreational skiing. Gerald's parents, both accomplished skiers, also offered individual and group ski instruction with much success through these years. Gerald was among their star pupils. He was skiing competently by age 5 and is now highly skilled at ski jumping and slalom events. After high school, Gerald attended college with vague intentions of becoming a lawyer, but he left joyfully after two years to help his parents expand the ski school enterprise. Gerald is now full-time director of the school, contemplating marriage with a girl he has known for over a year, and is planning further business ventures, including a retail sales outlet for ski equipment and resort wear.

Nina is the tagalong and by some years the youngest child of a large, comfortably situated family. All her older brothers and sisters are college graduates, and are either successful business and professional people or well-educated housewives who plan to go back to work when their children are a bit older. After doing poorly in high school, Nina entered a liberal arts college, disliked it, and flunked out. Next, she attended a business school to become a secretary, but was not interested in the curriculum and did not do well. She then asked her family to support her in beauty school, because she always liked to help her older sisters with their makeup and hairstyles and was so good at it that her older brothers repeatedly asked her to cut and style their hair. The parents, with little enthusiasm, agreed to support Nina in yet another training course. She made it handsomely through beauty school, worked for a time in a style and beauty shop, borrowed money from her family to start her own shop, and now operates it successfully with the help of five employees.

Dan, age 21, is a Native American. He was born and still lives with his parents and three younger sisters on a tribal reservation in America's Pacific Northwest coastal region. All of Dan's schooling took place on this reservation. Outdoor activity, especially boating, fishing, and horseback riding, occupied most of his attention throughout childhood and adolescence. Dan persisted sufficiently with his studies to graduate from high school and has always been respected by his teachers and classmates. Since grad-

uation, he has worked as a maintenance hand for a small charter boat fishing company. This work is seasonal because most charter business comes during the salmon runs from late spring to early fall. During the long winter months, there is little on the reservation to substitute for Dan's maintenance work. During these months, he has been extremely restless and bored. Dan believes that any permanent improvement in his work situation will require leaving the reservation, but he is uncertain about doing so. His parents prefer that he stay with the family, yet several of his best friends have moved out to establish themselves elsewhere. Recently, Dan has considered applying for an Indian Studies teacher-education program at the state university some 100 miles away. But neither college nor teaching much appeal to him. In short, Dan is both confused and anxious about the future. He is "on hold and counting."

Sue, now age 31, first became interested in accounting after visiting an Internal Revenue Service office as part of a junior high school occupational information course. It was clear to her that specialized college training was the best route to full certification and job opportunities in this competitive field. Though her parents were not wealthy, they began to save for her college program. Sue contributed to this fund by working summers and part-time during the high school years. She was admitted to a large midwestern university noted for its excellent business school. Sue excelled in classwork, though was forced to leave school before her junior year to replenish her financial reserve. Graduating a year later than originally planned, Sue became fully certified as a public accountant. She has since worked full-time, first in one, then another of the most respected accounting firms in the large metropolitan area where she lives. Sue is dedicated to her work and cannot seriously imagine doing anything else. At present she is laying the ground-work to start her own accounting firm.

Emil, now age 46, was the second of three children born to parents who sub-sequently immigrated to the United States from eastern Europe in 1938. His father, a watchmaker, established a jew-elry business in the capital city of an eastern seaboard state. As a child, Emil did not find his new life difficult, but he remained somewhat isolated from his peers and did not participate in school athletics or social activities. Emil was strongly attracted to music, however, and with his mother's support, began private lessons on the clarinet. He prac-ticed endlessly and soon won the admi-ration of several classmates who were starting a high school dance band. Emil joined this band, and gradually became proficient with the flute and tenor saxo-phone as well. After completing high school, Emil joined a second band which traveled a tri-state area for dances and shows. By age 21, Emil was a sea-soned musician. A year later he was re-cruited for the lead tenor chair in a na-tionally famous dance band. For the next several years Emil was a featured soloist with this band on the road, in concerts, and for recordings. Married first at age 29, Emil was divorced a year later be-cause road engagements complicated the marital relationship. A second marriage occurred three years later. But his work again became a source of much discord; the marriage was seriously threatened, especially after the birth of a daughter. Soon thereafter Emil resigned from his band at the end of a national tour. A brief period of despondency followed, but he rejoined his wife and daughter who by this time had moved to a moder-ately sized community in the southern United States. Unemployed for several months, Emil eventually studied for and

passed the state real-estate examination to become a licensed broker. He now deals in commercial properties in part-nership with two other experienced bro-kers. Though Emil plays music occasion-ally, his former vocation is now strictly a hobby.

These six descriptions, based upon the life circumstances of people whom we know, suggest several important points about career development. First, career development is remarkably varied and often differs by sex, socioeconomic level, racial and ethnic status, and place of residence. Second, vocational choice and commitment can reflect a wide range of influences such as modeling (Gerald), incidental learning (Nina), in-tensive practice (Emil), or even chance circumstances (Thelma). Third, delayed vocational choice may contribute much to general psychological discomfort and even to identity problems (Dan). Fourth, formal education or occupational train-ing is extremely important for career de-velopment in some cases (Sue), much less so in others, and for some may con-tribute few direct benefits (Gerald). Fifth, career commitments often change and can themselves require considerable readjustment (Emil). Sixth, satisfactory individual vocational adjustment may re-quire what is commonly viewed as down-ward vocational mobility (Nina). Finally, and perhaps most important, in almost all cases it is individuals who are instru-mental in determining their own career development, often under the most diffi-cult conditions (Thelma).

Ways of Viewing Career Development and Choice

Because career development and choice can be influenced by so many factors, including happenstance, it is difficult for psychologists to organize a coherent way of thinking about them. Presumably the roots of career development extend to the early childhood years. For most of us, this development assumes primary importance during adolescence. As noted in Chapter 1, occupational role contributes crucially to an individual's personal identity and status. Perhaps more than any other single event, landing and holding a job successfully is typically seen as a stamp of maturity and independence, the most legitimate American "rite of passage" into adulthood (Borow, 1976). A carefully considered career choice and suitable preparation are significant given the clear relationship between job satisfaction and mental health (Ausubel, 1954). Gallup Poll data over the past decade show that a large majority of Americans believe their work to be satisfying, though there is evidence of some decrease in the past year or so. Despite widespread job satisfaction, however, some 50 percent of Gallup Poll respondents indicate interest in career change.

Certain psychological hazards often affect job satisfaction. Skilled laborers, for example, confront boredom, a factor linked to absenteeism and alcoholism. Members of the helping professions, such as doctors and teachers, may experience "emotional burnout" from working intensively with demanding clients. For farmers, manufacturers, and many other important occupational groups, when the gap between personal effort and final product widens, so apparently does job dissatisfaction.

Social scientists seek a clearer understanding of how career development and choice occur in the hope that improved guidance will increase the likelihood that fulfilling work commitments will be made and practiced by more people. Studies have ranged from the influence of socialization practices that culminate in a general commitment to the work ethic, through the social and psychological determinants of vocational choice, to ways to predict occupational success

and how work is related to adult life (Tennyson, 1968).

Most psychological study has concentrated on the process through which individuals go to reach the point of specific vocational choice and commitment. Broad conceptual approaches to this process analysis can be grouped into four related categories: the trait-factor system, a sociological model, the personality-dynamics interpretation, and life-stage interpretations of vocational development (Osipow, 1968). Together, these approaches can broaden our perspective on the relations of family, school, and community to career development and choice.

Trait-Factor System

The trait-factor system is the traditional approach to vocational psychology. Its central premise is that through careful analysis and testing procedures, an individual's aptitudes and interests can be matched with society's occupational needs and opportunities. Once this match has been made, the individual's vocational problem is solved. Elaborate vocational testing procedures for measuring personal characteristics have been developed to effect this match, although it has become increasingly clear that the problem is very complex, and perhaps not feasible in technologically advanced societies. Elaborate personal testing and occupational opportunity analyses can help self-appraisal in relation to work, but we know that vocational attitudes and interests as well as society's job requirements can change. A trait-factor approach assumes both individual personality and occupational needs are static. In short, today's match may be tomorrow's mismatch.

An exemplary attempt to extend the trait-factor theory of vocational choice has taken the form of matching model personal orientations to occupational environments (Holland, 1973). Its premise is that children and youth gradually learn certain preferred styles or modes of coping with environmental tasks. Most persons can be classified by six fundamental personal orientations—realistic, intellectual, social, conventional, enterprising, and artistic. Each represents a bundle of capabilities, interests, aspirations, and coping mechanisms. Through a detailed personal assessment, it is claimed that inclination for career environments compatible with one's personal orientation or coping style can be determined. In effect, this again means matching personality "types" with occupational categories in ways that are suitable for career planning. This relatively new and much broader application of "matching" theory says little about the development of personal orientations. It is helpful, however, in pointing to the notion of classifying career options in relation to personality types. (One must, of course, first accept the personality typology as a sufficiently valid basis for career guidance.)

Personality Dynamics

Closely related to this more sophisticated version of trait-measurement theory is the personality-dynamics theory of vocational development and choice. Again, the basic idea is that personality style can be closely related to career entrance and involvement (Roe, 1956). The difference is the emphasis placed upon children's early development of motive structures as affected by socialization in the home. Ultimately, work comes to be viewed by an individual as a means of satisfying personal motives whose roots go back to early childhood. Three pervasive patterns of parent attitude thought to determine socialization practice are postulated: emotional concentration on, acceptance of, and avoidance of, the child. These socialization

patterns predispose the child to select from occupational clusters that relate to his or her past experience. For example, a background of warmth, support, and love will orient a child toward occupations that involve close working relations with people. In contrast, cold and rejecting parents presumably predispose a child toward impersonal occupations where one works with things, animals, or plants. If we accept this school of thought, vocational guidance will be incomplete and will likely be inaccurate unless the early life of the counselee is carefully considered.

Sociological Model

The sociological approach to career development is based primarily on the notion that many circumstances beyond an individual's immediate control affect career choice in important ways. The career choice process is complicated. Many events in one's life are not anticipated. New occupational roles rapidly and unpredictably emerge in a rapidly changing society such as ours; others disappear or grow scarce. Because vocational choice (including getting a job and having it continue to exist) may be influenced by such factors, as well as by chance, the task facing adolescents is to develop effective problem-solving techniques. These include a good general education (the *generalist* as opposed to the *specialist* notion of vocational preparation), flexible adaptational skills, and the ability to analyze opportunity structures.

Life-Stage Approaches

Life-stage accounts of career choice are usually based on the idea of sequences in occupational decision making that become more finely differentiated as individuals mature. One such account (Ginzberg, 1951; 1970) has the decision making occurring in three major sequential periods: *fantasy* choices (before age 11); *tentative* choices (11–17), and *realistic* choices (between 17 and young adulthood, when a final choice is made, though changes may occur at later points in life). Children in the fantasy period are said to believe they can become whatever they wish; they "translate" their impulses or needs into an occupational choice. During the transition period, young adolescents use their subjective interests, values, and self-perceived capabilities for this translation. Choices are by necessity tentative because they are not able, willing, or sufficiently informed to apply the sharp edge of reality to their thinking about occupations. As older adolescents or youth seriously seek the best fit between their career preparation and the goals and factual conditions of permanent work, they have moved into the more mature realistic period. This begins with serious exploration of alternatives and ends with a specific choice and commitment.

This sequential process of career development has been observed in such different groups as upper-class males and females and males from lower socioeconomic backgrounds, with two major variations (Ginzberg, 1970). One variation is in the *pattern* of choice. Some people, for example, show a singleness of purpose (Sue). This is most frequent for individuals with specific or pronounced capabilities that surface fairly early in life. In contrast, other persons begin with broad, general interests which are narrowed during adolescence. The second variation in this stage scheme is the *timing* for a crystallization of occupational choice. In a normative sense, this choice will occur around age 20, but it may take place much earlier or considerably later.

A similar life stage interpretation of career development is built more specifically from self-concept theory (Super, 1963; 1970). Career development is seen as a process of developing and implementing self-knowledge and understanding. The characteristic way in which one perceives and evaluates the self and the surrounding world provides the basis for thinking about work and life style. Three major questions dominate such thinking: "Who am I?", "What is possible for me?", and "Where do I belong?" (Wurtz, 1974). The answers to these questions require the development of an integrated and, hopefully, adequate view of the self *and* of the world of work. This view must be tested against reality and finally converted into a gratifying and realistic vocational choice. This development is said to occur in stages of vocational development extending from an initial crystallization of vocational *preferences* to eventual *plans for advancement* within a given vocation. The self-concept approach provides for the influence of observational learning during childhood and reflects the importance of children's identification with adult work models and concepts of career development (Super, 1963). The main theme, however, is how individuals implement their own self-concepts through vocational channels. Experiences that result in self-clarification and self-understanding are presumably linked to adequate vocational choice and career development.

Taken together, these four approaches represent an attempt to make sense out of the still rather mysterious process of career development and choice. All four stress the theme of linking our personal skills and aspirations with demands of the real world. Yet their limitations are widely acknowledged, especially for interpreting psychological processes and weighing the many influences that are part of the development of career behavior through time and beyond the point of initial occupational choice (Borow, 1976). Scholars have continued to flirt with the popular idea that such processes and choices do evolve in stagelike progression (for example, Ginzberg, 1951; Havighurst, 1964). Yet the often unpredictable and circumstantial nature of career choice and involvement for many youth causes us to question the extent to which rational planning and decision-making may dominate the process. In other words, the variety of channels through which youth develop a pattern of work behavior raises a question about the power of any *single* theory to account for all persons. We must recognize that most youth will eventually make several career choices, not simply one. This is not to say, however, that careful attention by personnel workers to the complexities of career development is useless for assisting children and youth toward satisfactory work adjustments. The issues of where, how, and how much to assist remain with us.

Basic Factors in Occupational Choice and Entry

Because career development can be viewed in so many different ways, none of which is applicable to all individuals, some authorities (such as Jepsen & Dilley, 1974) have argued for a synthesis in terms of *psychological decision theory*. Such theory attempts to coherently describe the specific factors that influence choices. Vocational decision making is analyzed by three components: the decision-maker (the person), the decision-situation (social context), and relevant information (what the person possesses and what can be provided from the environment). Alternative decisions, or choices, can be constructed from this information, together with the desired and probable outcomes (consequences) of the action. Within a counseling program, the preferred strategy is to help the decision-maker become aware of promising courses of action in tune with his or her needs, values, and expectations.

Consistent with this approach is a consideration of four personal factors that seem most important for shaping immediate occupational choice and entry, if not one's entire vocational life (Blau et al., 1968). Applied to any given individual, these include the amount and accuracy of occupational information, technical qualifications, social role characteristics, and preferred reward-value hierarchy. As we examine these factors it can be helpful to think how parents, teachers, and other adults with whom children and youth come into contact may contribute to career development.

Occupational Information

The more we know about career possibilities, the wider is our range of choices. Unfortunately, many youth, especially early school leavers and disadvantaged youth, are often naive and uninformed about their options. Fantasies about glamourous occupations such as professional athletics and show business may be firmly held. Credentialing requirements may be poorly understood. The message, of course, is very clear: it is important not only that older children and youth know the range and the kinds of opportunities that may be available for them, but also that they have some awareness of the nature of a job as it may relate to job satisfaction. Such information is now available. For example, eight factors seem essential to the job satisfaction of clerical and craft workers of both sexes (Ford & Borgatta, 1970): (1) The work itself is interesting. (2) The job is not wasteful of time and effort, that is, there is an efficiency factor. (3) Some freedom in planning the job is available to the worker. (4) Some latitude exists in how the job is actually done. (5) The job provides opportunities. (6) Feedback is given about job performance. (7) Lenient and not too close supervision is provided. (8) The job is worth putting effort into. Remarkably little difference between males and females exists about what makes a job attractive, although there is some difference in satisfaction by level of job. Higher occupational levels assign more value to the intrinsic nature of the job— for example, how interesting the job is— and whether it provides opportunity for self-expression; lower levels are more likely to value extrinsic values, such as pay, security, and the company of co-workers (Ronan, 1970).

These differential job values have been shown to appear as early as the ninth grade as a function of social class and possibly race (Shappell & Hall, 1971). In one study, inner city males and females stressed the objective qualities (extrinsic) that they would look for when they went to work, while suburban males were more likely to expect self-satisfaction from their work. The group with the highest expectation of need satisfaction (from among groups of inner-city boys and girls and suburban boys and girls) were the suburban boys. Over all, regardless of social class and race, males more than females were attracted by jobs that included risk, opportunity for advancement, and prestige, and that had to do with things rather than people. The personal satisfaction aspect of work, however, was more likely to be stressed by females than by males. These results are consistent with our discussion of socialization patterns in Chapter 9.

Technical Qualifications

The importance of technical qualifications seems self-evident. In a technological society, youth with the best training generally will find it easiest to fill a job. They are also most likely to be hired, barring employer bias (such as bias against females, blacks, or young

people generally). The questions, then, are about the quality and amount of training and where training can best be implemented. Child labor laws in America prevent serious on-the-job training until age 16 or so. Even then, training opportunities may be limited to jobs that few other people want or that have little long-term promise. Although a majority of Americans apparently view the primary purpose of education as a means to "get a better job," schools generally are inadequately equipped to provide thorough vocational training, even the desirability of a vocational orientation is debated. Colleges and universities have also come under attack for their often ambiguous occupational benefit (Bird, 1975).

The availability of meaningful work opportunities to develop technical qualifications for full employment seems to have lessened over the years. This has meant an increase in the tenuous and trivial nature of work experience for youth before ages 19 or 20 (Havighurst & Gottlieb, 1975). Relatively few young people get full-time work that leads them directly into an adult career and even part-time work is hard to come by for many youth. There has been a huge increase in the numbers of unemployed youth, largely because of a proportionate decrease of unskilled jobs in the U.S. labor force. Moreover, the jobless rate among young blacks and other minorities is about twice that of young whites. Perhaps as a result, there has been a dramatic rise in military enlistments by blacks over the past several years (Wilson, 1976). Apparently many minority youth have decided they have a better chance of finding careers in the army, for example, than in civilian industry. Larger numbers of such youth are clearly qualifying for more highly technical jobs in the military sector of American life.

The difficult employment picture for youth is not limited to America. Rather, it extends throughout the world. In 1977, for example, the International Labor Organization reported a record 7 million unemployed youth in the world's 24 richest countries. This joblessness is blamed upon social indifference, weak employment and training policies for youth, and inadequate vocational education. General economic conditions, the ebb and flow of recession or prosperity, also affect this problem. The "double bind" in job seeking seems pervasive: youths seek work experience but are all too often rejected because they have none.

Social Role Characteristics

That different occupations convey different amounts of social prestige and power is widely known and well buttressed by research (for example, Hodge, Siegel, & Rossi, 1968). Physicians, scientists, and Supreme Court justices have higher prestige than businessmen and those who work with their hands. Even within the same occupational group, such as teaching, a prestige hierarchy exists. College professors seem to enjoy higher status than high school teachers, who, in turn, are often more esteemed than elementary and "preschool" teachers. Unfortunately, this probably reflects the generally low prestige that Americans have traditionally associated with persons who care for the young.

Generally speaking, youth more often express occupational aspirations for higher-prestige occupations (Borow, 1976). What they aspire to and what they actually expect to achieve, however, can be quite different. One large-scale survey of American adolescents (Douvan & Adelson, 1966) disclosed that over half the males surveyed aspired to professional and semiprofessional jobs, less than 30 percent preferred skilled trades and crafts or other manual trades, and only about 15 percent wanted to pursue a job lower in status than their fathers'. Thus the general pattern, consistent over many studies, is upward striving. How firm adolescent's actual expectations for successful striving are cannot be determined from these data. But a realistic view of occupational opportunity suggests that many youths must necessarily revise their thinking and accept lower-prestige jobs. To illustrate, the occupational class distribution for 1970 indicated that only 14 percent of the actual work force held professional and technical positions. Taking this statistic as a rough estimate of job availability, the demand for professional status among youth far exceeds the need or supply. Less prestigious and poorer-paying jobs may eventually be taken as a last resort, or as a function of "drift" from one employment situation to another. The latter pattern is most likely among youth with limited education. Significantly, the U.S. Department of Labor has expressed concern that many less-appealing jobs may be rejected or go unfilled, especially if the social welfare system is successfully tapped by disenchanted or otherwise picky workers. The unemployment "problem," then, may reflect in part a reluctance or refusal of persons to accept jobs that are available but that are deemed undesirable.

Reward-Value Hierarchies

An individual's reward-value hierarchy is also important in determining what sort of job will be taken given the opportunity, and how happy he or she will be once settled in the job. A person desiring social prestige may take a low-paying job if it has high prestige, rather than a less prestigious job with higher pay. If adventurous, another person may choose in one direction; if security is valued more strongly, job choice will lie in yet another direction. Many authorities consider reward-value hierarchies to be closely related to personality, but the research findings are not yet sufficiently clear that firm vocational guidance can be given on the basis of personality data (Elton & Rose, 1970).

In general and until recently, salary and security have been the strongest reward values throughout America's labor force. Survey data from youth in the 1970s, however, suggest an increase in the value of intrinsic job factors—challenge, responsibility, achievement, autonomy, opportunity for self-improvement, and the social value of work (Havighurst & Gottlieb, 1975). This is more characteristic of college than noncollege populations, perhaps because of the greater initial economic security of families from which many college students come. Such signs of an emerging ethic of social responsibility among youth are heralded as a genuine value change within American society. Influenced by this ethic, an increasing number of youth will seek careers that are helpful to others and useful to society (Getzels, 1972).

We caution once more against sweeping generalizations. No single value structure is shared by the entire youth population. And, of course, we must also keep in mind the broader national picture of social and economic needs. In the 1960s, for example, it seemed that the demand for elementary and secondary school teachers would never be met. Today, employment opportunities in public education are extremely limited. Teaching is a buyer's market, the increased social commitments among youth wishing to teach notwithstanding.

These comments about occupational choice and entry highlight the importance of both self-understanding and accurate knowledge of the occupational scene. Concepts of self and work are formulated only gradually, however, and are subject to many influences. Thus we now turn to the question of major social influences on career development.

Major Social Influences

Career development is influenced by a constellation of many interacting factors related to the "accident of birth" (Miller & Form, 1964). Birth establishes family, race, ethnicity, physical make-up, social class, sex, place of residence, and to a large extent general educational opportunity. It is not possible to do justice to all these factors in this section. We choose to focus largely upon parental influence, sex differences as affected by social influences, and briefly on peers. Schools are considered in some detail because of their potential for comprehensive career guidance and education.

Parental Influence

One way to think about parental influence on the career development of children and youth is in terms of the "inheritance" of occupational orientation or even a specific occupational level (Caplow, 1954). Such inheritance may be direct—for example, grooming children for and eventually placing in their hands a business such as farming, independent retailing, or an apprenticed craft. More often this inheritance is less direct but nonetheless forceful (for better or worse). We refer to the psychological aspects of home life: parental modeling of attitudes and work preferences, patterns of reinforcement, extent and nature of parent–child interaction, achievement press, support for education, and the like. Depending too largely on social class, the combined weight of such forces can establish clear directions for career planning and choice. Many middle-class parents, for example, quickly dismiss the manual trades for their children. They expect their children to rise socially through education and suitable work experience. The range of acceptable occupations may be restricted accordingly. Over time, a system of family encouragement, financial backing, and even pressure affects the growing child. Attitudes consistent with specific occupational orientations (for example, the entrepreneurial or bureaucratic, discussed in Chapter 3) may shape children's perceptions and values. The quality of interpersonal relationships in the home often seems to create a basis for moving toward or away from work situations that require personal-social skills and interests for success (Luckey, 1974). (The *personality dynamics* perspective on career development is relevant here.)

To the extent that career development and achievement motivation are related, we would expect that socialization practices linked to such motivational development could at least partially account for individual differences in occupational level. Effective socialization by parents of four basic adjustment tendencies and coping styles in their children seems especially important in American society today (Borow, 1976). First is a capacity for self-reliance, or the ability to use personal resources for independent decision making and problem solving. The second is impulse control, the ability to delay gratification as in "work before play." The third is active mastery behavior and the development of a sense of personal control over the environment. And the fourth is achievement motivation itself, with its characteristic outcome of working to attain standards of excellence. These characteristics neither guarantee nor are uniformly required for satisfactory occupational attainment and adjustment, but as general capacities they seem to have wide application to the work situations in which most youth will eventually find themselves.

The importance of social skills, of course, cannot be overlooked. A failure to continue or advance in some occupations may be due less to cognitive than to social incompetence. Teachers, for example, rarely are "fired" or voluntarily leave their profession because they lack subject matter knowledge or intellectual skills. Rather, they quit teaching most often because they are unable to cope effectively with the social aspects of teaching—pupil interaction and management, cooperation with colleagues and administration, and so on (Evans, 1976).

Vocational development and adjustment depend much upon the cumulative home experience of children and youth. This experience is the basis from which gradually emerge general adaptational skills and maturity of outlook about work. A recent study of college students is typical of many findings supporting this point. Students who measured highest in vocational maturity and success in solving vocational choice problems were those who had also had the most successful psychosocial adjustments as children and adolescents (Munley, 1975). Specifically these adjustments developed a basic sense of trust, autonomy, initiative, industry, and personal identity. Some may argue, perhaps with justification, that such characteristics are biased in favor of the so-called middle-class value system. Few disclaim these characteristics for healthy psychological development, however, and they seem to us to transcend any specific social class.

Sex Differences in Career Development

Previous comments about sex differences and sex-role stereotyping in the schools are pertinent to career development. We wish to stress two basic points. First, social conditions and attitudinal barriers have in the past inhibited many women from pursuing and maintaining achievement-directed behavior outside the home (O'Leary, 1974). Among these inhibiting forces is a strong societal belief about the "proper" role of women as wives and mothers. Expressions of doubt or skepticism by males (and even by females themselves) about women's competence in positions of leadership is another such force. Still another is active attempts by male-dominated unions and business firms to prevent women from competing with men for preferred jobs. And, unlike males whose identity may evolve primarily as worker and only secondarily as husband or father, many females experience role conflict in the familiar career-vs-homemaker bind. This conflict is not easily resolved and may have a dampening effect upon any female's career orientations.

Such forces are not unique to the adult world. They operate as early as junior high school. One study of ninth grade boys and girls differing in race, social class, and IQ (Entwisle & Greenberger, 1972) showed that boys, in particular, held quite conservative opinions about women's work roles. They were generally negative about the idea of women working outside the home and even more opposed to the prospect of women holding "men's" jobs. Girls were generally more liberal, but their opinions were still laced with traditional thinking. Adolescents higher in IQ tended to be more liberal, as did blacks; but middle-class white boys, even those with higher IQs, were the least liberal group in this study. Peer-group pressures emanating from males with such conservative views may shape the occupational aspirations of females to a considerable degree.

The second basic point about sex differences in career development concerns motivational dynamics among women. We have already referred to the "fear of success" syndrome and how it may operate to the disadvantage of females in achievement situations. Beyond this, substantial data suggest an apparent preference among women for occupa-

tions high in affiliative or person-to-person contact value. Consistently over the years, females have exceeded men in preferring work that involves helping others; males more often seek money independence and leadership opportunity (Davis, 1964). Adolescent females are noted for the importance they attach to satisfying interpersonal relationships as a primary source of self-esteem; adolescent males more often cite personal achievement as the basis for their self-regard (Douvan & Adelson, 1966). As late as the early 1970s, studies (such as Gottlieb, 1974) have found college women still preferring the helping professions—teaching, nursing, social work—and not expecting salaries equal to men's. Exceptions to the general case abound, of course, but the overall picture does not indicate a major turnabout in the career development pattern of females. We do observe an increased *employment* rate among young women beyond age 19 or so in the past several years. However, employment barriers still seem to operate selectively against younger girls, especially minority and less-educated females (Havighurst & Gottlieb, 1975).

To champion a break from the traditional patterns of discouraging women from career planning and involvement and stereotyping them into selected career categories is to raise a number of important social issues. Among them are the possible effects of widespread career employment for women upon the general economy on work opportunities for men, on marriage and the nuclear family, on childbearing and care, and on a host of other aspects of American social life. But the most basic issue is the right of self-determination and self-realization through career involvement for any person, regardless of sex (or race). As one writer (Hausen, 1974) has observed, support for women's career development is not an attempt to find a place for every woman in the labor force. Instead, it is an affirmation of her uniqueness, worth, and dignity as an individual and for her right to freedom of choice in personal and professional lifestyles (O'Leary, 1974).

A Word about Peer Group Influences

We have suggested that the adolescent peer culture may affect the direction and extent of career aspiration among the young. This likelihood increases as the period of adolescence is prolonged by extended credentialing requirements for occupational entry. Yet it is extremely difficult to speak with certainty about the degree of clout exerted by peers as compared, say, to parents, teachers, and other adult role models. The reader will recall from Chapter 4 our generalization that parents seem generally more influential in affecting their children's important life decisions, value choices, and goal aspirations, while peers strongly affect the more superficial aspects of social life, such as preferences for clothing, music, argot, and games. This is not to reject the many indirect ways peer-group association may influence occupational development and decision making. Sex-typed attitudes about work, friendship patterns, peer-group achievement status, and general normative values can operate selectively to influence both self-image and occupational aspirations (Pietrofesa & Splete, 1975).

These influences may become most pronounced around the ninth and tenth grades (Hollander, 1967). Students who remain in school to complete graduation requirements seem especially sensitive to peer-group influence about further educational planning.

One careful analysis of such influences points up the significance of the social context of the school in which peers interact (Bain, 1974). Specifically, the class composition of a student body is strongly associated with students' desire and planning for both college attendance and occupational pursuits. Youths

from any given social class are more likely to make college plans if they attend higher socioeconomic level schools, least likely if they attend lower-class high schools. This finding seems somewhat independent of parental aspirations for their children and the quality of formal educational programming in a particular school. That is, extent of college planning may be explained most adequately for many youths by their personal friendships and reference-group identification. But another important factor can be an adolescent's self-perceived intellectual competence and personal resources. Such perception is shaped in large part by social comparisons, that is, by how well children and adolescents think they measure up to the prevailing level of achievement within their peer group. Even when performing well in an absolute sense, some students may question their competence for college if the level of peer-group achievement is high. Similarly, where peer-group achievement level is low, some adolescents who perform "better than average" may develop an inflated sense of competence. If so, a rude awakening can occur when they are confronted with higher standards and do poorly, for example, on college entrance exams.

We respect the potential power of peer-group forces to affect the nature and extent of career development among youth. Perhaps the single most important mechanism of influence is social pressures, supportive or otherwise, to remain or continue in some form of educational setting pertinent to occupational preparation. In general, the stronger the school commitment—motivation for competence, involvement in school activities, and cumulated school achievement—the greater the range of career opportunities and options (Kelly & Pink, 1971). Less-committed youth tend not to pursue education beyond high school. As a consequence they face early a more limited job market and often are less well prepared than their peers in continued education, whether in college, trade schools, or other post-high school vocational-technical training programs.

The School and Career Development

We have shown how career success may depend upon general educational attainment. But this does not speak to the efforts undertaken in schools to promote specific career planning, preparation, and choice. Vocationalism in the public schools has long been controversial. It began with the manual training movement prior to 1900, from which a more generalized vocational education policy evolved. This meant special curricula within secondary schools to equip students with marketable skills, a qualification for further training, or for many families, a homemaking and consumer education (Lecht, 1974). Despite many changes in its scope and techniques, vocational education has never been free from severe criticism or charges of ineffectiveness. School vocational programs have been viewed as either too specific or too general, a dumping ground for incompetent or otherwise difficult students, anti-intellectual or excessively academic, contributing to job obsolescence, reinforcing the economic status quo, and failing to help America's disfranchised youth improve their lot in life (Grubb & Lazerson, 1974). At worst, such programs have been seen as furthering racial and sex discrimination while at the same time contributing little to solving the nation's unemployment problem. Students themselves, especially non-college-bound youth, have also voiced regular criticism, perceiving school personnel as little interested in anything but the business of college preparation (Betz, Engle, & Mallinson, 1969).

Justly or not, vocational education has had a turbulent history and erratic financial support. The effectiveness of existing programs continues to be seriously questioned and the issue of how to improve an allegedly dismal state of affairs has come to the fore. Some authorities, for example, establish more refined counseling procedures to promote realistic vocational choices (Hanson & Sander, 1973). Others advocate simulation techniques to directly involve students in decision-making processes central to career planning (Johnson & Myrick, 1972). Still others advocate more state and federally subsidized work-study programs, manpower training programs, Job Corps and Neighborhood Youth Corps programs, and so on (Tolbert, 1974).

Career education These emphases are neither mutually exclusive nor incompatible. But strong protagonists for positive career development among youth (such as Marland, 1971; Ottina, 1974) argue persuasively for a more comprehensive, integrated approach to career education in the schools. The premise is that all educational experiences—curriculum, instruction, counseling—should prepare the individual for economic independence and increase appreciation for the dignity of work. All students must be provided with increasing options for occupational choice. Barriers to job skill attainment, real and imagined, are eliminated, as is the "artificial" separation between academic and vocational aspects of life. The relevance of school is increased by dealing more extensively with career planning, enhanced by career guidance and placement services.

More specifically, career education accepts four major obligations (Ottina, 1974). The first is to acquaint elementary school children with the career-oriented world in which they will live as adults. Second, junior high students are provided with a deeper study of two or three major career fields or occupational clusters in which they express interest (such as marine science, transportation, hospitality and recreation, and personal services). Third, senior high students are prepared for one or more careers that may lead them to one of several possible options: immediate job market entry, short-term post-secondary technical programs, or four-year colleges and universities and beyond to graduate training. All post-secondary experiences include continued guidance and counseling. Fourth, career education is designed to provide a way for adults to reenter formal education to upgrade their skills in their established career field or to gain entry to a new one.

Though not a new idea, career education is just beginning to make its presence known in some parts of the United States. For example, a recent survey (McLaughlin, 1976) indicates that formal career-education policies existed (1974–1975) in only about one-third of America's public school districts. Even then, broadly implemented programs are not commonplace. Full services are provided for possibly as few as 3 percent of pupils in these districts. Accordingly, it is much too early to assess the impact of career education. Many obstacles to its proper implementation remain to be overcome (school custom and tradition, legal and financial difficulties, and the schools' admissions-accreditation rules) (Law, 1974). However, persons who see a stronger link between schooling and working as a good thing can take heart in the promise of career education; it deserves a trial. But its ideological basis should be made explicit. According to some critics, for example, career education implies a commitment to the "corporate social order—high productivity, spiraling wages, automation, increasing economic growth, accelerating rates of social change, systematic administration, complex large scale organizations and a technical approach to the resolution of human problems" (Nash & Agne, 1973, p. 373).

Perhaps. Certainly any approach to vocationalism in a capitalist economy suggests that the worth of individuals may be judged by their productivity and lifetime contribution to economic expansion. We suggest that problems of socialization for work are much too complex for any educational system to solve alone. A frontal attack on employment practices and opportunities for youth is also needed. As a beginning, two broad approaches may contribute to this end (Havighurst & Gottlieb, 1975). One involves programs to encourage employers themselves to hire and train more youth. A second requires the development of entirely new job situations for youth outside the present economy. Consistent with this is the idea of a National Youth Service, to include a voluntary, or even compulsory, involvement in social-action programs, conservation and public-works programs, and the like. Much can be gained by a greater and more directly instrumental work involvement for youth that is coordinated as fully as possible with formal learning experience.

Two Dilemmas about Career Guidance and Education

It is comforting to think that as socialization practices improve for career development among youth they will be able to experience an orderly and successful progression toward choice, entry, and eventually, success and satisfaction in a vocational role. Choices should not be forced prematurely, however, especially in periods when job opportunities and requirements are rapidly changing. This problem represents a major adolescent dilemma or conflict between two basic developmental tasks (Rogers, 1969). The first is identity seeking (Appendix A), which, by definition, is an exploratory process. The second is reaching a specific vocational choice, which, by definition, is an entrenching process. All things considered, we place the higher priority on identity seeking, especially during early and middle adolescence, thus encouraging individuals to test themselves in a wide variety of situations and to learn the intricacies of self-evaluation and self-understanding.

College-bound youth probably have an advantage over their non–college-bound counterparts in identity seeking. They are, in effect, buying more time for self-development and self-exploration. Non-college youth, in contrast, often find themselves forced to make highly specific choices about vocational roles simply to survive. This group of young people needs much more attention from the schools than has been given them in the past. As we suggested earlier, a wider range of options for meaningful work experience is imperative for at least two reasons: to channel the development of individual competence and to harness youthful energies for constructive social purposes. We are encouraged by some creative action along these lines. Various communities throughout America, for example, are experimenting with programs using youth as teachers of younger children, social-service personnel, entrepreneurs, communications specialists, and the like (Tyler, 1974). The common ingredient of successful youth programs is participation that requires responsible action and decision making in a context of accountability where youths experience directly the consequences of their own behavior.

The overriding goal of school–community youth-involvement programs is growth in positive attitudes toward self, work, and adultlike involvement in social and economic problem solving. This raises a second dilemma associated with vocationalism and career education: the extent to which youth commit themselves to the work ethic itself. Data show that most contemporary youth hold generally positive attitudes toward work (Havighurst & Gottlieb, 1975). Yet the value of achievement is apparently un-

dergoing serious examination, especially among males. An increasing number of young people seemingly reject the American work ethic out of hand. They want nothing to do with the "rat race" that has produced ulcers, cardiovascular tension, and overconsumption of alcohol by their elders. Typically, such youth come from advantaged, liberal families. They do not choose to pay the price for economic security, power, status, and prestige that their parents have paid. Thus, some are high school dropouts, and many more (often gifted and creative people) are college dropouts. Some experts believe that the combined, free, anti-establishment thinking of this group will lead to "the greening of America" (Reich, 1970). Certainly, their liberalizing and sometimes disturbing behavior has produced thoughtfulness and often unease in American society. However, others believe that as this liberal, rebellious, and intelligent segment of society drops out, their logical and "predestined places" in the social order will be taken by conservative and equally intelligent young people from the working class (Berger & Berger, 1971). Thus, instead of the "greening of America," the "blueing of America" will occur.

We tend not to view this issue in either-or terms. There is room for much variation in a pluralistic society. The extent to which we are governed by the work ethic, however, largely determines the life style we model and reinforce in our dealings with children and youth. They, in turn, are faced with a task of selecting among conflicting values and life goals in relation to work and productivity. This dilemma can be thought about in terms of the classic tug-of-war between Dionysian and Apollonian qualities in human relations. To be Dionysian (after Dionysus, the Greek god of wine, vegetation, warmth, moisture—thus, fertility) is to be warmly, loosely, vividly alive and open to sensory experience. In other words, if we are Dionysian, we relish life as warm-blooded mammals. To be Apollonian is to sponsor competence in a wide range of activities. Apollo, another Greek god, was the father of the Pythian games (our modern Olympics); he was also the god of song, music, and poetry. He bested the satyr, Marsyas, before a jury of the nine Muses. The oracle of Delphi, the seat of ancient mythological wisdom, was his priestess. She knew the future of all who consulted her. Thus, Apollonian qualities are the uniquely human characteristics of thought, creativity, and of biological experience channeled through learning and technical skill. The result is all that is uniquely, intelligently, and artistically human. Apollonian qualities are skill, expertness, and wisdom—in short, competence.

Possibly the ideal socialization product is a person who combines both Dionysian and Apollonian qualities—individuals who are warmly and emotionally alive and rejoice in life, yet who are patient, in our culture are achievement oriented, are thoughtful, and subject themselves willingly and eagerly to learning so that they may be competent. This once more brings sharply into focus the issue of preferred goals of socialization and methods for accomplishing them first discussed in Chapter 3.

One way to think about life style in relation to work is the extent of involvement one desires or thinks is necessary for personal fulfillment. One scholar (Katz, 1966) has proposed a rough scheme for this purpose. Three work modes along a continuum of involvement are proposed. For one, the *vocational* mode, fulfillment and success generally requires complete, wholehearted dedication, and long-term commitment to the work situation. A second, the *occupational* mode, has persons occupying, but not possessed by, a job. Work is less demanding and essential for personal growth and satisfaction. A third mode is simply *employment*. Persons work to live; they are busy and are paid but work does not figure strongly in their psychological development and functioning. It is plausible to argue that our personal values are perhaps the key to how involved we wish to become in work or leisure. If so, it may behoove adolescents to explore early their own value preferences in relation to career opportunities. Basic value orientations such as altruism, status and recognition, materialism, and self-expression are pertinent to this exploration (Rosenberg, 1957). An increasing amount of attention is being paid to this in the form of *values clarification* activities for children and youth. This process is also related to more general moral development, the topic of Chapter 11.

SUMMARY

Chapter 10 has discussed closely related patterns of achievement and career development. Having first distinguished between achievement behavior and achievement motivation, we examined their developmental trends again to stress the comparatively early emergence and stability of achievement-related characteristics. From school age onward, most of what we know about achievement among children and youth comes from the study of their academic performance, measured by tests and grades. The principle that experiences have a cumulative effect seems to hold for such performance. Continued success or its apparent lack is evident as early as the primary grades. In addition to learning aptitude, such personality characteristics as self-esteem and intellectual achievement responsibility are often important for understanding these general trends.

We again stressed social factors that may account for the increased range of achievement differences among children as they grow older. Socioeconomic background is one factor, though it is necessary to look for more specific parenting behavior that may contribute to children's achievement orientation. Parental teaching styles, management techniques, and affect expression were identified as possible influences. Sex differences in achievement were also reviewed, with emphasis upon dynamics such as fear of success among both males and females.

School underachievement was considered next, with attention to the onset of chronically low academic performance among otherwise capable students. This pattern also seems to have its origins, or at least is expressed, in the early school years. Though its causes are obscure, two common approaches to the analysis of underachievement were the personal-deficit view and the problem of the match. Each view has its own implications for attempting to "correct" achievement difficulties should a value judgment be made to do so. These general strategies were discussed with particular emphasis upon meeting the needs of children and youth whose achievement difficulty can be traced to home–school discontinuities in values, language use, and learning styles. From this, a transition to the more general compensatory education movement was made. Compensatory education has been designed both to provide remedial experiences and to prevent progressive academic difficulties among economically disadvantaged and often culturally different children and youth. Some aspects of compensatory education's controversial history were reviewed, and optimism was expressed about its overall impact on the schools and society.

Career development was discussed as a life-long process of decision making whereby individuals seek a best fit between their occupational preparation and opportunities in the world of work. Six case examples were presented to illustrate the wide diversity of personal and situational factors that influence career choice. These examples suggested an overview of some major orientations for psychological study seeking to understand and facilitate career development and choice. The most clearly developmental orienta-

tion is the life-stage approach, although its utility and accuracy are not yet verified. Recently, some attempts have been made to integrate alternative views of career development in terms of psychological decision theory. We suggested several important components for occupational decision making, including an understanding of technical qualifications and reward-value hierarchies for given vocations.

The extent and direction of social influences on career development are perhaps determined most fundamentally by the accident of birth. Children "inherit" from their parents a psychological atmosphere variously conducive to career planning, preparation, and social mobility. This atmosphere is thought to affect the development of personality characteristics that have wide generality for adult work situations, including impulse control, sociality, and achievement motivation. Sex-role stereotyping appeared again as sex differences in career development. Ways in which this stereotype has delimited vocational opportunities for females were noted as well as females' normative preference for occupations that emphasize interpersonal relationships. Peer influences on career development were examined primarily as mutual reinforcement for continuing or leaving the school or other formal training agencies.

Chapter 10 concluded with a discussion of approaches and issues about schooling and career development. Though Americans commonly think of schooling as a means to desirable and secure employment, vocationalism in schooling has a turbulent and somewhat dismal history. Most recently master plans or blueprints for career education have emerged, intended to integrate the academic and occupational preparation functions of schooling. As yet, career education has not been undertaken sufficiently widely to say much about its impact. Supporters tend to view career education as the salvation of American education and the work force. Critics demur, emphasizing issues about pluralism, life style, and the work ethic in American society.

REFERENCES

Asbury, C. A. Selected factors influencing over- and under-achievement in young school age children. *Review of Educational Research*, 1974, *44*, 409–428.

Atkinson, J. W., & Raynor, J. O. (Eds.) *Motivation and achievement.* Washington, D.C.: V. H. Winston, 1974.

Ausubel, D. P. *Theory and problems in adolescent development.* New York: Grune & Stratton, 1954.

Bain, R. K. School context and peer influences on educational plans of adolescents. *Review of Educational Research,* 1974, *44*(4), 429–446.

Ball, S., & Bogatz, G. Research on Sesame Street: Some implications for compensatory education. In J. Stanley (Ed.), *Compensatory education for children, ages 2 to 8.* Baltimore: The Johns Hopkins Press, 1973.

Bar-Tal, D., & Bar-Zohar, Y. The relationships between perception of locus of control and academic achievement: Review and some educational implications. *Contemporary Educational Psychology,* 1977, *2,* 181–199.

Barton, K., Bartsch, T., & Cattell, R. B. Longitudinal study of achievement related to anxiety and extraversion. *Psychological Reports,* 1974, *35,* 551–556.

Barton, K., Dielman, T. E., & Cattell, R. B. Child rearing practices and achievement in school. *Journal of Genetic Psychology,* 1974, *124,* 155–165.

Bednar, R. L., & Weinberg, S. L. Ingredients of successful treatment programs for underachievers. *Journal of Counseling Psychology,* 1970, *17,* 1–7.

Berger, P. L., & Berger, B. The blueing of America. *The New Republic,* 1971, *164* (14), 20–23.

Betz, R. L., Engle, K. B., & Mallinson, G. G. Perceptions of noncollege bound, vocationally oriented high school graduates. *Personnel and Guidance Journal,* 1969, *47,* 988–994.

Bird, D. *The case against college.* New York: McKay, 1975.

Blau, P. M., et al. Occupational choice: A conceptual framework. In D. G. Zytowski (Ed.), *Vocational behavior: Readings in theory and research.* New York: Holt, Rinehart and Winston, 1968.

Bloom, B. S. *Stability and change in human characteristics.* New York: Wiley, 1964.

Borow, H. Career development. In J. F. Adams (Ed.), *Understanding adolescence* (3rd ed.). Boston: Allyn and Bacon, 1976.

Brophy, J. E. Mothers as teachers of their own preschool children: The influence of socioeconomic status and task structure on teaching specificity. *Chld Development,* 1970, *41,* 79–94.

Caplow, T. *The sociology of work.* Minneapolis: University of Minnesota Press, 1954.

Cole, M., & Bruner, J. S. Cultural differences and inferences about psychological processes. *American Psychologist,* 1971, *26,* 867–876.

Crandall, V. C. Achievement behavior in young children. *Young Children,* 1964, *20,* 76–90.

Crandall, V. C., Katkovsky, W., & Crandall, V. J. Children's beliefs in their own control of reinforcements in intellectual-achievement situations. *Child Development,* 1965, *36,* 91–109.

Davis, J. A. *Great aspirations.* Chicago: Aldine, 1964.

DeVos, G. A. Achievement and innovation in culture and personality. In E. Norbeck, D. Price-Williams, & W. M. McCord (Eds.), *Personality: An interdisciplinary approach.* New York: Holt, Rinehart and Winston, 1968.

Douvan, E., & Adelson, J. *The adolescent experience.* New York: Wiley, 1966.

Educational Programs That Work. Washington, D.C.: Office of Education, Health, Education and Welfare, 1976.

Elton, C. F., & Rose, H. A. Male occupational constancy and change: Its prediction according to Holland's theory. *Journal of Counseling Psychology Monograph,* 1970, *17,* No. 6, Part 2.

Entwisle, D. R., & Greenberger, E. Adolescents' views of women's work role. *American Journal of Orthopsychiatry,* 1972, *42,* 648–656.

Erikson, E. H. *Childhood and society* (2nd ed.). New York: Norton, 1963.

Evans, E. D. *Contemporary influences in early childhood education* (rev. ed.). New York: Holt, Rinehart and Winston, 1975.

Evans, E. D. *The transition to teaching.* New York: Holt, Rinehart and Winston, 1976.

Feather, N. T., & Raphelson, A. C. Fear of success in Australian and American student groups: Motive or sex-role stereotype? *Journal of Personality,* 1974, *42,* 190–201.

Feldhusen, J. F., Thurston, J. R., & Benning, J. J. Longitudinal analysis of classroom behavior and school achievement. *Journal of Experimental Education,* 1970, *38,* 4–10.

Ford, R. N., & Borgatta, E. F. Satisfaction with the work itself. *Journal of Applied Psychology,* 1970, *54,* 128–134.

Freeman, R. B. *The overeducated American.* New York: Academic Press, 1975.

Getzels, J. W. On the transformation of values: A decade after Port Huron. *School Review,* 1972, *80,* 505–519.

Getzels, J. W. Socialization and education: A note on discontinuities. *Teachers College Record,* 1974, *76,* 218–225.

Ginzberg, E. *Occupational choice.* New York: Columbia University Press, 1951.

Ginzberg, E. Toward a theory of occupational choice. In R. Roth et al. (Eds.), *The psychology of vocational development.* Boston: Allyn and Bacon, 1970.

Gordon, E. W. Programs of compensatory education. In M. Deutsch, I. Katz, & A. Jensen (Eds.), *Social class, race, and psychological development.* New York: Holt, Rinehart and Winston, 1968.

Gottlieb, D. *Youth and the meaning of work.* Washington, D.C.: U.S. Government Printing Office, 1974.

Grabe, M. D. Peer priorities and the impact of academic achievement. *Contemporary Educational Psychology,* 1976, *1,* 314–318.

Grubb, W. N., & Lazerson, M. Vocational education in American schooling: Historical perspectives. *Inequality in Education,* 1974, *16,* 5–18.

Halverson, C., & Waldrop, M. Relations between preschool activity and aspects of intellectual and social behavior at age 7 1/2. *Developmental Psychology,* 1976, *12* (2), 107–112.

Hansen, L. S. New research in career education. *Phi Delta Kappa Newsletter,* 1977, *21* (5), 10.

Hanson, J. T., & Sander, D. L. Differential effects of individual and group counseling on realism of vocational choice. *Journal of Counseling Psychology,* 1973, *20,* 541–544.

Havighurst, R. J. Youth in exploration and man emergent. In H. Borow (Ed.), *Man in a world of work.* Boston: Houghton Mifflin, 1964.

Havighurst, R. J., & Gottlieb, D. Youth and the meaning of work. In R. J. Havighurst & P. H. Dreyer (Eds.), *Youth.* Chicago: University of Chicago Press, 1975.

Heckhausen, H. *The anatomy of achievement motivation.* New York: Academic Press, 1967.

Heilbrun, A. B., Jr., Piccola, G., & Kleemeier, C. Male sex-gender identification: A source of achievement deficit in college females. *Journal of Personality,* 1975, *43,* 678–692.

Henderson, R. W. Environmental predictors of academic performance of disadvantaged Mexican-American children. *Journal of Consulting and Clinical Psychology,* 1972, *38,* 297.

Hermans, H. J. M., ter Laak, J. J. F., & Maes, P. C. J. M. Achievement motivation and fear of failure in family and school. *Developmental Psychology,* 1972, *6,* 520–528.

Hodge, R. W., Siegel, P. M., and Rossi, P. H. Occupational prestige in the United States, 1925–1963. In D. G. Zytowski (Ed.), *Vocational behavior: Readings in theory and research.* New York: Holt, Rinehart and Winston, 1968.

Hoffman, L. W. Fear of success in males and females: 1965 and 1971. *Journal of Consulting and Clinical Psychology,* 1974, *42,* 353–358.

Holland, J. L. *Making vocational choices: A theory of careers.* Englewood Cliffs, N.J.: Prentice-Hall, 1973.

Hollander, J. Development of a realistic vocational choice. *Journal of Counseling Psychology,* 1967, *14,* 314–318.

Horner, M. S. *Sex differences in achievement motivation and performance in competitive and noncompetitive situations.* Unpublished Doctoral Dissertation, University of Michigan, Ann Arbor, 1968.

Horner, M. S. Toward an understanding of achievement-related conflicts in women. *Journal of Social Issues.* 1972, *28,* 157–176.

Jensen, A. R. Personalities and scholastic achievement in three ethnic groups. *British Journal of Educational Psychology,* 1973, *43,* 115–125.

Jepsen, D. A., & Dilley, J. S. Vocational decision-making models: A review and comparative analysis. *Review of Educational Research,* 1974, *44,* 331–349.

Johnson, R. H., & Myrick, R. D. MOLD: A new approach to career decision-making. *Vocational Guidance Quarterly,* 1972, *21,* 48–52.

Kagan, J., & Moss, H. *From birth to maturity.* New York: Wiley, 1962.

Kagan, S., & Zhan, G. Field dependence and the school achievement gap between Anglo-American and Mexican-American children. *Journal of Educational Psychology,* 1975, *67,* 643–650.

Kasl, S. V. Are there any promising biochemical correlates of achievement behavior and motivation? The evidence for serum uric acid and serum cholesterol. *Review of Educational Research,* 1974, *44*(4), 447–462.

Katz, M. A model of guidance for career decision-making. *Vocational Guidance Quarterly,* 1966, *15,* 2–10.

Kelly, D. H., & Pink, W. T. School commitment and student career flows. *Youth and Society,* 1971, *3*(2), 1971.

Kifer, E. Relationships between academic achievement and personality characteristics. *American Educational Research Journal,* 1975, *12*(2), 191–210.

King, F., et al. An investigation of the causal influence of trait and state anxiety on academic achievement. *Journal of Educational Psychology,* 1976, *68,* 330–334.

Kowitz, G. T., & Armstrong, C. M. Underachievement: Concept or artifact? *School and Society,* 1961, *89,* 347–349.

Krauss, P. E. *Yesterday's children: A longitudinal study of children from kindergarten into the adult years.* New York: Wiley, 1973.

Lavin, D. E. *The prediction of academic performance.* New York: Russell Sage, 1965.

Law, G. Strategies for change through career education. *Inequality in Education,* 1974, *16,* 37–49.

Lecht, L. A. Legislative priorities for vocational education. *Inequality in Education,* 1974, *16,* 19–27.

Lenney, E. Women's self-confidence in achievement settings. *Psychological Bulletin,* 1977, *84,* 1–13.

Luckey, E. B. The family: Perspectives on its role in development and choice. In E. L. Herr (Ed.), *Vocational guidance and human development.* Boston: Houghton Mifflin, 1974.

Madsen, M. C., & Kagan, S. Mother-directed achievement of children in two cultures. *Journal of Cross-Cultural Psychology,* 1973, *4,* 221–229.

Maehr, M. L. Culture and achievement motivation. *American Psychologist,* 1974, *29,* 887–896.

Maehr, M. L., & Sjogren, D. Atkinson's theory of achievement motivation: First step toward a theory of academic motivation? *Review of Educational Research,* 1971, *41,* 143–161.

Marland, S. *Career education.* Washington, D.C.: U.S. Government Printing Office, 1971.

McCandless, B. R. *Children: Behavior and development* (2nd ed.). New York: Holt, Rinehart and Winston, 1967.

McClelland, D. C. *The achieving society.* New York: Free Press, 1961.

McClelland, D. C. What are the effects of achievement motivation training in the schools. *Teachers College Record,* 1972, *74,* 129–145.

Mead, M. *Male and female.* New York: Morrow, 1949.

Medvene, A. M. Occupational choice of graduate students in psychology as a function of early parent-child interactions. *Journal of Counseling Psychology,* 1969, *16,* 385–389.

Miller, D., & Form, W. *Industrial society* (2nd ed.). New York: Harper & Row, 1964.

Miller, G. W. Factors in school achievement and social class. *Journal of Educational Psychology,* 1970, *61,* 260–269.

Munley, P. H. Erik Erikson's theory of psychosocial development and vocational behavior. *Journal of Counseling Psychology,* 1975, *22,* 314–319.

Nash, R. J., & Agne, R. M. Career education: Earning a living or living a life. *Phi Delta Kappan,* 1973, *54,* 373–377.

Nimnicht, G., & Johnson, J., Jr. (Eds.) *Beyond compensatory education.* Washington, D.C.: U.S. Government Printing Office, 1973.

Nord, W., Connelly, F., & Daignault, G. Locus of control and aptitude test scores as predictors of academic achievement. *Journal of Educational Psychology,* 1974, *66*(6), 956–961.

Nuttall, E. V., et al. The effects of family size, birth order, sibling separation and crowding on the academic achievement of boys and girls. *American Educational Research Journal,* 1976, *13,* 217–224.

O'Leary, V. E. Some attitudinal barriers to occupational aspirations in women. *Psychological Bulletin,* 1974, *81,* 809–826.

Ollendick, T. Level and n achievement and persistence behavior in children. *Developmental Psychology,* 1974, *10*(3), 457.

O'Shea, A. J. Low achievement syndrome among bright junior high boys. *Journal of Educational Research,* 1970, *63,* 257–262.

Osipow, S. H. *Theories of career development.* New York: Appleton, 1968.

Ottina, J. An introductory overview of career education. *Inequality in Education,* 1974, *16,* 35–36.

Palmer, F. *Symposium on early intervention.* Annual Meeting of the American Association for the Advancement of Science, Denver, Colorado, 1977.

Passow, A. H. Compensatory instructional intervention. In F. N. Kerlinger (Ed.), *Review of research in education* (vol. 2). Itasca Ill.: F. F. Peacock, 1974.

Phares, E. J. *Locus of control: A personality determinant of behavior.* Morristown, N.J.: General Learning Corporation, 1973.

Pietrofesa, J. J., & Splete, H. *Career development: Theory and research.* New York: Grune & Stratton, 1975.

Purkey, W. W. *Self-concept and school achievement.* Englewood Cliffs, N.J.: Prentice-Hall, 1970.

Puser, H. E., & McCandless, B. R. Socialization dimensions among inner-city five-year-olds and later school success: A follow-up. *Journal of Educational Psychology,* 1974, *66,* 284–290.

Ramirez, M., & Price-Williams, D. R. Achievement motivation in children of three ethnic groups in the United States. *Journal of Cross-Cultural Psychology,* 1976, *7,* 49–60.

Reich, C. *The greening of America.* New York: Random House, 1970.

Robinson, J. E., & Gray, J. L. Cognitive style as a variable in school learning. *Journal of Educational Psychology,* 1974, *66,* 793–799.

Roe, A. *Psychology of occupations.* New York: Wiley, 1956.

Rogers, D. (Ed.) *Issues in adolescent psychology.* New York: Appleton, 1969.

Romer, N. The motive to avoid success and its effects on performance in school-age males and females. *Developmental Psychology,* 1975, *11,* 689–699.

Ronan, W. W. Relative importance of job characteristics. *Journal of Applied Psychology,* 1970, *54,* 192–200.

Rosen, B. C., & D'Andrade, R. The psychosocial origins of achievement motivation. *Sociometry,* 1959, *22,* 185–218.

Rosenberg, M. *Occupations and values.* New York: Free Press, 1957.

Rotter, J. B. Generalized expectancies for internal vs external control of reinforcement. *Psychological Monographs,* 1966, *80*(1), No. 169.

Rutkowski, K., & Domino, G. Interrelationship of study skills and personality variables in college students. *Journal of Educational Psychology,* 1975, *67,* 784–789.

St. John, N. Thirty-six teachers: Their characteristics and outcomes for black and white pupils. *American Educational Research Journal,* 1971, *8,* 635–648.

Schultz, C. B., & Pomerantz, M. Some problems in the application of achievement motivation to education: The assessment of motive to succeed and probability of success. *Journal of Educational Psychology,* 1974, *66,* 599–608.

Shappell, D. L., & Hall, L. G. Perceptions of the world of work: Inner-city versus suburbia. *Journal of Counseling Psychology,* 1971, *18,* 55–59.

Shaw, M. C. Underachievement: Useful construct or misleading illusion? *Psychology in the Schools,* 1968, *5,* 41–46.

Shaw, M. C., & McCuen, J. T. The onset of academic underachievement in bright children. *Journal of Educational Psychology,* 1960, *51,* 103–108.

Slaughter, D. T. Parental potency and the achievements of inner-city black children. *American Journal of Orthopsychiatry,* 1970, *40,* 433–440.

Stein, A. H., & Bailey, M. M. The socialization of achievement orientation in females. *Psychological Bulletin,* 1973, *80,* 345–366.

Stennet, R. G., & Fienstra, H. J. Late bloomers: Fact or fancy? *Journal of Educational Research,* 1970, *63,* 344–346.

Super, D. E. *Career development: Self-concept theory.* Princeton, N.Y.: College Entrance Examination Board, 1963.

Super, D. E. A theory of vocational development. In R. Roth et al. (Eds.), *The psychology of vocational development.* Boston: Allyn and Bacon, 1970.

Tennyson, W. W. Career development. *Review of Educational Research,* 1968, *38,* 346–366.

Tolbert, E. L. *Counseling for career development.* Boston: Houghton Mifflin, 1974.

Tyler, R. (Ed.) *New roles for youth in the school and the community.* (Report of the National Commission on Resources for Youth) New York: Citation Press, 1974.

Wilson, G. C. *Report on Army personnel statistics. Washington Post,* October 18, 1976.

Wurtz, R. *Self-concept theory and career guidance.* Address delivered at American Personnel and Guidance Association Conference, New Orleans, 1974.

Yee, A. H. Source and direction of causal influence in teacher–pupil relationships. *Journal of Educational Psychology,* 1968, *59,* 275–282.

Zigler, E. Child care in the seventies. *Inequality in Education,* 1972, *13,* 17–28.

Zigler, E. F., & Child I. L. (Eds.) *Socialization and personality development.* Reading, Mass.: Addison-Wesley, 1973.

chapter 11

Moral development

Walter, at age 16, is a convicted murderer. Shortly after being apprehended by police while committing a fatal assault on a 12-year-old girl, he confessed to seven other senseless but premeditated killings. The facts of each case have been corroborated by careful homicide investigation. After formal charges were brought against him, Walter's case was tried in the juvenile court system of the large eastern state in which he lives. Found guilty, Walter is now in jail. He talks freely, even boasts about his deeds. He claims no guilt or remorse. Asked why he performed such deadly acts,

Walter has replied, "Nuthin' else to do." And asked how he felt during the act of murder itself he has said: "It's like an actor on stage—when the dude dies it's like watching a show—the best part!"

Some 1600 miles from Walter's jail cell lives Carla, age 15. The same day that Walter's case went to trial, Carla was riding a bicycle around the perimeter of a lake situated near her home. Two preschool boys playing tag around the entrance to a boat dock caught her eye. One boy tripped, fell off the dock, and quickly disappeared into the murky water. The second boy, apparently frightened, hid behind a tree. Though unable to swim, Carla dismounted from her bicycle and plunged into the water after the first boy. She surfaced once, coughing, only to submerge again after several gasps for breath. Suddenly and miraculously, Carla came up a second time pulling the child by his hair. Meanwhile, another alert passerby had wrenched a supple tree limb from a smaller tree near the water's edge. Using this as a lifeline, he pulled both Carla and the young boy to safety. Carla was cited by police for her altruism, but refused a monetary gift from the boy's parents on the grounds that a life saved was reward enough.

These true accounts are each unusual indications of differences in the value that apparently can be placed upon human life. For Walter, it is cavalier disregard, if not contempt. For Carla, it is supreme. One cannot help but wonder what factors in their psychological makeups predisposed them to behave as they did. Neither wonderment about their acts, nor the acts themselves, imply that Carla is steadfastly virtuous, or that Walter is hopelessly and forever immoral, across all of their life's activities. But we cannot easily dismiss the implications of such differences for the study of moral development.

Until recent times, the study of morality has been more a matter for philosophers and theologians than for psychologists. Preoccupied with pragmatism—what *is*—many psychologists have not concerned themselves with *oughts*, *shoulds*, or moral rights and wrongs. Science is an objective, hardheaded concern with facts, not values, they have said.

This position has now changed. As one authority put it: "The barbarities of the socially conforming members of the Nazi and the Stalinist systems and the hollow lives apparent in our own affluent society have made it painfully evident that adjustment to the group is no substitute for moral maturity" (Kohlberg, 1964, p. 383). The moral connotations of the Vietnam conflict, Watergate, corporate price-fixing, and the recent incidents of bribery by government and corporate officials for political and business favors have also done much to sensitize Americans to perplexing ethical questions. A growing number of psychologists have occupied themselves, constructively we think, with values and morality. Their thinking and research are our concern in this chapter. We begin by providing some necessary definitions and clarifying certain assumptions that provide a basis for studying morality from a psychological viewpoint. Developmental aspects of moral behavior are examined and a discussion of major social influences on moral development follows, with special attention to moral education in the schools. Chapter 11 concludes with some dilemmas in moral development and socialization. This chapter is based upon concepts and data about morality that reflect a Western view of human affairs and Western values favoring individualism and logic. What we say may not apply to other views or ways of thinking about the world and social organization.

DEFINITIONS

Morality and Moral Principles

We ordinarily think about morality as reasoning, feeling, and, ultimately, acting (and justifying one's actions) in accordance with moral rules or principles. Normally this involves an examination of and choice from among alternative principles. These principles or rules are designated *moral* because they concern how we *should* or *ought* to conduct ourselves according to enlightened self-interest and the interests of other people. A moral situation is encountered anytime the consequences of our acting (or failing to act) may affect the welfare of others and our own sense of self-esteem or respect. Moral decision making is marked by a capacity to rationally consider alternative courses of action and anticipate as far as possible both their short- and long-term consequences. For one scholar, moral decisions are distinctive because they concern "areas of life in which people typically, though not always, experience inner conflict between the desire to do what they believe they ought to do and the desire to do something else" (Beck, 1971, p. 28). Similarly, another scholar emphasizes decisions (choices) of principle— *oughts*—that are both universalizable and can be justified by moral goodness or rightness (Hare, 1964). "Universalizable" means that if we hold a given moral opinion about an act performed by one person (Walter's criminal assault on the young girl), we must apply that same opinion about similar acts performed by like persons in equivalent situations. In any case, for most moral philosophers, autonomous and freely determined moral thought is itself the essence of morality—not necessarily behaving unequivocally according to specific virtues. This distinction between a capacity and willingness for conscious moral reasoning on the one hand, and absolute virtue on the other, is extremely important for the forthcoming discussion about moral education.

This distinction, however critical, still says nothing about the source and nature of moral principles themselves. Here divergent views come into play. Different clues to the origins and qualities of moral principles have been offered by observers of human nature throughout history. For one, there is the absolutism of the Ten Commandments. Religion and humankind's relationship with deities have figured prominently, though not uniformly, in moral thinking. Francis Bacon once wrote, "All good moral philosophy is but a handmaiden to religion." Other clues suggest an intuitive process of drawing primordial moral insights from nature. William Wordsworth put it briefly, if vaguely: "One impulse from a vernal wood may teach you more of man, of moral evil and of good than all the sages can." Or, as Ernest Hemingway wryly asserted: "What is moral is what you feel good after and what is immoral is what you feel bad after."

Psychologists, like others, have struggled mightily with the problem of what constitutes moral maturity, a necessary task for conceptualizing goal states in moral development. To illustrate, one pair of psychologists has formulated four criteria or principles to assess the maturity of moral judgments: concern for the sanctity of the individual, concern for welfare of one's larger social community as a whole, capacity to see and reason about both sides of an issue, and judgments based upon the spirit, rather than the letter, of the law (Hogan & Dickstein, 1972). Such criteria probably cannot tell the whole story of moral maturity, but they are compatible with many of the higher-order principles professed as basic "goods" by individuals noted for their moral thinking (Table 11.1).

The values of justice and human dignity pervade these moral goods. But the issue here is twofold. First, what is the basis upon which we determine for ourselves the validity of moral values and principles? Second, how do we come to integrate such principles into our own thought and behavior? These are the questions that psychologists attempt to answer through scientific inquiry. In the process, it has become increasingly clear that morality itself has two faces that do not always fit harmoniously.

TABLE 11.1   Some Principles or Moral Goods Expressed by Thinkers about Morality

Be guided by the considered claims of prudence, temperance, courage, and justice (Greek-Aristotle)

Do justly, love mercy, and walk humbly with thy God (Judaic—Old Testament)

Do unto others as ye would have others do unto you (Christian—Jesus)

Act on a principle that thou canst will to be law universal (Categorical Imperative—Immanuel Kant)

Act so as to bring about the greatest happiness to the greatest number (Utilitarianism—John Stuart Mill)

As I would not be slave, I would not be master (American Political Creed—Abraham Lincoln)

Absolute morality is the regulation of conduct in such a way that pain shall not be inflicted (Philosophy of Evolution—Herbert Spencer)

That line of action is alone justice which does not harm either party to a dispute (Hindu—Gandhi)

It is best to do to others what will strengthen you even as it will strengthen them, that is, what will develop their best potentials even as it develops your own (Principle of Mutuality—Erik Erikson).

Two Faces of Morality

First, and more important in the long run, morality is the development, formulation, and expression of intentions or conscience that are internal and that focus a person's outlook on life. Morality also involves the direct representation of a person's personal construction of social values. Second, and sometimes more pressing than the first face, each of us must assume objective obligations and responsibilities to our community and to the order of things in our society. The first face of our morality, our intentions or conscience, forces us to judge our personal society. As we know, the norms of some societies are false or evil, and the highest morality is to reject and combat them.

Behind the second face of morality, adherence to social norms and responsibilities, also lie human values. The first face is the values themselves. If we decide to abide by the norms of the group within which we live, we are implicitly agreeing that conformity to its norms makes possible the realization of values that lie behind them. We must then go still further and analyze the values and decide whether they are themselves sound.

This abstract matter can perhaps be clarified by example. Some years ago, in the 1950s, we knew a young man, Gary we shall call him, who was a prominent political and social campus leader. He was president of both the student council at his university and of a prestigious campus residential social club for males. Gary was thoughtful and principled. He did battle for civil rights, for full social and political rights for commuting students, for freedom of press for the campus newspaper, for student rights (and responsibilities), for the evaluation of faculty instruction, and for other issues that were indicators of high principles.

One night after a dance, Gary, his date, and some of his fellow club members and their dates, all under 21, were found drinking and engaging in sexual activities in a local motel. Penalties for these students would be set by the student council and the administration. Possibilities ranged from expulsion to forfeit of a certain number of academic credits. Gary—persuasive, articulate, and well respected by the university authorities—was in a good position to help his friends (and himself) because of his student council role. His friends put heavy pressure on him to use his influence in their behalf.

His personal representation of the first face of morality in our definition was that under no circumstances did one use an elected office for personal gain or for the special interests of any group, including his own social group. His representation of the second face of morality was that campus social clubs are good things, that they promote social development, that loyalty to friends is important, and that he was indeed close friends with the others who were in trouble. Driven by this conflict of principles to analyze the values behind his club, he came to the conclusion that for his group these values were close to personal self-gain, pleasure-seeking, and a loyalty to individuals that suggested gang psychology. Gary finally concluded that such values were less worthwhile than his principled dedication to the democratic process that had put him into the presidency of the student council. Reluctantly, Gary resigned from both his club and the student council (the latter resignation was not accepted) and worked with council and the administration on appropriate penalties for his and his friends' behavior (penalties that proved to be mild).

This example helps us to see the importance of reciprocity in human morality: I see your point of view, I honor it and respect it, and I facilitate it so long as the integrity of others is not destroyed in my so doing. I also respect custom and law, but, ultimately, my orientation is "to conscience as a directing agent and to mutual respect and trust" (Kohlberg, 1966, p. 7). In other words, reciprocity is essential if the value of human dignity is to be achieved. Together with a concern for equality and the welfare of others, reciprocity also provides the basis for *justice*, a moral principle that many believe is universally valid (Kohlberg, 1968). This principle itself poses a moral issue inherent in the example of Gary and his friends. Is it "just" for an educational institution to claim the right to control or sanction sexuality among consenting people?

To conclude, it is both simple and accurate to speak of these two faces of morality as the ethics of *personal conscience* and *social responsibility*, respectively (Hogan, 1970; 1975). A balance, or "golden mean," between the two faces, however difficult to establish, is perhaps the most complete state of moral maturity. If I act exclusively on personal and moral intuitions I may too often overlook the rights and privileges of others in the social collective. If I take my dictates for moral action strictly from social convention, contract, or law, I may fail to see how such dictates may unjustly affect a given individual. Mature moral development and behavior, then, can easily represent a persistent tug-of-war between these two ethics.

Different Assumptions About Morality

Having sketched out some major points of definition, we can now delve more deeply into the complexities of moral development. For centuries scholars have debated humankind's basic morality. Historically as well as currently, there are three major ways in which morality is construed, or assumptions on which its definitions are based (Hoffman, 1970). First, there is the conception of *original sin*, the "killer-ape" view of man. Evil begets evil. Second, there is the notion of *innate goodness*, the "fallen-angel" view of man, which sees humans as inherently pure, though corruptible. And third, there is the *tabula-rasa*, or blank-tablet, viewpoint. Nothing has been written on this tablet; beginning with infancy, humans are infinitely malleable.

At one time or another the major monotheistic religions, Christian, Islamic, and Judaic, have embraced the notion of original sin. Classical psychoanalytic theory, first mentioned in Chapter 9, also embodies this concept. Human personality structure is determined originally by basic instincts to seek pleasure and avoid pain. Moral chaos would result from such indulgent gratification unless it is checked. A counterforce, the conscience, is necessary to counteract the expression of these powerful biological drives (see Appendix A).

Humanists from Rousseau onward seem to embrace the fallen-angel point of view. Given the chance to grow freely, humans will seek to realize themselves and will move toward self-fulfillment and the constructive. Many modern cognitive-developmental psychologists, including Piaget, fit well into the fallen-angel school.

Learning theorists, including behaviorists, are more often tabula-rasa theorists. Their view of the nature of man is empirical and neutral. As earlier stated, behaviorists have traditionally shied away from making value judgments. Such judgments are inevitable, however, if one seeks to apply learning principles to modify behavior in practical settings, whether homes, classrooms, or prisons.

Those who embrace the original-sin view and those who take the tabula-rasa view are both likely to endorse active training and teaching programs for both the cognitive and the moral development of children. The original-sin people believe such training in morality is essential "to keep the beast in check." The tabula-rasa people consider teaching and training essential so that the end product of development is a person who functions usefully in society. Both the original-sin and the learning theorists, in other words, depend heavily on learning (arranged experiences) as major shapers of the end social product. This is as true for sex typing and sex identification (Chapter 9), as for cognitive development (Chapters 8 and 10) and moral behavior, as we see in this chapter.

Those who assume the innate goodness of man, on the other hand, place their faith in keeping "hands off"—in unarranged experiences. Rousseau advocated simply letting *Emile* grow naturally until puberty. Such thinkers as Piaget and his American disciples see moral development (like cognitive development) as a function of maturation within a context of general age-related experience. Humans act on their environment and the natural environment acts on them. They take from it what they need and what is suitable, and mature in accord with this interaction of biological development and learning. Those who take this view have little confidence in teaching either cognitive or moral development. They do not consider the environment unimportant. They know that a malign or unduly circumscribed environment can distort or retard either moral or cognitive development, but they argue that an artificially enriched or accelerated environment will accomplish little.

We wish to emphasize that moral development, like other streams of development, is both product and process. As a product within a democratic society, satisfactory moral development is thought to include several basic characteristics such as conformity within sensible limits to the social conventions of right and wrong behavior, impulse inhibition or self-control of human desires, a capacity for experiencing guilt, a perception of authority as rational, and reciprocity or consideration of others which may extend to acting for the benefit of others (as did Carla) (Hoffman, 1970; Staub, 1975). Given the personal-liability basis for America's legal system, such development will also include an acceptance of responsibility for one's own actions. The reader will recognize that the presumed product of moral development is a combination of thinking (cognition, reasoning, judging), feeling (affect), and acting (overt behavior). We turn to the process of moral development to examine, in turn, the cognitive, affective, and behavioral components of morality (Kohlberg, 1964; Adkins, Payne, & O'Malley, 1974). Each component has become the focus of particular theories in psychology. Moral thinking and judgment have attracted psychologists with a cognitive-developmental bent (Chapter 8). Emotional underpinnings of morality have long been the point of interest among psychoanalytic theorists. And behaviorists, in particular, have concerned themselves with the principles that govern moral conduct.

DEVELOPMENTAL CONSIDERATIONS

Cognitive Component of Morality

Psychologists with a cognitive-developmental bent, beginning with Piaget (Chapter 8), have led in studying the knowing and thinking component of morality. As in the study of intelligence, these psychologists generally view moral development as a series of qualitatively distinct stages of moral reasoning or judgment. The acquisition and progressive refinement by children of concepts of rules and justice and their reasons for making decisions that may affect the rights and property of others are the central concerns. As in the cognitive-developmental view of intelligence, several forces are said to work in combination to sustain the pattern of change through time: maturation, equilibration, and massed age-related experience, especially reciprocal social interaction with peers.

The Piagetian Viewpoint

Piaget's conception of moral development is based largely upon the study of children's play (specifically, how they conform to, develop, and may change the rules for their games) and clinical interviews with children about naughty deeds and their consequences. A typical Piagetian interview, for example, would involve presenting a young child with a pair of stories and asking for an explanation about why the story character's behavior may be wrong and why one act may be more wrong than another:

Story A: "There was a little boy named Peter. His father had gone out and Peter thought it would be fun to play with his father's ink-pot. First, Peter played with the pen, then he spilled some ink which made a little blot on the tablecloth."

Story B: "A little boy who was called Paul once noticed that his father's ink-pot was empty. One day when his father was away Paul thought of filling the ink-pot, to help his father, so that his father would find it full when arriving home after work. But while Paul was opening the ink-bottle, he tipped it over. The ink spilled out and made a big blot on the tablecloth."

Most children respond by saying that both boys were "wrong" because they shouldn't touch father's ink-pot. If they go further to say that Paul was especially wrong because he made a *big* spot on the tablecloth, their moral judgments presumably are influenced by the outcome of a misdeed, rather than the intention. In contrast, when children begin to differentiate intent in making moral judgments, distinguishing among pure accidents with no intent to disobey, carelessness, conscious efforts to harm persons or property, and good intentions gone wrong (as Paul's), they are said to have reached a more mature level of morality.

Piaget's description of moral development is more complex, however. It begins with a recognition of young children's egocentrism. Until about school age, they are unable to see anyone else's view and thus assume that all points of view are the same—like theirs. During this period of development children operate in terms of *moral realism.* This means that children believe that all rules are sacred and unalterable. Morality is *heteronomous,* determined totally by external powers, such as parents or other authorities. Things are seen as either black or white. Justice, especially any retribution for wrongdoing, is *imminent;* if one behaves badly, then something bad will happen — an accident or an inescapable, arbitrary punishment. For example, suppose Elizabeth disobeys her mother by refusing to clean up after play, then later falls and skins her knee. According to Piaget, the knee skinning will be perceived by young children as an inevitable punishment that results from the act of disobedience.

Later in the elementary school years, Piaget claims there is an important shift from moral realism to *moral relativism.* Laws are no longer seen as sacred and immutable, but as social arrangements that come about through reciprocal agreements and that are for the good of all those affected by them. Thus, rules are modifiable by human needs, including social change. Morality becomes *autonomous.* Motives are accounted for in making judgments about right and wrong. Children can take the role of another and view an event from other's perspectives, not just their own. In short, advanced cognitive development enables children to become more morally mature.

Despite the methodological imperfections in Piaget's strategy for gathering data from children (see, for example, Armsby, 1971), his major predictions about age changes in moral judgment have been fairly well supported by data from several different cultures. Those supported by the strongest evidence are regular changes with age in the following:

1. *Intentionality.* That is, acts are judged not so much according to their consequences as by the intention the person had. For example, the older child will regard it as worse to break a cup while stealing a cookie from the cupboard than to break a dozen by accidentally bumping into the tea cart. The younger child will judge the latter act, which destroyed more, as the worse of the two.

2. *Relativism in judgment.* The older child considers behavior in its context, the younger child in terms of absolute right and wrong.

3. *Independence of sanctions.* The older child behaves properly because of his own decision, the younger child because of fear of punishment or retribution.

4. *Use of punishment as restitution and reform.* Punishment should be meted in the form that makes up for the harm done or that helps the individual to learn to be better in the future.

5. *Use of reciprocity.* The points of view and the needs of others are taken into account in moral judgment and action.

6. *Naturalistic views of misfortune.* Ills that befall oneself and others are not necessarily the result of bad behavior, but occur for any one of a number of realistic reasons.

Piaget's overview of the development of moral judgment is not as rich in detail as may be necessary for a thorough understanding of morality. But his work has contributed toward this end in at least three important ways (Rest, 1974a). First, Piaget has clarified the domain of morality for psychological study as "those aspects of human experience and functioning that pertain to the rules of cooperation, to social arrangements whereby the interests and welfare of individuals are reciprocally interrelated in terms of obligation and rights" (Rest, 1974a, p. 64). Second, Piaget has documented some important qualitative differences in the moral thinking of younger and older children. Growth proceeds toward a more rational and comprehensive system of concepts and principles for processing information about human motivation and conduct in the moral realm. And third, Piaget's use of the *methode clinique*, with ingenious stories and tactics for probing and analyzing children's thought, has provided a new dimension to the study of morality.

The Kohlbergian Viewpoint

Following Piaget's lead, others have explored more deeply, and with adolescents and adults, the complexities of moral reasoning. Notable among these explorers is the influential Harvard cognitivist, Lawrence Kohlberg. Based on a relatively small number of studies. Kohlberg has advanced a developmental theory of children and youth as moral philosophers. His method, similar to Piaget's, involves a series of complex, hypothetical moral dilemmas about stealing, mercy killings, and the like. Interview data obtained largely from pre-adolescents, adolescents, and young adults have been analyzed to reveal certain important characteristics of moral thinking that are more differentiated than Piaget's heteronomy—autonomy distinction. In fact, Kohlberg's data are arranged in a sequential-stage model that parallels concrete and formal operational thought (Chapter 8). Specifically, three levels of morality are postulated, each with two stages, for a total of six stages (see Table 11.2). Kohlberg argues that these levels emerge successively from premorality, an early stage in which the child does not comprehend "goodness" or "badness" according to rules or authority.

Within level I, the "preconventional" level, are two kinds of primitive morality, each representing progressive stages of moral development. Stage 1 is the *punishment-and-obedience orientation*, typical of very young children. Conformity, for example, is largely a function of avoiding punishment: "I should not hit my baby sister because I will get spanked!" Gradually, if moral development proceeds on course, this stage is abandoned for stage 2, called by Kohlberg *naive instrumental hedonism*. At this stage the child (or individual) behaves "morally" to obtain rewards, to have his or her own favors returned, to store up "brownie points," and the like. The orientation is egocentric; no real insight about the broader bases for human moral behavior is shown. Children may express concern for what is "fair," but typically this is done in a self-serving way.

Level II morality, the "conventional" level, also has two stages. Stage 3 is conceived in terms of *interpersonal concordance*, or the "good boy and nice girl" orientation. Moral behavior in this stage is good behavior if it pleases other people, helps them, or results in their approval. We can think of this as a morality of social reinforcement. Conformity to stereotypes or to majority opinion is typical of this stage, presumably because it is the "thing to do." From this extrinsic orientation emerges stage 4, or the *law-and-order orientation*. Again, conformity is very strong, but apparently out of respect for authority, the absolute worth of fixed rules, and preservation of the social order. A person may argue, for example, that stealing is wrong because "It's against the law," or, "It is one's duty to obey society's rules." In a sense this is similar to stage 1 behavior, because the person conforms to avoid being censured by authorities. But stage 4 conformity is also motivated by a desire to avoid the guilt or shame that may occur if one fails to abide by accepted rights and duties.

"Postconventional" morality—level III—is marked by the support of moral prin-

TABLE 11.2 Summary of Kohlberg's Stages of Moral Development

Level and Stage	Content of Stage		Social Perspective of Stage
	What Is Right	*Reasons for Doing Right*	
LEVEL I— PRECONVENTIONAL Stage 1—Heteronomous Morality	To avoid breaking rules backed by punishment, obedience for its own sake, and avoiding physical damage to persons and property.	Avoidance of punishment, and the superior power of authorities.	*Egocentric point of view.* Doesn't consider the interests of others or recognize that they differ from the actor's; doesn't relate two points of view. Actions are considered physically rather than in terms of psychological interests of others. Confusion of authority's perspective with one's own.
Stage 2—Individualism, Instrumental Purpose, and Exchange	Following rules only when it is to someone's immediate interest; acting to meet one's own interests and needs and letting others do the same. Right is also what's fair, what's an equal exchange, a deal, an agreement.	To serve one's own needs or interests in a world where you have to recognize that other people have their interests, too.	*Concrete individualistic perspective.* Aware that everybody has his own interest to pursue and these conflict, so that right is relative (in the concrete individualistic sense).
LEVEL II— CONVENTIONAL Stage 3—Mutual Interpersonal Expectations, Relationships, and Interpersonal Conformity	Living up to what is expected by people close to you or what people generally expect of people in your role as son, brother, friend, etc. "Being good" is important and means having good motives, showing concern about others. It also means keeping mutual relationships, such as trust, loyalty, respect and gratitude.	The need to be a good person in your own eyes and those of others. Your caring for others. Belief in the Golden Rule. Desire to maintain rules and authority which support stereotypical good behavior.	*Perspective of the individual in relationships with other individuals.* Aware of shared feelings, agreements, and expectations which take primacy over individual interests. Relates points of view through the concrete Golden Rule, putting yourself in the other guy's shoes. Does not yet consider generalized system perspective.
Stage 4—Social System and Conscience	Fulfilling the actual duties to which you have agreed. Laws are to be upheld except in extreme cases where they conflict with other fixed social duties. Right is also contributing to society, the group, or institution.	To keep the institution going as a whole, to avoid the breakdown in the system "if everyone did it," or the imperative of conscience to meet one's defined obligations. (Easily confused with Stage 3 belief in rules and authority; see text.)	*Differentiates societal point of view from interpersonal agreement or motives.* Takes the point of view of the system that defines roles and rules. Considers individual relations in terms of place in the system.

TABLE 11.2   (continued)

Level and Stage	Content of Stage		Social Perspective of Stage
	What Is Right	*Reasons for Doing Right*	
LEVEL III—POST-CONVENTIONAL, or PRINCIPLED Stage 5—Social Contract or Utility and Individual Rights	Being aware that people hold a variety of values and opinions, that most values and rules are relative to your group. These relative rules should usually be upheld, however, in the interest of impartiality and because they are the social contract. Some nonrelative values and rights like *life* and *liberty,* however, must be upheld in any society and regardless of majority opinion.	A sense of obligation to law because of one's social contract to make and abide by laws for the welfare of all and for the protection of all people's rights. A feeling of contractual commitment, freely entered upon, to family, friendship, trust, and work obligations. Concern that laws and duties be based on rational calculation of overall utility, "the greatest good for the greatest number."	*Prior-to-society perspective.* Perspective of a rational individual aware of values and rights prior to social attachments and contracts. Integrates perspectives by formal mechanisms of agreement, contract, objective impartiality, and due process. Considers moral and legal points of view; recognizes that they sometimes conflict and finds it difficult to integrate them.
Stage 6—Universal Ethical Principles	Following self-chosen ethical principles. Particular laws or social agreements are usually valid because they rest on such principles. When laws violate these principles, one acts in accordance with the principle. Principles are universal principles of justice: the equality of human rights and respect for the dignity of human beings as individual persons.	The belief as a rational person in the validity of universal moral principles, and a sense of personal commitment to them.	*Perspective of a moral point of view* from which social arrangements derive. Perspective is that of any rational individual recognizing the nature of morality or the fact that persons are ends in themselves and must be treated as such.

From moral stages and moralization: the cognitive-developmental approach by Laurence Kohlberg in *Moral development and behavior: Theory, research, and social issues,* edited by Thomas Liekona. Copyright © 1976 by Holt, Rinehart and Winston. Reprinted by permission of Holt, Rinehart and Winston.

ciples whose truth and worth are essentially independent of any authority, including persons in positions of power who hold them and the individual's personal association with these authorities (or groups). Stage 5, the first stage of moral judgment and behavior within this level, is defined as the *social contract and legalistic orientation.* Persons at this stage of development consider their contracts with others as morally binding.

Moral action is viewed in relation to individual rights and standards for behavior that have been achieved by critical discussion and consensus with society. An individual accepts and abides by democratically accepted law. Conformity is less a matter of avoiding legal sanctions than it is that of avoiding the loss of respect of impartial observers who judge behavior in terms of community welfare. Agreements between people, formalized legally or not, are considered obligatory. Even the law, however, is not considered forever absolute; it can be changed through rational means in the interest of social utility.

The final and most advanced stage in moral development (level III) is stage 6—the *universal-ethical-principle orientation*. At this pinnacle in moral development, abstract and ethical principles (for example, the golden rule) are taken as indications of universal morality. They are "self-chosen" in the sense that individuals select principles to guide their behavior that consistently and logically represent their belief in the sacred nature of human life and the ultimate value of respect for the individual. Conformity to these principles occurs to avoid self-condemnation: "I could not live with myself if I did (such and such)." Hence a form of judgmental behavior rendered by personal conscience rather than social convention and laws is typical of stage 6.

Having defined these progressive stages, Kohlberg further maintains that: (1) these levels and stages of moral development are strongly cognitively determined; (2) each is a unique emergent from the one preceding it, in that it is qualitatively different; (3) the sequence of moral development is invariant and goes on from the first through the sixth stages (although not all and perhaps not many people reach stage 6, or even stage 5); (4) the developmental process is similar in all cultures (although it may not go as high in some cultures as in others); (5) a greater consistency between one's moral beliefs and actual behavior in situations involving moral conflict will occur at higher stages of development (especially stage 6); (6) moral development is irreversible; and (7) each stage is unitary (that is, in all areas of morality, the individual will judge—and tend to behave—according to the general principles or beliefs of that stage (Kohlberg,

1968; Kohlberg & Turiel, 1971). The reader will recognize how similar these ideas are to the general underlying principles of the cognitive-developmental view of intellectual development (Chapter 8).

Research generated by Kohlberg's original contentions has supported the general features of this stage-sequence model more often than not. Logic, of course, leads us to predict that moral judgment should be closely related to both intelligence and chronological age. Firm evidence shows that older and more intelligent children are more advanced in their moral reasoning than are younger and less intelligent ones (Rest, 1974a). And the progression of developmental change, as determined by comprehension of successive stage reasoning, does proceed upward, but with some tendencies for children to show occasional regression (Holstein, 1976; Kuhn, 1976). Children reportedly will *prefer* levels of reasoning higher (vs lower) than their own, although their comprehension of advanced moral principles quickly wanes beyond the next higher level (Rest, Turiel, & Kohlberg, 1969). There are also strong indications that moral maturity requires the development of role-taking skills (perspectivism) and, eventually, the ability for formal operational thinking (postconventional morality) (Moir, 1974; Tomlinson-Keasey & Keasey, 1974). Taken together, these data point consistently to the importance of cognitive-intellectual ability in the development of moral thinking.

But Kohlberg, like all theorists, is not without his critics (Aron, 1977; Gibbs, 1977; Kurtines & Greif, 1974). These criticisms fall into several related categories. One charge is that Kohlberg's claim of universality is ethnocentric or culturally biased, and other equally valid conceptions of moral maturity are not accounted for by his scheme. A second criticism alleges methodological problems, including weaknesses in Kohlberg's cumbersome and difficult to score interview technique. A third set of criticisms questions the limited data base for the theory itself. It is argued, for example, that Kohlberg and his followers have generalized about cultural universality far too widely from a small number of studies. Nor have the actual data from these studies always been presented for public inspection. Finally, the explanatory power of the theory has also been challenged on several grounds: a weakness in accounting for individual differences in moral development, ambiguity about the mechanisms that facilitate stage transition, unproved assumptions that if people are stimulated to reason "maturely" about moral problems they will naturally embrace principles of justice, and so on.

Interested readers may seek the details of such criticisms. Meanwhile, pending further validation research, we believe it is premature to offer a final verdict about the stage-sequence model. It does, however, seem a plausible approximation of developmental trends in moral thinking. The theory is useful as well for thinking about "moral education." At present, perhaps the greatest hazard of the theory is how easily it can be misused, especially for simplistically labeling children and youth (and adults!) as one or another "stage-thinker" (Aron, 1977).

One final issue about the Kohlberg theory is that the entire stage-sequence description of moral judgment has been formed from the study of what children and youth *say* about abstract stories of moral conflict involving fictional people. This leads us to ask: As children and youth increase in their moral judgment maturity do they also *behave* more morally? Data about the moral-judgment–moral-action relationship are neither extensive nor strongly positive. As the

reader can appreciate, it is extremely difficult even to gather data about real-life moral conduct, much less correlate it with elaborate interview protocols from large numbers of young people. There is some evidence to suggest lower levels of moral reasoning among chronic delinquents, higher levels among principled student activists, and modest positive relationships between children's moral reasoning scores and their moral conduct as perceived by others (peers, teachers) (Rest, 1974a). In addition to these modest relationships, supporters of the theory strongly maintain that when individuals reach postconventional morality, they tend to behave more consistently with their moral principles (Kohlberg & Turiel, 1971). All youth and adults surveyed, however, apparently do not reach this most advanced stage of principled morality. Estimates about the percentage of consistent stage 6 thinkers will, of course, vary with age (Kohlberg, 1975; Kurtines & Greif, 1974). We would expect no such thinking during childhood. By age 16, only about 7 percent of individuals studied have shown principled thinking. Among college age and adult subjects the percentage rises. But the incidence of stage 6 thinking is still less than 20 percent, even among subjects who are fully capable of formal operational thought. Such figures may be partly an artifact of measurement; higher percentages of advanced moral thinkers are reported when different assessment procedures are used (Rest, 1976).

However incomplete is the cognitive-developmental picture of moral development, it has certain important distinctive characteristics (Kohlberg, 1975):

1. Moral development consists of age-linked sequential reorganizations in moral attitudes and reasoning.

2. Major aspects of moral development are culturally universal.

3. Moral principles are viewed as structures that arise through the experience of social interaction with others.

4. Motivation for morality is activated by universal human concerns about acceptance, competence, and self-esteem.

5. The extent of environmental influences is determined by the general quality of cognitive and social stimulation over time.

It follows that the structures of moral development will provide a basis for thinking uniformly about moral problems at a high level of generality. But is morality really a unitary characteristic of human beings? There is room for doubt about this. For example, people often seem to apply different principles in their business and professional lives from those they use in their relations with their spouses, sweethearts, children, and friends. The pressure of urban evening traffic can devastate the moral behavior of usually high-principled men and women, as can extreme internal and external stresses of all sorts. The Kohlberg view of morality demands that individuals have full information about issues concerning them to behave in the ways demanded by moral development stages 5 and 6. Is it humanly possible to be well informed about all the issues that demand our moral commitment? Perhaps it is more realistic to think that our level of moral judgment and behavior will vary not only according to the pressures and temptations in our current situation but also according to our available information.

Thus, it can be argued that individuals are likely to both judge and behave at different moral levels. This would mean that humans typically will perform specific discriminative moral behaviors depending on the situation rather than act according to a unitary, universal, generalized moral process. A *capacity* for mature moral reasoning, then, may

be a necessary, but insufficient, condition for principled moral conduct. And a cognitive-intellectual analysis of moral reasoning does not provide much insight about the *feeling* component of morality. To what extent can the psychological study of affect and morality help us form a more complete picture of moral development?

Affective Component of Morality

We can begin our answer to this question by identifying three feeling states that figure strongly in moral development. These are *guilt* (moral anxiety), *empathy* (first discussed in Chapter 2), and *trust*. Partly because complex human emotions are so difficult to measure consistently and accurately we again are somewhat limited in our scientific knowledge about them. Under laboratory conditions, certain physiological measures of emotional response are possible (the well-known "lie detector" procedure in police science). But psychologists must frequently resort to verbal self-report measures of affect. This usually involves some form of questioning that requires children to report their feelings or how they think other people are feeling in familiar situations. Obviously, this requires that children be able to recognize (or recall) and put into words their various emotions—not an easy task even for adults. Despite such methodological limitations we have learned some important things about emotion and moral development, especially guilt and empathy. (It can be argued that trust is as much a belief or expectancy as a feeling state, but we include it in this section for reasons stated below.)

Guilt

Guilt is usually defined as self-criticism and remorse following a transgression or violation of a standard for behavior to which a child or youth feels obligated to conform (Ausubel, 1955; Hoffman, 1970). In effect, then, guilt is self-inflicted punishment, a form of psychic pain. Though experienced consciously, guilt is not something that can be easily controlled, turned on or off like water from a tap. Instead, given certain conditions of learning, guilt seems to occur automatically, although of an intensity varying with how severe a misdeed is in relation to the strength of the value that has been violated. The importance of guilt for morality is that it eventually becomes *anticipatory*. That is, "twinges" of self-reproach can precede a contemplated transgression, or one may begin to anticipate the negative affect that would follow a wrong act. To avoid self-reproach and remorse is to guide one's behavior in accordance with accepted values or standards. Even the thought of violating a moral standard may trigger a guilt response. Guilt thus serves an important self-regulatory function.

The matter of a balance between too little or too much guilt, however, is delicate. Little or no guilt would suggest that a person is not under control by internal sanctions. Rather, externally-based sanctions, as in fear of detection, punishment, or social rejection, would be required. In their absence (or disregarding them when present) and unrestrained by internalized moral principles, an amoral, if not immoral, pattern of behavior could easily develop. On the other hand, excessive or chronic guilt may result in extreme self-control and asceticism, at the expense of spontaneity and general well-being. Guilt has long been recognized as a breeding ground for neurosis, for example. Thus the issue concerns too much or too little of a good thing. In its most positive sense, guilt is a warning signal for our "sense of accountability" or "moral obligation." It helps us to curb hedonistic or irresponsible desires whose expression could bring harm to other people.

How does guilt develop? No one knows for sure, although it is plausible to suggest several important requisite conditions before guilt can serve a self-regulatory function (Ausubel, 1955). First, children must have a capacity for experiencing psychic pain. In its most rudimentary form, this pain may take the form of a child's general apprehensiveness or insecurity from disapproval by parents or significant others for having violated an important moral rule. Second, children must themselves come to accept moral values and resolve to abide by them. Third, they must develop a sufficient ability to recognize any discrepancy between their behavior and that which is consistent with internalized moral values.

The processes by which children come to internalize and behave in accordance with moral values are debatable. Many psychologists believe in the power of identification, discussed in Chapter 9. From the psychoanalytic perspective, satisfactory psychosexual and moral development, including guilt reactions, go hand in hand. An overwhelmingly important condition for both aspects of development is the same-sex parent, although ultimately both parents affect moral identification. This identification occurs in about the same way as gender identification. It represents the incorporation of parental standards as one's own, in the form of the *superego*, or superself. Out of the pattern of parental rewards for good behavior, children are said to develop a view of the ideal self. From experiences with punishment for bad behavior the conscience develops. Together, the ego ideal and conscience act as a moral watchdog, as it were. In view of the strong role accorded to identification models by psychoanalytic thinkers, it follows that the quality of children's moral development will depend largely on the degree to which their parents and others important to them are moral.

Many learning theorists take a more straightforward view of guilt. Rather than postulate such personality structures as the superego, they prefer to explain guilt in terms of conditioning (Chapter 2) and to explain conformity to moral values in terms of imitation learning and reinforcement, including vicarious reinforcement. In the final analysis it is mostly a matter of applying the vocabulary of learning psychology to moral development (see, for example, Hill, 1960; Eysenck, 1960).

But this is not to overlook cognition. Indeed, it seems probable that conditioning and punishment learning work in some way to associate guilt or "moral anxiety" with certain internal monitors for behavior (Aronfreed, 1976). We can only guess about the nature of these internal monitors, but their net effect is self-criticism and regulation. Again, self-criticism presumably will have a strong basis in feeling, but it also requires a cognitive awareness of rights and wrongs, or standards of desired behavior. Just what the appropriate "mix" of affect and cognition is and how it develops to produce moral behavior are among the most basic questions in developmental psychology.

In any case, developmentally speaking there is little evidence to indicate the presence of guilt feelings in many children much before age 4 or 5, and perhaps even later. To establish this, we must rely upon certain behavioral indicators such as children's critical self-references, seeking to confess wrongdoing, and adult's inferences about guilt in the children they know. As the daughter of the senior author, then age 5, said some few minutes after throwing an unpunished tantrum and threatening to "tear up the house": "Daddy (sobbing), I'm sorry! I feel so bad to myself!"

Measuring guilt is somewhat easier, but not necessarily more valid and reliable, in older children and youth. There

are few data about developmental trends beyond the elementary school years. Wide-ranging individual differences in professed guilt, however, are clearly evident throughout adolescence and beyond. Yet there is some question about the generality of guilt among individual children and youth. Many psychologists have assumed that guilt is unitary, that is, if I am high in guilt in one area (such as sexuality) I will be high in other areas as well (such as authority relationships and work responsibilities). This seems not to be the case and has prompted some authorities (for example, Adkins, Payne, & O'Malley, 1974) to wonder if guilt is really an important determinant of moral behavior. Our own subjective and clinical experience tells us otherwise, but we must admit the empirical basis for the guilt–moral-behavior relationship is inconsistent. While we encourage more lucid insights into this relationship, we say with assurance that guilt is only part of the affective story about morality. There is still the important matter of empathy.

Empathy

In simplest language, empathy means "feeling with someone else." If we are moved to tears by the tears of another, we empathize. If we are pleased to the point of experiencing a warm, visceral glow when good things happen to someone else, we are again empathetic. Empathy has been defined more technically as the "involuntary, sometimes forceful experiencing of another's emotional state—elicited either by expressive cues that directly reflect the other's feelings or by other kinds of cues that convey the affective impact of external events on him or her" (Hoffman, 1975a, p. 138).

Though our opening examples were of sadness and happiness, most research about empathy and its role in moral situations has involved distress. An empathic reaction to another person's misfortune, discomfort, or pain is thought to provide a basis (motive) for aiding that person. Aiding and other forms of action to benefit others are called *prosocial behavior*. As discussed in the next section, prosocial behavior may occur for reasons other than empathy. For the time being, however, we concentrate exclusively upon the development of the empathetic response.

As with guilt, we cannot say with absolute confidence exactly how empathy develops, but we have reason to believe that classical conditioning is a primary mechanism. Pleasant (unpleasant) affect that accompanies our gratifying (painful) past sensory experiences is elicited by content as delight (distress) cues from another person similar to those associated with the observer's own experiences (Hoffman, 1975a). To illustrate, Lonnie may fall from a swing, cut his head, and cry. Later, he may see his sister, Donna, fall and cry. The sound of the cry, the sight of blood, or other distress signals from Donna that are reminiscent of Lonnie's own earlier painful experience now evoke some degree of the agony (or at least a memory of it) that occurred initially in his fall.

Some theorists (such as Sullivan, 1963) place the origins of empathy in early infancy. That is, empathy is said to bridge the emotional communication between the nurturing caregiver and the nursling. It does seem logical to think that empathic development will be better aided by early kindliness toward and soothing gratification of the infant than, say, rude handling or neglect. Possibly the attachment process works in this way (see Chaper 3), but empathy probably develops only gradually from infancy onward.

Psychologists who study empathic development do not wholeheartedly agree about the conditions for empathy. In general, however, the data indicate three developmental requisites (Feshbach & Roe, 1968; Hoffman, 1975a; Selman, 1971). One, of course, is an initial capacity for emotional responsiveness. A second, as suggested above, is previous experience with affects that are empathized. To this extent, empathy may be facilitated by wide-ranging emotional experiences, including hardship. As one psychologist (Allport, 1961) has observed, some degree of experience with social rejection, discrimination, and even persecution may provide an emotional underlay for empathic tolerance and understanding. This is not to argue for programmed hardship, but it does suggest that role playing for both positive and negative social-emotional experiences may contribute in important ways to empathic responsiveness. And a third requisite is development of a cognitive sense of others, to include eventually the ability to take their roles or perspectives.

This third requisite itself shows a developmental sequence, beginning with a firm awareness of others as existing separately from oneself at about age 11 or 12 months (person permanence). During the preschool and certainly by the early school years children overcome their egocentrism and clearly distinguish their thoughts, perceptions, and feelings from those of other people. They show an ability to take the role of another in immediate situations that may involve feeling states in response to a variety of cognitive and verbal cues. Still later, beginning perhaps as early as middle childhood, children may think both about themselves and others beyond immediate situations into the future or other projected situations. At this point, they can begin to *anticipate* the feelings of others based upon a more complete concept of total life experience, their own and that of others. In effect, this may provide the basis of consideration of others that we consider so necessary in mature morality. Cognitive factors, including the ability to discriminate and comprehend emotional states, are thus crucial in the development of empathy.

Indications of empathy can be observed in rudimentary form very early in life. Megan, age 2, seeing a bandage on her mother's finger, patted her, saying, "Poor Mommy!" But with age, empathic responses become more differentiated and "pure." As with guilt, individual differences in empathic behavior are clear by school age. Girls often show stronger empathy than boys, and there is some indication that the greater the similarity between observer and person being observed, the more likely is empathic arousal. Thus, children may empathize more with peers of their same sex and race than otherwise (Feshbach & Roe, 1968). All told, we admit that the psychological study of empathy is itself in a rather primitive stage of development. To our knowledge, however, no one denies the significance of empathy for moral development.

Trust

We emphasize the affective dimension of trust because of the strong sense of well-being and security that defines a condition of trust. Trust can also be seen as a cornerstone for healthy psychological adjustment. Moral maturity would seem difficult, if not impossible, under conditions of psychopathological development. But it is accurate also to think about trust, especially interpersonal trust, as an *expectancy* or generalized belief that we can rely upon the word or promise of others (Katz & Rotter, 1969). Whatever the romantic emphasis we place on trust, it seems both important for any conception of moral development and closely tied to empathy as discussed above.

Among the strongest proponents of trust as a foundation for healthy personality development is Erik Erikson (1963).

According to his thought, our basic tendency to be optimistic and trusting as contrasted with cynical and mistrusting is learned during the first year or two of life. The basic condition for trust development is consistently acceptant, benevolent, and responsive parental care. Again, the learning process involved is probably classical conditioning. Trust is automatically learned from repeated pairings of comfort and relief (ministered by friendly and loving caregivers) with signals of distress made by infants. When they cry, someone soon comes to relieve their distress. When hungry, they are promptly fed. They are spared arbitrary separations and abandonments. When curious, they are introduced to the stimuli that elicited their attention, and these stimuli are found not to be hurtful. From such treatment, a general propensity arises to the effect that the world is basically safe and people are generally good.

As the reader will recall, and if Erikson is correct, learning to trust occurs during the developmental period that Piaget calls the sensorimotor stage (see Chapter 8). Babies exposed (with regard to their safety and comfort) to more and more complex stimuli and situations that demand problem-solving skills indeed become "masters of the thing." They learn to deal autonomously with their physical world. Trust and competence, then, may well be closely linked, with one feeding the other in a benign cycle. It is easy to see that overprotective parents, themselves likely to be mistrusting, lead their children to mistrust themselves (that is, their "radar" tells them their caregivers do not think they can cope). Their behavior also leads to mistrust of their environment, which, because of the behavior of those who look after them, they come to see as dangerous and unpredictable. Neglect, unpredictability, and rejection by caregivers would seem logically to produce the same result, as would sharp restriction of freedom for the children to explore the world around them.

"Blind" and realistic trust must be distinguished. We know that there are many situations in which children and youth (and adults) can be taken advantage of if they place their absolute trust in a manipulative other. On the other hand, persons of all ages seem to receive more reward, and live more comfortably, if they are basically trusting. An open, friendly, confident social approach typically elicits similar behavior from others. We like to think that trust begets trust. And a world in which trust is not valued as the basis for social and economic relationships would be threatening and unpleasant. Anxiety and trust probably are linked, although there is no firm evidence to support the link. It seems logical that highly anxious people will be less trusting, both of themselves and of others, than less anxious people. The relations between trust and dependency may well be complex. Do dependent individuals trust others but not themselves? Do excessively independent persons trust only themselves, and not others?

In sum, the present evidence — not altogether firm — suggests that moral development will involve some mix of affects that establish a generalized orientation toward others and basic self-regulatory functions. We have discussed this mix in terms of guilt, empathy, and trust. But just as it is not enough to reason or make intellectual judgments about moral situations, neither is it enough simply to feel about them. Ultimately, our general pattern of moral conduct must be considered. Thus we now turn to the behavioral component of morality.

Behavioral Component of Morality

We have stressed decision and choice in moral development. Buttressed by affect, decision and choice will often mean actively responding in situations so as to implement a moral principle, such as working to achieve human rights for an oppressed minority. At other times it will mean choosing not to act where to do so would be to violate a moral value. Thus, we all have many opportunities to lie, steal, and cheat others, but usually (if not always) choose not to. Either way, volition is assumed to be involved. In this section we discuss three behavior patterns that are expressed volitionally, though in childhood they seem more subject to external than internal controls. The first is impulse control or resistance to temptation; a choice not to succumb to self-serving enticements that have moral connotations. A second behavior pattern is altruism — sharing, giving, donating, or otherwise aiding others for their benefit. And the third is cooperation — in one sense a form of altruistic behavior, but in a broader sense working jointly with others for mutual benefit while emphasizing fairness to all participants.

Resistance to Temptation

The longstanding interest by psychologists in the development of individual differences in children's resistance-to-temptation behavior perhaps reflects their traditional "thou shalt not" approach to morality. This is apparent in Freud's work, for example, where resistance to temptation is considered a principal indicator of moral identification. We would expect to see some relationship between this indicator and guilt, as discussed earlier. Evidence on this point is not extensive, although moderately positive correlations between guilt measures and children's self-inhibition behavior in contrived laboratory settings have been reported (Hoffman, 1970). A typical procedure has children perform dull or boring tasks in the presence of various temptations (attractive, but "prohibited" play toys, or another person's unattended candy that could, but "should not" be eaten). An unseen observer then records whether the child deviates (performs a forbidden act), and if so, how quickly. Children who do not deviate, or who deviate only after an extended period of time, are judged stronger in their resistance to temptation. Similarly, the temptation to resist cheating for self-aggrandizement may be measured by a "peeping" test. Children are asked to make "correct" notations on a paper-and-pencil task, but with their eyes closed. A high score is possible only by looking, and thus affirms cheating.

Using these and other measures, psychologists have observed wide-ranging individual differences in children's resistance-to-temptation behavior as early as age 5 and throughout the ensuing school years (Sears, Rau, & Alpert, 1965). Some children seem never to deviate, or if they do, only after a long period of conformity. Others deviate quickly. These children also show different responses after their deviant acts. Some, usually those who resist longer, will show remorse or apologize, freely confessing their "sins." Others seemingly keep their feelings bottled up or otherwise refuse to admit their deviation (even to the point of lying about it). And still others will attempt to project the "blame" onto someone or something else.

It is logical to presume that children's home experiences dispose them to these different behaviors. Unfortunately, reports about how childrearing practices and resistance to temptation may be related are often ambiguous and contradictory. Clearer are findings from laboratory study about the relationship of mild punishment to deviation behavior. In general, differences in resistance-to-temptation behavior are associated with three conditions (Adkins, Payne, &

O'Malley, 1974; Aronfreed, 1976; Fry, 1975). One is threat of punishment (warnings about the negative consequences of "misbehavior") or actual punishment if deviation occurs (verbal rebuke, sounding a loud aversive buzzer, flashing a red light). A punishing stimulus seems most effective if presented in the early stages of transgression. A second condition is the use of rational, organized appeals to reason. Children who are given understandable reasons in advance why they should not deviate are less likely to do so. A third condition is children's general mood state. Children who are helped to think happy thoughts seem less likely to deviate than those whose mood reflects sadness and unpleasant thoughts.

As indicated in Chapter 2, both punishment and cognitive appeals may interact with children's chronological age. In general, cognitively-oriented controls (providing good reasons for not deviating) seem more effective with older (age 7 or 8 and beyond) than younger (kindergarten age and below) children. Punishment, if strong and quickly administered, can be effective with younger children under conditions of low cognitive appeal, but relatively ineffective when rational appeals are stressed. It all becomes quite complex. But then few serious students of development will expect simple prescriptions about modifying the behavior of so intricate an organism as the human being. At any rate, children's age-related ability to comprehend adult prohibitions is a significant variable in self-control (Adkins, Payne, & O'Malley, 1974; Parke, 1974).

Just as punishment and reasoning may affect impulse control, so does the behavior of models whom children observe in laboratory settings. Summarizing the research about modeling impact, one authority (Hoffman, 1970) has noted that deviant models can quickly disinhibit children's impulse expression. That is, given the opportunity to watch someone else violate a prohibition, especially if there are positive consequences (or no negative consequences) for doing so, most young children will follow the leader. Where a model resists, children may behave likewise, but not as consistently and perhaps only where strongly positive vicarious reinforcement is experienced (the model is seen being rewarded for good behavior with attractive incentives). And the consistency of a model's word and deed is also extremely important. For example, models who pay lip service to resistance, but then deviate, may be speedily imitated. Actions, it would seem, speak louder than words.

We cannot say whether findings about self-control or its lack in laboratory conditions can be generalized to the natural settings in which children grow and develop. But these findings at least suggest clues or hypotheses about what *may* work in the home, classroom, or play group. There is a further question about the extent to which children's capacity for resistance to temptation takes form in behavior *consistently* from one setting to another (Adkins, Payne, & O'Malley, 1974). "To what extent will children who resist or deviate in one moral situation tend to behave similarly in other moral situations?"

The answer to this question is equivocal. There is some evidence to suggest that consistency in situational moral behavior increases with age, especially as the ability for advanced moral reasoning develops. At the same time experimental research suggests that impulse control *does* fluctuate to some degree. This depends not only on children's past learning histories, but also on their perceptions of the situation, including other persons who may be present and any existing reinforcement contingencies. In the language of learning psychology (Chapter 2), moral development—especially self-control—can be viewed as the process (and result) of

progressive discrimination learning where judgments become finer and finer and responses are differentially reinforced. Consequently, the kind of specific learning experiences and opportunities that a child has will largely account for moral development as conceived by behaviorists. At the risk of oversimplification, an "immoral" person would most likely be viewed as one for whom the reinforcements for immoral behavior are greater or more consistent than are reinforcements for "moral" behavior.

Yet learning theorists seem rarely to talk about something as general as the "moral" person. Rather, they talk about responses within specific situations along a continuum of morality as defined by society. For example, a given husband or wife may be the model of fidelity in their home community and therefore moral in that setting. Yet, the same husband or wife may engage in extramarital affairs while traveling alone on business trips. Many people (including the person's spouse) would likely label this extramarital behavior as immoral. From an S-R learning viewpoint, these two situations, home and travel, may represent quite different cues and reinforcement contingencies that govern the class of responses involved in fidelity. However sensible this interpretation, it may be fallacious to suggest an extreme either-or dichotomy about moral behavior, that is, a general trait vs a situationally specific set of responses. The issue stands clear, however, and accentuates the need for still further and more sophisticated research about moral behavior.

Altruism

Altruism is most broadly defined as behavior carried out for the benefit of another (Rushton, 1976). Strictly speaking, however, "genuine" altruism is beneficence in the absence of anticipated or expected rewards, reciprocal favors, or social pressure (acting to avoid the disapproval of others). At issue, then, is motivation or intention in helping behavior. We distinguish between *expedient* altruism and what might be called *intrinsic* altruism. Much of what appears as "altruism" may simply reflect social conformity or a desire to reap certain rewards for oneself by behaving kindly toward others. Expedient altruism may also represent nothing more than a means of escaping social sanctions or punishments that may result from selfish or antisocial behavior. In contrast, intrinsic altruism occurs in the absence of external rewards or obvious personal gain. One may even give up valued personal possessions or privileges for the benefit of others without the slightest expectation of reciprocal behavior. Thus, intrinsic altruism is non-self-centered behavior, even though a feeling of satisfaction for acting altruistically may occur.

It is often difficult to discriminate between these two forms of altruism at the surface level of behavior. Even in carefully controlled laboratory studies of altruism, psychologists usually must rely upon careful inference about the motive states underlying such behavior. To sharpen their inferences, laboratory psychologists have largely confined themselves to the study of two types of altruistic behavior: rescue and donation (Bryan, 1975). In rescue situations, children are confronted with an "emergency" where they are led to believe that another person (unseen and unknown to them) is hurt or in distress. In such situations, children *do* something to assist a person in need. Rescue behavior is thus measured by the form and speed of an attempted helping response. In a typical donation situation, children are given options of giving away certain prizes or goodies they have acquired by playing games. They usually are left alone in the presence of a box intended as a receptacle for a gift to a needy other. The quantity of material contributed then serves as the index of altruism. Children in this type of situation must give up something they want for charity. Still other approaches to measure altruism (Rushton, 1976) include ratings of how considerate children may be of others in competitive game situations; teacher and peer sociometric techniques (see Chapter 4), and naturalistic observation of children's sharing and helping behavior. Experimental methods to study rescue and donation, however, have provided the greatest amount of information about altruistic behavior.

Based upon these methods, what do we know about children and youth as Good Samaritans? Rudimentary forms of sharing may occur in children as early as age 2, but altruism seems to increase only slightly during the preschool years (Hartup, 1970). From kindergarten onward, sharing behavior increases markedly. It probably parallels the cognitive development that results in decline of egocentrism and increased emotional development, independence, and widened experience, particularly the cognitive development that enables the child to receive satisfaction from helping others and from sympathizing and sharing with them. Children of 13 and 14 years are able to show selfless behavior, including the appreciation of points of view of others, nearly as well as college-aged young adults (Fry, 1967); these young adolescents are much more like college-aged students than they are like 9- and 10-year-olds. This trend also seems to parallel children's growth in understanding certain norms or values, such as social responsibility (one *should* help dependent others) and equality of resource distribution (a variation on the theme of justice).

Age and rescue behavior are also positively correlated from the late preschool to the preadolescent years. Some studies, however, have noted a sharp decline in helping behavior after this time (for example, Staub, 1970). Others (such as Yarrow & Waxler, 1976) report no consistent age–prosocial-helpfulness relationship. Thus the developmental trend for sharing is clearer than that for helping. Possibly, older children are more subject to conflict between the value of social responsibility and other strongly held and widely-shared values in America, such as competitive achievement and independence. Conflict, or opposing patterns of motivation, may lead to less predictable behavior. But the broader question concerns the generality of altruistic behaviors. Like resistance to temptation, altruism will vary according to situational factors and may not reflect a general moral trait or characteristic. It is simply too early to tell given the available research data.

Sex differences in altruism are infrequently observed, but when they are, the advantage goes to girls. Though not completely understood, these sex differences may result from girls' more frequent experiences with nurturant and helpful adults and the traditional emphasis upon girl's "appropriate" sex role behaviors: expressivity, sensitivity, and sympathetic responses (Bryan, 1975). Even so, extremely powerful modeling effects on children's altruism in contrived settings have been observed for both boys and girls. Both the amount and direction of altruism are affected by models. Again, as in so many other areas of behavior development, certain model characteristics (such as nurturance and power) and the consequences of a model's pronouncements in support of the desired behavior work together to increase the probability of imitation by children (Staub, 1975). In general, it would appear that models who are competent in demonstrating helpfulness, verbalize the importance of personal re-

sponsibility, and express positive affect at having acted altruistically have the potential to make a real difference in children's altruistic tendencies. Even so, children obviously must have ample opportunity to practice their altruism. And we are still unclear about the point at which expedient and intrinsic altruism diverge, with the latter coming to dominate the moral dimension of human interaction. A strong case can be made, however, for empathy as the motive state out of which intrinsic altruism and sympathy for others gradually evolve (Hoffman, 1975a). If so, an ability to empathize can be considered as prerequisite to intrinsic altruism. Until children become truly allocentric (other-centered) in their perspective we may not expect to see much selfless sharing and helping. That children share toys and other objects with others as early as the second year of life without prompting, guidance, or praise, however, is striking testimony to the prosocial nature or capacity of even very young human beings (Rheingold, Hay, & West, 1976).

Cooperation

Cooperation, like altruism, is an important behavioral component in moral development. Piaget, for example, conceives of autonomous morality as a morality of cooperation or reciprocity (Piaget, 1932/1948). As we have seen, when this stage of moral development is reached, children no longer view rules as rigid and unchangeable, but rather as set up and maintained by reciprocal social agreements. Thus, rules become subject to modification according to human needs and changing situations. Cooperation, then, may be one aspect of moral relativism.

Cooperation includes an element of altruism: "I will give up some of my prerogatives for doing things my way and grant you the opportunity to do them your way." But cooperation differs to the extent that it is tinged with enlightened self-interest: "If we work together, we will get done what I want (which happens also to be what you want). Working alone, neither of us can accomplish our aims." Thus cooperation is both constructively adaptive and a means for compromising conflicting viewpoints and desires for the welfare of all concerned. Its importance for the efficient workings of democratic society can hardly be overemphasized.

Cooperation probably begins in infancy. Its first manifestations may be during the dressing operation, when the baby learns to move his body so that diapers may be more easily pinned or arms more easily inserted into sleeves. The most successful toilet training appears to be an instance of parent–child cooperation, with each accommodating to the other. More mature forms of cooperation are developed through children's play (see Chapter 4). Our best evidence, however, is that efficient and completely successful cooperation in working for common goals is not common among children before ages 4–6 years (Cook & Stingle, 1974). This is not surprising, given the level of problem-solving ability and communication skills required in most cooperative activities. According to some reports (Meister, 1956), however, patterns of cooperation at these ages, and perhaps until about age 11 or 12, are usually based upon authority hierarchies. That is, one child may become more dominant than the other(s) in determining what tasks are to be done, how they will be done, and who will do them to reach a goal. Divisions of labor by mutual negotiation, where participants consider themselves equals, come later in the elementary school years. Even then, if children believe that any forthcoming rewards for "cooperation" may be based upon individual, rather than a collective team effort, com-

petitiveness may occur at the expense of group progress. In fact, faced with a choice between cooperative and competitive responses, American children seem more often to show competitive action as they grow older. This is somewhat more likely for boys than girls, although the data about sex differences are far from consistent. Racial, ethnic, and social class comparisons have also yielded ambiguous results. Crystal clear, however, is the finding that greater peer-group cohesiveness, friendliness, and productivity result from cooperative action when goal structures are arranged to foster such interdependence (Hartup, 1970).

In American society, there is an uneasy compromise between cooperation and competition. Traditionally, we are a competitive society. Of necessity, we are an interdependent society, and interdependence demands cooperation. That this does not come easily for American children (or adults) was illustrated in the discussion of cooperation and the peer group in Chapter 4. Children in other societies often seem to be more harmoniously cooperative and less self-destructively competitive than children in United States society. The distinction between bureaucratic and entrepreneurial families has already been discussed. To review, breadwinners—family heads —in bureaucratic families are employed in multilayered institutions, such as large, stockholder-owned companies, school systems, and agencies of the government. Entrepreneurial families are in business or in practice for themselves and must thus be more ruggedly self-sufficient and competitive. One study indicates that early adolescents (boys, in this case) from bureaucratic families incorporate more of the ethic of cooperation and reciprocity than adolescents from entrepreneurial families (Berkowitz & Friedman, 1967).

It has also been shown (see Chapter

4) that cooperative behavior is learned and its frequency sharply increases when significant adults model it, then give reinforcement when it occurs. We have also seen that cooperativeness is associated with leadership and popularity, and thus has implications for self-esteem and other kinds of learning that occur in social interactions.

It seems logical that cooperativeness and trust are closely related. To cooperate with other persons, we must be able to trust them. The greater the degree of our trust, the more frequently we choose to coexist, or be interdependent, or cooperate. Competence is also related to cooperation since we are more likely to cooperate with those whom we believe know what they are doing than with those whom we believe are inept. Competence can be more subtly tied to cooperative, socially constructive behavior. One trio of authors worked therapeutically with 15- to 17-year-old institutionalized delinquent boys (Shore, Massimo, & Ricks, 1965). Their treatment was an academically oriented therapy, in which they tried to increase the boys' academic competence while giving them generous response-independent reinforcement. It was found that as the boys' academic skills improved, their self-esteem grew. With improvement in self-esteem, the boys' attitudes to authority also improved and their behavior (with particular reference to cooperativeness) became more acceptable. This change came in an orderly sequence: first improvement in competence, then in self-esteem, then in attitudes to authority—and finally, and only then, improvement in behavior.

It seems clear that the principles for developing cooperation are about the same as those for developing any other kind of social behavior: appropriate models, clear instructions, opportunity to practice, and rewards for cooperating. But we agree with others (such as Cook & Stingle, 1974) that United States cul-

ture may suffer from a "cooperation deficiency." A strong emphasis upon individualism and competitive achievement in United States homes, schools, and businesses may come at the expense of opportunities for learning and participating in satisfying cooperative activity with others. Perhaps an ethic of enlightened self-interest and social responsibility should be more strongly emphasized in the American socialization process. Both altruism and cooperation seem more likely to occur if children and youth are helped to see that what is good for them is also good for their neighbors.

Concluding Remarks

We have considered several cognitive, affective, and behavioral aspects of human development that fit, in one way or another, a general conception of morality. But these various components cannot be fitted together easily or neatly. Their interrelations are complex and not altogether consistent. We have noted the difficulty in validating a *general* trait of morality. And it is clear that situational factors affect morality. Yet moral judgment, affect, and conduct do seem sufficiently interdependent to support the principle that all aspects of development interact. Studies (Hoffman, 1975c; LaVoie, 1974; Rubin & Schneider, 1973) show moral judgment, empathy, and altruism to be positively correlated across different situations. Certain learning conditions, especially contact with models, also are consistently associated with patterns of moral conduct (Hoffman, 1975b).

It would be nice to advance a master framework or model for an accurate synthesis of the many facets of morality. One theorist, for example, virtually equates moral development with ego (self) development. That is, moral development, interpersonal development, and the development of self-concept and inner life are thought to proceed together as a single, integrated structure (Loevinger, 1975). Another theorist prefers to think about an integration of character structure — our general orientation toward the social rules that presumably govern our behavior (Hogan, 1975). This viewpoint conceptualizes character structure in terms of five distinguishable dimensions:

1. *Moral knowledge:* knowledge of relevant social rules, including values that enable moral judgments.

2. *Moral positivism and moral intuitionism:* a set of attitudes about how different kinds of rules should be used for regulating social affairs. Positivism concerns utilitarian ethics (law as an instrument of social reform and serving the common good). Intuitionism, in contrast, places emphasis upon what a given person perceives as good or right with lesser regard for established norms and conventions.

3. *Socialization:* the extent to which rules and values of one's reference group(s) are internalized, that is, accepted as personally obligatory and binding.

4. *Empathy:* the capacity and willingness to behave in accordance with the needs and expectations of others, whether or not they correspond with the social rules.

5. *Autonomy:* the capacity to decide moral matters independently from social or peer group pressures and the dictates of authority.

Morality viewed as character structure in this way is obviously both a matter of degree and subject to many differing combinations. Thorough moral knowledge and ethics of responsibility, with high socialization, empathy, and autonomy, are said to comprise moral maturity. High socialization and autonomy, but low empathy, would define a strict, harsh, Old Testament moralist. In contrast, low empathy and socialization in concert with high autonomy would produce a stubborn, commanding, zealous reprobate. This five-dimensional model possibly comes as close as any to portraying the multifaceted nature of moral development, though it is somewhat ambiguous about the precise nature of moral *reasoning*. However, it implies that failure to attend to any one dimension of character structure is to fall short of the ideal moral maturity. And it is natural to question the extent to which social influences affect the course of this complex interplay of personality dimensions.

MAJOR SOCIAL INFLUENCES

The study of social influences on moral development has concentrated on parental socialization techniques, including affectional relationships, modeling, application of parental controls, and the use of such influence techniques as reasoning and induction (Jessor, 1975). The relationships of these parent-controlled variables to the affective and behavioral components of morality are somewhat clearer than they are to the moral judgment component. We begin with the most secure generalizations about socialization influences, comment briefly on peer-group contributions, and then refer to data about school and the mass media.

Parenting

Most studies about parental childrearing practices and children's moral development are correlational, so we cannot make direct cause–effect statements on the subject. However, the correlational studies have shown a fairly reliable or consistent pattern of relationship between what parents do, or say they do, and the level of their children's morality. Among the most reliable of these patterns is the apparent outcome of power assertion versus nonpower assertion (Hoffman, 1970; 1975c). As indicated in Chapter 3, power-assertive parents manage their children by force, physical or emotional, even to the point of abusing their children. A less obvious and somewhat different form of power assertion is love-withdrawal, a punitive technique, in the same way that power assertion is usually punitive. In love withdrawal, however, anger is more controlled, the variables are more psychological than physical or emotional, and the time span is indefinite. For example, children usually know that if they are to be spanked (power assertion), it will be done and over with. But they may have no idea when love withdrawal will end—in an hour, in a week, or, as with one mother and her adolescent son we know, in five years. Power assertion ordinarily ends positive interaction between parent and child while it is going on, but it endures for only a short period. Depending on the parent and the child and on how forgiving each is, positive parent–child interaction may be resumed almost immediately after a spanking, for example. Love withdrawal also ends parent–child interaction (positive or negative) for its duration, and its duration is indefinite.

There is no conclusive research evidence about the effects of love-withdrawal techniques on moral development, though a clear negative relationship is reported between more explicit power assertion and such development (Hoffman, 1970). What seems most impressive, however, is the growing number of studies that support a positive relationship between *induction* techniques and morality, including altruism, guilt, and resistance to temptation (for example, Hoffman, 1975b, c; Leizer & Rogers, 1974).

Induction means reasoning. It is a democratic way to deal with moral behavior, and it may be self-oriented or other-oriented. In *self-oriented induction*, one may say "Don't cheat because sooner or later you will be caught in your own deception, and cheating keeps you from learning what you are supposed to." In *other-oriented* (victim-centered) *induction*, the child or youth is told, "Don't pull the puppy's tail, it will hurt him," or "Say thank you because Mrs. Smith's feelings will be hurt if she thinks you don't appreciate what she did for you." Victim-centered induction includes parental encouragement of children's reparation or restitution when appropriate, assisting children to make thoughtful apologies, and showing concern for the feelings of one against whom their children have harmed. Other things being equal, other-oriented induction is logically more conducive than self-oriented induction to promoting moral development, since it is levied against egocentrism. It also seems likely that other-oriented induction techniques are more effective in developing empathy (feeling with others).

Finally, when rule infraction does occur, but a parent believes some punishment should follow, it may be important not to "punish first and ask questions later." This idea may be especially important for older children and youth whose understanding of fairness and ability to express their side of the story should be respected. One study, for example, suggests that mothers who investigate the circumstances of their adolescent son's misbehavior fairly and completely *before* a punishment is selected, may be more effective in promoting mature self-control among these boys than are mothers who impulsively "shoot from the hip" (LaVoie & Looft, 1973).

Cutting across these different ways

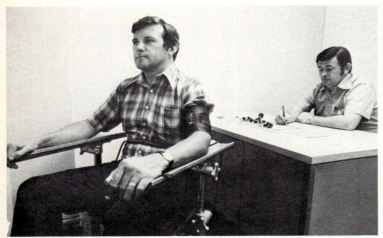

© 1971, Arthur Sirdofsky

Michael Weisbr

Ford Foundation

Michael Weisbrot

Michael Weisbrot

Michael Weisbrot

© 1969, Lawrence Frank, from Black Star

parents rear their children is the variable of affection. Affection is less likely to accompany power-assertive techniques than non–power-assertive techniques of childrearing, but there is much individual variation. Some parents who use much physical discipline, for example, are also loving; and some equalitarian, induction-technique parents are rather withdrawn and impersonal with their children. There are also social class differences: economically disadvantaged and poor parents are more likely to be power-assertive than better-educated and more affluent parents. On the whole, however, rational discipline in a context of a nurturant parent–child relationship seems important for moral development, especially in boys. And, as we saw in Chapter 3, this general pattern is also associated with children's growth in autonomy or instrumental competence.

Nurturance, praise-giving, and firm standards for behavior may provide much of the desired climate for growth in moral judgment (Fodor, 1973). Comparatively few studies of direct parent influences on moral reasoning have yet been done. The limited data do, however, suggest some interesting relationships between parents' and children's levels of moral reasoning. Again, and for unknown reasons, the relationships are more clear for parents and their sons, as compared to daughters (Holstein, 1976; Haan, Langer, & Kohlberg, 1976). Moreover, both male delinquents and their mothers have demonstrated lower moral levels than comparably intelligent mothers and their nondelinquent sons (Hudgins & Prentice, 1973). There is some hint of evidence that mothers may change their form of moral reasoning as children get older, to better stimulate the offsprings' thinking about moral matters (Denney & Duffy, 1974). In general, however, the extent of parental impact on children's moral reasoning is still an open research question.

In sum, even though social science research data must be viewed tentatively, we can speak with some assurance about the likelihood of ill effects of power assertion and the likely positive outcomes of induction in a nurturant setting. A disciplinary approach based upon high power-assertive tactics by parents is associated more with children's fear of external detection and punishment, much less with an autonomous, self-regulated moral orientation. Parental help in anticipating and assessing the consequences of the child's behavior upon others seems a common ingredient in the development of moral maturity. In addition, recent laboratory studies suggest the importance on moral development of modeling cooperation and altruistic acts, promoting direct and vicarious reinforcement for self-control, training children to verbalize the positive consequences of nontransgression, and providing wide-ranging opportunities for role taking (Kanfer & Zich, 1974; Staub, 1975). To these have been added further suggestions: reciprocal communication with children and youth (to include dialogue about moral dilemmas and conflict resolution); helping children become self-confident and skilled about helping others; encouraging introspection among children about the reasons they do or do not conduct themselves in a moral manner (self-understanding); and swift disapproval for actions that are morally wrong, followed by a crisp explanation of why the actions are wrong. In real life, "some power assertion may be needed for the voice of reason to be heard" (Hoffman, 1970, p. 341).

No set of guidelines, however firm their empirical support, can guarantee moral development. Parents, however skilled in their implementation, are only one influence in children's moral development. Children and youth may respond well or ill to even the best-intentioned parents. In short, individuals themselves contribute to their own moral development. And, of course, the moral climate beyond the home must be considered, including the peer group and the schools.

Peer Influences

The data about peers and morality mostly have involved the role of peer interaction in fostering advanced moral judgment. Long ago, Piaget suggested that interactions with peers are prime sources of the disequilibriums that result in moral growth. Young children are morally absolutist—in a stage of objective morality. In this stage, they have a one-way respect for authority and believe that rules are sacred and unchangeable. Their rules are likely to be derived from uncritical acceptance of what their parents or other caregivers have laid down for them as being right and proper. But expanding social interaction with peers can, in many ways, serve the leveling function described in Chapter 4. Children may discover many exceptions to their parent's moral rules within their peer-group activities. For children to be accepted in their peer group (a crucial condition for social development), they usually must move away from a one-way conception of rules toward reciprocity. Other persons must be respected and sometimes given way to. Only then will they respect you and sometimes give way to you. For successfully socialized children and youth, mutual respect emerges from this necessary reciprocity, much of which is learned in games. The child eventually learns that moral rules and laws are themselves products of group agreement. Since rules and laws are derived from group agreement, they are subject to change and, as such, require analysis, thought, and action.

A number of predictions can be made from such a theory, among them that children who are leaders within their peer group will be more successful in learning mutually respectful reciprocity than nonleaders, because of the centrality of the formers' group roles. This learned reciprocity will result in, and perhaps cause a higher level of, moral development among boys and girls who show high leadership than among those low in leadership. One thoroughgoing study of fifth- and sixth-grade children clearly supports this prediction: the children's stage of moral reasoning was positively related to the quantity and quality of their social participation (school clubs, friendship circles, leadership roles) whether judged by teachers, peers, or themselves (Keasey, 1971). Further evidence suggests that adolescents lower in moral reasoning level are more susceptible to peer-group conformity pressures (Fodor, 1971). Peers may also serve as effective models for facilitating children's sensitivity to the importance of intentionality in making moral judgments (McMannis, 1974). And an intimate "chum" relationship, especially during preadolescence, is an important catalyst for developing a broadened sense of humanity, or concern for the welfare of others (Mannarino, 1976).

On the whole, then, peer-group influences can be positive, if most of the group's members are children from homes where a desirable course of moral development has already been established. But peer-group experiences can also run counter to moral conduct, as delinquent gangs aptly illustrate. Delinquent children or youth can conceivably disinhibit their peers under certain conditions (low risk of detection, strong reinforcement for misconduct), as shown in laboratory studies of modeling. At the grass roots level, this may be something akin to the one bad apple that spoils the entire barrel. At worst, tyranny, as exemplified by William Golding's *Lord of the Flies*, may develop in the absence of more mature moral forces. And group contagion (see Chapter 4) can occasionally entrap normally well-behaving children (and adults), as lynching gangs and other forms of mob action reveal. Fortunately, these actions are relatively infrequent. The vast majority of children and youth seem unseduced by the presence and actions of morally immature or retarded peers. At issue, however, is the total social context that supports moral behavior. Much peer interaction occurs within the school, so it is logical to examine schooling and moral development.

Schooling and Moral Development

In Chapter 5 we discussed the school as socializer, with moral development being one of three major dimensions of emphasis for children and youth. Recounting the *importance* of school for moral development has far outweighed the production of any evidence about *actual impact* of schooling on such development. According to one authority (Kohlberg, 1966), the traditional approach to moral or "character" education in America's schools has lacked a coherent psychological framework for planning and stimulating moral growth. Rather, a "bag of virtues" approach has been emphasized, with teachers haphazardly and sometimes inconsistently stressing conformity to moral prescriptions through exhortation, preachment, and injunction. In the final analysis, this may result in equating "effective discipline" with character education. That such an approach does not work is revealed by the many alleged moral ills of our society. If so, what are the alternatives?

Americans committed to individualism and democracy are quick to reject any alternative that smacks of moral indoctrination or group pressures that subjugate personal needs and freedom to state interests. In the U.S.S.R., for example, it is apparently believed that optional personal (moral) development can occur only through productive activity in a social collective—contributing to the common good while discounting individual values and preferences. Total, unwavering allegiance to the collective defines this socialist morality. Strong emphasis is placed upon group criticism, self-criticism, and group-oriented rewards and punishments. As one observer of the Soviet scene has noted, widespread use of procedures for criticizing self and others in public is the socialization practice that clashes most sharply with the American pattern (Bronfenbrenner, 1963).

Given the general ideological objection to this alternative, and assuming that the schools *should* do something more than exhort children, is there any "morally acceptable" blueprint from which to guide activities for moral education? A growing number of psychologists and educators seem quick to agree. Two approaches, in particular, are heralded: the cognitive-developmental approach and values clarification. We briefly consider these in turn.

The Cognitive-Developmental Position

The cognitive-developmental approach takes stimulation of the individual child's moral judgment and character development as the basic aim of moral education. In practice, the approach has been conceptualized in Kohlberg's theory of moral development (Kohlberg, 1975). The approach is morally justified on the grounds that since we know (a) what constitutes the normal, natural course of human moral development, (b) and education is a means for promoting maximum personal development, (c) then moral education is a matter of facilitating growth toward moral maturity in the direction that we know children and youth already are going. The emphasis is *cognitive*—a concern for pupils' ability to make moral judgments and formulate moral principles of their own from within a constellation of intellectual activities. It is claimed that values as such are not taught, nor do they need to be. Instead, children and youth will come eventually to recognize and internalize moral principles of inherent worth. The focus is on the development of logical thought structures by which moral problems can be analyzed, interpreted, and judged; problem-solving and decision-making skills take precedence over any conformity to external sources of value, moral conduct, or feeling states. Certain cognitive tools, however, are seen as better than others. The more mature moral thought is—comprehensive, systematic, internally consistent, and principled—the better.

Teachers, as facilitators of moral thinking, are said to contribute to pupil growth in two related ways. One is by directly modeling moral judgments just beyond that stage in which a pupil presently functions. This is usually referred to as the "plus 1 approach," meaning that whatever stage students are in, they will be best stimulated to change by reasoning that reflects the next immediate stage in the overall sequence of moral development. The second way in which teachers catalyze upward movement is by providing relevant moral dilemmas for discussion with the classroom group. Any differences in reasoning that emerge from within the group can then be juxtaposed to create disequilibrium among lower-stage pupils (Turiel, 1974). If all goes well, conflict resolution gradually will occur, bringing students to successively higher stages of moral reasoning. This will take much time and teacher skill in correctly assessing or diagnosing stage thinking, "programming" just the right amount of conflict, and exerting only indirect influence by Socratic questioning, reflective thinking, and other group-discussion techniques. The main objective is to facilitate development as far as possible, or to "stretch the mind" in such a way that a learner will search for and discover more logical and principled modes of coding and analyzing moral experiences. Kohlberg himself confesses, however, that some persons may never reach the highest stages, even with appropriate experience. This suggests that certain intellectual limitations, such as an inability to achieve formal operational thought (Chapter 8), may prevent the achievement of full moral maturity as defined by Kohlberg.

What are the effects of the cognitive-developmental approach to moral education? Impact research has been neither extensive nor uniformly rigorous. Nor, as yet, is the approach widely practiced in American schools. What studies have been published, however, range across a variety of settings to include primary grades, high schools, college students, Sunday Schools, and even prisons (Arbuthnot, 1975; Purpel & Ryan, 1976; Rest, 1974b; Selman & Lieberman, 1975). Results of these efforts are mixed. We can be encouraged by evidence that some persons who experience moral dilemma often do advance in their ability to perform higher-level reasoning; others do not. For some the change is immediate, with an apparent "relapse" after time passes. For others, real advances do not show up until as much as a year later. And, as this book is written, we cannot state with any confidence that increased moral judgment skills have any effect on actual behavior outside of the educational setting. Nor is it likely that this kind of data will come easily. There are enormous difficulties in attempting evaluation research in this area of human functioning, especially in reliably sorting out formal school experience effects from home, peer-group, and general cultural experiences. We encourage interested readers to keep abreast of this interesting and potentially productive approach to moral education by reading the literature that is sure to appear in future years.

Values Clarification

Though in some respects compatible with a cognitive-developmental orientation to moral education, *values clarification* involves children and youth in a self-examination process focused on priorities for personally defined "goods" that can be integrated into daily life. In other words, values clarification is a process of coming clearly to know or recognize what one thinks is worthy in life, choosing those for which one cares most, and acting consistently with reference to those value choices (Raths, Harmin, & Simon, 1966; Simon, Howe, & Kirschenbaum, 1972). This approach requires that seven criteria be met for something to be called a "value": Choosing (1) freely, (2) from alternatives, (3) after thoughtful consideration of the consequences of each alternative; *Prizing* (4) cherishing, being happy with the choice, (5) willingness to affirm the choice publicly; and *Acting* (6) doing something with the choice, (7) repeatedly in some pattern of life. Here, as in the Kohlberg approach, rational, cognitive activity is presumably the basis for coming to grips with valuing.

The method of values clarification involves novel and entertaining learning activities from which value issues leading to decisions about personal preferences are raised. Certain basic questions pervade most discussions: how we choose to live our lives, what career we seek and why, how leisure time is used, what kind of a person we wish to be, what kind of people we admire, and how we would prefer to behave in different situations. But moral dilemmas or conflicts, including any standards by which one might determine right or wrong and how one *ought* to behave, are

not addressed. By implication, then, all values are equally valid. If the criteria for valuing are met, any outcome is "acceptable." Thus the salient feature of values clarification is the means for individual choice and commitment. Authoritarian or rigid moralizing is explicitly rejected by this approach. Teachers must be accepting, nurturant, and trusting. Students are encouraged to lead themselves out of confusion and uncertainty within the vast maze of values that surround them in a pluralistic society. Once the journey into a dawning of values has been made, clarifiers are said to be more positive, purposeful, enthusiastic, and proud about themselves and their life styles.

Does values clarification work? Again, little research evidence exists about the impact of this experience. Students we know who participate usually report enjoying values-clarification activities. Participants in this experience often feel more positively about school as well. But firmly documented effects are still wanting. Philosophically, the approach appeals to humanists in education and psychology (Appendix A) and supporters of informal discovery modes of learning and teaching. Values clarification also seems to appeal to ethical or moral relativists, those who believe that no absolute standards or moral values exist. Thinking relativistically about moral values assumes that my values are no better (or worse) than yours. All of us are entitled to our own opinions. No way exists to "prove" that my opinions are more (or less) moral than yours. In this sense, values clarification differs markedly from the cognitive developmentalist perspective with its emphasis on ultimate and inherently worthy moral principles such as justice.

As scholars (such as Lockwood, 1975) have noted, the basic objection to moral relativism is that it can be an instrument for justifying almost any activity in which a person or social group may wish to engage. While it must again be stressed that values clarification is primarily a "therapeutic" process of self definition in terms of personal goods, the connotation of relativism gives us pause. Strictly speaking, if Stalin or Thomas Aquinas reaches their values according to the seven stated criteria, they are equally and acceptably "clarified." This is not to dismiss the importance of introspection and a systematic examination of personal value priorities in conjunction with other people, as provided by values clarification. And, of course, if we can safely assume that human beings are, by nature, good and will naturally seek to clarify and commit themselves to values that insure a balance between their personal and the larger common good, the dangers of extreme relativism fade away. Otherwise, many will seek more than values clarification for the fundamental ideas necessary for practicing any morality: empathy, anticipation of consequences, respect for human dignity, and the like (Oliver & Shaver, 1966; Peters, 1970; Wilson, Williams, & Sugarman, 1967). The problem, however, is that unless such moral principles are themselves examined and accepted by volition, we still cannot speak about moral education. Any effort to foist a value or principle upon another is, in effect, an attempt at moral indoctrination.

The issue is delicate. Despite a growing literature on moral education, there is still much apprehension, even confusion, about which way to go. And to choose not to go in any direction itself is a moral decision with more than fleeting consequences.

Concluding Remarks

In this brief section, we have stressed only two of the more visible and much-talked-about approaches to moral educa-tion. Important clues to further thinking can be gleaned from still other sources. For example, the potential of cooperative instruction for pupil's prosocial development can be cited (Johnson et al., 1976). Specific training for social perspective-taking skills, an important component of moral development, can be successful (Chandler, 1973). Children also seem to benefit from joint participation in making up rules to govern their own behavior in game and school situations (Merchant & Rebelsky, 1972). Mini-courses in values education have been proposed, as have more general discussion materials for the moral aspects of public issues (Beck, 1971). Still other authorities (for example, Scriven, 1975) propose a straightforward *cognitive* approach to moral education, to emphasize the skills of moral analysis. This will include first, acquiring and comprehending the "facts" of moral issues; second, the ability to reason logically about moral truths and their application; and third, a competency in the study of ethics.

In general, then, most educational leaders seem favorably disposed toward some form of moral education. Indeed, such education inevitably "comes with the territory" (Purpel & Ryan, 1976). But agreement about the content and method of moral education is presently lacking. However conceived, it seems futile to speak about moral education until a firm concept of *moral existence* is attained (Peters, 1970). If we define moral being strictly by a moral code of some kind, the result is an authoritarian approach to moral education. If we take the romantic view that children and youth can "go it alone" and decide morality all by themselves, then we abdicate any responsibility for moral guidance and leave the bulk of moral education to chance. This leaves only a middle-of-the-road position that most moral philosophers seem to prefer: guidance in moral thought and action by those who understand and can deal with the complexity of humankind's moral affairs. Teachers are in a strategic position to model moral decision-making and conduct their own affairs morally. If any single principle is most significant for this purpose, it is *mutuality:* a relationship of trust and mutual strength that allows both pupil and teacher to develop their respective strengths (Erikson, 1964). For teachers, this will require both a genuine commitment to pupil welfare and a secure personal moral development of their own.

A Word about the Mass Media

In Chapter 5, we suggested that modeling effects from certain television viewing often seem to become manifest in children's aggressive behavior. At least, opportunities for learning many antisocial behaviors (including aggression) by observation are rampant throughout television programming. By definition, most (if not all) criminal behavior modeled on television and motion pictures is immoral. Thus one cannot help but wonder what the impact of such episodes is on the moral thinking of children and youth. To be sure, many programs seem to make a moral point, as in "crime does not pay." But all too often, the message is, "Don't get caught." In other words, the real problem with crime is being found out and punished — not moral grounds for the reason why crime and other harmful acts are wrong. Moreover, if Piaget is right about young children attending primarily to the *consequences* of acts and not *intentions,* they may easily miss the moral points of programs even when they are explicit. In other words, from a cognitive-developmental perspective, any moral symbolism or rationalizations of television

programs will probably be too abstract for them to comprehend. This problem of matching program content and presentation to the cognitive capacities of young viewers seems poorly handled by most producers of children's television programs.

It is unlikely that American commercial television will ever be coherently used as anything but "entertainment," and certainly not as a medium for moral education. This medium is rich in its potential to portray prosocial behavior, as is the cinema. And, occasionally, we see magnificent stories of a moral nature such as the films, *A Man for All Seasons* and *Beckett.* Just as children may learn about a wide range of antisocial and immoral acts from the media, so can they learn about moral and prosocial behavior. The supporting empirical evidence for this point is limited. A few well-executed studies, however, point to televised modeling influences on children's behaviors that are important for total moral development: resistance to temptation, sharing, cooperativeness, giving positive reinforcement to others, and willingness to help others in need (Coates, Pusser, & Goodman, 1976; Friedrich & Stein, 1973; Wolf, 1973). Educational television programs about positive interracial relations reportedly influenced play preferences and patterns of young white children to more frequently include nonwhite peers (Gorn, Goldberg, & Kanungo, 1976). Such influences are not uniformly seen in all studies, however. For example, benefits of prosocial viewing seem to accrue when adults and children view together, with some planned follow-up activity designed to reinforce the "lessons." Taken as a whole, however, we cannot dismiss television as a potential force in shaping children's moral concepts and beliefs, if not their actual behavior.

SUMMING UP MAJOR DILEMMAS ABOUT MORAL DEVELOPMENT

There is perhaps no more complex an area of human development and socialization than morality. Among the more essential questions involved are these: When does conformity become mindless submission? How can we bring up our children to conform in a reasonable way yet, at the same time, be original and creative? (By definition, originality and creativity constitute nonconforming behavior.) How can children and youth learn to conform to a reasonable degree, yet maintain their respect and tolerance for harmless but sometimes annoying nonconformities of others? Are there biological factors in development that contribute to or mediate in any way the extent to which individuals become sensitive or insensitive, responsive or unresponsive to the moral aspects of human life?

Behavioral Conformity as a Moral Matter

Derived from such questions is this one: if we can and do teach children and youth to conform—to respect law, order, and custom—are we simultaneously denying them the opportunity for spontaneity, originality, curiosity, and creativity? In American society, it seems that we often punish nonconformers. The lack of continuity in American life, the nuclear family structure built around the all-too-fragile husband–wife pair, and the breathless pace of United States society may cause us to cling to conformity for personal security. If we are lost in the group, we cannot be singled out and held responsible. We may be lost, but we are secure in our anonymity. Nonconformity also threatens our bureaucratic, republican structure, which, with all its unwieldiness, impersonality,

and other weaknesses, may still be necessary for a democracy to survive.

For such reasons, nonconformers are likely to be punished by their peers and the authority figures in their lives. To be punished is to have one's integrity threatened. Anger and continued, often destructive, rebellion are the end result of nonconformity for many. Such people may be the ones who bomb, burn, and assassinate. Moderates—the ones who see the merits in both sides of the case—are often punished by those in the extreme ideological groups at the left and the right. Moderate people are thus often forced into radical positions, probably driven more often to the right than to the left in our society, because, on the whole, leaning toward the right is safer and less controversial.

In any case, a degree of conformity for the collective social good, as in much of law, seems necessary for a moral existence. On the other hand, unquestioning obedience to authority can itself reach the point of serious moral violations, as the now-famous Milgram experiment has revealed (Milgram, 1974). A large majority of young adults participating in this study continued to obey an experimenter's request to administer electric shock to another person (the experimenter's confederate, unknown to the participants), up to a point marked on the apparatus as the highest and lethal level of shock. In contrast, only about one-third of the subjects broke with the experimenter and refused to administer the shocks (which, incidentally, were followed by increasing, though false, cries of pain from the stooge). It is this loss of autonomy and failure to act in resistance to immoral dictates that seemingly undermine those persons who may verbally profess to hold values about the wrongness of inflicting injury upon others. As an aside, of course, we can go further and question the morality of such experimentation itself—however instructive the results. It is a classic example of the dilemma about means and ends.

Rationality of Authority as a Moral Matter

If democracy is to thrive, those who administer it—the authorities—must be perceived by those in the ranks as rational, basically well-intended people. But what of urban slum, rural black, or Chicano children and youth whose depressing conditions are often clear to authorities who are not kind, rational, well disposed, nor fair? Among such authorities are many police, landlords, teachers, and welfare workers. They are the dominant power figures, more powerful than parents, to whom poor children are exposed.

More affluent children and young people are also frequently confronted with irrational authority: teachers who are grossly unfair; police who assume guilt; public officials who cheat, steal, and lie. It may be that the disposition to see authority as rational goes back to earliest childhood, perhaps to the early development of trust discussed earlier in this chapter. If so, there is danger in too much as well as in too little trust. It is no better to be a gull than a cynic. Pollyanna cannot survive any more successfully in today's complex society than an utterly alienated, despairing, and cynical member of, for example, the hard-drug culture.

Impulse Inhibition as a Moral Matter

We have seen that there is agreement that one aspect of advanced moral judgment and behavior is the ability to delay gratification so as to opt for a later, larger reward rather than for an immediate, smaller reward. Carried to its extreme, as it sometimes is in our culture

(where there is still a Puritan streak), this attitude may mean that you never have any fun *now*. Or it could also mean a denial of the impulsive "spur of the moment" behavior that often makes life exciting.

Having done a considerable amount of traveling, we have often encountered frail, elderly women (more often than men) who have saved all their lives for the "chance to see Paree." But they have saved so painfully and for so long that they no longer have either the energy or the talent for enjoying *Paree* when they finally get there. Further, they have often waited until they lost the partner with whom they wished to share *Paree*, so they see it in loneliness.

On the other hand, we often see children and young people who greedily and recklessly grasp the here and now, much like Aesop's grasshopper in the fable of the grasshopper and the ant. Addiction to either drugs or alcohol often implies inability to cope with the frustration and the denial that are part of the human condition, and inability to postpone immediate gratification. Moreover, it usually implies a loss of independence to the point of organizing one's life around the acquisition of drugs. Little room is left for autonomous judgment and action for the benefit of others (save subsidizing the drug merchant). How do we bring up our children with a capacity for simply *being*; for having fun, for turning loose, for acting like happy, carefree Dionysian people sometimes, yet for the most part adhering to an Apollonian ethic? In the Apollonian way of life, planning occurs, things are accomplished, and to *do* is a central motive. Dionysians enjoy things now, and there are occasions when this is both useful and necessary. Apollonians are more likely to wait to enjoy the larger thing later, but if they wait too long, they may lose it forever.

Some thoughtful youth (and some not

so youthful) deplore the competitive, impersonal, materialistic fabric of American life. A surprising number of our brightest young people on the highest moral development level carry their distaste for the conforming American way of life to the point of dropping out. This can be a loss to everyone.

Perhaps a major American task at all levels, from elementary school through big business, industry, and government, is to modify the American system so as to allow more room within it for individual expression and happiness. In the long run, the culture will profit (even in so crass an index as the gross national product) if everyone is a bit happier and is given a bit more leeway as a biological, emotional human being. In other words, we can predict that unhappy workers will produce fewer products of poorer quality than happy workers, even with all the technology in the world; and more of them will be social casualties.

Consideration for Others as a Moral Matter

Consideration for others is closely related to impulse inhibition and needs little additional discussion. Consideration for others often, perhaps usually, demands impulse inhibition, because "What is good for me can be bad for you." The issue in childrearing and education is to develop respect for others and a lively sense of reciprocity and consideration, but not at the risk of losing personal autonomy and a balanced freedom to enjoy life on one's own terms.

A Biology of Morality?

A final issue is the possible contribution of biological factors to the genesis of moral behavior (Eysenck, 1976). To the extent that moral behavior is influenced by conditioned learning (Chapter 2), especially external sanctions that are applied initially to inhibit impulsivity, and subsequently result in a generalized moral anxiety (conscience), certain biological or genetically determined factors may mediate patterns of moral conduct. One is a constitutionally-linked resistance-to-stress factor, or a constitutional predisposition to react in certain ways to need frustration. The less able people are to tolerate frustration, the less likely may they learn deferred gratification or impulse control.

A second, perhaps closely related factor is low cortical arousal. Cortical arousal seems linked to, and may be a predisposing condition for, low conditionability. This means a relative imperviousness to "normal" reactions to gratifying or aversive stimulation and consequent high sensation seeking. In extreme cases, a pattern of rather indiscriminant "thrill seeking" without fear or guilt from usual social controls (to which most of us are responsive) may evolve. Such is the dynamic often attributed to the so-called sociopathic or psychopathic individual: self-service without regard for the consequences of one's actions for others, lack of self-recrimination, pathological egocentricity, an apparent incapacity for love or meaningful and reciprocal interpersonal relations, poor judgment, failure to learn from experience, and so on. Inevitably, a diagnosis of psychopathy is more than a little subjective. But such was the clinical assessment of Walter, whom we introduced at the beginning of this chapter. And it is not outside the realm of possibility that his biological makeup includes such things as low cortical arousal.

Even if biology is somehow implicated in many cases of moral development gone wrong, it can neither be used to excuse nor tell the complete story of variations in morality. The study of biology, however, may lead us to a more complete understanding of individual differences in moral behavior. For the present we emphasize both the tenta-

tiveness of the foregoing ideas and the moral issue of what might be done to ameliorate stunted moral development when it is clearly diagnosed.

Our discussion of moral development has been built upon two aspects of morality. Most generally, the highest morality consists of (1) personal principles of justice and reciprocity based upon empathy, mutual respect, and regard for the integrity and rights of human beings and (2) realistic acceptance of social responsibility. The psychological study of morality and moral development has been influenced by some fundamental assumptions about human nature: a belief in humankind's innate depravity or in humankind's inherent purity and goodness, or in the tabula rasa, or a nuetral, blank-slate human nature. A belief in innate depravity leads logically to concerns about how children can be socialized to hold their impulses in check, to conform in harmony with the larger social order. Inherent goodness implies interest in the natural unfolding of capacities for mature moral thinking and prosocial action. The blank-slate view leads to an analysis of how children and youth learn morality or immorality, since conditions of the environment will determine the story either way.

Going beyond these initial philosophical differences about the moral nature of humankind, we have described from the current psychological literature three interrelated components of moral development and behavior: cognitive, affective, and behavioral. The theories of Jean Piaget and Lawrence Kohlberg were used to illustrate the cognitive component, with their emphasis upon moral judgment or reasoning—how individuals think about moral conflicts and problems. As in the study of intellectual development, the cognitive-developmental approach to morality is built upon the notion of fixed or invariant stage-sequence growth toward maturity. Kohlberg's theory was discussed in most detail, including descriptions of three successively higher levels of development—preconventional morality, conventional morality, and principled morality—each of which is further differentiated into two periods for a total of six stages. Many questions about the accuracy and universality of this theory remain to be answered. But the theory provides a useful way to

SUMMARY

account for age differences in moral judgment and a tentative basis for arranging environmental experiences that may facilitate natural growth.

A second component of moral development is clearly more affective than cognitive: the roles of guilt, empathy, and trust. These affects are extraordinarily difficult to study scientifically, but all three seem to develop fairly early in life, at least in rudimentary form. By age 5 or 6, many children will give evidence of self-reproach and remorse, although wide individual differences can be observed among them. Empathy, like guilt, seems to reflect the influence of conditioning, as well as certain cognitive achievements, including an ability to take the role or perspective of other people. A basic sense of trust, with probable origins in the primary caregiver-infant relationship, is a further indication of interrelated moral development. Without trust, it seems unlikely that human affairs could be conducted on a mature moral basis.

Behaviorally-oriented psychologists concentrate mostly on a third component of moral development: moral conduct. More care has been exercised in the laboratory observation of response patterns believed pertinent to morality than is possible in naturalistic study. Children's self-control under conditions of temptation has been extensively studied. Children as young as age 5 vary in their resistance-to-temptation behavior, presumably reflecting individual differences in conditionability and socialization history. To the study of self-restraint can be added a growing literature on positive forms of social behavior: altruism and cooperation. Age-related trends in two types of altruistic behavior, rescue and donation, were discussed. Children's cooperativeness has been most frequently studied in contrast to competitiveness. American children, more so than children in many other cultures, are apparently socialized more for competitiveness than cooperation. How this emphasis may work against moral relationships in an interdependent society was discussed.

Our familiar examination of major social influences continued in Chapter 11, with attention to parenting, peers, and the schools. Most data about parenting and children's moral development are correlational, thus limiting our knowledge about cause–effect relationships. Among the most reliable findings, however, is a negative association between parental power assertion and children's level of moral judgment and behavior. And a growing number of studies point to the importance of induction techniques for promoting moral development, especially when they occur in a climate of emotional warmth, encouragement, and acceptance. Peer-group influences are even more difficult to establish. Both positive and negative peer modeling effects can be observed. Peer group impact seems to vary according to the strength of personality characteristics (autonomy, dependency, personal conscience) as influenced more profoundly by earlier home experiences.

As for schools, we have concentrated more heavily on issues about moral education than upon data about the effects of schooling on moral development. The reason is simply stated: virtually no large-scale research about morality and schooling has been conducted in America.

But this lack is no measure of educators' interest in moral education. On the contrary, this interest has grown considerably in the past few years, as indicated by a glut of literature on the subject. This literature certifies the need for a coherent and morally justified blueprint for moral education, but opinions differ widely about the specifics of content and method. To illustrate some differences and issues in moral education we discussed two approaches, the cognitive-developmental position and values clarification.

We concluded Chapter 11 by referring to certain dilemmas or matters of unresolved debate about moral development and behavior. These were the relation of behavioral conformity and morality, the issues of rational authority and morality, and of impulse inhibition-expression, and the importance of considering others in moral relationships. As a final bit of frosting on the cake of uncertainty about morality we addressed certain questions about the biological foundations of moral development. Resistance-to-stress and ease of cortical arousal were discussed as possible sources of individual differences in response to socialization for moral conduct.

REFERENCES

Adkins, D. C., Payne, F. D., & O'Malley, J. M. Moral development. In F. N. Kerlinger (Ed.), *Review of research in education* (vol. 2). Itasca, Ill.: Peacock, 1974.

Allport, G. W. *Pattern and growth in personality.* New York: Holt, Rinehart and Winston, 1961.

Arbuthnot, J. Modification of moral judgment through role playing. *Developmental Psychology,* 1975, *11,* 319–324.

Armsby, R. E. A reexamination of the development of moral judgments in children. *Child Development,* 1971, *42,* 1241–1248.

Aron, I. E. Moral philosophy and moral education: A critique of Kohlberg's theory. *School Review,* 1977, *85,* 197–228.

Aronfreed, J. Moral development from the standpoint of a general psychological theory. In T. Lickona (Ed.), *Moral development and behavior: Theory, research, and social issues.* New York: Holt, Rinehart and Winston, 1976.

Ausubel, D. P. Relationships between shame and guilt in the socialization process. *Psychological Review,* 1955, *62,* 378–390.

Bandura, A. *Social learning theory.* Englewood Cliffs, N.J.: Prentice-Hall, 1976.

Beck, C. *Moral education in the schools.* Toronto: Ontario Institute for Studies in Education, 1971.

Berkowitz, L., & Friedman, P. Some social class differences in helping behavior. *Journal of Personality and Social Psychology,* 1967, *5,* 217–225.

Bronfenbrenner, U. Soviet methods of character education: Some implications for research. *American Psychologist,* 1963, *27,* 550–565.

Bryan, J. H. Children's cooperation and helping behaviors. In E. M. Hetherington (Ed.), *Review of child development research.* Chicago: University of Chicago Press, 1975.

Chandler, M. J. Egocentrism and antisocial behavior: The assessment and training of social perspective-taking skills. *Developmental Psychology, 1973, 9, 326–332.*

Coates, B., Pusser, H. E., & Goodman, I. The influence of "Sesame Street" and "Mister Roger's Neighborhood" on children's social behavior in the preschool. *Child Development, 1976, 47, 138–144.*

Cook, H., & Stingle, S. Cooperative behavior in children. *Psychological Bulletin, 1974, 81, 918–933.*

Denney, N., & Duffy, D. Possible environmental causes of stages in moral reasoning. *Journal of Genetic Psychology, 1974, 125, 277–283.*

Erikson, E. *Childhood and society* (rev. ed.). New York: Norton, 1963.

Erikson, E. *Insight and responsibility.* New York: Norton, 1964.

Eysenck, H. J. Symposium: The development of moral values in children. (VII) The contribution of learning theory. *British Journal of Educational Psychology, 1960, 30, 11–21.*

Eysenck, H. J. The biology of morality. In T. Likona (Ed.), *Moral development and behavior.* New York: Holt, Rinehart and Winston, 1976.

Feshbach, N., & Roe, K. Empathy in six- and seven-year-olds. *Child Development, 1968, 39, 133–145.*

Fodor, E. M. Resistance to social influence among adolescents as a function of level of moral development. *Journal of Social Psychology, 1971, 85, 121–126.*

Fodor, E. M. Moral development and parent behavior antecedents in adolescent psychopaths. *Journal of Genetic Psychology, 1973, 122, 37–44.*

Friedrich, L. K., & Stein, A. Aggressive and prosocial television programs and the natural behavior of preschool children. *Monographs of the Society for Research in Child Development, 1973, 38*(4), No. 151.

Fry, C. L. A developmental examination of performance in a tacit coordination game situation. *Journal of Personality and Social Psychology, 1967, 5, 277–281.*

Fry, P. S. Affect and resistance to temptation. *Developmental Psychology, 1975, 11, 466–472.*

Gibbs, J. C. Kohlberg's stages of moral judgment: A constructive critique. *Harvard Educational Review, 1977, 47, 43–61.*

Gorn, G. J., Goldberg, M. E., & Kanungo, R. N. The role of educational television in changing the inter-group attitudes of children. *Child Development, 1976, 47, 277–280.*

Haan, N., Langer, J., & Kohlberg, L. Family patterns of moral reasoning. *Child Development, 1976, 47, 1204–1206.*

Hare, R. M. Adolescents into adults. In T. Hollins (Ed.), *Aims in education: The philosophic approach.* Manchester, England: Manchester University Press, 1964.

Hartup, W. W. Peer interaction and social organization. In P. H. Mussen (Ed.), *Carmichael's manual of child psychology.* New York: Wiley, 1970.

Hill, W. Learning theory and the acquisition of values. *Psychological Review, 1960, 67, 317–331.*

Hoffman, M. L. Moral development. In P. H. Mussen (Ed.), *Carmichael's manual of child psychology.* New York: Wiley, 1970.

Hoffman, M. L. The development of altruism motivation. In D. J. DePalma & J. M. Foley (Eds.), *Moral development: Current theory and research.* Hillsdale, N.J.: Lawrence Erlbaum, 1975. (a)

Hoffman, M. L. Altruistic behavior and the parent–child relationship. *Journal of Personality and Social Psychology, 1975 31, 937–943.* (b)

Hoffman, M. L. Moral internalization, parental power, and the nature of parent–child interaction. *Developmental Psychology, 1975, 11, 228–239.* (c)

Hogan, R. A dimension of moral judgment. *Journal of Consulting and Clinical Psychology,* 1970, *35,* 205–212.

Hogan, R. Moral conduct and moral character: A psychological perspective. *Psychological Bulletin,* 1973, *79,* 217–232.

Hogan, R. Moral development and the structure of personality. In D. J. DePalma & J. M. Foley (Eds.), *Moral development: Current theory and research.* Hillsdale, N.J.: Lawrence Erlbaum, 1975.

Hogan, R., & Dickstein, E. A measure of moral values. *Journal of Consulting and Clinical Psychology,* 1972, *39,* 210–214.

Holstein, C. B. Irreversible, stepwise sequence in the development of moral judgment: A longitudinal study of males and females. *Child Development,* 1976, *47,* 51–61.

Hudgins, W., & Prentice, N. M. Moral judgment in delinquent and non-delinquent adolescents and their mothers. *Journal of Abnormal Psychology,* 1973, *82,* 145–152.

Jessor, S. Recent research on moral development: A commentary. In D. J. DePalma & J. M. Foley (Eds.), *Moral development: Current theory and research.* Hillsdale, N.J.: Lawrence Erlbaum, 1975.

Johnson, D., et al. Effects of cooperative versus individualized instruction on student prosocial behavior, attitudes toward learning, and achievement. *Journal of Educational Psychology,* 1976, *68,* 446–452.

Kanfer, F. H., & Zich, J. Self-control training: The effects of external control on children's resistance to temptation. *Developmental Psychology,* 1974, *10,* 108–115.

Katz, H. A., & Rotter, J. B. Interpersonal trust scores of college students and their parents. *Child Development,* 1969, *40,* 657–661.

Keasey, C. B. Social participation as a factor in the moral development of preadolescents. *Developmental Psychology,* 1971, *5,* 206–220.

Kohlberg, L. Development of moral character and moral ideology. In M. L. Hoffman & L. W. Hoffman (Eds.), *Review of child development research* (vol. 1). New York: Russell Sage, 1964.

Kohlberg, L. Moral education in the schools: A developmental view. *The School Review,* 1966, *74,* 1–30.

Kohlberg, L. Stage and sequence: The cognitive-developmental approach to socialization. In D. Goslin (Ed.), *Handbook of socialization theory and research.* Skokie, Ill.: Rand McNally, 1968.

Kohlberg, L. The cognitive-developmental approach to moral education. *Phi Delta Kappan,* 1975, *56,* 670–677.

Kohlberg, L., & Turiel, E. Moral development and moral education. In G. Lesser (Ed.), *Psychology and educational practice.* Glenview, Ill.: Scott, Foresman, 1971.

Kuhn, D. Short-term longitudinal evidence for the sequentiality of Kohlberg's early stages of moral judgment. *Developmental Psychology,* 1976, *12,* 162–166.

Kurtines, W., & Greif, E. B. The development of moral thought: Review and evaluation of Kohlberg's approach. *Psychological Bulletin,* 1974, *81,* 453–470.

LaVoie, J. C. Cognitive determinants of resistance to deviation in seven-, nine-, and eleven-year-old children of low and high maturity of moral judgment. *Developmental Psychology,* 1974, *10,* 393–403.

LaVoie, J. C., & Looft, W. R. Parental antecedents of resistance-to-temptation behavior in adolescent males. *Merrill-Palmer Quarterly,* 1973, *19,* 107–116.

Leizer, J. I., & Rogers, R. W. Effects of method of discipline, timing of punishment, and timing of test on resistance to temptation. *Child Development,* 1974, *45,* 790–793.

Lickona, T. (Ed.) *Moral development and behavior: Theory, research, and social issues.* New York: Holt, Rinehart and Winston, 1976.

Liebert, R. M., & Schwartzberg, N. S. Effects of mass media. *Annual Review of Psychology,* 1977, *28,* 141–174.

Lockwood, A. L. A critical view of values clarification. *Teachers College Record,* 1975, *77,* 35–50.

Loevinger, J. Issues in the measurement of moral development. In W. H. Holtzman (Ed.), *Moral development: Proceedings of the 1974 ETS Invitational Conference.* Princeton, N.J.: Educational Testing Service, 1975.

Mannarino, A. P. Friendship patterns and altruistic behavior in preadolescent males. *Developmental Psychology,* 1976, *12,* 555–556.

McMannis, D. L. Effects of peer-models vs. adult-models and social reinforcement on intentionality of children's moral judgments. *Journal of Psychology,* 1974, *87,* 159–170.

Meister, A. Perception and acceptance of group power relations in children. *Group Psychotherapy,* 1956, *9,* 153–163.

Merchant, R. L., & Rebelsky, F. Effects of participation in rule formation on the moral judgment of children. *Genetic Psychology Monographs,* 1972, *85,* 287–304.

Milgram, S. *Obedience to authority.* London: Tavistock Publications, 1974.

Moir, D. Egocentrism and the emergence of conventional morality in preadolescent girls. *Child Development,* 1974, *45,* 299–305.

Oliver, D., & Shaver, J. *Teaching public issues in the high school.* Boston: Houghton Mifflin, 1966.

Parke, R. D. Rules, roles, and resistance to duration: Recent advances in punishment, discipline, and self-control. In A. D. Pick (Ed.), *Minnesota Symposium on Child Psychology.* Minneapolis: University of Minnesota Press, 1974.

Peters, R. S. Concrete principles and the rational passions. In J. M. Gustafson et al. (Eds.), *Moral education.* Cambridge, Mass.: Harvard University Press, 1970.

Piaget, J. *The moral judgment of the child.* New York: Free Press, 1948. (Originally published, 1932.)

Purpel, D., & Ryan, K. (Eds.) *Moral education: It comes with the territory.* Berkeley, Calif.: McCutchan, 1976.

Raths, L., Harmin, M., & Simon, S. *Values and teaching.* Columbus, Ohio: Merrill, 1966.

Rest, J. R. The cognitive-developmental approach to morality: The state of the art. *Counseling and Values,* 1974, *18,* 64–78. (a)

Rest, J. R. Developmental psychology as a guide to value education: A review of "Kohlbergian" programs. *Review of Educational Research,* 1974, *44,* 241–259. (b)

Rest, J. R., Turiel, E., & Kohlberg, L. Relations between level of moral judgment and preference and comprehension of the moral judgment of others. *Journal of Personality,* 1969.

Rheingold, H. L., Hay, D. F., & West, M. J. Sharing in the second year of life. *Child Development,* 1976, *47,* 1148–1158.

Rubin, K. H., & Schneider, F. W. The relationship between moral judgment, egocentrism, and altruistic behavior. *Child Development,* 1973, *44,* 661–665.

Rushton, J. P. Socialization and the altruistic behavior of children. *Psychological Bulletin,* 1976, *83,* 898–913.

Scriven, M. Cognitive moral education. *Phi Delta Kappan,* 1975, *56,* 689–694.

Sears, R., Rau, L., & Alpert, R. *Identification and child rearing.* Palo Alto, Calif.: Stanford University Press, 1965.

Selman, R. L. Taking another's perspective: Role taking development in early childhood. *Child Development,* 1971, *42,* 1721–1734.

Selman, R., & Lieberman, M. Moral education in the primary grades: An evaluation of developmental curriculum. *Journal of Educational Psychology,* 1975, *67,* 712–716.

Shore, M. F., Massimo, J. L., & Ricks, D. F. A factor analytic study of psychotherapeutic change in delinquent boys. *Journal of Clinical Psychology,* 1965, *21,* 208–212.

Simon, S., Howe, L., & Kirschenbaum, H. *Values clarification.* New York: Hart, 1972.

Staub, E. A child in distress: The influence of age and number of witnesses on children's attempts to help. *Journal of Personality and Social Psychology,* 1970, *14,* 130–140.

Staub, E. *The development of prosocial behavior in children.* Morristown, N.J.: General Learning Press, 1975.

Sullivan, H. S. *The collected works of Harry Stack Sullivan.* New York: Norton, 1963.

Tomlinson-Keasey, C., & Keasey, C. B. The mediating role of cognitive development in moral judgment. *Child Development,* 1974, *45,* 291–298.

Toner, I., Holstein, R., & Hetherington, E. M. Reflection-impulsivity and self-control in preschool children. *Child Development,* 1977, *48,* 239–245.

Turiel, E. Conflict and transition in adolescent moral development. *Child Development,* 1974, *45,* 14–29.

Wilson, J., Williams, N., & Sugarman, B. *Introduction to moral education.* Baltimore: Penguin Books, 1967.

Wolf, T. M. Effects of televised modeled verbalizations and behavior on resistance to deviation. *Developmental Psychology,* 1973, *8,* 51–56.

Yarrow, M., & Waxler, C. Dimensions and correlates of prosocial behavior in young children. *Child Development,* 1976, *47,* 118–125.

Yussen, S. R. Characteristics of moral dilemmas written by adolescents. *Developmental Psychology,* 1977, *13,* 162–163.

chapter 12

Human development and social challenge

Throughout this book we have emphasized both what is known and what is unknown about human development and socialization. We identified many issues associated with parenting and child care, peer relationships, schooling, and the mass media. These issues ranged from single parenting and family structure through early educational intervention and sex-role stereotyping to career guidance and moral education. Theoretical psychological issues have also been discussed, such as the nature—nurture controversy, the critical-periods hypothesis, and different views about human intelligence. By no means have we exhausted all the issues about human development. To further extend our issues orientation we now address some important aspects of human development and behavior that pose unique social challenges. Social challenges are problems of human experience whose eventual solution is in the best interests both of individuals and of society as a whole. We will discuss three: exceptionality in development, aggression and social deviance, and racial prejudice.

In the United States, these are challenges because of our professed commitment to the democratic ideal—itself defined by certain core values that should guide the socialization process: individuality, respect for the rights and property of others, equal opportunity for the pursuit of happiness, and so on. Translated into socialization practice, for example, the values of individuality and equal opportunity mean assistance for each and every person to achieve maximum, positive development. Similarly, the value of respect for the rights and properties of others inevitably requires the individual to make some adjustments to society and to refrain from discriminatory acts against others. We examine first the topic of exceptional development, then discuss the critical social problems of aggression and racial prejudice.

EXCEPTIONAL DEVELOPMENT

Understanding children whose development is exceptional has long challenged both psychology and society in general. In one sense, of course, all children are exceptional because all are unique individuals with idiosyncratic tastes and talents. However, the term *exceptional* has taken on a special meaning in psychology and education. It refers to children whose developmental status is sufficiently different from the normal pattern that special learning opportunities are advisable for them to maximize their growth potentials. Exceptional children and youth show a wide range of characteristics and needs. Some are remarkably advanced or precocious in their intellectual development. Others are remarkably delayed or retarded. Still others show debilitating physical or sensory handicaps, for example, sensorimotor impairments. And still others show deep emotional disturbances or fail to develop normal capacities for language communication and mastery of specific academic tasks such as reading. Whatever the form or basis for exceptionality, such children usually present especial problems of socialization to their parents and society. They nearly always require differing levels or kinds of educational services in the schools. And since each category of exceptionality represents a relatively small percentage of the childhood populations, their life circumstances and growth patterns are something of a mystery to many adults.

We cannot do justice in this chapter to all categories of exceptional development. We will discuss two related forms of exceptionality: giftedness and mental retardation. Both exemplify some major issues that apply to almost all categories of exceptionality. The gifted and the retarded are both important subjects for continuing psychological research and are also extremely important for the work of educators. We discuss each form of exceptionality in terms of historical context, definitions, major characteristics, and selected socialization issues.

The Gifted

Historical Context and Definitions

Early interest in intellectually gifted children is recorded in ancient Greece (Kirk, 1972). Plato, for example, proposed that gifted youngsters should be raised to develop their abilities fully, and thus provide optimal leadership for the Greek state as adults. Through the following centuries, only occasional interest in giftedness is recorded. After about 1850 this interest became more sustained with the beginning of studies of *genius,* which at that time, often connoted both intellectual prowess *and* psychopathology. Treatises such as "The Degenerative Psychosis of Genius" (Lombroso, 1891) were not uncommon. A strong belief that intellectual brilliance was inherited also prevailed, as noted in a famous British work, *Hereditary Genius* (Galton, 1892/1925).

During the early 1900s, interest in giftedness shifted from that rare breed of highly superior adults to include the larger category of intellectually gifted children and youth. Louis Terman's landmark longitudinal study in California of children and youth with IQs of 140 and above was instrumental in producing this shift. Terman's study now fills five separate volumes; the first volume was published in 1925. Following Galton's lead, Terman was able to show that intellectually gifted individuals are often superior, or at least above average, in all major aspects of development, including physical and psychological health.

The study of creativity also originated in the early 1900s. However, the great surge of interest in creativity and giftedness occurred in the 1950s, spurred by Guilford's important distinction between convergent and divergent thinking (Chapter 8). As we have seen, creativity research focused upon personal-social and cognitive process factors, and eventually included a strong concern for education and training. Highly creative children and youth do not always perform with equal excellence on measures of intelligence. In effect, then, the interest of creativity contributed to an expanded concept of giftedness (Albert, 1969).

Recently, a broad-ranging interest in *talent* has emerged. Talent refers to further abilities highly regarded by society, but not always included in the more general concepts of intellectual giftedness or creativity (Getzels & Dillon, 1973). Exceptional mechanical or social-leadership skills are examples. With today's thrust toward full development of all human resources, the identification and nurturance of nonacademically talented children and youth suggest an even broader notion of giftedness.

These shifts of interest and changing ideas about giftedness are paralleled by research definitions of gifted persons. As we have suggested, early definitions were based heavily upon exceptional achievement as shown in adulthood. Genius, for example, was determined by worldly accomplishments and not much thought about as a potential that might be discovered and cultivated in childhood. Another Galton study, *English Men of Science* (1875), is a classic example.

As standardized intelligence tests came into use, giftedness was defined in more relative terms, as a top percentage (the top 2 percent or less) of the general population in psychometric intelligence. During the past several decades, however, many working definitions have appeared. Well-meaning professionals have incorporated increasingly broader criteria to indicate *potential* for giftedness: high measured intelligence, *or* high academic aptitude, *or* high levels of creativity, *or* exceptional talents, *or* definitions that combine some or all of the foregoing

(Getzels & Dillon, 1973). The general working definition that follows, for example, indicates the many faces of giftedness, but restricts the term to genuinely exceptional potential and the consequent educational needs:

> Students with superior cognitive abilities include approximately the top 3 percent of the general school population in measured general intelligence and/or in creative abilities or other talents that promise to make lasting contributions of merit to society. These students are so able that they require special provisions if appropriate educational opportunities are to be provided for them (Martinson, 1973, p. 193).

Characteristics of the Gifted

Since the late 1800s, most studies of talented individuals have focused on the intellectually gifted. These studies have two major outcomes. First, they refute the common lay stereotype that persons of superior intelligence are usually, if not necessarily, defective or deficient in some other way—physically feeble, socially inept, maladjusted, and the like. As mentioned earlier, Terman's longitudinal studies of over 1,400 gifted children revealed their all-around positive development well into middle-age or beyond, for most of them. Terman's work has been criticized on methodological grounds (for example, Hughes & Converse, 1962), but the main findings have been replicated by other researchers and no sound contradictory data have yet appeared. One recent review of the research literature about gifted children and adults, for example, concluded by referring to this group as "a population which values independence, which is more task and contribution oriented than recognition oriented, which prizes integrity and independent judgment in decision making, which rejects conformity for its own sake, and which possesses unusually high social ideals and values"

(Martinson, 1972, p. 84). This seems to hold generally, not uniformly or completely, for gifted persons, who, of course, also have no monopoly on such characteristics. And while gifted persons may show some commonality in development, they also show heterogeneity in learning styles, ability profiles, and personal-social characteristics (Robinson, Roedell, & Jackson, 1977).

The second major outcome of studies about the gifted has been to establish a composite picture of individual, demographic, and family background characteristics that indicate a high probability for giftedness. On the basis of past statistical evidence, persons are more likely to develop giftedness if they are male, born to older and well-educated parents of middle-to-upper socioeconomic status, high in the birth order of a small family, and their fathers are professionals or semiprofessionals (Payne, 1974). Again, we hasten to stress that this is a generalization, and in this case partially an artifact of researchers' choices of subjects for study. Females, for example, have been underrepresented in gifted child research for reasons we do not clearly understand. Studies of representative populations indicate very little difference in the number of gifted males and females (Hitchfield, 1973). There is some telling evidence, however, that particular types of giftedness, such as extreme precocity in mathematics and science, consistently favor males (Stanley, 1973). In addition to a relative neglect of gifted females, selectivity in research samples and methods has also left a knowledge gap about giftedness among nonwhite children, especially those from lower socioeconomic backgrounds. Even with poor and spurious selection criteria, however, most authorities agree that gifted individuals come from all walks of life. We think it reasonable to conclude that all racial, ethnic, sexual, and socioeconomic groups produce individuals with abilities so outstanding as to be considered gifted. Until a better research base is established any composite picture of gifted children or youth must be critically examined and held only very tentatively.

Recently, two related research thrusts have received increased attention. Both involve special procedures for identifying giftedness. It has long been observed that the subjective impressions of parents and teachers can be unreliable or misleading for this purpose. One thrust, consistent with the idea of *talent,* is the search for children and youth who show superior *specific* abilities. Many intellectually advanced children do not show a pattern of overall giftedness, or equally superior skills, across the broad range of intellectually functioning. The *Study of Mathematically Precocious Youth* at Johns Hopkins University exemplifies this approach. The young participants in this study are generally quite bright, but they are best described as genuine "math whizzes." To illustrate, one 12-year-old has completed a college-level computer-science course with honors. A second is a self-taught calculus master. Another 13-year-old has completed 4 1/2 years of precalculus mathematics in 60 2-hour Saturday morning sessions. The Johns Hopkins study now includes some 2,000 such children whose life circumstances are being monitored as they move into advanced mathematics courses and other programs of accelerated learning (Stanley, 1976).

The second related research thrust attempts to identify children high in general intellectual potential as early as the preschool years. The reasons for this research direction are straightforward and practical:

Early identification creates the opportunity for early intervention. The parent who is aware of a child's special abilities can plan intelligently for appropriate, challenging educational experiences. The educator who has direct information about a child's advanced abilities can develop programs geared to the child's actual level of competence rather than to a level calibrated on the basis of chronological age alone. Since intellectually advanced children have skills beyond those usual for their age, their educational needs are radically different from the needs of their same-age peers. The earlier those needs are identified, the sooner educational programs can be tailored to fit them (Robinson, Roedell, & Jackson, 1977, p. 5).

The authors of this quotation are currently conducting a longitudinal early-identification project at the University of Washington in Seattle. Special testing procedures, parental report information, and behavioral observations are used to select children for study. Some children are placed in a preschool program carefully designed to nurture their development. In general, the children selected show performance measures of general intelligence, spatial reasoning, reading skill, and/or memory of double the "normal rate." Thus most of these 3- and 4-year-old children demonstrate cognitive proficiencies similar to children twice their age. The study also includes some children whose measured abilities are somewhat less advanced, but who give evidence of potential for extraordinary intellectual abilities. The earliest tentative finding from this project is that preschool screening procedures, including parental involvement, can be effective in identifying children who give every indication of exceptional giftedness. To date, however, attempts at still earlier identification, for example in infancy, have not been fruitful (Willerman & Fielder, 1974). And, of course, the long-term implications of early identification and nurturance of exceptional talent remain unclear.

Some Issues in the Study of Giftedness

We need a greater research commitment to gifted children and youth. The benefits of early identification, for example, will depend upon the suitability of any intervention procedures for the gifted. This in turn raises the issue of education for the gifted.

Educational programs Educational programs for gifted children have typically involved one or a combination of three approaches: ability grouping, enrichment, and acceleration. Ability grouping places the gifted into special classes or tracks or, in the extreme, in special schools. Arguments for this practice include the mutual stimulation among gifted pupils and freedom to implement special instructional procedures to allow for a more rapid pacing and differentiation of learning activities. Such grouping may seem undemocratic, and may cause a loss both to the students who are grouped and to those who are left. The success of such programs is difficult to judge. Students going through at the higher tracks often give favorable reports, though some believe that their programs should be even more demanding (Klein, 1958). Obviously, grouping itself is no magic solution; such post-grouping arrangements as quality teaching and curriculum must also be guaranteed (Getzels & Dillon, 1973).

Enrichment refers to instructional procedures and curriculum experiences beyond the customary for a particular subject, grade, or age. It does *not* include advanced placement in or vertical acceleration through a school program. In practice, enrichment takes one of several forms (Stanley, 1976). First, and perhaps most common, it may consist simply of busywork—more, but not qualitatively different, performance options or requirements. A second form of enrichment may involve advanced work, but work that is not specifically tailored to students' special talents. Math whizzes, for example, may not desire or necessarily profit by enriched social studies. A third form of enrichment is a more gen-

eral, even intensive cultural stimulation than is normally the case in most schools. Expanded opportunities in music, art, dance, drama, creative writing, and foreign language learning illustrate this approach. If provided to students with specific talents in these areas, cultural enrichment can be educationally relevant. One can argue, of course, that such opportunities should not be restricted to the gifted, nor is there any evidence to suggest that children with special academic talents in mathematics or science will be suitably enriched in this way. The remaining enrichment alternative is an opportunity to learn advanced material of in-grade subject matter pertinent to a child's special aptitudes. With this alternative there is a continued risk of moving ahead during one year of schooling, only to encounter normal grade level activities the next. A continuing plan of academically relevant enrichment is therefore imperative to avoid progressive boredom or repetitiveness.

Such a continuing plan is more accurately called academic *acceleration,* a third educational alternative for gifted children and youth. Acceleration can take several forms: permitting bright children access to school programs earlier than their chronological age-mates, general grade-skipping, or selective and progressive movement into higher school levels in a subject area for which exceptional expertise has been developed. Research about the effects of acceleration is more consistently positive than for the other alternatives we have discussed Getzels & Dillon, 1973; Stephens & Evans, 1973), yet acceleration is used the least. One reason for this is inherent in the bureaucratic administration of many schools. To accelerate children is administratively "inconvenient" or "too expensive." Also, teachers may be ill-prepared or reluctant to meet the challenge of instruction for accelerated students. There may also be fears, possibly more perceived than real, among both parents and teachers that acceleration will create problems of social-emotional adjustment for younger gifted children who move into contact with older students. Some worry about what will be done with or for youth who complete their formal education in less than the prescribed compulsory school attendance period. On balance, we think the potential benefits of acceleration outweigh the risk of harm. Yet the issue persists and requires careful analysis for any individual case.

Some additional issues. Other issues about the gifted, less specifically related to schooling, are important. For example, little is known about childrearing practices and family relationships for gifted children and youth. Some authorities (e.g., Robinson, Roedell, & Jackson, 1977) have observed that parents may experience ambivalence about having a gifted child. Parental pride in their children's accomplishments may be countered by parental anxiety about inabilities to meet children's special needs. Parents may experience embarrassment about their children's public displays of precocity (a 3-year-old reading from the menu in a French restaurant). Other parents may champion their children's cause so zealously as to offend their neighbors. Yet secure, competent parents can and do derive much satisfaction from watching their children's pattern of giftedness unfold. Parent education about the gifted, counseling services for parents about any unique socialization problems they may face, and strategies for joint parent–teacher planning of home–school learning experiences deserve serious attention.

To conclude, one thing is certain: much remains to be learned about the gifted (Bernal, 1974; Gallagher, 1975; Getzels & Dillon, 1973; Newland, 1976; Wittek, 1973). The most basic question may be the precise nature of giftedness itself. True, gifted children seem generally to learn both more and faster than their less-gifted peers. Why this occurs is simply not understood. Many teachers with whom we have discussed the matter seem to think gifted children learn differently from other children, but as yet no firm evidence exists on this point. Such aspects of psychological development as self-concept, sex role, and moral development among the gifted are also relatively unexplored at the time of this writing. And giftedness among children who are culturally different, or are from economically disadvantaged backgrounds, or reside in rural areas has been badly neglected by psychologists. These are but a few promising directions for future research. Gifted children and youth represent an invaluable human resource in need of better understanding and nurturance. We have sketched out a few of the important issues about them. Perhaps you, the reader, will be inclined to contribute in some way to a firmer knowledge base about giftedness and human development.

The Mentally Retarded

Historical context and definitions Like the gifted, mentally retarded children and youth are mentioned in the written records of early Greek and Roman civilizations (Kott, 1971; Rosen, Clark, & Kivitz, 1976). Retarded persons, however, were generally rejected, uncared for, or even actively exterminated in ancient times. Throughout the Middle Ages they were stigmatized in various ways. Retarded individuals, for example, were often exploited as jesters or fools for the pleasure of the aristocratic class.

The organized Churches were actually the only consistent source of protection for the mentally retarded until the 1800s, although some religious leaders viewed the retarded as being "possessed by demons." It was about this time that asylums for the retarded were created for general caretaking and segregation from society at large. Gradually, thereafter, more positive social attitudes toward the mentally retarded developed. Forward steps were taken from mere caretaking to more reasoned treatment of the retarded, including education for them. These changes were spurred in large part by Jean Itard's work in France with an apparently mentally retarded feral child. Itard's procedures fell short of training this child for total sufficiency, but the child's progress was so great that Itard's work was widely and highly acclaimed. Itard's student, Eduard Seguin, began the first residential school for the retarded in Paris in 1837. Seguin also helped establish the first residential institution for America's retarded in 1848. This institutional movement expanded greatly during the next 50 years.

The twentieth century brought some disillusionment about such institutions and their impact. They made little progress in assisting the retarded toward a "normal life." Perhaps, as a result, public schools gradually became more active in dealing with the less severely retarded. Strong views about retardation as hereditary (along with insanity and criminality) seemed to provide a "justification" for such extreme measures as the sterilization and forced segregation of huge numbers of retarded persons. More humane attitudes and improved scientific studies of the retarded slowly reduced these practices. When many retarded persons assisted constructively to meet America's domestic humanpower needs during the Second World War, their traditional image as a "menace" to society was shattered.

Today, various social institutions, including the public schools, are intensely involved with almost all forms of mental retardation. Strong efforts are made to place the mentally retarded in regular community settings wherever appropriate. This community integration helps make their lives more normal and further educates the general public about their capabilities and contributions. Legal activity has occurred to specifically guarantee the civil rights of all retarded individuals.

Definitions An acceptable definition of mental retardation has been extremely difficult to formulate. At issue, of course, is adequacy of mental functioning. It has been popular to think in terms of three levels of such functioning: *mild*, or educable for self-sufficiency in a very basic sense; *moderate*, or trainable to the point of elementary self-care; and *severe*, or totally dependent. However, full agreement about the precise details of a definition has never been achieved. One "official" definition, perhaps the most widely accepted, includes the American Association of Mental Deficiency's (AAMD) three interrelated criteria for classifying the mentally retarded: "Mental retardation refers to significantly *subaverage general intellectual functioning* existing concurrently with deficits in *adaptive behavior* and manifested during the *developmental period*" (Grossman, 1973, p. 11, italics added).

Subaverage general intellectual functioning means a performance of two or more standard deviations below the mean on a standard intelligence test such as the Stanford-Binet (see Appendix B). The developmental period extends from the prenatal period to age 18 years. Adaptive behavior is age- and culture-dependent; it refers to general standards of personal independence and social responsibility. For example, an elementary school-age child unable to perform self-help skills (dressing, feeding) would be viewed as deficient in adaptive behavior.

The AAMD definition has been the most widely accepted for over a decade. Dissenters, however, make a strong case for further refinements (Peterson, 1974). Among the most notable disagreements are: (1) the term *mental retardation* should be discarded because it is both educationally irrelevant and carries a stigma of social incompetence; (2) there is a question of cultural and ethnic fairness arising from social norms, languages, and dialects different from those of the white middle class, which often provide the standards for normality; (3) a distinction is necessary between *mental subnormality* (individuals socially incompetent) and *educational subnormality* (individuals intellectually inadequate for regular classroom education, but to whom academics can still be of value with the assistance of special education services; (4) the strong reliance on standardized tests is questionable, particularly given their limited cultural and ethnic generalizability; and (5) the AAMD definition connotes a prediction of social incompetence in adult life, a prediction appropriate only when dealing with the lower extremes of mental handicap.

Accordingly, an alternative definition, more applicable to trainable and dependent retarded persons, has been formulated (Dunn, 1973). Moreover, the term *general learning disabilities* is preferred to *mental retardation* for educable children and youth who will some day become self-sufficient.

Mentally retarded individuals include not more than that 1 percent of each ethnic or racial subgroup who are so deficient in general intellectual ability that their inability to care for themselves, coupled with their disruptive behavior in some cases, is so severe, when compared with their age mates in the community, that they require assistance, care and protection in excess of that which average parents can be expected to provide during their childhood, or that which average communities should be able to provide during their adulthood (Dunn, 1973, p. 67).

The 1 percent of the general population referred to in this definition is further divided into three categories. A majority (75 percent) are *mildly retarded* (IQ of 68 to 52). A much smaller group (20 percent) are *moderately retarded* (IQ of 51 to 36). The remainder (5 percent) are *severely* or *profoundly retarded* individuals (IQ below 36). These percentage figures and IQ ranges are only general approximations (Dunn, 1973).

Characteristics of the Retarded

Perhaps the most striking characteristic of mental retardation is its diverse, often unknown, causes. As many as 95 percent of the cases are classified as "cause unknown." For gross descriptive purposes, this group is often known as the "cultural-familial" retarded, signifying a suspected interaction between hereditary and environmental influences. Those children whose retardation has a more specific cause also tend to be more severely handicapped. These better-known causes include both genetic and environmental syndromes. We recall from Chapter 2, for example, Danny's *Down's Syndrome* (chromosomal aberration). Genetically influenced syndromes such as *phenylketonuria* (progressive retardation caused by enzyme deficiency for normal metabolism) also belong in this category. Problems in prenatal development, discussed in Chapter 6, are widely associated with mental retardation. Environmental insults at birth (anoxia, or lack of oxygen resulting in the death of brain tissue) and thereafter (as in lead and mercury poisoning) are further causes. The interested reader will want to consult more advanced and comprehensive sources for details (Robinson & Robinson, 1976).

Developmentally speaking, a prognosis about mental retardation with known cause is often possible at birth or, in some cases, even before (see Chapter 6). Except for strong inferences from family history analysis, prediction is poor for the larger category of unknown ("cultural-familial") causes. The earliest possible diagnosis is, of course, essential for intervention procedures to have maximum therapeutic effect. Unfortunately, however, retardation is often accompanied by other dysfunctions, such as deficient motor control and sensory functioning. The single most common indicator is delayed development. Normal landmarks in motility (rolling over, pulling to a stand, walking, skipping), language development, perceptual-motor coordination, and social development are reached slowly and tediously—if reached at all. In the absence of extraordinary therapy, children who show gross retardation have but slim chances to achieve full adult maturity.

Beyond this, it is difficult to generalize about characteristics of mentally retarded children and youth. As a group, such children show individual differences on the same order as do their more normal counterparts. The persistent policy of classifying these children can too easily result in stereotypic thinking about them. Commonalities among all children, retarded or otherwise, are often overlooked. The mentally retarded, like all children and youth, have common physical and psychological needs. They are social beings. They are persons of worth and dignity. Their specific characteristics will depend upon the cause and severity of their retardation. But these characteristics will also depend upon the sociocultural context in which they develop, including any special treatment or educational programming for their benefit. As one psychologist has observed (Stroud, 1966), the main problem with the retarded is that we treat them as retarded.

Some Issues in the Study of Mental Retardation

Early diagnosis and intervention   Among the most important issues about mentally retarded children and youth are early diagnosis and care, including attempts to facilitate their long-term development in the direction of normalcy. Much work is underway to perfect valid means to identify, as early as possible, children who are at risk for developmental retardation or disability. Thorough medical examination, of course, is crucial for all newborns. The phenylketonuria syndrome, for example, can be predicted by urinalysis and prevented by quick diet control. Neonatal assessment procedures are currently receiving much attention, and there is increasing attention to actual behavior possibly indicative of central nervous system pathology (Tronick & Brazelton, 1975). The results of such assessments often provide direction for therapeutic interaction methods. Down's Syndrome infants, for example, can show significant advances in development if intensive and sustained intervention procedures are begun at birth (Hayden & Dimitriev, 1975). Though initially expensive, these programs can ultimately yield rich benefits, since retarded individuals who achieve greater self-sufficiency are less likely to require even more expensive life-time institutional care.

As yet, advanced intervention programs, such as the Down's preschool program, are largely experimental and involve comparatively few children. It appears that more conventional residential care (state hospitals, public and private institutional facilities) continues to provide a major source of "treatment" for mentally retarded children and youth, especially, of course, for the more profoundly retarded. Recent social policy has favored a trend away from large central institutions to smaller commu-nity-based facilities in which greater pa-rental and community involvement can occur to benefit the retarded (Balla, 1976). Proponents argue that this trend relieves much of the dehumanization al-leged to occur in many large institutions. The trend is also consistent with more enlightened views about normalizing the life circumstances of retarded individ-uals. And, as indicated earlier, there is increased legal effort to protect retarded persons against unnecessarily restrictive living conditions. In general, it appears that retarded children receive better care in smaller institutions. But, as one ob-server (Balla, 1976) has documented, considerable variation exists in the qual-ity of care. And there is little evidence to indicate that residents actually behave much differently in institutions of differ-ent sizes. Clearly, better documentation of institutional practices and their im-pact is required for judicious social pol-icy decisions to benefit the retarded (Berkson & Landesman-Dwyer, 1977).

Meanwhile, concerned professionals continue to place much faith in the promise of early and sustained home-based and preschool intervention for re-tarded children. Among the most widely discussed early intervention projects in America is the "Milwaukee Project" (He-ber, Garber, Harrington, Hoffman, & Fa-lender, 1972; Heber & Garber, 1973; Trotter, 1976). This project, begun in the 1960s and still underway, has the objec-tive of preventing progressive decline in intellectual functioning among children at risk for *cultural-familial* mental retar-dation. This type of mental retardation, as we noted, has no apparent physical cause and is found chiefly among eco-nomically depressed urban and rural populations. Because of its general inter-est and potential significance for social-policy formulation, we discuss the Mil-waukee Project in some detail.

Because the measured intelligence of a mother is the best single indicator of her offspring's intelligence, maternal IQ was the basic criterion for selecting the participants in this longitudinal study. Forty newborn infants and their mothers (IQ less than 75) were assigned to either an experimental (special treatment) or control (no treatment) group. All partici-pants were black and lived in Milwau-kee, Wisconsin. The selection criteria were intended to minimize cultural, ra-cial, and ethnic differences within each group. Black families in the area were not highly mobile, which further in-creased the stability of the sample.

The intervention program had two principal components: maternal rehabili-tation and infant and early childhood stimulation. An important feature of the maternal program was preparing the ex-perimental mothers for employment op-portunities. Project investigators be-lieved that the home environment would improve as an indirect effect of the im-proved employment potential, increased earnings, and self-confidence of the mothers. A second major feature for mothers was training in general home and family care: budgeting, nutrition, family hygiene, and so on. The criterion for success of the maternal rehabilitation component was reliable maternal em-ployment. "In home" maternal behavior changes, however, did not lend them-selves to objective measurement.

The stimulation program for experi-mental children was divided into in-fancy and preschool age periods. For both periods, individualized and pre-scriptive instructional techniques were utilized in a day-care and early educa-tion center: intensive teacher–child con-tact 7 hours per day, 5 days per week, 12 months per year until the children were eligible for first grade. Initially in-fants had one teacher each to provide a consistent mothering figure. Gradually this ratio was changed to include more individuals. The curriculum for infants included activities for perceptual-motor development, sensory discrimination, receptive and expressive language experience, and such general cognitive experience as problem solving with manipulative toys.

The preschool program began when the experimental child reached two years of age. Building upon the infant program, this curriculum had three learning areas: (1) a language program to develop skills in vocabulary, auditory attention, comprehension, and the like; (2) a reading program; and (3) a math/problem-solving program including exploratory materials for inquiry-skill development. Throughout the entire stimulation program, control children were contacted *only* for testing on the same schedule as were the experimental subjects.

This testing program included many different assessments to provide a comprehensive picture of the children's development: (1) developmental schedules of infant adaptive behavior; (2) experimental learning tasks to reveal response strategies; (3) measures of language development; (4) measures of social development, including mother–child interactions; and (5) standardized tests of general intelligence.

Program results were marked. By the end of the preschool period (with children about 6 years of age), the experimental subjects were performing significantly better than controls in all areas of assessment. In measured IQ, for example, experimental children consistently surpassed controls by 20 to 30 points, beginning about age 2. Recent follow-up data reveal that the experimental children at 9 years of age were maintaining a 20 point IQ advantage over their controls and still performing in the normal IQ range (Trotter, 1976).

This project has been hailed as an outstanding example of successful intervention. It is offered as strong evidence for the plasticity of measured human intelligence, thus supporting environmentalist claims about improving human potential. But, as the reader may suspect, the Milwaukee Project is not without its critics (Page, 1972; Throne, 1975). The most severe criticism is the lack of *treatment specification*. That is, many different things occurred simultaneously—some planned, some perhaps spontaneous—without any means of linking specific program components to specific outcomes. This leaves other investigators in the lamentable position of not knowing what specific aspects of the intervention were effective. What should be included in later intervention projects? Other questions about the equality of the two groups of infants and measurement of their development have been raised as well. On the face of it, however, the Milwaukee Project has met its primary objective (at least to date). Many children with a prognosis of cultural-familial retardation apparently can be helped toward more advanced functioning given the appropriate circumstances for learning. An issue for further research, of course, is the extent to which this outcome can be repeated for similar children in different communities. If it can be repeated, the basic social issue clearly requires a commitment of resources to such a purpose.

Public school programs for the retarded School programs for retarded children and youth are included within the domain of special education. As with the gifted, alternatives for special education abound. Programs for the retarded range from regular classroom placement through self-contained special classes and teaching systems in regular schools to segregation in completely separate schools. Expanded educational services, including preschool and "postschool" programs, sheltered workshops, and specific vocational training, are on the increase as educators respond to legislative and judicial demands that *all* exceptional children be provided with suitable educational programs at public expense until they reach adulthood.

The objectives, content, and methods of instruction for retarded children vary considerably, usually according to some scheme for categorizing their needs and limitations. In American public schools, the most common approach requires an assessment of general measured intelligence. Descriptive labels are then used to group these children for instruction and care. To quote one authority:

Most popular are the terms *educable mentally retarded* (EMR) and *trainable mentally retarded* (TMR). EMR children generally are defined as having IQs from 50 or 55 to 75 or 80. They are expected eventually to achieve academic work at least to the third-grade level and occasionally to the sixth-grade level by school-leaving age. TMR children with IQs of 25 or 35 to 50 or 55 are not expected to achieve functionally useful academic skills. Self-care and social adjustment within a restricted environment are the goals of their school experience. Children with still lower IQs previously tended to be known as *custodial mentally retarded,* but fortunately that terminology is no longer in use. Presently they tend to be known as "right to education children," although hopefully a less awkward term will soon emerge. Some educators have recognized the learning problems of the *dull normal* or *slow learning* child (IQ = 75–89), but the present consensus tends to be that special education is neither necessary nor desirable for this group, except for those with specific learning disabilities (Robinson & Robinson 1976, p. 371).

Where competently delivered, educational services for educables have been generally adequate for their stated purposes; less confidence is expressed about the results of conventional school programs for trainables (Dunn, 1973). However, the refined application in recent years of *precision teaching,* a system of instruction based upon principles of conditioning and reinforcement (Chapter 2), has shown much promise for both educables and trainables (Haring, 1974). The search for "better ways" continues, as does debate about a number of important issues (Moss, 1974). One such issue is how best to meet the need for parental education and involvement in special education. Another concerns any effects of labeling on the self-concept of retarded children. Still another is the extent and nature of public school responsibility for the care, if not instruction, of severely handicapped children. And there is also the problem of the sex education of mentally retarded children and youth, an issue complicated by frequent negativism among parents about their retarded offspring's sexuality (Dupras & Tremblay, 1976).

A final issue, as yet unmentioned, is the move in special education away from segregated classes for mildly retarded children and youth to their integration into normal classroom life with nonretarded peers. This practice, known as "mainstreaming" (Kirk, 1972), is motivated in large part by dissatisfaction with segregated classes or special grouping for the mildly retarded (Budoff & Gottlieb, 1976). As implied above, one source of this dissatisfaction is the possible negative effect of labeling and segregation on retarded children's self-images. Another source, more strongly reinforced by research evidence, is that special classes are not superior to regular grade placement for these children's educational development. These ideas, along with the availability of improved procedures for individualized instruction, have led an increasing number of special educators to support mainstreaming. But mainstreaming requires certain conditions to achieve its anticipated benefits. Administrative support is imperative. Teachers must be both receptive and capable of managing the mainstreamed classroom. The "normal" children with whom the mentally retarded are mainstreamed must be prepared to accept and interact positively with their new classmates. Otherwise, retarded children may merely trade one set of problems (segregation) for another (mainstreaming). We worry especially about the social relations of retarded children. Data indicate that many retarded children—notably those low in physical attractiveness and social competence—are not socially acceptable to their peers (Siperstein & Gottlieb, 1977). At its worst, this constitutes a form of prejudice.

As this book is written, none of these issues about educating the retarded has been resolved, nor are they likely to be in the near future. Each of them, however, is clearly related to conditions for the general development and welfare of retarded children and youth. Again, we encourage our readers to consider how they might somehow contribute to further understanding and improving the life patterns of retarded children and youth.

Parents of the retarded certainly deserve our sensitive concern and support. Giving birth to and rearing retarded children can often be a trying emotional experience, even though much gratification may come from helping them develop (Robinson & Robinson, 1976). Parents of the retarded face numerous practical problems, such as difficulty in managing child behavior, medical expenses, restrictions on leisure activity and entertainment, and disrupted sleep. Improved counseling techniques and parental education for skillful child management in the home are but two promising directions for assisting parents of retarded and other at-risk children such as the

emotionally disturbed (O'Dell, 1974; Tavormina, 1974).

AGGRESSION AND SOCIAL DEVIANCE

A second, quite different, social challenge is the nature and management of aggression and social deviance—especially juvenile delinquency. The common denominator for both patterns of behavior is their antisocial character. In one sense, both patterns are normal. Most children and youth are aggressive or delinquent at some time in their development. If chronic and intense, however, these patterns may reflect emotional disturbance or serious personality disorders. Either way, they create much conflict, both among the young and between the young and their elders. However, the challenge is not limited to children and youth. Parents can behave aggressively toward their children, even to the point of severe child abuse. Thus we examine aggression of both children and parents from a psychological perspective.

Aggression

Aggression, discussed in Chapter 5 (mass media), is unquestionably a major concern for most American parents and teachers (Ziv, 1970). Parents often see aggressive behavior as a danger to their children, a threat to themselves, or both. More often than not, teachers also consider aggressive behavior as disruptive, a threat to their efforts to maintain order and group control, and something which usually requires direct action. Extreme youthful aggression, in the forms of vandalism against school property and of actual physical violence against teachers, has become a serious nationwide problem (Bayh, 1975; McPartland & McDill,

© 1973, George W. Gardner

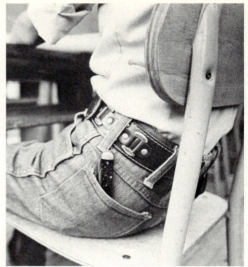

Kenneth Karp

Kenneth K

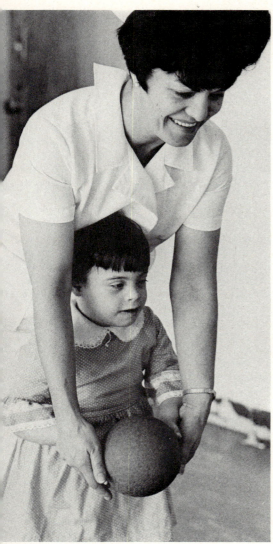

anne Szasz

Michael Weisbrot

1977). We examine in detail the meaning of aggression, along with some background factors and the relationship of frustration and punishment to aggression. Subsequently, guidelines for living with aggression are suggested. The section concludes by discussing how aggression may be sustained across generations of Americans, at least in part, by adult violence toward children.

The Meaning of Aggression

There are at least three problems in defining aggression. The first is deciding how to limit the term. Two broad approaches have been taken to solve this problem (Bandura & Walters, 1963). The most conservative approach limits the meaning of aggression to observable behavior, including the effects or consequences of aggression. For example, acting-out behaviors, either *verbal* (yelling, shouting, threatening, ridiculing) or *physical* (hitting, kicking, throwing objects at another person), are clear to any observer. The effects of such behaviors can usually also be observed: pain or injury to another person, destruction of property, and the like.

A more risky approach to defining aggression actually is an extension of the first—including in the definition the apparent *intention* or *motive* of the aggressor. One person, for example, may deliberately set about to cause pain to another. Including a judgment about intent or motivation requires that we *infer* such motivation from the aggressive behavior observed. Intent, of course, cannot be directly observed. To be sure, a person may admit verbally to another that his intent was to injure. Even then, however, it is an assumption that such an admission is true. Correct inference about the motives of others is a difficult matter. In children's play situations, for example, it may be impossible to determine whether one child strikes another

accidentally or intentionally. Knowing the exact social context in which the striking behavior occurs increases the probability of correct inference. However, the difficulties associated with inference in explaining or analyzing behavior underline the need for caution. Otherwise, children may be unjustly accused, blamed, or punished for aggression that is, in fact, misinterpreted by an observing adult.

A second problem in defining aggression is to distinguish between aggression whose goal is harm to others for harm's sake, and aggression that is designed to achieve an instrumental goal (to get something done, to protect something, or to reach some desired outcome). Examples of instrumental aggression include aggression to gain possession of material goods, to win a prize in competition with others, or to achieve control or power over another's activities. Such instrumental aggression *may* include harm to others. It frequently occurs, however, when a child or a youth wishes to obtain desired goals quickly, perhaps because no constructive alternative to aggression exists.

Third and final is the problem of whether and to what extent aggression is *situational* (is specific to certain social settings and conditions) or *general* (represents a basic tendency for children or youth to show a certain level or kind of aggression across a wide variety of settings). For example, some children seem to behave aggressively wherever they are—school, church, or playground. Other children, in contrast, rarely behave aggressively and then only in certain stressful situations. The issue is whether aggressiveness is a pervasive personality characteristic or a set of responses to very specific conditions. Behaviorally-oriented psychologists are inclined to accept the latter view. Other psychologists emphasize the instinctual nature of aggression and thus usually lean toward the personality trait viewpoint. This underlines the role of "theory" in guiding one's interpretation of behavior (see Appendix A). Both possibilities are plausible and not necessarily incompatible.

When general aggression seems to characterize a given child's behavior, many psychologists assume that strong feelings of hostility toward others must exist, whatever the cause of this anger. Again, other psychologists doubt that hostility is necessarily involved. Either way, "inner feelings" are difficult to assess just by looking at an individual's behavior. Situational aggression directs attention to the circumstances that lead to acting-out *and* any consequences of aggression that promote or maintain the behavior. For example, we might observe that Duncan, age 6, is aggressive only when other children make unfair demands on him for sharing toys. In such a self-defense situation, an aggressive response may be not only appropriate but also desirable.

There is some evidence to indicate individual differences in aggression-proneness. Further, indications of suffering from a victim seem to influence the frequency and intensity of further aggression. High-aggressive boys, for example, have been observed to aggress more when their victim's pain cues are low. Victim-suffering, it seems, may serve as an index of "successful" aggression among such boys (Perry & Perry, 1974).

Some Background and Developmental Factors in Aggression[1]

Most people in our society appear to value reasoning rather than brute force to solve personal conflicts. This belief is reflected in American childrearing prac-

[1] The role of televised violence in children's aggression was discussed in Chapter 5.

tices. American parents generally seem to discourage their children's direct aggression, or acting-out behavior, and encourage rational means for problem solving. However, the specific form that such discouragement takes varies widely. One source of variation is the age of the child (Feshback, 1970). For example, very young children are often permitted to occasionally hit, bite, and throw objects during expressions of rage. These direct aggressive acts by older children are usually vigorously discouraged by their parents. Many parents, however, resort to physical punishment in dealing with children's aggression, ostensibly for the purpose of reducing or eliminating the undesirable behavior. Unfortunately, it is probably true that angry adults often act out their own aggression on their children, sometimes with little or no justification. By so doing, they provide a model of aggression to their children, with the effect of eventually increasing rather than reducing childhood aggression.

The effects of disapproval and various forms of punishment on children's aggressive behavior are not easily predicted. Generally, however, physical aggression among children gradually decreases in frequency throughout the preschool years (especially among girls). This decrease does not mean that aggression subsides. Rather, verbal aggression (yelling, name-calling, swearing, and threats of physical aggression, tattling, and reproving) becomes more frequent during the late preschool years. During the primary-grade years, most children learn how to substitute competitive striving for extensive verbal and physical outpourings of aggression. Yet some children, more often males than females, show a strong, stable pattern of aggressive behavior through childhood and into adolescence (Kagan & Moss, 1962). During adolescence, of course, direct forms of aggression can become very serious for both society and the individual. For example, physical assault, property destruction, and theft are criminal acts. This anticipates the aggression–delinquency relationship discussed below.

To conclude, a prolonged pattern of aggressiveness over the developmental years may indicate that parents tolerate, or even approve of and reward, their children's aggressive behavior. Frequent aggressiveness can result in many problems, especially in school, where acting-out behavior is inappropriate. This leads logically to a study of conditions under which aggression can be managed or controlled. What have psychologists learned about these conditions?

The Management of Aggression

First, we must establish a rationale for the management of aggression. Again we refer to the democratic ideal. Allowed to flourish, aggression often results in harm to others or interferes with their rights. Moreover, children and youth who frequently act aggressively toward their peers often end up being rejected by them. Peer rejection cuts off aggressive children from many valuable social contacts, to say nothing of likely harm to their self-esteem. Unfortunately, further retaliation (the vicious circle) is often the result of aggression. A basic task for child and youth workers, then, is to determine how aggression may be channeled so that both society and the individual benefit, if possible, rather than suffer.

To accomplish this requires a serious study of factors that promote more or less aggressiveness in children and youth. Constitutional factors conducive to aggression such as hyperactivity, low threshold or tolerance for pain, and strong emotional reactivity must, of course, be considered. Although constitutional factors are rarely subject to direct control, medical procedures may be effective in extreme cases. Interesting

work has begun, for example, on the neuropharmacology of aggression (Avis, 1974). Specific drug therapy is apparently effective in changing some, but not all, forms of aggressive behavior.

More immediately, parents and teachers can exert some control over the conditions under which aggressive behavior often increases. For example, opportunities to imitate aggressive models may actually promote aggression (Davids, 1972). By models we refer to both adults and other children who are themselves violent (live or viewed on film) and who threaten, coerce, ridicule, and manhandle other people. The effects of models can be particularly strong if the aggressive behavior modeled is successful and leads to desired outcomes (Feshback, 1970). Situations where children's aggression is allowed to go unchecked are likely to foster more acting out. These include settings where basic standards for conduct are not applied clearly and consistently and where children get their way by bullying and intimidating others. Any direct encouragement and reward for children's aggression will be likely to increase its occurrence. Wherever possible, positive reinforcement for aggression should be removed or avoided entirely if aggression is to be minimized.

The role of frustration   Frustration is usually defined as an unpleasant emotional state that results when individuals are unable to achieve some desired goal. A popular, long-standing view in psychology is that frustration frequently leads to aggression and that some degree of frustration probably underlies all forms of aggression (Dollard et al., 1933). While this view does not fully explain aggression, it is clear that when frustration leads to anger, aggressive behavior is a likely outcome.

An obvious practical implication of the frustration–aggression relationship is to avoid any prolonged or excessive frustration of children to prevent needless aggression. Conditions that typically produce frustration in young children, or at least serve as antecedents to aggression, include confining them to small spaces, requiring them to remain quiet or sit for long periods, prodding them always to "hurry up" their activities, providing inadequately for rest periods and snacks, changing routines frequently and unexpectedly, unfairly removing privileges, and inflicting physical discomforts, including corporal punishment.

Of course, like death and taxes, a degree of frustration tolerance does seem necessary for all children and youth. Helpful adults will assist children to deal with their frustrations constructively wherever possible, rather than allowing outpourings of aggression. The degree to which frustration is relevant to a given situation or task may be important for this purpose (McCandless, 1967). Many learning tasks, both in and out of school, are frustrating to children and youth because of their complexity and the practice that is required for mastery. This kind of frustration is normal and can be expected in the early stages of many new learning activities. But helpful teachers will not add irrelevant sources of frustration to this more relevant or "natural" frustration. Vague, poorly organized presentation strategies by teachers, requirements of children for which they are ill-prepared, poor planning, distracting noise, substandard lighting and room temperature control, and inconsistent discipline can all be sources of irrelevant classroom frustration.

Punishment and aggression The relationship of punishment to aggression also merits our attention. Punishment inflicted by any authority figure, for example, can often inhibit children's direct expression of aggression while in the presence of the punisher. But harsh punishment also often leads to increased aggressive behavior directed toward other objects or persons, especially in the absence of the original punisher (Berkowitz, 1973). This is *displaced aggression*. Aggression (in retaliation to a punisher) is not directed toward the original punisher. Instead, it is expressed toward some less-threatening figure or object, a smaller child, a toy, or even a pet animal. To explain displaced aggression, some authorities (for example, Bandura, 1969) emphasize a facilitating modeling effect produced by a punishing adult. Parents who both permit and punish aggressive behavior frequently have highly aggressive children (Feshback, 1970). Some frustration is probably produced by this pattern of parenting, especially for children whose parents respond to aggression inconsistently—allowing it on some occasions, only to unpredictably punish it on others.

There is also danger in the consistent use of strong punishment. Punishment may not only stop or inhibit the behavior toward which it is directed, but stop *all* behavior. The net effect may be inhibited, passive, nonspontaneous children for whom constructive social, cognitive, and motor development is difficult because they seldom display behavior that can be rewarded. Constructive socialization proceeds best using selective reinforcement, emphasizing positive and developmental, rather than negative and repressive, interactions with significant others.

Catharsis and aggression A widely held belief in American society is that aggressive behavior may be dissipated or reduced through *catharsis*, that is, by the free expression of aggression either vicariously (in fantasy or by watching others act aggressively), or openly through play, verbalizing one's feelings, or actual aggressive responses toward something—striking a Bobo doll or smashing a junk car with a sledge hammer, for example. It is commonly argued that cathartic expression of aggression reduces the tendency to perform other aggressive acts, or produces feelings of satisfaction or relief from tension. A belief in catharsis often underlies the practice of helping children to become less aggressive (and hostile) by acting out their feelings in doll play, shooting toy guns, finger painting, physical exertion, or related forms of vicarious experience (such as watching cartoons in which the characters behave aggressively).

Though the notion is appealing, there is little research evidence that catharsis works in these ways (Berkowitz, 1970). In fact, tactics for cathartic expression may even promote higher rates of aggression among children. Of course, most people will agree that aggressive doll play or mild competitive games are less destructive than striking one's peers. It should not be assumed, however, that such activities will necessarily reduce children's "aggressive feelings" or cause them not to act out against other children. Cathartic activities are best viewed simply as means for channeling aggression *away* from human targets.

This view can be used to distinguish constructive and destructive ways of expressing anger. We do not advise that children or youth "bottle up" their anger and be prevented from emotional catharsis. Not expressing anger may have its own negative consequences, such as psychosomatic disorders, impaired cognition, and deceptive interpersonal relationships (Holt, 1970). But neither should we conclude that catharsis is a cure-all for unwanted aggressive behavior.

A clinical note about self-awareness can be added as well. It seems wise for children, youth, and adults to learn to recognize their feelings of hostility and anger, accept their hostility and anger without anxiety and guilt, and, at the same time, handle such feelings in personally and socially constructive ways.

These are known as *coping techniques*. One cab driver, for example, diminishes the frustration of urban traffic by asking himself (or his passenger), "I wonder what happened to that poor devil this morning?" when honked at or yelled at irrationally. Similarly, a teacher we know practices isometric exercises at the first sign of irritability or anger.

Violence Against Children

Concentrating on the development and management of children's aggression, we referred in passing to how punitive actions by parents may predispose or activate similar aggression among their children under certain circumstances. We now address specifically the problem of aggression, or coercive power, directed toward children by their parents or caretakers—intentional actions that result in physical injury, sexual molestation, emaciation, or, occasionally, death. Child abuse extends beyond physical injury to include psychosocial deprivation (such as poverty) and psychologically abusive practices in institutions such as the schools, juvenile courts and detention centers, child welfare agencies, and the like.

In this section we discuss *individual abuse* by parents of their children in the home setting. This abuse takes many forms. Some parents "indirectly" abuse their children by failing to provide adequate physical care and nutrition. Others act in more directly outrageous ways to harm their offspring. Consider, for example, the following incidents of child abuse that have come to our attention in recent months.

Danielle, age 5, whose right arm was axed off at the elbow by her father as "punishment" for rummaging through his chest-of-drawers without permission.

Tommy and Teddy, twin boys, age 10, who were tethered in their beds for five days without food and with water only once a day after failing to do their Saturday chores "satisfactorily."

Lonnie, age 2, whose mother scalded his buttocks with boiling water, ostensibly for playing with "forbidden" *objets d'art* placed on the coffee table in the family living room.

Beverly, age 3, now incapacitated by permanent brain damage from repeated, savage beatings by her stepmother who said she "was sick and tired of her whining around calling me Mommy."

Bernard, whose mother died giving him birth and who had since lived with his grandmother, was kicked to death at age 6 in the men's room of an automobile service station by his father after they had spent a Sunday afternoon together at the zoo.

Child abuse in recent years has become all too commonplace in America and other "advanced" societies throughout the world. No one knows the exact magnitude of the problem. Marshalling the best sources of data available, experts in the study of child abuse (for example, Alvy, 1975) estimate that some 700 children die each year at the hands of their parents or foster parents. All told, it is believed that from one to four million children are physically abused in one way or another by caretakers during any given year, with another seven million subjected to the abusive conditions of poverty.

Statistically speaking (Gelles, 1973), the incidence of child abuse is greater in, but certainly not limited to, the working class. The abusing parent is most often the mother, perhaps because of a predominance of female-headed households in America, although a greater number of *severe* abuses may come from a father, stepfather, or other adult male living in the home. The early years of life (3 months to 3 years of age) are the most dangerous period for children of abusing parents. Very young children, of course, are the most physically vulnerable to physical force. Infants lack the skills to maintain meaningful social interactions with easily frustrated parents. Moreover, infants can create economic or other hardships for their families, to which parents may respond primitively and punitively.

Sensitized to this disgraceful state of affairs, professional child workers have increasingly concerned themselves with attempts to explain, control, and prevent child abuse (Fontana, 1971; Gil, 1970; Kempe & Helfer, 1972; Maurer, 1973). We briefly examine their progress.

Explaining Child Abuse

Three major related pathways for exploring child abuse have been created in recent years (Parke & Collmer, 1975). The first and perhaps most prevalent pathway is the *psychiatric model*, which presumes some form of psychological defect(s) among parents who abuse their children. Studies based upon this model concentrate on differentiating the personality characteristics of parents who do, as compared to parents who do not, abuse their children. The most general and reliable finding from such studies is that abusing parents as a group are low in empathy and stress-tolerance, easily aroused to aggression, and have themselves often been abused as children by their own parents (Spinetta & Rigler, 1972). Though somewhat helpful in understanding the abuse syndrome, knowing about such characteristics does not tell us anything about the conditions under which abuse-prone parents may act out against their children. In addition, not all abusing parents fit this clinical picture.

Hence a second pathway or approach to the problem of explanation has been formulated, a *sociological* interpretation of abuse in which cultural values and the social organization of family and community take precedence over individual differences. According to this view, patterns of child abuse have their roots in the cultural sanction of violence as a way to resolve interpersonal conflicts. Who can forget the embarrassing truth made explicit in the 1960s, namely, "Violence is as American as cherry pie!"? Survey data clearly show that physical punishment is both frequently used and often preferred by many American parents as a childrearing tactic. Corporal punishment is easy, swift, and often *does* inhibit children's behavior. It can be further reinforcing because it releases parental frustration. And it is widely modeled by authority figures (police, television characters, and even some teachers) all easily observed by parents and their children.

Though child abuse does appear more often in cultures that also sanction corporal punishment for childhood socialization, we cannot claim a cause–effect relationship between these two variables. Other factors and conditions must be taken into account in the sociological analysis of child abuse. One important condition is the stress produced by the discomfort and frustration of limited economic resources. Child abuse occurs across all socioeconomic levels, but its incidence is often higher in families with marginal and unstable economic situations, where it may simply be symptomatic of an inadequate support system (for example, comfortable living space, secure employment, access to day care) (Garbarino, 1976). Family size and family–community relationships may also figure strongly in an abuse pattern. For example, abuse is more likely to occur both in larger (four or more children) than in smaller families and in families who are "socially isolated" from other people (whether by choice or circumstance).

These factors, however plausible in making sense out of child abuse, do not tell the complete story. Still another approach to this problem is the *social-situational* model. In addition to the conditions mentioned above, this approach identifies specific situational factors, including the characteristic interaction patterns among family members, especially husband and wife, inconsistency in disciplinary tactics used by parents, the intensity of physical pain with which children respond to punishment, the extent to which parents are able to "justify" corporal punishment as a means for shaping "moral conduct," reaction of the spouse to abusive acts, and children's contribution(s) to their own abuse. How children may provoke abusive treatment from parents is important to our theme about interaction and how individuals may contribute to their own development. Some children are apparently more likely than others to become targets of abuse in a particular setting that increases the probability of negative child–parent interaction. For example, children who are unwanted, suffer from genetically-determined anomalies, are temperamentally incompatible with their parents, are chronically ill, or are simply physically unattractive and ill-coordinated may be more probable candidates for abusive treatment. If so, another form of vicious cycle may occur: abuse contributes to behavior patterns and an appearance of neglect and harmful treatment that, in turn, elicits further abuse (Bakan, 1971). Such cycles underline the need for sensitive parent education about alternatives to corporal punishment in children socialization. Figure 12.1 presents a summary of how social context and aspects of the individual parent or caretaker may interact to produce a pattern of child abuse.

Controlling and Preventing Child Abuse

Both short- and long-term social action programs are important in any attempt to control and prevent child abuse, as is explained succinctly in the following quote:

Short term control involves some type of crisis intervention which may prevent an imminent case of abuse from occurring. Telephone hot lines, crisis nurseries, and day care drop-off centers are examples of short-term control. Similarly, temporary removal of the abused child from the home may be viewed as another form of short-term control. However, in light of the large number of abused children reported annually, removal and placement cannot be viewed as an economically feasible solution to the abuse problem. Long-term control has the more ambitious aim of restructuring the social interaction patterns of the family members that may be the cause of abuse or the modi-

fication of either the child's or the parent's attitudes, values, personality, and/or behavior which are viewed as causing the abuse (Parke & Collmer, 1975, p. 556).

The specific nature of long-term intervention and control will vary with the change-agents' preferred way of interpreting child abuse. If a psychiatric approach is used, then the preferred intervention strategy will be a modification of parental personality. Psychological counseling, individual psychotherapy, or various forms of group (family) therapy may be used. They may focus upon parental affect, behavior, or both. Such strategies are typically both expensive and time-consuming. Even when effective, such therapies are difficult to provide on a wide

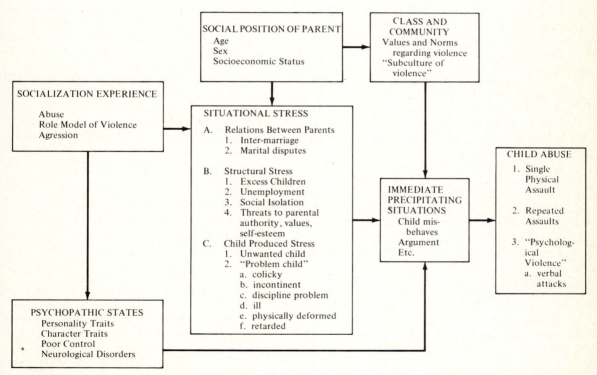

Fig. 12-1 A social-psychological model of the causes of child abuse. (From R. J. Gelles, Child abuse as psychopathology: A sociological critique and reformulation. *American Journal of Orthopsychiatry*, 1973, *43*, 611–621. Reproduced by permission.)

scale. It is unlikely that psychiatric intervention will ever become a dominant solution to the child-abuse problem.

Proponents of the sociological perspective (such as Gil, 1970) argue for massive changes in social philosophy and values, eventually eradicating poverty by providing a guaranteed income, comprehensive health and social resources, improved family life education, acceptable housing, maternal support and comprehensive cultural-recreational facilities. The idea is that as living conditions improve, the reasons for abusive child-rearing (stress, frustration) will disappear. The recommendations are both noteworthy and promising, but few authorities seem convinced that simply eliminating poverty (even if possible) would also eliminate child abuse.

Thus, the social-situational approach to child abuse analysis has considerable practical appeal. This requires actually modifying the home context in which child abuse occurs, emphasizing behavior change in both parents and their children. Training parents in the skillful application of behavior-modification techniques (O'Dell, 1974), or even to act as therapists for their own children (Johnson & Katz, 1973) may be involved. Techniques for anger control for parents, increasing parental sociability, and increasing parental recognition of the harmful effects of their abusiveness are also recommended. Group participation experiences for child-abusing parents can be used, for example, as in *Parents Anonymous*. Such experiences can include additional child-care instruction and a provision for emergency parent-aide support services. People are working hard to remove the blight of child abuse from American family life. Information about the successful impact of these efforts is scarce and inconclusive, but we can be encouraged by some hopeful prospects of curbing such violence against the young.

Social Deviance Among Youth: The Crisis of Juvenile Delinquency

Part and parcel of the general issue of aggression in American society is the peculiar problem of juvenile delinquency. Four points can be made to begin our discussion of this problem. First, perhaps the most central feature of what we call "delinquency" is its antisocial character. To paraphrase one authority (Thornburg, 1971): Juvenile delinquency can be described as norm-violating behavior. Legally, juveniles are delinquent if they violate the law and are convicted by a court for doing so. Behaviorally, they are delinquent if they commit aggressive acts contrary to social norms or demands. In both cases their activities are antisocial.

This definition of delinquency can be made more precise. For example, it is important to differentiate between "true delinquency" and "pseudodelinquency" (Glueck, 1966). True delinquency occurs repeatedly. If the offenses are committed by youths past the statutory juvenile court age of 16, they are punishable as either felonies or misdemeanors. Pseudodelinquency, in contrast, involves occasional deviation from acceptable norms for conduct; it is not a chronic or habitual pattern of criminal acting-out. Without the distinction between true delinquency and pseudodelinquency, practically every juvenile could be classified as delinquent. Authorities generally agree that juvenile delinquency is no either-or affair. Most individual children and youth behave delinquently at some time and in some fashion during their childhood or adolescence. Our serious social challenge is the more frequent and felonious behavior of the young.

Second, the juvenile delinquency rate in America (and in most industrial nations of the world) has risen progressively since the Second World War. This increase, moreover, is disproportionate to juvenile population growth over the same time span (White House Conference on Youth, 1971). In 1960, for instance, approximately 20 delinquency cases per 1,000 juveniles (ages 11–17) were reported; in 1968, roughly 29 per 1,000 were recorded. At the present time, about 3 percent of the juvenile population is referred to juvenile courts during a single year, and over twice this number has been in some kind of trouble with the police (Gibbons, 1970). Some authorities estimate that a more accurate rate for true delinquency is about 10 percent of the juvenile population. Statistics presented by the U.S. Senate Sub-Committee to Investigate Juvenile Delinquency (Bayh, 1975) suggest that violent juvenile crime in America has increased by nearly 250 percent since the early 1960s. During the same period, crimes directed by youths against property increased over 100 percent. By 1975, 50 percent of all violent crimes (homicide, rape, personal assault) and 80 percent of all property crimes (robbery, burglary, vandalism) were committed by persons under 25 years of age.

Third, juvenile delinquency is an extremely complex phenomenon that has multiple causes. Much of the research about delinquency has been aimed at dispelling many popular myths about the causes of delinquency. Simple explanations based on the singular impact of slum conditions, low intelligence, working mothers, the mass media, and "bad genes" have been abandoned by students of delinquency in favor of more sophisticated hypotheses mentioned below.

Finally, some youth (and these are most often advantaged, intelligent youth high in moral judgment) may commit legally delinquent acts because of sincere, well-thought-out convictions that the social order is wrong. Examples of such official delinquencies by individuals and groups are civil disobedience over issues of racial discrimination, the draft, napalm, the Southeast Asia war, ecology, and so on. Such actions are technically considered delinquent or criminal because they violate existing law, but these matters do not enter into our discussion of "true" delinquency.

Some Mediating Factors in Juvenile Delinquency

As with other behavior patterns discussed in this book, patterns of delinquency are mediated by many factors. We shall consider three such factors; age, sex, and social class.

Age At least two basic generalizations about the relationship of age to delinquency patterns have strong factual support. First, a disproportionate number of total criminal offenses occur among the juvenile population, as compared to other age groups. In the home county of one of the authors, for example, well over one-half the felonies from 1965 to 1975 (including murder, rape, auto theft, and assault) were committed by juveniles. Second, from preadolescence onward, juvenile delinquency becomes progressively more diverse and serious. According to one report, for instance, the frequency of offenses against persons (murder, rape, assault) and property (robbery, vandalism, forgery), and disorderly conduct increases steadily with age (Freedman, 1966). Other reports indicate crimes of aggression increase "precipitously" to about age 19, increase less sharply thereafter, and decline rapidly after age 25 (Ausubel, 1954; Bayh, 1975).

Reasons most commonly advanced to account for these generalizations include the frustration–aggression hypothesis discussed earlier in this chapter, alienation among youth, delayed maturation (including retarded moral development), differential association by juveniles with delinquent models, the unadulterated audacity of the young (often manifested in thrill-seeking and nose-thumbing at the adult establishment), and just plain desire for money (Ausubel, 1966; Bandura & Walters, 1959; Freedman, 1966; Gibbons, 1968; Glueck & Glueck, 1968; Gold, 1970; Richards, 1966; Short, 1976). Fortunately, there is much evidence to indicate that for many delinquent youth, antisocial and criminal behavior is temporary. Juvenile delinquency does not necessarily lead to adult criminality. This, of course, is no reason for society to take delinquency lightly or to exempt the young from being held accountable for their own actions.

Sex   There are marked sex differences in delinquency throughout adolescence. Boys generally begin delinquency earlier and engage in it more frequently than girls. Juvenile court records, for example, currently indicate that for every female referral there are from four to five male referrals, and males are usually younger at the time of their first referral. Moreover, the basis for court referral is usually different for the two sexes. Boys, for example, are more often referred for theft, assault, vandalism, and other direct, aggressive offenses than are girls. Delinquency among girls, in contrast, is more likely to take the form of sexual promiscuity, petty shoplifting, running away form home, or "general incorrigibility."

There has been considerable speculation about an increase in female gang delinquency in recent years, but little hard evidence exists. We have been impressed, however, with more frequent press reports (perhaps reflecting sensationalism) about females in groups assaulting and "shaking down" both younger children and elderly persons. Females, it seems, also engaged in more

extortion and theft within schools than in years past. Some of our colleagues are quick to suggest this is an accompaniment of women's liberation. Others see it simply as further evidence of a crisis in American family life. Whatever the dynamics, sex-related delinquency patterns undoubtedly reflect differences in cultural conditioning, motivation, opportunity, and the degree to which society tolerates deviant behavior among young males and females. It is apparent, however, that differences exist in the antecedents of delinquency for boys and girls. Family tension and conflict, for example, are often more important factors in female (as opposed to male) delinquency.

Social class   A traditional and popular view of delinquency is that such behavior is primarily a product of deprived socioeconomic conditions. Delinquency does occur among juveniles of the lower social class, but it is by no means limited to this stratum of society. Currently, middle-class delinquency is also commonplace, although it may be more often "hidden" than is lower-class delinquency, going undetected or unreported by legal authorities.

Despite the absence of a definitive relationship between social class and delinquency, official records indicate that middle-class delinquency is relatively less serious (Gibbons, 1968). One extensive analysis of delinquency by the offenders' social class (Chilton, 1967), for example, disclosed that middle-class youths are comparatively "underinvolved" in robbery, truancy, larceny, and vagrancy, while somewhat "overrepresented" in traffic violations, vandalism, joyriding, and violations of liquor and curfew ordinances. Lower-class youth more frequently commit offenses that result in personal gain and in injury (or the threat of injury) to property and people. Finally, there is some indication that *habitual* misconduct is less likely among middle-class juveniles than among lower-class juveniles. This last point may be the clearest of the social-class distinctions.

Not much is known about upper-class delinquency, perhaps because it is even more hidden than middle-class delinquency. Some research exists, however. One authority reports that upper-class boys in private school settings report more delinquent acts and a more permissive attitude toward deviance than do their upper- and middle-class counterparts in the public schools (Vaz, 1969).

To sum up, factors such as age, sex, and social class combine to influence patterns of delinquency in complex ways. Age, sex, and social-class differences in both the kind and the frequency of delinquency can be observed. Caution must be exercised, however, in generalizing about these differences, because of widespread differences in detecting, reporting, and prosecuting juvenile delinquents from one community to another and probably from more-advantaged to less-advantaged children and youth. The latter are more likely to be caught and if caught, prosecuted (McCandless, 1970).

Approaches to the Explanation of Juvenile Delinquency

There are many approaches to the explanation of juvenile delinquency in United States culture. Some explanatory concepts have already been mentioned. These and other concepts can be conveniently divided into three broad interpretive frameworks, analogous to the explanations for child abuse discussed earlier. For delinquency, however, these are the biogenic, psychogenic, and sociogenic perspectives (Gibbons, 1970).

Faulty biology, hereditary defects, or body build and temperament are viewed as principal predisposing factors in delinquency by those who take the *biogenic* perspective. Supporters of the *psychogenic* perspective differ among themselves widely on theoretical details, but most stress that delinquency is a symptom of maladjustment or psychic conflict, usually rooted in faulty parent–child relations. Those who take the *sociogenic* perspective typically view delinquency as behavior learned normally within a given social structure, including gangs that may evolve into a delinquent subculture. It is the broader social environment—not psychic disturbance or genetic disorder—that is the generating factor in delinquency according to the sociogenic viewpoint.

Some authorities lean strongly toward the first two perspectives (for example, Glueck & Glueck, 1968; Silverberg & Silverberg, 1971), while others definitely favor the third (for example, Burgess & Akers, 1966; Gibbons, 1970). Even within a given approach, however, there is rarely clear agreement about causation. For example, authorities who hold the sociogenic view of working-class delinquency differ in the extent to which they stress such variables as (1) avenues for status that are denied to lower-class males (opportunity failure); (2) social-class value conflicts; (3) a matriarchal family tradition in lower-class life; and (4) various forms of economic and social deprivation. Other variables receive attention in sociogenic interpretations of middle-class delinquency, including the quest for masculinity, a lack of commitment to adult roles and values, status inconsistencies produced by rapid upward social mobility, and various forms of exploitation by the parents of juveniles (for example, excessive pressures for achievement) (Elkind, 1967; Pine, 1966). Different forms of delinquency probably occur for different reasons and at present, authorities do not agree that a universal theory of criminal behavior can account for these different forms.

Delinquency and the Schools

Our comments about juvenile delinquency and schooling are organized around delinquency and school achievement, including the manner in which the school may contribute to patterns of delinquency; and the role of the school in coping with the delinquency challenge.

Delinquency and school achievement A prominent relationship between school maladaptation and delinquency has long been observed by psychologists and educators (Silverberg & Silverberg, 1971). Persistent truancy frequently marks the initial step in school maladaptation and delinquency. And, as with school dropouts (Chapter 10), a disproportionate number of retarded readers are found among groups of juvenile delinquents, especially boys. Studies (for example, Hunt & Hardt, 1965) consistently reveal that many chronic delinquents have a relatively low level of conceptual functioning. This includes difficulties in abstract-linguistic school tasks, a heavy dependence on concrete thought, impulsivity, low deferred gratification, and low attentiveness. Obviously, such characteristics impede rather than facilitate school progress, and may contribute to frustration or failure in academic endeavors.

Many authorities (for example, Schafer & Polk, 1967), especially those who adopt a sociogenic view of delinquency, believe that negative school experiences act forcefully to orient youth to patterns of delinquency. They argue that school represents an overwhelming obstacle to goal or status attainment for many youth who are ill-equipped or unmotivated for the successful pursuit of school activities. Delinquency, therefore, may be a common response of youth to this developmental hazard. It is perhaps significant that among school dropouts who are also delinquent the incidence of delinquency is greater *before*, as compared to *after*, their leaving school (Elliot, 1966).

The school's role in delinquency prevention The causation of delinquency is far more complex than might be indicated by critics who blame the schools for the problem of antisocial behavior. Indeed, one must beware of making the United States system of public education a scapegoat for this and other social ills. There is, however, sufficient evidence to suggest that the schools contribute, often unwittingly, to patterns of delinquency. To again cite the important Bayh Report (1975), several aspects of school practice have been linked to increased delinquency. One is the often punitive, authoritarian means for excluding youth from school by suspensions or expulsions. Often, such youth return to avenge themselves for real or perceived ill-treatment. In addition to this "pushout problem" we can note the increased presence of youthful but well-organized gangs within school systems (mostly urban), whose activities are sanctioned implicitly because of fear and incompetence among school authorities. Untreated racial tensions, another sore spot in many schools, can erupt in ugly violence. And far too many violations of due process, such as violations of students' rights to fair hearings, can cause deep resentment among already hostile youth.

We mention these factors, not to absolve youth from their responsibilities for proper school conduct, but as cues for possible solutions to the school delinquency problem. Unfortunately, schools generally appear to have been slow to move in the direction of delinquency prevention. As late as 1972–1973, for example, a broad survey of 219 school districts for evidence of this revealed only *two* comprehensive, fully operational delinquency prevention programs (Knudten, 1976).

Positive steps to combat the surge of school delinquency can and are being taken, however, in several related ways. First, and most obvious, negative conditions for learning and human interaction that exist within the schools must be eliminated. Such conditions have been mentioned repeatedly throughout this book. Second, the school can be a principal setting for the early identification of potential delinquents. Methods for this purpose, including delinquency-prediction scales, have been developed by behavioral scientists. In our opinion, these methods merit far more attention by educators than they have so far received. Third, the school is in a key position to exercise full cooperation, if not leadership, in implementing community-wide programs for delinquency prevention and treatment. These could be police–school liaison efforts, urban-life education programs, work-study programs, or community-based family education (Wenck, 1976).

Several conditions must be met by school personnel for community-wide programs to succeed. These include a commitment to rehabilitation (as opposed to punitive action), means for involving youth themselves in delinquency prevention and control, provision for highly skilled youth workers, effective channels for communicating the facts about delinquency to the community at large, and procedures for the continual evaluation of ameliorative efforts (Kvaraceus, 1966).

The evaluation of delinquency-prevention programs has been particularly weak in the past (Dixon & Wright, 1974). Where evaluation data are available, it appears that several of the more popular approaches to prevention have had little positive effect. These include recreation programs, social casework, and counseling for delinquents as individuals or in groups. Stronger results have been shown for community treatment programs that use volunteer help, youth service bureaus, and educational and vocational projects. But no single social institution working independently of others is likely to have much impact on delinquency (Schuchter, 1976).

Serious problems of poverty—often the wellspring for delinquency—and the excessive involvement of poor youth in America's criminal justice system, suggest that even a radical redistribution of resources to schools and other community services may have little impact over the long haul. Instead, it can be argued that youth need alternative routes for entering the world of work and should no longer be confined by compulsory attendance in formal school settings (see Chapter 10). At least, we need to assess fairly the school as only one of many interrelated social institutions that have a stake in delinquency prevention and social welfare.

RACE RELATIONS AND HUMAN DEVELOPMENT

Throughout the foregoing chapters we have stressed the importance of social context and growth-sustaining conditions for human psychosocial development. We continue with this theme by discussing a nemesis to such development for millions of American children and youth: racial and ethnic prejudice. Since the Declaration of

Independence in 1776 the American ideal has been that race or ethnic status should be irrelevant for the pursuit of happiness, judging individual worth, and the like. That this ideal has fared poorly is self-evident. Conflicted race relations, manifested in sustained prejudice among white, economically advantaged Americans against their racially or ethnically different fellow citizens, have only recently undergone serious examination and corrective legislative action. Even as this book is written, we see far too many examples of frustrated attempts among racial and ethnic minority group persons to better their life circumstances.

Americans are still experiencing serious reverberations from the 1954 Supreme Court decision mandating school integration and from subsequent civil rights legislation of the 1960s. Progress toward equal opportunity and social integration has been made, but it is still not uncommon to hear that many young minority group Americans—especially blacks, Puerto Ricans, Chicanos, and Native Americans—are not much better off socially and economically than they were several decades ago. In American culture there has been and still is a clear relation between race and ethnicity on the one hand, and poverty and disadvantage on the other. Children of many racial and ethnic minority families often suffer doubly—once because they are discriminated against by reason of skin color, language, dialect, or even religion, and again because many of them are poor. Stereotypes about the poor and ignorant are applied to them. Some teachers, for example, seem to expect these children not to learn well, nor to be active, ambitious, friendly or cooperative. Exaggerated notions about "loose" sexual behavior are also held about some minority groups, and perhaps about the poor in general.

We now consider in more detail prejudice, segregation–integration, and efforts to improve race relations within the schools.

Racial and Ethnic Prejudice

Literally, prejudice implies a preconceived and unreasonable judgment or opinion, usually unfavorable, marked by suspicion, fear, intolerance, or hatred of a person or group of persons. Sociologically, prejudice is usually more apparent among members of majority groups, although stereotyped beliefs about "outgroup" persons are common among all groups who differ in skin color, religion, geographical residence, language, or other cultural traditions. Behaviorally, prejudiced persons usually maintain a social distance from the prejudiced-against others, and, in the negative extreme, actively disparage, derogate, or seek to harm them. From what research data can be marshalled about the topic, it seems that most forms of prejudice are learned in much the same way other social attitudes are learned (see Chapter 2). Children or youth are most likely to be prejudiced if they have prejudiced models; if reasons for prejudice have been made explicit (that is, if they have been taught); if they have expressed, rehearsed, and practiced prejudice; and if they have been rewarded for prejudiced behavior.

For example, in studies whose subjects have ranged from second-graders to senior medical students and noncollege adults from the south and the north, whites living in the south are more prejudiced, or at least admit to being more prejudiced, than those living in the north. However, education affects their prejudice more than it does northerners'. The well-educated southerner, for instance, has been shown to lose prejudice more readily than the well-educated northerner (McCandless, 1967).

Such research findings reflect a learning point of view about race prejudice. Prejudice is "normal," in the sense that it is learned. If conditions are correct, it can also be unlearned. But there is another interpretation of prejudice, based upon psychodynamic theory, which maintains that prejudice is simply one of many manifestations of an unhappy and maladaptive personality. Prejudice is "scapegoating" or "projecting"—attributing to others the hatred and fears persons have of themselves and about their own impulses. There are research data to support this point of view, just as there are data to support the learning point of view. For example, one study of boys in an interracial summer camp revealed that living with persons of a different race has no overall effect on people, but that there are differential changes, with some (boys, in this case) staying the same in prejudice, others greatly reducing prejudice, and still others increasing prejudice (Mussen, 1950). On the whole, those who lost prejudice during the camp experience had enjoyed camp more and seemed to be more open, well-adjusted boys, whereas those whose prejudice increased had not enjoyed their experience and seemed to have a chip on their shoulders and believed the world was against them.

The psychodynamic point of view closely links prejudice and authoritarianism, prejudice being seen as simply one manifestation of an authoritarian and rigid personality. This point of view is best expressed in a classic study to which we refer the interested student (Adorno, Frenkel-Brunswik, Levinson, & Sanford, 1950).

Our opinion is that both theories of prejudice are plausible and can account for different instances of prejudice. The feelings of some prejudiced people we know are so intense that it is difficult to account for them by a straightforward, cognitive learning theory. They seem to be rooted in basic personality structure.

On the other hand, we have seen in our own classes many young people who seemingly shed prejudice immediately after being exposed to simple anthropological, psychological, and sociological information. Thus, for many, prejudice is no more than a certain form of learning, or a lack of learning.

Development of Racial Awareness and Prejudice

We wish to emphasize six points about developmental aspects of racial awareness and prejudice. First, though based on rather slim evidence, it seems that awareness of one's own race and ethnic group is evidenced by most children by age 4, and often as early as age 3; and negative attitudes toward members of other races are apparent among children as young as 5 (Stevenson, 1967). (A firm awareness of physical attributes and gender also occurs about this time—see Chapters 6 and 9.) Related to this development is some historical evidence that black children begin to take a dim view of negritude and that white children begin to exhalt whiteness. More recent studies (for example, Hraba & Grant, 1970) of racial preference and identification indicate a more positive picture of racial identity, especially among black children. Such findings are consistent with corollary evidence that racial attitudes, focus of pride, and stereotypes have shifted rapidly in the 1960s and 70s. Yet researchers (for example, Lerner & Karson, 1973; Maykovich, 1972; Trubowitz, 1969) continue to report the existence of negative racial stereotypes about minority groups among many white children. There are indications of increased negativism with age among black children toward white children as well. These reports indicate that children's attitudes seem less prejudiced or stereotyped than those of the adults with whom they associate. However, on the whole the picture is not particularly pretty or encouraging.

A second related point, also tentative, is that prejudicial racial attitudes are learned in a three-stage process (Allport, 1958). During stage one, *pregeneralized learning,* children do not clearly understand the concept of race or ethnicity or even what their attitudes about minorities should be. Yet vague feelings about color may exist, i.e., white is good and black, brown, or yellow is not. A primitive basis for evaluating others is therefore present. Terms such as "nigger," "spic," or "slant eye," also poorly understood, nonetheless have negative connotations. Gradually, words are clearly associated with racial categories and the die is cast for more strongly held attitudes about racial or ethnic "outgroups." This leads to stage two in the development of prejudice, a *verbal rejection* of the unfavored status. Negative opinions are expressed about racially different others in compartmentalized fashion. As the sheep in George Orwell's *Animal Farm* bleated: "Two legs bad! Four legs good!" Stage three in learning prejudice is marked by a finer *differentiation* of concepts and beliefs, presumably to rationalize them and derive the benefits of social acceptability. Certain individuals may become exempt from the more generalized racial stereotype, as in "Some of my best friends are Negroes" or "Of course, *she* isn't like the others, you know."

The third point about the development of prejudice in children is the fairly clear relationship of such prejudice with a parental childrearing orientation low in, if not largely counter to, humanistic values. Power assertion, including inconsistent punishment, low use of reason in explaining and enforcing home rules, and a seemingly cold indifference of parents toward their children, is correlated with childhood prejudice. Parental indifference seems to have its most direct effect on children's self-esteem; the more negative are attitudes toward self the more likely prejudicial attitudes toward others will occur. We emphasize that prejudice can be the outcome of direct tuition even in the most benevolent families. But the cold, power-assertive parent seems to contribute more to a view of humanity among children that predisposes them to adopt a prejudicial stance toward others. This point is consistent with the psychodynamic interpretation of prejudice discussed earlier.

Fourth, certain environmental "supporting mechanisms" also figure strongly in the development and maintenance of prejudice (Ehrlich, 1973). These include properties of the contact situation (or its lack) that affect attitude formation and change. Interethnic contacts among children and youth, for example, are determined largely by spatial segregation (integration) at the neighborhood, school, and playground levels. In segregated communities, these contacts—if and when they occur—tend to be formal, structured, and somewhat artificial. Consequently, there may be little opportunity to learn about the common humanity shared by members of different racial and ethnic groups through extended and personalized activities. In other words, social restraints in interracial contact seemingly provide a context for sustaining ethnic and racial stereotypes and prejudices. To these supporting mechanisms can be added inputs from the mass media, especially television, many of which represent minority groups in token or frivolous fashion.

A fifth major point about the development of prejudice is its apparent relationship to a young person's level of cognitive sophistication (Glock et al., 1975). The greater the cognitive skill, the less likely are prejudicial attitudes and behavior to exact their toll in personal relationships among members of majority–minority racial and ethnic groups. This cognitive-skill–prejudice relationship is not fully understood. But more cognitively advanced children and youth seem less willing to accede to overgeneralizations, exaggerations, or caricatures about racial differences. They are able to recognize and deal factually with relative differences. They discriminate more accurately and fully the "truth content" of any stereotype. Such young people also seem better immunized against intolerance of racial and ethnic differences because of greater sensitivity and insight in understanding the origins of or reasons for these differences. In statistical terms, we can state simply that general intelligence and racial and ethnic tolerance are positively correlated. Thus, in addition to the strong influence of social learning we again note the importance of cognitive-intellectual factors in interpersonal relationships.

Sixth and finally, many minority group members seem to be prejudiced against themselves (McCandless, 1967). From the psychodynamic perspective this is tantamount to identification with the aggressor (Appendix A). A minority group that suffers from prejudice may incorporate the prejudice of the powerful group to the degree that its members reject themselves and other members of their racial or ethnic group. Indications of this have been documented among both blacks and Jews. We suspect that this form of maladaptive adjustment is rapidly disappearing, although the evidence is not extensive. We can refer to one study (Maykovich, 1972), the data from which reject the idea of a "mirror image"—that minority members will accept the negative stereotype. Major research reviews (for example, Zirkel, 1971) also suggest a shift in the direction of more positive self-views among minority children, with the possible exception of Native Americans (about

whom, incidentally, very little is known).

To conclude, it seems that the first five or six years of life are extremely important, though not conclusive, for the formation of racial attitudes. Thereafter, prejudices become increasingly stable and selectively reinforced. One scholar summarizes the matter:

A directional set is given to the mind during the preschool years by the reaction of parents in terms of direct instruction, indirect instruction, or behavioral cues; the comments of peers; exposure to stereotypes in literature; spontaneous color associations; and observation of role occupancy. The processes of selective perception, reinforcement, subsidization to self-image, and cognitive closure help give these attitudes their final form as the child grows older. Although the mechanisms which transmit attitudes are similar for all children, the extent of these feelings and the reactions to them is affected by the child's psychological and sociological environment and his (her) racial membership (Porter, 1971).

Race Relations: Where Are We Now?

Prejudices against various ethnic and racial groups continue to develop and manifest themselves in conflicted race relations, as most of us can confirm by our personal experiences. But it is difficult even to suggest preliminary and tentative answers about where America is in its race relations as we approach the 1980s. Newspaper headlines, news magazine articles, and our associations with friends of different races, temperaments, and racial and ethnic makeups, cause us to vacillate from depression to hopefulness. That our reactions are mirrored in others is indicated by a survey reported from the Institute for Social Research at the University of Michigan earlier in this decade (Truax, 1971). Though this survey dealt largely with white–black relations, its general tone likely applies to other minorities as well.

In this survey, thousands of American white and black people, ranging in age from 16 to 69 and representing 15 major cities, were questioned about attitudes of whites toward blacks (on whom race relations seem most dramatically focused in America). Three important survey questions were revealing. The first question was: "What is the main cause of the urban riots?" Answers ranged from the extremely prejudiced, such as ". . . agitators . . . those violent, communistic black leaders" to the other extreme of antiprejudice, such as the answer "Dissatisfaction. Blacks are dissatisfied with the way they live, the way they are treated, and their place in the social structure of America."

The second question was: "What should city government do to prevent such disturbances?" Prejudiced answers: "Ship them all back to Africa"; "Lock up all the trouble-makers and show them we mean business." An antiprejudiced answer: "Not only promise but actually improve conditions, education, housing, jobs, and social treatment to such a point that something is actually physically there to show them that the city government realizes their problem and is actually doing something concrete about it."

The third question: "Have the disturbances helped or hurt the cause of blacks?" Prejudiced answer: "Hurt. Whites are starting to wise up to what a danger these people can be. They are going to be tough from now on. People are fed up with giving in and giving them everything their little black hearts want." Antiprejudiced answer: "They have helped, because they have forced white people to pay attention and have brought the subject out into the open and you can't ignore it anymore."

There were two general conclusions from the survey data. First, despite some extremely prejudiced attitudes among whites, the white population is not monolithically racist. Whites are often inconsistent in both their tolerance and prejudice. For example, 86 percent of the whites questioned said they would not at all mind having a black as supervisor in their job. On the other hand, 51 percent opposed laws to prevent racial discrimination in housing, although 49 percent said they would not at all mind having a black family with about the same income and education move next door. This suggests that for many whites, social-class discrimination is as important as race discrimination, or even more so.

The second, more tentative, conclusion from the survey was that schools below college level (as well as churches) exert little effect on prejudiced attitudes. Rather, they seem almost to seek to preserve the status quo. There is little to indicate that either Protestant or Catholic churches exert much influence in promoting racial tolerance, the efforts of the clergy notwithstanding. It was shown, however, that antiprejudiced attitudes were associated with college attendance.

Findings from this massive University of Michigan survey permit cautious optimism. According to the researchers, white and black attitudes moved closer together on many questions of principle during the 1960s. But general measures of feeling toward the other race have shown no dramatic changes. Increased cross-racial contacts in various social settings have occurred, however, with evidence of stronger friendship patterns among nonprejudiced members of different racial groups.

School Desegregation and Race Relations

Few will deny that improving racial harmony is a problem that involves virtually all social institutions, including organized government, business and labor, religious and educational organizations, and so on. But aside from legal mandates against discriminatory housing and employment practices, school desegregation has been viewed as perhaps the most promising means to equalize educational opportunity and enhance race relations. In major urban settings, the primary mechanism for this, often resisted by parents regardless of racial or ethnic identity, is busing. In other settings, these means include changes in school-attendance boundaries, straightforward voluntary movement into schools dominated by one or another ethnic or racial group to achieve a better "balance," and "magnet" programs — schools with special curricula to attract ethnically heterogenous groups of students. What have we learned about the impact of such policies on children and youth?

An extensive interpretive review of over 120 studies of segregation, desegregation, and integration of racial groups (St. John, 1975) helps to answer this question. Most of these studies were conducted during the 1960s and early 1970s. As a group they are flawed in method and focus mostly on school achievement for black minorities in both voluntary and forced desegregation situations with whites. Considering the difficult research problems involved, it is remarkable that the following patterns of findings have appeared.

1. Blacks often, but not always, show achievement gains following their integration into predominantly white schools. They seldom, if ever, show decreased achievement. Achievement among white students seems unaffected much one way or the other when they remain as the majority. But white achievement is lower in black majority schools.

2. Where measures of black self-esteem have been taken, it appears that *if* changes occur in this attribute, the long-term results of integration are often in the direction of higher self-regard. This may be a by-product of improved achievement, increased attention by faculty to black's educational needs, greater sense of black unity, or still other factors. There are notable exceptions to this pattern, however, with a few studies showing decreased self-regard among black students following their integration with whites, especially academic self-concept in the face of higher standards for achievement.

3. As compared to blacks in segregated schools, blacks integrated with whites may report higher educational and occupational aspirations, but they often do not. Where aspirations are encouraged, it is usually in school situations where white students are in the majority. Perhaps modeling effects and increased competitive striving account in part for these changes where they occur.

4. Many studies indicate an increase in anxiety among blacks who experience desegregation. This is clearest in the short-term; few studies deal with longer-term trends in anxiety. The effect is understandable, since a drastic change in school environment may elicit general fears, insecurity in peer relations, perceived pressures to achieve, and even a heightened fear of failure. When it occurs, the overall effect of increased anxiety seems not to be totally negative, given points 1–3 above.

5. The impact of desegregation upon interracial attitudes and behavior appears both confusing and disturbing. Unfortunately, where changes are observed they are often in the direction of increased hostility and intolerance among whites and blacks alike. This effect seems more likely in forced rather than voluntary desegregation. Though poorly understood, the social context in which school desegregation occurs may make some difference, as suggested by our earlier comments about mixing pupils from different socioeconomic levels.

These preliminary findings about racial integration in American schools may or may not hold up as further and more carefully designed research is conducted. In the meantime, we must conclude that the benefits of integration do not come without some social costs. Perhaps children and youth of all races or ethnic groups need a better psychological preparation before integration occurs. Certainly what occurs after desegregation is crucial. Interracial mixing as such is not enough. Positive human relations must be modeled and practiced by faculty, students may require special group-relations training, and parents of minority children and youth must also be integrated within the home–school support system. Unfortunately, there are still too many indications that teachers themselves may practice insidious ethnic and racial discrimination in many American schools (Grainger & Young, 1976).

Concluding Remarks

From this brief treatment of race relations and development, one conclusion necessarily emerges: we are acutely lacking in firm, clear, consistent knowledge about the challenge. We have also seen that race and ethnicity are very much interrelated with social class, politics, and economics. From this discussion and data presented in previous chapters (especially in Part II), it is clear that, in the long run, it is not good for people to be poor, whatever their racial or cultural identity. Moreover, the presence of the very poor in American society may be as unfortunate for the affluent, but usually in more subtle and long-range ways, as it is for the poor themselves.

We argue for the American ideal: race, sex, religion, color, and creed should have no bearing upon judgments about people. We believe that extensive and intensive racial and social-class interaction is good for everyone. Our reasons are not entirely idealistic. From our

knowledge about intellectual, cognitive, social, and personal development, we surmise that openness to new and varied experiences will facilitate human growth along all dimensions. For many Americans, there is little opportunity for any extensive racial and ethnic interaction unless there are firm legal steps to assure it. Prosperous white surburbanites can learn as much from extensive multiracial and ethnic interaction as can the encapsulated residents of San Francisco's Chinatown or segregated dwellers in Spanish Harlem. Is there any substitute for well-digested breadth of experience?

Finally, we commend the efforts of many educators to promote interracial harmony and understanding during the critical and formative early school years. For example, multicultural curricula, emphasizing parent participation, have been developed for use in nursery schools (Evans, 1975). Positive interracial attitudes among children have been fostered by preschool programs that are designed to organize interracial associations and to increase children's knowledge about racial differences (Crooks, 1970). The systematic use of multiethnic readers in schools is also associated with positive attitude changes among white children toward their black counterparts (Litcher & Johnson, 1969). Experimental procedures have been designed that successfully reduce prejudice among elementary school children (Katz, 1973) and modify the racial preferences of kindergarten pupils (Hohn, 1973). There is hope. On the other hand, attempts to reduce prejudice, such as specialized curricula and controlled reinforcement procedures, do not always succeed (Best et al., 1975; Dent, 1975).

Permanent and progressive positive changes in race relations will probably depend on the degree to which members of all races agree upon, commit themselves to, and work actively to attain, harmonious racial integration both in and out of the schools. There also remains the continuing dilemma of a balance between social integration on the one hand and a collective national identity (regardless of race or ethnicity), combined with a clear sense of identity based on one's unique racial or ethnic heritage, on the other.

Cultural differences vs cultural deficiency. Certainly the practice of respectful race relations must occur at the local community and school levels. An attitude most helpful toward this end is full appreciation of cultural differences as opposed to a view of the culturally different as somehow deprived or deficient, and therefore inferior. Recall from Chapters 8 and 10, for example, the cumulative-deficit hypothesis so widely held among many psychologists and educators. According to this hypothesis, vast numbers of children and youth (usually members of minority ethnic groups) fail to develop normally. Instead, they manifest certain personal deficits (cognitive and motivational) that progressively interfere with the course of development, especially as such development is affected by formal education.

In recent years, however, many authorities, notably Cole and Bruner (1971), have objected to this view of development among poor minority children and youth. They argue that cultural deprivation is more accurately a "special case of cultural *difference* that arises when an individual is faced with demands to perform in a manner inconsistent with his past cultural experience" (Cole & Bruner, 1971, p. 874). This argument is based on an analysis of the cumulative-deficit hypothesis, which, it is reasoned, can be contradicted on several grounds.

First, according to the "doctrine of psychic unity" (Kroeber, 1948), we recognize that different conclusions about human existence can be reached depending

upon the way we organize our experience. In the final analysis all ways of organizing experience are arbitrary. Thus, the dominant view of "cultural deprivation" may simply be an artifact of how majority culture experience is organized. Second, consistent with our comments in Chapter 7, all peoples are thought to be equivalent in their functional linguistic ability. As such, we cannot attribute any less cognitive ability than is necessary for the complex development of language to any cultural or ethnic group. Third, the "situation-bound" nature of psychological experimentation and study can be criticized. Psychologists (and behavioral scientists generally) too often fail to account for the complex interaction of cultural and social variables that affects human behavior differently in different situations at different points in time: "Groups ordinarily diagnosed as culturally deprived have the same underlying competence as those in the mainstream of the dominant culture, the differences in performance being accounted for by the situations and contexts in which the competence is expressed" (Cole & Bruner, 1971, p. 870).

This third contention further shows the need for a careful examination of the competence–performance relationship. In their study of learning and development, psychologists ordinarily strive to maximize children's performance (intellectual or otherwise), after which inferences are drawn about the children's underlying competence. But, too often, a psychologist's (or an educator's) view of competence is both situation-blind and culture-blind. When this is so, at least two steps are needed: (1) determine whether a given competence in fact is expressed in a given situation; and (2) determine the significance of that situation for a child's "ability to cope with life in his own milieu" (Cole & Bruner, 1971, p. 874).

Two important implications for

school personnel flow from this line of thinking. First, they need to recognize and accept the idea that educational difficulties can be analyzed in terms of cultural differences (rather than learner pathology). Such a change in outlook among teachers, for example, should lead to a more positive attitude toward minority-group pupils in the schools. If so, the pupils themselves would also benefit. Second, the right road to education for minority-group pupils may be less a demand that teachers create new intellectual structures in such pupils than a task of more skillfully *transferring* these pupils' existing skills to classroom activities.

The position summarized here deserves careful attention. If the argument is correct, the suggestion about skills transfer is most relevant. However, there is a major educational problem yet to be solved: how best to develop, and communicate to teachers, valid ways for achieving this transfer. Given existing cultural differences, we must ask if the present, general cultural experience of Americans with diverse racial and ethnic heritages, permits finding an acceptable common ground for universal education. How far must (should, can) we take cultural pluralism and still retain a genuine sense of common humanity and national unity in America? We conclude this chapter (and book) with these questions as one form of challenge to our readers, who, in the final analysis, must seek their own answers and contribute in their own positive way to better race relations for all.

SUMMARY

Chapter 12 presented three aspects of human development and socialization, each of which poses a unique social challenge to American democracy: exceptionality, aggression, and racial and ethnic prejudice. Intellectual giftedness and retardation were used to illustrate problems and issues of exceptional development. Both the gifted and the retarded have shared a history of neglect and misunderstanding. Even in the twentieth century only gradual progress has been made toward dispelling myths about individuals with accelerated or delayed mental development. More extensive research on both populations has changed fundamental concepts about them. The meaning of giftedness has been expanded from rare genius to include a diverse range of talented individuals. Similarly, the meaning of retardation has been redefined to distinguish among differing degrees of intellectual incapacity.

Psychological studies have revealed that the gifted and the retarded, as groups of individuals, are heterogeneous in their personal characteristics. This prevents easy generalizations about them. As a group, however, gifted children and youth seem to enjoy good-to-superior physical and mental health. They seem also to strongly value autonomy and initiative. Studies of background factors in giftedness often point to the advantage of middle-to-upper socioeconomic status,

small families, and high birth order. Current research trends consistent with the notion of providing for maximum development of the gifted are early identification and stimulation and programs to cultivate special abilities, for example, mathematical talent. These trends are especially important for understudied segments of the childhood population such as females, racial and ethnic minorities, and the economically underprivileged.

Similarly, early identification and intervention are sorely needed to assist the retarded toward more normal development. Though reliable early identification or prognosis for retardation is feasible, much remains to be learned about its causes. Even so, carefully planned and executed programs to assist the retarded can produce impressive results. But again, and as for the gifted, public policies for educating the retarded are not uniform in philosophy, method, or financial commitment. Recent legislation about "education for all" and efforts in schools to "mainstream" retarded children and youth are but two current issues that fit our notion of exceptionality and social challenge.

Aggression and social deviance form the second aspect of human development and socialization that creates a social challenge in American society. We have differentiated aggression by intentions and consequences, its general or situational nature, and broad developmental trends. Recognizing the existence of widespread aggression in American society, psychologists have been particularly concerned with understanding the conditions under which it occurs. This study has drawn some general guidelines for the management of aggression. Special attention has been given to subtle ways in which aggression is positively reinforced, the relationship of punishment and aggression, the catharsis hypothesis, and the frustration–aggression hypothesis. These matters provided a background against which to couch our comments about violence by adults against children. Several different approaches to the problem of explaining child abuse were summarized, emphasizing their implications for controlling and preventing this growing problem. Finally, the meaning and some important background factors in juvenile delinquency were examined.

Several different approaches are taken to explain delinquency, though none is completely satisfactory. One consistently clear finding, however, is the relationship between school maladaptiveness and delinquency. The school's role in delinquency prevention was considered, with brief reference to other social action programs for this purpose. Though some positive results can be reported for delinquency prevention programs, the overall picture is grim. We can say with assurance that the social challenge of reducing and preventing delinquency among youth has not been well met in America.

Chapter 12 concluded with a discussion of a third social challenge: humane race relations. We defined race relations as the way in which members of different racial and ethnic groups get along, including their power relations and interpersonal contact. The American ideal has race as an irrelevant factor in determining life's pathways. In practice, American society is still far short of this ideal. Racial prejudice filters into institutional practices and personal-social relations among racially different people. We considered the development of prejudice, assuming that prejudice can be directly learned or unlearned. But prejudice can also be symptomatic of deeper personal and social maladjustment. Firm knowledge about the origins of prejudice is limited, but by age 4 or 5 most children are aware of their own racial and ethnic group and may even show out-group prejudice. Socialization factors and prejudice were examined along with some important correlates of racial tolerance, including higher education and cognitive skills.

Problems about race relations seem most clearly focused on black–white relations. From attitude surveys we concluded that such relations, though often tenuous, are by no means hopeless. Some improvement has occurred, particularly among college youth and middle-aged people. Fairly or not, the bulk of the social challenge to improve race relations has fallen on America's schools. From studies of the impact of busing and school desegregation, it appears that minority-group children and youth may often benefit academically, with no corresponding academic liabilities for the white majority. Evidence about personal-social outcomes is extremely ambiguous, with little encouragement about improved interracial attitudes. Scattered field experiments have shown, however, that desirable effects can be achieved. Many dedicated professionals continue to work to improve race relations. We argue that racial and cultural prejudice and discrimination must give way to the humanistic attitude of appreciating cultural differences and the principle of mutuality as discussed in Chapter 11.

REFERENCES

Adorno, T. W., Frenkel-Brunswik, E., Levinson, D. J., & Sanford, R. N. *The authoritarian personality.* New York: Harper & Row, 1950.

Albert, R. S. Genius: Present-day status of the concept and its implications for the study of creativity and giftedness. *American Psychologist,* 1969, *24,* 743–753.

Allport, G. W. *The nature of prejudice.* Cambridge, Mass.: Addison-Wesley, 1958.

Alvy, K. T. Preventing child abuse. *American Psychologist,* 1975, 921–928.

Ausubel, D. P. *Theory and problems of adolescent development.* New York: Grune & Stratton, 1954.

Ausubel, D. P. Psychological factors in juvenile delinquency. *Catholic Education Review,* 1966, September, 91–101.

Avis, H. H. The neuropharmocology of aggression: A critical review. *Psychological Bulletin,* 1974, *81,* 47–63.

Bakan, D. *Slaughter of the innocents.* San Francisco: Jossey-Bass, 1971.

Balla, D. Relationship of institution size to quality of care: A review of the literature *American Journal of Mental Deficiency,* 1976, *81,* 117–124.

Bandura, A. *Principles of behavior modification.* New York: Holt, Rinehart and Winston, 1969.

Bandura, A., & Walters, R. *Adolescent aggression.* New York: Ronald, 1959.

Bandura, A., & Walters, R. Aggression. In H. W. Stevenson (Ed.), *Child psychology.* Chicago: University of Chicago Press, 1963.

Bayh, B. *Our nation's schools—a report card: "A" in school violence and vandalism.* Washington, D.C.: U.S. Government Printing Office, 1975.

Berkowitz, L. Experimental investigations of hostility catharsis. *Journal of Consulting and Clinical Psychology,* 1970, *35,* 1–7.

Berkowitz, L. Control of aggression. In B. M. Caldwell & H. N. Ricciuti (Eds.), *Review of child development research* (vol. 3). Chicago: University of Chicago Press, 1973.

Berkson, G., & Landesman-Dwyer, S. Behavioral research on severe and profound mental retardation (1955–1974). *American Journal of Mental Deficiency,* 1977, *81,* 428–454.

Bernal, E. M. Gifted Mexican-American children: An ethno-scientific perspective. *California Journal of Educational Research,* 1974, *25,* 261–273.

Best, D. L., et al. The modification of racial bias in preschool children. *Journal of Experimental Child Psychology,* 1975, *20,* 193–205.

Budoff, M., & Gottlieb, J. Special class EMR children mainstreamed: A study of an aptitude × treatment interaction. *American Journal of Mental Deficiency,* 1976, *81,* 1–11.

Burgess, R. L., & Akers, R. L. A differential association: Reinforcement theory of criminal behavior. *Social Problems,* 1966, *14,* 128–147.

Chilton, R. J. Middle-class delinquency and specific offense analysis. In E. W. Vaz (Ed.), *Middle-class juvenile delinquency.* New York: Harper & Row, 1967.

Cole, M., & Bruner, J. Cultural differences and inferences about psychological processes. *American Psychologist,* 1971, *26,* 867–876.

Crooks, R. C. The effects of an interracial preschool program upon racial preference, knowledge differences, and social identification. *Journal of Social Issues,* 1970, *26,* 137–144.

Dent, P. L. The curriculum as a prejudice reduction technique. *California Journal of Educational Research,* 1975, *26,* 167–177.

Dixon, M. C., & Wright, W. E. *Juvenile delinquency prevention programs.* Nashville, Tenn.: George Peabody College for Teachers, 1974.

Dollard, J., et al. *Frustration and aggression.* New Haven, Conn.: Yale University Press, 1933.

Dunn, L. M. Children with moderate and severe general learning disabilities. In L. M. Dunn (Ed.), *Exceptional children in the schools.* New York: Holt, Rinehart and Winston, 1973.

Dupras, A., & Tremblay, R. Path analysis of parent's conservation toward sex education of their mentally retarded children. *American Journal of Mental Deficiency,* 1976, *81,* 162–166.

Ehrlich, H. J. *The social psychology of prejudice.* New York: Wiley, 1973.

Elkind, D. Middle-class delinquency. *Mental Hygiene,* 1967, *51,* 80–84.

Elliot, D. S. Delinquency, school attendance, and dropout. *Social Problems,* 1966, *8,* 307–314.

Evans, E. D. *Contemporary influences in early childhood education* (2nd ed.). New York: Holt, Rinehart and Winston, 1975.

Feshback, S. Aggression. In P. Mussen (Ed.), *Carmichael's manual of child psychology* (vol. 2). New York: Wiley, 1970.

Fontana, V. J. *The maltreated child* (2nd ed.). Springfield, Ill.: Thomas, 1971.

Freedman, M. K. Background of deviancy. In W. W. Wattenberg (Ed.), *Social deviancy among youth.* Chicago: University of Chicago Press, 1966.

Gallagher, J. *Teaching the gifted child* (2nd ed.). Boston: Allyn and Bacon, 1975.

Galton, F. *English men of science.* New York: Appleton, 1875.

Galton, F. *Hereditary genius* (2nd ed.). London: Macmillan, 1925. (Originally published, 1892.)

Garbarino, J. A preliminary study of some ecological correlates of child abuse: The impact of socioeconomic stress on mothers. *Child Development,* 1976, *47,* 178–185.

Gelles, R. J. Child abuse as psychopathology: A sociological critique and reformulation. *American Journal of Orthopsychiatry,* 1973, *43,* 611–621.

Getzels, J. W., & Dillion, J. The nature of giftedness and the education of the gifted. In R. Travers (Ed.), *Second handbook of research in teaching.* Skokie, Ill.: Rand McNally, 1973.

Gibbons, D. C. *Society, crime, and criminal careers.* Englewood Cliffs, N.J.: Prentice-Hall, 1968.

Gibbons, D. C. *Delinquent behaviors.* Englewood Cliffs, N.J.: Prentice-Hall, 1970.

Gil, D. G. *Violence against children: Physical abuse in the U.S.* Cambridge, Mass.: Harvard University Press, 1970.

Glock, C. Y., et al. *Adolescent prejudice.* New York: Harper & Row, 1975.

Glueck, E. T. Distinguishing delinquents from pseudodelinquents. *Harvard Educational Review,* 1966, *36,* 119–130.

Glueck, S., & Glueck, E. T. *Delinquents and nondelinquents in perspective.* Cambridge, Mass.: Harvard University Press, 1968.

Gold, M. *Delinquent behavior in an American city.* Belmont, Calif.: Brooks-Cole, 1970.

Grainger, R. C., & Young, J. C. (Eds.) *Demythologizing the inner-city child.* Washington, D.C.: National Association for the Education of Young Children, 1976.

Grossman, H. J. (Ed.) *Manual on terminology and classification in mental retardation: 1973 revision.* American Association on Mental Deficiency, 1973.

Hallahan, D. P., & Kauffman, J. M. *Introduction to learning disabilities.* Englewood Cliffs, N.J.: Prentice-Hall, 1976.

Haring, N. G. (Ed.) *Behavior of exceptional children: An introduction to special education.* Columbus, Ohio: Merrill, 1974.

Hayden, A. H., & Dimitriev, V. The multidisciplinary preschool programs for Down's Syndrome at the University of Washington Model Preschool Center. In B. Z. Friedlander, G. Sterritt, & G. Kirk (Eds.), *Exceptional infant: Assessment and intervention.* New York: Brunner-Mazel, 1975.

Heber, R., Garber, H., Harrington, S., Hoffman, C., & Falender, C. *Rehabilitation of families at risk for mental retardation: Progress report.* Rehabilitation Research and Training Center in Mental Retardation. Madison: University of Wisconsin, 1972.

Heber, R., & Garber, H. *Rehabilitation of families at risk for mental retardation: Progress report II: An experiment in the prevention of cultural-familial retardation.* Paper presented at the Third International Congress of the International Association for the Scientific Study of Mental Deficiency, The Hague, Netherlands, September 4–12, 1973.

Hitchfield, E. M. *In search of promise.* London: Longman, 1973.

Hohn, R. L. Perceptual training and its effects on racial preferences of kindergarten children. *Psychological Reports,* 1973, *32,* 435–441.

Holt, R. R. On the interpersonal and intrapersonal consequences of expressing or not expressing anger. *Journal of Consulting and Clinical Psychology,* 1970, *35,* 8–12.

Hughes, H. H., & Converse, H. D. Characteristics of the gifted: A case for a sequel to Terman's study. *Exceptional Children,* 1962, *29,* 179–183.

Hunt, D. E., & Hardt, R. H. Developmental stage, delinquency, and differential treatment. *Journal of Research in Crime and Delinquency,* 1965, *2,* 20–31.

Johnson, C. A., & Katz, R. C. Using parents as change agents for their children: A review. *Journal of Child Psychology and Psychiatry,* 1973, *14,* 181–200.

Kagan, J., & Moss, H. *Birth to maturity.* New York: Wiley, 1962.

Katz, P. A. Stimulus predifferentiation and modification of children's racial attitudes. *Child Development,* 1973, *44,* 232–237.

Kempe, C. H., & Helfer, R. E. (Eds.) *Helping the battered child and his family.* Philadelphia: Lippincott, 1972.

Kirk, S. A. *Educating exceptional children* (2nd ed.). Boston: Houghton Mifflin, 1972.

Klein, M. M. What honor students think. *High Points,* 1958, *40,* 5–32.

Knudten, R. D. Delinquency programs in schools: A survey. In E. A. Wenk (Ed.), *Delinquency prevention and the schools: Emerging perspectives.* Beverly Hills, Calif.: Sage Publications, 1976.

Kott, M. G. The history of mental retardation. In J. H. Rothstein (Ed.), *Mental retardation: Readings and resources* (2nd ed.). New York: Holt, Rinehart and Winston, 1971.

Kroeber, A. L. *Anthropology.* New York: Harcourt, 1948.

Lane, P. E. Introduction: Federal definition of LD: Last chance to make your input. *Journal of Learning Disabilities,* 1977, *10,* 66–67.

Lerner, R. M., & Karson, M. Racial stereotype of early white children. *Psychological Reports,* 1973, *32,* 381–382.

Litcher, J., & Johnson, D. Changes in attitudes toward Negroes of white elementary students after use of multi-ethnic readers. *Journal of Educational Psychology,* 1969, *60,* 148–152.

Lombroso, C. *The man of genius.* London: Scott, 1891.

Martinson, R. A. Appendix A: Research on the gifted and talented: Its implications for education. In S. Marland, *Education of the gifted and talented.* Report to the Subcommittee on Education, Committee on Labor and Public Welfare, U.S. Senate, Washington, D.C., 1972.

Martinson, R. A. Children with superior cognitive abilities. In L. M. Dunn (Ed.), *Exceptional children in the schools* (2nd ed.). New York: Holt, Rinehart and Winston, 1973.

Maurer, A. (Ed.) Violence against children. *Journal of Clinical Child Psychology,* 1973, *2,* 2–51.

Maykovich, M. K. Stereotypes and racial images: White, black, and yellow. *Human Relations,* 1972, *25,* 101–120.

McCandless, B. R. *Children: Behavior and development* (2nd ed.). New York: Holt, Rinehart and Winston, 1967.

McCandless, B. R. *Adolescents: Behavior and development.* Hinsdale, Ill.: Dryden, 1970.

McPartland, J. M., & McDill, E. L. (Eds.) *Violence in schools.* Lexington, Mass.: Heath, 1977.

Mussen, P. H. Some personality and social factors related to changes in children's attitudes toward Negroes. *Journal of Abnormal and Social Psychology,* 1950, *45,* 423–441.

Newland, T. E. *The gifted in socio-educational perspective.* Englewood Cliffs, N.J.: Prentice-Hall, 1976.

O'Dell, S. Training parents in behavior modification: A review. *Psychological Bulletin,* 1974, *81,* 418–433.

Page, E. B. Miracle in Milwaukee: Raising the IQ. *Educational Researcher,* 1972, *1*(10), 8–16.

Parke, R. D., & Collmer, C. Child abuses: An interdisciplinary analysis. In E. M. Hetherington (Ed.), *Review of child development research*. Chicago: University of Chicago Press, 1975.

Payne, J. The gifted. In N. G. Haring (Ed.), *Behavior of exceptional children: An introduction to special education*. Columbus, Ohio: Merrill, 1974.

Perry, D. G., & Perry, L. C. Denial of suffering in the victim as a stimulus to violence in aggressive boys. *Child Development*, 1974, *45*, 55–62.

Peterson, D. Educable mentally retarded. In N. G. Haring (Ed.), *Behavior of exceptional children: An introduction to special education*. Columbus, Ohio: Merrill, 1974.

Pine, G. J. The affluent delinquent. *Phi Delta Kappan*, 1966, *48*, 138–143.

Porter, J. D. R. *Black child, white child: The development of racial attitudes*. Cambridge, Mass.: Harvard University Press, 1971.

Richards, C. V. Discontinuities in role expectations of girls. In W. W. Wattenberg (Ed.), *Social deviancy among youth*. Chicago: University of Chicago Press, 1966.

Rimm, D. C., & Somervill, J. W. *Abnormal psychology*. New York: Academic Press, 1977.

Robinson, H. B., Roedell, W. C., & Jackson, N. E. Early identification and intervention: Preschool and early childhood education. In *Annual Yearbook, National Society for the Study of Education*. Chicago: University of Chicago Press, 1977.

Robinson, N. M., & Robinson, H. B. *The mentally retarded child: A psychological approach* (2nd ed.). New York: McGraw-Hill, 1976.

Rosen, M., Clark, G. R., & Kivitz, M. S. Introduction. In M. Rosen, G. R. Clark, & M. S. Kivitz (Eds.), *The history of mental retardation: Collected papers* (vol. 1). Baltimore: University Park Press, 1976.

St. John, N. H. *School desegregation*. New York: Wiley, 1975.

Schafer, W. E., & Polk, K. Delinquency and the schools. In *Task force report: Juvenile delinquency and youth crime*. Washington, D.C.: U.S. Government Printing Office, 1967.

Schuchter, A. Schools and delinquency prevention strategies. In E. A. Wenk (Ed.), *Delinquency prevention and the schools: Emerging perspectives*. Beverly Hills, Calif.: Sage Publications, 1976.

Short, J. F., Jr. (Ed.) *Delinquency, crime, and society*. Chicago: University of Chicago Press, 1976.

Silverberg, N. E., & Silverberg, M. C. School achievement and delinquency. *Review of Educational Research*, 1971, *41*, 17–34.

Siperstein, G., & Gottlieb, J. Physical stigma and academic performance as factors affecting children's first impressions of handicapped peers. *American Journal of Mental Deficiency*, 1977, *81*, 455–462.

Spinetta, J. J. The child abusing parent: A psychological review. *Psychological Bulletin*, 1972, *77*, 296–304.

Stanley, J. Accelerating the educational progress of intellectually gifted youth. *Educational Psychologist*, 1973, *10*, 133–146.

Stanley, J. Identifying and nurturing the intellectually gifted. *Phi Delta Kappan*, 1976, *58*, 234–237.

Stephens, J. M., & Evans, E. D. *Development and classroom learning*. New York: Holt, Rinehart and Winston, 1973.

Stevenson, H. W. Studies of racial awareness in young children. In W. W. Hartup & N. L. Smothergill (Eds.), *The young child*. Washington, D.C.: National Association for the Education of Young Children, 1967.

Stroud, J. *Issues and problems about mental retardation*. Speech delivered at the University of Washington, College of Education, May, 1966.

Tavormina, J. Basic models of parent counseling: A critical review. *Psychological Bulletin*, 1974, *81*, 827–835.

Terman, L. M. *Genetic studies of genius* (vol. 1). Stanford, Calif.: Stanford University Press, 1925.

Thornburg, H. D. *Contemporary adolescence: Readings.* Belmont, Calif.: Brooks-Cole, 1971.

Throne, J. M. The replicability fetish and the Milwaukee Project. *Mental Retardation,* 1975, *13,* 14–17.

Tronick, E., & Brazelton, T. B. Clinical uses of the Brazelton Neonatal Behavioral Assessment. In B. Z. Friedlander, G. M. Sterritt, & G. E. Kirk (Eds.), *Exceptional infant* (vol. 3). New York: Brunner/Mazel, 1975.

Trotter, R. Environment. *APA Monitor,* 1976, 7(9).

Truax, D. (Ed.) Campbell reports on race studies: White attitudes toward Black people. *ISR Newsletter,* 1971, *1*(10), 4–6.

Trubowitz, J. *Changing the racial attitudes of children.* New York: Praeger, 1969.

Vaz, E. W. Delinquency and the youth culture: Upper- and middle-class boys. *Journal of Criminal Law, Criminology, and Police Science,* 1969, *60,* 33–46.

Wenck, E. A. (Ed.) *Delinquency prevention and the schools: Emerging Perspectives.* Beverly Hills, Calif.: Sage Publications, 1976.

White House Conference on Youth. *Profiles of children: 1970.* Washington, D.C.: U.S. Government Printing Office, 1971.

Willerman, L., & Fielder, M. F. Infant performance and intellectual precocity. *Child Development,* 1974, *45,* 483–486.

Wittek, M. J. Reflections of the gifted by the gifted on the gifted. *Gifted Child Quarterly,* 1973, *17,* 250–253.

Zirkel, P. A. Self-concept and the "disadvantage" of ethnic group membership and mixture. *Review of Educational Research,* 1971, *41,* 211–225.

Ziv, A. Children's behavior problems as viewed by teachers, psychologists, and children. *Child Development,* 1970, *41,* 871–879.

appendix A

Major perspectives on development

In their efforts to achieve sensible explanations of the what, when, and how of development, psychologists present, test, verify, and often refute hypotheses. Verified hypotheses are the stuff of psychological theory. Psychological theories are more or less organized, integrated, and internally consistent formulations of relationships or principles of human behavior. These theories vary considerably in scope, comprehensiveness, and utility. They also vary in their heuristic value, that is, their power to generate further inquiry. In this book, theory is underplayed. Not only are most theories highly abstract, but several plausible alternative theories about human development exist. Suddenly to grapple with their abstract nuances and often competing explanatory concepts can be a frustrating and sometimes confusing experience for many students. However, a study of theory can also be exciting, because theories help us make sense out of the human experience and provide clues about how to improve the human condition.

Readers may nonetheless legitimately ask, "Why devote an appendix to a topic as abstract as theoretical perspectives on human development?" We offer two reasons. First, to a considerable degree, the way we look at things determines what we find out about them, what conclusions we draw, and how valid and useful are our conclusions. The practical implications can be enormous. For example, consider the implications of different views of metropolitan planning: the view taken by a highway engineer in contrast to that of an ecologist; or, consider the view of automobile design taken by a style-conscious body designer and that by a safety-oriented Ralph Nader.

So it is with different ways of looking at human development. Different psychologists value and look for different things; they see children, youth, and adults from different theoretical perspectives; they study different phenomena, often seek different goals, and are likely to reach different conclusions depending upon the way they look at developmental patterns.

The second reason for exploring different views of development is our belief that it is valuable for students to examine carefully their own perspective on development; or, if they do not have a clear perspective, to strive to establish one. Students often can best examine their perspective, or establish one, by carefully considering the perspectives of professional psychologists whose life work is the study of development and behavior. In the process of establishing or examining a personal view of development and behavior, it usually becomes necessary to make our assumptions and beliefs explicit, consider their validity, and systematize our observations of children and youth. We believe that these actions in themselves are educational. Certainly, they are essential for those who practice the behavioral sciences and the helping professions, as the following quote suggests:

> Yet, of course, all [persons] are theorists. They differ not in whether they use theory, but in the degree to which they are aware of the theory they use. The choice before the [person] in the street and the research worker alike is not whether to theorize, but whether to articulate this theory, to make it explicit, to get it out in the open where it can be examined. Implicit theories—of personality, of learning [of development], and indeed of teaching—are used by all of us in our everyday affairs. Often such theories take the form of old sayings, proverbs, slogans, the unquestioned wisdom of the race. Scientists on the other hand explicate [their] theory (Gage, 1963, pp. 94–95).

We do not wish that all readers become scientists, only that they become more aware of both formal and informal (or personal) psychological theory. Equally important, readers should become aware that psychologists, no matter how dedicated to scientific objectivity, neither conduct research nor theorize in a social vacuum. Psychologists, like anyone else, are selective and make value judgments about what they do.

In this appendix, we discuss four major schools of thought about human development and behavior: the psychoanalytic, behaviorist, humanistic, and cognitive. The first three perspectives are examined in detail. Because ideas from cognitive-developmental psychol-

ogy have already figured so strongly in
this book, especially in Chapter 8, we
"revisit" them more briefly. We emphasize each perspective's meanings for the
nature and applications of psychological
study.

THE PSYCHOANALYTIC PERSPECTIVE

Definition

The psychoanalytic tradition in developmental psychology is most closely associated with the work of Sigmund
Freud and his followers. The historical
influence of Freudian psychology, technically called *psychoanalysis*, has been
enormous. Its impact on psychological
thought is still clearly visible in many
discussions of human development, especially emotional development. Certain
departures from classical psychoanalytic
theory have occurred, resulting in the so-
called *neoanalytic* psychologies, one of
which we mention later. However, we
concentrate mainly on the ideas that
make up the classical view. The following excerpt sets the conceptual tone for our
comments about Freudian psychology:

Psychoanalysis began . . . in a therapeutic
setting. It was characterized from the beginning by a specific method of observing human behavior (i.e., the physician listens to
the verbal expression of the patient's flow of
thought, and attempts to comprehend empathically what patients wish to communicate about their psychic state) and by a specific mode of theory formation (i.e., the
physician attempts to bring order into the
data which he has obtained about the inner life
of the patient). . . . Therefore it can be said
that psychoanalysis is a science based predominantly upon a method of clinical observation. It interprets empirical data, and thus
its starting point is always observation of
people: of things people say, things people
say they feel, and things people say they do
not feel. . . . Psychoanalysis is not a method

of "pure" observation—if such a thing actually exists in science—but observation and
theory are closely interwoven: *observation
forming the basis of theories and theories influencing the direction and focus of observation* (Kohut & Seitz, 1963, pp. 113–114, italics added).

We would add that *both* psychoanalytic therapy and research typically
call for the observation of children in
formal as well as in free-play settings.
Especially for youth and adults, the behavioral data used in addition to speech
content include style of speech (blocks
and hesitations, for example), bodily
posture, gaze meeting and avoidance,
blushing, perspiring, trembling, relaxa-
tion, and so on.

Practicing psychoanalytic psychologists seem to believe that theoretical
knowledge and observational attitude are
so completely integrated that an awareness of any dichotomy between theory
and observation disappears (Kohut &
Seitz, 1963). Yet they also maintain that
psychoanalytic hypotheses must be
checked against both direct observations
and verbal reports of persons being studied. The latter commitment is supposed
to establish the scientific component of
psychoanalysis. But fusing theory and
observation creates the possibility that
subjectivity will prevail over objectivity
in studying behavior. Evidence gathered
from this perspective may therefore represent art or intuition more than science.

Characteristics of the Psychodynamic Perspective

The data obtained from people through
methods of free association, interviews,
and special tests have produced an extraordinary viewpoint about human development. We begin by discussing the
general features of this view, then describe its developmental aspects.

First, the psychoanalytic tradition is
preoccupied with aberration and disease,

rather than with normalcy and health. The data about disturbed human beings are organized to explain normal as well as abnormal behavior. Furthermore, psychoanalytic theory and therapeutic practice are grounded more in the clinical than in the experimental method of studying behavior. Subjects for clinical study have usually been advantaged middle- and upper-class adults whose childhoods are reconstructed in the clinical settings. It is true, however, that many variations of psychoanalytic method exist, particularly among adherents of neoanalytic theories (for example, Erikson, 1963).

Second, the psychoanalytic focus on childhood experiences indicates a belief that early life experiences, notably parents of neoanalytic theories (for example, damentally determine total personality development. Emotional experiences and the early socialization of human instincts are especially important. Instincts for sexuality, self-preservation, and aggression are among the most significant "raw material" for human motivation.

Third, consistent with the first two characteristics, psychoanalytic adherents are more likely to concentrate on the individual than on the culture, on events that have been traumatic rather than on positive growth experiences, and on how personality is structured more than on how change occurs in human development. Because the affective characteristics of personality are viewed as all-important (corner B of the model presented in Chapter 1), the intellectual components of behavior often become secondary. Despite this, psychoanalytic thinkers maintain that the principal goal of therapy is the development of rational thought. But for psychoanalysts, rationality seems mostly a matter of learning socially acceptable ways to meet basic instinctual needs, resolving emotional conflicts, and achieving self-understanding. In fact,

some view psychoanalysis as essentially a psychology of conflict and anxiety.

Fourth, much of the conceptual structure of psychoanalytic thought is based on the premise of unconscious mental life. Dreams, hypnotic behavior, slips of the tongue, selective forgetting, and sudden flashes of insight (the "Aha!" experience) are used to infer a mental life that is outside of our conscious awareness. This premise about the unconscious raises two related questions: if the idea of an unconscious mental life is necessary to explain behavior; and in the absence of behavioral definition, how can one possibly study the unconscious scientifically?

Fifth, psychoanalytic psychologists are deterministic. Freud was one of the first to argue that all behavior has a cause (is determined) and can be explained by general principles of behavior. Moreover, this determinism includes two basic assumptions about personality development: personality is determined by a complex organization of psychic forces and personality develops in a series of distinct, age-related, predictable stages.

Three Major Personality Components

Three basic components of personality organization are assumed: the *id* (seat of biological drives); the *ego* (basis for reality contact and problem-solving behavior); and the *superego* (the moral "watchdog"). The psychoanalytic emphasis upon personality *dynamics* comes from the fluid, incessant interplay of these components with each other and with the external world of reality. Dynamism occurs as the *id* constantly strives for expression (one's biological instincts constantly seek gratification); as the *ego* seeks practical, socially acceptable ways to delay, substitute, or otherwise handle basic motivations and conflicts between the id and the superego;

and as the *superego*, one's conscience and ideal self-concept, restricts the id and monitors the ego processes.

Libido, a basic energy force that Freud assumed was constantly being produced from the time of birth, underlies this personality structure. It builds up in each individual like steam builds up in a pressure cooker or a boiler. If the steam or energy is not released, there is danger of explosion. People do not physically explode, but Freud's theory says that high energy levels cause pain and discomfort, while low energy levels are associated with pleasure. Anything that increases libidinal energy leads to tension and unhappiness. Anything that decreases libidinal energy leads to feelings of contentment and well-being. As the reader has probably guessed, the id dominates infant behavior—it is the biological given. Ego and superego development is a slow, complex process, the outcome of which is largely determined by experiences during the first six years of life. The experiences that lead to the resolution of conflicts about sexuality in relation to one's parents and the resulting sex-role identification (Chapter 9) are among the most important factors forming adult personality.

Stages of Psychosexual Development

The classical deterministic psychoanalytic view of development suggests five successive stages that characterize individual personality development in all cultures. This sequence of stages represents the gradual transformation of the human being from a narcissistic, pleasure-seeking, impulse-dominated infant to a reality-oriented, self-controlled adult. This transformation may not be successful, however, if the circumstances for development are not "right." In other words, it is possible for persons to become fixated at one or another stage of development, after which their subsequent development is stunted. The central task for developing individuals is learning to control basic impulses (such as the drive for sexual gratification) and satisfy needs within the social constraints of their environment. Conflicts, frustrations, and satisfactions experienced during these stages contribute decisively to personality development. These experiences revolve successively around *oral*, *anal*, and *genital* functions in the early years. Such functions are associated respectively with problems of dependency, aggression, and interpersonal relations (Langer, 1969). A period of latent sexuality follows from about ages 6 to 12, whereupon puberty (Chapter 6) marks the final, *genital* stage of development. We now consider these stages in more detail.

The oral stage. During the first few years of an infant's life the oral system is extremely important. Children's first experiences with satisfaction and discomfort and with pleasant and unpleasant human relations are associated with the mouth and the feeding process. During this **oral stage,** libidinal energy is pleasantly released through oral activities—eating, sucking, swallowing. Relaxed and generous treatment during the oral stage is thought to produce childhood and adult personalities characterized by cooperative, peaceful, friendly, optimistic, and sharing and giving traits.

Children who are deprived of food or otherwise harshly treated during the oral period seem to suffer from a build-up of libidinal energy and tend to be overwhelmed by fears and anxieties. According to Freudian theory, infants who are not sufficiently gratified or pleased during the oral stage tend in later life to spend a lot of time trying to compensate or make up for deficiencies suffered during the oral stage. Overeating, overdrinking, and excessive smoking are often thought of as forms of oral compensation. People who seem to devote an undue amount of energy defending against the anxiety and insecurity associated with oral deprivation are sometimes said to be fixed or fixated at the oral stage. In addition to the more obvious oral behavior, orally fixated adults are sometimes seen as miserly, arrogant, aggressive, impatient, competitive, suspicious, depressed, and cynical.

The opposite of deprivation, over-protection and overgratification, during the oral stage can also lead to *fixation.* Over-protecting parents sometimes tend to keep their children from moving on to later developmental stages. Without encouragement to develop, children may become orally fixated in a different way. Such people tend to be overly dependent. They put too much trust in others, expect others to do everything for them, and have unrealistic feelings of security and self-confidence. Orally deprived children, on the other hand, tend to become prematurely dependent on themselves and self-sufficient, while at the same time remaining insecure and uncertain. In this manner, Freudian theory explains how similar personality traits (dependence) may have completely different origins, just as very different-appearing behaviors may have similar origins.

The anal stage.   The *anal stage* overlaps the oral stage and lasts from about 1 year or 18 months to around 4 years. During this period children are asked to submit to the will of their parents, to forego their own pleasure and learn to give in to the demands of society. This can be seen most vividly during toilet training (in Western societies). During the anal stage children begin to gain control over their muscles, including the muscles that control elimination. Release of libidinal energy in the anal stage is associated with muscle control, and pleasure is derived from activities like urinating and defecating. The trait of *autonomy* (self-determination or self-will) is thought to develop or be blunted during the anal stage.

The *anal character* (fixation at the anal stage) may, according to Freud, be the result of too early or overly strict and harsh toilet training. The anal personality is characterized by excessive orderliness, stinginess, and obstinacy. Too strict toilet training is also thought by some people to inhibit or hold back the natural exploratory interest of chil-

dren by causing them to be filled with shame in matters related to the elimination of body waste. In such cases, children may regress, or move backward developmentally, to the oral, dependent stage and fail to develop self-confidence and independence. In children who never give in to parental training, adult traits of wastefulness, unpunctuality, extravagance, and vacillation (indecisiveness) are thought to occur.

Anal fixation, like oral fixation, is also thought to occur through either deprivation or overgratification. Such overgratification might be the result of parents not imposing limits and affectionately giving in to all of a child's demands. Fixation due to this type of indulgence might produce a personality with overpowering self-confidence, insensitivity to needs of others, and extreme social dominance. Fixation due to overindulgence during the anal stage probably occurs less often than fixation due to deprivation for two reasons. Parents almost always have to put some limits on their children in order to protect them from bodily harm. And even if parents are overindulgent, children soon learn that other adults and even other children require them to stay within certain limits.

The phallic stage.   Between 3 and 5 or 6 years of age children become increasingly aware of their own sexuality. Young boys and girls find out that they are physically different from each other. The pleasant release of libidinal energy during this stage is often associated with self-manipulation or stimulation of the genitals (the male's penis, or phallus, and the female's vagina). Freud calls this the *phallic stage,* but he has often been criticized for overemphasizing the male aspects of development and minimizing the importance of female development. The changes that seem to take place during the phallic stage do, however, apply to both males and females. During this stage children are interested in their own sexuality as well as that of others, and they usually begin to build up a warm relationship with the parent of the opposite sex.

According to Freudian theory, overly harsh and restrictive treatment during the phallic stage may impair or damage self-confidence, curiosity, and ambition and produce anxiety about the body and its natural functions, particularly in the area of sexual behavior. Fixation due to overgratification at this stage is probably relatively rare in the United States because parents and society tend to discourage childhood sexuality.

The Oedipus conflict. A child's attachment to the parent of the opposite sex results in what Freud saw as one of the most important aspects of development. If normal development is to continue, boys must give up the intense relationship they may have had with their mothers. Girls must do the same with regard to their fathers. Presumably, giving up this relationship represents a major struggle or conflict for young children. Freud called it the *Oedipus conflict.*

Oedipus was a tragic character in Greek mythology. As a child, he was separated from his parents and reared by other people. As a young man, he met his father (whom he did not know) and killed him in an argument. Later, Oedipus returned to his home kingdom of Thebes where he met his mother, the queen Jocasta. Not knowing she was his mother, Oedipus fell in love with and married her. For these mistakes, both Oedipus and his mother (wife) suffered terribly.

Freud used the story of Oedipus to symbolize the type of love-hate relationship he thought all children go through with their parents (even though children may not recognize what is happening, as Oedipus did not).

A resolution or solution to the Oedipus conflict usually takes place between 5 and 6 or 7 years of age. The conflict is resolved by a compromise. A young boy soon realizes that he cannot actually replace his father, but that he can capture a good deal of his mother's love by imitating the values and behavior of his father. Girls are supposed to follow the same developmental pattern, but Freud thought this happened later in girls than in boys. In resolving her conflict, a young girl will imitate much of her mother's behavior in an attempt to capture her father's love. In this manner, boys and girls begin to develop their own value systems and behavior patterns, borrowed in part from their parents. Boys tend to develop their father's type of masculinity, girls their mother's femininity.

When the Oedipus conflict is successfully resolved, boys presumably take a natural,

easy, proud attitude toward their maleness, girls toward their femaleness. If, for one reason or another (such as unduly harsh, rejecting, or overprotective parents of either sex), the Oedipus conflict is not resolved, young children may continue their strong attachment to the parent of the opposite sex—perhaps at the expense of developing their own masculine or feminine identity. Failure to resolve the Oedipus conflict has been suggested as one explanation for homosexual behavior and for problems of sexual performance such as impotence on the part of the male and frigidity on the part of the female. Again, as with earlier stages, similar behavior may have very different origins: One girl may conceivably become homosexual because she had a strong, tender mother and a weak father; another because her father was harsh and rejecting but to a lesser degree than her mother.

The latency period. Following the resolution of the Oedipus conflict, infantile sexuality seems to recede or become less important. This marks the beginning of the *latency period* (from age 6 to 12). Latency, from the Latin word for "hidden," suggests that sexuality is still present but hidden by other interests. During this developmental stage much attention (libidinal energy) seems to be directed at learning skills and the further development of a set of values and standards. As children begin to leave the home more often, they start to learn from people other than their parents. Freud believed that during this period boys seek the company of other boys and find masculine models or heroes among older men. Similarly, girls tend to stick together during this period and begin to imitate and learn from older women other than their mothers. Freud called latency the "natural homosexuality period" that comes before the reawakening of sexual interest.

The genital stage. The period of latency ends when children begin to reach physical and sexual maturity during puberty. Secondary sex characteristics (including fully developed sex organs and breasts, facial hair for males and the monthly menstrual cycle for females) develop during puberty, and libidinal energy is once again focused on the genitals. During this *genital stage,* growing children become aware of the fact that relations with the opposite sex can be pleasant.

The genital stage brings with it several problems. As adolescents become aware of their own sexuality, they may become self-conscious about their growing bodies and secondary sex characteristics. They may worry that they are developing too slowly or too rapidly. They may also have trouble deciding between the comfortable existence of childhood and the responsibilities of adulthood. These and other problems during the genital stage sometimes lead to emotional upsets, moodiness, and rebellion against authority. But if the previous stages have been handled relatively well, adolescents will usually be prepared to make the adjustments required by the genital stage and move into adulthood (McCandless & Trotter, 1977, pp. 10–13).[1]

Some Implications of a Psychoanalytic View of Human Development

Freud and his followers have profoundly influenced developmental psychology and the psychology of adjustment. Though many psychoanalytic ideas are difficult to test empirically, the general perspective has been a rich source of hypotheses, especially about affective relationships within the family and their impact on behavior (Bronfenbrenner, 1963). Early childhood experiences are seen as crucial for character formation, including the development of basic attitudes toward authority and the opposite sex. Extremes in socialization technique, such as overindulgence or restrictiveness, are seen as equally problematic for healthy development. However, only very general guidelines for "appropriate" childrearing flow from this theoretical perspective. Parents should be warm and accepting, yet firm; thick-skinned and reserved, yet able to communicate empathically with their children at a mo-

[1] From B. R. McCandless and R. Trotter, *Children: Behavior and Development* (3rd ed.). New York: Holt, Rinehart and Winston. Copyright © 1977. Reproduced by permission.

ment's notice. The behavior of children and youth, however erratic and conflicted, must be seen as a result of competing interests, such as the pleasure-seeking and pain-avoidance of the individual against the pressures and demands of society to conform for the good of the social order. Later psychoanalytic writers, including Freud's daughter, Anna, maintain that conflict and turmoil are not only part and parcel of normal growth, but essential for continued growth throughout adolescence and young adulthood.

The psychoanalytic perspective on development has unquestionably appealed to and influenced a broad segment of our society, including psychologists. But accepting this perspective implies ways of thinking about development and socialization that are quite different from the other perspectives to be discussed in this appendix. Some of the more important of these implications are:

1. The stage-sequence pattern of psychological development from oral to genital development proposed by Freud must be accepted more on faith than on strong empirical verification through modern research methods. Freud's original contention that the pattern is universal (applies to children everywhere) has never been verified. Modern psychoanalytic thinkers, however, believe that this stage-sequence pattern holds for children in *Western* cultures. Even then further reservations are made. A notable example is that for the Oedipal conflict to occur, a particular social context (an intact nuclear family organization) must exist. Another basic idea of classical psychoanalysis—latent sexuality in middle childhood and preadolescence—is also suspect in light of contemporary knowledge (Chapter 9). For objective scientists, the final authority is observed fact. The full facts about psychoanalytic theory have yet to be established.

2. Classical psychoanalysis is biased, toward the abnormal and the pathological. To explain behavior from this perspective, one first looks for any developmental problems, conflicts, and anxieties that an individual may have. Then inferences are made about possible motives that underlie unproductive or nonconstructive behaviors. Psychoanalysis further implies that few if any people are truly psychologically healthy. Most "normal" people experience a variety of psychological problems throughout life; when these "normal" problems begin to interfere with daily life—to affect the quality of work, play, and love—psychoanalytic thinkers speak about more extreme psychological sickness.

3. The psychoanalytic view of human development leads one to concentrate on interpersonal intervention for emotional first aid (such as mental health service or psychotherapy) rather than on broader social intervention (such as better academic practices within the schools or a guaranteed annual wage). Within psychoanalysis the emphasis is much more on adjusting the individual to things as they are than on promoting social reform that will make individual life and development less arduous. Socially speaking, psychoanalysis has traditionally been a status-quo theory.

4. Persons holding the psychoanalytic viewpoint are inclined to think of the developmental course as basically terminating with the resolution of basic sexual conflicts and the accompanying repression of early childhood experiences at around the age of 6 to 8 years. One cannot, therefore, be very optimistic about the possibility of fundamental change during later childhood, youth, maturity, and old age. What change is possible requires deep therapy, a luxury unavailable to most persons. Many psychodynamicists make an exception of the stage of adolescence, with its vortex of new drives (libidinal and aggressive). During adolescence, they argue, earlier problems and unresolved sexual conflicts may be reactivated and possibly healthily resolved.

5. Classical psychoanalysis tends to hold caretakers and their childrearing practices responsible for all aspects of children's psychological development. Socialization influence is seen mostly as one-way, from caregiver to child, with little emphasis upon interaction effects. Thus, the often dramatic and constructive, but sometimes destructive, role of individuals in their own development is neglected by psychoanalytic theory. Moreover, parent and sibling relationships are generally seen as more important for psychological adjustment than, say, peer-group factors.

6. Because personality formation is determined mostly by historical (infancy and early childhood) forces, psychoanalysis, like behaviorism (see next section), leaves no room for free will. Even more than behaviorism, the psychoanalytic position may foster an attitude that people have little personal responsibility for their own behavior. That is, problems are perhaps too easily seen as the fault of biology and "oppressive" socialization over which individuals can say they have no control.

7. Implicit in the analytic position (and particularly in classical psychoanalysis) is a preoccupation with data coming mostly from verbal reports (and overt behavior, including words, shown by children in play). This may lead to neglect of nonverbal behavior and possibly make the entire psychoanalytic system (including therapy) inappropriate for individuals who are unable or unwilling to make full use of elaborate expressive language skills.

8. If we think in psychoanalytic terms we are likely to be equally interested in the individual case (a clinical understanding) *and* general theoretical

principles of explanation. However, we are unlikely to gather data from *large samples of people,* partly because the basic psychoanalytic technique is exceptionally time-consuming, complex, and expensive. This means that generalizations about behavior and development are based upon comparatively small samples of subjects. Alternatively, larger groups of subjects are drawn for study by their psychological adjustment status (such as type and extent of fears, sexual maladjustment, neurosis) with an attempt to establish causation by an after-the-fact exploration of such variables as feeding, weaning, toilet training history, sibling rivalry, and father absence. Causation, of course, can never be proven after the fact. Simply because one thing follows another does not establish cause–effect.

9. Psychoanalytic views on child-rearing seem to include more emphasis on *what not to do* rather than on *what to do.* Do not deprive the infant of the breast, do not rigidly schedule feedings, do not wean or toilet train "too early," do not separate the child from its mother until at least the age of 3, and so on. Although psychoanalysis is rich in its emphasis on explanations (again, largely from after-the-fact analyses of how development has gone wrong), few specific cues for positive behavior management can be extracted from this theory. In fairness, however, a general principle of management derived from psychoanalysis should be mentioned: help developing individuals to express or channel their instinctual impulses in ways that are socially acceptable, or in ways that are at least not destructive to the self and to others (see Chapter 12, discussion of *catharsis*).

A Word about Neoanalytic Psychology

Classical psychoanalysis still dominates the thinking of many psychologists. However, there have been significant extensions, modifications, and reformulations of Freud's basic ideas. These modified positions de-emphasize biological instincts, especially sexuality, as driving forces in human behavior, and place greater stress upon the developmental contributions of cultural and interpersonal influences. Notable among these positions is Erikson's (1963) stage theory of psychosocial crises. Erikson's work has broad appeal throughout psychology for several reasons. First, his ideas constitute one of the few integrated views of development across the entire life span, from birth to old age. Second, he proposes explicit criteria to define the "healthy" personality, at least within technologically developed societies such as the United States. Third, much of what Erikson says is compatible with principles of social learning and certain aspects of cognitive-developmental theory. Erikson's picture of development also reflects the principle of cumulative learning so heavily stressed by behaviorists, even though his assumptions about the predetermined course of development are not likely to be accepted by them. And finally, Erikson's concern for selfhood, especially the development of a firm personal identity during adolescence, is consistent with the humanistic psychologies.

Erikson defines socialization as a series of eight stages, each representing a central psychosocial problem or task. For an individual to proceed satisfactorily through successive stages, the crisis associated with each stage must be adequately resolved. These crises, or conflicts in development, are seldom completely resolved. Yet a reasonably successful resolution at one stage serves both as a bulwark against later frustrations and as a solid base from which to master each successive developmental problem at a time favorable for its solution. In other words, Erikson holds that each unique crisis exists in its purest, clearest form at a particular stage in development. If the problem is dealt with appropriately at that time, the foundation for progress to the next stage has been established.

Erikson further believes that achievements in one stage are not necessarily permanent. New demands continually face the developing child; past achievement alone may be insufficient to meet these demands. Nonetheless, a pyramiding of successful stage-related accomplishments becomes the best insurance that subsequent crises will also be resolved. Finally, crisis resolution at each stage results in a basic personality characteristic. Of course, the degree to which a characteristic is developed depends upon the nature of the child's experiences during a given stage. Erikson's concern is with the preponderance of the "favorable" over the "unfavorable," and with the general life style a child develops to cope with reality.

Table A1 presents a summary of Erikson's eight stages. Interested readers are encouraged to study the theory as it evolved and is applied in Erikson's writings (see references).

Concluding Remarks

This brief overview of the psychodynamic perspective of human development has been provided because, historically, the psychoanalytic (and especially the Freudian) approach has been important. Few hard facts about either development or behavior have emerged from psychodynamic practice and theory, partly because of the imprecise and subjective approach to socialization research taken by many psychologists of this persuasion (see Chapter 3).

On the other hand, analytic psychology has played an important role—many say the most important role—in stimulating research into the experiences of earliest childhood. Freud was vitally important in establishing the notion that all behavior is caused and is thus lawful.

Analytic psychologists have succeeded in interesting the intelligent lay public in psychology to a degree equalled by no other school of psychology. Many areas of human behavior previously taboo for research have been opened (or vital assistance has been given to opening them) by dynamic psychology. Examples include sexuality in general (and childhood sexuality in particular) and the phenomena of death and grief. Analytic psychology has exerted an important effect on the "harder-headed" psychologies and has been instrumental in making them include more in their scope and be more relevant to real-life human problems. Analytic psychology seems also to have stimulated people to be more aware of themselves and the implications of their own behavior. As psychologists, we assume that this is good. Psychoanalysis must also be commended for its enlightening views on psychological conflict, father absence, the nature of anxiety, and the aggressive acting-out behavior of children and youth (see Chapter 12). In these areas, psychoanalysis has generated much research and a healthy ferment among psychologists of many theoretical persuasions.

THE BEHAVIORIST PERSPECTIVE

Definition

We can consider ourselves behaviorists if we believe that psychology is "the study of observable behavior and that the methods employed are the methods of science, namely, controlled systematic observation including experimentation. . . . Behaviorists will identify themselves with carefully controlled and executed experiments in which the stimulus variables are appropriately manipulated, exact controls are executed, and the resulting behavior can be accurately observed and measured" (Lundin, 1963, p. 258).

TABLE A.1   Erik Erikson's Eight Stages of Human Development

Stages (Ages are approximate)	Psychosocial Crises	Radius of Significant Relations	Psychosocial Modalities	Favorable Outcome
I. *Birth through first year*	Trust vs. mistrust	Maternal person	To get To give in return	Drive and hope
II. *Second year*	Autonomy vs. shame, doubt	Parental persons	To hold (on) To let (go)	Self-control and willpower
III. *Third year through fifth year*	Initiative vs. guilt	Basic family	To make (going after) To "make like" (playing)	Direction and purpose
IV. *Sixth to onset of puberty*	Industry vs. inferiority	Neighborhood; school	To make things (competing) To make things together	Method and competence
V. *Adolescence*	Identity and repudiation vs. identity diffusion	Peer groups and out-groups; models of leadership	To be oneself (or not to be) To share being oneself	Devotion and fidelity
VI. *Early adulthood*	Intimacy and solidarity vs. isolation	Partners in friend-ship, sex, compe-tition, cooperation	To lose and find oneself in another	Affiliation and love
VII. *Young and middle adulthood*	Generativity vs. self-absorption	Divided labor and shared household	To make be To take care of	Production and care
VIII. *Later adult-hood*	Integrity vs. despair	"Mankind" "My Kind"	To be, through having been To face not being	Renunciation and wisdom

Adapted from E. Erikson, *Childhood and society* (2nd ed.). New York: Norton, 1963; and *Identity: Youth and crisis.* New York: Norton, 1968.

The roots of behaviorism in American psychology go back to John Watson (Watson, 1913). He was instrumental in turning psychology away from "mentalism" (theories involving propositions or assumptions about the mind not subject to open verification through objective observation) and philosophy. Watson championed the idea that psychology should be a science dealing only with natural events (human and animal behavior) whose occurrence could be observed and empirically stated. Watson also clung stoutly to the scientific principle that psychology and its data were public, not private, events.

Moreover, Watson maintained that within psychology, as in all science, the ultimate objective is prediction and control. For psychology, overt *behavior* is the subject of prediction and control. Finally, Watson and his followers agreed that the scientific or technical language employed must be designed to achieve unambiguous communication among those who work in the field (Watson, 1930; Skinner, 1953).

Characteristics of the Behaviorist Perspective

Behaviorism can be distinguished in many important ways from the other major perspectives on human development.

Before examining these ways, we wish to make three introductory points. First, for simplicity and the ease of control in laboratory research, many behaviorists have preferred to work with animals rather than human beings. Most of the major learning theories that have dominated psychology are built on data from the study of rats, cats, pigeons, and monkeys (see Hilgard & Bower, 1966). Many important ideas in developmental psychology, including the critical-periods hypothesis and clues about behavioral genetics, have come from animal study (see Chapter 2). Though many behaviorists continue to work with animals, others have become intently involved with human subjects of all ages. Complex real-life problems such as language and behavior disorders have become topics for behavioral analysis. It remains true, however, that many of the behaviorist's methods and guiding principles for child study have been derived from animal research.

Second, behaviorists have traditionally seemed happiest when they have discovered an empirical law or have formulated a comprehensive theory that integrates several empirical laws. In short, their orientation has been to basic science and the advancement of knowledge. Historically, this goal of seeking the truth about learning (and development) has dominated any concern about practical applications or finding solutions to social problems. This picture has greatly changed in the past several decades. Today, behaviorism is a rich source of principles for the design of environments and learning materials for behavior modification. Ironically, behaviorism is now maligned by persons who believe that these principles should *not* be used, or who fear that they will be misused.

Third, several "suborientations" exist within contemporary behaviorism. One is the so-called "radical" behaviorism of psychologists such as B. F. Skinner (1953). Psychologists taking this view concentrate upon describing and quantifying actual, observable behavior, and precisely documenting the conditions under which specific behavior changes occur. Another subgrouping of behaviorists is less stringent about the basic datum for scientific study, and allows inferences about how symbolic thinking (words and images) may supply an intervening process between stimulus and response (see Chapter 2). They stress the power of social-learning principles based upon observational learning and modeling, more than upon reinforcement (Bandura, 1974). References for further study about details (and disputes) within behaviorism are provided at the end of this appendix. Here we consider only the general, broadly applicable characteristics of behaviorism. These may be stated in the form of seven interrelated points.

Characteristics of Behaviorism

First, the principle about which behaviorists most universally agree is that human development is overwhelmingly a function of learning. Development changes primarily as a result of experiences within the environment. Learning, as defined in Chapter 2, refers to behavior change as a result of experience or practice. The following quote from a representative behaviorist view of development illustrates this strong learning emphasis:

[P]sychological development refers to progressive changes in the behavior of a biologically changing organism in response to a succession of environmental events which, for the most part, are products of the culture. Progressive changes in behavior may take many forms simultaneously: (1) changes in terms of the *number of responses to the same object.* When presented with a cube, a young infant will most likely put it in his mouth. Later he may also throw it on the floor, put it in a box, and stack it on other cubes, etc. (2) Changes may be increases in the *length of the sequence of behavior* (chains) which defines the ultimate response. The tinkle of a bell may produce a turning of the infant's head toward the object. Later the same stimulus will bring about head turning, grasping, and bringing-to-mouth behavior. (3) Progressive changes may be increases in the *number of other responses in operation* at the same time. In the initial stages of walking practically all the child's responses are engaged. Later he walks with ease and at the same time talks and uses his hands effectively to do other things, as in fielding a baseball. (4) Developmental behavior changes also include *increases in skill* (shaping of the topography) in any of the behaviors described above. Compare, for example, the awkward gait of a two-year-old and the smooth strides of a six-year-old (Bijou & Baer, 1965, pp. 20–21).

Second, behaviorists insist on precise methods, clear behavioral and situational definitions of concepts, and the belief that a concept has no meaning unless it can be translated into very specific, measurable terms. The concept *dependency*, for example, is at a very high level of abstraction. Behaviorists, if they use the concept at all, will tie it carefully to behavior. For a given behaviorist, dependency in 3-year-old Nolan may be defined as (1) frequency of his attempts per unit of time to sit on his parent's lap when he is in a strange situation; (2) frequency per unit of time that he wishes to hold the hand of the responsible adult in specified situations; (3) duration of crying when he is separated from caregivers; and so on. Note that both the *situations* and the *behavior* are so defined that observers possess clear ground rules for their observations. Thus two or more different observers, operating according to these situational and behavioral definitions, can achieve perfect or near perfect agreement about how many dependent behaviors occurred of each kind and in each situation. Finally, the data are gathered in

such a way that quantitative indication of frequency (or "amount") can be made for statistical analysis. In short, behaviorists are *empiricists*. They rely on observed facts as the final authority. They depend first on experience and experiment and only then on theory and conjecture, the latter often reluctant and sometimes scanty or reduced.

Third, behaviorists are likely to concentrate on comparatively simple situations and simple behaviors. For this reason, the behaviorist tradition has often been described as a concern with the "molecular" (vs "molar") aspects of human behavior. Their belief is that only situations and behavior that can be precisely manipulated experimentally will in the long run lead to the prediction and control they espouse. Understanding, prediction, and control will be most economically achieved by working from the simple to the complex. Behaviorists also believe that the laws and interrelations they find while working with simple phenomena will also apply to more complex phenomena. Most behaviorists are reductionists in their attempts to explain behavior. They *reduce* any accounting of complex ways of behaving to fundamental, parsimonious concepts and principles of learning, such as S-R associations, response chains, and reinforcement (Chapter 2). An example of this approach was cited in Chapter 8, when we discussed the attempt by certain behaviorists to explain intellectual development using conditioning principles.

Fourth, because behaviorists are prone to work with simple rather than complex phenomena, many are given to working in laboratory situations where they (typically) manipulate one variable at a time to see what occurs, rather than carry out their studies in the natural environment with all its complexity and unpredictability. We must again emphasize, however, that in recent years "applied behaviorism" has become increasingly popular. Many behaviorists have taken up the study of children in natural settings, especially the school. For example, entire systems for academic instruction have been built from principles of behaviorism. These include systems for preschool and primary education as well as college level courses (Bushell, 1973; Keller, 1968). Such principles have also been applied to problems of psychotherapy and criminal behavior (Stolz, Wienckowski, & Brown, 1975).

Fifth, almost all behaviorists exhibit a burning interest in the learning history of the organism with which they are working, whether it be a pigeon or a preschooler. It is an article of faith with behaviorists that the behavior of every organism at a given time depends partly on the environmental context in which it occurs and partly on the organism's learning history. Of particular interest is a person's history of *reinforcement*; the individual's past experience with rewards and punishments, including the frequency and consistency with which given behaviors have been rewarded, punished, or ignored.

Sixth, though individual subjects are often studied singly to describe their behavior in response to controlled conditions, behaviorists are more interested in general laws than in individual differences. The importance of individual differences is not denied, but not many behaviorists have devoted much attention to such differences. The behaviorist typically searches for generalizations, principles, and "laws" that are universally applicable to behavior. This, as we will see, is in sharp contrast to the humanistic perspective, which takes a lively interest in the individual case. When behaviorists do deal with individual differences, they concentrate on such an individual's reinforcement history and present state—for example, excitement or low blood sugar. However, certain outgrowths of behavioristic psychol-

ogy—programmed learning and other technological advances in education—are firmly oriented toward the individual. That is, these techniques are designed to provide for individualization in instruction.

A seventh and final point is the present growing effort to incorporate concepts of cognitive psychology into behavioristic interpretations of learning and development. Especially pertinent are the developments of symbolic activity (representing experience through language) and self-regulatory capacities (anticipating or predicting events and "summoning" responses in advance) (Bandura, 1976). These developments permit problem-solving, without actually having to concretely act out all possible alternative solutions. Thinking, including self-control through self-administered reinforcements and reflection upon rules for guiding personal behavior, thus becomes a legitimate focus of study for cognitively oriented behaviorists. Admittedly, only the result of thinking, not the covert act itself, can be observed. But thoughts can be observed and counted by persons doing the thinking. Furthermore, explicitly verbalized thinking provides a fruitful medium for exploring the nature of symbolic activity. Readers will recall that cognitive-developmentalists value highly this approach to child study (Chapter 8). Symbolic behavior, then, seems rich in potential for facilitating a rapprochement among psychologists from diverse theoretical persuasions.

In sum, behaviorists' foremost interest is in S–R (Stimulus–Response) variables. S variables are the properties in the environment and response-produced cues that affect behavior. More formally stated, S variables are events in the individual's social or physical environment that are either contemporaneous with any behavior being observed or that have occurred in the past. R variables refer to overt observable behavior. They are any specific act or series of acts that are described by classical or instrumental conditioning (Chapter 2). Many behaviorists go further to include O (Organismic) variables. These are variables that indicate the state of the organism, including anatomical and physiological properties (Spence, 1963).

Implications of a Behaviorist Perspective

As a rule, behaviorism applied to development is not oriented to an ages–stages relationship as is psychoanalytic theory (or cognitive-developmental theory—Chapter 8). Rather, the idea of increasingly precise learning sequences is stressed, for example, children's left–right discrimination (Chapter 2). Apart from biological status, most normative data are interpreted primarily to indicate what children and youth have learned in their natural environment, not necessarily what they may be capable of given different environmental circumstances. Except for organic deficits, any particular pattern of behavior, however exemplary or deviant, will be explained by learning principles, not the instinctual drives or ego–superego conflicts of psychoanalysis. Notable attempts to translate the vocabulary of psychoanalysis into learning-theory terminology have been made (for example, Dollard & Miller, 1950). Increasingly, a certain mellowing has occurred within behaviorism about incorporating ideas associated with cognitive processing, observational learning and imitation, and expectancies (Bandura, 1976; Travers, 1977). But within behaviorism, the bottom line for development is *cumulative learning* (Gagné, 1968). Children's development is a continuous and progressively more differentiated set of organized behavioral sequences. In a real sense, then, children are shaped by their environment to behave for better or worse, richer or poorer, in sickness or in health.

Given these ideas, we suggest some implications for the student of development who chooses to view behavior from this perspective. We recognize a certain amount of risk in drawing implications; shades of meaning may not be considered in the same way by other authors.

1. Since learning is the preeminent concern of behaviorism, one taking a behaviorist perspective is vitally concerned with how learning occurs, including the conditions that promote and interfere with it. This encompasses all kinds of learning, from comparatively simple pecking behavior of pigeons to the complexities of formal academic learning. A study of the learning process and the conditions affecting it requires attention to environmental influences (patterns of reinforcement and models of behavior for imitation learning, for example). It is, after all, the environment that is most subject to manipulation or change; the individual's biology generally is not. For any individual's behavior, whether considered "good" or "bad," the environment (S variables) is essentially the unit for analysis. Just as the environment can produce desirable behavior, so can it produce undesirable behavior.

2. A closely related point is that all behavior is lawful. If all the facts were or could be known, all behavior could be understood, predicted, and controlled. It follows from this deterministic view that human beings are not free agents. Behaviorists are logically compelled to reject the philosophic and religious notion of free will. Humans are controlled by the forces in their environment. The issue involves seeking an understanding of *how* we are controlled and how control, including self-control, can be exercised for positive ends. For such reasons, many think of behavior-

istic psychology as mechanistic and lacking idealism.

3. Behaviorists take a strict view of the concept of science. In general, they believe that if something is not observable, it is not a matter for science and cannot (and perhaps should not) be studied. Accompanying this view is a strong preference for meticulous, precise research methodology and definitions. This preference may lead to intolerance of psychoanalysts and humanists, for example, and of those who study relatively abstract concepts such as imagination, imagery, the creative process, or other loosely defined aspects of personality development. Accordingly, behaviorists are inclined to break down any and all behavior into its specific parts (R variables). Since they are data bound, behaviorists may not give the role to "the dream and the spirit" that many would like.

4. Perhaps because behaviorism is deterministic and demands that clarity and precision prevail in research, behaviorists are likely to be attracted to formal, structured, didactic training approaches for changing behavior. Such approaches can be defined, and are subject to manipulation so that their effects can be observed. Thoroughness, efficiency, and clarity prevail. Behaviorists have worked extensively to devise effective means for achieving important behavioral goals where other approaches have failed, notably in the schools and institutions for the retarded and emotionally disturbed.

5. While the psychodynamic and humanistic perspectives apply mainly to corner B (personal-social) in the model of development advanced in Chapter 1, a behavioristic approach seems to offer considerable promise for understanding corner C (academic-cognitive achievement). In other words, if behaviorists are correct in their understanding of behavioral development, they may provide a great thrust forward in providing us with the means for developing individual competence.

Competence seems essential (although not sufficient) for a satisfactory, working life in United States culture. And if behaviorism can help to promote competence while at the same time not interfering with "happiness" (a difficult notion to define), then behaviorism can also make tremendous contributions to our understanding of mental health.

Concluding Remarks

We, the authors, both come from a professional psychology background based on the empirical study of child development and the philosophy of science known as logical positivism. We therefore feel comfortable with the behavioristic tradition. In our opinion, the contributions of behaviorism to the understanding of behavior and development are both numerous and significant.

But despite our general affinity for the methods of behaviorism in psychology, some major criticisms of this approach to human development must also be considered. These criticisms can be grouped into three categories (Lundin, 1963). First, behaviorism is often charged with reflecting a narrow, simplistic approach to the study of human behavior. By focusing primarily on responses or response patterns that are amenable to empirical investigation, the behaviorists have missed the larger, fuller spectrum of behavior that is uniquely human. This preference is simply an outgrowth of the behaviorists' concept of scientific study. Behaviorists argue that it makes better sense to start with comparatively simple behaviors that can be objectively studied and over which some control of environmental conditions can be established. In so doing, the relationship between environmental events and behavior may be observed more clearly. Once these relationships are described, one is likely to be equipped for the task of studying successively more complex behavior. Few, if any, human activities are mastered successfully by jumping in at a complex level before developing the necessary background skills. The study of human behavior would seem to be no exception. Admittedly, however, progress may be slow and frustrating.

A second criticism is that the behaviorist has invested heavily in animal study. Critics often maintain that information derived from such study either is restricted in value or is irrelevant for the understanding of human behavior. In a historical sense, this criticism is at least partly justified. We know of no serious student of behaviorism who equates human behavior with animal behavior or who actually believes that information gained from the study of less complex organisms automatically applies to human beings. However, there seems to be no sound reason to deny oneself the possible insights that may come from animal study. If for no other reason, animal studies provide rich hypotheses for the study of human behavior. Even more important, many basic principles coming from laboratory animal studies hold very precisely for human beings of all ages (Skinner, 1953). But behaviorists have a responsibility to communicate the limitations of data gathered in controlled laboratory and other experimental settings.

The third criticism refers to the behaviorists' preoccupation with overt behavior and their relative neglect of covert, internal behavior or "under the skin events." This neglect is sometimes taken to imply that behaviorists do not care about feelings or emotions. From our experience, it is not lack of concern for human feelings that prevails among behaviorists. Rather it is a problem of dealing with abstract concepts of behavior that have few, if any, referents in objective space and time. For example, in behavioral terms what is meant by such popular terms in psychology as "the unconscious," "inferiority complex," "conscience," and "self-confidence"? Are such terms necessary to describe and explain behavior? If such concepts cannot be defined behaviorally, the behaviorist has little recourse but to abandon them or try to objectify them so that scientific methods of study can be applied. Many behaviorists have grappled with this task in promising ways (for example, Bijou, 1975; Staats, 1971).

Perhaps the reader, like ourselves, will find much of value in the behavioristic perspective. Its methods and associated learning principles together provide a powerful framework to analyze and modify behavior. As others have noted (for example, Travers, 1977), many behaviorists, if too "purist" in their approach to human development, may miss the significance of inner processes of thinking and feeling that all of us can validate by our own subjective experience. Nor can we be assured that the principles of associative learning stressed by behaviorists, for example, are useful or valid for explaining certain aspects of development such as native language development (Chapter 7), major transitions in intellectual processing (such as concrete to formal operational thinking) and cognitive style (Chapter 8), and moral reasoning (Chapter 11). And, of course, applied behaviorism—putting the methods of behavior modification to work in schools, psychiatric clinics, and prisons—carries with it an important set of ethical issues about behavioral control that must be carefully thought through and consensually resolved (see Bandura, 1969). All things considered, however, many major ideas about behavior change generated within behaviorism have proven enormously helpful in the study of human development.

THE HUMANISTIC PERSPECTIVE

Definition

The central tenet or core feature of humanistic psychology is that it attributes to human beings a "measure of dignity and excellence consistent with [their] high evolutionary status and accomplishments" (Maddi, 1963, p. 180). The humanistic goal is to study the best in humans. Humanistic psychologists stress affection for humankind, respect for individuality, and a passionate interest in people's behavior as human beings. As a prominent spokesperson for humanism in psychology has put it: "There should be a stout affection for human beings coupled with a consuming interest in their emotions and evaluations, their imaginations and beliefs, their purposes and plans, their endeavours, failures, and achievements" (Murray, 1959, p. 5).

Humanistic psychologists mostly concern themselves with human potential, uniqueness, and dignity; behavior that is singularly human; and methods of study based on their affection for and joy in human nature. Higher "needs"—justice, order, and love—and the pursuit of intrinsic and ultimate values of perfection, goodness, beauty, and truth are taken as realities for study (Maslow, 1968). Humanistic psychology is often regarded as a protest against the alleged extremes of both behaviorism and psychoanalysis and has therefore been described as the "Third Force" in major psychological thought. Its popularity has seemed to grow in parallel with increasing urbanization, technocracy, and bureaucracy in modern society.

Characteristics of Humanistic Psychology

As though they were the spokes of a wheel around this core definition, a number of related characteristics of humanistic psychology can be distinguished (Maddi, 1963; Child, 1973). First is the idea that conscious rationality, intent, and decision making characterize human behavior more than does the irrationality of uncontrollable, unconscious impulses. Humanistic psychologists argue that human beings, to some degree in early childhood and more fully in youth and adulthood, are thinkers and active planners and their lives are more a reflection of this thinking and planning than of their emotions, impulses, or instincts. Philosophically, humanistic psychology fits nicely with the premises of cognitive-developmental theory discussed in Chapters 8 and 11.

Second, human behavior reflects more the *operation of internal forces* and *self-initiating tendencies* than the influence of external factors. For humanists, this implies that individuals are basically responsible, self-determining, freely choosing, and active in shaping their own growth and environments. Humans do not passively react to conditions of their upbringing or the social forces that impinge upon them. This idea is similar to the religious and philosophical notion of free will and is also related to the point advanced in Chapter 1 about children and youth as factors in their own development. However, many humanistic psychologists stress the interaction of conscious rationality and emotionality, especially in such "peak experiences" as insight, wonderment, or awe about a person's self or subjective experience. In fact, the "emotional-cognitive flashes," intuitions, hunches, and new ways of experiencing and understanding the self are highly valued for purposes of personal growth (Maslow, 1968).

These two characteristics of humanistic psychology are further illumined by the words of an exemplary protagonist of this approach. This statement also illustrates how democratic philosophy is intertwined with humanism.

Up to now the "behavioral sciences," including psychology, have not provided us with a picture of [humans] capable of creating or living in a democracy. . . . They have delivered into our hands a psychology of an "empty organism," pushed by drives and molded by environmental circumstance. . . . But the theory of democracy requires also that [humans] possess a measure of rationality, a portion of freedom, a generic consequence, appropriate ideals, and unique value (Allport, 1955).

Third, humanistic psychology emphasizes human uniqueness, both as individuals and as a species. To most humanistic psychologists, little is gained for an understanding of humans by studying the white rat, the pigeon, or even the nonhuman primate. Indeed, the typical humanistic psychologist is likely to ask, "Is psychology the study of laboratory animals?" If humans are to be understood, their uniqueness and wholeness must be defined and used as a springboard for psychological study.

Humanistic psychologists are much more likely to stress the psychology of normality and excellence than they are to concentrate on abnormality and pathology. Theirs is a psychology of positive growth, prosocial rather than antisocial behavior, and "self-actualization" rather than depression and defeat. Curiosity, creativity, imagination, and subjective experience intrigue them, although they often also show a lively concern for social and cultural forces that debase human beings or otherwise prevent people from reaching their fullest potentials. This idea is expressed by the following statement:

Some theories of becoming are based largely upon the behavior of sick and anxious people or upon the antics of captive and desperate rats. Fewer theories have derived from the study of healthy human beings, those who strive not to preserve life as to make it worth living. Thus we find today many studies of criminals, few of law-abiders; many of fear, few of courage; more on hostility than on affiliation; much on the blindness in [humans], little on [their] vision; much on [their] past, little on (their) outreaching into the future (Allport, 1955, p. 18).

Fourth, humanistic psychology accents humans' future orientation, their continuing sense of purpose, and their tendency toward psychological growth. This implies that psychological growth, not decay, may well go on through maturity and until death. Given the chance, humans continue to grow toward successively higher levels of personal integration. Successive growth means that humans are continually involved in the process of discovering their true selves— defining their true sense of being and learning how to be fully human. Discovering both one's humanness and one's "specieshood" is implied by this aspect of humanism.

A comment about motivation and development is timely. To some degree, many psychologists of other persuasions (notably the behaviorist and the psychoanalyst embrace the classical notion of *homeostasis* in learning or development. According to classical homeostatic theory, organisms (including human beings of all ages) experience tension because of unmet needs. They are reinforced or rewarded for any behavior that reduces this tension. Thus one can maintain or return to a physical or a psychological "balance" that consists of a relatively low level of organismic tension. This low level of tension is thought to be the most satisfying state of existence. But, in line with their emphasis on successive growth and achievement on higher levels of personal integration, humanistic psychologists vigorously reject such a notion of homeostasis. Humanistic ideas have led to theory and research indicating that infants, children, youth, and adults are attracted by the novel; that they are curious and exploratory "by nature"; that they prefer complexity to simplicity; that they like to be surprised; and that boredom (lack of sufficient stimulation) is unpleasant, even punishing. The humanists believe such data show that human beings seek stimulation, and do not simply strive to reduce tension. They further argue that the more stimulus input an infant, a child, or a youth receives (short of being overwhelmed), the more they demand and thus the more likely they will become effective and knowledgeable forces in determining their own development.

Fifth, humanistic psychology emphasizes the persistent role of psychosocial conflict in development through time. Generally, conflict results when an individual or a group is faced with things or situations that call for mutually incompatible behaviors, either because of their nature or because of the learning history of that individual or group. The more important the possible outcome and the more equal the strength of the competing behavior cues, the more intense the conflict. Conflict can be comparatively minor and transitory, for example, among preadolescents, who struggle with a decision about how best to spend (or save) their weekly allowance. Or conflict can persist over time and involve basic aspects of psychological development.

The humanistic perspective identifies two such fundamental life conflicts. One is the perpetual conflict between a person's human propensities for pleasure-love-sex and the achievement of decisive, responsible real-world commitments. A second, perhaps more significant, lifelong conflict is the motivational clash between complacent, security-seeking adaptation to life's status-quo features and venturesome, creative, visionary action that can potentially improve and enrich

life in a changing world. The conflicts of our human experience vary in magnitude and depth throughout the full course of psychological development. But humanists have little patience for notions of predeterminism; they take a lively interest in and maintain a strong advocacy for joy and self-determination across the total life span.

Sixth, humanistic psychologists are keenly interested in the study of the single, unique case. This approach contrasts with most schools of psychology (except some of the traditional clinically oriented analytic psychologies). The usual psychological approach is to study large numbers of people, reducing data to what is true for the group and neglecting the individual. The study of the unique, single case is often termed the *idiographic* approach; the study of large groups and statistical treatment of the data by means, ranges, variances (heterogeneity or homogeneity), significant differences between experimental and control groups, and so on, is often called the *nomothetic* approach (see Appendix B). While many humanistic psychologists are interested in group differences, they are more likely than most psychologists to study the single case or the person or few persons who do not conform to the group tendency. Individual differences, in other words, intrigue most humanistic psychologists.

As a result, humanistic psychologists, like their psychoanalytic peers, are much more tolerant of subjective clinical data than are behaviorists. Nor are humanistic psychologists so much concerned with precision in methodology as with the viability and social importance of their ideas about growth and development. Things do not have to be crystal clear and precisely measurable before humanistic psychologists will agree to consider and study them. Nor do humanistic psychologists, as a group, see "much value in the behavioristic type of situational analysis . . . because it tends to oversimplify the subtlety and complexity of human interaction with the environment and restricts the range of stimulus meaning considered" (Maddi, 1963, p. 166).

Seventh, the literature of humanistic psychology shows that humanistic psychologists are an optimistic, and perhaps sentimental, lot. They are interested essentially in behavior that has important life significance and its broad, long-term implications for personal experience. As such, it is tempting to link humanistic psychology with Rousseauean philosophy, a philosophy based on the assumption that human beings are naturally good, are inherently capable of self-direction, and are invested with an innate sense of freedom (Kessen, 1965). To Rousseau can be traced the romanticism of the nineteenth century and beyond—a romanticism accompanied by devotion to nature, proud individualism, and obsession with liberty, freedom, and human rights. The pessimism and cynicism about humans often attributed to other psychological perspectives, especially psychoanalysis, are not apparent in the writings of humanistic psychologists. Optimism bordering on idealism pervades their writings, stemming in large part from their conviction that normalcy and competence are the natural topics for psychological study. In the extreme, such writings may convey a smugness about humanistics as the only pipeline to truth in understanding behavior (Child, 1973).

Eighth, humanistic psychology, like behaviorism, does not provide us with an explicit ages–stages description of uniformly sequential development. Rather, humanists speak of processes and trends, major differences between young and old, conflict-resolution strategies, and such topical matters as altruism, creativity, and phenomenology. The most common bond among human-

istic psychologists is concern for some concept of selfhood (see Chapter 1). These developments are thought to begin in earliest infancy with body-image formation (Chapter 6) and a primitive sense of interaction with the environment. They continue throughout life and, for humanists, serve as the core of human personality. Most recently, the idea of self-concept development has been reinterpreted in terms of a theory about the self, that is, a set of ideas and meanings which function to guide one's behavior in three ways: optimize the pleasure–pain balance of the individual over the life span, facilitate the maintenance of self-esteem, and organize the data of experience in a manner that can be coped with effectively (Epstein, 1973). In short, people strive to maintain and act in accordance with their own internally consistent self-view.

Humanistic psychologists have no corner on the study of self-development, nor does choosing to study such development necessarily make one a humanist. But the general topic of self-development mirrors humanism in psychology. Again, interested readers can consult a variety of sources for further information (see References).

Implications of the Humanistic Perspective

We now propose a set of implications for human development derived from the perspective of humanistic psychology.

1. A major motive for the study of human development at all ages is the pleasure, even the joy, the psychologist derives from such study. Accordingly, the principal orientation for humanistic study of development is normality, health, and positive well-being. For example, creativity (Chapter 8) and prosocial behavior (Chapter 11) are viewed as natural conditions of human beings in a

healthy state of psychological development. But humanistic psychologists are likely to neglect what can be learned from the study of exceptional development (for example, from the study of the retarded, the delinquent, the emotionally disturbed, the organically impaired) or from the study of nonhuman organisms. Consequently, such humanists arbitrarily limit or close off possible sources of understanding the broad spectrum of human development.

2. Within humanistic psychology, emphasis is placed on the individual's potential for constructive growth and ever higher levels of personal and social integration. A belief in humans' power to develop their innate potentials underlies this emphasis. No person, however unpromising he or she may appear, is written off in advance because of genetic or experiential predeterminism. The concern for ultimate, long-term development may result in some neglect of the here-and-now. However, there undoubtedly is agreement among the humanists about the futurity issue (see Concluding Remarks).

3. The humanists express a strong interest in the unique individual of whatever age, and place less emphasis on the group or the average. Uniqueness and honesty in modes of expressing internal growth forces are encouraged and respected.

4. Humanistic psychologists focus on behavior and on traits that are "big and important," such as *self-actualization, creative self-awareness,* and *constructive growth tendencies.* Unfortunately, these global terms are often poorly defined, sometimes causing communication and research difficulties. Related to such imprecision is the idea that, as in psychoanalysis, behavior is best understood in relation to an individual's perceptions, feelings, fears, and motivations at any given moment. In practice, this leads to a preoccupation with affect (as opposed to cognition), despite the strong theoretical concern for man's rationality.

5. Humanistic psychologists profess strong interest in ethics and values. Values that promote the "good life" as perceived by humanists (personal freedom, for example) are endorsed. Values that are believed harmful to people (competition for status, for example) are usually rejected. Openness, nonauthoritarianism, autonomy, and freedom from anxiety are examples of other valued concepts of behavior. Paradoxically, some intolerance of any other view of what human beings should be often accompanies this concern. In any case, humanistic psychology seems as much a philosophy of being as an attempt to explain and predict behavior.

6. Humanistic psychology implies an interest in human welfare, with attendant goals of understanding and correcting environmental forces and conditions that distort or interfere with positive growth. This includes campaigns to eliminate allegedly abusive educational practices and restrictive childrearing practices. Some humanistic psychologists become involved with dramatic, sometimes revolutionary, means for achieving ideal ends—liberation movements, free schools, encounter groups, and the like. Occasionally this may reflect impulsiveness, expediency, opportunism, or simply a popularized orientation to psychological study.

7. The flair within humanistic psychology for generalized ideals, global human traits, and social reform may be accompanied by a neglect or even a rejection of taut, carefully specified methods of studying human behavior and of those who develop and evaluate programs for improving individual psychological functioning. Some humanistic psychologists show a rather cavalier approach to the scientific method, for example, and are impatient with or indifferent to the slow, tedious, painstaking

process of making bit-by-bit additions to scientific knowledge.

8. This final point is perhaps not so much a negative criticism as it is a question. Where do most humanistic psychologists stand today in relation to the issue of the *being* (and/or?) *becoming* person? Traditionally, humanistic psychologists have been preoccupied with long-range goals, plans, and ever-higher levels of personal-social integration. For example, G.W. Allport's classic work is titled *Becoming; Basic Considerations for a Psychology of Personality.* A central theme of "becoming" is that humans continually strive for unattainable goals and are never completely fulfilled or completely achieve unity of purpose.

The current humanistic position about *being* is perhaps less clear. A psychology of being seems as important in today's complex and harried world as a psychology of becoming. There are times in all lives (probably some time during each day, throughout life) when simply enjoying the here-and-now seems vital for psychological health. Moreover, it is plausible to argue that the best indication of *becoming* human at later ages is the degree of *being* human at earlier ages. Indications are that humanistic psychologists are now concerned with being. Two of the most prominent, Carl Rogers and the late Abraham Maslow, had close affiliations with Esalen, one of the leading groups working to help people toward a happier *being*, including full self-acceptance, sensitivity in interpersonal relationships, and Dionysian joy.

Concluding Remarks

Our assessment of the humanistic perspective on human development should be clear. We do not wish to do without a healthy infusion of humanism. It makes the study of human development more fun; it induces the enjoyment of each in-

fant, child, or youth worked with or studied; it leads to a healthy regard for and appreciation of individual differences; and it motivates the pursuit of important rather than trivial issues to think about, organize, and study.

But neither do we want too blithe a humanism to interfere with scrupulous empiricism and precise research methods, nor lead us to careless analysis of concepts and development of definitions. An urgent humanistic position can also lead to shortsighted "remedial" action or to expediency. But the humanist's emphasis on study of the *whole person,* how humans seek fulfillment through love and creative accomplishment and the conflicts they experience along the way make humanistic psychology an appealing perspective on human development.

COGNITIVE-DEVELOPMENTAL PSYCHOLOGY REVISITED

General Overview

"Cognition" means knowing. The reader recalls from Chapter 8 that the major thrust of Jean Piaget's theory of cognitive-intellectual development is to understand how humans come to know and organize their thinking about the world. This includes a study of thinking *processes* and the way in which concepts originate in sensorimotor acts and concrete experience. The essence of development is a sequentially governed cycle of assimilation and accommodation. What humans assimilate (take in) from the environment is determined by their cognitive capacities at any given time. By acting on this information, higher levels of thinking are constructed. Thus the environment provides a *setting for*, but does not *cause* development. In other words, the environment provides the nourishment or content for cognitive "digestion," thus powering self-directed growth (Langer, 1969).

Over the past several decades, the cognitive perspective on human development, thinking, and motivation has undergone something of a renaissance. Or, as one authority (Dembar, 1974) has suggested, it is perhaps more accurate to say that psychological theory has come full circle because the study of cognition—including attention, perception, memory, language, and thought—has been a fundamental task for psychology since its birth as a behavioral science in the late 1800s. Watsonian behaviorism did much to overshadow cognitive psychology during the 1920s. Skinner and others sustained psychology more as a science of human behavior than as a broader science of human experience. But, a strongly behavioristic S–R orientation seems inadequate to explain the full complexities of human functioning, especially language and reasoning. Of course, many cognitive psychologists continued their study of memory, perception, and problem solving relatively unaffected by behaviorism. Their cause was greatly aided during the 1950s by the "discovery of Piaget," who had been working vigorously all along toward a comprehensive theory of cognitive-intellectual development.

Other breakthroughs in psychological study have also strengthened the cognitive movement. For one thing, advances in linguistics have forced a reconceptualization of language development and the language–thought relationship (Chapter 7). For another, cognitive sources of motivation, such as curiosity arousal and the "need" to resolve contradictory information, have shown their significance (Berlyne, 1965). Also, there have been innovative studies of concept learning and problem solving, including strategies for sorting and classifying information, as in cognitive style (Chapter 8). And there has been an attempt to identify mental operations as they are performed within the complex structure of human intellect (Guilford, 1967).

Much of this cognitive renaissance can be summarized by the growing popularity of human information-processing theory (Rumelhart, 1977). Roughly speaking, this theory is built from an analogy of the human being with the computer. To understand how a computer works, one must chart the information flow sequentially from input to output. This is precisely what must be done to understand how humans take information from the environment, transform it into thought patterns, and translate these patterns into self-directed or self-initiated behaviors. Several phases in information processing are studied: sensing, recognizing patterns, understanding language, remembering, and reasoning (Rumelhart, 1977). To many of our professional colleagues, psychology has "gone cognitive." Not all cognitivists work within a developmental framework, of course, but it seems reasonable to say that the study of human cognitive activity is clearly the "Fourth Force" in American psychology.

Many esteemed psychologists can be found among the leaders of this "fourth force." Jerome Bruner (1964), for example, maintains that human cognitive development is an evolutionary process in the use of representational modes, that is, means for identifying relationships between objects, events, or ideas and their signs or symbols. Infants and very young children are said to represent experience through motoric action. Older preschool and young school-age children come to use imagery to represent their experience as thought. Symbolic representations (for example, language) are used increasingly with age, and eventually become the dominant mode for thinking. Similarly, Heinz Werner (1957) interprets cognitive development from a perspective on stages of perceptual activity that progress from global and undifferentiated through analytic and selective to integrated and synthetic. Like Piaget, these theorists emphasize orderly, sequential, interactive development. They share a belief that development includes changes in the organization of complex integrating processes (stages). This clearly distinguishes cognitive-developmentalists from behaviorists, for example, who see development as the continuous acquisition of discrete or atomistic behaviors (linear, quantitative growth) (Cooper, 1977).

Implications of the Cognitive-Developmental Perspective

Piaget's theory (Chapter 8) provides a strong exemplar of the cognitivist perspective. We are concerned here with some tentative implications of the Piagetian approach to parallel our discussions of the other major perspectives.

1. Cognitivists look primarily at the rational and pre-rational variables of human development and behavior. They often seem to think less about the emotional aspects of human motivation than about describing problem-solving processes. Cognitivists, in other words, are likely to think mostly about Apollonian rather than Dionysian human existence. In the extreme, this preoccupation with rationality may cause neglect of personal-social aspects of human development. Yet cognitivists ultimately will attend to a principal goal of psychology: full explanation of all behavior (but especially intellectual behavior).

2. The cognitive-developmental position, at least in Piaget's version, emphasizes the natural environment—the informal, unarranged learning experiences presumably common to all mankind. Formally arranged experience and teaching are secondary to humans' experience of actively initiating and constructing their own learning. In fact, structured,

organized, didactic approaches for learning are not much favored by most Piagetians, especially if "out of tune" with a learner's existing cognitive structures. Consistent with this orientation is their philosophical position about human development, which is more akin to Rousseau's than is the behavioristic view.

3. Cognitive-developmental psychologists believe in invariant and perhaps biologically determined sequences of development that apply to all of mankind. A central task is to prove this invariance. This may come at the expense of understanding individual and cultural differences. While this task of identifying transcendent commonalities for all people and all cultures is valuable, the unique case so beloved of the humanistic and the psychoanalytic psychologists, and the joy of dealing with the unique case, are likely to be lost to the cognitivist.

4. For similar reasons, cognitivist psychologists pay less attention to individual and cultural differences. They also pay little attention to sex differences. In research literature, it is not surprising that we find few sex differences in the behaviors studied by Piaget and his followers, but many sex differences in the behaviors that intrigue humanists and psychoanalytic psychologists. Only in such research areas as paired associate and discrimination learning are we as unlikely to find sex differences as we are in the kinds of thought in which Piagetians are most interested.

5. Cognitive developmentalists typically think in fixed stages and categories rather than in flexible processes and agents for developmental change. Thus, we suggest, they are likely to neglect some important forms of human learning and the potential for change that is shared by human beings of all ages. In Chapter 2, we suggested the implications and potential of alternative and more economical   sequence-relevant   ap-

proaches to human development. Cognitivist psychologists are not likely to place much value on the potential of such approaches.

6. It follows that cognitivists are not likely to think much about intervention as a way of "improving" or speeding human development. Basically, cognitivists believe that individuals will profit from experience only when they are maturationally ready (that is, when children's assimilation readiness is developed to somewhere near their ability to accommodate). In other words, the traditional cognitive-developmentalist believes that one cannot (and probably should not try to) accelerate the developmental process through arranged experiences (learning) (Kohlberg, 1968). Maturation, general age-related experience, and self-directed equilibration are the key factors.

Similarly, cognitivists are more likely to be observers and testers of behavior (looking for *capacity,* as it were), than experimental manipulators of behavior. Neither do they seem much interested in the history of the organism. Cognitivists concentrate their attention mainly on the behavior of the infants, children, youth, or adults when they are faced with a problem to be solved.

Concluding Remarks.

In our judgment, cognitive psychology provides a good and necessary foil for traditional psychoanalytic psychology. Some cognitive psychologists, however, go as far in dramatizing the rational, problem-solving, and "intellectual" aspects of human development and behavior as do the analytically-inclined in emphasizing the instinctual, emotional, and noncognitive aspects. On the other hand, cognitive-developmental psychology seems to fit well with the humanist position. Humanists proclaim a strong interest in (but often pay relatively little attention to) the rationality of human life

and the transcendence of mind over matter.

Behaviorism and cognitive-developmental psychology have overlapped all too little. Psychologists from these schools of thought have not often brought their mutual skills to bear on the study of developmental processes, although much constructive cross-fertilization has occurred recently. Both behaviorists and cognitive developmentalists profess interest in a sequence-relevant concept of development. It seems to us, however, that behaviorists are less age-conscious in their study of children and have less interest in *invariant* growth sequences or chronologically fixed developmental stages based on broad assumptions about maturation and general age-based experience. Fortunately, many behaviorists now recognize the appeal and descriptive validity of Piagetian developmental stages. They have begun to examine areas of Piagetian theory for purposes of empirical investigation. These aspects include concept definitions, that is, how change from one Piagetian stage to another can be defined and how it occurs, and whether the change from one to another Piagetian stage may be speeded up or slowed down. Many behaviorists and behavioristically-oriented educators are eager to prove that intervention designed to improve the human intellectual condition will work. Cognitive-developmentalists seem less optimistic. Even so, it is difficult to exaggerate the impact of cognitive-developmental theory on the field of psychology as a whole.

CONCLUSION

Having reviewed these major perspectives, we neither intend nor are we able to claim that any one of them is necessarily better or more correct than the others. The important issue is the usefulness of each for analyzing various aspects of development. Each perspective differs somewhat in preferred methods for studying behavior and in judgments about the important questions to study. Analytic and cognitive-developmental psychologists find the stage concept of development important and useful. This concept, together with notions about personality structure or logical thought structure, is basic for any analysis of behavior. Behaviorists, in contrast, prefer the language of learning theory to explain development; stimulus–response relationships are a principal unit of analysis. Humanists differ, and believe an individual's self-concept and perceptions are fundamental for describing and explaining psychological development. The distinctiveness of these perspectives is mostly a matter of how observations of human development are codified, interpreted, and used to account for commonalities and differences in human development through time. If we value parsimony and precision, we probably will come to think behavioristically about development. Humanistic and cognitive-developmental psychology are perhaps easiest on our vanity, with their emphasis upon rationality, initiative, and self-realization. On the other hand, psychoanalysis and the various ego psychologies that flowed from it (see Hall & Lindzey, 1970) offer what is perhaps the most elaborate and colorful network of explanatory concepts, useful *if* one is convinced of predeterminism in development.

We have, of course, sketched out only the most general aspects of these perspectives. Interested readers can consult an impressive literature for a more complete and differentiated picture of these master frameworks for studying human development (see References). In the final analysis, we prefer to think about these frameworks as tools for use in breaking new ground for psychological study. If useful, these tools will be maintained, sharpened, and adjusted as new research tasks are confronted. As they become less useful, they may even be discarded, better ones taking their place. It is interesting, for example, to ponder the future of the frameworks we have examined. What will be the status of psychoanalysis, behaviorism, humanistic psychology, and cognitive-developmental psychology in the year 2001? 2051? 2101?

No one can say. But if the past is any indication, we can be sure that changes in psychological theory will occur. Meanwhile it is important to remember that although developmental psychologists of various theoretical persuasions differ on many basic issues, they also agree on many equally important ones. All developmental psychologists, for example, seem to agree that human development is an orderly progression through time, hierarchical by nature, and cumulative in its outcomes. They also are concerned with *both* heredity and environment, though emphasizing different aspects of heredity and environment. For instance, all four perspectives begin with the basic assumption that genotypic structures form or provide a basis for integral units of development. From point of birth, psychoanalytic and cognitive-developmental theories stress biology, maturation, and internal forces more than do behaviorists and, to some extent, humanists. Behaviorists and humanists stress the power of environmental forces.

We mention these points to caution the student of human development against an unneeded and counterproductive polarization of theories. We can learn much from, and perhaps eventually integrate, many important aspects of these different theoretical perspectives. To assess their usefulness in helping us to make sense out of human development, we offer a simple bit of advice: "If the shoe fits, wear it!"

RECOMMENDED SOURCES FOR FURTHER STUDY

A.   General References.

The following books contain overviews of major theories and concepts of learning or development. All are excellent sources of bibliography for still deeper study.

Ammon, P., Rohwer, W., & Cramer, P. *Understanding intellectual development.* Hinsdale, Ill.: Dryden, 1974.

Baldwin, A. L. *Theories of child development.* New York: Wiley, 1967.

Hall, C., & Lindzey, G. *Theories of personality* (rev. ed.). New York: Wiley, 1970.

Langer, J. *Theories of development.* New York: Holt, Rinehart and Winston, 1969.

Lerner, R. M. *Concepts and theories of human development.* Reading, Mass.: Addison-Wesley, 1976.

Muuss, R. E. *Theories of adolescence* (3rd ed.). New York: Random House, 1975.

Wepman, J. M., & Heine, R. W. (Eds.) *Concepts of personality.* Chicago: Aldine, 1963.

B.   Further Sources of Study for Major Perspectives on Human Development

1.   The Psychoanalytic Perspective

Bettelheim, B. Psychoanalysis and education. *School Review,* 1969, *77,* 73–86.

Brown, J. A. C. *Freud and the post-Freudians.* Baltimore: Penguin Books, 1961.

Field, K., & Schour, E. The application of psychoanalytic concepts of personality development in the educative process. *American Journal of Orthopsychiatry,* 1967, *37,* 415–416.

Freud, S. *An outline of psychoanalysis.* New York: Norton, 1963.

Silverman, L. H. Psychoanalytic theory: The reports of my death are greatly exaggerated. *American Psychologist,* 1976, *31,* 621–636.

2.   The Behavioristic Perspective

Bandura, A. *Principles of behavior modification.* New York: Holt, Rinehart and Winston, 1969.

Berlyne, D. E. Behavior theory as personality theory. In E. F. Borgatta & W. W. Lambert (Eds.), *Handbook of personality theory and research.* Skokie, Ill.: Rand McNally, 1968.

Bijou, S. *Child development: The basic stage of child development.* Englewood Cliffs, N.J.: Prentice-Hall, 1976.

Skinner, B. F. *About behaviorism.* New York: Knopf, 1974.

Thoreson, C. E. (Ed.) *Behavior modification in education.* Chicago: University of Chicago Press, 1973.

3.   The Humanistic Perspective

Bugenthal, J. (Ed.) *Challenges of humanistic psychology.* New York: McGraw-Hill, 1967.

Buhler, C., & Allen, M. *Introduction to humanistic psychology.* Belmont, Calif.: Brooks/Cole, 1971.

Rogers, C. *On becoming a person.* Boston: Houghton Mifflin, 1961.

Sargent, S. S. The humanistic approach to personality. In B. B. Wolman (Ed.), *Handbook of general psychology*. Englewood Cliffs, N.J.: Prentice-Hall, 1973.

Severin, F. (Ed.) *Humanistic viewpoints in psychology*. New York: McGraw-Hill, 1965.

4. The Cognitive-Developmental Perspective

Eliot, J. (Ed.) *Human development and cognitive processes*. New York: Holt, Rinehart and Winston, 1971.

Flavell, J. H. *Cognitive development*. Englewood Cliffs, N.J.: Prentice-Hall, 1977.

Piaget, J., & Inhelder, B. *The psychology of the child*. New York: Basic Books, 1969.

Sigel, I. E., & Cocking, R. R. *Cognitive development from childhood to adolescence: A constructivist perspective*. New York: Holt, Rinehart and Winston, 1977.

Varma, V. P., & Williams, P. (Eds.) *Piaget, psychology and education*. Itasca, Ill.: Peacock, 1976.

REFERENCES

Allport, G. W. *Becoming: Basic considerations for a psychology of personality*. New Haven: Yale University Press, 1955.

Bandura, A. *Principles of behavior modification*. New York: Holt, Rinehart and Winston, 1969.

Bandura, A. Behavior theory and the models of man. *American Psychologist,* 1974, *29,* 859–869.

Bandura, A. *Social learning theory*. Englewood Cliffs, N.J.: Prentice-Hall, 1976.

Berlyne, D. E. Curiosity and education. In J. Krumboltz (Ed.), *Learning and the educational process*. Skokie, Ill.: Rand McNally, 1965.

Bijou, S. W. Development in the preschool years: A functional analysis. *American Psychologist,* 1975, *30,* 829–837.

Bijou, S. W., & Baer, D. M. *Child Development II: Universal stage of infancy*. New York: Appleton, 1965.

Bronfenbrenner, U. Developmental theory in transition. In H. W. Stevenson (Ed.), *Child psychology*. Chicago: University of Chicago Press, 1963.

Bruner, J. S. The course of cognitive growth. *American Psychologist,* 1964, *19,* 1–15.

Bushell, D., Jr. The behavior analysis classroom. In B. Spodek (Ed.), *Early childhood education*. Englewood Cliffs, N.J.: Prentice-Hall, 1973.

Child, I. L. *Humanistic psychology and the research tradition: Their several virtues*. New York: Wiley, 1973.

Cooper, R. C. *Principles of development*. New York: Paper Book Press, 1977.

Dembar, W. N. Motivation and the cognitive revolution. *American Psychologist,* 1974, *29,* 161–168.

Dollard, J., & Miller, N. E. *Personality and psychotherapy*. New York: McGraw-Hill, 1950.

Epstein, S. The self-concept revisited: Or a theory of a theory. *American Psychologist,* 1973, *28.*

Erikson, E. *Childhood and society* (2nd ed.). New York: Norton, 1963.

Erikson, E. *Identity: Youth and crisis*. New York: Norton, 1968.

Gage, N. L. Paradigms for research on teaching. In N. L. Gage (Ed.), *Handbook for research on teaching*. Skokie, Ill.: Rand McNally, 1963.

Gagné, R. Contributions of learning to human development. *Psychological Review,* 1968, *75,* 177–191.

Guilford, J. P. *The nature of human intelligence*. New York: McGraw-Hill, 1967.

Hall, C., & Lindzey, G. *Theories of personality* (Rev. ed.). New York: Wiley, 1970.

Hilgard, E. R., & Bower, G. H. *Theories of learning.* New York: Appleton, 1966.

Keller, F. S. Goodbye, teacher. *Journal of Applied Behavioral Analysis,* 1968, *1,* 79–89.

Kessen, W. (Ed.) *The child.* New York: Wiley, 1965.

Kohlberg, L. Early education: A cognitive-developmental view. *Child Development,* 1968, *39,* 1013–1062.

Kohut, H., & Seitz, P. Concepts and theories of psychoanalysis. In J. M. Wepman & R. W. Heine (Eds.), *Concepts of personality.* Chicago: Aldine, 1963.

Langer, J. *Theories of development.* New York: Holt, Rinehart and Winston, 1969.

Lundin, R. W. Personality theory in behavioristic psychology. In J. M. Wepman & R. W. Heine (Eds.), *Concepts of personality,* Chicago: Aldine, 1963.

Maddi, S. R. Humanistic psychology: Allport and Murray. In J. M. Wepman & R. W. Heine (Eds.), *Concepts of personality.* Chicago: Aldine, 1963.

Maslow, A. H. Some educational implications of the humanistic psychologies. *Harvard Educational Review,* 1968, *38,* 1–12.

McCandless, B. R., & Trotter, R. *Children: Behavior and development* (3rd ed.). New York: Holt, Rinehart and Winston, 1977.

Murray, H. A. Preparation for the scaffold of a comprehensive system. In S. Koch (Ed.), *Psychology: A study of a science, 3.* New York: McGraw-Hill, 1959.

Rumelhart, D. E. *Introduction to human information processing.* New York: Wiley, 1977.

Skinner, B. F. *Science and human behavior.* New York: Macmillan, 1953.

Spence, J. T. Learning theory and personality. In J. M. Wepman & R. W. Heine (Eds.), *Concepts of personality.* Chicago: Aldine, 1963.

Staats, A. W. *Child learning, intelligence, and personality.* New York: Harper & Row, 1971.

Stolz, S. B., Wienckowski, L. A., & Brown, B. S. Behavior modification: A perspective on critical issues. *American Psychologist,* 1975, *30,* 1027–1048.

Travers, R. M. W. *Essentials of learning* (4th ed.). New York: Macmillan, 1977.

Watson, J. B. Psychology as the behaviorist views it. *Psychological Review,* 1913, *20,* 158–177.

Watson, J. B. *Behaviorism.* New York: Norton, 1930.

Werner, H. The concept of development from a comparative and organismic point of view. In D. B. Harris (Ed.), *The concept of development.* Minneapolis: University of Minnesota Press, 1957.

Statistical and measurement considerations

Throughout this book we used such statistical terms as *correlation, statistical significance, means, standard deviations,* and so on. A full comprehension of research findings in psychology—whatever the specific topic—usually requires understanding such terms. In Appendix B we therefore briefly explain this basic terminology for readers unfamiliar with it. This familiarization can also be helpful for reading and understanding reports of original research upon which much of this book is based. Readers should recognize, however, that ours is a "bare-bones" treatment. A variety of textbooks provides a deeper and more comprehensive discussion of statistics and principles of psychological measurement. (See the list at the end of the appendix.)

CORRELATION

A correlation coefficient is an expression of the relationship between one thing and another–the degree to which two things vary together. The correlation between height and weight in a sample of 50 young men can be illustrated as follows: First, array the men in order of their height, with the shortest man to the left, the tallest man to the right. Put a card over each man's head indicating his weight. Observation will show a tendency for the shorter men to be lighter, the taller men heavier. A number of men will be heavier than those taller than they, and vice versa. But, for the group as a whole, greater height will go with greater weight. In other words, height and weight will covary–will be positively correlated with each other.

Correlation coefficients, theoretically, can range from perfect positive (+1.00) to perfect negative (−1.00). The condition of a perfect positive correlation would be met if, in our illustration, the tallest man was the heaviest, the next tallest the next heavy, and so on down the line to the shortest and the lightest man. The more interchange in weight status between men of different height (as, the third from the shortest man is found to be the third from the heaviest), the lower the correlation. If there is no covariance between height and weight, but simply a chance relation, the correlation is zero. If the shortest man were the heaviest, the next shortest man the next heavy, and so on, until the tallest man was revealed to be the lightest, the condition for a perfect negative correlation would be fulfilled.

PREDICTION THROUGH CORRELATION

The principal purpose in calculating a correlation coefficient (r) is to predict one variable from another. Knowledge of a man's height is more useful if it also helps to predict his weight than if it gives no information about him other than how tall he is. Correlations are likely to lead to deceptive inferences about causality: If two things are correlated with each other, it is tempting to say that one "causes" the other. Correctly, we should assume only that they are related, but should also be encouraged to look for the reasons for the relation. In general, tall men are heavier than short men for the rather elementary reason that they have more bones to cover and coordinate with muscle and fat. There is simply more to them. But their height did not cause their weight.

A simple calculation is useful in appraising the predictive value of a correlation coefficient. It is easy (but incorrect) to assume that the rather high correlation of .70 between a test of reading achievement and intelligence for fourth-graders means that all the brighter children read better than those less bright. This correlation indicates a substantial relation between reading and intelligence. Hence, knowledge of the children's intelligence helps to predict their standing in reading ability among other children of their age. But the relation is by no means a perfect one. To determine how much of the total variance of reading (all the factors that influence, or determine, reading skill) is accounted for by intelligence, one multiplies the correlation between the two by itself: .70 × .70 is equal to .49. Translated, this means that 49 percent of the variance of reading in our sample of fourth-graders is accounted for by the children's intelligence. To put it in other words, the .70 correlation between intelligence and reading accounts for 49 percent of the possible range of factors that enters into making a perfect prediction of where a child stands in his reading group. But 51 percent of the variance remains unaccounted for when we know only the intelligence-test scores of a group of children. Of this unaccounted-for 51 percent of the variance, a certain amount is explained by the amount of practice children have had; some is due to parents' intelligence; some can be accounted for by the number of books in the home libraries; some by motivation; some by study efficiency; some by the acuity and coordination of vision; some by testing errors; and so on.

The average correlation of about .50 that has been found between the intelligence of parents and children indicates that only 25 percent of the variance of children's intelligence can be accounted for by the brightness of their parents. A correlation of .20 between children's strength and their speed of response means that only 4 percent of the variance of speed of response is accounted for by strength, leaving 96 percent to be predicted from knowledge of other factors and measurement problems.

Much faulty generalization results from failure to calculate how much of the variance of one variable is due to another with which it is correlated. A correlation of .70 looks reassuringly high, but still leaves us with 51 percent of the variance unaccounted for. Thus, one must search for still other factors that may be correlated with a given variable. As indicated in Chapter 8, for example, many factors are correlated with a variable such as children's intelligence. These correlates include, but are not limited to, parental intelligence. Other correlates are birth order, family size, general socioeconomic status, schooling, and characteristics of the individual, including physical and mental health, motivation, and self-esteem. Even these correlates do not account for all of the variation in human intelligence. In any case, the correlation coefficient simply describes the direction and magnitude of a relationship between two or more variables. It does not establish anything about causation.

SOME GENERAL MEASUREMENT CONCEPTS

A *concept* is the general term for the class of behavior you are reading about or which the author of a research paper has studied. Illustrative concepts — expectation — have been discussed in Chapter 6; other examples include cognitive style, creativity, anxiety, and so on.

A *population* is the group an author has studied and on which he reports. A population may consist of 27 hooded rats, 8 babies 4 days old, 10,000 Chicago fifth-grade children, or 100 fathers and mothers of first-graders.

A *normal distribution* is one that lies between the ends of a continuum, and is shaped approximately like a bell. Figure A.1 illustrates a normal distribution.

It can be seen from the figure that there are few (perhaps only one from a large population) at either end A or end B of the continuum. Most people (or cases, or subjects) fall between the ends. To use height as an illustration: Very few ninth-grade boys are only 5 feet tall (end A of the continuum); an equally small number are 7 feet tall (end B of the continuum). The average American ninth-grade boy is about 5 feet 5 or 6 inches tall. This figure is arrived at by hypothetically measuring all ninth-grade American boys, adding their heights together, and dividing by the total number of boys who have been measured. You will, for reasons that have been discussed, arrive at a figure somewhat too great: chronically ill, seriously retarded, some economically disadvantaged boys who have had poor nutrition and hence are not as tall as they may have been with better diets, will not be attending school.

In a normal distribution, as indicated in Figure A.1, the *mean*, or average, and the *median*, or midpoint, are the same. By *median* is meant that point in the distribution above and below which exactly one-half the population falls. Means and medians are different from each other when the distribution is *skewed*, or abnormal. If we compute the average annual income of five men picked at random, we may obtain figures as follows: $3,000, $4,000, $5,000, $6,000, and $1,000,000. Our mean, in this case, is $203,600. It is ridiculous to assume from the data collected that the average American male earns more than $200,000 a year. By chance, we have secured a *biased* sample.

In such a case, the *median*, or midpoint, probably gives a more accurate, or at least a more meaningful, picture of the true state of affairs in the United States: the median is $5,000 and our sample includes two men who earn more than this and two who earn less. Income and education figures for developing countries are often more meaningfully represented by medians than means; in such countries, there are typically few very wealthy men and women and few very highly educated, but a great mass who are desperately poor

and/or illiterate. Including those who fall at or near the high-income end of the continuum (the very wealthy, the exceptionally well educated) makes our mean misleadingly high.

Authors frequently speak of relatively *heterogeneous* or *homogeneous* populations. By heterogeneous, they mean that the population includes great differences among its members; in other words, ends A and B of the continuum in Figure A.1 are widely separated. In a homogeneous population, all the members are relatively similar to one another—the ends of the continuum are close together. A population including children from ages 3 to 13, boys and girls, Black, Puerto Rican, and Appalachian, with some of the children coming from very poor homes and others from very wealthy homes, would be more heterogeneous for almost any conceivable dimension than a population of fifth-grade boys in a rural Illinois elementary school.

When authors talk of their results having high *variance*, they mean that some children changed not at all or perhaps actually regressed, while others changed a great deal. For low variance, changes tend to be similar in amount and in the same direction. Variance is often expressed as the *standard deviation* (SD). The standard deviation is a statistical term—a figure used to indicate how variable a population or a set of results is. About two-thirds of a population is included in the portion of the curve drawn in Figure A.1 that falls between a score or a measurement one standard deviation below the mean, and a score or a measurement one standard deviation above the mean.

When we move from secondary sources of information (textbooks and reviews of research) to primary sources (original research reports) we encounter a number of even more specific statistical terms. Without having studied sta-

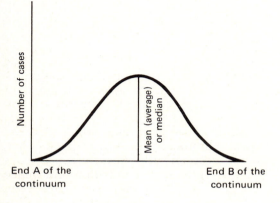

Fig. A-1 Diagram of a normal distribution.

tistics directly, it is difficult—indeed, impossible—for most of us to make much sense of these terms. Thus we must take the author(s) on faith (most editors will check to see that the authors' statistical procedures are legitimate). Even so, it is important (and we are inclined to think it is mandatory) to know in an elementary way the meaning of *levels of statistical confidence* or *statistical significance*. We now consider this important idea.

LEVEL OF STATISTICAL CONFIDENCE

A central task of science is to discover lawfulness in its subject matter. Developmental psychologists seek to determine lawfulness in human structure, growth, and function. Statistics are among the tools used to demonstrate lawfulness. Among other tasks assigned to statistics is that of providing an estimate of the confidence that can be placed in our findings. We are particularly interested in whether we can assume that they occurred for reasons other than chance.

Ordinarily, we speak with "confidence" of results that are statistically significant. In this volume, statistical significance refers to any result at or below the .05 (or 5 percent) level of confidence. Such a figure (which may also be referred to as p for probability, $p = .05$) indicates that the results to which it refers are of such magnitude that they would occur by chance only five times in a hundred. The .01 ($p = .01$) level of confidence tells us that results like ours would be expected through chance once in one hundred times; the .001 level of confidence once in a thousand times.

In our earlier example, a correlation of .70 was postulated between intelligence and reading achievement for children in two fourth-grade classrooms. To establish the significance or the level of confidence for this correlation, we can consult a table or go through certain computations. Either of these procedures shows it to be significant at less than the .001 level. That is, a correlation of this magnitude, based on a population of this size, would be expected to occur by chance fewer than once in a thousand times.

For another illustration, suppose that the investigator's purpose is to test the effectiveness of an accelerated reading program. By a process of random selection, one-half the children in four classes of fourth-graders are assigned to an experimental group. The remaining children constitute a control group. The purpose of the study is to see whether the experimental children can be significantly advanced in reading skill over children remaining in the regular reading program by supplying individual instructions and enriched reading materials. Some safeguard must be introduced, however, so that it can be said that any superiority they show is due to the reading program and not to the Hawthorne effect (improvement in performance as a result of taking part in an experiment). This safeguard is introduced by giving the control children an amount of individual attention equal to that given the experimental youngsters, but social rather than instructional in nature; and supplying them with attractive materials that differ in content from those regularly used, but are at the same level of difficulty. Otherwise, the experiences of the two groups are the same.

The children are tested for reading achievement before and after the study. The experimental (accelerated) group does not differ from the control group at the beginning of the study, but has gained a full grade level at its end, while the control group has gained only a half year. Statistical computations relating to this differential gain result in a numerical expression of sufficient size to have occurred by chance only once in one hundred times. In practice, we proceed from this indication of lawfulness to the conclusion that the accelerated reading program was responsible for the difference in experimental and control group gains.

Faulty generalization often results from overconfidence in expressions of statistical significance, such as placing too much faith in a single experiment or study that shows significance at the .05 or .01 level. Less often, insufficient, hence faulty, generalization is made because of skepticism about the level of confidence of a finding.

This can become confusing, even to a rather sophisticated reader. In a study by Dennis and Sayegh[1] the experimental subjects gained significantly in developmental age (at the .03 level). This means that there are but three chances in one hundred that such gains could have come by chance alone. In other words, there are ninety-seven chances in one hundred that the enriched experiences given to five experimental babies were associated with and probably caused by the treatment administered to them by the experimenters. It is difficult to secure a result significant at this level with such a small number of subjects. One's chances of obtaining statistical sig-

[1] W. Dennis, and T. Sayegh. The effect of supplementary experiences upon the behavioral development of infants in institutions. *Child Development,* 1965, *36,* 81–90.

nificance increase the bigger one's sample is. But Dennis and Sayegh's control group also increased more rapidly in developmental age than would have been expected during the experiment (the authors are vague about the exact level of significance of the gain). We are told only that "the gains of the control group were smaller. . . . By the sign test, which was used in the case of the experimental group, the change in rate of gain of the control group has a very low level of significance" (p. 88). We are left with the understanding that the experimental group of five babies improved significantly more than the control group of eight babies. But we are not given data sufficient to decide for ourselves (it should be added that the authors are sympathetic to the Dennis and Sayegh point of view) whether or not there was *really* a statistically significant difference between the children given the extra hour of experience each day for fifteen days and those who did not have this experience.

To conclude, an understanding of statistical significance, correlation, and other statistics such as mean and standard deviation usually is ample for reading textbook treatments of psychological development. Eventually, however, many students will go beyond the standard textbook level to more technical reports in research journal articles and monographs. For those who do, we recommend the following additional sources of information about research methods, psychological measurement, and statistics.

RECOMMENDED SOURCES FOR FURTHER STUDY

Ferguson, G. A. *Statistical analysis in psychology and education* (4th ed.). New York: McGraw-Hill, 1976.

Kerlinger, F. N. *Foundations of behavioral research* (2nd ed.). New York: Holt, Rinehart and Winston, 1973.

Lemke, E., & Wiersma, W. *Principles of psychological measurement.* Skokie, Ill.: Rand McNally, 1976.

McCall, R. B. *Fundamental statistics for psychology* (2nd ed.). New York: Harcourt, 1975.

McGuigan, F. J. *Experimental psychology: A methodological approach* (2nd ed.). Englewood Cliffs, N.J.: Prentice-Hall, 1968.

Wright, R. L. D. *Understanding statistics: An informal introduction for the behavioral sciences.* New York: Harcourt, 1976.

Glossary

ACCOMMODATION A process of adjusting or modifying one's cognitive structures, because new, more accurate information is discrepant with old, less complete information.

ACHIEVEMENT Record of accomplishments (test scores, relationships, works of art).

ACHIEVEMENT MOTIVATION A learned and generalized predisposition to seek success.

ACTUALIZATION FUNCTION OF SCHOOLS Role of schools in enhancing self-esteem and social development of students as well as increasing critical thinking abilities.

AGE-RELEVANT DEVELOPMENTAL CONCEPT Approach to the description and analysis of developmental change that uses age as the primary index by which to order behaviors.

AGGRESSION Physical or verbal behavior that tends to hurt or destroy.

ALTRUISM Consideration and acting for the benefit of others.

ANACLITIC IDENTIFICATION A generalized imitation of another person, usually a primary caretaker, which is reinforcing or comforting to the child.

ANDROGENS Male hormones that regulate sexual and, in some aspects such as aggressiveness, psychological development.

ANDROGYNY (PSYCHOLOGICAL) The adoption and integration of the full range of human character traits despite cultural pressures to regard some traits as exclusively masculine or feminine.

ANXIETY Generalized feelings of uneasiness or dread, usually without objective cause.

APOLLONIAN NATURE OF MAN A view of human nature that emphasizes the thinking, *cognizing*,[1] symbolic, and appreciative activities of man, along with a stress on planning ahead, *motivation to achieve*, delay of gratification, and inhibition of impulses.

"APPLIED BEHAVIORISM" The study of behavior in natural settings rather than in laboratory situations.

ARTICULATION Production of speech sounds.

ASSIMILATION The process of making new information part of one's existing cognitive structure.

[1] Italicized words or phrases are defined elsewhere in the glossary.

ASSOCIATIVITY Piagetian notion of the child's realization that parts of a whole may be combined in different ways without effecting a change in the whole or the end result.

ASYMPTOTE The highest point of a plotted set of data, after which the function or curve levels out, indicating the stable level of a particular variable (such as *intelligence* or some other aspect of development).

ATOMISM A research strategy, typified by *behaviorist psychology*, which holds that large concepts of human development can be analyzed into elementary units without loss.

ATTACHMENT An affectional tie that one person forms to another person that endures over time.

ATTENTION A process by which the individual responds selectively to only certain elements from among the stimulus array to which he or she is exposed.

It is conceived as having two phases:

1. *Orientation reaction.* A behavioral vigilance, to identify stimuli.
2. *Selective scanning.* The individual selects and studies a part of the environment.

ATTENTION SPAN The range of stimuli that an individual's attention can encompass, in terms of either number or time.

AUDITORY DISCRIMINATION Ability of the individual to distinguish between sounds, particularly language-relevant sounds.

AUTHORITARIAN PARENTAL CONTROL A style of parenting that stresses obedience and control, with little verbal give and take.

AUTHORITATIVE PARENTAL CONTROL A style of parenting that combines firm, rational control with warmth, receptivity, and encouragement.

AUTONOMY Concept of self-directedness closely related to *independence*, the development of which is encouraged by peer groups and older siblings, who represent somewhat different *norms* to those of the parents.

AVERAGE A statistical term indicating a value in a distribution of scores around which all the other values are dispersed. Also used to mean the standard or typical case. See also *mean*.

AVERSIVE CONTROL   Form of behavioral management through negative reinforcement and punishment.

BEHAVIOR MODIFICATION   A method of changing human behavior by means of conditioning procedures.

BEHAVIORAL STABILITY DILEMMA   A persistent issue in developmental psychology, dealing with the relative continuity of traits and behaviors, including aspects of personality and *intelligence,* in individuals over their developmental span.

BEHAVIORIST PSYCHOLOGY (BEHAVIORISM)   A school of psychology, originated by John B. Watson, that emphasizes the study of behavior by rigorously controlled experiments.

BIOLINGUISTICS   Scientific discipline concerned with maturational factors (anatomical and physiological) that set the stage for language development.

BODY IMAGE   An individual's perception of the physical self, derived from internal sensations and fantasies and from how one thinks one looks to others.

BUREAUCRATIC PARENTAL OCCUPATION   An influence upon developmental change, considered to transcend social class lines and characterized by parental salaried occupations with a high degree of job security. It affects a wide range of childrearing practices stressing egalitarian behavior and emphasizing social adjustment, or "getting along."

CAREER DEVELOPMENT   A lifelong process that includes home, school, and community experiences as they affect *self-concept, expectancies,* choice of life style, and, especially, means of earning a living.

CAREER EDUCATION   A master plan for school curricula for the purpose of preparing individuals for economic self-sufficiency and job satisfaction.

CATHARSIS   The expression and discharge of conscious or repressed emotions, often through artistic expression.

CENTERING   The tendency in children to focus attention on a single aspect of a situation or event and to ignore other relevant aspects, thus accounting for an inability to attain the operation of *conservation.*

CEPHALOCAUDAL PRINCIPLE   The principle that development, especially the embryological, progresses from head to "tail."

CHILD ABUSE   Coercive power directed toward children by parents or caretakers that results in physical injury, sexual molestation, starvation, and, occasionally, death. Most conceptions of child abuse extend beyond physical injury to include psychosocial deprivation and psychologically abusive practices in the home, school, and other settings.

CHILD–PEER INTERACTIONS   Conceptualization of experience with a continually widening group of peers in terms of the influence that this *primary group* exerts on social, academic, and vocational development.

CLASSICAL CONDITIONING (PAVLOVIAN CONDITIONING)   A procedure in which a stimulus that normally evokes a given response is repeatedly joined with a stimulus that does not usually evoke that response,

with the result that the latter stimulus will eventually evoke the response when presented by itself.

CLASSIFICATION   Piagetian notion of the child's ability to organize an array of objects into hierarchies or classes, including the tasks of multiple classification (simultaneous organization along a number of equivalent dimensions such as color and size) and of superordinate conceptual classification (simultaneous organization along a number of dimensions on different conceptual levels).

CLINICAL METHOD   A research technique that includes interviews, life histories, testing, projective techniques, case observations, and so on.

COGNITION   A general term for any process that allows an organism to know and be aware. It includes perceiving, reasoning, conceiving, judging.

COGNITIVE STYLE   The mode in which a person organizes and classifies his or her perceptions of the environment.

COGNITIVE-DEVELOPMENTAL PSYCHOLOGY   A psychological approach to human development primarily concerned with matters of *intelligence,* thinking, logical processes, *language,* and competence or efficiency, as well as an emphasis on *epistemology.* Best represented by the *developmental stage theory* of Piaget.

COMMUNICATION STYLE   The unique way in which individuals use language to express thoughts and feelings, to relate socially to other people, to clarify ideas, and to describe experiences.

COMPENSATORY EDUCATION   An approach to education programs, typically aimed at the disadvantaged population, that incorporates remedial goals (attempts to fill social, cultural, or academic gaps in a child's education) and preventive goals (education during the early childhood years to forestall later academic problems).

COMPETENCE   The ability to perform an action; the *linguistic* notion of the child's grasp of the abstract properties of *language* and his or her means for interpreting and generating *linguistic* structures, as opposed to speech production or performance.

COMPETENCE STRIVING   Efforts directed toward the achievement of a feeling of effectiveness.

CONCEPT   A general term for the class of behavior one is considering, or which the author of a research paper has studied (for example, *frustration,* regression, *anxiety*).

CONCRETE OPERATIONS PERIOD   Piagetian developmental stage, from 7 to 11 years of age, during which the child begins to use operations such as *classification, reversibility,* and *conservation,* but can do so only by manipulating actual or concrete objects, and is unable to perform these operations in hypothetical situations or abstract terms.

CONFORMITY   A self-regulation of attitude or behavior brought about by social pressure to become like one's peers.

CONSERVATION   According to Piaget, the ability that develops over time to comprehend those aspects or relationships or phenomena that remain constant during and after transformations in appearance, configuration, or state.

CONTENTIVES Class name for nouns, verbs, and adjectives first used by the child in *telegraphic speech* utterances, an intermediate stage in grammatical development.

CONTROL GROUP In experimental studies, the group of subjects that receives no treatment and serves as a reference group against which change in the *experimental group* may be measured.

CONVERGENT PRODUCTION OR THINKING Thought aimed at finding a single logical solution to a problem.

COOPERATION *Prosocial behavior* that develops in infancy as the result of accommodations made between child and parents and that matures through children's games and other peer-group interactions.

CORRELATION COEFFICIENT (r) A statistical expression of the degree to which two measures vary together, ranging from perfect positive (+1.00) through zero, or no relationship (0.00), to perfect negative (−1.00). Casual explanations cannot be inferred from correlation, but one may predict the amount of *variance* that one variable contributes to another in a relationship by squaring the correlation coefficient (r^2).

CORRELATIONAL APPROACH An approach to the study of development that consists of descriptions of behavioral change in relation to *norms* for that behavior as well as to other factors—for example, family background, *socioeconomic status*, child–peer interactions, and *intelligence*.

COUNTERCULTURE A *culture* whose views and behaviors are opposite from those of the dominant one.

CREATIVITY A pattern of motives, attitudes, and traits associated with the production of original works, also carrying the implication of outstanding quality.

CRITICAL PERIOD The only point in time when a particular environmental event can have its exclusive or maximum effect upon development.

CROSS-CULTURAL STUDY A type of experimental design in which comparable data are acquired from two or more different cultures for the purpose of testing theories about individual or group differences in development and behavior.

CROSS-SECTIONAL STUDY A type of experimental design in which a number of individuals at different stages of development are studied simultaneously, as a means of drawing general inferences about the progress of development.

CUE OR DISCRIMINATIVE STIMULUS *Behaviorist* designation for a stimulus or pattern of stimuli capable of eliciting a particular behavior or class of behaviors because of association of that stimulus with *reinforcement*. The concept is central to the notion of *stimulus control* of behavior.

CULTURE The established customs, roles, and learned behaviors of a group of people that are passed on from generation to generation.

CULTURAL COMPETENCE Notion within the *behaviorist* concept of child development that emphasizes the shaping power of arranged experience for the child in order that he or she may develop maximal skills and environmental mastery. Essentially in keeping with a *determinist* perspective.

CUMULATIVE-DEFICIT HYPOTHESIS A part of the *critical-periods* perspective: deficiencies or distortions of experiences may pile up and interfere with future development, perhaps in a geometric fashion.

CURIOSITY A tendency to be attracted by the novel and the strange, and, in its developed form, to seek knowledge. See *epistemic curiosity*.

DEPENDENCE A general concept applied to the relation of an individual to another or to society, as receiving aid without which he or she is presumably unable to maintain himself. See *independence*.

DETERMINISM The philosophical position, embodied in *behaviorism*, that people are controlled by the forces of their environment, and hence are not free agents to act as they please—a position repudiated by the religious and philosophical doctrine of free will and the principles of *humanistic psychology*.

DEVELOPMENTAL INTERACTION Conceptual approach used to connote the multiple aspects of physical-motor, personal-social-emotional, and cognitive-intellectual-achievement development that together contribute to the child's psychosocial development.

DEVELOPMENTAL STAGE THEORY A theory that regards development as an invariable series of qualitatively different periods. Stage theorists include Piaget, Freud, Erikson, and Kohlberg.

DEVELOPMENTAL TASKS Age-related tasks to be mastered for continued progress toward higher levels of maturity. Such tasks have their source in physical *maturation*, cultural pressures, and personal values and aspirations.

DIALECT A *language* system differing to a greater or lesser degree from standard English in terms of grammatically different additions, deletions, and word combinations, as well as the possible incorporation of grammatical rules and vocabulary from non-English linguistic systems.

DIFFERENTIATION Developmental process in which behavior becomes increasingly complex and integrated.

DIONYSIAN NATURE OF MAN Conceptualization of human nature that emphasizes the enjoyment of and capacity for immediate sensory experiences, a lack of impulse inhibition, motivation to enjoy present experiences on their own terms rather than wait for future gratification, cultivation of deep interpersonal relationships, and a general "back to nature" orientation.

DISCOVERY LEARNING Active, usually self-guided, explorations of the environment that result in self-formulated knowledge from first-hand experience.

DISCRIMINATION LEARNING SET Acquisition of the ability to perceive differences among stimuli and to respond differentially to these stimuli in terms of a *problem-solving process,* with the most highly developed form of this set being *insight learning.*

DISEQUILIBRIUM *Cognitive-developmental* concept referring to the feeling of uneasiness experienced by an individual in response to newly assimilated information that is not in agreement with past knowledge. By means of *accommodation,* individuals seek to eliminate this unsettling condition by learning about the source of error in their prior knowledge and achieving a more accurate perception of reality.

DIVERGENT PRODUCTION OR THINKING Ability to operate on the given elements of the environment in a fluent, flexible, and elaborative fashion to achieve end results that are unexpected and original. According to some theorists, this kind of operation is central to the concept of *creativity.*

DOWN'S SYNDROME A genetic disorder that results in a particular form of mental retardation.

EFFECTANCE MOTIVATION A need to make sense of the environment and to be effective in relation to it.

EFFECTIVE CULTURE Those aspects of behavioral uniformity and diversity which affect individuals and groups within a larger social configuration, operating as mediators of developmental change and transmitted to the child by the *primary group.*

EGO According to Freudian theory, the part of the psyche that handles transactions with the external environment according to the *reality principle.* The ego mediates between the demands of the *id* and the *superego.*

EGOCENTRISM Piagetian concept of the child's inability to understand that others have needs and points of view which differ from his or her own. This results in a tendency to evaluate objects and events solely in terms of one's own perspective. With the achievement of *formal operations* and the ability to simultaneously consider multiple points of view, egocentrism is dissipated.

EIGHT STAGES OF MAN Erikson's neopsychoanalytic theory postulating a series of eight developmental crises that each person must face in the course of development.

EMPATHY Capacity for understanding another individual's thoughts or feelings by being able to take his or her psychological perspective; a necessary precursor for the development of *altruism* and *morality.*

ENTREPRENEURIAL PARENTAL OCCUPATION An influence upon developmental change, considered to transcend *socioeconomic class* lines, characterized by parental occupations involving self-employment or work on a commission basis that often includes risk-taking and competition. It affects a wide range of childrearing practices that emphasize *independence* training, mastery of skills, self-reliance, and ample use of psychological techniques of discipline.

EPISTEMIC CURIOSITY Activity directed toward gaining, coding, and storing information in the form of symbolic responses that can guide behavior on future occasions. Believed to be motivated by conceptual conflict or conflict due to discrepant thoughts, beliefs, attitudes, or observations. Because of this conflict, individuals seek information to buttress, support, develop, or refine their prevailing thought, and resolution is considered to be intrinsically reinforcing.

EPISTEMOLOGY The branch of philosophy concerned with understanding the origin, nature, methods, and limits of knowledge, particularly with reference to human thought. Typified by the developmental research of J. Piaget.

EQUILIBRATION In Piaget's theory of development, the process by which *accommodation* and *assimilation* are brought into balance by the reconciliation of new and past experience.

EQUIVALENCE Piagetian notion of a child's ability to understand that objects which differ along one or more dimensions (varying size and texture, for example) may still be similar along some other dimension (such as weight). Also the concept that a change along one of these dimensions (shape) does not necessarily mean that the other dimensions (texture and weight, for example) will also change. This concept is synonymous with the concept of covariance.

ESTROGENS Female hormones that regulate sexual development and are associated with maternal behavior.

ETHNICITY The *culture,* religion, and *language* traditions of a people or cultural group, such as Italian Americans or Jews, as distinguished from the concept of *race or racial group.*

ETHOLOGY The science of comparative behavior, in which various species are observed in their natural habitats for evidence of characteristic ways of behaving and adaptability.

EXCEPTIONALITY IN DEVELOPMENT Any pattern of human development sufficiently different from the *norm,* whether advanced or delayed, to require special assistance in the developmental process.

EXPANSION TECHNIQUE Type of adult influence on the child's grammatical development, in which the adult responds to the child's two- or three-word utterances by formulating complete and grammatically correct versions of the child's presumed ideas, using the child's utterance as the skeleton of the more complete expression.

EXPECTANCY A learned disposition whereby an organism anticipates that a specific situation will be brought about by a given response to a stimulus.

EXPERIMENTAL GROUP In experimental studies, the group of subjects that is exposed to a particular treatment or independent variable, in contrast to the group of subjects receiving no experimental treatment (*control group*).

EXPERIMENTAL METHOD Techniques of studying development by testing hypotheses and gaining information through manipulation of variables.

EXTENDED OR KINSHIP FAMILY A family in which father, mother, grandparents, and uncles and aunts live together or in close proximity, providing many substitute parents for young children.

EXTENSION TECHNIQUE Type of adult influence on the child's grammatical development in which the adult responds to the child's two- or three-word utterances by contributing a related idea, thus carrying the child's idea into a wider range of meaning and experience.

EXTINCTION The gradual weakening of a conditioned response resulting from the withholding of the unconditioned stimulus or the instrumental reward.

FACTOR ANALYSIS A statistical method of finding the smallest number of factors that can account for all the correlations among a set of variables.

FALLEN ANGEL VIEW OF MAN View held by *humanistic* and *cognitive-developmental psychology* that man is essentially good. *Morality* should therefore not have to be taught, because it is inherent, although a malign environment could deflect a positive course of development.

FETUS The unborn offspring of an animal in its more advanced state of development. In human beings, from the end of the third month of pregnancy to birth.

FORMAL CULTURE Broadly shared guidelines held to within a given group of people, involving both uniformity and the allowance of diversity in the behavior of its participants. These formal characteristics may not, however, apply precisely to a particular person or group within that *culture* (see *effective culture*).

FORMAL OPERATIONS PERIOD (PERSPECTIVISM) The last of Piaget's periods of cognitive development (from adolescence through adulthood) during which the individual learns to think simultaneously of two or more operations and, as a consequence, is able to carry out systematic experiments, to consider hypothetical objects and events, and to understand abstract principles.

FRUSTRATION A stress state that results when an individual is unable to achieve a desired goal. Considered by some theorists to be closely related to the induction of *aggression*.

FUNCTION WORDS Class name for prepositions, conjunctions, and articles ("up," "to," "on," "in," "but," "and," "the") that are combined with *contentives* to form complete sentences by the young child.

GENERATIVE GRAMMAR A theory developed by Chomsky and of central importance to *linguistics*, that there is an innate and universal human mechanism by which developing individuals actively structure the *language* spoken in their community, permitting them to create and understand sentences which they may never have heard before.

GENETICS Study of the way in which hereditary characteristics are transmitted from one generation to another.

GENOTYPE The sum of the individual's genetic endowment. Conceptualized in an interactive *nature–nurture* point of view by the equation: genotype $\times$ environment = phenotype.

GIFTED, INTELLECTUAL Those individuals with superior cognitive abilities that comprise approximately the top 3 percent of the general school population in measured *intelligence* and/or creative abilities or other talents that promise to make contributions of merit to society.

GRAMMAR In *psycholinguistics*, the rules (sometimes formal but usually unwritten) used by the speaker of a *language* to construct sentences.

GUILT ORIENTATION A psychological predisposition for self-censure and remorse where wrong-doing is anticipated or actually accomplished.

HALO EFFECT A tendency to be biased in the estimation of a certain characteristic of an individual because of a positive or negative impression of another characteristic of the same individual.

HAWTHORNE EFFECT The condition in which performance of individuals is affected by their knowledge that they are participants in an experiment.

HETEROGENEOUS POPULATION A *population* that includes a wide variety of differences among its members on some measure or combination of measures.

HOLOPHRASTIC UTTERANCE One-word expressions that represent the earliest phase of grammatical development in the child and occur at about one year of age. These expressions are related to the actions of the child or actions the child desires of other people and require an awareness of context for understanding.

HOMEOSTATIC THEORY ("BALANCE THEORY") Theoretical notion used to deal with the construct of motivation, which states that organisms, including humans, are rewarded by or reinforced for tension that occurs because of some need, since they find it satisfying to have tension reduced.

HOMOGENEOUS POPULATION A *population* in which all members are relatively similar to one another on some measure or combination of measures.

HUMANISTIC PSYCHOLOGY The general psychological approach that emphasizes the special characteristics that differentiate human beings from other animals. Humanistic psychologists especially stress positive, constructive human capacities.

ID According to Freud, the unconscious and most primitive part of the psyche, comprising needs, drives, and instinctual impulses. The id operates according to the pleasure principle and is in constant conflict with the *superego*.

IDENTIFICATION General concept that may be defined in three ways:
1. *As behavior.* When a person behaves like some other person at a high level of generality and abstraction (mannerisms, *language* habits, values,

interests, and even thought processes).

2. *As motive.* Consciously or unconsciously a person is moved toward, or wishes to be (and usually then becomes) similar to someone else.

3. *As process.* The mechanisms through which the child comes to emulate a model.

IDENTITY FORMULATION   A major growth trend of the *self,* involving an awareness of group membership and the expectations, privileges, restraints, and social responsibilities accompanying that membership. It is a process through which a child gains knowledge of such matters as his or her name, race, sex role, and social class, and the meanings that these identifying labels have for the child's life.

IDIOGRAPHIC APPROACH   An experimental approach to development that focuses on the study of individual cases.

IMITATION   A process of *socialization* in which one person learns by copying the behavior of a model.

INCIDENTAL LEARNING   Learning without set purpose or special effort to learn.

INDEPENDENCE   The opposite concept to that of *dependence* behavior, whose form changes with age, in terms both of the objects of one's *dependence* and of the frequency with which such behavior is manifest. Conflict about independence–dependence relationships typically intensifies with the onset of adolescence, because of the value attached to independence in United States culture and the fear of parents that the adolescent "is not yet ready."

INDUCTION TECHNIQUES   Form of reasoning considered to be a democratic means of dealing with, and teaching, moral behavior and values to children and, at the same time, encouraging the child to assume a particular orientation to society. Parents may shape and foster two possible induction orientations:

1. *Self-oriented induction.* Similar in content to *shame orientation* in that it aims to encourage the child to conform to a social standard for his or her own good and to evaluate acts in terms of their ultimate benefit.

2. *Other-oriented induction.* Consists of pointing out to the child the consequences that his or her acts may have for others and of encouraging the child to develop *empathy* for others and to learn to curb *egocentric* impulses.

INFORMATION PROCESSING   The means by which humans receive and transform information from the environment into complex thought patterns and, ultimately, responses for acting on the environment. Information processing is a way to describe cognitive activity and includes *attention, perception,* memory, *language,* and reasoning.

"INNER SPEECH" OR "INNER LANGUAGE"   The self-communicative or intrapersonal aspect of *language,* typified by daydreaming, planning solutions to problems, and giving direction and organization to one's movement. It becomes increasingly more important as *cognitive development* progresses, particularly in the form of thinking that is characteristic of the Piagetian *formal operations period.*

INSIGHT LEARNING (ONE-TRIAL LEARNING)   The grasping of those relationships leading to the solution of a problem (sometimes after a single trial's exposure to the problem), based on perceptual reorganization of previous experience.

INSTRUMENTAL COMPETENCE   Baumrind's characterization of *socialization* as a product defined along the dimensions of social responsibility (presence or absence of achievement orientation, friendly or hostile behavior, and cooperative or resistive behavior toward peers and adults) and *independence* (dominant and purposive) versus tractability (submissive and aimless) in behavior. It is closely associated with an *authoritative parental control* style.

INSTRUMENTAL CONDITIONING   A form of learning in which a stimulus, having prompted a response that either results in positive reinforcement or is effective in preventing or removing an aversive stimulus, is subsequently more likely to prompt that response.

INTELLECTUAL ACHIEVEMENT RESPONSIBILITY   The extent to which individuals believe that they are responsible for the consequences of their behavior (success or failure) in *achievement* situations, and that these consequences are not due to chance, luck, fate, or the arbitrary behavior of other persons.

INTELLIGENCE   Broadly defined in terms of the ability of an individual to solve problems. Is determined by a complex interaction of heredity and experience. Intellectual development as *process* is viewed as the increasing complexity of cognitive processes, particularly in areas of ability to conceptualize, understand, and obtain knowledge; as a *product,* intelligence is conceptualized as a particular ability or score on an intelligence test at some point in time, such as an *intelligence quotient.*

INTELLIGENCE QUOTIENT (IQ)   Measure of *intelligence* obtained by dividing the individual's mental age (MA), as determined by his or her performance on a standardized test, by chronological age (CA) and then multiplying by 100. An IQ of 100 is considered average.

INTENTIONAL LEARNING   Behavioral or informational acquisition activity governed by a "closed" attention system, or set, in which the individual concentrates on one thing at a time and resists distraction until the job is completed. An example is the formal classroom learning situation.

INTERDEPENDENCE   Behavioral balance between the notion of personal *independence* and some degree of interpersonal *dependence.*

INVARIANCE DESPITE CHANGE (OBJECT CONSTANCY)   Piagetian notion of the child's ability to conceptualize objects and people as maintaining a constant identity, despite certain variations in their appearance because of changes of context and circumstance.

JUVENILE DELINQUENCY *Norm*-violating behavior, usually of an antisocial nature. Legally, juveniles are delinquent if they violate the law and are convicted for doing so. Behaviorally, they are delinquent if they express aggressive acts contrary to social norms.

KILLER APE VIEW OF MAN View of man's essential nature as basically evil or, at best, irrational, nonmoral, and antisocial. Moral training is essential "to keep the beast in check" and to civilize him, a view espoused by the major religions and by classical *psychoanalytic psychology*.

LANGUAGE A complex system for communication, composed of grammatical and semantic properties, as distinguished from speech (actual utterances), and functionally conceptualized in terms of receptive (language) aspects (the ability to understand and act on the communications that are received) and expressive (language) aspects (the ability to spontaneously produce various words, sentences, or constructions in one's language repertoire). Communication through language may be interpersonal or intrapersonal (*inner speech* or self-communication).

LANGUAGE DIFFERENCES DILEMMA A persistent issue in schools where there are large populations of children whose first *language* is not English. It involves the problem of helping these children to discriminate between those cases where their own *language* or English is more appropriate, without making them feel that their *language* or *culture* is inferior.

LANGUAGE–THOUGHT DILEMMA Persistent issue in *language* development concerned with the question of whether, on the one hand, the pattern of thought is a function of the structure of a given language (*linguistic-relativity hypothesis*) or whether, on the other hand, language is structured by logical cognition, serving only to express thought, as Piaget contends.

LEADERSHIP The exercise of authority to influence others in group settings. Associated with leadership is a cluster of qualities such as *intelligence*, sociability, assertiveness, and especially *competence*.

LEARNING Relatively enduring behavioral changes that come about as a function of experiences, both arranged and unarranged, encountered in adapting to one's environment.

LEARNING SET Readiness to respond in a certain way to a particular type of learning situation because of the acquisition of some *problem-solving* strategy.

LIBIDO Originally used by psychoanalysts to mean sexual desire, but later in the more general sense of vital impulse or energy. In the analytic concept of personality, libido is in ceaseless struggle with the *ego*, being held in check mainly by the *superego*.

LINGUISTIC PERFORMANCE The spontaneous production or use of grammatical forms of *language*, commonly described as speech, as distinguished from the underlying knowledge of language, conceptualized as linguistic *competence*.

LINGUISTIC RELATIVITY HYPOTHESIS Notion that thought or mental behavior is shaped by the particular *language* through which it is processed. The position represents one extreme in the *language–thought dilemma*.

LINGUISTICS Discipline investigating the structure and content of *language*, including *grammar*, sound combinations, and meaning, and providing the conceptual basis for *biolinguistics*, *psycholinguistics*, and *sociolinguistics*.

LOCUS OF CONTROL The way individuals perceive the world they live in. When a *reinforcement* is perceived by the subject as following some action of his or her own, but not being entirely contingent upon that action, in our *culture* it is typically perceived as the result of luck, chance, fate, or the actions of powerful others. Such an interpretation is labeled as belief in "external locus of control." If the person perceives that the event is entirely contingent upon his or her own behavior, this belief is labeled "internal locus of control."

LONGITUDINAL STUDY Developmental study that focuses on the change in the same person or group of persons over an extended period of time.

LONG-TERM MEMORY STORE Relatively permanent memory that has a seemingly unlimited capacity.

LOVE-WITHDRAWAL TECHNIQUES Techniques of child-rearing in which *punishment* is psychological, in the form of nurturance withdrawal, and may result in a poor parent–child interaction. There is little consensus as to the effect of these techniques on *moral development*.

MASTURBATION Achievement of sexual satisfaction by self-stimulation of the genitals.

MATURATION The process of developmental change that is extensively, if not totally, controlled by genetic or hereditary factors.

MAXIMUM-SUSCEPTIBILITY NOTION A concept within the *critical periods* literature that there is an optimal time for a particular experience to have an effect on development, and that if a child is either too young or old for the experience it will have little effect.

MEAN A measure of the central tendency of a set of scores, derived by adding all the scores and dividing the sum by the total number of cases.

MEDIAN A statistical term indicating that point in a distribution of scores above and below which exactly one-half the population falls.

"ME"–"NOT ME" DISTINCTION Piagetian concept, occurring during the *sensorimotor period*, of the development of the primitive notion of the self as an entity independent of its environment.

"MENTALISM" A theoretical position involving propositions or assumptions about the mind not subject to verification through objective observational techniques.

MENTAL RETARDATES Roughly 1 percent of the general population who are so deficient in general intellectual ability that they are unable to care for themselves or whose behavioral inadequacies make special supervisory care necessary.

MODELING In *social learning theory*, a form of learning whereby a person becomes able to perform action(s) by emulating another person. Occasionally, modeling refers also to the actions of a person being observed by another.

MORAL DEVELOPMENT The process by which an individual achieves behavioral conformity within societal limits of acceptability and learns to inhibit impulses when necessary or desirable.

MORAL IDENTIFICATION (INTERNALIZATION) Psychodynamic concept for the process by which the child incorporates parental standards and values as one's own, in the form of the *superego* or conscience.

MORAL JUDGMENT Judgment concerning whether an act is right or wrong. According to Piaget and Kohlberg, moral judgment is a function of and parallels development.

MORAL REALISM (ABSOLUTISM) According to Piaget, the attitude characteristic of small children that all rules are sacred and unalterable and operate in terms of a *morality* that is determined by others.

MORAL RELATIVISM According to Piaget, a late stage of *moral development* arrived at by the child through experience with peers and adults, in which he or she comes to view laws and social rules as arrangements that come about through reciprocal agreements and function for the good of all those affected by them.

MORALITY Development, formulation, and expression of internal intentions or conscience, focusing a person's outlook on life and involving a personal construction of social values and of the objective obligations and responsibilities that an individual has to his community.

MORPHOLOGY A study and description of word formation in a *language*, including inflection, derivation, and compounding, as distinguished from syntax.

MUTUALITY A principle of human interaction founded upon mutual *trust* and respect, which guides interaction in such a way that persons can develop their respective strengths and have no need to gain at another's expense.

NATIVIST–ENVIRONMENTALIST (RATIONALIST-EMPIRICIST) DILEMMA Persistent issue in *language* development, referring to whether universal, innate biological structures predispose the child to develop *language* (nativist or rationalist) or whether experiential factors, analyzed in terms of learning principles of environmental reinforcement (environmentalist or empiricist) explain *language* development.

NATURALISTIC, INDIGENOUS GROWTH Theory of child development, related to the philosophy of Rousseau, which emphasizes freedom in childrearing and educational practices and the belief that maximum socialization benefits can be gained by placing children in an enriched, benign, accepting, permissive, informally arranged environment, where a high value is given to the child's creative self-expression.

NATURE–NURTURE CONTROVERSY A highly controversial issue in psychology related to the relative importance of heredity ("nature") and environment ("nurture") in the development of behavior.

NEONATE A newborn infant.

NOMOTHETIC APPROACH An experimental approach to the study of development that focuses on the study of large groups and on statistical treatment of the data in terms of *means*, ranges of scores, *variances (heterogeneity* or *homogeneity)*, and significant differences between experimental and control groups.

NONVERBAL COMMUNICATION (BODY LANGUAGE) The way in which body position, gestures, facial movements, and eye contact are used to communicate mood, emphasize points made in spoken *language*, and otherwise transmit meanings that accompany verbal communications.

NORM In psychological testing, the average performance level for a given group of people; in social psychology, the standards or expectations for behavior upheld by societies; in developmental psychology, typical or average behavior that serves as convenient indices of development.

NORMAL CURVE The plotted form of the *normal distribution;* a bell-shaped curve.

NORMAL DISTRIBUTION The expected distribution of data in psychological research, with most cases clustered in the center and increasingly fewer cases as extreme ends of the curve are approached. The *median* and *mean* of the distribution are the same.

NORMATIVE-DESCRIPTIVE APPROACH An approach to the study of development in which behaviors are charted in relation to age changes (age at onset of behavior, age *norms* describing increases or decreases in behavior).

NUCLEAR FAMILY The typical family in the United States, in which one or both parents and the children live in their own home, with grandparents and other relatives frequently living some distance away.

OBESITY The excessive accumulation of adipose (fatty) tissue.

OBJECT PERMANENCE The Piagetian term referring to the individual's realization that objects continue to exist even when they are not visible. According to Piaget, the complete development of object permanence marks the beginning of the *preoperational period.*

OCCASIONAL QUESTION TECHNIQUE Source of adult influence on the child's grammatical development in which the adult, by replying to the child's statements with questions, aids the child in clarifying his or her utterances and in learning the relationship of the declarative and interrogative grammatical forms.

OPERATIONAL DEFINITION   A definition of an abstract concept in terms of the operations for observing it, so that other observers could duplicate the defined procedure.

ORGANISMIC VARIABLES   *Behaviorist* designation for the properties of the organism being investigated, including anatomical and physiological characteristics.

ORGASM   Sexual climax that can be produced in human infants of either sex. After puberty, however, sexual climax in the male is accompanied by ejaculation, the expulsion of semen and seminal fluid from the penis.

OSSIFICATION   The developmental process by which an infant's cartilage is hardened into the bones of later childhood and adulthood and, finally, the brittle bones of old age.

PARALINGUISTICS   The study of intonation in expressive *language*.

PEER "VERSUS" PARENTS DILEMMA   Cluster of issues that may cause conflict between parents and children regarding the child's choice of friends, dress, recreation, and so on. Peer influence often seems greatest during early adolescence.

PERCEPTION   Process of organizing, coding, and interpreting raw sensory input or experience, developed as a complex function of *maturation* and environmental impact and related to the development of cognitive processes.

PERCEPTUAL SET   A readiness to perceive stimuli in a certain way or to see things that might be lost to others in a competitive array of stimuli, as a function of past learning or the current state of the organism.

PERFORMANCE INTELLIGENCE FACTOR   A score on the Wechsler intelligence tests, based on items in which the role of language is minimized.

PERFORMANCE SET   Habitual mode of coping with particular kinds of situations.

PERMISSIVE PARENTAL CONTROL   Childrearing practices that stress nonpunitive parental attitudes toward the child; a positive acceptance of the child's impulses, desires, and actions; low control and emphasis on obedience to externally defined standards; and an attempt on the part of the parent to act as a resource for the child rather than as a directive agent.

PHENOTYPE   In genetics, the characteristics that actually appear in a living organism, such as hair and eye color.

PHONEMES   The smallest units of sound of a *language*.

PLAY BEHAVIOR   Classification of social interactions among young children (ages 2–5) at play into six categories of social involvement:
1. *Unoccupied behavior.* Smallest extent of social involvement, in which the child is occupied with watching anything that may be of interest.
2. *Solitary play.* Child acts alone, making no effort to associate with peers.
3. *Onlooker behavior.* Child watches other peers at play with sustained interest and occasional communication.
4. *Parallel play.* Child plays near, but not with, other children, using similar or identical toys but according to his or her own rules.
5. *Associative play.* Social interaction based on play activities of borrowing and lending, with children making no attempt to divide tasks or organize the activity in terms of groups.
6. *Cooperative play.* Groups are organized for some purpose, with leaders and task assignments.

POPULATION   The total group of cases or people toward which a study is directed, rather than the smaller *sample* that is observed or experimentally tested as representative of the total group.

POWER-ASSERTION TECHNIQUES   Techniques of child-rearing in which the parent manages the child by force, physical or emotional, and which may result in a poor parent–child relationship. Such techniques block the child, frustrate mastery and *competence* needs, and are not successful for instilling *morality,* because the child's attention is focused on the parent and on the *self* rather than on the consequences of the act that elicited the *punishment.*

POWER TESTING   A *psychometric* principle of test construction, in which an individual's score is a function of his or her ability to solve a series of problems arranged in order of increasing difficulty, with no time limit imposed.

PREJUDICE, RACIAL   A preconceived, usually unreasonable and unfavorable, judgment or opinion about persons not of one's own *racial group.*

PREOPERATIONAL THOUGHT PERIOD   The second of Piaget's four periods of intellectual development (approximately ages 2 through 6), during which a child becomes able to understand many complex events but lacks the ability to use mental operations. As a result, the child cannot coordinate thoughts into logical systems. For example, he or she cannot understand other viewpoints, think in an organized, self-directed manner, or understand *classification* or *conservation.*

PREPARATORY SET   Predisposition of the organism to act in a particular fashion because of motives or needs (hunger, thirst), instructions, or sense-modality preferences (taste, touch, smell, and so on).

PRIMARY GROUP   A constellation of people, consisting of family, neighbors, close friends, and classmates, that transmits the customs and values of the *effective culture* to an individual in terms of reward–punishment patterns, behavioral *expectancies,* and so on.

PRIMARY SOURCE   A scholarly article that reports original data, analyzes them, formulates results, arrives at conclusions, and sometimes makes recommendations for action based on these data.

PROBLEM-SOLVING PROCESS   The process involved in the determination of the correct sequence of alternatives leading to the successful performance of a task or the achievement of a goal.

PROCESS–PRODUCT DISTINCTION The distinction between the underlying trend or progress of development (process) and a particular manifestation of that growth trend (product). Exemplified by *intelligence*, which is both a trend in the growth of cognitive abilities (process) and a score on an intelligence test (product).

PRONUNCIATION Final phase of the Montessori three-period sequence for vocabulary development, in which the caretaker, pointing to the object or quality that was labeled during the naming phase and identified in the recognition phase, requires the child to describe that object or quality in response to the question, "What is it?"

PROSOCIAL BEHAVIORS Behaviors that are socially constructive and usually benefit both the person who engages in them and those who receive them. *Trust, altruism,* and *cooperation* are examples of this behavioral category.

PROTESTANT ETHIC Cluster of behavioral characteristics emphasizing *independence*, individualism, and the *work ethic*.

PROXIMODISTAL PRINCIPLE Idea that physical growth and motor control develop from shoulder and thigh toward fingers and toes.

PSYCHOBIOLOGICAL SEXUAL DEVELOPMENT Process by which an individual, regardless of cultural influence, must make certain behavioral adjustments to increased size and strength, to *maturation* of primary and secondary sex characteristics, and to the biological rhythms and pressures that follow *puberty* (menstrual cycle for girls and pressure toward sexual outlet for boys). With sexual maturation, the organism becomes susceptible to and influenced by new sexual reinforcers.

PSYCHOANALYTIC PSYCHOLOGY A psychological approach to human development primarily concerned with early life experiences, notably parent–child and sibling relationships, that are regarded as central to personality development. Particular emphasis is placed on emotional experiences and the early *socialization* of human instincts (sex drive, self-preservation, *aggression*), as well as on the phenomenon of the unconscious. Concentration is on the individual rather than the *culture*, on traumatic events rather than positive growth experiences, on the way in which personality is structured rather than on how changes occur in human development; and, while the aim is to understand and explain the normal personality, theoretical and therapeutic emphasis is almost solely on pathology.

PSYCHOLINGUISTICS The study of the relationship between *language* and the psychological characteristics of language users.

PSYCHOMETRICS Mathematical measurement aspects of psychological experiments; more recently, statistical treatment of mental test results.

PSYCHOSEXUAL DEVELOPMENT According to Freud, the different phases in sexual development, especially the mental aspects occurring between infancy and adolescence. These stages are the oral, anal, phallic, latency, and genital.

PSYCHOSOCIAL CONFLICT A condition that results when an individual or a group is faced with situations that call for mutually incompatible behavior, either because of the nature of the situation or because of the learning history of that individual or group. Conflict of this nature is often associated with *anxiety, independence-dependence,* and *aggression,* as well as *prosocial behaviors: trust* versus mistrust, *altruism* versus selfishness, *cooperation* versus competition.

PUBERTY The age at which secondary sex characteristics first appear and sexual organs become functional, marking the onset of adolescence.

PUNISHMENT The act of delivering an aversive stimulus to an organism because it has performed a disapproved action or because it has failed to perform an approved action; if successful, punishment inhibits or otherwise reduces the probability that the punished response occurs.

RACE OR RACIAL GROUP Concept referring to a subdivision of the human race characterized by distinguishable physical characteristics transmitted from one generation to another, as distinct from the more general cultural concept of *ethnicity*.

READINESS Possession of the prerequisite skills necessary for the mastery of a task at a new level of difficulty by virtue of *maturation* or specific learning experiences.

REALITY PRINCIPLE According to Freudian theory, one of the regulatory principles of mental functioning whereby an individual adjusts his or her behavior to the conditions of the environment by delaying, giving up, inhibiting, or changing drive and need satisfaction.

RECIPROCITY A basic component of human *morality* defined as the ability of an individual to see, respect, honor, and facilitate another individual's point of view so long as the integrity of others is not destroyed by this action.

REFLECTIVITY–IMPULSIVITY Dimension of *cognitive style*, particularly relevant to the *problem-solving process*. Defined as the tendency of children or youth to think carefully about problem solutions before volunteering a response (reflectivity) or the alternative tendency to respond quickly and thoughtlessly without taking sufficient time to think carefully about the nature of the information, the materials, or alternative responses (impulsivity).

REINFORCEMENT (RESPONSE-DEPENDENT REINFORCEMENT) The occurrence of some environmental event (positive, such as delivery of food to a hungry subject; or aversive, such as the delivery of painful electric shock) that is contingent on the emission of a given response by the subject. It has the effect of increasing or decreasing the probability that the experimental subject will repeat the response under similar environmental conditions.

REINFORCEMENT HISTORY *Behaviorist* conceptualization of an individual's past experience with rewards and punishments, including the frequency and consistency with which given behaviors have been rewarded or punished (or ignored), which gives the scientist a means of explaining individual differences in behavior.

RESISTANCE-TO-TEMPTATION Ability of an individual to inhibit or otherwise control his or her self-indulgent and other forms of self-seeking behavior in the presence of enticing conditions. This may take the form of self-denial or of deferring personal gratification to a more suitable time.

RESPONSE VARIABLE Dependent variable in psychological research that changes with changes in the stimulus variable.

RESPONSE-INDEPENDENT REINFORCEMENT Similar in concept to the *behaviorist* concept of *reinforcement (response-dependent reinforcement)*, but differing in that the delivery of the reinforcer is *not* contingent (or dependent) upon the emission of a particular response, but is spontaneous or unplanned and may be used to favorably influence a child's perceptions of himself and his environment.

SAMPLE A subgroup of *a population* that is used as representative of the entire population and from which conclusions are drawn that are said to be characteristic of the entire population.

SCHOOL ANXIETY Emotional tension related to academic progress, commonly experienced by children when they begin school. Usually decreases during years of middle childhood and beyond, except in those children whose academic progress is slower than that of their peers.

SCHOOL COMPOSITION DILEMMA Issues relating to the benefits and liabilities of unisexual versus coeducational schools. Arguments revolve around sexual behavior that may or may not be fostered in each setting, as well as on more clearcut issues relating to differences in rate of *maturity* and activity level for males and females.

SECONDARY GROUP A loosely constituted, peripheral constellation of people, including the members of an individual's political precinct, his or her church congregation, and other organization members with whom he or she associates infrequently or temporarily and who serve to transmit aspects of the *effective culture* to the individual.

SELECTIVE MODELING TECHNIQUE (GRAMMATICAL) A type of adult influence on the child's grammatical development, in which certain grammatical structures (singular–plural forms, active–passive forms, noun–verb forms, affirmative–negative forms) are used by the adult, who encourages or reinforces the child to produce the utterance.

SELF Central concept in the study of self-development. Controversy revolves around two central concepts:

1. *Self as object*. A person's attitudes, perceptions, feelings, and evaluation of himself as an object— what a person knows and thinks about himself or herself.
2. *Self as process*. Self is considered an amalgam of active processes of thinking, perceiving, and remembering.

SELF-ACTUALIZATION A central concern of *humanistic psychology*, dealing with the process by which an individual realizes and fulfills his or her potential.

SELF-CONCEPT The individual's knowledge and evaluation of the self.

SEMANTIC DEVELOPMENT Development of word meaning, the influence of meaning on *syntax*, and the relationship of meaning to action, all of which are sometimes referred to as vocabulary development.

SENSORIMOTOR DEVELOPMENT Piagetian developmental stage, lasting from birth to 18 months or 2 years, during which the infant learns to differentiate himself from objects and individuals; seeks stimulation and learns to prolong interesting visual stimuli through mental representation; and discovers, by means of manipulation, that an object retains its identity or meaning despite changes in location and point of view.

SEPARATION ANXIETY *Anxiety* occurring in a child between 13 and 18 months caused by actual or threatened separation from his or her mother.

SEQUENCE-RELEVANT DEVELOPMENTAL CONCEPT Approach to developmental change based on the idea that changes which ordinarily occur within extended time periods can be accomplished in a far shorter time through efficient training, as long as the individual is in possession of prerequisite skills.

SERIATION Piagetian notion of the child's ability to arrange a number of events or objects into a continuum such as "greater than," "less than," "more than," and "fewer than."

SET A tendency to behave toward certain stimuli in a predetermined way as a function of past experience or some need state of the organism.

SEX-ROLE STEREOTYPES Patterns of behavior that are considered to be culturally appropriate and valued for males and females, reflecting a complex interaction of biology (for example, menstruation and pregnancy in women) and learning experiences (for example, ascendance-submissiveness, or occupational choice).

SEX TYPING The acquisition of certain behaviors designated as masculine or feminine in a given culture.

SEXUAL ORIENTATION (SEX-OBJECT CHOICE) The sexual preference of individuals, directed exclusively toward persons of the opposite sex (heterosexual), equally toward persons of both sexes (bisexual), or exclusively toward persons of the same sex (homosexual).

SHAME ORIENTATION Construct common to both *social learning* (behaviorist) and *psychoanalytic* psychologies that hypothesizes a standard of *moral identification* primarily directed toward saving face and not getting caught in the commission of a transgression. Behavioral standards are seen as relative, with a lack of firmly internalized prohibitions of the sort found in *guilt orientation*.

SIGNIFIER–SIGNIFICANT DISTINCTION Piagetian notion of the child's acquisition of the conceptual difference between the word or label (signifier) and the object, event, or characteristic for which the word stands (significant).

SKEWED, OR BIASED, DISTRIBUTION A statistical concept referring to a distribution of scores that is not symmetrical or *normal*, in which *mean* and *median* are different from each other.

SOCIAL COGNITION The process by which humans come to know and to organize their knowledge about other people, including motivation, standards for social conduct, social role behaviors, and effects of one's behavior on other persons.

SOCIAL DEVELOPMENT Process concerned with child–peer interactions, as well as interactions with significant figures other than parents (aunts, teachers, older siblings), and the effect that these interactions have on the child's personality development.

SOCIAL ETHIC Cluster of behavioral characteristics that emphasize *cooperation*, cordial compromise, and "getting along."

SOCIAL LEARNING THEORY A behaviorally oriented theory of development that investigates the acquisition of traits, values, attitudes, and behaviors through the observation of models.

SOCIAL POWER The ability of one person to evoke submissive responses from other people.

SOCIALIZATION The process by which individuals learn the ways, ideas, beliefs, values, and *norms* of their particular *culture* and adapt them as part of their own personalities.

SOCIOBIOLOGY The study of how biological factors may serve as the basis for social behavior patterns across different species, with an emphasis upon understanding the evolutionary character of these patterns.

SOCIOECONOMIC STATUS, OR CLASS A stratification or categorization of society formulated on the basis of education level of the heads of the family, the father's or mother's occupation, characteristics of the part of town and the house in which one lives, and the source and size of family income.

SOCIOLINGUISTICS Scientific discipline, related to *linguistics*, concerned with the study of *language* or *dialect* differences associated with ethnic group, geographical, and social class factors, including a focus on the social origins of *communication style*, attitudes toward *language*, and various social implications of language use.

SOCIOMETRIC TECHNIQUES A method of mapping social groups to determine patterns of attraction (popularity), leadership, and rejection among the members.

SOMATOTYPE THEORY A body-type theory, proposed by Sheldon, relating physique to temperament and classifying individuals into three types: endomorph, mesomorph, and ectomorph.

SPEED TESTING A *psychometric* principle of test construction in which an individual's test score is a function of how many items can be successfully completed within a defined time limit.

STABILITY Trend in the development of *self* in which an individual's view of self, including self-regard, becomes better organized and more stable, leading to a greater capacity to resist and recover from environmental disorganization and to ignore appraisals by others of oneself that are incongruent with one's own view.

STANDARD DEVIATION (SD) A statistical term used to indicate how variable a population or a set of results is.

STATISTICAL CONFIDENCE, OR SIGNIFICANCE A statistical concept referring to the probability of an obtained result occurring for reasons other than chance (for example, because of the experimental treatment). Statistical significance generally refers to any result at or below the .05 (or 5%) level of confidence, indicating that such a result would occur by chance only five times in one hundred.

STATISTICAL NORMALITY Term used to connote a case or a behavioral instance considered to fall within one *standard deviation* above or below the *average* or *mean*. Also, more generally used to denote the quality of being average, or typical of, the general population.

STATISTICS A group of mathematical techniques used to demonstrate or ascertain lawfulness in research and provide an estimate of the confidence that can be placed in empirical findings to see whether they occurred for reasons other than chance.

STIMULUS CONTROL The regulation of behavior by the stimulus that is present during or associated with *reinforcement*.

STIMULUS VARIABLE The independent variable in psychological research. Changes in the stimulus variable cause changes in the *response variable*.

STRANGER ANXIETY Emotional response taking the form of crying and withdrawal from any unfamiliar person, reaching a peak somewhere between the ages of 7 and 9 months and disappearing by the age of 15 months. The response seems to be closer to fear than to *anxiety*.

STRUCTURE OF INTELLECT Guilford's theory of *intelligence*, devised from the technique of *factor analysis*, and composed of 120 factorial cells or combinations of cognitive products, contents, and operations.

SUPEREGO According to Freud, the partially unconscious part of the *ego* that incorporates parental and social standards of *morality*. The *superego* inhibits those impulses of the *id* that are most condemned by parents or society, and is thus in constant conflict with the *id*.

SYNTAX Aspect of *language* defined by rules for internal structure and form of sentence or phrase construction, applied spontaneously by the child prior to the application of word-form rules (*morphology*) in expressive (*language*) speech.

TABULA RASA VIEW OF MAN The belief that the mind of the newborn child is like a clean slate upon which experience writes. This attitude is typical of *behaviorist psychology*.

TELEGRAPHIC SPEECH Intermediate phase in grammatical development of the child, at around the age of 1½ years, marked by the use of two- and three-word sentences, solely made up of *contentives* (nouns, verbs, and adjectives) for communicating needs and observations.

TRANSITIVITY Piagetian notion of the child's ability to utilize the operation of *seriation* (organizing objects in an ordered series) with abstract derivations to solve problems of symbolic logic.

TRANSSEXUAL An individual who is physiologically of one gender but psychologically of the opposite gender ("a man trapped in a woman's body," or vice versa) and whose sexual orientation is toward individuals of the opposite psychological gender (for example, a psychologically female transsexual is sexually attracted to males, even though the transsexual is physically a male).

TRANSVESTITE An individual of one gender who dresses in the manner of the opposite gender for the purpose of achieving erotic stimulation, but whose sexual orientation may be either homosexual or heterosexual.

TRUST *Prosocial behavior*, defined as a generalized *expectancy* held by an individual or a group that the word, promise, or verbal or written statement of another individual or group can be relied upon (interpersonal *trust*). Thought to be learned during infancy as a function of positive interactions between the infant and caretakers.

UNDERACHIEVER A person who does not perform as well as would be expected from known characteristics or abilities, particularly from measures of intellectual aptitude.

VALUES CLARIFICATION The process of coming to know or recognize what is worthwhile in life, choosing those things for which one cares most and acting consistently on the basis of those value choices.

VARIANCE The square of the *standard deviation*, often used in primary sources to indicate the amount and direction of change in a set of results.

VARIANCE ACCOUNTED FOR (r^2) A statistical method of calculating the predictive value of a correlation, obtained by multiplying the *correlation coefficient* between two variables by itself.

VERBAL INTELLIGENCE FACTOR A score on the Wechsler intelligence tests, measured by items requiring verbal definitions and the ability to give logical answers to reasoning questions.

VERBAL LEARNING The learning of verbal information received by the individual in oral or printed form.

WORD FLUENCY [TALKING RATE] Component of *language* behavior dealing with the rate or frequency with which a child expresses his or her thoughts and feelings, asks questions, and initiates conversations with others, all of which are subject to the influence of *response-dependent reinforcement* techniques.

WORK ETHIC A set of enduring values organized around work as a basic good. The value cluster usually includes *independence*, thrift, self-sacrifice, future-orientation, *achievement*, and personal responsibility.

Index of Names

Youniss, J., 284, 315
Youth Poll America, 114, 140, 343, 351, 352, 363
Yussen, S.R., 449

Zahn, J.C., 305, 315

Zajone, R.B., 86, 104
Zelnick, M., 343, 353
Zhan, G., 402
Zich, J., 432, 447
Zigler, E.F., 379, 404
Zimmerman, S., 355, 361

Zirkel, P.A., 483, 494
Ziv, A., 463, 494
Zuckerman, M., 355, 363

Index of Subjects

AAMD, *see* American Association of Mental Deficiency
Accommodation, 274–275, 518, 533
Achievement, 366, 367–369
  and effectance motivation, 365
  female, 372–374
  importance of, in American society, 365, 367
  motivation
    vs achievement behavior, 366
    to avoid failure (*Maf*) 366, 364
    biochemical effects on, 26, 370
    and career development, 392
    defined, 366, 533
  patterns in young children, 367–368
  scholastic, 367, 374–375
    and class (socioeconomic), 370–371
    and juvenile delinquency, 478
    -personality correlation, 369
    after racial integration, 485
    and sex differences, 372–374

Achievement (*cont'd*)
  under-, 375–377
  and fear of success, 372–374
Action schemes, 276
Adaptive behavior, 113, 457
Addiction, 179, 196, 204–205
Adolescents, alcoholism among, 196
  cognitive development of, 281
  growth spurt in, 92–93
  health disorders of, 196, 201
  intelligence testing of, 265
  motivational drop among females, 364
  and nutritional problems, 205
  occupational aspirations of, 390
  and premarital pregnancy, 345–347, 351, 354
  pubertal changes in, 190–191, 340–341
  sexuality of, 344–356
Affluence, psychological hazards of, 17, 83, 133
Age, and individual differences in intelligence, 266–267
  and parental goal values, 95–96
  and peer-group dependency, 107, 109–110

Age (*cont'd*)
  -relevant developmental concepts, 43–48, 533
Aggression, 463–470
  background of and developmental factors in, 467–468
  and catharsis, 469–470
  constitutional factors, 468
  definitions of, 466–467
  management of, 468–470
  and peer modeling, 127
  prosocial, 109–110, 124
  and psychoanalytic theory of identification, 323
  and punishment, 469
  and sex differences, 323, 327
  and televised violence, 165–167
  verbal vs physical, 109
Alcoholism, 196, 442
  impact of, on pregnancy, 204–205
Altruism, 425–427, 429
  parent-fostered, 96
  sex differences in, 427
  in young children, 110, 426, 427
American Association for the Advancement of Science, 379
American Association of Mental Deficiency (AAMD), 457

GOLDEN GATE SEMINARY LIBRARY